Preventing Fraud and Mismanagement in Government

Preventing Fraud and Mismanagement in Government

Systems and Structures

JOSEPH R. PETRUCELLI,
CPA/CFF/CGMA/ABV, FCPA,
CVA, MAFF, PSA, CFE
JONATHAN R. PETERS, PH.D.

WILEY

Library of Congress Cataloging-in-Publication Data is available.

ISBN 9781119074076 (Hardcover)
ISBN 9781119220039 (ePDF)
ISBN 9781119220022 (ePub)

Cover Design: Wiley
Cover Image: © Pung/Shutterstock

Printed in the United States of America

10 9 8 7 6 5 4 3 2 1

Contents

Foreword

I T SEEMS LIKE GOVERNMENT CORRUPTION is in the news every day and the public's opinion of those representing us is very low. People are frustrated with politicians and their policies, but most of us just complain and go on about our business. My good friend Joe the "800-pound friendly gorilla" Petrucelli decided to do something about it. A dedicated accounting professional, Petrucelli put together this book based on his years of investigating various frauds and applied that to the problems we see in our government. Waste, fraud, and abuse of power are all things that thrive in the darkness but quickly wither in the light of day.

Government should be held accountable to the people, and the best way to do that is for the people to understand how government works. In many ways, the government is transparent in its reporting, but not transparent enough according to Petrucelli and his coauthor, Dr. Jonathan Peters. More transparency is only going to come about through understanding what all the information coming from our government representatives means. When there is understanding, there are questions, and where there are questions, transparency had better follow.

Fraud can be prevented, but it may have less to do with reminding people of their ethical responsibilities and more to do with procedures that let people know that they will be caught if they cheat. The concept of the 800-pound friendly gorilla—someone providing powerful oversight—should be applied to government as much as it is in well-run companies. Now Petrucelli and Peters are doing just that.

—Walter A. Pavlo, Jr.
President of Prisonology, LLC
Forbes.com Contributor
Coauthor of *Stolen Without a Gun*

Acknowledgments

T O WRITE A BOOK MEANS someone believes in your ideas and vision. Sheck Cho, Pete Gaughan, Connor O'Brien, and Wiley: Thank you for making this project a reality. To Brien Jones at NACVA, thank you for your continued support.

To my partner, Timothy Piotrowski, 35 years of friendship, respect, and strong core values—without your continual support this book would not have become a reality. To the Moth, as I know him, Walt Pavlo, living proof that one bad choice does not define a person's character. Thank you for all your support, the wonderful foreword, and the inputs you made to this book.

CSI students, faculty, and staff: Thanks for re-creating me and allowing me to share in your current and future successes. Your energy, your support, and the team spirit are second to none. To my coauthor, Jonathan Peters, your insight, your support, and all your efforts made this book a reality. Professor Pat Galletta: Thank you for taking time to proofread and for all you do for the students at CSI and allowing me to be part of that.

To Jonathan Capp, not only my drummer for life but my friend as well. Thank you for your support, the wonderful suggestions, and edits to help get the book to completion. To Bob Morrison, the smartest government accountant I know. Thank you for all your checking and cross-checking and for the long-standing friendship we continue to enjoy.

To Assemblyman and friend, Robert Karabinchak, thank you for your efforts to create accountable government, for continuing to fight for transparency, and for emphasizing the importance of creating "numbers that don't lie."

To my staff at PP&D, Lynn, Brian, Joe Z., Joe M., Priscilla, Mom, Jennifer, and anyone else I've missed, thanks for your loyalty and support. My second family.

To my Mom and Dad, thanks for all your support and making believe that "I think I can" means you can as long as you're willing to put the time and effort in. To my in-laws, thanks for all the years of support. To my two boys, Joey and Matt, I love you and enjoy watching you grow each and every day. Thanks for your support.

To my wife, Angela, who gives me the freedom to be me and reminds me of the importance of family. Thank you for your patience.

To all of those virtuous public servants who show up every day and work to make our government institutions. Your service inspires our work and your selfless dedication is one of the few things that keep us hopeful for the future of government enterprises. We hope you all achieve 800-pound friendly gorilla status and that you use that power to make our government institutions accountable and efficient.

Joseph R. Petrucelli

To Joseph Petrucelli, my coauthor, whose guidance and inspiration was critical to the completion of this work. His boundless energy and endless ideas drew out many concepts and thoughts from me that have enriched this work. My hope is that our writing will inspire further discussion as to the potential solutions for corruption and mismanagement in our government institutions.

To the public servants and elected officials that served with me or worked for the various public agencies I have served or work with. Your endless good and bad examples pepper this work and enriched our discussion, making it all the more accurate. I cannot say it has all been good, but it all has been informative and educational for me.

To my colleagues in the field of public finance and economics. The growing need for our services in government service is becoming more critical as society and elected officials defer key public finance decisions to a later date. We need to step forward into the policy debate and provide clear and objective analysis of our financial challenges. I hope, as a profession, we can develop tools and techniques to help our society pick through the political mire and help us all find reasonable solutions for our government financial challenges that are fair, practical, and equitable.

To my Mom and Dad: You are both at the core of my being. Dad, you still inspire me from Heaven with your life examples of honesty and integrity. You were an 800-pound friendly gorilla if there ever was one. Mom, you were my first and best copy editor. I hope this work reflects well on the time you spent working with me. All errors that remain are due to my flaws, not your training.

To Caroline and Adam, my children, you both continue to inspire me and make me try to be a better person and a better father. Sorry for all the lost time when I was typing and could have done more with you. Sorry for the missed meals when I was off working on government matters and attending town meetings. I hope that you both have long lives full of adventure and success; I have all the best dreams for you both. Maybe this book will convince you that public service is an honorable and important use of one's time.

To my wife, Nancy, the patient observer of this herculean effort and my endless sounding board for book topics and issues. You have been there through all of my years of government service and academic work. You put up with all that comes from being married to a crazy professor who actually serves as an elected official. Your integrity, wit, taste, and clarity of thought have made this work more precise, more fair, and more grounded in perspective.

Jonathan R. Peters

About the Authors

Joseph R. Petrucelli, CPA/CFF/CGMA/ABV, FCPA, CVA, MAFF, PSA, CFE (CPA in New Jersey, New York, Pennsylvania), is a well-known expert in the area of forensic accounting. He is a founding partner of PP&D Accounting Services Inc. and Fraud Forces Inc., where he provides forensic accounting, tax, and consulting services. He is called upon frequently as an expert witness on valuation, labor negotiations, and fraud. His client list includes large public agencies, major corporations, and multiple municipal unions and governments. He authored *Detecting Fraud in Organizations* (Wiley). He is a popular adjunct professor at the College of Staten Island of the City University of New York, where he teaches accounting-related courses on a regular basis and assisted in the development of a graduate-level forensic accounting course. He frequently lectures on fraud risk and ethics. He is a former New Jersey real estate commissioner and is actively involved in various nonprofit work.

Jonathan R. Peters, Ph.D. (Fair Haven, NJ), is a professor of finance in the Business School at the College of Staten Island of the City University of New York and a member of the doctoral faculty in the Ph.D. programs in economics and earth and environmental science at the CUNY Graduate School. He is also a research fellow at the University Transportation Research Center at the City College of New York. Dr. Peters has served as an expert on panels at the National Academies of Science and is a subject-matter expert in the areas of transportation finance, road pricing, and the privatization of public assets. He has recently published in *Research in Transportation Economics*, the *Journal of Public Transportation*, and the *Transportation Research Record* of the National Academies of Science. He also has served as a member of the Borough Council of the Borough of Fair Haven, New Jersey, for the past 10 years. He currently serves as president of the Borough Council.

Preface

"The tree of liberty must be refreshed from time to time with the blood of patriots and tyrants."

—*Thomas Jefferson*

THE 800-POUND FRIENDLY GORILLA SPIRIT is back, and joining him in writing this book is Professor Jonathan Peters. In *Detecting Fraud in Organizations*, the idea was to use the gorilla to deter, detect, and prevent fraud in all organizations but with a focus on the private sector. In this book, the same level of thinking will be applied to government and public entities. With the addition of Professor Peters, a whole other dimension will be brought to learning about the existence of mismanagement and fraud in the world of government.

The 800-pound friendly gorilla metaphor refers to creating a self-governing spirit. The gorilla lives in groups. The gorilla eats foliage, leaves, bamboo, and fruits, and it does not have to kill to eat. The gorilla will recklessly pound on its chest, hoping to scare off its enemy to avoid the fight. The gorilla cares for its young. Despite all this, the perception is often that the gorilla is strong and forceful in order to achieve its objectives. The author's reference to the 800-pound friendly gorilla is not a one-person focus but, rather, involves the spirit of all interested concerns. The 800-pound friendly gorilla that will be continually emphasized throughout this book is to remind the reader that it's not about catching fraud and mismanagement after the fact. It's all about setting the proper ethical self-governing tone in the people involved in the process, by ensuring that they understand the consequences of a bad choice before they make it. Good people do bad things, but maybe if they better understood the responsibilities and the resulting consequences of their actions, they might think twice before doing them.

With the continuing political and social unrest in other countries and at home, people are now faced with idiosyncratic risk. These unsystematic risks occur as a result of change due to the unique circumstances associated with specific microcosms, as opposed to any overall, or macro, perspectives. How much of a role government can or should play in our society and, in particular, with respect to spending and taxation is currently open for public and political debate.

With the continued focus on smoothing social justice and equality, the past and current surge in spending appears to be the means that government has chosen to quell public unrest. Identifying the societal preferences for government services and output will assist in the understanding of how we have arrived at this point. So, how and when did this surge in spending start? No greater set of societal, legal, and government change occurred than during the 1960s, only, perhaps, excluding the 1930s and the Great Depression. All the change was brought about by societal influences. Social movements will come and go, and if there remains a continual attempt to represent all manner of political beliefs and objectives, it is likely that government debt will continue to rise and may lead us down the path to government insolvency.

In the early 1960s, governments relied on increased revenues. Economic growth was strong. Unfortunately, by the early 1970s, when deficits began to pop up in governments, borrowing and other forms of financing became the preferred method of funding government shortfalls. It is interesting to consider the differences between national and state government finances and the flexibility that a national monetary system such as the Federal Reserve may offer in terms of public finance.

In this book, the public debt, including some of the behavior that led to the current $18 trillion U.S. national debt, will be examined. With government increasing taxes of all kinds, hiking fees such as entrance fees and road tolls, and creating new fees, while providing fewer services, one has to ask why the debt is continuing to increase.

And let's not forget the lowest cost of funds (interest rates) in history, massive financial system bailouts, and questions about inflation fighting. Yet governments and public entities, at all levels, tend to be awash in debt.

One could easily argue that in any government and/or public agency greed is a product of everyone. Starting with the public at large that wants big government when it comes to personal pocketbooks—for retirement needs such as Social Security, medical care, wars, and more—but doesn't want to pay for any of it, there's the problem of competing greed. The formula we need to examine is whose interests are being served and whether or not the intended needs being satisfied are those of the people that the government and/or public agency intended to benefit.

The conflict-of-interest formula: self-interest of the few/(divided by) self-interest of all should = (equal) 1. We need to have one-to-one correlations, which means everyone is on the same page and rowing in the same direction.

The Government Accountability Office (GAO), formerly the General Accounting Office, provides a unique perspective on this situation. The GAO is an excellent example of an 800-pound friendly gorilla at work. It independently examines the processes and standards of government entities at all levels. Its insight into the financial practices of the federal government is quite telling and provides us with some context for the scale of the challenge we face in reforming government financial practices:

> While federal financial management has improved since the federal government began preparing these statements, the GAO has been unable to render an audit opinion on the government's consolidated financial statement because of the following impediments:[1]
> 1. Serious financial management problems leading to financial statements from the Department of Defense that cannot be audited;
> 2. The federal government's inability to adequately account for and reconcile intragovernmental activity and balances between federal agencies; and
> 3. The federal government's ineffective process for preparing the consolidated financial statements.

This is pulled directly from the GAO's website. The authors will look to fully explore and explain these types of issues in an attempt to understand potential mismanagement and fraud. Only sound systems and structures built on independent integrity and ethics can correct the problems of the past and pave the way to a fiscally brighter future for government entities.

NOTE

1. http://www.gao.gov/key_issues/federal_financial_accountability/ issue_summary.

Introduction

PREVENTING FRAUD AND MISMANAGEMENT *in Government Systems and Structures* explores the dimensions of fraud and mismanagement that can and, unfortunately, do exist too often in government entities. Mismanagement is when people manage or control situations poorly. It can be associated with misconduct, corruption, malfeasance, and misuse and may or may not be fraud. Understanding mismanagement and the intent of the parties involved in it leads to skeptical thinking and close scrutiny.

Both of the authors have extensive experience with government entities— as elected and/or appointed officials and as government staffers and/or contractors. Applying their life experiences in dealing with government entities, the authors bring the reader not only an academic perspective but real-life examples and lessons learned in fraud and mismanagement. Through examples and well-explained overviews, the authors create a much-needed awareness of how mismanagement and fraud in government are precipitated, despite consistent oversight. The authors argue that only through keen awareness and sound adjustment of systems to the changing times can the journey to creating a more efficiently managed government begin. The premier issues of status quo apathy remain: that the general public accepts and, all too often, does not care about fraud in government. This attitude resounds on a daily basis, from the national to the local level. Without interest and at times ensuing outrage, mismanagement and fraud will continue in today's governments.

The words *greed* and *need* rhyme. The two words work hand in hand in developing an understanding of where mismanagement and fraud might exist in government. From the first breath we take, we learn to need. **Need** is defined as "a situation in which someone or something must do or have something."[1] Now let's define **greed.** Greed is "a selfish desire to have more of something."[2] Exploring greed and need in the context of a relevant range of the facts is a key step in correcting areas of mismanagement and fraud in government. The **"carrot and the stick"** comes to mind when thinking of the establishment of government policies within which a combination of rewards (carrot) and punishments (stick) are used to motivate and control. Once it's understood that a particular "carrot" motivates a person, it is not hard to control that person, as that person's self-interests are being satisfied.

The authors examine areas in which conflicting interests may be hidden in government systems and structures. A conflict of interest is defined as "conflict between the private interests and the official responsibilities of a person in a position of trust."[3] Examining the trust we bestow on others and the responsibilities assigned to parties we trust is where the focus needs to be placed in order to prevent fraud and mismanagement in government. Knowing where value (transferred into cash) and people can meet that value within the system and structures is key to developing an understanding of the potential for mismanagement and fraud.

PEOPLE ARE YOUR GREATEST RISK AND YOUR GREATEST ASSET

> *"We the People of the United States, in Order to form a more perfect Union, establish Justice, insure domestic Tranquility, provide for the common defense, promote the general Welfare, and secure the Blessings of Liberty to ourselves and our Posterity, do ordain and establish this Constitution for the United States of America."*

Sound familiar? It's the preamble to the U.S. Constitution. A self-check of unexpected morally guided systems and creation of balance among people are key in getting a good grasp on where fraud and mismanagement can occur in government. This is no different in private organizations, as it all comes down to the tone set at the top of the organizational structure.

Without the proper ethical spirit being instilled at the top and funneled all the way through to the bottom, fraud and mismanagement in government will continue to exist. Notice that the term *ethical spirit* is used, as it would be impossible to create a position of oversight everywhere to make sure people adhere to the higher principles. What the authors are counting on is that the readers of this book will become informed and assume the friendly watchdog tenor of that future 800-pound gorilla by holding those in public service accountable.

These are all familiar partnerships: president-Senate, president-Congress, president-voter, husband-wife, parent-child, board of directors–chief executive officers, manager-staff, and mob boss–soldier. What is the common theme? Besides their obvious relationship to one another, they are all just people. So the question becomes: "Whose interests are being served, their own or others'?"

In primary school, the familiar Latin motto was learned: "E pluribus unum." It translates into "One out of many." But are all people's needs met equally? How does government handle these differing needs? Is it the proverbial "squeaky wheel" that "gets the oil"? Is a beneficial outcome contingent upon a "horse trade," making an unethical act for political gain appear acceptable?

The **salad bowl** concept suggests that the integration of the many different cultures of U.S. residents combine like a **salad**, as opposed to the more traditional notion of a cultural melting pot. In Canada this concept is more commonly known as the cultural mosaic.

Crayola brand **crayons** were the first kids' crayons ever made, invented by cousins Edwin Binney and C. Harold Smith. The brand's first box of eight Crayola crayons made its debut in 1903. The crayons were sold for a nickel, and the colors were black, brown, blue, red, purple, orange, yellow, and green. The brand name Crayola was created by Alice Stead Binney (wife of Edwin Binney), who took the French words for chalk (craie) and oily (oleaginous) and combined them.[4] The idea is that the more colors in your box, the more diversity and, in turn, the more opportunity for creating a more diversified drawing. Yet in government this diversity comes with a cost and often creates distractions that can lead to diversions and ultimate division.

Government tends to mix all funding sources into one bowl in order to satisfy the vast variety of self-interests. It is this **fishbowl** thinking that creates the opportunity for fraud and mismanagement to exist. We like to call it comingling and related-party subsidies.

Government leaders live their lives in a fishbowl. Most of what they do is up for public perusal, broadcast around the world. They are public servants. As such, their lives are no different from that of the fish being viewed as it swims around in its bowl, subjected to the eye of beholder. National service requires a level of openness unheard of by leaders in the private sector of for-profit organizations and even nonprofit enterprises. Social networks and media demand a new level of transparency that fosters communication and interest. Generational shifts, technological advancement, revenue shortfalls, and political changes are just a few of the key shifts occurring at all levels of government to create the necessary awareness. This new complexity demands leaders with proactive vision in order to manage effectively.

Terms like *salad bowl, colored crayon box,* and *fishbowl* need to be replaced with one term that reflects a united self-interest. We all know a salad bowl creates diversity in taste, a full box of colored crayons gives a picture with a rainbow-like effect, and a fishbowl full of well-balanced fish with no conflicting interests such as hunger remain peaceful and soothing to view. Yet we know that with diversity comes challenge.

We often forget that the concept of the sum of the whole being equal to its parts can be problematic. This whole is based on some type of grouping, such as proximity or similarity, so the parts can be collected in an organized manner. As we know it, this creates consistency in order to attempt to achieve the whole. But does it really? We mentioned the beauty of what happens with combining vegetables in a salad bowl to enhance the taste. We know that having many crayons to choose from in creating that drawing make it more colorful. We know that a fishbowl full of fish that are well-fed live in peaceful harmony. It's all about balance.

Yet, once conflicting self-interests are introduced, they may become the overriding force in the decision-making process. An environment where mismanagement and fraud can flourish has been created. All it takes is for one fish to want to eat more than the food that is available (resources). Soon the fish seeking more food (resources) looks at the other fish as food, and that fish turns on yet another fish. Soon the only fish that's left to eat is the one that has eaten all the resources.

In an organized structure, everyone has to eat in order to maintain balance. Putting the proper policies and procedures in place that help avoid conflicting self-interests and maintain the resources allows the public entity to remain a viable ongoing concern.

There is no greater government advancement than policies and decisions that advance all people's interests. An adherence policy that requires the core mission and defined objectives of the whole group's interests, not just the parties benefiting, must be considered. This is the formula. The whole, in order to be a sum of its parts, must be balanced, with all interests and concerns addressed. Disneyland is not the only place where this can be achieved. When all interests and concerns are considered, a self-monitoring, ethical group of people can reduce more mismanagement and fraud than the best-defined internal controls.

If you accept our challenge, you will have a significant element to monitor in your everyday lives from this point on—identifying where these conflicting interests lie. Why is it that people, in general, seem to commonly oppose one another? The answer: Once you identify the potential greed and needs within relationships within a given process, you will be on your way to understanding why conflicting interest left unchecked will continue to enable fraud. The same level of thinking can be applied in determining where potential mismanagement and fraud can occur.

It is always easy to think that it is someone else who should intervene to identify, manage, and correct fraud, but the simple reality is that we all have a hand in government and public corruption, and we all need to lend a hand to control corruption. If not you, then who? If not now, then when? Remember the famous John F. Kennedy quote, "My fellow Americans, ask not what your country can do for you, ask what you can do for your country"? What can you do for your government? You can maintain some level of professional skepticism and, in doing so, help hold government accountable.

FOCUS OF THE BOOK

The authors review government and public entity systems and structures to understand their inner workings and where the opportunities for the kind of misstatement that leads to mismanagement and fraud lie. By continually applying the skeptical who, what, where, why, when, and how—the standard journalism formula for questioning—you will see how one can successfully expose those areas ripe with potential for fraud and mismanagement. Understanding and applying history, we will help the reader gain an understanding of the importance of developing sound structures and systems that can be put in place to mitigate fraud and mismanagement. Notice that the word *mitigate* is used. That is because, since no two people think and/or act alike, there is no 100 percent guaranteed method to stop fraud and mismanagement. One-size-fits-all "government issue" thinking does not work. All laws can do is mitigate some common forms of misbehavior. The most effective mitigation lies in maintaining a high standard of ethics.

Promoting ethical behavior in organizations through ethical leadership has been brought to the forefront in developing effective systems and structures to prevent fraud from occurring. As a result of many of these highly visible frauds, ethical behavior at the top levels of organizations is of interest. While companies such as Enron and Tyco typify corruption, there are examples of wrongdoing in a wide variety of organizations including, but not limited to, education, athletics, the media, as well as the boardroom. Our focus will be to shed light on the particular areas in the public/government entities.

Being a moral person involves acting with integrity and objectivity that is free from bias. The moral person is perceived as being a trustworthy person. Ethical leaders should exhibit traits such as integrity, honesty, and trustworthiness.

Specifically: The displayed moral behavior of public officials' and public employees' actions in their private lives should be consistent with the moral standards they publicly portray. Look to see if they do the right thing when no one is watching. Are their actions moral? Do they take responsibility for their actions? Do they show genuine concern for others? Do they put others' interests before their own? Do they apply their values when making behavior and management decisions?

The actions being displayed by public officials and employees must be consistently applied to all without bias. The communicated actions must be for the intended purpose of the entity interest and not the public official or employees.

Being a moral manager involves proactively promoting ethical behavior in others through the use of role modeling, communication, and formal reward systems, not only with a monetary perspective. Ethical leaders recognize that subordinates are searching for ethical guidance and that people in these authoritative positions can influence the ethical behavior of others in a positive or negative way.

Achieving ethical behavior is not just a matter of finding the few bad apples that commit fraud, but instead involves helping all the people in the public entity achieve high ethical standards, which can be accomplished through the demonstration of ethical leadership. "Actions speak louder than words."

Examining the visual actions and verbalization behavior by these trusted people is key in developing effective systems and structures—especially examining where these people have access to the organizational value within the organizational processes.

Through this book's exploration of varied histories, the reader will be amazed at how simple it actually is to commit fraud. At issue: Is it necessary to see the theft of money as the only form of fraud and mismanagement? No, because many of the frauds that are perpetrated do not involve money but, rather, theft of time, the gifting of jobs to the unqualified, and even hiring one person to do many jobs. While all of that reeks of a lack of ethics, it may not actually be illegal. Immoral, yes. Illegal, not always. One can consider why actions such as this have not been made illegal and who would have to pass laws making such hiring illegal. Laws cannot be relied on to legislate moral behavior. The law cannot be the driving force behind a free society that leads to the American dream. It is important to distinguish between the immoral (subjective) and illegal (definitive). Mismanagement may be the result of nothing more than poor work performance.

Some examples of behavior that are illegal (definitive) but morally acceptable (subjective) are: drinking under age, driving over the speed limit, smoking marijuana, cheating on a tax return, or splitting a cable signal to send it to more than one television.

Often the people breaking these laws do not think of themselves or others as immoral. Often the person who is involved in the mismanagement and/or fraud may not see the act as illegal. That in mind, it's important that definitive standards be established and applied to all equally to achieve a proper ethical tone.

Some examples of immoral (subjective), but not illegal behavior are: cheating on a spouse in a marriage, breaking a promise to a friend, or creating budget accounts that are not expected to be spent so funds are available for other expenditures that the public may not want. Many examples of mismanagement are immoral acts that may be self-serving or expedient.

People do not go to jail or get fined for doing these things. These acts may be morally wrong, though, depending on whom you're talking to. When examining behavior associated with potentially poor ethics, these often gray areas need to be examined closely. The immoral view is dependent upon who is viewing the behavior. Minor breaches in ethics that are not illegal serve as a reminder that often in government, or the public sector, the money is lost and debt grows because the person is viewing facts that are subjective and not definitive. These areas of moral judgment are the ones that create the subjectivity we examine in this book. The problem is that *immoral* can mean "criminal" to some and not to others. Only reasonable thinking applied by the whole group of interested parties can set a tone for an ethically balanced society and lead to the mitigation of fraud and mismanagement.

In government and public agency accounting, valuing some assets and liabilities on the balance sheet involves subjective judgment. For example, the management has some discretion with respect to what provisions they need to make for accumulated sick time. Often, the accounts in the government communications are intricately detailed records replete with explanations of past actions. The risk of material misstatement associated with accounting estimation varies as significantly as the complexity and subjectivity associated with the process being examined. The availability and reliability of sufficient relevant data, the number and reliability of assumptions made, and the degree of uncertainty associated with the assumptions are all key factors that increase the subjectivity and reliability of the findings.

Accounting is a social science involved in the studying, identifying, measuring, and analyzing of the assets of the government or other public-sector entity. Accounting assists in providing the decision making and control for stakeholders, with information previously recorded, in a systematic and useful manner. Accounting produces systematic, structured, and valuable quantitative information. That information is expressed in monetary units, explaining transactions that affect certain identifiable and measurable economic events that have an effect on the government and/or public entity. This is then communicated to interested parties.

Accounting provides information on economic and financial situations for the government and/or public entity at a given time and accumulates those results over a period of time. This means that the information becomes historical, or stagnant. While this information can aid the users in making decisions based on existing management controls in place, it will not lead to the needed projected future controls. Finance professionals will generally provide estimates of future financial conditions of an entity via various forms of financial forecasting. The combination of the historical and projected information would provide financial context for firm managers on a continuous basis.

Thus, sound decisions that are rational and lead to efficiency are made on an ongoing basis rather than from this type of historical perspective. Remember, mismanagement and/or fraud is best mitigated when the proper ethical tone is established while formulating the economic and financial information. This should be supported by continually updating the controls in place on an ongoing, as-needed basis.

 ## RULES: DO THEY STOP FRAUD AND MISMANAGEMENT?

There is a great debate in the accounting world between a rules-based approach and a principles-based approach when preparing financial statements. Without a rules-based approach, these authors think that the accountant's work product, when examined in a court of law, would expose the accountant's judgment to significant discussion of methods and thus increase liability.

Consistency, conservatism, and control lead to balance, while independence, integrity, and objectivity lead to ethics and sound, principled thinking. There needs to be some rule-based standard in order to have consistency and objectivity in financial communications. The English language has a vast range of words, each of which has one meaning, so that we can communicate with each other clearly. Imagine if people could choose the meaning of the words they use. There would be no way to understand each other. Unfortunately, in striving for consistency and objectivity, the opportunity for fraud and mismanagement still seeps in, because things and events often become predictable. Words like *routine* and *expected* need to be replaced with surprise visits, different thinking, and consistency in form rather than substance.

Substance over form in accounting is the concept that the financial statements and accompanying disclosures of an entity should reflect all the underlying realities of the transactions. The information appearing in the financial statements should not merely comply with the legal form. Principles-based thinking means it should make sense versus rules-based thinking that says, "This is the way to do it whether or not it makes sense." This thinking does not prevent fraud and mismanagement.

For example, someone intent on hiding the true purpose of a transaction could structure it to just barely meet Generally Accepted Accounting Principles (GAAP) rules, which would then allow that person to record the transaction in a manner that hides the true intent of the transaction. Conversely, International Financial Reporting Standards (IFRS), being more principles-based, make it more difficult for someone to justify hiding the intent of a transaction, if they apply the IFRS framework. Using the rules to make the transactions appear correct versus applying the rules with principles-based thinking that reflects the transactions' real intent prevents fraud and mismanagement.

It is important to abide by this one set of ground rules with respect to exposing mismanagement and fraud—that is, only a judge and jury can convict someone of fraud. Rule 2, as Mr. Miyagi said in *The Karate Kid*, is "Remember Rule 1." Another key point is that often mismanagement, errors, and other variables exist that may not rise to the level of criminal fraud. Therefore, understanding the requirements of what a judge and jury need to find to establish that someone is guilty of committing fraud is critical. It is all relative to the circumstances and the environment. In Colorado, marijuana is legal; in New Jersey, it's not. The determining factor is made by the societal views. No one is caught until others say it's wrong and bring it to light.

MIRD: THE FOUR CRITERIA TO PROVE FRAUD

Here we set forth the elements required to meet the burden of proof associated with fraud. **All—yes, all**—of the elements must be present to find fraud.

The first element necessary for fraud to be determined is that there must be a **material misrepresentation** made. Materiality is one of the judgment-based accounting principles that we discuss in other chapters with regard to developing the proper systems and structures within government entities to prevent fraud and mismanagement.

The second element necessary in determining fraud is that there must be **intent** "to deprive or defraud the true owner of his property."[5] Intent is not always easy to prove. There are two burdens of proof. Preponderance of the evidence, also known as *balance of probabilities*,[6] is the standard required in most civil cases.[7]

"Beyond reasonable doubt" "is the highest standard used as the burden of proof in Anglo-American jurisprudence and typically only applies in criminal proceedings."[8] These authors like to use accounting language that equates to the legal term *preponderance of the evidence* by comparing it to the "more likely than not" accounting standard for contingencies for probable, which is defined as 50.01 percent of the proofs on our side. We win. To tip the legal scale the accountant's way with a high level of confidence usually requires far more than 50 percent certainty. Just hitting 50.01 to 49.99 percent leaves a "flip the coin feeling" to judgment. On the other hand, the "beyond reasonable doubt" in accounting terminology would be equivalent to confirming the cash movement and "the money is in the bank," leaving no room for doubt. The bank being a third party verification source is considered a strong piece of evidence.

When dealing with criminal fraud, one should look to hold to the "beyond reasonable doubt" standard. In tandem, when dealing with mismanagement, the preponderance of the evidence, or lesser civil standard, is required to correct mismanagement in a government unit.

Fraud and mismanagement are often similar; and it often comes down to whether or not the act itself is a definitive or a subjective one. It's a matter of legal versus illegal. To clarify, mismanagement is the process or practice of managing ineptly, incompetently, or dishonestly but does not rise to a criminal classification.

One area of concern in the public entity is the mismanagement of funds. This often involves situations in which a person fails to follow the policies and/or guidelines with respect to the public entity's funds. Most mismanagement, based on the authors' experience, involves some form of negligence or neglect by the responsible party. In order to defend negligence, one must maintain due care. If due care is maintained by having well-established policies, mismanagement can be mitigated. There are many cases in connection with boards, authorities, municipalities, or places where there is some established agency/fiduciary type relationship. Some examples of these agency/fiduciary types of relationships can involve granting a power of attorney to an executor of an estate or giving voting power to legislate, as with the powers given to municipal councils, committees, or commissions. Mismanagement can occur by giving anyone the ability to authorize an act on behalf of another's interest.

Here are some fund mismanagement examples:

- Comingling funds with one's own personal accounts
- Providing information about the funds without the party's authorization (i.e., failing to maintain confidentiality)
- Using the funds for one's own personal use rather than their intended purpose
- Violations of fiduciary duties created by the person in accounting authority
- Failing to account for any transactions or changes in the account
- Violations of various policies and/or applicable laws

Intent is very difficult to prove, whereas errors are frequently attributed to following orders or an unintentional oversight. So, there is often a fine line between mismanagement and fraud. That is why these authors follow the rule that only a judge and jury can find someone guilty of fraud after considering all the relevant facts and circumstances.

The third needed element needed in the determination of fraud is **reliance**, "acting upon another's statement of alleged fact, claim, or promise."[9] The party that was harmed must prove that they relied on the statements or documents. **Relevance** in an accounting concept is when the information generated by an accounting system impacts the decision making of someone reviewing the information. Examining the relevance of the accounting transaction helps identify the areas that are being relied upon in developing sound systems and structures around these vulnerabilities.

The fourth and final element needed to draw a conclusion that fraud has taken place is **damages**. The party to which material was misrepresented (by another party) must be able to prove damages either to a level of preponderance of the evidence in civil matters or beyond reasonable doubt in criminal matters. These damages must be reasonable and estimable—one of the more critical of the four criteria, with respect to public entities. Unlike Enron or WorldCom, the public entity carries on and the taxpayers with the deep pockets are victims.

Damages are not always clear, and the past errors and poor judgments need to be quantified and learned from. One way to prevent public entity damages is by having well-established systems and structures in place with the proper people in oversight positions providing checks and balances.

You must have all four (MIRD) elements to meet the burden of proof.

As you can see, these are not easy hurdles to surmount. There is also a substantial investment required in order to address a fraud and mismanagement that may have occurred. These costs can include lawyers, expert witnesses, employee testimony time, the actual damages, and other costs.

The non-monetary losses are loss in morale, loss in operational efficiencies, and negative press. Now you know why many government fraud cases are never exposed or prosecuted, especially in high-profile and politically charged arenas like government.

The key is proactive rather than reactive thinking. Putting the systems and structures in place that keep people from making bad choices is the real mitigation factor when it comes to fraud and mismanagement. Successful measures include forward thinking like employee bonding and other potential insurance coverage, background checks and other fraud risk planning that mitigates the potential risks within the public entity processes.

 ## JUDGMENT

Another area that this book examines is how government acts when everyone is watching and when no one is watching. What would you do when no one was watching? Would you remain transparent, or would you start the justification process for a sense of entitlement? Add speculation, which is built on thought rather than documentary supports, and you now have a risky place that can allow fraud and mismanagement to exist. Recognize areas that are prone to speculation—especially if these areas have no examples of unsuspected 800-pound friendly gorilla monitoring. In addition to speculation, examine intense strain, extreme pressure, and external influences to further mitigate the risk of making an improper judgment. Any unsubstantiated judgment needs to be met with the appropriate level of professional skepticism. What a person will do when no one is watching can tell a lot about that person.

Positions of power can create opportunities for corruption. "Absolute power corrupts absolutely."[10] Where are the political checkpoints and where is the balance in government? Can they be overridden? These are the questions that the reader will be asked to draw upon in the book's examination of the long history of government decisions. In shining light on past mistakes, the opportunity is created to learn from them and generate more creative, productive forward thinking.

One usually remembers a wrong answer on a test as opposed to the ones that were right. Likewise, organizations can learn from past errors and streamline the management of problems in the future. The Fire Department of the City of New York is known worldwide for its expertise in disaster scene management and fire safety. In reviewing the long history of the department, it becomes evident that the firefighters have built on the experience of weathering past disasters, such as the 9/11 terrorist attacks, to continually improve their rescue and recovery techniques. It's something all fire companies do. This is just an example of great magnitude by virtue of the size of the organization and its emergency response capacity in a major city. In a world-class organization, improvement may not come overnight, and failure and challenge may be strong teaching tools. The same live-and-learn principle applies with fraud and mismanagement. For instance, the continual rise of debt costs, higher taxes, and overlap of services are the historical lessons that the public entity should take seriously. Planning needs to happen before unforeseen disasters ensue and not because of after-the-fact **learning experiences.**

Another key examination process in developing systems and structure resolves around the legal thinking of probable cause. Probable cause[11] is a requirement found in the Fourth Amendment to the U.S. Constitution that must usually be met before police may make an arrest, conduct a search, or issue a warrant. The reason this is relevant in government is that public officials have a greater potential for being criminally charged because they are involved with public funds as opposed to private matters. Public officials typically have a sworn or charged duty to work in good faith. As such, the bar for probable cause is somewhat lower in the eye of the public and the courts. Citizens, therefore, expect that a much higher level of transparency and adherence to policy will be practiced by officials in an effort to avoid being implicated. The problem that often is encountered during public-sector investigations is the claim that procedure was followed as they knew it to be correct, or they just didn't understand that a mistake was made. Such claims are not shields from liability or criminal charges.

The best defense against fraud is asking this simple question: What would a reasonable person think of the actions? Establishing the reasonable person thinking policy is a key step to avoiding bad decisions and choices. A jury of one's peers often judge the accused, and it is important that the accused can withstand that review. In the case of government, what would the public think of the acts that were performed? In the court of law the unclean hands principle doctrine[12] can cut both ways—whereby, if the defendant can show the plaintiff was unethical, the case can be dismissed. Too often, government officials and staff forget this principle and wind up implicated.

Another legal area of concern is the concept of **misprision**. Black's Law online defines this as "(1) a contempt against the sovereign, the government, or the courts of justice, including not only contempt of court, properly so called, but also all forms of seditious or disloyal conduct; (2) maladministration of high public office, including peculation of the public funds; (3) neglect or light account made of a crime, that is, failure in the duty of a citizen to endeavor to prevent the commission of a crime, or, having knowledge of its commission, to reveal it to the proper authorities." (See 4 Bl. Comm. 119–120.[13])

During a lecture, an attendee made one of the authors aware of a unique situation. The party had to defend himself as a result of reporting an illegal act of someone who was part of a court proceeding. The acts performed by the Certified Public Accountant (CPA) in this example were ordered in the judge's chambers. The tax returns were found to be false, and the judge instructed the CPA to report the matter to the Internal Revenue Service. The problem was that the party reported to the IRS that the CPA violated client privacy and knew about the misstatement as the appointed receiver. Since the instructions were in the judge's chambers and not on the record, the CPA was implicated and forced to defend the matter. Lesson learned. Anything that involves implicating others should be done through an attorney, and all applicable laws (whistle-blower, court jurisdiction specific,[14] etc.) and rights should be closely examined. Now, back to the notion that it's not what is said but what can be proved. Speaking to documents is a surefire remedy. The only approach should be a documented one that involves judgment.

A useful tool for accountants or nonattorney professionals, when faced with sensitive matters, is the use of a **Kovel letter**, named after the *United States v. Kovel* case. It can be extremely helpful in mitigating these sorts of exposures. The lawyer involved in the matter hires the accountant or nonattorney professional and, in effect, is doing the work as a subcontractor to the lawyer. By having a legal relationship to an attorney, the accountant and nonattorney professional have some degree of shelter from legal action through the protection of attorney-client privilege.

Knowing the applicable whistle-blower laws associated with the specific government entity being examined is also important. When making a judgment call in these gray areas or high-exposure matters, seeking Kovel and whistle-blower law protections can be the difference between being implicated and not. Being aware of these types of tools helps in managing the risks associated with the judgment decision you are making with regard to mismanagement and fraud in government. Ultimately, tips remain the most common method of uncovering mismanagement and fraud. This is true in politics more than in any other institution, as people are continually vying for power and tips can be a useful tool to defeat a rival.

If you encounter any mismanagement or potential fraud, seek legal counsel and report your findings to the appropriate level of authority. The fact that you have knowledge of the potential crime carries with it a concern that you could be implicated. Remember, whoever is getting blamed will look for someone else to blame. Make sure you have all your i's dotted and t's crossed before you accuse. Remember Rule 1: Only a judge and a jury can find fraud. Finally, one must live with oneself. So, if you find yourself in this position, you need to examine your role and relationship to the fraud being committed. How will you explain your actions to your children, your parents, your spouse, and your friends if you have a role in government abuse of power?

Remember your Constitutional Fifth Amendment: the right to remain silent and your right to an attorney, if you should ever be implicated or accused of fraud or mismanagement. In government, everything "can and will be used against you." We explore interviewing and interrogation methods later in the book, in the examination of the government unit.

The examination of the risks associated with these often-varying judgment calls and the basis on which people making these bad decisions are using the form of these often shaky rationales can hold a key to uncovering the potential areas for mismanagement and fraud in a public entity. The authors examine these speculative and intense areas of judgment by looking at the various processes of the governmental organization. Through this examination of government process, the reader will gain an understanding of the structure, purpose of its formation, control points, people within the entity with trusted responsibilities, and past history.

There should be a direct relationship between the amount of value that an individual has control over and the level of the system of checks and balances that will validate their integrity and performance. There are no greater areas of potential fraud and mismanagement risk than those that involve subjective thinking rather than definitive checks and balances.

STRUCTURES AND SYSTEMS

From the time we are born to our dying day, we learn things in organized ways. Whether it is the sequence of numbers from 1 to 10 or the alphabet from A to Z, without a method of organization, we have no means to establish baselines and maintain order. A simple form of control is that checks are prenumbered in sequential order to maintain control over the writing of them. **Structure,**[15] as defined by Webster online, is "the way that something is built, arranged, or organized: the way that a group of people are organized: something (such as a house, tower, bridge, etc.) that is built by putting parts together and that usually stands on its own." Examining the objectives is key to developing the right structure for any system to be effective in defining and adhering to its policies. Defining specific responsibilities in chain-of-command and sequential-type controls is needed to create accountability.

The greater the trust that is given to people in key control point areas and the value that is exposed to those people who are unchecked, the greater the opportunity for mismanagement and fraud to occur. **System,**[16] as defined by Webster online, is "a group of related parts that move or work together: a body of a person or animal thought of as an entire group of parts that work together: a group of organs that work together to perform an important function of the body." Once again, grouping together people who have perceived common interests is key in the pursuit of achieving the best interests of all. Unfortunately, there are often self-interest conflicts among the politicians, the public, the users, participants, and interested parties. In order to develop an understanding of the systems and structures that prevent fraud and misman-agement, let's examine the Brian Riedl memo. We have interjected *(italicized)* language in order to assist the reader in understanding the importance of knowing where these structures and systems are needed.

In **Brian Riedl's** Web memo on government waste, he identifies **Six Categories of Waste:**[17]

1. Programs that should be devolved to state and local governments; *an effective program would include: communication, efficiency, and having adequate internal controls and oversight in place.*

2. Programs that could be better performed by the private sector; *an effective program would have: a detailed cost benefit analysis, ways to create efficiency, and adequate controls and oversight in place.*

3. Mistargeted programs whose recipients should not be entitled to government benefits; *the deficiencies are lack of controls, poor segregation of duties, self-interest conflicts, political capital needed to get reelected.*

4. Outdated and unnecessary programs; *the deficiencies are caused by no one watching, no interest, no outrage, no checks, no independent political job selections (nepotism).*

5. Duplicative programs; the deficiencies are caused by the need for *home rule self-interest, no third party monitoring of unsuspected 800-pound friendly gorilla organizations and lack of properly communicated and well-defined policies and procedures.*

6. Inefficiency, mismanagement, and fraud. *Examine: MIRD rule focusing on the key deciding factor, the intent of the involved party.*

To simplify the accounting focus that can prevent mismanagement and fraud in the public entity and where these systems and structures should be placed, we need to understand where the value can be converted to cash or tangible benefit. These accounting areas are the receipt of funds, the receipts of goods and services, the paying of vendors/contractors, and payroll. Examining the policy effectiveness in these areas with 800-pound friendly gorilla oversight is key to creating greater efficiency and the fight to right past wrongs and abuses. History repeats itself if you let it. Forward thinking and "pay as you go" are not concepts that currently comprise core values of many government enterprises. The authors continually address these matters in this book.

According to the ACFE 2014 study, "Approximately 77% of the frauds in their study were committed by individuals working in one of seven departments: accounting, operations, sales, executive/upper management, customer service, purchasing and finance."[18] One could ask whether these areas are generally full of evil people and that is why fraud is concentrated in these functional departments. But that is not the case—the key issue is that these are all areas with strong access to value and control—and that tends to focus the attention of fraudsters on these areas.

In this respect, government is no different than private or public companies, as it has similar disciplines and functions. The core missions are different in that one is profit-oriented and the other is not for profit. But the monitor values are the same to the person potentially mismanaging and/or perpetrating the fraud. These are the accounting areas where cash value exists that clearly need the 800-pound friendly gorilla oversight.

 ## DEVELOPING SYSTEMS IN STRUCTURE BY ASKING THE RIGHT QUESTIONS

A quote from Milton Friedman, a Nobel Prize–winning economist, is helpful in questioning government intervention and/or oversight. He said, "One of the great mistakes is to judge policies and programs by their intentions rather than their results."[19] The effectiveness of systems that create structure needs to be assessed according to the results the systems generate.

Formulating questions that will secure these answers helps to create efficiency (preventing mismanagement?) and helps in preventing fraud. Keep in mind that this is not an all-inclusive list of questions, as, again, there is no one-size-fits-all way to uncover mismanagement and fraud.

System and Structure Question Approach Tool

Observation: Identify and note the issues and details.

- What is the goal of the policy or the objective of government? How were you able to reach your conclusion?
- Is the goal realistic?
- What is the name/title of the policy or objective?
- Who is going to be responsible for the policy and objective details?
- Are the policy and objectives committed to a written plan? If so, is the plan easy or difficult to understand? Is the plan made readily available for review?
- What people, places, or events does the policy plan describe, explain, or discuss?
- What type of policy is it (economic, social, political, or culturally related)?
- What influenced the policy or objective? How much lobbying surrounds the proposed policy?
- What citizens, groups, and constituents will you hear from?
- What is the timing of the policy?
- Are there details that suggest the time period the policy will be needed for?
- Does the plan include a detailed cost analysis and how it will be funded for the duration of the policy, including implementation costs?

Reflect: Generate and test hypotheses associated with the policy.

- How does the policy affect the feeling or mood of the citizen/country?
- Why do you think the initiators chose this particular policy?
- Whose interest does the governmental policy affect?
- Are there potential conflicts of interest that exist?
- What evidence and research support your policy?
- What percentage of citizens do you think this policy reaches?
- How do you think the policy might make the public feel?
- How does the policy make you feel?
- Does the policy show bias? If so, toward what or whom?
- What evidence supports your conclusion of the policy objectives?
- What is happening during the time period in which this policy is being developed and implemented?
- What did the public learn from reading and listening to the debates associated with the policy during its formulation and implementation?
- Does any new information you learned contradict or support your prior knowledge about the topic of this policy?

With respect to suspected fraud and mismanagement, asking who, what, when, where, why, and how questions with a high expectation of transparency is key in understanding government structure and operation. What other sources and resources might not have been considered that could clarify a policy to the public?

Napoleon Bonaparte said, "If you wish to be a success in the world, promise everything, and deliver nothing." The only successful government program is the one that meets clearly identified objectives. It should not operate solely along the lines of meeting what its administrators think people want but, rather, what serves the greater good of all people's interests, not any one specific interest.

An example of a failed government program is Prohibition. The United States attempted to prevent drinking by legislating moral behavior. Instead, the government caused a black market to arise—one that was characterized by organized crime and rampant violence. Prohibition was enacted in 1919 and repealed in 1933. As with any failed government policy, the people did not want to be controlled. That's why it failed. In this situation, government attempted to stymie the free market. Government was initially designed to keep people safe and preserve freedom. Telling people they could not drink was overstepping the bounds of "We the People." Think of it this way: If the government were to intervene in a sporting event to ensure a particular outcome, how would the sport advance? People in government have to be entrusted to have balanced oversight so those in the general public can make their own choices.

Government policies are not designed to affect behavior all of the time. That doesn't mean all government policies are mismanaged or fraudulent or not required. In the case of Prohibition, there were unintended consequences of regulating a drug—alcohol. There is always the potential of an unintended consequences with every program. The unintended consequence of welfare is to create long-term dependency in some cases. Same with unemployment, though it is in the short term. An unintended consequence of war is to create a private-sector industry that is dependent upon government spending. It is through understanding the potential consequences of the policy and actions of the public entity that we can institute the systems and structures that mitigate the mismanagement and fraud. Putting time limits on proposed policies, rather than giving people a sense of dependency and not adding requirements to get off these programs, creates dependency and with that the ability to control and potentially manipulate.

These consequences cannot be allowed to create distraction and the ability to divert and divide, three key ingredients that the fraudster and party's mismanagement need to gain cover.

AGFOT (ASSISTED GORILLA FRAUD OBSERVATION TECHNIQUES)

From this point on, your professional skepticism needs to be raised. While it is important to have faith and beliefs, it is equally important to remember that if it seems too good to be true, it likely is. You are up against a broad range of illegal, immoral, and questionable acts committed by people who seek to evade detection, especially from the dedicated fraud hunter. The hunter needs to have high ethical standards, a tough skin, tenacity, and a skeptical nature to fight a plethora of fraud activities. That 800-pound friendly gorilla must have the cleverness, savvy, and skill to take the corrupt party to task for its actions through the appropriate use of various legal and management tools, both inside and outside of the organization.

Let's define some key terms to be aware of when we are making our observations. **Corruption**[20] is defined by Webster as a dishonest or illegal behavior especially by powerful people (such as government officials or police officers). **Nepotism:**[21] The unfair practice by a powerful person giving jobs and other favors to relatives. **Mismanagement:**[22] to manage badly or carelessly.

The authors thought the West Virginia Supreme Court of Appeals summarized malfeasance in the appellate court decision nicely, as follows:

> **Malfeasance** has been defined by appellate courts in other jurisdictions as a wrongful act which the actor has no legal right to do; as any wrongful conduct which affects, interrupts or interferes with the performance of official duty; as an act for which there is no authority or warrant of law; as an act which a person ought not to do; as an act which is wholly wrongful and unlawful; as that which an officer has no authority to do and is positively wrong or unlawful; and as the unjust performance of some act which the party performing it has no right, or has contracted not, to do.
>
> *Daugherty v. Ellis, 142 W. Va. 340, 357–8, 97 S.E.2d 33, 42–3 (W. Va. 1956) (internal citations omitted.*[23]

Official misconduct[24] is defined as improper and/or illegal acts by a public official, which violates his/her duties to follow the law and act on behalf of the public good. Often such conduct is under the guise or "color" of official authority (trust).

Timing is everything. What are the varying issues surrounding the government units? What is the reason for delay or rush to implement? The publicly traded organization has to meet the expectation of the investors. So what are the external pressures faced by the government unit you are examining? Are there contributors and/or related concerns pushing the policy? The people in these positions dread public opinion with respect to raising taxes or user fees like tolls. The politicians should fear public opinion to create accountability and balance. Understanding these expectations is applying looking-beyond-the-numbers thinking. It is through managing these expectations that we can develop strong internal controls.

Lifestyle changes. Failing to examine the trusted people in the governmental areas of responsibilities that have access to the value is one sure fire way to enable fraud. Just ask Dixon, Illinois, residents, whose city's treasurer and comptroller, Rita Crundwell, embezzled $53.7 million over a 20-year period. Crundwell was the appointed comptroller and treasurer (conflicting responsibilities, which violates the segregation of duties control) of Dixon, Illinois, from 1983 to 2012, and is believed to have committed the largest municipal fraud in

U.S. history. During the same time period, Crundwell owned RC Quarter Horses, one of the best-known quarter horse breeders in the country. Crundwell won 52 world championships and was named the leading owner by the American Quarter Horse Association eight consecutive years before being arrested.

How could the treasurer of a small Illinois town with an annual budget of $6 to $8 million steal more than $50 million in 20 years? The answer is simple. No one was watching (no interest). Crundwell was a trusted person with the power to create accounts and write checks. Clearly there were no effective internal controls and/or segregation of duties. Crundwell had access to multiple funds and the ability to transfer between funds, and she found someone to cast blame on the state for not sending aid timely. The State delay in providing the anticipated aid to supplement the operation of the local government was a way for Crundwell to explain away shortfalls in the budget and cash flows and divert attention away from herself. This simple fraud is an example of how when people in a trusted position with access to value are left unchecked, fraud can occur. Monitoring lifestyle changes of trusted people with access to the value is a tool that if in place would have drawn attention and created a need for further professional skepticism. Something as simple as the implementation of an annual **background check** on trusted employees—or verification of public information and disclosure of documents on these trusted people—can often expose this type of fraud. However, someone needs to be applying the appropriate level of professional skepticism. In this case, there were no internal controls, and that cannot be allowed to happen.

Knowing how the government entity processes its cash flows, with continuous monitoring/safeguards in place to spot change, is key. Monitoring and verifying your people's activities (lifestyle) would have caught this fraud. In this case, the warning signs were there, yet no one was watching or questioning. Crundwell was a horse breeder, a very expensive hobby for a modest-salaried public servant. She was a trusted person with complete overriding control and authority. Again, one has to question where the internal controls (auditors) were. Again, remember the auditors rely on management and Crundwell was trusted management. Where were the mayor and/or elected officials (management) who should have been guarding the resources? Without the public asking the right questions and paying attention there is no 800-pound gorilla in the room ensuring accountability from its government. No interest. No outrage. No mitigation.

Now get ready for a different journey through the way government operates by understanding that the people in these trusted positions with access to value can and may commit acts of deceit and malfeasance. The authors will assist you in gaining an understanding of the importance of becoming an expert in identifying the Perspectives, Occupations, and Positions (POP) in an organization—the POP that provide the opportunity for mismanagement and fraud in government. Remember that value does not necessarily mean cash in government. The advancement of political interests by obtaining higher office is a valuable asset. Getting a job for someone or procuring inflated contracts for friends also has tremendous favor value. Government needs to have a process that continuously puts in place the 800-pound friendly gorilla checks and balances to ensure that the policies meet their intended purposes.

Once again, we draw no conclusions as to whether someone committed fraud, only a judge and a jury can find someone guilty of fraud. When reviewing the facts and circumstance surrounding any examination, use the evidences that are provable. Remember it is not our job to develop legal opinions, we only come to conclusions of accounting within a reasonable degree of accountant certainty.

 NOTES

1. http://www.merriam-webster.com/dictionary/need.
2. http://www.merriam-webster.com/dictionary/greed.
3. http://www.merriam-webster.com/dictionary/conflict%20of%20interest.
4. http://inventors.about.com/od/cstartinventions/a/crayons.htm.
5. http://thelawdictionary.org/.
6. http://definitions.uslegal.com/b/balance-of-probabilities/.
7. http://dictionary.law.com/default.aspx?selected=1586.
8. http://www.liquisearch.com/legal_burden_of_proof/standard_of_proof_-_united_states/legal_standards/beyond_reasonable_doubt.
9. http://legal-dictionary.thefreedictionary.com/reliance.
10. Lord Acton quote, http://www.brainyquote.com/quotes/authors/l/lord_acton.html http://www.quotationspage.com/quotes/Lord_Acton/.
11. http://www.law.cornell.edu/wex/probable_cause.
12. http://thelawdictionary.org/unclean-hands/.
13. http://thelawdictionary.org/misprision/.
14. Court Jurisdiction is important as the different courts may have different rules and regulations.
15. http://www.merriam-webster.com/dictionary/structure.
16. http://www.merriam-webster.com/dictionary/system?show=0&t=1420209360.

17. Brian M. Riedl. "50 Examples of Government Waste" (October 6, 2009), http://www.heritage.org/research/reports/2009/10/50-examples-of-government-waste.
18. http://www.acfe.com/rttn-summary.aspx.
19. https://bfi.uchicago.edu/post/milton-friedman-his-own-words.
20. http://www.merriam-webster.com/dictionary/corruption.
21. http://www.merriam-webster.com/dictionary/nepotism.
22. http://www.thefreedictionary.com/mismanagement.
23. http://encyclopedia.thefreedictionary.com/Official+misconduct.
24. http://legal-dictionary.thefreedictionary.com/official+misconduct.

CHAPTER ONE

Government and How It Works

"Every gun that is made, every warship launched, every rocket fired signifies in the final sense, a theft from those who hunger and are not fed, those who are cold and are not clothed. This world in arms is not spending money alone. It is spending the sweat of its laborers, the genius of its scientists, and the hopes of its children. This is not a way of life at all in any true sense. Under the clouds of war, it is humanity hanging on a cross of iron."

—*Dwight D. Eisenhower*

Topics:

National Government
State Government
Local Government
Agencies
Public Authorities
Public-Private Partnerships

Key questions:

Can government forms regulate morality?
What are political agents looking to do?
What are the forms of government?
Where are the best observation points in these entities to identify the risks
they face?

T HIS CHAPTER WILL INTRODUCE the reader to various operational and organizational aspects of government. It spells out how and why government functions the way it does, from a fiscal perspective, setting the foundation for the ultimate exploration of the potential for government fraud and mismanagement. The examination of the cash flow that migrates into and out of the various governmental units is key. Prime examples of activities that can create opportunities for mismanagement and fraud are: the strong centralization of activity in the federal government, the significant financial transfers between the federal and state governments, and the direct fiscal effect of state government on the municipal (local) level. These types of intergovernmental transactions should be subjected to strict professional scrutiny.

We will examine the key forms of government encountered in American society, the role each level of government plays in our lives, and its effects on our wallets. We will examine the primary sources of government revenue, spending, and capital infrastructure, and how government borrowing funds its long-term existence. The reason it is important to analyze the forms of government is that it establishes the environment in which the public entity must operate and leads to developing a better understanding of abnormal or deviant behavior. A key element in understanding why fraud happens is to understand the perspectives within which people operate in order to develop the appropriate systems and structures to prevent fraud and mismanagement.

One thing we are going to ask you to consider throughout this and all the chapters, is how the moral standards and structural practices of a public entity form and the behavior of the people who are involved in the process. We then ask you to think about how would you observe and verbalize your findings. When you are in the field, you need to actually develop creative ways to generate an opportunity to examine these people from two perspectives, exploring both their visual cues (how are their bodies reacting?) and verbalization (support-able/believable), preferably unexcitingly. Watching the trusted parties' visual cues and verbalization with respect to their actions will potentially generate warning signs requiring further reexamination.

This examination does not necessarily have to result in finding fraud. Nervous people may be nervous because they are not comfortable speaking in public. This thinking helps in designing systems and structures as you identify weaknesses that may need something as simple as training or support to make the nervous party comfortable. A solid approach is to watch people in action and monitor them as they speak. Remember to always document your findings.

Understanding the basics of the governmental structures and operations and the various types of governmental levels and entities is one of the key elements in developing an understanding of how potential misstatement and fraud can exist in the overall governmental structures. We look to explore the mechanisms that create and maintain the power of political entities and how these entities interact with the general public and each other. A particular emphasis is placed on public agencies and tiers of authority. A thorough under-standing of the hierarchy in any organization is imperative in following the flow of money and who enables access to cash resources. By examining the behav-ior surrounding the flow of money we begin to develop the necessary insight needed to institute the proper levels of internal control. It all starts by ensuring the correct ethical behaviors are in place. Remember the "Tone at the Top."

Governmental entities serve many functions in society. Knowing who the potential enablers and detractors are and their personality behavior is important in building systems and structures around them that lead to accountability and mitigate fraud and mismanagement.

TYPES AND FORMS OF LOCAL GOVERNMENT: AN EXAMPLE FROM NEW JERSEY

Government comes in many forms. Even at the local level, there are significant variations in the structures and operations in which people function. Each of the structures has its own inherent quirks, power structures, and process requirements. Therefore, an understanding of the broad variations gives insight into who has their hands on the levers of power, poised to push for good and/or corrupt purposes.

In New Jersey, there is a staggering number of municipalities per capita—565 for a population of 8.9 million. Right next door, to the east, is New York

City, one massive municipality of 8.2 million residents in the state of New York that is run by a singular governing body.

The types of local government, according to the New Jersey League of Municipalities, are borough, township, city, town, and village.

Each of the 565 varying types of municipalities in New Jersey is run according to one of 12 forms of government: Borough, Township, City, Town, Village, Commission, Council-Manager Act of 1923, OMCL Mayor-Council Plan, OMCL Council-Manager Plan, OMCL Small Municipality Plan, OMCL Mayor-Council-Administrator Plan, and Special Charters.

The first five forms are associated with a particular type of municipality. Each of these five types has a unique form of government historically associated with it. The next seven forms are "optional" forms of government available for adoption, with the exception of the OMCL Small Municipality Plan (which is available only to municipalities with a population of under 12,000), by all 565 municipalities.[1]

Government attempts to organize itself into various segments much like ants form eusocial colonies. It's within the concept of grouping communities where the conflict often arises, as smaller communities have different needs than larger. In explaining the decision making, or voting power, of different forms of municipal government, terms like "strong mayor–weak council" and "strong council–weak mayor" are often bandied about. At the end of the day, it's a form of division that is often created by one interest, not in agreement, with another. Unlike the ant colony that builds its lifestyle around the family unit and operates in a highly organized structure with defined roles, the governmental unit often finds itself with conflicting self-interests and roles that are not always clearly defined and with the overriding power in the hands of a few.

Think of it this way: Strong and weak are opposites, and, while they attract one another, they often create control conflicts. There's the stronger politically connected individual versus the weaker. There are the rich versus the poor. The rich feel they pay their fair share of taxes, and the poor think the rich do not pay enough. In order to develop sound systems and structure, there is a need to understand all interests involved.

New Jersey has 565 municipalities that are, in turn, run under the umbrella of 21 county governments. To further break down the myriad of New Jersey public agencies, the New Jersey Office of the State Comptroller identifies 55 state authorities, 205 local commissions[2] and authorities,[3] and 604 school districts,[4] not to mention the organizations that cluster under the state government itself. All of these entities were created to serve a population of 8.9 million people. Based on this data there is one public entity for every 6,160 people in the state.

The typical fraudster loves all this hierarchy and bureaucracy, as it has a high distraction potential. The fraudster knows how to sift through duplications and unearth what's buried in the past. Only through a meticulous cost analysis will New Jersey stop being crowned the king of property taxes, according to WalletHub.com. The more taxes or revenue the public entity receives, the more value exchange opportunity. The fraudster needs to be able to convert value to cash and remain undetected. When the public entity has greater cash flow (value), the risk for fraud and mismanagement opportunities becomes available to the trusted people who have access to that value. As long as the cash flow and revenues keep coming in, they are likely to remain undetected and fly under the radar.

Let's for a moment think about a hedge fund that is leveraged. As long as the money comes in and can provide a satisfactory return and remain liquid, there is no outrage or interest. It is not until there is no money to satisfy the existing obligations that people begin to question the funds management.

The need to raise taxes, borrow, and find quick-fix solutions are red flags and require a higher level of skepticism—just like the hedge fund that outperforms other, similar funds. These types of comparisons are useful. Comparing governmental units and looking for such red flags can mitigate fraud and mismanagement in government.

The economy and social well-being of the citizenry are further conflicting interests with the taxing of personal income or paying of *user* fees such as highway and bridge tolls, parking fees, or park entry fees. The conflict arises because people who are not users may subsidize people needing the service. Taxes involve a similar conflict in that people who work harder feel they are taxed too much, and the money is given to people who do not work as hard or use the system. This causes the hardworking person to question whether to continue to work hard or to learn ways to avoid the system. In general, people will do what they perceive is fair. The Laffer curve,[5] named after Arthur Laffer, is a supply-side economic theory in which taxes affect revenue in two ways: mathematically and economically. We will add that people will follow rules and pay as long as they feel that it's fair.

Figure 1.1 applies some of the Laffer curve thinking. It assumes the public entity has a zero tax and this generates no revenue. People will not work for no pay. There are conflicting interests between raising the tax rate to generate revenue and who pays for the services. The mathematic and economic

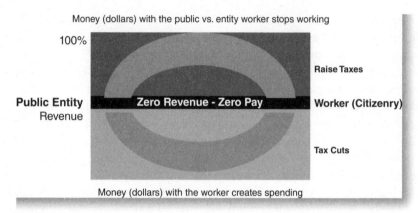

FIGURE 1.1   Circular Laffer curve

variables are in conflict. The Laffer curve suggests that, as the public entity raises taxes (fees) from low levels, tax (fees) revenue collected by the public entity also increases. The Laffer curve also shows that as tax rates increase to a certain point, people will begin not working as hard or not working at all, thereby reducing tax revenue. Eventually, if tax rates (fees) reach 100 percent, then all people will probably choose not to work, because everything they earn will go to the public entity. If the fees become too high, the users will stop using.

So, as we move forward with government policy, one has to ask the hard question: Just how much money should the government raise and how many services should they provide? With the burdensome debt structure public entities face, and the need for the creation of multiple funds to satisfy these debts, you have the potential breeding environment for fraud to remain undetected. Both conditions offer the needed distraction that fraudsters look for to perpetrate a scheme to breach the process for their own gain. Subsidies, grants, and aid are all distractions that enable the movement of funds and are areas that need behavior examination and audit personality testing.

Let's take Enron as an example of the case of having multiple funds and the ability to transfer and move money between funds. Andrew Fastow, chief financial officer of Enron, was a genius in his ability to set up related-party entities to move losing assets off the books. Remember the POP: Fastow had the perspective, occupation, and position to perpetrate a fraud.

Let's take funds and interactions related to government authorities—state, local, school boards, and so on. Taxes are allocated across these entities, and fees are utilized (allocated) across various public entities. All these entities afford the fraudster the opportunity to divert, distract, and divide. More important, they provide the means to gain access to the needed value to exchange for the fraudster's own benefit.

When there are competing self-interests such as when the government raises taxes, leading to a reduction in the household or firm income, and thus a reduction in consumer consumption of household goods and industry spending on labor and capital, this is clearly a divisive act and causes conflict. The competing perspective is that the government knows what's best and needs your tax dollars to fulfill the greater good, which can often be also interpreted as rewarding political donors and supporters. The taxpayers' thinking is, "Why are you spending and requiring me to pay more for your interests?" Thus, the tax function alters the channels of spending and creates alterative demand scenarios that would not occur if the households and firms purchased goods from the market based upon their individual choices. The key word is *choice*. Once choice is eliminated, you have conflict.

Just how do the choices of government impact particular spending and consumption patterns? We can examine a basic service that is generally seen as a public good provided typically by a government agency or authority and in many cases receiving a public subsidy. We will look at a mass transit system such as a municipal bus service or heavy rail system that goes by various names around the world: metro, subway, the "T," the underground, and such.

 ## POLITICS, PUBLIC OPERATIONS, AND LOSS

In the private sector, we examine costs for the entity and also the potential revenue. By comparing the functional form of these two measures, one can establish the point at which the firm covers its costs and thus produces a profit. These parallel relationships formulate a correlation that can be analyzed and assist management in critical decisions.

In terms of costs, it is common to find a certain amount of fixed costs and some additional amount of costs that vary as production increases or decreases. In a general model, we would specify the amount of fixed costs and also the variable costs per unit. It would be common to find public goods having a high amount of fixed costs, with limited additional variable costs for each additional unit of production. One could examine a service such as mass transit—where we have a very high level of fixed costs to deploy and operate the system on a daily basis, and the additional cost of adding another rider is very low. With massive stations, railroad cars, buses, operations costs, and a huge capital stock—none of which is really tied to the level of ridership on a given day—we can see that we are going to add variable costs at a slow rate for each additional rider, but we have to reach a high level of ridership to cover all of our fixed costs.

In our example, we make these assumptions:

- Fixed costs are $100 million per year.
- Variable costs are $3 per rider.
- Demand will be around 33 million riders per year.

Putting a fare structure in place and calculating total revenue as the ridership times the fare per rider produces the general estimate of the break-even point. If we examine existing demand, we find that pricing the rides at about $6 per ride will produce about 33 million rides, and at that point we can solve for the break-even point—which is 33.3 million rides annually priced at $6 per ride. There is where the baseline water mark would be established if this was a profit-making firm in a competitive market. Figure 1.2 illustrates this point.

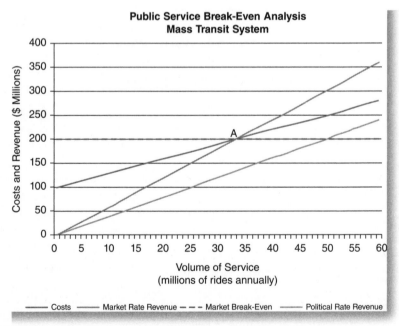

FIGURE 1.2   Break-even analysis for mass transit with market-based fare

The agency produces at Point A and breaks even on costs at $200 million annually and provides 33.3 million rides. If ridership exceeds that level then the entity has a profit, and if ridership is below that level then the entity loses money and requires a subsidy—or it will have to increase the fares to cover costs.

But this is a public service. Being a public service, the politicians may want to establish rates for the service that are below the operating and break-even costs. This causes two problems. First, by lowering the price, we create additional demand for the service—as the price is lower than the true cost of delivery—and that encourages consumption. Take as an example what would occur with ice cream consumption on a hot day if we lowered the price: excess consumption. Second, the low price causes a structural loss for the public authority, which is then forced to seek a subsidy to provide that service.

Now you have politics in play. The elected officials see that there is political value in keeping the fare low, as that creates a concentrated group of beneficiaries (transit riders) who then will work to maintain that pricing structure. This situation may very well be sustained for a considerable period, as the transit users and elected officials may work in coordination to use the tax system to provide ongoing subsidies for the entity. They may also attempt various short-term patches to the finances of the entity to continue the service as long as possible.

In our scenario, we posit a fare that is $4 per ride based upon the desires of the elected officials to offer a cheap ride, for political expediency. This price is maintained as long as the governmental sector can provide a subsidy to cover the cost. In our example, ridership would have to increase to 100 million riders annually to have the transit agency break even. This may not occur, as there may not be demand for that many rides at $4 per ride. Thus, the actual ridership may settle into some interim range—say, 60 million rides annually—and the agency will suffer a $40 million per year loss ($280 million in costs and $240 million in revenue).

Figure 1.3 provides an illustration of this point. Ridership would have to be at Point B for the entity to break even with a $4 fare. The agency would now have a total cost of $400 million and revenues to match. However, it is likely that ridership will fall somewhere between Points A and B and thus some degree of subsidy will be required. Further, it is possible that additional investment may be required to provide more than 33.3 million rides, and that may alter the cost curve as we increase the volume of service.

One way to measure transportation cost efficiency is by gaining an understanding of the term *load factor*. Think of the load factor as a way to measure how crowded a public transit vehicle must be before additional service needs

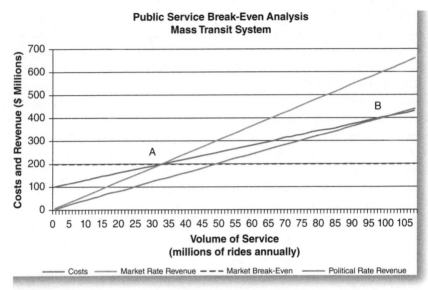

FIGURE 1.3   Break-even analysis for mass transit with discounted fare

to be added. "The industry standard load factor for crowding is 1.25. In other words, in a low-floor 40 foot bus that has 38 seats, the bus will be described as crowded if more than 48 people are on board (38 seats + (38 · 0.25)) = 48."[6]

In the public entity we have subsidized service revenue and unsubsidized cost with respect to the services being performed by the public entity. The tipping point is north or south of the break-even costs. Developing an understanding of the tolerable level of dollars for the provided services by the public users and/or subsidizers is an important tool in making the necessary management decisions. In New York City, this exact scenario is currently being played out. The Metropolitan Transportation Authority (MTA) is the largest mass transit system in terms of ridership in the United States; with a transit fare set at about 58 percent of costs and over 7.8 million rides per day inside New York City alone, the MTA loses over $10 million a day operating its system, or $2.7 billion each year. Part of this gap is covered via dedicated taxes that subsidize transit services as well as tolls on bridges and tunnels that are set above the cost of the service. This has also been sustained by the agency over time by borrowing additional funds to close this gap and to fund capital expenditures; as a result, the MTA has now accumulated $36 billion in debt that consumes 17 percent of revenue to fund on an annual basis.

Size and complexity are potential complexities that the fraudster uses to generate access to value and remain undetected. Government budgets allow for surplus, carry forward and over to future periods. Expenditures are not accrued in some instances and liabilities are not always exact, as we use estimates that require judgment. These people's responsibilities need to be closely analyzed if we are to prevent fraud and mismanagement.

Whenever people are left unchecked, there is fraud risk exposure. When the budget the public entity puts forth does not materially impact a taxpayer or user, no one checks. As the economic or cash flow contracts, these same taxpayers and users become interested. No interest, no outrage. The larger the base, the longer the materiality impact will take to reach the taxpayer and user. Size and complexity offer more cash flow and a means to keep oiling the squeaky wheel when someone asks questions. What often happens is that the public entity throws more money their way to shut down the inquiry. Events such as Superstorm Sandy and the subprime lending crisis create increased budgetary spending. That increased budgetary spending generates financial scrutiny that cannot be shut down by simply throwing money at the inquirers, thus exposing the Fraud as a result of the increased financial scrutiny.

The public entity needs to understand the costs of the service and a simple break-even analysis that leads to the determination of the tipping point at which the public will no longer tolerate the level of dollars for the service being provided. "Life, liberty, happiness" are the foundation of the Declaration of Independence. For many public entities, the three magic words are "supply, demand, and price." In any transaction between a provider and a user, the price of the good or service is determined by supply and demand. Therefore, supply and demand are in turn determined by the conditions which people will accept and operate within. Subsidy is a provocative decision on the part of a government as it changes the economic decisions and relative competitiveness of a region because it twists the economic incentives of the region—with certain services subsidized and others taxed to provide these same services. In the realm of policy, subsidy has assumed an almost mythic value, and political leaders are quick to assume that all subsidies are good. We caution the reader to consider carefully what services and goods to subsidize, as the role of government in setting the table for commerce is very important. In New York City, the massive success of the transit system has created a corresponding massive need for subsidy (Figure 1.4)—and the current elected officials are struggling to find revenue sources to fill the gap in funding.

Having a myriad of government entities creates a morass of officials performing similar, even duplicate, functions. With so many separate bureaucracies at work, there ends up being a massive duplication of effort in

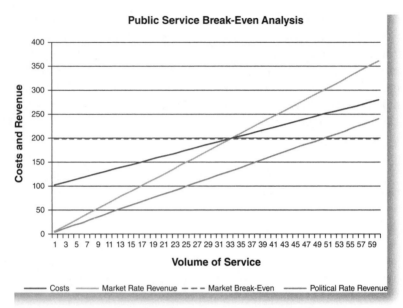

FIGURE 1.4   Break-even analysis for mass transit with subsidy

performing the same simple task, such as buying a garbage truck. It also creates the need for a web of consultants, legal advisors, and contract workers, some of whom have a vested interest in maintaining the status quo, because doing so bears the potential for maximizing their income via the system.

Benjamin Franklin said, "In this world nothing can be said to be certain, except death and taxes." Most Americans' largest financial burden is taxes. The country, as a whole, doesn't earn enough money to pay its total tax bill for the year until April 15, tax day. The varying states' taxing rates and methods makes it even worse. *The more revenue there is, the more debt that can be incurred. That alone fuels a greater potential for fraud and mismanagement.* The more revenue that is available, the greater the cash flow available to the entity, and this affords the fraudster the ability to create transfers and other expenditures while remaining undetected. Without money, there is no value to gain access to. Cash flow needs to be examined closely and the level of trust surrounding the cash flow needs to be examined closely. So understanding the various forms of government gives greater insight into potential enablers and detractors. By examining the enablers' and detractors' behavior that is deviant or abnormal, you're creating a solid defense for the individual taxpayers' and users' wallet in the end.

In most areas of the United States, individuals and firms operate in a world of distinct forms of government. The United States has three primary areas of government: federal, or centralized; state, or a subdivision of federal; and local, or a subdivision of state. At the local level, there is a further subdivision into county and municipal forms of government, as highlighted in the New Jersey example.

These forms of government provide an imbedded structure of operations and supervision designed to protect societal interests, but are also ripe for abuse at the hands of the unethical.

 ## GLOBAL FORMS OF GOVERNMENT

With international trade or commerce, various government structures in foreign countries are encountered. While these forms of government are not in the average American's realm of experience, their functional structures have, in many cases, been in place for centuries. The key is to learn how often one person can influence others to gain control. We feel examining the various forms of government will assist the examiner in developing additional soft skill perspectives beyond the normal accounting methodologies and standards.

Any system built on absolute control creates the opportunity for override, so fastidious scrutiny is needed to keep it in check. In an **absolute monarchy** form of government, also referred to as absolutism, the monarch rules without restriction, laws, constitutions, or legally organized opposition.

Similarly, in a **dictatorship,** the ruler or a small clique has absolute power and operates without being restricted by a constitution or laws. Cliques should be closely examined for the makeup of the people in control. While defining forms of government, one can speculate how fraud and mismanagement can potentially come into play. For instance, terms like "absolute" or "the implication of no rules" imply that there is no structural guard to keep fraud and mismanagement at bay.

Dictators will often resort to force or fraud to gain tyrannical political power, which they will maintain through the use of intimidation, terror, and the suppression of basic civil liberties. Dictators are masters at employing techniques like the use of mass propaganda in order to sustain their public support. The point is to understand how to create absolute power by understanding the language and applying it in your review. Is there intimidation or suppression of the controls and procedures within the process? Is there bias or misleading information surrounding the process? If these are present, then further examination is necessary.

In a **constitutional monarchy,** the government is guided by a constitution whereby the monarchy's rights, duties, and responsibilities are written laws or established by custom. This operates on the assumption that the constitution will not be circumvented. What makes any constitution secure is communicating what the exact responsibilities and duties are and having systems in place to enforce them. The emphasis needs to be on ensuring that the people understand these responsibilities and know where the potential overriding authority lies, as well as the consequences for failure to adhere to the established laws.

In an emirate form of government, a sultanate is given the supreme power. The ruler of a Muslim state is an emir. The emir, ruling as an absolute monarch, may have absolute overlord or sovereign authority with constitutionally limited authority. Again, the effective system focuses on the absolute power and the specific limits that are in place. In the monarchy form of government, the supreme power is in the hands of a monarch who reigns over a state or territory. This is usually for his/her lifetime and is an established right through heredity. It's a form of nepotism, or entitlement. Nepotism is when favor is granted by those with power or influence to family or friends, typically by giving them a prestigious job. Again, with no term limits people are left in authority for long time periods. Without a change in leadership, a sense of entitlement begins, along with a full understanding of the power and what is needed to remain in power and continue to satisfy the interests of those in power.

The monarch is a supreme ruler—such as a king, queen, or prince—with constitutionally limited authority. Where is the person who enforces the limited power? What systems are in place to enforce these restrictions? These are some of the questions that need to be addressed with respect to safeguarding the resources.

In an oligarchy form of government, the control is exercised by a small group of individuals whose authority is generally based on their wealth or power. Oligopolies, as they are referred to in the market, occur when a few companies control the market. The cable companies are good examples of this. This sort of control by an entity can result in various forms of collusion, reducing competition and hiking prices for consumers. There is the possibility for similar outcomes in government organizations with oligarchical control. In government, it's called horse trading when both sides expect equal concessions in order to give one side the advantage. The idiom "You scratch my back and I'll scratch yours" comes to mind.

In a **parliamentary monarchy,** an established state is headed by a monarch who is **not actively involved in policy** formation or implementation but, rather, acts in a **ceremonial capacity.** The governmental leadership in the parliamentary system is carried out by a cabinet and headed by a prime minister, premier, or chancellor drawn from a legislature (parliament). Again, the focus is on the required duties and responsibilities, as it is with any position of control.

It is interesting to note the complex role that a monarch has in a parliamentary monarchy. In the case of the United Kingdom, the queen has specific ceremonial roles and also has the right of consultation with the elected government. Specifically, she has the right to be consulted, the right to encourage, and the right to warn. Essentially the queen provides a very high level of supervision of governmental activities. She is also asked to approve laws through what is called royal assent. While this is granted in the vast number of cases, it still has some impact on policy. These rights, while seemingly minimal in terms of power over elected officials, can, in fact, have persuasive impact on public policy and governmental actions. For instance, if the queen asks to delay action or review a particular law, it sends a strong message about her concern with the actions of the government. In that situation, the elected officials may find themselves in a pitched public debate with a beloved and respected monarch with 60-plus years of public service and deep institutional knowledge of her country. This is the type of fight that most elected officials will quickly lose interest in pursuing in most cases.

In contrast with the role of the queen, the actions of the president of the United States are generally viewed as political and partisan as opposed to the queen's role, which is viewed as objective and informed. This discussion brings to the reader an understanding of the core role of effective management and supervision in creating a sensible government. It is not that the queen is that involved on a day-to-day basis, but she could be the 800-pound (really, an 80,000-pound) friendly gorilla at any moment. It creates a need for internal vigilance and careful thought in establishing governmental policies and practices.

The presidential form of government is one in which the executive branch exists separately from a legislature. The term in U.S. government is the executive (president) and the legislative arms (the House of Representatives and the Senate). The problem is that the executive branch is typically not accountable to the legislative branch. Lots of negotiation between the two branches, with often conflicting interests, occurs, and, as with any negotiation, there is the potential for backroom dealing.

Gaining an understanding of the approval process in any organization or authority is key in identifying where the value is exposed. In the U.S. presidential form, the executive does not have to agree or have the support of the legislative branch. Therein a perfect setting for conflicting interest is established. It is in such a setting that the opportunity for fraud and mismanagement can percolate.

A president coming through a political process commonly has the support of only roughly a third of the people voting, based upon the electoral process—as Table 1.1 illustrates. No president has been elected in the past two decades with even 30 percent of the total vote—with the exception of Barack Obama, who just squeaked by that rate in 2008—and he could not repeat that performance in 2012. As such, his moral suasion is limited, and there may be very vocal opposition to his opinions and positions. Also, the president lacks the long institutional memory that would add credence to his opinions.

In a **communist** government, the **state plans** and controls the economy and a single authoritarian leader often rules or a particular party holds power. The state plans the controls for the economy via the role of central planner. The core of this concept is that the state knows better than its people in terms of public policy, and the population needs to follow the central planner's directives. There are mandated state controls that are imposed, which eliminates or limits private ownership of property or capital. Are these controls applied evenly or is a nepotism effect precipitated? Are all concerns addressed or is this one-size-fits-all thinking? The goal in this form of government is to create a classless society, so all goods are equally shared by the people. In a **Marxist**

TABLE 1.1 Presidential Voting Rates, 1988 to 2012

Election Year	Winner's Share of Popular Vote	Total Vote Turnout	Total % of Americans Who Voted for President Elect
1988	53.4%	50.2%	26.8%
1992	43.0%	55.2%	23.8%
1996	49.2%	49.1%	24.2%
2000	47.9%	51.3%	24.6%
2004	50.7%	55.3%	28.0%
2008	52.9%	57.5%	30.4%
2012	51.1%	57.5%	29.4%

government, the political, economic, and social principles were developed by the nineteenth-century economist Karl Marx. A quote that comes from the *Communist Manifesto*, published in 1848, says, "Workers of the world, unite!" Marx viewed the world from the struggling workers' perspective and their interests, which contrast with those of capitalist business. Marx's perspective was that these conflicting interests would incite class warfare within the society.

It is important to consider that Marx was writing in the 1840s in England and his perspective was based in part on the abuses that the newly emerging manufacturing sector was heaping on the workers: child labor, unsafe work practices, and generally difficult working conditions in the new factory economy. How his critiques have influenced capitalist and mixed economies as well as communist or socialist economies over the past two centuries is still the subject of heated debate. Suffice it to say that his critiques shaped social policy and labor standards in capitalist economies. These same changes have impacted communist countries, which are, in fact, just a form of authoritarianism or oligarchy.

The common notion in the 1840s in England was that the workers would always be taken advantage of by the business owners; a balance of power that could be established, in part, through the use of labor unions and governmental sanctions was not possible. Again, conflicting interests rear themselves as the driving force behind conflict. No matter what the public entity or form of government, this is the area that bears the forbidden fruit, and, accordingly, the appropriate controls and oversight are necessary.

In the Marxist-**Leninist** government, communism was expanded by Vladimir Lenin from the doctrines of Karl Marx. Lenin saw a policy of extending a country's power and influence through diplomacy or military force being the final stage of capitalism. Lenin shifted the focus from the workers' struggle to the developed versus underdeveloped countries. For us fraud examiners, the focus remains on examining the competing interests. The main distinction between a developing country and one that is underdeveloped is that a developing country has an industrial base and capital. There is a lot of truth in the title verse "Money makes the world go 'round" from the musical *Cabaret*. Where there is money, there are competing forces. Where there are competing forces, self-interests are not in balance.

Maoist theory and practice followed Marxism-Leninism. It was developed in China by Mao Tse-tung. The policy stated that a **continuous revolution** was necessary for leaders of a communist state to communicate with their people. A revolution is forcible overthrowing of a government, because people are demanding change. Hostile takeovers come to mind, where two sides are in disagreement with one side determining the only solution is to advance their interest by gaining full control. The word *forcible* in the world of handling the risks of fraud and mismanagement cannot replace the sound concept of keeping balance. The way to keep balance is to have ethical people in power who are well-trained, communicative, and transparent, steering clear of any hint of a conflict of interest. There is no need for absolute control or overthrowing if the systems are maintained with balance amongst all those concerned.

The public servant needs to operate like a fish in a bowl, always visible to the public he or she serves, never using force to get the message across. All force does is create animosity and mistrust. First, understanding why the need for force may develop is critical in creating a way to resolve these potential conflicts before the boiling point is reached.

In the **socialist** form of government, the planning, producing, and distributing of goods is controlled by the central government. The thinking in this form of government is that such central control of government will lead to fairer, more equitable distribution of property and labor. History, however, shows that this form of government has resulted in dictatorships over workers, establishing a ruling elite. Again, this idea of concentrating all the power in the hands of the few, left unchecked, can lead to fraud and mismanagement. As some see it, socialism has crept into many of our existing elected forms of government, with the governmental entities taking on various aspects of social policy and economic control. In the United States, for instance, there is an ongoing debate about the role of various public programs and their limitations on free enterprise. From farm subsidies to Obamacare to unemployment policy, the U.S. government continues to vacillate between more and less socialist-centric policies. European and other developed countries around the world have settled on socialism for many public matters, such as health care, child care, and worker standards.

The old proverb "Give a man a fish and you feed him for a day; teach a man to fish and you feed him for a lifetime" invokes a proactive perspective. Governments that teach people life skills that enable them to break free from reliance on public assistance and/or entitlements, such as nepotism, leads to cost-effectiveness and efficiency. The theory: The better trained the employee, the more efficient. Continual training is a critical ingredient in the recipe for prevention of fraud and mismanagement. The better-trained employee closes the loophole through which fraud and mismanagement can seep. Since he or she met the first hurdle in the battle, he or she recognizes it exists.

Confederacy is a union made by forming a compact or treaty between states, provinces, or territories that creates a central government with limited powers. The forming entities retain supreme authority over all matters, except those delegated to the centralized governmental unit.

In a **constitutional** government, the operations are based on an authoritative document (constitution) that sets forth the system of fundamental laws and principles. This lays out the operating nature, functions, and limits of that established governmental unit. A federal form of government (federation) is one in which the sovereign power is formally divided—usually by means of a constitutional writing that is established by a central authority and a number of constituent regions, or states, colonies, or provinces so that each region retains some management oversight over its internal affairs. The confederacy form differs in that the central government exerts influence not only on the individuals but on the regional unit as well. Understand the responsibilities and powers with which these individuals have been entrusted.

Democracy is a form of government in which the supreme power is retained by the people, but it is usually exercised indirectly through a system of representation and delegated authority that is periodically renewed. In a constitutional democracy form of government, the sovereign power of the people is spelled out in a governing constitution. In a **Democratic republic**, the power rests in the body of the citizenry, which is entitled to vote for officers and representatives who answer to it. In a **federal republic,** the powers of the central government are limited by the states, colonies, or provinces and maintain a certain degree of self-governing. The sovereign power remains with the voters who chose their governmental representatives. In a republic form of government, the people elect representatives to vote for them on legislation.

Parliamentary democracy is a political system in which the legislature (parliament) selects the government: a prime minister, premier, or chancellor and cabinet ministers. This form of government is largely based on the strength of the party in an election. In this form of government, both the people and the parliament can hold the governmental representative accountable. The parliamentary governing body is an executive branch that comprises a cabinet and its leader. That leader is a prime minister, premier, or chancellor who is nominated to the position by a legislature or parliament. The leader is held accountable to the cabinet. This type of government can be dissolved and shut down at will by the parliament (legislature) by means of a no-confidence vote or the leader of the cabinet.

Ecclesiastical is a form of government administered by a church. In a **theocratic** form of government, a deity is recognized as the ruler. The deity's laws are interpreted by ecclesiastical authorities (bishops, mullahs, etc.). The government is subject to religious authority. Religious fraud through power manipulation can exist in both civil and criminal cases. This is a distinct diversion from the U.S. Constitution, in which church and state are separate. In a theocracy, the religious rules of a particular group are then applied as de facto laws. This opens the door for a tremendous amount of power to reside with religious officials, as they apply their religious opinion as the law of the land. The fraud can be carried out in the name of a religion or within a religion. The fraud can be a result of false claims being made such as something being kosher that really is not.

A great example of this kind of theocracy was the governorship of Brigham Young, president of the Church of Jesus Christ of Latter Day Saints, or the Mormon Church, from 1847 to his death in 1877, in what was known as the Utah Territory. Brigham Young was appointed territorial governor by President Millard Fillmore in 1851 and he served until 1858. Young had strong control over both the Mormon Church and the Utah Territory. In his capacity with both, he had great latitude in his dealings with the federal government as well as the Native Americans and travelers in the region. Much controversy surrounds this period and the actions of Young with respect to pioneers on the Oregon Trail that may never be fully understood. What is known, though, is that a series of incidents occurred in which travelers were harassed and killed due to their non-Mormon status. It was, however, clear, that Young had strong control over the Utah militia and various regional public safety organizations. History dictates that he used these government entities to promote his vision of a Utah territory that was firmly under the control of him and his church. Finally, after an extended period of hostility with the U.S. government, he was replaced by non-Mormon Alfred Cumming, of Georgia. The intent with the replacement was to minimize the control of the Mormon Church on territorial government. Power left unchecked, creates the ability to centralize self-interests and separation from the interest as a whole. It is these types of segregations in specific groups that create territorial power players who then develop overriding control and division. Proper levels of skepticism and questioning create that necessary balance. Where these potential centralized power players are meant, we will use a more familiar term, *power broker*. Power brokers are people who exist to influence people to vote towards a particular elected official or referendum in exchange for political and/or their own financial benefits.

When it comes to tax fraud or money laundering, the problem is that religion can become a communication inhibitor and offer the fraudster cover. Religion is often cloaked in altruistic appeals to higher beings. Who's going to question God's leaders? Those appeals and/or surrenders to a supreme heavenly power often give way to people, or believers, shedding their guard and exposing their vulnerabilities. The other problem is that affinity groups, like religions, share common interests. The knowledge of those common interests in itself is a convenient, powerful hook to reel people into the fold.

Affinity fraud is a common component of various investment scams, such as a Ponzi scheme,[7] as identifiable groups are at the core. Various religious or ethnic communities, the elderly, or professional groups are commonly coerced or played in such a confidence scheme. The fraudsters who promote affinity scams frequently pretend to be active members of the group. They enlist respected **enablers**, vital members of the community or the religious leaders from within the group. They ask these enablers to spread the word about the scheme so it convinces those people that it is a legitimate and worthwhile investment. This technique actually can help conceal the fraud, as there may be strong social pressures to avoid affinity conflict; even if the fraud is detected, affinity group members may be resistant to exposing the fraud, as it may incite shame on valued leaders or the group as a whole. Also, given the economic damage that exposure may bring to the members of the group, there may be a desire to ride the wave and, hopefully, jump off before a scandal ensues. The result: less engagement and visibility in putting a stop to the fraud.

Let's change the term from fraudster to lobbyist, or someone who is attempting to influence decisions made by officials in a government for a specific concern. Examine why there is such a strong lobbying effort for or against a decision. Measure the economic benefits to those lobbying the interest versus the general public. This creates outside-the-numbers thinking and awareness that is necessary to establish proper controls. You now have the unsuspected 800-pound friendly gorilla monitoring. Taking into account the interests of the lobbying party versus the public reaffirms that the value is identified at the point of conflict. With any conflict, one party wants more than the other. Otherwise, there would be balance, settlement, and no conflict. Where there are groupings of people with common interests, skepticism must be present to create balance, rather than the development of one-dimensional thinking.

In an **authoritarian** government, state authority is imposed on many aspects of citizens' lives. Some central authority has the sole right to make and enforce laws or sanctions. The authoritarian form of government can be created under some delegated authority over a small component of governmental action or with the expansive power of an authoritarian government, such as North Korea. By delegating authority to an entity, without election, the government gives wide enough latitude in the operation of these entities, as they are not subject to external review or control. This can be done on a very limited basis. For instance, imagine if the power of overseeing traffic violation trials was granted to an arm of the Department of Motor Vehicles. In theory, the administrative law judge who might be hearing a case on a moving violation offense is actually an employee of the state Department of Motor Vehicles, where appeals of his or her decision are heard by a panel at the same agency. In many other cases involving the use of an administrative law judge, that judge may have been a former lawyer of the agency for which she/he works. This relationship between the judge and the agency for which he or she works may spur a lack of objectivity in the judicial process.

Enforcing speed limits, building code compliance, and tax payment are all examples of masked authoritarian thinking. If you don't pay taxes or if you fail to abide by a speed limit, there are the consequences of being fined and/or imprisoned. While we have separated the government forms, every one of them has to have an authoritative (rule-based) form, in one way or another, to maintain order. It is critical that the people subject to these rules find them fair. Another key element is that the control mechanisms remain transparent and open to interpretation with the appropriate flexibilities. The proper oversight of these same entities needs to include we emphasize reasonable checks and balances over the powers delegated to the entity. Notice the use of the word *reasonable*, since there is no absolute, sure-fire solution to stop fraud and mismanagement. It's a continual work in process.

The **totalitarian** form of government seeks to subordinate the individual to the state by controlling not only all political and economic matters, but also the attitudes, values, and beliefs of its population. The fraudster finds ways to control their surroundings and to develop enablers and detractors. Allowing this thinking does not work in managing fraud risk, as any locked or controlled environment is static and, with enough planning, can be overridden. In the authoritarion type of government the opposite is true.

In an **anarchic** form of government, there is no authority. This is a result of having no system or structure in place. The lack of structure is an impetus to law and disorder. Where no systems and structure exist, or where they do exist but are not monitored, the environment breeds potential for fraud and mismanagement. Fraudsters love to leave things unreconciled, in disarray and in a confused state. This all comes about when the proper levels of control and oversight are not put into place.

Countries such as Haiti and Somalia have government systems that have bordered on anarchy at certain points in time. At those times, government functions essentially ceased and the society fell into disarray. A common outcome is that essential government activities may then fall to nongovernmental organizations (NGOs), such as Doctors Without Borders, the United Nations, or UNICEF.

The intent of this discussion was not to expound upon a comprehensive list of all government forms, as there are forms of government at the local level in New Jersey to draw upon in the initial example. Reviewing these government form definitions creates an awareness of who is ultimately responsible, what the approval abilities of any given government are, and their core policy missions and objectives. Think of these as the perspectives/purpose of the government or public entity being examined in detail to understand the complex linkages and interrelated parties. The emphasis here is on the importance of the accountant, or an examining party, in gaining the correct understanding of the government and how it operates as a means to the end of preventing fraud and mismanagement.

Heaping more divisionalized[8] structure, such as authorities, special-purpose districts, and public-private partnerships on top of the already overriding structures of federal, state, and local government, creates the distraction that provides a fertile growing site for fraud and mismanagement, inadvertent or not. All of these entities have various powers that are delegated to them by some form of government charter or authorization, which can often conflict. For instance, given the structure of the U.S. Constitution, unless the federal government retains a right or role, then that role is ceded to the state government or, ultimately, the people. Counties, cities, and other local forms of government are creatures of the states, and, as such, their particular charters or legislative authorization limits their authority. Therefore, we find that a multilayered governmental structure is found in most regions of the United States. The bulk of these entities have revenue, fee or taxing of residents, workers or firms such as taxing itself, or fee-charging, bonding, and other spending via individual financial practices. These myriad separate entities create an ideal environment in which conflicting interests develop and can lead to the necessary divisiveness needed to enable fraud and mismanagement.

REVENUE FUNCTIONS WITHIN GOVERNMENTAL AND PUBLIC ENTITIES

In terms of understanding the role that these various governmental agencies play in our society and their ultimate potential for fraud and abuse, it is useful to examine and understand their revenue functions and funding (bonding) capability. No matter what form the governmental or public entity takes, it needs revenue sources to operate. Greed needs sources of fuel like money and power. There also needs to be a strong understanding of the leadership structure and any governmental protections afforded to the decision makers, specifically with respect to the abilities to override, veto, or circumvent the intended purpose to expose the potential opportunities for fraud and mismanagement. Greed needs to position itself by gaining access to value. From the perspective of fiscal discipline, the detachment of the supervision of a particular entity from legal or political oversight creates significant opportunity for mission creep, politicization of policy decisions, diversion of resources to pet projects, and an overall lack of responsiveness to needs outside of the organization. These pet projects are often created by divided interests or those that stand to benefit from public funding in some way. They typically look to find ways to circumvent the public interest, encourage red tape entanglement, and create the necessary distractions so that the special interest is fueled with the financing. These projects need to be held to the highest level of transparency if fraud and abuse are to be prevented. One method to increase supervision is the requirement of a referendum or some other voting initiative in order to approve the funds for a project.

For example, in the past, if a school budget referendum failed in New Jersey or the spending plan was not approved in the school elections, formerly held in April, the budget did not go back to the voters, but instead was sent for revision and approval to the municipal governing body to cut. What would then generally happen is that the board of education members would **lobby** the municipal government, with the help of teachers and parents (enablers), and this would lead to few if any cuts actually being made.

Now board elections are held in November in New Jersey, and as long as the board stays within a 2 percent levy cap in budget spending, the budget is automatically approved and there is no referendum. The past procedure came with the types of external pressures that are often outside the scope of a traditional financial analysis and need to be examined. It is these types of overrides that prevent the ultimate checks and balances (the vote) from occurring and undercut the role of the voters in creating accountability in the governmental organizations. The idea of appointed commissioners, elected officials, and other policy makers overriding the direct will of the people is no different than overriding the internal controls that ensure the credibility of the financial numbers. Vetoing represents the ability to override. Any override should be allowed to take place only when accompanied by the proper level of support. Management needs to have systems and structures in place to ensure transparency and accountability, as there are often conflicting views.

Sometimes entities are shared between states. Then a real question arises as to who has ultimate control and authority when beyond state borders. Without proper supervision and voter interest and awareness, government agencies can divert from their core mission and charter. Incredible as it may seem, this actually can and does happen for a variety of reasons. For instance, in the case of bi-state agencies, such as bi-state bridge operating authorities, which are agencies that have a federal charter to operate between states, we find that the federal government in 1987 repealed the oversight provision from federal law. This action, though, did not ensure that the individual states had the proper legislative oversight for the same agencies (GAO Report). This essentially left these agencies as sovereign entities in their realm of operation, answerable to no one and subject to their own whim as the only control action.

In most governmental roles, the oversight of government activities is done at the hands of elected officials. Elected officials, or politicians, serve at the will of the voters who elect them to office. The form of government, its responsibilities, and supervising authorities are key elements in understanding the potential for risk that can be created. While there is a lot of literature available in the field of political science that examines what motivates elected officials, a healthy understanding of the daily life of an elected official should be examined along with that politician's access to the government resources as well as that of his or her constituents. This is necessary to create a healthy level of skepticism that must be introduced to understand the meaning of Lord Acton's dictum "Absolute power corrupts absolutely." It is these often conflicting behavior signs that should generate red flags if the proper 800-pound friendly gorillas are monitoring.

For ease of discussion, let's assume that elected officials make decisions in light of the political desire to retain their office, or what those who examine matters in forensic accounting term *self-interest analyzing*. As such, we would expect them to make decisions that are politically expedient, or decisions that make most voters happy as opposed to unhappy. Other motivations—such as altruism, honesty, fairness, personal legacy, quest for higher office, desire for additional political power, desire to punish a political enemy or rival—are catalysts to various forms of corruption and government fraud. It is the study of these often-conflicting self-interested parties and motivations that provide the necessary information to develop systems and structures to improve government efficiency and prevent fraud. The more the public watches the actions that motivate and surround these trusted public servants, the greater the chance of preventing them from making bad choices.

In the case of public agencies, public authorities, and special-purpose districts, the **oversight** may be provided by appointed directors or supervisors with a significant bureaucratic layer protecting sitting directors from public scrutiny or control. Usually, these directors or supervisors are appointed by elected officials and serve for a given fixed term. Examining the relationships between these elected officials and the appointed party is a simple tool for preventing potential collusion or bias from occurring in the established system and structure.

The proper ethical tone needs to be established from the start by these parties. These same parties need to avoid bad choices by making decisions that have integrity, are independent, and are objective. Starting any process with a clear bias or special interest is setting a bad standard of practice. Unfortunately, our existing systems are rife with examples of appointees who lack objectivity. In fact, it is almost a requirement that appointees have some "special" connection with the elected official who appoints them to a particular commission. Further, it is commonly found that these directors have some link via prior government or private-sector service in the field of interest. Just examine the rotating door of the U.S. Treasury, the Federal Reserve, and Goldman Sachs to see this sort of potential for conflict of interest played out on a regular basis. Or you could just say "any one of a number of major investment banking firms."

Once appointed, there is generally a recall provision for these director-type positions. These positions may also be subject to political oversight. In practice, the elected officials often find it expedient to allow a significant amount of autonomy for these directors and to use this separation of power for political gain, thus claiming a lack of political control for unpopular decisions made by the authority or agency.

Another example of an entity that does not have a lot of voter or elected official control is the Federal Reserve System. The Federal Reserve Board functions with a high level of autonomy from the U.S. government due to its board structure[9] whereby the seven directors are appointed for a 14-year term on a rotating basis—one every two years. As such, the president of the United States has very limited control over the board and its policies, since directors, by law, may serve only one full term. Theoretically, the president, with just cause, can remove a director. But, based on our research, this has never been done. This high level of autonomy has come under fire in recent years, with the Reserve Board being sued over a lack of transparency in its financial dealings during the 2008 financial crisis.

Recently, Bloomberg Business[10] reported that more than half of Americans want the Federal Reserve abolished. Congress established the Federal Reserve Board in 1913 to promote national monetary goals and policy for the good of the people. This focus on national interest was intended to be promoted by its makeup of seven board members and 12 reserve bank presidents.

However, without independent audit and supervision, as well as a much more diversified brain trust, it appears that the over 50 percent of American people may be right to be concerned.

Entities with concentrated control, supervision, and policy are areas where the skepticism and systems and structures need to have a high level of accountability. The Federal Reserve Transparency Act of 2015 directs the Comptroller General (GAO) to complete, within 12 months of its enactment, an audit of the Board of Governors of the Federal Reserve System (Federal Reserve Board) and of the Federal Reserve Banks, and submit to congress, within 90 days of audit completion, a detailed report of audit findings and conclusions. Without this type of transparency and full disclosure rules in place to govern the Fed's monetary policy decision making, it is likely that the American taxpayers could continue to be on the hook for trillions in bailouts and loan defaults, as history has shown.

At the end of the day, there is generally some form of government sanction and control for these various agencies. The elected officials, or directors, at the helm advance the operational aspects of their mission. Government entities pass laws or rules. They set regulations over various aspects of society, which often have various inherent self-interests. They confirm treaties, regulate commerce, subsidize certain activities, contract for certain services, and allocate resources. In this book, the financial and revenue aspects of government activity are explored. So discussion of the rule/law-making aspect of government is limited and focus homes in more on the basics of government finance.

THE FEDERAL GOVERNMENT

"A wise and frugal Government, which shall restrain men from injuring one another, which shall leave them otherwise free to regulate their own pursuits of industry and improvement, and shall not take from the mouth of labor the bread it has earned. This is the sum of good government, and this is necessary to close the circle of our felicities."[11]

—*Thomas Jefferson, founding father, principal author of the Declaration of Independence, and third president*

Since the time Jefferson was president, the federal government has had a role in protecting one interest over another. There need to be assurances that government creates a balance between the interested parties that are paying and those receiving. The federal government's role in providing goods, services, and regulatory oversight is broad and pervasive in modern American society. Either by a direct provision of services or funding via federal programs—like Social Security and national defense—or by funding through state or local entities for national programs (highway funding and mass transit systems, for example), the federal government is a major component of governmental activity and, thus, the national economy. In many cases there is a high degree of fiscal federalism in federal spending. This is where funds are transferred to the states or local governments to provide either specified services or as a block, or comprehensive grant, with broad spending latitude at the local level. Funds collected at the federal level are disbursed back to state and local governments to administer federal programs or promote local programs consistent with federal goals. These funds may be made available as an unconditional transfer to the local government. In this instance, no real requirements are placed on the receiving government. A second method would be to pass through the funding on a conditional basis. In this instance, the receiving government is given a set of requirements and conditions that must be agreed to in exchange for the funding. An example is the New Jersey Department of Environmental Protection's Green Acres Program funding. A municipality is granted or loaned funds, at low interest, in order to preserve land for passive or active recreation. That funding is contingent upon an agreement with the municipality that the land must be preserved forever. No development may encroach upon the deeded property.

For instance, while the president will submit a budget proposal to Congress, Congress ultimately has the so-called power of the purse. The executive and legislative branches control the federal budget, with the budget proposal coming from the executive branch (president and White House), with final funding decisions made by the U.S. House of Representatives and the U.S. Senate. Final approval of the federal budget is subject to presidential veto. But that provides limited oversight on the overall spending package. The primary sources of funding for the federal government's budget are derived from a number of fees and taxes. The primary source is the federal personal income tax and the federal corporate income tax. In addition, receipts from special retirement contributions, such as Social Security and other excise taxes, or taxes on specific goods such as fuel taxes, provide over 95 percent of federal receipts.

TABLE 1.2   Federal Government Revenue Sources—1990 and 2011

Source of revenue	1990	2011 (Est.)	1990%	2011%
Individual income taxes	466.9	956.0	45%	44%
Corporation income taxes	93.5	198.4	9%	9%
Social insurance and retirement receipts	380.0	806.8	37%	37%
Excise taxes	35.3	74.1	3%	3%
Other	56.2	138.4	5%	6%
Total federal receipts	1,032.0	2,173.7	100%	100%

Table 1.2 provides an overview of the split of revenue sources by area in 1990 and 2011. The relative pattern of funding by source has remained very stable over the past 20 years. Tax and fee types and revenue policy are discussed in detail in Chapter 2.

A further confounding issue is the matter of federal spending—which has generally exceeded federal revenue sources. Figure 1.5 provides a perspective on the overall level of spending at the national level in the United States. You can see that the level of federal revenue collection has tended to fluctuate with the level of economic activity and thus has weakened in recessions and strengthened during economic booms. Federal spending has a quite different structural pattern, with strong growth in spending, averaging 5.57 percent per year from

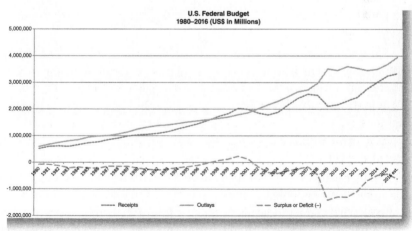

FIGURE 1.5   U.S. Federal Budget Receipts, Outlays, and Surplus/Deficit

1990 to 2010. That was caused by spending increases in statutory programs and a general bias toward overspending on the part of government officials. The net result is a general revenue shortfall in the federal budget that is funded through additional borrowing to attempt to cure the structural deficits. A structural deficit occurs when a country, state, municipality, or other entity posts a deficit. Expenditures greater than revenues equals deficit, regardless of how the economy is doing.

We will continually explore the anomalies that are encountered, the importance of planning for unexpected events, and how to avoid unanticipated expenditures. It is imperative in the establishment of any financially sound system that the assumptions used to determine revenues and government spending be constantly monitored and improved upon. It is the failure to have fail-safe practices in place in the event of a specific type of fiscal collapse that responds in a way that will cause harm. Failing to have well-established, reasonable reserves for the unexpected and future obligations, opens the floodgates of fiscal imbalance that can lead to mismanagement and fraud.

The more confusion caused by events like 9/11 and the subprime lending crisis, the more opportunities there are for potential mismanagement and fraud. Table 1.3 and Figure 1.5 for receipts, outlays, and surplus or deficit support the idea that revenue follows changes in events, whether they are positive, like the advancements in the economy or the technology boom, or negative, like the unprecedented real estate property appreciations prior to the subprime lending financial crisis. The oversight needs to be in place with rising positive advances as well as with negative declines. There is an imminent need to apply conservative and well-documented assumptions. That means lower revenue estimates must be made to lower higher costs in fiscal projections.

Inadequate monitoring of the necessary internal controls surrounding the various revenues continually slaps the taxpaying American with higher taxes. Those taxes and hidden, or ineffectively communicated, fees and/or other revenues feed the growing revenue needs of government to meet its established polices and agenda. The $1.032 trillion of inflation-adjusted receipts equals $1.776 trillion,[12] leaving a gap of $397 billion (2,174 less the 1,776), which represents 38.6 percent or an average of 3.5 percent (38.6/11) per year above the inflation-adjusted amount. Is it potential mismanagement or fraud? There is a need to develop systems and structures that provide accountability and transparencies to the average constituent. Table 1.3 provides an overview of the U.S. Federal Government receipts, outlays, and surplus or deficit from 1980 to 2016.

TABLE 1.3 Summary of Receipts, Outlays, and Surpluses or Deficits: 1980 to 2016

Year	Receipts	Outlays	Surplus or Deficit (−)
1980	517,112	590,941	−73,830
1981	599,272	678,241	−78,968
1982	617,766	745,743	−127,977
1983	600,562	808,364	−207,802
1984	666,438	851,805	−185,367
1985	734,037	946,344	−212,308
1986	769,155	990,382	−221,227
1987	854,287	1,004,017	−149,730
1988	909,238	1,064,416	−155,178
1989	991,104	1,143,743	−152,639
1990	1,031,958	1,252,993	−221,036
1991	1,054,988	1,324,226	−269,238
1992	1,091,208	1,381,529	−290,321
1993	1,154,334	1,409,386	−255,051
1994	1,258,566	1,461,752	−203,186
1995	1,351,790	1,515,742	−163,952
1996	1,453,053	1,560,484	−107,431
1997	1,579,232	1,601,116	−21,884
1998	1,721,728	1,652,458	69,270
1999	1,827,452	1,701,842	125,610
2000	2,025,191	1,788,950	236,241
2001	1,991,082	1,862,846	128,236
2002	1,853,136	2,010,894	−157,758
2003	1,782,314	2,159,899	−377,585
2004	1,880,114	2,292,841	−412,727
2005	2,153,611	2,471,957	−318,346
2006	2,406,869	2,655,050	−248,181
2007	2,567,985	2,728,686	−160,701
2008	2,523,991	2,982,544	−458,553
2009	2,104,989	3,517,677	−1,412,688
2010	2,162,706	3,457,079	−1,294,373
2011	2,303,466	3,603,056	−1,299,590
2012	2,449,988	3,536,951	−1,086,963
2013	2,775,103	3,454,647	−679,544
2014	3,021,487	3,506,114	−484,627
2015	3,249,886	3,688,292	−438,406
2016 est.	3,335,502	3,951,307	−615,805

Short term deficits in government budgets may occur due to unforeseen random events (storms, earthquakes and such), but it appears that the Federal deficit is based on normal spending patterns that are ongoing, exceed existing revenue sources and not unforeseen in any way.

Figures 1.6, 1.7, and 1.8 provide some quick reference points to monitor with respect to why the Federal Reserve needs to continue to print money and the federal government needs to continue to deficit spend (government spending in excess of revenue that are funded through borrowing rather than taxation). Both actions occur when there is a lack of accountability. These

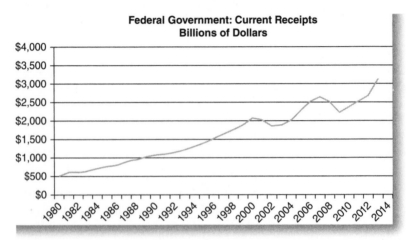

FIGURE 1.6   Federal government: current receipts

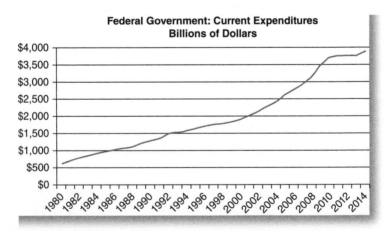

FIGURE 1.7   Federal government: current expenditures

offer those 10,000-foot general information views. The details are discussed as the potential areas where fraud and mismanagement can come into play are revealed.

Figure 1.6 illustrates how the receipt of money is an area where there is a need for monitoring and oversight. The revenues continue to grow, yet we continue to borrow and operate in deficit. The deficit is a result of outlays exceeding receipts.

Figure 1.8 provides a concise picture of the general net budgetary deficit conditions since 1980. Please note the location of the zero point on the graph—located toward the top of the graph. With the vast bulk of federal budgets over the past 30 years having a strong budget shortfall—26 of 30—only four had a surplus.

Thinking needs to be expanded in this area of spending from past and present expenditure focus to what is due in the future. Given the off-balance-sheet liabilities that can exist, such as pension and sick-time liabilities in the public entity, it is becoming necessary to monitor the working capital base needed to fund all past, present, and future spending to enable the government and public entity to remain an ongoing concern.

Figure 1.8 shows how allowing the public entity to operate in deficit breeds fraud and mismanagement. With a deficit you once again afford the fraudster a means to distract attention and assign blame. There is no money available, so the only solution is to raise taxes or fees. The people for whom you are raising taxes and/or fees have no say and, if they do, the next answer is bankruptcy. Bankruptcy is the great equalizer—who is going to pursue an entity that is bankrupt, as there are no funds?

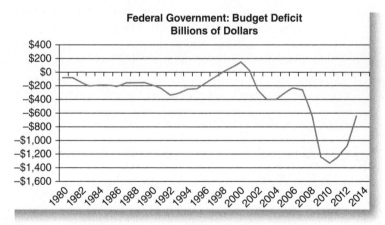

FIGURE 1.8 Federal government: budget deficit

The allowance (reserve) accounting concept is the idea whereby the public entity sets, or allocates, sums of money to be reserved for a specific purpose like collectability issues and or some other purpose that is based on someone's judgment. If the fraudster over- or underallocates, there are impacts to the budget and the opportunity becomes available to convert value for the fraudster's own benefit. Examine any reserves or allocations closely, especially those across related public entities.

Overspending is spending more than the expected or allotted amount, which enables fraud and mismanagement to occur. The entity should not be allowed to spend more than a line item and cover that budget deficit by transfer or other means. That deficiency should be required to be made up in the next budgetary period. While these entities have these systems in place, they are not preventive in terms of why the overspending occurred and what actions are being put in place to prevent reoccurrence. Proactive systems would monitor at the point the budget is overexpending and not wait till the year-end to correct.

If the money needs to come from somewhere else, the place it was taken from in the current year was either overbudgeted or needs to be adjusted in future periods. This type of one-shot adjustment at a specific period like year-end defeats the whole purpose of budgeting, which is to have people stay within their means and be accountable. If it is an extraordinary or unusual event that caused the over-expending, it should be documented and serve as the basis for adjustment in future periods. The people involved in the budget should be required to document the overage and/or surplus in the account. Only with sound budgeting and monitoring can the public entity prevent fraud and mismanagement. This simple exercise of correcting and monitoring spending and revenue shortfalls, if they exist, is a tool that is necessary to ensure that sound systems and structures are in place

This pattern of structural shortfalls in annual budgets leads to an accumulation of debt or shortfalls in funds needed by the U.S. federal government. Debt is one way the government can develop the needed working capital. The governmental or public entity simply issues bonds and notes. The federal government has generally favorable borrowing conditions that allows it to raise significant amounts of cash via the issuing of bonds that are well received by investors in the financial markets. Over time, the historical shortfalls lead to a structural national debt that now tops $18 trillion.

Figure 1.9 provides a perspective on the national debt from 1950. The national debt was at roughly $1 trillion in 1980. Even as late as 1986, the national debt was in the range of $2 trillion. Since 1986, the national debt has risen to $6 trillion in 2006 and now sits in the range of $18 trillion (2015).

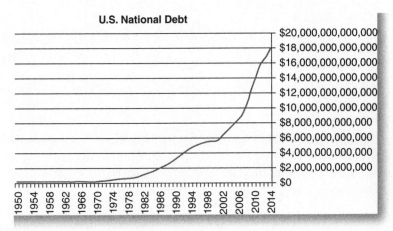

FIGURE 1.9 U.S. national debt

This year's estimated budget shortfall ($1.2 trillion for Fiscal Year 2015) is expected to compound this problem.

Debt can be manipulated, as it is debt and liability on a balance sheet; it is that debt that is sold or a transaction that is created to shift the debt so it can become a revenue source. Any organization using long-term borrowing as a means to fund operation shortfalls should be flagged and closely examined.

There are two types of governmental securities: nonmarketable securities such as savings bonds, various series (A, B, EE, etc.) bonds, and private shares, and marketable securities, such as Treasury bills and bonds that can be purchased and resold to the public. The nonmarketable securities, such as savings bonds, must be held until maturity and can't be resold to another party. Typically, these types of governmental securities are viewed as risk-free assets, since the actual return equals the expected return. Risk in any asset is viewed as the difference between the actual returns and the expected return. This makes the government security attractive to people who are averse to the risks associated with the stock market or other volatile investments. This creates a pool of money available to fund government debt. It is the ability of the public entity to borrow that creates opportunities for deficit spending and/or reallocation of funds for other purposes than the ones established by the government form.

Table 1.4 gives an overview of the funding categories of the national debt. Roughly one-third of the debt is held by government entities in nonmarketable securities—essentially IOUs from the federal government to other "trust funds," such as Social Security and federal pensions. The other two-thirds is held in tradable securities, with a significant portion held in bills and notes. Those bills and notes have a maturity of less than 10 years.

TABLE 1.4   Structure of the U.S. National Debt, January 2015

Marketable Securities		
Bills	$1,412,887	7.8%
Notes	$8,239,915	45.6%
Bonds	$1,589,165	8.8%
Treasury inflation-protected	$1,063,727	5.9%
Floating-rate notes	$163,991	0.9%
Federal financing band	$13,612	0.1%
Total marketable securities	**$12,483,297**	**69.0%**
Nonmarketable securities		
Domestic series	$29,995	0.2%
Foreign series	$264	0.0%
State and local government series	$113,684	0.6%
U.S. state savings	$175,638	1.0%
Government account series	$5,277,355	29.2%
Hope bonds	$494	0.0%
Other	$1,567	0.0%
Total nonmarketable securities	**$5,598,997**	**31.0%**
Grand total	**$18,082,294**	**100.0%**

Source: U.S. Treasury,
http://www.treasurydirect.gov/govt/reports/pd/mspd/2015/opds112015.pdf

Foreign governments and other international entities hold $6.1 trillion of the national debt. This is roughly one-third of the total debt outstanding. Obviously, these foreign owners and sovereign governments expect to have this value returned to them at some point in the future—and will also expect ongoing interest payments from our government to compensate them for lending us these funds.

Studying the people in an organization and their self-interested behaviors is important and forms the basis for developing sound systems and structures. Are these people risk averse or risk takers? How much debt has accumulated under their control? Understanding the reasons for the debt, matching the debt to the purpose, and making sure the financial information supports the debt are important design features in the system and structure that needs to be developed. Auditors tend to rely on management's (the politicians and the government employees) oversight of the internal controls with a historical verification perspective. A simple example of this issue is the entity's balance sheet, which shows the financial position of the government for a snapshot period at a given date. What this means is that it is expected to remain stagnant until the next update, which is often not as frequent as necessary to provide the entities with an accurate picture of the current financial position. This may be due to the varying timing of the receipt of revenues and other transactional events that occur in unsystematic ways. Given the significant lag in transactional events, opportunity for exposure to fraudulent activity exists during the intervals between those fiscal snapshots. Knowing the public entity's ability to pay debt and ensuring that all obligations are reflected, whether or not due for payment in the current period, is critical in the development of long-term cash flow planning to satisfy capital needs.

Fiscal Discipline

National governments differ from state and local governments in that the ability of the national government to borrow money extensively, or tax via inflation by printing money (seigniorage),[13] provides the national government with significantly more fiscal flexibility. This flexibility has been demonstrated in recent years, as the U.S. national debt has increased dramatically while the federal government has not faced any major fiscal constraints from outside forces. Rather, the only real limitation has arisen from internal political unrest that came from the politicization of the debt ceiling for the federal government. While it's rare, ratings companies do sometimes report downgrading the U.S. debt rating. The most recent downgrade transpired in 2011, when Standard & Poor's took the U.S. bond credit rating from AAA to AA+. This change appeared to have little impact on borrowing ability or interest costs for the U.S. government. The point is that the U.S. Treasury remains just as safe as it was before the downgrade. The downgrade was apparently a response to the federal government increasing the debt ceiling. The federal government is giving the arrogant perception that it is too big to fail, and therefore the downgrade is symbolic in that it recognizes the fact that there is no one to bail out the federal government (unlike the federal government's bail out of AIG and other banking institutions).

The downgrade does in fact reflect a deteriorating financial condition and should not be taken lightly. Downgrades often lead to higher interest rate borrowing costs and can impede the ability to raise funds through future bond issues. These financial indicators need to be closely examined.

Understanding this flexibility in borrowing also exposes a potential to the system. Financial entities may attempt to get the national government to function as a backstop "lender of last resort" to preserve institutions. By having the ability to expand its borrowing volume with little impact on bond rating creates the illusion that this backstop is low cost or free. Private entities may then attempt to leverage against these public resources.

Understanding arbitrage is critical in identifying and/or preventing fraud and mismanagement. Arbitrage is the simultaneous purchasing and selling of an asset in order to profit from a difference in the price that occurs between two or more participants. The term *tulip mania* refers to a large economic bubble, or tulip, that occurs when asset prices deviate from their intrinsic value. The term came into play when tulips were being sold at prices significantly above the tangible value as a result of the expectations and demands associated with these tulips. So what happens when the tulip bursts? Who was crazier, the tulip lover who refused to sell for a small fortune or the one who was willing to splurge?[14] Typically, it is the government that is called in to bail us out of a financial crisis related to speculative bubbles and uncollateralized optimism. So is it these often external influences that exist outside the public entity that need to be watched and monitored before the actual burst takes place. This creates proactive forces that prevent the misuse of debt to enable fraud and mismanagement.

These leveraging-type actions, such as using credit without tangible collateral, are available to government. If left unchecked, they pose significant financial risks and create opportunities for fraud and mismanagement. Basically, the Federal Reserve and the government can purchase an asset by paying on account, like in the margining of a stock, by making a small down payment and borrowing the rest. This type of leveraging fails to collateralize and create tangible deliverables but, rather, relies on intangible or intrinsic ones. It is a breeding ground for financial crisis and structural imbalance in our financial system. It requires significant oversight to manage unsustainable growth spurts that are perceived to occur, giving the false perception of continuing indefinitely. The old adage "If it seems too good to be true, it probably is" comes to mind.

Structure of Federal Debt

Government spending policies set the scale of the national debt and programs and the revenue tools used to fund current and capital operations. Sound fiscal policy dictates that debt be used to support capital expenditures and that current revenue should fund current expenditures. Borrowing to fund current expenditures is not considered fiscally responsible. However, at the federal government level, this is common practice.

A second consideration is the term structure of the debt, where, in a fiscally responsible organization, one would suggest that the length of term on the debt should match to some degree the length of life span of the asset purchased. As such, for long-term capital investment, a long-term structure is rational and, for short-lived assets, or current expenditures, should be funded with a shorter repayment term. Proper fiscal planning would dictate that a debt be funded with a structure of payments that will allow the debt to be retired with a reasonable and affordable payment. Obviously, one can take on such a high level of debt that it is unlikely to be paid off in the term that is the basis of the spending, as is the case with the federal government. In such a case, it is logical to see funding terms that reflect the estimated time to amortize the debt.

In a February 2015 U.S. Treasury briefing, the Treasury Borrowing Advisory Committee reported that the weighted-average maturity of the U.S. debt portfolio in 2015 had increased to 68 months, from a low of 49 months in 2008. This new ratio compares favorably to our historical pattern of weighted-average debt maturity being in the 60- to 70-month range from 1985–2004. However, they also reported that 67 percent of the U.S. debt portfolio was maturing within five years and only 13 percent had maturity greater than 10 years. This is in sharp contrast to peer countries of the United States, such as the United Kingdom, where 34 percent of the debt will mature within five years and 46 percent had a maturity greater than 10 years. It is obvious that the U.S. federal government has a structure of borrowing that is not in line with the long-term financing of this debt, and that exposes the U.S. government to refinancing risk. As stated in the Treasury briefing, the U.S. debt situation is concerning, considering that "near term rollover risk is higher than other major government bond issuers."[15]

Given that the national debt now sits at a multi-trillion-dollar level and the federal government continues to run budgetary shortfalls, it seems that the appropriate term structure of the national debt would be funded in the 30- to 50-year range. This would raise the annual costs of funding the debt by forcing reduction through required amortization of principal but would limit the exposure of the government to interest rate spikes that could drive the cost of the debt even higher. The existing national debt is currently funded with a relatively short-term structure—with 67 percent of the debt requiring refinancing within five years, according to the February 2015 U.S. Treasury Borrowing Advisory Committee reporting as cited in footnote 20 of the report. It is this type of balloon financing structure that requires refunding of debt prior to payoff. This is no different than if a homeowner had a note that was ballooning (maturing) in five years. One major concern in balloon-type financing is the potential risk caused by interest rates going up—where the borrower is at risk for not being able to meet these higher costs. Government is subject to the same types of risks. The U.S. Department of Treasury knows this is a matter of concern. Affordable ways of funding the national debt have been explored. In February 2015, the Treasury Borrowing Advisory Committee reviewed the opportunity to increase the weighted-average maturity of the national debt, due to the current market conditions. The reality is that long-term borrowing rates are currently not much higher than short-term rates.

Yet, based upon the existing term structure of interest rates, as shown in Figure 1.10, if the U.S. Treasury tried to shift the maturity date on the national debt, a rather significant increase in borrowing costs would follow. However, doing so would provide a more sustainable and prudent funding base for the national debt. In general, it is anticipated that longer-term rates will be somewhat higher than short- and medium-term rates. This is due to the fact that lenders are taking on more risk to lend for an extended period of time. This difference in interest rates would impact the cost of borrowing if there is an increase in the terms of the loan or bond. For example, if the funding was just shifted for the one- to five-year maturity segment of publicly held debt ($8.2 trillion in January 2015, or 45.6 percent of the national debt) to 20-year average maturity, the cost of borrowing for the public segment of this one category would rise from $85 billion a year to $197 billion. That's an increase of $112 billion each year. By not implementing this funding change, there is a saving on current expenditures for borrowing costs. But Americans could face a spike in costs in future years if the cost of borrowing goes higher.

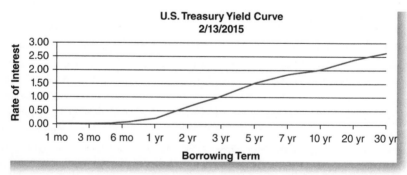

FIGURE 1.10   U.S. Treasury yield curve, 2/13/2015
Source: http://www.treasury.gov/resource-center/data-chart-center/interest-rates/Pages/TextView.aspx?data=yield

Focusing on maturity risk—not only in terms of matching the assets and liability maturities but also with regard to the governmental inflows and outflows of cash—is critical in preventing potential fraud and mismanagement. A debt of $18 trillion was not incurred overnight. Only with reasonable maturity matching can a long-term solution be developed to address the huge debt problem many governmental units face.

STATE GOVERNMENTS

State governments provide many useful functions that, in some cases, are rooted in the colonial charters granted prior to the Revolutionary War. Given the depth of these roots in the history of the United States, there is some variation in the organizational structure and practices by state. We will attempt to provide a basic overview of state government and the various financial practices that are generally observed across the United States. Organizational structures and practices may vary by state and region.

State governments, in general, are organized with an elected governor, or head of the executive branch, and two legislative bodies—typically an assembly and a senate. There are, however, some U.S. states that have unicameral forms of government that are operated under the umbrella of one legislative chamber. Unlike the federal government, both state assembly and senate bodies are representative of population, as opposed to the U.S. Senate, in which each state is represented by two senators regardless of population. These three groups—executive (governor), assembly, and senate—formulate a state budget and spending/taxation plan for the particular state.

States vary in terms of their particular laws and taxes, as they have varying competing interests and goals. For instance, states like Delaware function as tax havens, with favorable corporate taxes. Others, such as Alaska or Kansas, may favor certain industries, such as farming, mining, and petroleum. Therefore, our discussion here is a general one and limited in applicability to any given state. In terms of financial resources, the state governments generally rely on income taxes, sales taxes, excises taxes, and fees as primary sources of revenue. These funding sources may be dedicated for special purposes or poured into the general fund. In the United States, there is significant interest in special-purpose funds, as opposed to general fund sources. With that comes an overriding focus on taxes as dedicated from users for particular purposes. This is in sharp contrast to the European model, where there is limited ability to segregate revenue for special purposes and most revenue pours into the general fund.

Once the revenue has been collected, there is an allocation process in which political powers-that-be decide on the allocation of resources. In the case of the general fund, the political discussion can be intense, where various pet projects and special interests are duking it out for the same fixed pool of funds. For dedicated sources of funding, even those provisions are not absolute. State legislators are experts at breaking open "lockboxes" that contain dedicated funds. Finally, the state governments generally have a bonding capability that can be used to finance revenue shortfalls.

State bonding capability is not unlimited and is tied to revenue sources that are dedicated to repaying the bonds. Bonds are not a revenue source. They are a source of cash flow, but they need to be considered as a revenue-smoothing tool to provide for uneven spending patterns on government projects.

State-level borrowing is limited, to some degree, by state statute. These limits can be set by the state constitution or by legislative act. In a number of states, the limit is set based upon a percentage of the value of all property in the state. Other states limit the level of spending on debt service (the amount paid for principal and interest on borrowing annually), which effectively caps the debt level for a given bond rating. Some states have no expressed cap on debt but have historical patterns of borrowing that function as general guidelines for debt issuance. Some states limit borrowing to some ratio of the total general fund revenue and/or may limit the term of borrowing to some maximum number of years. Finally, certain states require voter referendum to issue debt. As we can see, there is considerable variation in the levels allowed, authority for issuing, management, and maturity of state debt.

The level of debt is also capped from a functional perspective based upon the lenders and the bond rating appetite. Given that the rate of interest charged is based upon the overall state bond rating and the financing duration, you can see that as a government gets further in debt, the cost of borrowing tends to increase. Correspondingly, as the financial future of the state seems brighter and revenues improve, the cost of borrowing falls. States have to manage this relationship in a complex and dynamic way, balancing borrowing costs and bond volume against their natural aversion to raising taxes or fees.

As illustrated in Figure 1.11, as the quality of bonds declines, the cost of borrowing goes up—across all maturities. If an entity has a AAA rating from Moody's or S&P, one would expect to pay 1.65 percent for 10-year notes, 2.45 percent for 20-year bonds, and 2.60 percent for 30-year bonds. As quality declines, the rates increase. As an entity adds to the total outstanding debt or

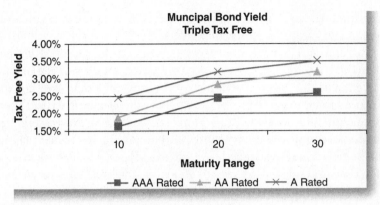

FIGURE 1.11   Municipal bond yield, triple tax free

the revenue sources decline, the bond rating will decline, due to the concern about ability to pay. This then adds to the financial burden of holding an existing level of debt. That, in turn, curtails the ability to issue further bonds if the revenue pool is fixed. This relationship functions as a built-in limiter on government entities and caps their issuance of additional debt. For a fixed 20-year debt of $100 million, the cost of borrowing goes from $2.45 million annually for AAA-rated securities to $3.20 million annually for A-rated securities—a 30.6 percent difference in the cost of borrowing. Please note: These costs examined here are only for the best categories of borrowing—the "A" quality; there are lower grades of bonds such as B rating all the way down to D, with similar breakdowns inside each group. Thus, even at the high investment grade level, there is considerable variation in borrowing rates and this may be even greater in lower-grade issues.

 ## LOCAL GOVERNMENTS

"All politics is local," as former Speaker of the U.S. House of Representatives Tip O'Neill was known to be fond of saying. Local government provides many key services and goods to local communities that are in many cases poorly understood by local voters. Local government can be grouped into county and local municipal government. Counties, in many cases, are rooted in the colonial period with the establishment of many dating back to the mid-seventeenth century on the East Coast of the United States. County government may be organized under a board of elected "freeholders," who supervise local county-level spending. Cities or towns have various terms for their leaders. *Mayor* is a common title for the top official, with *aldermen, council members, commissioners,* and *committee members* being the titles of some of the legislative body members. The various forms of government were listed earlier in this chapter. There are various forms of authority, including those in which executive power lies within a committee, for example, most schools in New Jersey operate independently from Municipal or county government. Thus, looking at the ethical tone at the top of these public entities and who has access to the resources, whether it be goods and/or services or value created by these goods and services, is important in any structure, especially on the local level.

Local municipal government comes in many organizational forms, usually in step with any given municipality's size. There are cities, boroughs, townships, villages, and hamlets within larger municipalities. In addition, there may be independent school, transportation, water, sewage, and other boards for local needs. In some cases, the city government overlays the county government and is coterminous—such as in San Francisco, which is both a county and a city. In New York, the city government overlays five counties and assumes most county functions under the city government. In the case of functional boards, such as transportation, these entities may function across county and municipal boundaries and serve and tax across the region.

The role and scope of local government have been hotly debated in the past 100 years in the United States. Local government suffers as the last in a great line of government entities that, in many cases, have rule-making authority. In general, municipal governments are creatures of the state. This means that local governments are many time subjected to comply with additional federal and state laws and agency policies. A simple example is environmental regulation, for which the federal, state, and even county government can promulgate rules that must be implemented by local government. Examples of such environmental regulation are recycling, water quality, leaf composting, and storm-water runoff. The local government may be charged with implementation and the accompanying cost to implement various regulations without discussion or power to refuse. As such, the local government may be "crammed down" on with what is known as an unfunded mandate.

Further, the types of services provided by local government vary considerably across the nation and even within states. Hospitals, public health facilities, libraries, museums, mass transit systems, courts, roads, drainage systems, parks, police, firefighters, ambulance services, recreation, schools, building regulations, public housing, public open space, recycling, pools, beaches, and many more things fall within the possible range of local public services provided in any given town.

Selecting that mix of services to provide and also the funding mix of revenue tools to provide for long-term support of these systems is an ongoing discussion in most municipalities. What is deemed "necessary" and "critical" is the basis of many public debates and exposes the conflicting interests. Suffice it to say, many "necessary" expenditures are not all that necessary and many "critical" services are not always of a true crisis nature. It is common to see mission creep and scope issues crop up in local political debate. Typically, the management of local government will continue to see expanded roles for their organization that are far broader than their true mission. Every public service typically requires capital investment and training for staff. Be it a tactical assault team for the police, expanded firefighting skills, training and/or equipment, a new sport, or even an additional language class offered at the local high school, each expands the role of government and typically incurs costs. Most bureaucrats are resistant to reducing their functional roles to accommodate change. This leads to more, not less or stable, capital and operations costs—more roads, more sports, more equipment. All told, costs of municipal services end up rising. Visit your local or county government and suggest abandoning anything—a road repaving, a wanted tennis court … whatever. Experience the process. It's not easy.

Considerable power rests at the local level, with many key planning and functional issues left to the local governments. With funding issues, more and more responsibilities will be initiated by the federal and state entities, as they divest themselves of the funding responsibilities that are often attached to these policy mandates. In particular, the determination of land use matters at a local level is of critical interest in terms of power and corruption. Major private projects see their most significant political support or opposition at the local level. Surprising to many, major private projects, such as the building of a shopping mall, may have very little federal or state oversight, leaving the supervision and policy decisions to the local government. Interestingly, some of these decisions may be optimal for a given local government, but may impose significant direct public costs or external burdens on other local, state, or even federal entities.

Yet local governments' elected officials and bureaucrats may lack sophistication or the scale of operation to hire experts in all areas. So they may rely on the skills of hired consultants, local knowledge, or past practice to choose a course of action. This creates a political operating environment that can be a prime breeding ground for corrupt practices. In the best-case scenario, the local government makes a wise choice based on good counsel from prudent providers or staff. In the worst-case scenario, the local government relies on poor advice and information in rendering a decision and/or relies on a corrupt provider to guide the entity.

PUBLIC AGENCIES

Public agencies are typically authorized by national, state, or local governments with some statutory responsibilities that leave them somewhat detached from the elected officials in terms of day-to-day operations. A public agency is defined as "the government of the United States; the government of a state or political subdivision thereof; any agency of the United States, a state, or a political subdivision of a state; or any interstate governmental agency."[16] A **public agency** is typically affiliated with a local branch of state, county, local (municipal), or federal government. A **private agency**, which is usually a state-licensed entity, either nonprofit or for-profit, serves as an agent to a government entity. An example is the private inspection facilities in New Jersey that perform car inspection services.

Public agencies are typically chartered to provide some limited service or supervision that is specified in the organizing documents. These agencies can also have powers delegated to them by federal or state statute, and must operate within the scope of particular laws and enforcement provisions. These entities then usually operate under an appointed director, typically appointed by the president of the United States for federal agencies. The Senate, in some cases, may confirm the director. Once appointed, the director and administrators may have broad latitude in decision making and policy actions, with limited recourse by elected officials to discipline the agency or remove the director. Finally, the agency may have rule-making authority, which essentially gives it the power to make regulations. Those regulations have the teeth of actual laws and, as such, the agency can then enforce rules with legal authority.

The reason for separation of elected officials from agency control is an interesting and complex matter. Some agencies are established to remove the day-to-day operations of critical government functions from the highly politically charged environment of the statehouse, town hall, or capitol. Issues such as national security may guide us to seek the assistance of a structure such as the Central Intelligence Agency (CIA). By operating as a separate agency, the

CIA director can exert considerable control and operational guidance over the organization without seeking direct approval from the president or Congress. The need to remove the agency from political entanglements in policy may also guide us toward an agency structure. Independent watchdog agencies such as the Federal Trade Commission (FTC), the Environmental Protection Agency (EPA), and the Securities and Exchange Commission (SEC) may be organized as independent agencies, in part, to insulate the rule-making and enforcement activities from the political sphere of government. As further protection from political interference, for federal government agencies that are considered regulatory in nature such as the FTC or SEC, it is policy that their agency heads can be removed from office only with good cause. In agencies that are not considered regulatory, such as the EPA, the director serves at the will of the president.

One key control measure over an agency is the question of funding. A government agency may have a high degree of autonomy in terms of daily action, but it still needs to obtain funding for operations and capital projects. This generally requires interaction with elected officials and offers some degree of operational control over the agency, as there is generally interest on the part of the director to obtain requested funding. This gives rise to the public budget hearing that occurs in many cases, with elected officials grilling directors and agency staff over policy and operational decisions.

Agencies responsible for taxation and fee-based operations have considerably more latitude in terms of their interaction with elected officials. If the revenue created by their taxes or fees is sufficient to fund all or part of agency operations, then the agency may well have the economic power to avoid serious supervision and control by elected officials. For instance, the General Services Administration (GSA) of the federal government functions as the "government landlord" through the Public Building Service (PBS) arm of GSA for federal buildings. Federal agencies that occupy GSA properties pay rental fees to the PBS and that revenue is then used to pay for the building operations and capital improvements. In addition, the GSA operates the federal vehicle pool of 210,000 vehicles, with individual agencies paying for the use of these vehicles.

It is important to consider that the agency does not have to have a net income (known as profit in the private sector) to benefit from revenue and fees. Generally, an agency with significant revenues and cash flows can divert a segment of that revenue to fund particular projects that may be politically unpopular and difficult to fund through a budget allocation from the elected officials. By taking advantage of an internal revenue stream, one may be able to create a larger shortfall in a politically strong area (say, the GSA vehicle pool—a real no-brainer for the elected officials in terms of funding) while funding the controversial project without recourse to the general budgetary allocation.

At agencies with a high degree of financial independence and strong agency statutory authority, the level of independence from oversight may be astounding. This autonomy may be most easily shown by the chair and board of the Federal Reserve System (Fed), as stated in their own policy.

"The Federal Reserve Act requires the Federal Reserve Board to submit written reports to Congress containing discussions of the conduct of monetary policy and economic developments and prospects for the future." This report, dubbed the *Monetary Policy Report*,[17] "is submitted semiannually to the Senate Committee on Banking, Housing and Urban Affairs and to the House Committee on Financial Services, along with testimony from the Federal Reserve Board Chair."

This requirement is achieved by reporting twice a year to these committees. However, the Fed operating policies are largely independent of any political discussion, as the Federal Reserve does not seek funding from Congress. It actually pays a net dividend from Federal Reserve bank operations to the U.S. Treasury as a residual payment after all Federal Reserve System costs are paid. In 2012, this amounted to $88.9 billion paid to the U.S. Treasury. Thus, any significant expenditure deemed necessary by the Fed board or regional banks is deducted prior to this transfer. This simple fact may explain the generally informative, but emotionally detached, presentation made by the Fed chair to Congress. He or she is well aware that her agency has little to no risk in terms of budget or practice due to the testimony given. The head of an agency without revenue powers knows full well that his or her answers may subject his or her agency to political retribution through the budget process.

 ## PUBLIC AUTHORITIES

The Office of the New York State Comptroller defines "public authorities" as corporate instruments of the state created by the legislature to further public interests. These entities develop, operate, and maintain some of New York's most critical infrastructure, including roads, bridges, and schools.[18] Public authorities are typically authorized by nation, state, or local authority and are usually chartered to provide some limited service or role in a given region. Federal authorities are chartered by the federal government and include authorities such as the Tennessee Valley Authority—an electric power, waterway, and economic development entity. State authorities include many mass transportation authorities, airport operators, turnpike authorities, power systems, water systems, sewage systems, and the like. Local governments may band together and seek state charter for local authorities as needed. They may also provide separate boards to supervise particular government entities, such as housing authorities.

An authority is a completely separate branch of government with no operational ties to the organization from which it is created. It is different than an agency in two key respects: It may have a budget that is separate from the authorizing entity, and it may have the ability to issue its own debt. The New York State Comptroller's office[19] defines the differences between state agencies and authorities as follows:

> Unlike traditional State agencies, many authorities conduct business outside of the typical oversight and accountability requirements for operations including, but not limited to, employment practices, contracts and procurement procedures, and financial reporting.

Key aspects of all of these public authority entities are that they are typically run by a charter (compact) and that they have a board of directors, a chairperson, and executive management. Included in the charter is, in most cases, the authority to charge fees and provide for the issuing of bonds, usually with some range of cap on the amount of bonds issued. The bonding limits set boundaries on the activities of these entities and protect the chartered entity from unlimited activities or scale with respect to the authority. The role and scope of authorities is considerable, and governments across the United States have ceded considerable amounts of government function and power to public authorities.

In December 2014, the comptroller of the State of New York reported that there were 1,180 public authorities in New York State alone with a wide range of power and issues related to policy and supervision delegated to these entities. This growth in authorities in the state is dramatic. It started with the first, the Port Authority of New York and New Jersey, in 1921, and saw an average increase of 12.67 authorities per year over the following 93-year span. These authorities employed 153,502 people and collected $59.8 billion in revenue in 2012.

Public authorities have a number of odd characteristics that make them similar to government in some aspects and private corporations in other ways. Generally, they have some form of financial and activity reporting but may claim exemption from various forms of government oversight. Further, their unique status may in fact preclude the public from pursuing the entity in court under unclear statutes and various aspects of government sovereignty. In some cases, federal and state law is ambiguous, or even silent, with respect to public authorities.

GOVERNMENT VIA CONCESSIONS, FRANCHISES, AND CONTRACT WORK

This is not an actual form of government, but in fact consists of private entities that act under the governmental umbrella to provide goods and services. These arrangements are authorizations for work that occur under all of the forms of government previously specified. Government does not function only through its standing agencies and departments. Government, in many cases, hires outside private corporations and firms to provide government services. These private firms may be hired in a number of ways to serve public needs, including straight billing of fees for service, standing contracts that are renewed regularly via resolution, and ongoing concession. All of these modes of purchase or lease have limitations and challenges for the governmental entity, and proper standards of practice need to be applied in the contracting process. Appropriate performance standards and enforcement provisions need to be included in the contract. In addition, the governmental entity needs to be prepared and equipped to hold the contract provider accountable as needed to maintain compliance. Failure to include these clauses or failure to act in situations of nonperformance exposes the governmental entity to additional risk.

Some of the classic forms of government corruption involve the use of private contract abuse to funnel money from government sources to politically connected private-sector firms. A classic example of this is the Tweed Courthouse in New York City, which was constructed in the 1870s using various corrupt and connected firms. Costs rose from an initial estimate of $250,000 to a final cost of more than $12 million ($200 million in today's dollars), and construction dragged on for 20 years, from 1861 to 1881. The key reason for these overruns was the extensive graft and kickbacks that were paid to individuals connected to William Magear "Boss" Tweed of Tammany Hall—the local party boss.

Another more recent phenomenon is the migration of public ownership into private entities that function under government license or franchise. These entities are given a contract to provide some form of service or operation under the auspices of the franchising governmental entity. For example, in some states and also in European countries, toll roads have been transferred or created by private entities that have been given some franchise agreement. The control over the entity is limited and is largely dictated through the contract terms of the operating agreement.

Are these governmental entities or private enterprises? A number of interesting questions arise. Given their government sanction and contract, it could easily be argued that their activities should be subject to public scrutiny and public bidding laws. The problem occurs when the controls break down and public interest is not there. Given that they function under sanction of the government, it should be determined whether or not the service provided is exclusive to the selected firm and other firms are excluded from the market. These authorities that tend to "float under the radar" bear less accountability.

Oversight and proper contract design is the key to a successful concession contract. These concession contracts have many detailed terms and have to be negotiated with an eye to detail and with clear objectives. Contracts can be deficient in key details and also potentially can undervalue the asset leased. For example, in 2008, the city of Chicago sold a concession to operate parking meters in downtown Chicago. The concession agreement was for a term of 75 years, and the concessionaire was the same firm that leased a number of the public parking garages in Chicago. This contract was subject to an investigation by Chicago's Office of the Inspector General in 2009. The report found that Chicago had been paid roughly 46 percent less for the lease of the asset than the full value of $2.13 billion.

Perhaps some of the lessons to learn with regard to private concessions may come from outside the United States. European governments have a long history of providing public services through concession agreements. In many countries, the history and framework of Roman law discourages the use of a quasi-governmental agency such as a public authority that would be standard practice in the United States. Projects are undertaken via either the public sector (true government) or the private sector (private company). The European governments have also developed laws and standards of practice to ensure contract compliance and protection of the public. In particular, governments may place constraints on the length of concession contracts, impose limitations on increases in prices for concession services, and set operational quality standards. We explore these practices in later chapters.

 ## PUBLIC-PRIVATE PARTNERSHIPS

A partnership is an organization in which two or more entities manage and operate a project. Both are equally responsible for the debts incurred by the project. This business relationship is between a private-sector company and a governmental agency for the purpose of completing a project that will serve the greater good of the public. Public-private partnerships (also known as PPP, P3, or P^3) can be used to finance, build, and operate projects for things such as public transportation, parks, and convention centers. Financing a project through a public-private partnership can allow a project to be completed sooner or make it more financially feasible.

This PPP concept is currently all the rage in Washington and in various state capitals. This model of providing public services relies on a private-sector firm to organize and perform the work under contract with the governmental entity. The form and relationship can be complex, with various portions of the work provided by the private sector and with various roles for government incorporated into the project.

PPP infrastructure-type projects can be grouped into four broad categories as identified by the World Bank: management and operating contracts, leases, concessions, and joint ventures. Using these general forms, government can contract to have a private entity perform a given management service, can lease or otherwise transfer the operations of a government asset to a private operator, or can partially or fully divest itself of ownership of a government asset.

Typical examples of divesting or joint ventures would be a government selling or leasing a noncore asset that can be operated as a private entity through the use of fee revenue or some sort of government payments. In many areas, the government has built a utility service—such as electricity, water, or sanitary sewers. The government can maintain these assets through the use of public funds—or in some cases can decide that it is optimal to lease or outright sell the asset to a private operator. This operator then has a contract to provide a given level of service or it may fall under additional regulation—such as public utility service law—that controls its prices and service levels. This may be important for government entities that have limitations on their capital spending and bond issuance. Thus, by transferring the asset to a private owner, selling a part ownership in the project, or leasing out the assets, they can then tap into the ability of the private partner to borrow and invest in the asset.

The most basic form of concession is privatization of an existing public asset—such as a toll road or electrical grid. This is called a *Brownfield* project— as the project has been constructed and is in place and operating. This type of project is very attractive to private investors if the terms of the lease are reasonable, because they are purchasing or leasing what is known as a going concern. A going concern has a known volume of sales and usage, a known cost structure, and known operating conditions. As such, the potential private leaser of the property is better able to evaluate the expected cash flows and capital needs—and this gives greater value to the project.

As an alternative, governments can grant concessions to construct new facilities or assets. These types of contracts are known as *Greenfield* projects—as these assets are being built on a "green field" (i.e., one that has not previously been built on). Given that the asset is not yet in place, operating conditions, costs, and revenues are much less established. Further, the costs of construction are unknown and the potential exists to have significant cost overruns or delays in the project. As such, private leaseholders are going to discount the value of the project to account for this risk and will generally negotiate for more favorable terms in the lease contract to protect the private firm from unforeseen outcomes. These could include government financing of the project, government guarantees, and progress payments for meeting certain construction milestones.

In all of these models of PPP, the government sector has to perform a careful analysis of the value components that are being transferred to the private sector. In many cases, governments look to transfer assets in a poor state of repair, as that is the situation that motivated them to consider privatization—a desire to avoid the significant capital investment to upgrade existing facilities. In those cases, the contract terms will be reflective of the poor asset conditions. If the government is leasing an asset in a good state of repair and one with a strong revenue stream, then the value of the lease in terms of payments to the government should be high. It is very important to be aware that the terms and conditions that are specified in the contract will be subject to minute analysis by the private-sector partner—and they will expect to hold the government to all the terms of the lease. Further, one should expect that the private leaseholder will try to take all liberties allowed in the contract to minimize costs and maximize cash flow to the private operator.

Be aware that private-sector experts are more than willing to work in the service of government and public organizations. However, private firms participate based upon the desire for revenue and ultimately, profit. As such, projects need to provide a good level of projected return if one wishes to engage the help of private firms. PPPs are not a magic solution to revenue or cost issues in the provision of government services, but they offer alternative methods of project delivery and operations.

One of the more interesting forms of PPP is known as DBOM in the world of transportation and public infrastructure. **DBOM** stands for **Design, Build, Operate, and Maintain**. In this model of PPP, the private operator receives a contract to bring a capital project from the design phase all the way through the operation and maintenance of the project for a period of time. In traditional contracting for a capital project, a single firm under government contract may complete the design, and then the project is publically bid for construction. After completion of the project, the asset is turned over to the government entity for operations and maintenance. In a DBOM contract, the government issues a contract with general performance goals for a system. It allows contractors to bid for the whole package of designing the system in detail, building it, and then operating and maintaining it for a fixed period. In return, the private owners would receive revenue from the project and/or a series of payments for the construction and services provided. The operating and maintenance contract has a limited period of service and after completion of that period the asset is generally turned over to the government entity for a new contract to be reformed or for municipal or other potential operating purposes.

As an example of this concept, in 1996, New Jersey Transit contracted to construct a new light rail system in Hudson and Bergen counties in the state of New Jersey. This system, called the Hudson–Bergen Light Rail System (HBLR), opened in 2000. As opposed to the traditional method of providing rail transit services with agency-owned assets and operations, the HBLR was built using a DBOM contract, with the firm 21st Century Rail being awarded a contract to construct and operate the system for a period of 15 years from the start of operations. The private operator was then responsible for the staffing, operations, and other maintenance costs for the system during this contract period. This allows significant flexibility in terms of operating and staffing practice as compared to traditional government operations.

Overall, this method of project delivery is seen as one that provides the correct set of incentives for the private contracting firm, if the contract terms are well-defined. Given that the designer of the project is the same entity that will build and operate the project, cost and design decisions should be made that reflect the overall long-term cost of delivering the service. For instance, cutting corners and doing shoddy work on a component of the project—say, a bridge section on the line—would represent a significant financial risk to the DBOM contractor. That's because the failure of the bridge or significant repair costs would be borne by the DBOM contactor. In sharp contrast, if a contract is just a construction contract, the private contractor has little incentive to ensure that the project components will be in good working order past a relatively short warranty period (generally one to five years). Also, the DBOM contractor has incentive to expend more effort on design aspects and selecting materials that will have long life and minimal maintenance needs, as the contractor will be operating the system for that extended period. Finally, the DBOM contactor has incentive to deliver the project in a timely manner so that operation and maintenance payments can be procured.

In contrast, some traditional government contracts have been subject to significant cost overruns and long-delayed project delivery. For example, the Wollman Rink ice skating rink in New York City was a textbook case of project delay, in which, starting in 1980, a projected two-and-a-half-year renovation of the facility stretched to six years with no end in sight. Finally, real estate developer Donald Trump stepped forward in 1986, and under his firm's supervision and construction management, the renovation was completed in three months. Another example is the famous Central Artery/Tunnel Project, also known as "The Big Dig" in Boston. This initial project cost was estimated at $2.8 billion, with a construction period estimated to run from 1991 to 1998. The project was finally completed in 2007, after 16 years under construction and at a total cost of $14.6 billion. New York City's East Side Access project, a new transit link in Manhattan, was initiated in 2006, with an estimated $6.3 billion in costs and a forecasted completion date of 2013. Current projections from the project sponsor, New York's Metropolitan Transportation Authority, are for a 2023 completion date, with a total cost of $10.178 billion. These are examples of traditional governmental contracting practices that have gone awry and why PPP contracts are viewed in many cases as better project management practice as well as control risk for the government entity.

One key advantage that PPP projects can offer to the public sector is project administration and cost control. Current practice in public contracts relies on the lowest qualified bidder to provide the service. This can result in somewhat less efficient or experienced bidders winning the contract. Meeting the minimum bid criteria and offering the lowest price does not ensure quality work. By using a PPP contract, the PPP contract winner can negotiate a price with a given qualified contractor and manage costs through an ongoing relationship with the contractor. Given that no long-term relationships can be formed in the public competitive bid process, there is little social pressure to perform well and no real penalty for poor performance, outside of the contract penalties and warranties that often do not carry significant contractual consequences. Companies such as Macquarie Bank of Australia, which have multiple PPP contracts, can develop ongoing relationships with construction, maintenance, and financial companies.

Another advantage is that the contract terms can shift some of the risk for cost overruns to the private contractor and provide incentives for early delivery and cost control. By specifying the contract payment schedule and various targets for construction and system performance, the governmental entity can provide incentives for the PPP constructor or operator to achieve certain outcomes and project goals. In public-sector administration, it is rare to find significant penalty clauses or benefits for project management and success. With the ownership and administration tied to government service, who would be the valid payer if a bureaucrat failed to achieve project goals? Would Nevada be forced to pay Nevada a project penalty if a highway project ran over in terms of cost or was not delivered on time? With a proper PPP contract, the governmental entity can place rewards and penalty clauses that can potentially increase or reduce profit for the PPP contractor. Most contracts routinely include liquidated damage clauses in the bid specs. These terms can provide incentive to manage costs and also promote on-time or early project delivery. The impact can be dramatic. According to the American Association of State Highway and Transportation Officials (AASHTO), the Hudson–Bergen Light Rail was completed for $2.2 billion on budget and with a project time savings estimated at eight years, as compared to a traditional multiple contract design/bid/award/construct process.[20]

There has been a long history of private assets providing contracted services for public benefit. The electric company, water supply entities, sewer authorities, and telecommunications companies are, in many cases, private entities that provide key regional infrastructure. In some cases, these same services may be provided by government entities. Privatization offers governmental units the opportunity to lease (in most cases a lease is used as opposed to outright sale) a public asset to a private operator in exchange for a single lump sum or a series of structured payments.

These leases can be for a considerable period of time and may include price escalation clauses that increase the value of the lease. A prominent example of this type of contract was the lease of the Chicago Skyway to a private concern led by Macquarie Bank of Australia and Cintra transportation systems of Spain. Cintra S.A. is one of the largest private developers of transport infrastructure in the world. Its full name is Cintra Concesiones de Infraestructuras de Transporte. Cintra is one the largest private toll operators in the United States. The City of Chicago leased a municipally owned toll highway to this private concern for a period of 99 years. The lease terms included favorable allowances for toll increases as well as terms and conditions for road operations. In exchange, the City of Chicago received a one-time payment of $1.83 billion in 2006. The private concern is responsible for maintenance and operation of the roadway and in exchange keeps all toll and other revenue.

One key advantage of PPP is the opportunity for the private entity to bond against future fee increases. In traditional agency or authority funding models, bond purchasers will generally allow an agency to bond against future revenue generated by existing fees but are resistant to additional bonding against the planned increases in these same fees. Fearing that the agency in question will lose the political will to increase fees as scheduled in future periods, bond purchasers and bond rating agencies are reluctant to approve lending against any future of the value of future fee increases to be bonded against in the current period. This allows a greater front-end payment and thus can be an inducement to government entities to lease assets and achieve the maximum short-term payout, which can be disposed of in various ways by the current elected officials. As this process essentially delivers the value of future fees into the hands of today's politicians, one must consider the various aspects of public finance in these decisions.

Clearly, this form of lease allows a government entity to capitalize on the value of a publicly owned asset and obtain a potential cash windfall. However, it is very important to carefully negotiate the terms of a long-term lease, as any errors or omissions in the lease will typically require additional cash payments or other compensation to the concessionaire to correct these errors. Also, the level and frequency of price changes need to be considered carefully. Granting an exclusive operating agreement to a private firm can create incentive to price-gouge. The Europeans have a more conservative view on privatization contracts, with French and Spanish road concessions generally containing lower price escalation clauses and shorter lease terms. These factors reduce both the risk of contract error and also the lump-sum cash value of these leases. Finally, given the move toward lump-sum payments for these concessions, one must be concerned that the elected officials who are the stewards of these public funds will develop a long-term strategy for their use. Utilizing a lump-sum payment from a concession agreement to satisfy a short-term budget need is not prudent. Unfortunately, if history teaches us anything, we find that elected officials have a very difficult time planning for long-term capital management.

One of Cintra's biggest public-private partnerships involved a 75-year lease infrastructure deal for the Indiana Toll Road in 2006. Cintra and minority partner Macquarie of Australia paid $3.85 billion to Indiana to operate the 157-mile roadway.[21] The leases allowed Cintra to collect the toll revenue through the year 2081. The problem with the agreement in Indiana was that it allowed the toll rates to more than double from $14 to $32 within the first five years, calling for a 2 to 3% inflationary adjustment for the remaining 70 years. Toll rates are indexed to the rate of inflation.

Overall, PPPs offer many interesting alternative methods of project finance and project delivery for elected officials to consider. The problem is it offers immediate, onetime cash fixing and also removes the responsibility for maintaining and repairing the existing infrastructure from the government entity but it also may place significant costs on facility users. With various risks and components of value, we caution their broad use and application without careful evaluation of contract terms and project specifications. A careful transparent cost study with proper projections and with high levels of professional skepticism is a must. Unfortunately, given the value at risk, it is difficult for government entities to hire competent and objective valuation experts to negotiate the deal for the public entity. This is due in part to the extensive specialization of valuation consultants on the "buy" side of the market, where the larger paychecks for valuation consultation are in the hands of the purchaser (leaser) of public assets. Finally, any PPP project should be carefully evaluated for market power and the creation of de facto monopolies by the granting of an exclusive government contract for a given service.

 ## CONCLUSION

As we have seen, there are myriad forms of organizations that can provide government or public services in our society. The various roles and forms of service provision need to be carefully explored by elected officials and policy makers. The behavior that surrounds these public-entity forms is critical in formulating a plan to mitigate fraud and mismanagement.

There is considerable pressure to expand the role of government and add costs and services based on political pressure. The problem is that people do not want to pay for these services. These expansions may seem on the surface to be benign, but may in fact cause structural cost increases for the government entity, and require the application of a high level of skepticism.

Careful consideration of the method and cost structure of each form of government service should be examined and decisions should be driven in large part by long-term costs and the ability to provide the service effectively. Clearly documented, well-defined language along with the properly trained people and controls surrounding the authorization process are essential.

All governmental entities should consider whether or not a service or expenditure is clearly a government matter or could be performed more effectively or provided more efficiently as a private expenditure. Government should be cognizant of the particular line of business and what is involved. Should the United States have the Export-Import Bank of the United States (Ex-Im), which is the official export credit agency? The Ex-Im is an independent, self-sustaining executive branch agency with a mission of supporting American jobs by facilitating the export of U.S. goods and services. The salient issue is whether or not government should perform a function itself or outsource it to others. The authors remind the reader that many individuals in the private sector would love to have their personal expenditures shifted to the government; only with prudent practice and sound judgment can proper balance be maintained between public and private costs. Any government intervention or partnership should never lead to the creation of monopolistic or oligopolistic precedents. It should not inhibit market entry by limiting open market participation and/or steering to political or related-interest parties, either. Utilities, cable companies, and sports authorities that create limited markets are arenas in which the potential for fraud and mismanagement thrives. Free market and skeptical oversight are critical in ensuring that a proper ethical tenor thrives.

In conclusion, the exact public-entity forms and responsibilities vary considerably across states and regions in the United States and in other countries. Regardless of the form, the behavior needs to be examined for any deviant or abnormal patterns. The sheer number, variety, and overlapping nature of public entities makes the job of ensuring accountability and preventing fraud in the public sector a challenging task. While this may prevent people from identifying silver bullets, a general approach can be developed and applied in any one of the scenarios described in this chapter. Well-trained independent public servants working within well-developed compacts (constitutions, charters) that clearly define responsibilities and duties and have a no-tolerance-for-override policy, ensure transparency, and have the public's support are what create adequate controls and balance. It is a well-developed system and structure with the proper ethical tone that ensures the mitigation of fraud and mismanagement.

NOTES

1. http://www.njslom.org/types.html.
2. http: //www.nj.gov/comptroller/news/docs/authoritiescommission.pdf.
3. Readers with a strong interest in governmental entities are advised to read the enabling statues that create these organizations. Naming and the definitions of these entities are somewhat subjective.
4. http://www.state.nj.us/education/data/fact.htm.
5. http://www.laffercenter.com/the-laffer-center-2/the-laffer-curve/.
6. http://publictransport.about.com/od/Transit_Planning/a/Load-Factor-Low-Floor-Vehicles-Need-A-Lower-One.htm.

7. A Ponzi scheme is a fraudulent investment operation where an individual or organization is paid returns from new investors' capital, rather than from profit earned by the investments.

8. Divisionalized organizational structure is that the divisions can act with a high degree of autonomy to address specific issues by the power (authority) they have been given.

9. The Federal Reserve Act establishes both 14-year terms for members of the board and four-year terms for the chair and adds: "each member shall hold office for a term of fourteen years from the expiration of the term of his predecessor, **unless sooner removed for cause** by the President."

10. http://www.bloomberg.com/news/articles/2010-12-09/more-than-half-of-americans-want-fed-reined-in-or-abolished.

11. Thomas Jefferson, http://www.brainyquote.com/quotes/quotes/t/thomasjeff130495.html#EbhxrksstgU0eGeK.99.

12. http://data.bls.gov/cgi-bin/cpicalc.pl The inflation number utilized the U.S. Bureau of Labor Statistics Inflationary calculator.

13. Seigniorage is the difference between the value of money and the cost to produce it. If it costs the U.S. government $0.05 to produce a $1 bill, the seigniorage is $0.95, or the difference between the two amounts.

14. http://www.businessweek.com/2000/00_17/b3678084.htm.

15. http://www.treasury.gov/resource-center/data-chart-center/quarterly-refunding/Documents/February2015TBACCharge1.pdf.

16. Fact Sheet #7, U.S. Department of Labor, www.dol.gov/whd/regs/ ... /whdfs7.pdf.

17. http://www.federalreserve.gov/monetarypolicy/mpr_default.htm, accessed 1/22/2015.

18. Public Authorities, Office of the State Comptroller, www.osc.state.ny.us/pubauth/.

19. http://www.osc.state.ny.us/pubauth/whatisauthority.htm.

20. http://transportationfinance.org/projects/hudson_bergen_lrt.aspx.

21. http://www.landlinemag.com/Story.aspx?StoryID=24861#.V2gaH_nF-fg.

CHAPTER TWO

Public Finance and How Government Creates Cash Flow

"I know no safe depository of the ultimate powers of the society but the people themselves; and if we think them not enlightened enough to exercise their control with a wholesome discretion, the remedy is not to take it from them, but to inform their discretion by education. This is the true corrective of abuses of constitutional power."

—*Thomas Jefferson*

Topics:

Taxation
Revenue
Fees
Spending
Levers on Value

Key questions:

Is cash king or is it power?
Where should we put the checks and balances?

UNDERSTANDING GOVERNMENT FINANCE—in terms of how the various entities generate the necessary funds needed to meet the expenditures, is necessary to maintain services and accommodate public policy—is critical in creating sound systems to prevent fraud and mismanagement. Today's society is built on credit and debit cards and the ability to pay through phones, PayPal, and other technologies. Yet, government deficits continue to rise. In this chapter, we continue to work to bridge the communication gaps that often continue to gape between the professionals and the general public by guiding you through the byzantine maze of how government generates sufficient cash to continue providing services to the citizenry.

As we stated in chapter 1, watching the trusted parties' visual cues and verbalizations with respect to their personality behavior surrounding their financial responsibilities potentially generates warning signs that require further examination. These visual and verbal representations can help you in determining opportunities that may exist that enable you to see how one can gain access and convert cash for their own benefit. By maintaining an environment that includes physical, unsuspecting (policing) observations surround the actions and verbalizations of the parties surrounding these policies, procedures can be put in place so that fraud and mismanagement cannot occur in the public entity. Reviewing past examples of past control weaknesses, overrides, and oversight will help in your development of sound systems and structures. To improve your soft skills, examine past inappropriate or questionable behavior and follow it through to see if the financial position of the public entity was affected.

GOVERNMENT FINANCE 101

Governments need resources to provide and maintain services. In the private sector, one may use firm income (historically retained earnings), bonding, borrowing, and other debt forms, such as owner equity, to fund future operations. For governments, though, there are three main revenue sources: fees, taxes, and borrowing. Over any given span of time, each of these funding mechanisms can be used in a mixed manner by various governmental units, depending upon current economic conditions, capital and operational needs, and political whim, to fund needed operations.

As we explore the various financial tools that governmental entities can utilize to fund current operations and capital investment, one would be wise to consider the full range of options that are available and also the political horse trading that typically goes into a public finance decision. Simple and fair methods of revenue collection may be shunted aside as political insiders seek to avoid burdens on their constituents. The lack of revenue may drive the need for additional borrowing or implementation of less fair or expensive-to-collect forms of revenue generation. Only by completely understanding the full spectrum of options and examining the final financial solutions can we truly understand the strong political influence of vested interests in the realm of public finance.

Even simple public finance issues—where there are clear beneficiaries and also clear sources of revenue to fund public projects—can be subject to considerable debate and political rancor. In the following case, we study a government service that has long been established as a public-sector good: roads and mass transit. But the political decisions as to who should pay and how much to pay have yet to be resolved in Washington, D.C., and in many state capitols. The massive and ongoing debate around transportation funding also provides us with good insights into how the national and state debates interact and overlap in terms of public finance.

CASE STUDY: TRANSPORTATION FINANCE

One of the basic functions of government is to provide the public infrastructure: streets and highways that deliver public services, create economic growth, and maintain the quality of life of its citizenry. Some governments, for political reasons, are resistant to increasing taxes, so they employ other forms of finance. For instance, a gasoline tax, at a fixed rate per gallon, was implemented in many states in the 1920s to address the needs for better roads. The tax was very popular at the time. That's because it was part of the push for what was dubbed the Good Roads Movement, in which state governments across the nation invested heavily for the sake of improving road infrastructure. In the past 20 years, however, this situation has reversed. The federal government, in particular, has become politically resistant to increasing the federal gasoline tax from the current rate of 18.4 cents per gallon. This has led to a dramatic decline in purchasing power of the funds for transportation infrastructure. A national debate has ensued over how to fund transportation projects while there is a massive increase in structurally substandard bridges and roads across the nation. Perhaps we are looking at the beginning of a Bad Roads Movement. For years, government has been using these funds for purposes other than bridges and roads and the intended purpose of the tax.

The Federal-Aid Highway Act of 1956, known as the National Interstate and Defense Highways Act (Public Law 84–627), was signed into law on June 29, 1956, by President Dwight D. Eisenhower for the construction of 41,000 miles of interstate highway that was slated for completion within a 10-year period. At the time, it was the largest public works project in American history.[1] The reason "Defense" was named in the act designed for road construction was because funds were being diverted from the U.S. Department of Defense. This type of separated funding is often what allows for transferring between funds. In other words, it approves the funding of projects beyond the original scope for which the funds were raised and dedicated. Yet the demand for resources has far outstripped the supply of funds that were generated to complete transportation projects and maintain up-and-running systems.

> "The Highway Trust Fund is facing an estimated $168 billion short-fall over the next decade, and, absent any general fund transfers, will run out of funds by mid-year 2015, due to increased spending and an eroding gas tax."[2] The gasoline tax only pays for half of the state's needs in highway spending.[3]

The answer seems to be raising revenues by increasing the tax rates, finding new names for the taxes by calling them fees, and other one-shot gimmicks. The skepticism needs to be applied on the spending side, not on the revenue, to make decisions to raise taxes transparent and justifiable. Understanding why there is the need to raise revenue to meet spending is important in developing changes to policy and procedures that could be put in place to smooth increases and put less burden on the citizenry. It, however, requires planning, directing, and controlling (all key terms in effective management).

In addition to federal fuel taxes, there are state fuel taxes. Table 2.1 addresses only the federal taxes. Selected for examination are the highest toll user fees based on Tax Foundation data from the 2011 Census. Delaware is ranked number one in total user fees and taxes and covers 78.6 percent of

TABLE 2.1 Share of State and Local Road Spending and Road-Related Fees and Taxes

State	Share of State & Local Road Spending Covered by User Fees and User Taxes, 2011						Road-Related User Fees and User Taxes Collected by State, 2011 in Millions						
	Tolls & User Fees	Rank	Fuel Taxes	License Taxes	Total, User Fees & User TAXES	Rank	Tolls & User Fees	Fuel Taxes	License Taxes	Total, User Fees & User Taxes	Total, State-Local Road Spending	Share Covered	Rank
California	4.40%	20	38.70%	21.30%	64.40%	4	$651.10	$5,705.50	$3,132.00	$9,488.60	$14,726.50	64.40%	4
Connecticut	0.10%	49	30.90%	12.60%	43.60%	29	$1.80	$477.80	$195.30	$674.80	$1,548.40	43.60%	29
Delaware	48.10%	1	21.20%	9.30%	78.60%	1	$258.30	$113.80	$50.00	$422.10	$537.20	78.60%	1
Florida	15.10%	6	38.40%	15.30%	68.80%	3	$1,235.80	$3,151.80	$1,253.60	$5,641.20	$8,200.40	68.80%	3
Hawaii	0.80%	37	30.20%	46.40%	77.30%	2	$4.40	$170.50	$261.80	$436.70	$564.60	77.30%	2
Massachusetts	18.20%	5	25.80%	14.70%	58.70%	6	$467.90	$660.80	$378.10	$1,506.80	$2,564.80	58.70%	6
New Jersey	32.80%	2	12.10%	13.60%	58.50%	8	$1,414.90	$524.20	$587.50	$2,526.60	$4,318.10	58.50%	8
New York	29.10%	3	14.60%	12.80%	56.50%	11	$3,212.20	$1,609.40	$1,414.70	$6,236.40	$11,029.30	56.50%	11
Pennsylvania	9.60%	12	22.90%	9.30%	41.80%	33	$859.10	$2,064.20	$834.30	$3,757.60	$8,995.40	41.80%	33
Texas	10.00%	9	28.40%	17.60%	56.00%	13	$1,096.80	$3,108.40	$1,924.10	$6,129.30	$10,939.10	56.00%	13
U.S. Average	8.30%		26.90%	15.20%	50.40%								

Source: Tax Foundation calculations from U.S. Census Bureau, State and Local Government Finance 2011.

its road spending through the federal tax and user fees. California is ranked number one in spending with respect to state and local roadways, and only 64.4 percent of the needed road spending is covered through federal taxes and user fees. So where does the other needed percentage come from, the state fuel tax? The point is that the taxes and fees are user-based, yet they are not sufficient to cover all the infrastructure costs necessary to maintain the roadways. That means the money needs to be raised some other way. If revenue falls short of covering expenditures, the next place to generate funds is through debt (borrowing). The simple accounting principle that requires the expenditures and the revenues to match needs to be applied. Infrastructure replacement, repair, and maintenance are very costly, and adequate fees need to be collected to fund them. Zero-based budgeting or controlling the budgets more effectively come to mind in order to accomplish this. It's a simple concept: Expenditures must be justified for each new period. Delays cost money. Simple inflation proves that point.

Although fuel taxes and user fees result in significant revenue being raised by the public entities, it still creates huge deficits as a result of the costs required to maintain these infrastructure systems. Why? These are the value points that require a high level of skepticism. Ask simple questions. Labor (toll collectors) has been replaced with E-ZPass technology. Did increased technology actually lower the cost of collection or did we just substitute capital for labor costs? Where have those funds been diverted to? Those funds were raised for a specific purpose and should remain in the accounts for which they were created. They should not be allowed to be stretched to meet the established policies and procedures of some other, unrelated purpose. Road maintenance needs to take place on an ongoing basis and not be put off until the roads have been so neglected that they cost billions to restore to full functionality.

Further, there is significant pressure to impose new and increased fees on vehicle owners to support other components of the transportation system such as mass transit. Although one can consider the impact of private vehicles and trucks on congestion in a region, it is important to also consider the aspects of user fees as opposed to general taxes. We will explore the various funding sources for government projects in the next chapter, but the question as to whether transit users should provide the bulk of funding for mass transit services via transit fares or whether these services should be supported from other tax resources is still an open policy discussion. Currently, the federal and many state governments divert some portion of fuel taxes to funds for mass transit systems. This creates further political turmoil, as some users (drivers) are overburdened with tax costs and some users (transit riders) are recipients of subsidy. These users are thus likely to attempt to influence the political process to change the outcomes to favor their particular group. We will discuss further aspects of subsidy of public services later in this chapter—in particular, goods with social benefits to their use.

There are conflicting interests concerning where gas taxes, auto fees, and other "dedicated" revenues should be spent. Should the spending be dedicated to *cars* or to *roads* or to *transit*? Putting all these possibilities together such that all transportation is evaluated and budgeted as one unit creates the ability to divert, distract, and divide. The roads and mass transit being subsidized create conflicting interests. *Subsidizing* creates the ability to gain access to value within the public entity. It is a form of financial aid or support with the intent to support economic and social policy. When people are subsidizing a benefit that does not benefit them, there is separation of interests. The ones requiring the subsidy are benefiting from the subsidy. With any division, you no longer operate under the majority consensus. The focus is on satisfying the group that gets to that 50.01 percent, "more likely than not" thinking or the necessary approvals. This puts the value in the hands of the people with power.

The purpose of our analysis and presentation here is to illustrate the complex interactions and various payer/recipient classes in any taxation or fee-based public service or infrastructure. Fee-based systems argue that the user pays, the user gets. Broad-based tax policies argue that all benefit and the general fund pays. In between is the model of dedicated taxes with lockboxes or other means of diversion control. All have valid arguments—but a broader discussion of the mode of payment and tax burden is warranted, as it is always easy to say that someone else should pay. Our examples here are intended to illustrate this complex environment.

The authors are well aware of the various issues surrounding the subsidy of mass transit and the multiple funding sources that provide for transportation infrastructure, but the literature is far from clear in establishing a good understanding of the relative costs and relative tax or fee burden of transportation infrastructure. One of the authors is currently working on a study to examine the burden of road infrastructure costs by level of government (local, county, state, and federal) and the related fee and tax revenue sources. It is not clear that the user sets are overlapping in many geographic areas—that is still to be established from the literature. Thus, heavy users of mass transit may be quite distinct from heavy users of private automobiles. Also left undiscussed are the municipal and public benefits of road infrastructure, where most municipal services are provided via the road network—fire, police, ambulance, trash, recycling, and such. Delivery of private services like utility maintenance and goods delivery (UPS, FedEx, U.S. Postal Service, and truck delivery [appliances and furniture, for example]) all utilize the road network. So, nondrivers logically should contribute to road infrastructure, as they benefit from the provision of roads even if they do not drive.

Governments can stretch the limits of funding purposes to divert resources to the general fund. As a glaring example of this, the authors point to the sale of a stretch of untolled road in New Jersey from the state (owned by the New Jersey Department of Transportation) to a toll agency (the New Jersey Turnpike Authority). This sale is questionable in terms of the value of the asset sold versus the price paid. This sale was not an "arm's-length" transaction, and, as such, one should consider if the purchase was prudent and appropriate for the agency.

A *New York Times* article dated May 3, 1991, stated, "The Florio administration hopes to help balance its next budget by selling one of the state's busiest stretches of highway, the 4.4 miles of Interstate 95 between the George Washington Bridge and the New Jersey Turnpike, for $400 million."[4] The buyer was a related party—the New Jersey Turnpike Authority. The way it was paid for? If you guessed new debt, you guessed right. The bond debt term is $400 million at an interest rate of at least 7 percent. At the time, it was claimed that these costs would be paid without imposing tolls on that stretch of road. Instead the toll payers on the rest of the turnpike would have to pay back the bond debt. Even at 7 percent interest only, with no payment of principal, there's an additional interest cost of $28 million annually. Using a simple present-value inflation of dollars from the 1991 debt of $400 million, it would equate to $689 million in 2015, unless the debt was retired through diversion of toll resources.

It is clear, from a New Jersey state government perspective, that this deal is very favorable. The government sold an asset, with no direct revenue and significant costs to another entity, for $400 million. From the perspective of the purchasing agency, the Turnpike Authority, there was little to no value transferred. The road was in place and the costs of operations and capital became a burden to the toll authority, since there was no established plan in place to increase the revenues to generate additional funds to pay for the increased costs as result of the sale.

These one-shot revenue solutions to resolve systematic shortfalls of other, unrelated areas in government by simply diverting revenue from or adding debt to another governmental entity are examples of bad decision making. This distracted the Turnpike Authority from its core mission, which is to maintain the toll roads under their supervision. Now the Authority has an additional asset to maintain with the same revenue stream and more debt.

THE BASIC RULES OF FORENSIC ACCOUNTING

In Joe's previous book, he created the ten Forensically Accepted Generally Accepted Accounting Principles Assumptions (FAGAAPA), and we are especially referring to Principle 8, the Whatever I Need principle, which focuses on revenue recognition. This is an example of creating a revenue stream from debt; it is clearly a violation of sound accounting practices and a circumvention of sound, principle-based thinking. What caused the need to create $400 million in revenue? What could be done to prevent this for future generations? The one-shot thinking needs to be replaced with how the problem can be fixed going forward—proactive thinking. The goal is not to use the proverbial "kick the can down the road" approach. There is no better thinking than for an entity to engage in long-term planning for all short-term actions that are often taken by the various governmental units.

Let's roll the time forward to the 2008 Lehman Brothers collapse. Repo 105 is the name given to Lehman Brothers' accounting maneuver that attaches a short-term repurchase agreement to a liability. In this maneuver, the credit balance is moved from the balance sheet as debt and classified as a sale or revenue in the income statement, as credits to the income statement are revenues. The cash obtained through this "sale" is then used to pay down debt, allowing the company to appear to reduce its leverage by temporarily paying down liabilities to allow for a stronger-appearing company balance sheet. Then, after the company's financial reports are published, they are able to borrow the necessary cash and repurchase its original liabilities.

What makes the Florio acquisition similar is that new debt is established on a related entity—the New Jersey Turnpike Authority—and a revenue flow is created in a different entity, or the state itself. These extremely creative accounting and financing techniques are what cause increases in tolls, fees, and taxes. They are also why the money runs out.

Rule: Debt is a credit balance in government funds and financials, which is a financing activity which generates an inflow of funds. Debt provides the liquidity a fraudster needs to gain access to cash. Understanding the mind-set employed in using debt to replace onetime revenue fixes that generate the necessary cash flows for onetime budget fixes or structural deficits is an area in which skepticism needs to be applied. Ask questions. Why is debt load increasing? Has there been a refinance? Or, in government terms, has there been a refunding? This often results in reduced interest cost and the potential to add funds related to a financing cash flow. Also, at a later date, when that debt is no longer required to be paid, there will be an additional cash flow. Follow the debt fund savings to see where those funds are being used. New Jersey has a cap on annual increases in spending, but its debt falls outside of the cap. So how is it a true financial cap? Watch what the public entity does with the savings resulting from refunding and debt payoff. This is another area in which there needs to be far more transparency to foster better control.

A simple follow-the-money accounting application is necessary to maintain sound systems and structures that prevent fraud and mismanagement in the governmental units system. A careful examination of the new debt terms should be performed to ensure that in the refunding process the terms of the debt were not extended. Such an extension can result in the refunding amounts simply stretching the debt out over a longer period of time.

After we follow the money you need to learn the three ways to value an asset. The first is the asset approach, in which a review of the governmental unit assets and liabilities is used to develop a value. With a sale of $400 million and a debt of $400 million, applying the simple accounting formula of assets less liabilities equals fund balance, it is clear there is no value. But that includes examining the budgets of both the state and its related authorities as a whole.

The second approach is the market approach, which relies on the current value that someone who is not under duress would be willing to pay and that the transaction would be viewed at arm's length. This approach looks to the real marketplace at the time of the transaction to determine the asset's real current value. We refer to it as "as of date valuation," which means the value of the asset as of a certain date. Accountants like to think of this method as a substitution approach. This is accomplished by finding comparable sales or transactions that are representative of the asset being valued or sold.

The final methodology is the income approach. This takes a look at the core reason for the acquisition and how it will make money. The transaction was made and will have no creation of new revenue; therefore, without a revenue generation feature, again, there would be no value under this methodology. If there is a related-party transaction among governmental units, transparency and detailed examination need to be applied, along with the avoidance of one-shot revenues and short-term fixes.

When, and if, a particular government revenue tool is limited from use due to political or social pressure, the elected officials must then consider alternative forms of finance to meet given revenue and spending targets. Simple taxes, with low cost of collection, as with excise taxes, may be supplanted by more complex fee systems or multiple smaller revenue sources. This creates added pressure on governmental entities to raise fees further to cover additional administrative costs to complex tax systems. To further expand on the matter of revenue and spending tools, the major revenue sources that provide government cash flow will be outlined.

Cost of Collection

The cost of collection results from taking the necessary actions to realize promises to pay. The cost incurred to collect a debt is a typical cost you should be familiar with. An example is when people do not pay their mortgage and the bank has to take collection action. In the public entity, collection action typically arises from some form of tax or user fee that requires collection action to secure the funds owed.

Any taxation or user fee system has costs associated with the collection of the revenue. These costs can be broken down into administrative, compliance, and societal categories. When one is considering a tax or fee, these subdivisions of cost should also be taken into account.

Administrative costs are the costs incurred by the agency collecting the tax or fee. They include direct costs of collection, such as cash management, fee collection systems, forms, payment of administrative staff, and the like. Taxes, such as the federal income tax, have extremely low administrative costs for collection. This is due in part to the significant burden that the tax authority imposes on the taxpayers to complete the tax payment process (a compliance cost, which we explore in the next section). However, a major component of the efficiency of the tax is that the taxing authority collects a rather significant amount of revenue from a small base of users. This tends to minimize the number of tax collection transactions and, thereby, the cost of collection and policing. For example, the Internal Revenue Service (IRS) reported that it spent $11.7 billion in 2009 to collect $2.3 trillion in income taxes. This is an administrative cost of roughly 0.5 percent of revenue. The 92,577 employees of the IRS collect an average of $25.3 million in taxes per employee per year.

The IRS is also quite efficient in its operations and practices, as it collects the tax revenue through various automated sources, such as paycheck deductions.

This delivers revenue in a pooled fashion to the IRS and, essentially, adds costs to payroll systems that are considered compliance costs on the part of the users. The IRS does not collect from each worker after it is paid. It collects in bulk from the payroll systems. The owner of the firm is, in essence, required to perform work for the IRS—without compensation.

Compliance costs are the cost of collecting revenue that are placed on the payer of the tax through either additional expense in supervising the collection of the tax or through additional work required to complete forms and submit tax payments. The IRS forces tax payers to complete form work or hire professionals to assist in completing the required paperwork to pay the income tax. This reduces the package of costs that are paid by the agency, but may not impact the total costs of collecting the tax. It is possible that a tax agency may choose a low administrative cost method of collecting taxes as that lowers the annual budgetary cost of administering the tax—even if that method has high compliance and social costs. As we examine various forms of taxation and fee systems, we will continue to reflect on these issues and look to explore how the method of collection is selected.

Social costs are costs that are imposed on nontaxpayers in the process of paying the tax. For instance, if a particular fee is levied on trucks at a border crossing and that causes additional delay for the trucks, that fee may well impose a pollution cost due to additional idling of trucks at the border crossing. These costs are not borne by the taxing or fee authority or the trucking company. They fall outside the direct participants in the taxing process and, as such, are social costs. Theoretically, one could also find a social benefit to a tax system. For instance, if the same truckers bought lunch from vendors during the border crossing delays, that could be viewed as a social benefit of the taxation system. Another example of social cost would be if drivers diverted from a toll system. The influx of traffic in the abutting neighborhoods, for the sake of drivers avoiding paying a tax or fee, would create pollution and/or add risk for accidents and injuries. The social cost would be lower quality of life, damaged infrastructure from added traffic, and strain on municipal services (cost), such as police.

One can clearly see that the various players in the taxation and fee collection game could have radically different perspectives on how the mix of costs should be developed. Individuals outside of the system would prefer low to no social costs and perhaps social benefits from a taxation system.

It's interesting to note that an individual or group outside the system (not paying for taxes or the required fees) may seek to create a system that produces social benefits for themselves, at the expense of the taxpayers in the system. In effect, they have designed a tax system that produces external benefits that accrue to a group of nontaxpayers who then become a built-in advocacy group for extending or perpetuating the policy, as this group is not paying for it, but enjoys the benefit.

Taxing and fee authorities will be tempted to have low administrative costs and look for a fee system that incurs the lowest administrative collection costs. This reduces the budgetary needs to pay for the collection system. So it may prove to be easier to implement and maintain funding for the collection process. Further, a low administrative cost may be seen by elected officials as proof of good government operations. By the same token, any attempt to manage the total cost of collection may be seen as reducing the efficiency of government. Adding to the administrative costs of collection to reduce compliance costs may be seen as wasting public funds and reducing the net revenue production of the tax or fee. Remember that a taxing authority may have little to no incentive to reduce compliance and social costs, unless it is controlled in some way or forced to consider these aspects of its revenue systems.

Taxpayers (users of the tax system) will look to have a more balanced view of the mix of administrative and compliance costs. To them, a very efficient system, but one that carries with it higher administrative costs may not be preferable to one that has lower administrative and compliance costs. In cases where the user pays both of these costs—either through higher taxes or fees to pay the administrative costs or through more extensive paperwork and compliance efforts in their own organizations—the user base would have the incentive to go with the package that incurs the lowest total administrative and compliance costs. It is hard to argue the idea that users might also tend to choose low administrative cost taxes, as they may feel that they can manage their compliance costs as a component of the entity's operations. They may also be suspicious of a taxing authority's ability to maintain their administrative process and keep compliance costs low.

Table 2.2, from Peters & Kramer (2003),[5] provides information on various forms of taxation and reports administrative and compliance costs. The table also provides various estimates of social costs for these same tax systems. As shown, different types of tax systems have distinctly different levels of

TABLE 2.2 Toll System Performance Benchmarks: Comparison to Alternative Taxation Systems

Tax	Year	Revenue	Administrative Costs	Compliance Costs	Total Tax Collection Costs
General Taxes					
Federal Income Tax	2001	$ 2,129,000,000,000	$ 8,772,000,000	$69,831,200,000	$ 78,603,200,000
% of tax collected			0.41%	3.28%	3.69%
National Gas Tax	1996	$ 19,653,800,000	$ 51,000,000		$ 51,000,000
% of tax collected			0.26%		0.26%
National Gas Tax	1999	21,236,659,000	$ 55,107,389		$ 55,107,389
% of tax collected			0.26%		0.26%
State Fuel Taxes	1999	$ 29,000,000,000	$ 290,000,000	$ 580,000,000	$ 870,000,000
% of tax collected			1%	2%	3.00%

Toll Systems

Garden State Parkway *	2002	$194,851,414	$36,317,215	$33,709,294.62	$70,026,510
% of tax collected			18.6%	17.3%	35.9%
Massachusetts Turnpike	2001	$ 214,352,000	$ 39,835,440		$39,835,440
% of tax collected			18.6%		18.6%
New Jersey Turnpike	2001	$433,868,929	$48,548,749		$48,548,749
% of tax collected			11.2%		11.2%
Pennsylvania Turnpike	2002	$375,750,731	$54,700,000		$54,700,000
% of tax collected			14.6%		14.6%
Orlando - Orange Ct. Exp.	2002	$146,200,000	$26,700,000		$26,700,000
% of tax collected			18.3%		18.3%
All Tolls	2000	$ 6,596,425,000			

* GSP Compliance costs estimated by Peters & Kramer (2003)

administrative, compliance, and social costs. Income taxes, as previously outlined, tend to be very administratively efficient, but bear some significant compliance costs. The U.S. federal income tax is administered by the IRS with 0.41 percent administrative costs and an estimated 3.28 percent compliance costs. The bottom line is the IRS has shifted 89 percent of the cost of collecting the federal income tax to users, leaving the IRS to bear only 11 percent of the total costs for collection.

Tax Collection Example—Fuel Taxes

Fuel taxes are collected at the national and state levels. They provide a basis for the funding of the nation's transportation systems, such as highways and transit systems. These taxes are collected generally on a fixed price per gallon at the refinery, distributor, or importer level. For instance, Oregon collects all of its fuel taxes from approximately 300 entities. At the national level, the IRS collects $21 billion in fuel taxes from approximately 1,800 entities: The refinery, distributor, or importer collects the tax at the metered fuel distribution points as they fill the tank truck that actually delivers the fuel to the various fuel stations. In the case of gasoline, the federal tax is currently 18.4 cents per gallon. The distributor then passes this cost along to the fuel station, which then charges the final fuel purchaser a price that includes the federal and state taxes. States have similar methods, and, because of those methods, extremely low administrative costs are associated with collecting fuel taxes. The IRS collects the national fuel taxes for an administrative cost of 0.26 percent of the revenue collected. States have similar rates in the range of 0.25 to 1 percent of revenue collected.

Compliance cost estimations are usually based on taxpayer surveys or studies and, as such, may be subject to some variation in reporting. The 3.28 percent compliance cost estimate for the federal income tax is based upon IRS estimates. Alternative estimates by the Tax Foundation place the compliance costs for federal income taxes at 15 to 24 percent of the tax revenue collected. A cold, hard look at compliance costs by objective observers may be warranted.

Fuel taxes can provide us with an interesting insight into the question of compliance costs. As we outlined earlier, they are generally collected at the refinery, importer, or distributor. Their effort represents the majority of compliance costs, as users who purchase gasoline just pay a higher price that's rolled into the payment transaction. Some states provide an allowance for the cost of collecting the tax and any evaporation (shrinkage) of fuel that occurs in transit. So a supplier that collects the tax is given compensation for compliance costs. This is generally in the 1 to 3 percent range of the tax collected. There was a good test of the true level of compliance costs in Texas in 2001. There, distributors are given a 2 percent allowance for collection and shrinkage. Discussions about changing that process and moving payment of the tax to another entity were met with resistance from the distributors. Apparently, the 2 percent allowance was more than adequate to compensate them for the cost of collecting the tax. It, in fact, had a positive impact on the distributor's profitability. So it seems clear that fuel taxes can be collected with an administrative and compliance cost of 2 to 3 percent of revenue collected.

Other forms of fees and taxes bear various levels of costs of collection that should be examined and put into perspective as to the general efficiency of the tax system as well as the desire to structure user pay systems. Table 2.2 also illustrates the various costs for collection fees on toll roads. In general, Peters & Kramer found administrative costs for toll road systems in the range of 12 to 22 percent of revenue collected. Peters & Kramer also revealed administrative costs of 20 percent, user compliance costs of 9 percent, and social costs of 8.3 percent on the Garden State Parkway in 2001. In the end, the total tax collection costs represented 37.3 percent of revenue. Various forms of taxes can also have very high costs of collection. For instance, Transport for London (TfL) runs the London Congestion Zone, a cordon toll that spends roughly 36.4 percent of the revenue from the congestion zone fees on the administrative costs of collecting the charge. This is due, in part, to the fact that TfL uses photographic recognition of license plates that enter central London and then has to perform character recognition on each plate photograph and bill. This results in roughly 15 to 20 million transactions to manage and collect each year.

Enforcement and Compliance: Tax Evasion

Any tax or fee system will also be subject to evasion and compliance issues. One must consider the type of tax or fee that is applied and then also how payers may fail to make payments. Failure to pay may result from operational inefficiency: The user may not know that he or she should pay, or there may be some form of malfeasance at play. Users may seek to avoid payment based on several perceptions. For one reason or another, they may feel the fee or tax is unfair and rationalize some sort of evasion for not paying. Or they may just be looking to minimize or avoid cost to their family. In the end, evasion and nonpayment will occur at some rate and need to be policed and managed to minimize the loss to the revenue-collecting agency.

Policing and management of nonpayment is a complex process, in that the taxing authority needs to consider the relative costs of pursuing noncompliance versus the potential revenue to be obtained from the delinquent taxpayer. This is, in part, due to purposeful evaders, where the taxpayer is actively looking to avoid payment. These evaders look to disguise their activity or obstruct collection, and their methods can be quite varied and creative.

Income and other tax evasion is pervasive in certain countries. Greece is well known for having a massively inefficient tax collection system that is subject to large-scale evasion. Artavanis, Morse, and Tsoutsoura (2012) estimated that 31 to 48 percent of Greece's federal annual budget shortfall is caused by tax evasion[6] or avoidance. It is important to remember that tax evasion is more attractive when people perceive that there will be less enforcement. In the United States, for instance, the vast majority of taxpayers pay their taxes as required and even incur significant compliance costs in the process because they know the penalties for noncompliance are stiff. It's not because U.S. residents are any more moral than Greek citizens. The IRS polices tax evasion on a regular basis, and American people know that. This virtuous or wicked spiral is important to consider when implementing and modifying tax and fee structures. Once a pattern of evasion is established, it is expensive and difficult to reverse that pattern.

Taxing and revenue authorities should consider tax and fee collection a leaky bucket, within which they look to maintain the general integrity of the revenue collection, but understand that the tax collection system will leak a bit and that is just a by-product of the process. The goal is to keep any small holes in the bucket small while patching the most draining leaks. Trying to patch every hole can lead to a much greater strain on administrative costs with only mild spikes in revenue collection to compensate. The result is a net reduction in usable net revenue production from the tax.

Burden of Taxation

Who pays a given tax is of interest to taxing authorities, elected officials, and the public. Some forms of taxation have various impacts on particular groups or classes of taxpayers. Of special interest is the burden of taxes—the particular costs as they impact households and firms. Taxes that are narrowly focused, such as specific excise taxes, impact the users and producers of particular goods so that they become burdensome to a particular user class.

Virginia's General Assembly levied the first known colonial tax in 1619—a poll tax[7] in Jamestown. The tax was paid to allow a voter to register to vote in several colonies. "The first attempt to tax income in the United States came in 1643 when several colonies instituted a 'faculties and abilities' tax."[8] The tax collectors in these periods would personally visit every household and calculate the tax owed on the spot. Virginia recognized the ability to tax property. Again, to this day, the ability to pay has served as the foundation of the various taxing and fees that are now in existence.

There are different taxing structures. But to understand them it is key to first understand the types of tax rates. The marginal tax rate is the rate of tax paid on the next dollar of income. If it is applied to a deduction, then it is paid on the next dollar of savings. The average tax rate is when you take the total taxable income and divide it by the average tax. The effective tax rate differs from the average tax rates in that all income, whether taxable or not, is factored in and divided by the average tax rate. An average rate is required due to the fact that there are multiple tax rates—regular income tax, capital, and alternative minimum—that can be applied, depending on the income type.

A progressive rate structure is one in which the effective rate paid increases as a portion of the total income as income rises. The tax rate increases at the various levels of total income as income rates. The federal personal income tax system is an example of a progressive tax system.

On the other hand, with a proportional tax structure, the tax of the average remains the same as the tax base increase. Examples are sales taxes, real estate taxes, personal property taxes, and some excise taxes, such as the gasoline tax, since the gasoline is taxed at a constant price per gallon. This means that the marginal and average tax rates are the same at all levels of the established tax base, because the same rate is applied on a constant basis. Sales tax is a fixed-rate tax and is always applied at the same rate, regardless of a person's earning level. Example: John buys a car for $10,000 and earns $1 million a year. Joe buys the same car for $10,000, earning $20,000 a year. Both paid sales tax of $700 ($10,000 · 0.07), assuming a 7 percent sales tax rate.

Taxes that impact lower-income users and place a greater burden on low-income households are considered regressive taxes. Here, the average tax rate exceeds the marginal tax rate—the exact opposite of the progressive tax. So the tax paid per dollar of income decreases as income rises. Taxes such as fuel taxes and sales taxes are proportional in terms of rate—everyone pays the same tax per unit—but regressive in total burden.

With sales taxes, the lower-income households may have a greater amount of household income consumed and, thus, pay a greater percentage of household income on sales taxes. Whereas higher-income households may consume quite a bit more, but not in direct proportion to their additional income. Considering this, high-income households may well pay a lower average percentage of income in sales taxes than low-income households.

Social Security is an example of a regressive tax, as there is a cap on the tax. As one earns more income, the average tax rate goes down. The reason is that $118,500 is the maximum amount on which the 6.2 percent Social Security tax rate is paid. So, if an individual's income is doubled, or $237,000, the tax remains at $7,347. If we divide that $237,000 into the $7,347, the average tax rate is 3.1 percent ($7,347/$237,000), or half of the 6.2 percent assessed on everyone earning below the $118,500 threshold. This is considered a regressive tax.

By examining consumption patterns and the relative use of certain goods, we can explore the regressive nature of certain taxes, such as fuel, tobacco, alcoholic beverages, and tolls. Given that certain households consume certain goods at higher rates as compared to their income, when one examines the actual level of tax dollars collected by income cohort, one can see that certain taxes may actually have a changing burden by income. Consider fuel taxes in this scenario. Low-income households have less fuel consumption (and thus lower taxes) due to the use of mass transit, and higher-income households spend lower percentages of income on fuel (and taxes) as income rises. However, the low income households are also subject to the increasing user fees associated with utilizing the mass transit systems, which affects their ability to pay other necessities. The public entity needs the ability to pay in the formulation of taxing and user fee policies. One needs to consider the compounding aspects of these fees and taxes and also the questions of user pay versus public subsidy in the provisioning of any public service. The public entity needs to think about usage and necessity, with a full understanding of how to fund on an ongoing basis.

Figure 2.1 shows the tax implications as a result of the various tax structures. The more income you make under a progressive tax structure, the more taxes you pay. With the proportional structure, the same tax rate is paid over the established base, or constant. For example, price per gallon is the base and the gasoline tax rate is applied at the same constant tax rate. The regressive is higher the income, the lower the average tax rate due to the cap on the base taxable amount.

The U.S. Congress Joint Committee on Taxation keeps tabs on how much money the U.S. Department of Treasury does not collect due to tax deductions,

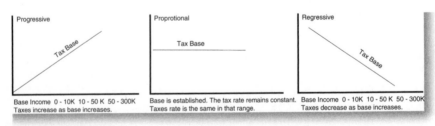

FIGURE 2.1   Different Tax Bases

tax credits, and exclusions. These tax breaks from 2014 to 2018 resulted in $4 trillion in uncollected taxes.[9] The most costly contributor to the tax break, the health insurance care perk, is estimated to be $785 billion. The next biggest tax break is the mortgage interest deduction, at $405 billion in lost taxes.[10] Capital gains were estimated at $633 billion in investment gains on sales of investments and dividends. Pension plans comprise another perk account that amassed $399 billion in lost taxes in five years. The step-up in basis attributable to an estate results in another $175 million in tax breaks, further reducing the revenues. The estimated uncollected capital gains from the sale of homes is $149 million.[11]

Staggering numbers like these are what create the necessity of diverting funds from other governmental sources to meet the infrastructure and policy needs. These deductions do not affect the average taxpayer. The health care and pension exemptions benefit the private employers, as they create a current tax deduction. Since the governmental unit pays no tax, there is no tax benefit. The public employee benefits, since the money contributed reduces the individual's current taxes. However, public employees eventually incur tax consequences in the later years of their lives when they retire. There is no guarantee of that money or guarantee-defined benefits being there. One only needs to look at Detroit and New Jersey Governor Chris Christie's threat in April 2016 to allow Atlantic City to fall into bankruptcy if the unions fail to negotiate for more conservative wage and benefit packages. Using the threat of bankruptcy to create compromise when the public official cannot negotiate fairly and openly or regulate negotiations is problematic. In the article "Why America's First National Supermarket Chain Just Filed for Bankruptcy, Again,"[12] Great Atlantic & Pacific Company (A&P) decided to default rather than pass the costs on to the customer. The article says that "A&P is blaming the unwillingness of its biggest cost center, its employees, to negotiate their way out of what will be an event in which at least half the company's employees will be laid off." Whether A&P or the public entity, there is a price taxpayers are willing to pay, and, when it gets to that point, it seems to be the only time the public holds the elected official accountable. Again, a no-interest-no-outrage mentality instigates extreme measures, like bankruptcy.

On the other side of the coin, these types of reductions force people to work longer and compete in the job market longer, not because they want to, but because they have to as a result of the impending decrease in benefits and increase in health care costs.

The matching principle of accounting works. If Christie and other governors appropriately funded these liabilities, where would the pension liability really lie? It seems to be the goal to divert attention by giving perceived tax relief in one area when, in reality, it's being paid for in another or telling public workers that their benefit plans are not financially stable. The revenues need to be matched with the purposes for which they were designed. One-shot revenues should support one-shot needs. Giving tax deductions while knowing you'll need to create revenue somewhere else that will spur another cash flow need is mismanagement. An easier manipulation of fund balance exists when giving the public entity the ability to mismatch the timing of debt to create artificial cash flow readings. Maturity mismatching is one of them.

Maturity Mismatching

In considering the issuance of debt to fund capital expenditures for a governmental entity, one significant concern is the question of how long it will take to fund the debt. If government mismatches the timing, there is an opportunity to create fraud and mismanagement. In general, it is considered good practice to match the maturity length of the debt to the expected life span of the asset financed. This allows the governmental entity to pay for the capital asset within a time horizon that is matched to the asset's life.

By not matching the correct debt maturities, the public entity is increasing the cash need of the current year's budget for a new school building with a life span of 70 years by using a shorter 30-year term; the reason being the principle reduction is lower on a 70-year term.

In contrast, the public entity reduces the budget cash needs by using a 30-year term to finance a police car with a life expectancy of three to five years. The reason is a 5-year term requires larger principle payments. These both lead to net financial positions being incorrectly stated by the public entities. Shorting the term increases the cash flow needed to settle the debt, and lengthening the term reduces the cash flow needed to satisfy the debt.

In finance, a commonly applied method of determining the financing term is to consider the useful life span of the asset and implement a funding method that reflects that life span. This is known in the finance field as maturity matching, or the hedging principle. As stated by Keown, Martin, & Petty, "An important rule of thumb for financing a firm's assets is something called the hedging principle. Very simply, this principle suggests that the firm's long-term asset investments should be matched with long-term sources of financing such as long-term debt or equity."[13]

One of the most widely respected graduate texts in financial practice, Brigham & Ehrhardt's *Financial Management: Theory & Practice*, places special emphasis on this point by stating it very simply and with extra emphasis on this issue:

> After a firm chooses the total amount of debt in its capital structure, it must choose the maturities of the various securities that make up its debt ... For all these reasons, *the safest all-around financing strategy is to match debt maturities with asset maturities.* In recognition of this fact, firms generally place great emphasis on maturity matching, and this factor often dominates the debt maturity decision.[14]

These standards provide the reader with good and solid advice as to the structure of borrowing within their entity. Fund operational expenditures out of current revenue: Keep paying for this year's expenditures out of current revenue sources. For capital investments, generally match the funding terms to the life of an asset. Say, for a fire truck—which has a practical working life of 20 years—one could easily argue for a 10- to 20-year bond funding mechanism. For very long-lived assets such as buildings, bridges, and roads, 30- to 70-year funding is not unreasonable to consider. Finally, for real estate acquisition, one could argue for very long terms, as the asset essentially has an unlimited life.

In practical terms, most public finance can run in short-term spans of 1- to 30-year financing terms or longer. Bonds with a life/maturity of more than 30 years are difficult to get issued, since the maximum term in the marketplace is typically 30 years. Generally, if longer financing is needed, the process of bond refunding can be used instead. Here, a given issue is retired with the proceeds of a new bond issue, which was issued for the explicit purpose of refinancing existing debt. Thus, an entity can pay down on a 30-year issue and then refinance the balance on a new bond issue, stretching the term at the same time and extending the repayment period.

The authors have extensive experience in working with public entities. They have been involved, on a regular basis, in discussions and debates over public finance issues. They caution the reader to get a broader perspective on the use of debt and maturity matching. They have seen that debt and maturity matching are critical matters that hold significant risk for public entities. Common practice, in their opinion, is not always good practice. In several cases, the authors have encountered what they deemed can be a distinct disconnect in the use of the maturity matching principle. They have found that it is common practice for local governments to use short-term borrowing and annual refinancing for a good portion of its debt through the use of bond anticipation notes, since short-term rates are attractive and may not require principal reduction.

Bond anticipation notes (BANs) are short-term instruments that are intended to provide "bridge" funding in preparation of a full bond issue. In practical use, local governments use BANs as an ongoing funding source, refunding them annually. This exposes the government to interest rate risk and any dislocations that can occur in the financial markets. The authors believe this practice has become common due to the low cost of borrowing in the short-term market as well as the generally favorable borrowing conditions that allow refinancing without significant costs. One should not be fooled by this success. It comes at a significant risk, as governments can have significant capital projects funded with a minimal one-year financing.

FISCAL FEDERALISM

One particular challenge to operations and good financial practice is the issue of fiscal federalism. Fiscal federalism is the process by which the central government provides funding via grants or transfer payments to other levels of government to pay for services and capital projects. These funds may be provided freely from some central pool of resources and allocated by the local government based upon local desires and controls. If the federal government provides these resources through an unconditional grant that is provided either in cash or by transfer at some point, then the local government functions with little federal constraint. Call this centralization of funds "fishbowl accounting." These grants create potential conflicts of interest among the government agencies vying for these centralized funds. The risk for fraud lies in the development of secret agreements being made by the people in control, who are usually trying to gain an advantage for somewhere else. We like to call this the "horse trade risk," which we define as the risk associated with people advancing their self-interests to gain access to value, for their own personal financial benefit. Both end up gaining advantage over the larger group. Example: Steven Spielberg's movie *Lincoln* demonstrates a jobs-for-votes bargaining scenario wherein enough votes are secured to abolish slavery. The political "incentives" and language may be different today, but the process is not an unfamiliar one.

Take a look at the case of Rod Blagojevich, former governor of Illinois. The case involved pay-to-play and horse trading types of allegations. The horse trading allegation was that Blagojevich, while holding public office as governor, solicited (via bribery) the 2008 appointment to the U.S. Senate seat left vacant by President-elect Barack Obama. The value is created when multiple parties are vying for a position. This is no different than supply and demand. The greater the demand, the higher the price.

PFDA

Rule: Examine grants closely to make sure that the grant (favor) suits the purpose, not some other conflicting interest. Look at any close relations and the potential for the horse trade risk as a way to preserve the systems and governmental structures to prevent fraud. Grants should be based on need, rather than a tradeoff interest rationale where "You scratch my back, and I'll scratch yours."

The central government may also choose to have control over a local government by using the access to federal funds as a tool to discipline the local government into conforming to federal goals. Example: The federal government provides national fuel tax revenue to the states to fund transportation projects, but commonly requires conformity to national standards with mechanisms such as vehicle emission inspections. The receipt of the federal funds is contingent upon compliance with things such as the inspections. These federal funds come with covenants like constraints that give rise to additional costs in order to comply with them. These grants run out of money, which means that these funds will need to be replaced (usually by increasing taxes and/or fees). These both raise issues in accepting a grant, because remember that the intent of a grant is to subsidize (temporarily fix). Therefore, the public entity has to put in place a plan on how it is going to pay for the services if the grant funding was to cease. This is no different than if you lost your job and did not have reserves to carry you over until you found a replacement job.

The use of fiscal federalism can allow local governments to take actions that are locally desirable but may fail to meet national needs. If federal dollars are available to promote regional development or public infrastructure, local governments may invest in projects that tightly serve local needs, while not using national goals to set their spending patterns. This opens the door for local governments to use fiscal mismanagement to promote their local goals using federal resources.

In most cases, the federal government may not have limited control or supervision over these spending practices, so local entities can divert resources as they see fit. This calls for well-defined and communicated policies and objectives with checks and balances surrounding the specific spending allowed by the subsidy, with surprise visits to test compliance.

User Fee versus Tax

One of the ongoing debates in Washington and in many state capitols focuses on reliance on taxes versus user fees for revenue. With many politicians committed to avoiding any tax increases, there is extra pressure to impose fees on users of a government service to pay directly for that service. This concept has been stretched and twisted in politics to include almost any government charge.

The tests for what is truly a user fee as opposed to a tax is multifaceted in nature. First, the fee should be charged only to entities that directly use a given public service, and users can choose not to consume the good or service in question. Second, this fee should have an extremely high percentage of the revenue raised and dedicated to the direct provision of the service consumed. Third, the user should not have paid through an alternative tax or fee mechanism for the service consumed. Finally, the fee should be set to provide adequate revenue for the service provided and not greater than the minimum necessary to fund the service. These standards provide some measure of good practice with regard to employing user fees.

In practice, the term *user fee* is applied to almost any fee. As former U.S. Secretary of Commerce Malcolm Baldrige Jr. was known to say, "If it is a Democratic proposal, it is a tax; if it is Republican, it is a user fee."[15] While this is just an opinion, it highlights the fundamental sloppiness (or weakness) inherent in the definition of fee versus tax policy. It is not simply the political party that proposes a given fee that determines whether that particular fee is a user fee or a tax. These tests, stated above, instead, provide a good benchmark by which the various forms of government-sponsored revenue tools can be evaluated.

With continual shortfalls in government budgets, there's always a possibility that there will be additional pressure to implant additional charges under the guise of user fees to generate more revenue. Such charges must be evaluated according to the tests put forth above to determine whether they are taxes or user fees. Given the generally high cost associated with collecting various types of fees, one must consider the alternative form of financing available for a given service, and if the user fee tests fail, then perhaps a more general, low-cost source of revenue should be used to provide the service. One must examine the burden of taxation and the alternative method that could be used to fund a given government service. By monitoring cost controls, and usage and efficiencies that are in place surrounding the tax or user fees, you are creating real government accountability.

The concept of a user fee, however, is very appropriate for those ancillary or discretionary services that may or may not be provided by the government. With a service that benefits a certain small segment of the whole population, a user fee may provide benefits to the group that is provided with the service. For example, a town wants to provide for a community garden that serves the individuals who lease plots. Given that specific residents will get access to the particular service, at the exclusion of others, it seems fair that the services provided to that plot are charged to leaseholders. Further, the government sector can organize and provide services to a plot holder as a consolidated group expenditure. Doing it this way provides each leaseholder with services at lower-than-usual cost per person. This is no different than buying goods in bulk as a group, which typically leads to lowering of the costs. For instance, water supply, fencing, and plowing of the garden in the spring can all be provided as a collective service sharing amongst the consolidated group, leading to the development of an at-cost user fee equally shared amongst the users.

The governmental entity also affords the consolidated group with an advantage in borrowing for capital investment at a lower interest rate cost. As an ongoing and established financial entity, a government can borrow based on its general financial conditions and typically at a tax-free rate. This allows the governmental entity to provide capital investment for the community garden at a lower rate than one would pay in the private sector as an individual.

A true user fee system can benefit the users of a service by providing services to a collective group as opposed to individuals and can provide lower-cost public financing. The actual users benefit with minimal to no impact on the taxpayers in a town or region.

The authors will argue that underinvestment in public capital that benefits particular user groups may be much more hurtful than applying a user fee to provide for the given capital or service. Take, for instance, New York City's High Line Park. This park facility was created in western Manhattan on an unused elevated freight rail line and opened in 2009. The positive impact of this facility on the revitalization of the district has been widely touted. This element of public capital has provided a core base of amenities in a former industrial zone and has stimulated various private investments in the area. If carefully chosen, this process has the potential to actually provide a net positive impact on local tax revenue that may more than offset the additional costs of providing the amenity. However, projects must be very carefully chosen—and public capital investment may well be necessary, but not be sufficient—there must be a component that includes successful redevelopment planning.

Pigouvian Taxes and Subsidies

Any fee or tax that is proposed as a partial solution to outside parties (taxpayers or users) for things that are bad for you and that are produced for consumption may very well be labeled a Pigouvian tax. Economist A.C. Pigou argued in 1920 that any good that causes damage to outside parties should be taxed to pay for the damage caused or to help pay for the social costs of consuming a given good. Pigou highlights the costs related to alcohol consumption and taverns. He pointed out that there is a significant social cost imposed by alcohol consumption, such as policing and prison costs. These costs can be partially or fully recovered by a tax on consumption of the particular good such that revenue is produced to offset the needed social costs. Further, the increase in price of the good caused by the Pigouvian tax would decrease the quantity consumed of the good and, therefore, reduce social costs, theoretically.

Carbon taxation and the cap and trade proposal are two good examples of applying Pigouvian taxes. Carbon taxation has been proposed to reduce the consumption of fuel and other products that produce carbon dioxide and carbon monoxide. These greenhouse gases are considered social ills and, as such, should be controlled. Carbon taxation has been politically controversial, but one could argue that by placing a tax on a good, producers with a strong need to use the good are much better off than going with some form of regulation that bans the use of a particular fuel or product. The use of a Pigouvian tax on carbon allows consumption of fossil fuels. It just imposes an additional cost on producers and encourages efficiency.

Cap and trade is another controversial proposal that has its roots in Pigouvian taxation. Here, in an effort to reduce global pollution, the proposal is to cap the production of these pollutants at a given level and allow producers of these pollutants to trade volumes of pollution. This allows the producers who can reduce emissions effectively—say, by migrating from coal as a fuel to natural gas and reducing sulfur dioxide in the process—to trade these reductions to producers who have a very difficult time reducing their pollution level. These costs would be placed on the "dirty" firms and would precipitate higher cost for their product, discouraging consumption. By allowing the trading of credits, one would get the needed reduction in pollution with the minimal amount of disruption to the economy in terms of output and jobs. The government could also ramp down the cap on a given pollutant over time to reduce the overall level so that it would be necessary for firms that need to maintain their level of pollutant output to purchase credits.

Goods could also provide social benefits from consumption. So it may be beneficial to provide a Pigouvian subsidy on their consumption as incentive to consume more. Goods such as mass transit use or education may have positive social impacts. Mass transit use reduces the level of automobile use. Less use of automobiles reduces air pollution and traffic congestion. By subsidizing mass transit use via a Pigouvian subsidy, the cost of mass transit travel is lowered, thereby encouraging use and reduction in a region's carbon footprint. Two key questions with respect to a Pigouvian subsidy that need to be answered are: What is the source of revenue to use to subsidize the goods? and How much will it cost to subsidize?

In the case of mass transit, these systems routinely lose money on operations and capital investments. They generally are provided with a tax subsidy, so that the fare for a rider is significantly lower than the full cost of providing the service. Typically, mass transit systems in the United States lose 35 to 60 percent of the cost of the ride. These costs are covered by some form of dedicated tax or subsidy. The metric commonly used is known as farebox recovery, which is the ratio you get by dividing the fare charged by the cost of providing the ride.

One could argue that education provides an additional example of the need for a Pigouvian subsidy, where consumption of education may be lower than socially optimal if the service was provided to the user at cost. The value of an education is best realized over a long span of time, with significant value accruing to the individual over the course of his or her career. By subsidizing the education of a low-income student, we lower the price of the good and encourage consumption. Society then recovers the cost of the subsidy over the life span of the individual through the income tax system.

GOVERNMENT REVENUE SOURCES

Taxes

Taxes are mandatory charges that governmental entities apply to various activities based upon political and revenue needs. They can be broadly grouped into excise, income, property, and sales tax categories. Various levels of government have the authority to collect these fees based upon statutory authorization. Of key importance to any tax mechanism is an enforcement and collection process that yields the desired revenue and also punishes, or intercepts and collects, revenue from individuals and entities that do not wish to pay the given tax or levee. Tax systems with weak enforcement provisions are generally not desirable, as the payer base can typically observe tax evasion on the part of some

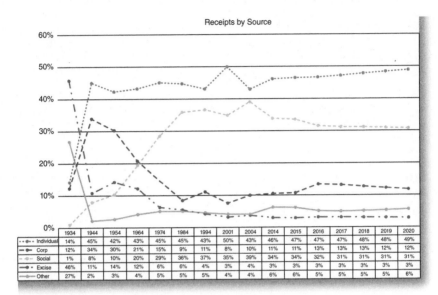

FIGURE 2.2 Amount of Federal Tax Receipts by Source
Source: http://www.taxpolicycenter.org/taxfacts/displayafact.cfm?Docid=203

users. If they are not intercepted, then the rate of evasion should be expected to increase. It is important to remember that taxes are a compelled payment, not a voluntary one.

Figure 2.2 shows the shift in the way the U.S. government has raised revenue from citizens in the form of taxes since 1934 to fund its operations.

As illustrated in the chart, in 1934, the personal income taxes raised 14 percent of the revenue and the Social Security tax 1 percent for a total of 15 percent of the revenues raised to fund the U.S. Government. Excise taxes, estate and gift taxes, and custom duties provided the bulk of federal revenue (72.5 percent) in 1934. In 2014, the personal income tax raised 46 percent of the revenue and Social Security tax 34 percent for a total of 80 percent of revenue to fund the U.S. government, according to the Tax Policy Center numbers.

Various forms of taxes have been proposed and implemented to provide revenue for government services. When examining the various aspects of taxation, one must consider the political environment in which they are created. These fees (taxes) place various burdens on different segments of the population and the business community. How and why the taxes are applied and the societal fairness of the tax burden are elements that need to be considered in light of the overall revenue goal.

Excise Taxes

Excise taxes are taxes that are applied to specific goods at a given rate. How and why these particular goods are subject to these taxes are interesting questions to examine.

Some excise taxes, such as those for tobacco or alcohol, are applied to artificially raise the price of certain undesirable goods to discourage their consumption, hence their common name, vice taxes. They have the added feature of raising revenue for the government. Other excise taxes are applied on goods to produce revenue for particular services and to provide needed investment dollars. For example, in the 1930s, hunters lobbied for excise taxes on hunting equipment to provide a stable base of resources to purchase wildlife refuges and fund other conservation efforts. To this day, guns, ammunition, fishing poles, bows, arrows, and other equipment are excise taxed at the federal level to provide for wildlife conservation funding (Pittman–Robertson Act of 1937 and extensions).

The fuel taxes mentioned previously also fall into that category, where funds generated by the fee at the national and state levels are then deposited into a segregated fund within the governmental entity to provide for a given service. However, these fiscal segregations are not absolute. The diversion of resources from their stated purpose, for various reasons, is always a possibility.

In addition, new legislative mandates may inspire new excise taxes to produce revenue to fund specific federal or state programs. For instance, in 2010, the federal government placed a 10 percent excise tax on indoor tanning services to fund, in part, universal health care. Interestingly, spray-tanning and self-tanning systems and procedures were excluded from the tax. One can imagine the day, given creeping legalization, that marijuana sales are fully taxed as part of the overall set of goods subject to excise taxation. That will provide a massive new source of revenue for national and state governments. When that point is reached, there will probably still be an illicit trade in marijuana, but it would be similar to cigarette or alcohol bootlegging, which is the illegal production and/or import of what is a legal product for the specific purpose of avoiding the taxes.

Tobacco products and alcoholic beverages were and are taxed at the federal and state levels. At the federal level, these taxes are administered and collected by the Bureau of Alcohol, Tobacco, Firearms and Explosives. At the federal level, these are generally excise taxes, with various forms of tobacco products taxed at a unit rate that varies by type of tobacco—cigarettes, snuff, chewing tobacco, pipe tobacco, and such. Further differentiation in tax is seen in cigars, for which the tax is a percentage of price. In this case, it's a rather steep 52.75 percent of the sales price. But, it is capped at a maximum of $402.60 per 1,000 cigars. This taxation policy results in the odd fact that cigars that cost more than 78 cents are taxed at a lower tax rate than cheap cigars and that no matter how expensive a smoke, the maximum tax is 40.3 cents per cigar.

Alcohol is even stranger, with the tax adjusted to reflect the alcohol content of the beverage in question. Separate rate classes for beer, wine, and distilled spirits are augmented with the rates varying by the proof (alcoholic content) of the beverage. Oddly, naturally sparkling wine (aka Champagne) is taxed at $3.40 per gallon—more than three times the rate of basic still wine at $1.07 per gallon. If the sparkling wine is artificially carbonated, then there's a 10-cent discount on the sparkling wine tax, up to $3.30 per gallon. In addition, there is a very significant credit for small producers in the wine and hard cider category, with a credit generally available for smaller-scale producers. For wine, this is a 90-cent credit per gallon for the first 100,000 gallons per year, and a decreasing credit up to 250,000 gallons.[16]

IRS Publication 510 provides a list of the various federal excise taxes and the current rates for the particular goods.

Property Taxes

Property taxes are extensively used by local governments to fund government operations and provide municipal services, such as recreation and police protection. An assessment is made of the value of the property under consideration, and the property is then taxed on an annual rate based on that value. Many variations exist on this theme. Some towns favor certain types of land use with lower taxation rates and programs providing tax subsidies and protections for certain classes of taxpayers. Property taxes tend to be major funding sources for local schools as well as municipalities, especially in New Jersey, and they are widely applied, the local school tax comprising approximately 60 percent of the total tax bill. While the Municipality's taxes comprise a far lower 20 to 30 percent or so, with the remainder being the county tax in the 10 to 15 percent range. The Municipalities (local) have the unpleasant task of not being able to vary according to income, and, unless some measures of control are implemented, they may have disproportionate impacts on low-income households, making them regressive taxes in nature.

Establishing appropriate value is difficult in some cases, as real estate markets can be "thin" from a market perspective. Thin markets lack a significant number of similar transactions and, as such, the assessment of value may suffer from few comparable sales. Real estate is a spatial commodity in that each property is unique in terms of location, topography, site, proximity to schools and businesses, and more. This creates variation in value that needs to be captured in the assessment process so that the municipality can accurately tax the full spectrum of properties in a fair way. Superior properties may transact infrequently, as owners seek to retain them. Poor properties transact more frequently, for the opposite reason, leading to a lower average value of transacted properties as compared to the full base of properties in a given community.

Property taxes are collected typically by a given local entity and then distributed to the various appropriate revenue groups. In New Jersey, for example, property taxes are collected by the local municipal government (which, for ease of discussion here, will be called a town) that runs the assessment and collection process for the other entities. The town then funnels that money to the various entities—county government, school board, library board, and the like. The town assumes full mathematical value of the tax collected based on its tax rate and retains no discount for uncollectable revenue or the cost of assessment or collection. As such, the local town (municipality) has essentially been burdened with the administrative cost of collection that the other governmental entities avoid and do not pay for.

There has been considerable discussion on the mix of taxes and the rate of taxation that is used in local government to provide for various services. Some towns use sales and special-purpose taxes as well as income taxes to provide funds for local services. Any form of taxation is subject to political challenge and limitation. In some states, local budget increases are capped by state law, as are increases in tax rates. These caps create the need for alternative means to fund the public entity. This makes the user fee attractive as they often fly under the citizen's radar. These user base fees are supposed to operate at break-even. Unfortunately, a creative public entity can start allocating to other funds and misdirect the funds to be used to fund unrelated purposes.

An example the authors have seen is when the public entity allocates costs amongst related entities to a user fee associated with, as an example, a sewer utility operated by the same government management team and/or raising the fees based on allocation of these costs. These allocated costs appear to be higher as a result of the allocations made and create a perceived need to increase the user fees. The increase in user fees generates more revenue. The additional revenue in turn does not address the customary sewer infrastructure and instead generates additional surplus. This surplus can be shifted elsewhere to fund an unrelated budget. Once a capital purchase is selected, say a dump truck that will be used by both the town and the sewer authority, the cost is then allocated more heavily towards the sewer authority—even if the capital is being used equally or more by the town. This then creates the need for additional fee revenue in the sewer authority to support this cost. Again, the regulations allow the funds to be used elsewhere and commingled so it is not illegal. So, once again, who is the fraudster? Is it the public entity utilizing these loopholes or the legislature that created them? Examine all cost allocations for reasonableness. Allocation means judgement and where there is judgment there needs to be high levels of skepticism.

One of the most famous caps on property taxes is California Proposition 13, under which voters in California decided, based on a ballot initiative, to limit property tax increases to 2 percent a year and to base value, for assessment purposes, on the date of property purchase. The net impact of this legislation is to protect property owners from large increases in property taxes and to favor long-term residents and keep them in their hometowns. The objective: As the market values in some areas have increased dramatically, property taxes have been held for those longtime homeowners at their historical purchase value. It's one way of doing it. Other states provide subsidies and tax credits to certain residents (such as senior citizens) to protect affordability for a given group of homeowners.

The unfortunate outcome of these caps on rates and subsidies is a revenue shortfall from the property tax mechanism that must be collected from other property taxpayers (existing tax rates on other users rise more) or through additional taxes on other goods (sales, income, and such).

Personal Income Taxes

In 1913, the United States passed the 16th Amendment and enacted the income tax. It was designed to replace revenues raised from tariffs, and it was intended to be applied only to the wealthiest taxpayers.

Personal income is taxed by various governmental entities and provides a significant component of funding for the federal and many state governments. The key aspect of an income tax is that it collects a certain tax on your income subject to various considerations related to how that income is generated. In particular, the tax effects related to regular income as opposed to capital gains—with capital gains having various favorable rates as compared to regular income subject to some limitations—are taxed at progressive rates.

Income taxes have a few favorable aspects. First, they tax at higher levels when individuals experience high-income periods, unlike property taxation, which taxes at the same rate regardless of income status. The

TABLE 2.3 Regular Personal Income Tax Rates for the Federal Income Tax in 2014

Single Filing Status		
10%	on taxable income	from $0 to $9,075
15%	on taxable income	over $9,075 to $36,900
25%	on taxable income	over $36,900 to $89,350
28%	on taxable income	over $89,350 to $186,350
33%	on taxable income	over $186,350 to $405,100
35%	on taxable income	over $405,350 to $406,750
39.6%	on taxable income	over $406,750
Married Filing Jointly or Qualifying Widow(er)		
10%	on taxable income	from $0 to $18,150
15%	on taxable income	from $18,150 to $73,800
25%	on taxable income	from $73,800 to $148,850
28%	on taxable income	from $148,850 to $226,850
33%	on taxable income	from $226,850 to $405,100
35%	on taxable income	from $405,100 to $457,600
39.6%	on taxable income	over $457,600

Source: http://www.irs.gov/uac/SOI-Tax-Stats-Individual-Income-Tax-Rates-and-Tax-Shares

structure of tax rates in the United States generally provides a degree of progressiveness, whereby the rate of taxation rises over a portion of the income scale. So lower-income households face lower marginal rates as compared to higher-income households. The regular federal income tax rates ranged from 10 to 39.6 percent on married couples earning over $456,600 in 2014. It is important to remember that all households can use all rates on each particular block of income and that Social Security taxes capped out at $117,000 in 2014. Considering that, the U.S. federal tax rates are mildly progressive as compared to income.

Capital gains are an additional source of personal income taxation. Capital gains are taxed at a more favorable rate. If investors own a particular security or asset for a given length of time, they are taxed at a lower maximum rate on the increase in value. Capital gains or losses represent the change in value in a capital asset, which is taxed at a given rate. Stocks, bonds, and real estate are simple examples. If one purchases a property for $400,000 and sells it for $600,000, the difference in value—in this case, $200,000—would generally be subject to capital gains taxation. The federal tax laws favor long-term ownership of assets

TABLE 2.4   Federal Tax Rates by Income Category (Married Filing Jointly)

Income Class	Short-Term CG and Ordinary Income	Long-Term CG
$0 to $18,150	10.0%	0.0%
$18,150 to $73,800	15.0%	0.0%
$73,801 to $148,850	25.0%	15.0%
$148,851 to $226,850	28.0%	15.0%
$226,851 to $405,100	33.0%	15.0%
$405,101 to $457,600	35.0%	15.0%
over $457,600	39.6%	20.0%

Source: http://www.irs.gov/uac/SOI-Tax-Stats-Individual-Income-Tax-Rates-and-Tax-Shares

by reducing the rate of taxation on assets held longer than 12 months. In the case of most capital gains, the short-term rate is the same as regular income and long-term rates are 10 to 20 percent lower than ordinary income rates. For high-income households, these capital gains rates are highly favorable in terms of tax burden. Table 2.4 provides an overview of tax rates on capital gains by holding period and income.

Tax Burden—Income Taxes

Given the hot political debate on taxation policy, it is interesting to note the overall burden of taxation (who pays) and compare it to income classes. Based upon the 2011 reporting by the IRS, the authors developed Table 2.5, which reflects that 78.9 percent of income tax filers in 2011 represented all taxpayers in the 15 percent or lower marginal tax bracket. The average adjusted gross income for these tax bracket filers was $29,928, and the average federal tax paid was $1,605. The top income class, which is the 35 percent bracket, had an adjusted gross income of $1,295,722 and paid an average tax of $328,665. Overall, the top 35 percent marginal tax bracket paid an average marginal tax rate of 25.4 percent of adjusted gross income, considerably lower than the top rate of 35 in 2011. The 16 to 33 percent marginal tax bracket had an average gross income of $48,102 and paid an average tax of $18,848, or 39.3 percent of their adjusted gross income, which is higher than the marginal tax rates, as illustrated in Table 2.5.

The top 35 percent of earners can typically write off more for charity and have other allowable expenditures. They have more to spend and understand the need to develop resources to shelter income through trusts or other deferral vehicles. The real effect of the personal income tax falls on the middle-class

TABLE 2.5 Tax Classified by Marginal Tax Rate and by Filing Status (Tax Year 2011, All Individual Income Tax Returns)

Tax Bracket	(Returns/Total Returns)		Total Adjusted Gross Income	(Total AGI/ Returns) Average AGI	Total Taxes Paid	(Total Taxes/ Returns) Average Total Tax	(Total Taxes Paid / Total AGI) Average Tax
	Filed Returns	% of Tax Filiers					
0–15%	114,642,063	78.9%	$3,431,054,060,000	$29,928	$184,016,945,000	$1,605	5.4%
16%–33%	29,590,693	20.4%	1,420,706,060,000	48,012	557,727,290,000	18,848	39.3%
35%	922,346	0.6%	1,195,104,424,000	1,295,722	303,143,255,000	328,665	25.4%
	145,155,102	100%	$6,046,864,544,000	$41,658	$1,044,887,490,000	$7,198	17.3%

taxpayer, as the resulting adjusted gross income is taxed at a higher rate. If taxes are raised in the (16 to 33 percent) middle tax brackets, these payers have less to spend on necessities. Ultimately, this hurts the economy because they will have less to spend. Imbalances such as these create deficits and inequality.

Cost of Collection—Income Taxes

In all of our discussions of various revenue tools, it is useful to consider the relative cost of collection and administration for the various tax and revenue mechanisms. Income taxes provide a useful starting point for this discussion. The IRS—whatever you may feel about its policies—is a very effective revenue-generating system. It reports a cost of operations in the range of .41 to .53 percent of revenue. In 2013, the IRS reported an $11.6 billion budget to collect $2.855 trillion in revenue. While this represents the administrative costs of collecting the tax (cost to the agency), additional costs are incurred by the public to comply with the tax collection system.

General estimates of the cost of tax compliance, due to the need for record keeping, paid consultants, and filing of paperwork, appears to be in the 3 to 4 percent range of revenue collected. These costs are foisted onto the public and are not directly observable as costs of the tax collection system. They are often buried in household and business type expenditures.[17]

Tax revenues should be developed for the sole purpose of funding government operations, which, in turn, pay for specific things the government wants to accomplish in line with the policies of a reasonable person's needs. Any imposed tax should maintain a voluntary system that keeps the citizens' freedoms in check and is always completely transparent. It should keep the cost of collection down, encourage economic growth and investment, and reward hard work and savings efforts. It should reduce the required paperwork from the taxpayer. It should encourage exports and not subsidize imports that compete against domestic products. And it should eliminate bureaucracy (red tape) and promote business friendly legislation. In the authors' opinion, there is no greater revenue generator for the government than when public entities create policies that spur job creation. Government needs to set the table for economic growth—via good and reasonable policies—and let the private sector select the proper industries and products to develop. In simplest terms, let the government set the table and have the private sector cook the meal.

State and Local Income Taxes

States and local governments may apply income taxes on households and corporations. These taxes range from about 2 to 9 percent on income. These rates vary considerably by state, and this offers an opportunity for firms, in particular, to handle the tax burden through aggressive tax management. These taxes may also alter the competitiveness of a state or region to attract and retain certain types of business. Much of the discussion about the burden of taxation and collection process from the previous federal taxation discussion applies to state income taxes as well.

See Appendix Table A.1 for the top ten 2014 state tax rates along with estimated population figures on July 1, 2014. As you can see, the high and low tax brackets vary significantly from state to state, as do the population figures.

Sales Taxes

Many states and municipalities apply a sales tax to the cost of goods or services. These taxes are assessed by the final seller of a good or service and charged to the purchaser of the good. Interim sale of goods is not taxed under a general sales tax, but only the final transaction. In the United States, sales taxes are applied to many goods and are generally used by states and local government to provide revenue for the general fund and specific project funding. The rate of taxation varies.

Fine Revenues

Governmental entities can assess fines against firms and individuals for the purpose of punishing transgressions and also to raise revenue like the Consumer Financial Protection Board (CFPB)[18] assessed against GE Capital in the amount of $225 million for deceptive credit card practices.[19] The Securities and Exchange Commission charged Avon with a Foreign Corruption Practice Act (FCPA) violation that led to Avon's agreeing to pay $135 million to settle the SEC and criminal charges.[20] NewDay Financial agreed to a $2 million fine after the CFPB alleged that the mortgage lender was involved in an improper kickback scheme and used deceptive marketing practices that targeted veterans. There are also seizures that the Internal Revenue Service, Drug Enforcement, and other agencies obtain as a result of criminal activity or noncompliance.

Fine revenue tends to be expensive to enforce and collect. One should consider the cost of collection and net revenue in any fine type system. The simple example of a traffic ticket which may appear on the surface as a low cost revenue source—until one considers the full cost of policing and court costs. These all contribute to the fishbowl of varying revenue streams. The question that needs to be asked is whether or not these revenues are matched and the payments are made for the intended purposes, which is to enforce compliance. What are the controlling oversight factors in place in the government system and structure to avoid potential fraud and mismanagement of these funds?

Fees

Governments apply fees to goods and services that they provide based in part on the idea that user pay is appropriate. They are commonly called *user fees*. Fees such as park admission costs, road tolls, driver's licenses, and vehicle registrations form a component of government funding that is growing due in part to a desire by elected officials in many areas to avoid raising taxes. Fee revenue can allow the government to provide special services to particular entities based on a cost recovery model of operation. People have options with user fees, whereas with taxation they do not.

Fees have several advantages, as they can be targeted to produce revenue from people who want a particular service. In many cases, a government can actually provide useful services to the public at lower cost than private-sector providers or individuals. For instance, in many areas of the United States, household water supply is provided by individual well drilling and pumping by homeowners. In regions with sufficient population density, the government can use the ability to borrow funds at favorable rates coupled with their organizational skills to build a general water supply system. Users can then pay for their access to and use of these systems based upon their volume of use. Fees can be set to encourage conservation and recover costs. The net effect is that a system that serves particular users can be funded while not burdening all taxpayers with the cost of a service some are not using.

Fees are generally more expensive to collect as compared to income taxes, as the transactions tend to be more discrete, the fee collection process more frequent, the size of transaction smaller, and the policing of evasion more important. The fee collection process can range from simple collection of a sewer or water fee on a quarterly basis up to a mass transportation or road toll collection system where users may have hundreds of millions of individual transactions per year representing fees in the $1 or less range. Careful consideration of the cost of collection and evasion should be conducted in the discussion of fee-based systems. A common range for cost of collection is 10 to 20 percent. In London, the London Congestion Zone—an area-based road toll—spends more than 40 percent of revenue on revenue collection.

Many economists believe a value-added tax, or consumption tax, maintains freedom and, in turn, a healthy economy. It is the most difficult to manipulate. It means the person buying knows that if he or she buys that good, it is subject to tax and the consumer of the good can decide whether or not to pay the tax. It's no different than the taxes on cigarettes or liquor. The greater the value, the greater the tax. If you can afford a $1 million yacht, you can afford the tax, as opposed to the person who is trying to buy necessities.

Government has to develop taxation and other revenues that revolve around the funding purposes and not this fishbowl, one-size-fits-all type thinking. As demonstrated, the ranges, the methodologies, and the types of taxes and fees do not replace sound monitoring of spending and funding of the intended purpose for which the funds were raised. Allowing any manipulation of funds through transfers and/or any other, similar alternative measures will create a potential environment in which fraud and mismanagement can occur in the public entity. Appendix Table A.2 is a list of the ways government revenue can be raised through taxes, fees, or other labeling. Knowing how the governmental unit creates its revenues (inflows) and matching the intended purpose is a major step in preventing fraud in mismanagement. Joe's Principle 2, the Show Me the Money principle, relies on a separation-type principle of thinking.

Rule: Apply FAGAAPA principle 2, Show Me the Money, and analyze the uses to determine whether the fees are being utilized for the intended policy or directive for which it was put into place. Is the fee likely to be continued, avoiding one-shot-solution thinking and the economic, social, political, and extraordinary circumstances that put the revenue (inflow) at risk?

As with any entity, government needs to maintain cash flow for operating working capital. Current assets (liquid) need to meet current liabilities (appropriation/expenditures) to enable the continued services it was designed to provide to its citizenry.

Transfer Payments

The federal and state governments are, in many cases, engaged in programs whereby they provide residents with government resources in the form of transfer payments. Transfer payments are payments from government sources for social protection and income support. Programs such as Aid to Families with Dependent Children, farm subsidies, Social Security payments, and unemployment insurance provide government aid to families and, in a sense, are reverse taxes. Households and individuals qualify for the aid payments based upon the rules and operational practices of the various programs.

The level and scale of transfer payments is often the subject of intense political debate. Recently, the political rancor that surrounded extending unemployment benefits to provide longer periods of coverage has been very intense. Traditionally in the United States, unemployment insurance is provided for 26 weeks, as opposed to European nations, where extended coverage beyond 26 weeks is common. President Obama and the Democratic leadership were looking for a longer period of coverage due to the recession of

2008; however, the Republican majority was resistant to extending benefits longer than 99 weeks of coverage.

Transfer payment programs are subject to the threat of people altering behavior to maximize both eligibility and payments from programs. Politicization by users and participants in pushing for the programs or pressuring elected officials to expand or extend programs creates the potential for implementing unsound fiscal policies. Farm programs and subsidies are intensely political. In certain key states, there are strong farm interests. Because of the makeup of the U.S. Senate, those interests have disproportionate power relative to population size in the political debate. Just an interesting side note: There is a growing scrutiny over the existing, grandfathered farm assessment in New Jersey, which offers a significant slash in property taxes to those owning five or more acres of land and using a certain percentage of it for farming. While it may be unethical, it is not illegal, due to an old law, for those in the upper income bracket with enough property to qualify for and take advantage of this special assessment. It can save them up to millions of dollars in taxes, by virtue of farming, say, honey on a small section of their property, or growing and selling Christmas trees or firewood to utilize this loophole in the law. This means someone with a large estate puts a small farm within the acreage and they get their tax burden significantly reduced.

Utilizing the T account approach (from Joe's first book) in the world of transfers means there must be an examination of the account where the funds came from and the account where the funds went into. Following the accounts affected by transfer and determining whether a transaction is a normal recurring one or a onetime anomaly is an effective control. Ask why the transfer is being done. These transfers often require journal or adjusting entries and are not like the writing of a check or the depositing the revenues, which go through the bank during the year as expected revenues and appropriations. Question these journal and adjusting entries. The need to transfer is typically the result of a potential underestimation of an amount in one place versus an overestimation of an amount in another, an unexpected event, and so on. These diversions warrant examination to prevent fraud and mismanagement. If funds can be transferred readily, then it means budgeted expenses are not being fully expended and skepticism should be applied. If it's a one-time transfer, examine why with the proper levels of skepticism.

Bonding and Borrowing

Bonding and other forms of borrowing present an opportunity for governments and agencies to raise funds without increasing fees or taxes. The downside to these forms of finance is that they are not revenue tools but, rather, are a way to provide smoothing of costs for particular types of projects, by spreading the costs over longer durations of time.

Borrowing can take the form of issuing bonds or notes, or borrowing from financial intermediaries. In any form, the borrowing is subject in most cases to some form of financial review of carrying capacity and creditworthiness. Government and agency bonds are generally rated by the financial rating agencies and are then sold into the markets at rates based upon the tax status and bond rating. In most cases, these issues are considered to be tax-free issues, which lowers the borrowing costs for the entity.

The **bond rating** is generally conducted by one of the three major rating agencies—**Fitch, Standard and Poor's**, and/or **Moody's**. Standard & Poor's and Moody's rate more than 80 percent of all municipal and corporate bonds. These firms evaluate the fiscal health of the issuing organization, the existing bonding and borrowing levels, and the risk and ability of the project to raise the needed funds. Combining these factors, the rating agency produces a general bond rating that is then used by the financial markets to set the value of the bonds and therefore the implied cost of the acquiring funds—basically, the cost of interest.

A bond rating is performed as a function of credit risk evaluation. A bond rating does not constitute a recommendation to invest or the risk consideration of the investor. These rating agencies perform updates of the public agencies ratings periodically. These ratings reflect and capture a specific time period (snapshot view). With any snapshot view there always remains the risk of an unforeseeable factor that can change the rating drastically.

Atlantic City's continued treat of bankruptcy and Detroit and Scranton actual bankruptcy, serve as proof of how quickly public entity finances can change. While there can be many factors that go into the investment decision-making process, the bond rating is often the single most important factor affecting the interest cost of the bonds.

To assist you in understanding the assigned rating for general obligation bonds, here are the factors that the rating agencies typically assess:

- ▦ Economy
- ▦ Debt structure
- ▦ Financial condition
- ▦ Demographic factors
- ▦ Management practices of the governing body and administration

The same criteria are also used to analyze revenue bonds and lease obligations, although additional credit criteria are considered (e.g., users and user charges for utilities). The covenants and protections offered by the bond documents are highly important and offer an additional consideration to the final determination equation. These rating agencies use mathematical ratios to compare an issuer to others (benchmark). There is the inherent problem that judgments must be made in the rating process, and, accordingly, the rating is not a scientific evaluation—it is subjective.

The rating categories in Table 2.6 are driven by the ability of the entity seeking to borrow funds to pay its financial commitments. The stronger the reserves (fund balance) and the greater the ability to raise revenue and be in a sound financial position that the public entity can demonstrate, the lower the cost of funds. The cost of funds is one of the most important considerations for a public entity that is borrowing. The better the rating, the lower the cost of funds. The typical rating agency's expectation is for the public entity to maintain adequate reserves to generate a strong rating, which in turn lowers the cost of funds (borrowing costs). In order to maintain reserves, the public entity must ensure the planned projects can fund themselves and that effective controls are in place to manage current and future spending.

Table 2.7 should serve as a red flag, since it represents non-investment-grade risk, which should be examined with extreme caution, as the chance for default is greater.

The need to maintain bond ratings and the impact of new or additional issues on the overall financial situation in which a given entity functions puts a strong constraint on fiscal behavior. In reality, the ability of the bond market to discipline the financial behavior of governments may represent an even greater threat than voter outrage. In fact, voters may be dedicated to a fiscally imprudent course of action. The final straw that draws a governmental entity into fiscally responsible behavior is its bond ratings and the reaction of the financial sector to fiscal distress, and is often the result of a downgrade rating by one of the rating agencies, which brings the financial concerns to light.

Generally, governmental entities have access to the bond and borrowing markets with a high degree of flexibility. This allows governments to flex their spending and capital investments in many ways. This is both useful and appropriate, as expenditures at the state and local level may vary significantly over time. Entities that abuse their ability to pay and ignore financial limitations may be shut off from additional borrowing or may see their rates increase due to a financial downgrade of their borrowing, or a lower credit rating. In the most extreme cases, borrowing is cut off and the governmental entity moves onto a cash exchange for all expenditures. This severely limits the expenditures category to cash on hand or drives the entity to raise additional funds.

TABLE 2.6 Understanding Ratings

| Rating Description | Rating Agencies | | | Credit Risk Information |
	Moody's	Standard & Poor's	Fitch	
Prime	Aaa	AAA	AAA	Strong ability to pay and capacity to meet financial commitments.
High Grade	Aa1	AA+	AA+	A weaker ability to pay.
High Grade	Aa2	AA	AA	
High Grade	Aa3	AA−	AA−	A strong ability to pay but has more risks due to result of changes in circumstances and economic conditions than the earlier categories.
Upper Medium	A1	A+	A+	
Upper Medium	A2	A	A	
Upper Medium	A3	A−	A−	
Lower Medium	Baa1	BBB+	BBB+	Has the means to meet its financial commitments. Surrounding economics or changing circumstances are more likely than not to lead to a weaker ability to pay financial commitments.
Lower Medium	Baa2	BBB	BBB	
Lower Medium	Baa3	BBB−	BBB−	

Investment Grade

TABLE 2.7 Understanding Ratings

Rating Description	Rating Agencies			Credit Risk Information
	Moody's	Standard & Poor's	Fitch	
Non-Investment-grade speculative	Ba2	BB	BB	
Non-Investment-grade speculative	Ba3	BB–	BB–	The public entity has near-term vulnerabilities. The entity has some major ongoing type of uncertainties and exposure that will more likely than not affect the public entity's ability to meet its financial obligations.
Highly Speculative	B1	B+	B+	
Highly Speculative	B2	B	B	
Highly Speculative	B3	B–	B–	
Substantial risk, extremely speculative, default likely	Caa	CCC	CCC	The public entity has near-term vulnerabilities. The public entity has some major ongoing type of uncertainties and exposure that will likely affect the public entity's ability to meet its financial obligations.
	Ca	CC	CC	Public entity is highly vulnerable.
		C	C	Public entity is highly vulnerable, may be in bankruptcy.
				The public entity failed to pay one or more of its financial obligations (rated or unrated) that became due. Defaulted.

Not Investment Grade

C	D	D	
e, p	pr	Expected	Preliminary ratings used when obligations are pending receipt of the final documentation and legal opinions.
WR			Rating withdrawn for reasons including: debt maturity, calls, puts, conversions, etc., and or other reasons (e.g., change in the size of a debt issue, refunding/refinancing), or the issuer defaults.
Unsolicited	Unsolicited		This rating was initiated by the ratings agency and not requested by the issuer.
	SD	RD	This rating is assigned when the agency believes that the obligor has selectively defaulted on a specific issue or class of obligations but it will continue to meet its payment obligations on other issues or classes of obligations in a timely manner.
NR	NR	NR	No rating has been requested, or there is insufficient information on which to base a rating.

These types of flexibilities create override-type thinking that requires a higher level of skepticism, which often consists of simply asking the right question. Controls such as segregation of responsibilities, authorization, sign-off by third parties deemed independent, and other strong measures need to be placed around these areas of cash inflow that potentially lack oversight.

Remember these rating decisions are judgment-based and date-specific, which means they can change on a spur of the moment. This is why in your soft skill arsenal you should make sure you remain cognizant of external influences, like rating agencies and the immediate impact they can have on a public entity's financial condition.

Bonding or borrowing is generally more orderly and helps organizations undertake many logical projects with high costs and long life spans. For example, a school district is building a new school for $70 million. This asset has a long term life of 30 to 50 years and will produce benefits for the region for the life of the asset. It may also lower costs of operations, as a new asset may have better efficiency and lower maintenance costs. Utilizing the bond or lending markets is highly appropriate, as a large-scale capital expenditure is not logically placed into one year's operating budget. It is logical for this expenditure to be paid for over time by current and future users of the asset, due the extended usefulness of the asset; this benefits both current students and, perhaps, even their children's children. Immediate expensing of the asset would create fiscal distress for current taxpayers, who would see their current taxes spike radically. Future users would essentially ride free on the value if all payments were expended in the current period, as in this case the asset has long-term benefit.

An alternative scenario is to have the school district save money out of current taxes for an extended period and then have the school be restricted from these accumulated funds for other than the benefit of the interest of the funding parties. Logic and practice indicate that this is probably an imprudent course of action, as local politics and temptation will be too great, and these funds would likely be raided prior to the date for some other expenditure, current or capital, in the 30 years leading up to the date of construction. Governmental entities have proven to be painfully inept at predicting costs of projects. So, it is usually highly unlikely that they would accumulate the actual appropriate level of funding necessary to replace an asset.

A simple, direct solution exists: Bond or borrow the amount of money needed for the project. The governmental entity knows what to borrow, since the project would likely have been bid on and, through the bid, a firm, basic cost for the facility would have been established. Then borrow the appropriate amount and set the terms and conditions for repayment subject to a strong fiscal plan and a given payment structure. If the entity cannot afford to commit to the payments, this is a strong indication that the entity might not have the resources to pay for a particular project. It is better to identify shortfalls early on, prior to the incurrence of further debt, making it all the more important for you as the examiner to understand the entity's ability to pay the debt back.

It is very risky to assume that revenue will flow in to fill the gap in funding. Numerous examples exist where governmental entities took on debt with the expectation of future revenue. This is especially the case if there is a failure by the government to create a forward look, rather than a pay-as-you-go plan. In any case, a bonding or borrowing model allows for more clear definition of the financial expectations for the project.

Management planning needs to include an analysis of the multiple changes in circumstance that can potentially occur within the public entity. Things, like an elected official not being re-elected, or an elected official that has been in elected positions for a long time, who may have become complacent or the other side of the coin empowered to rationalize themselves into gray areas. Other changes in circumstances may include demographic, economic, societal, technological, regulatory, and so on. Therefore, as an examiner, it is important to pay attention to the external pressures that are out there. As examiners, we need to make sure that there are policies and procedures in place to handle the unexpected.

BOND STRUCTURE

Bonds are generally split into two categories—revenue bonds and general obligation bonds. Revenue bonds are a broad category where the expected repayment of the bonds is obtained from project revenue. In later chapters, we will see that the words *project revenue* are very broad at certain agencies and, as such, bond proceeds may cross-subsidize a broad range of operations within the issuing firm.

General obligation bonds are backed by the tax base of an existing municipal or agency area. They are the only method of financing for projects that have little to no revenue prospects. Government services, such as schools, prisons, environmental projects, and public roads are usually funded with general obligation bonds.

Revenue Bonds

Revenue bonds are bonds backed by the revenue produced by the project. The mere name "bond revenue" calls for further examination. A high level of skepticism should be applied. Who, how, and when can increases be implemented, and does the entity have the ability to pay these increased debt instruments from the anticipated revenue to be generated from the project? It is extremely important to determine the future revenue stream that needs to be generated to pay back these bonds. It is common for large-scale capital projects that have the potential to produce revenue to need interim financing. This allows the construction of large-scale projects such as toll roads that are then paid for over time by the user base of the facility.

In addition, revenue bonds may be issued by public organizations in a pooled fashion—whereby the bond proceeds fund various project investments inside the organization. These pooled bonds blend the various revenue aspects of projects to create bonds that have repayment and risk characteristics that are more palatable to the financial markets than stand-alone bonds on a financially frail project.

For example, the New York State Thruway Authority (a toll road entity) has been further tasked with maintaining and operating the Erie Canal system (a waterways project). The Erie Canal produces little revenue and does not cover its capital and operating costs via user fees. As such, the Erie Canal would be unable to issue revenue bonds to provide for capital investment—as those bonds would not be purchased in the market or would have extremely high rates of interest due to the poor financial conditions of the canal system. By pooling canal capital projects with the Thruway Authority, which has a strong revenue stream and stable operating costs, the bond market evaluates the issue based on the total revenue and cost perspective of the blended entities. This creates a situation where the market is very willing to lend based upon the blended project revenue.

Obviously, the terms are less desirable than if the Thruway Authority Projects were funded on a stand-alone basis, because the bond rating firms will evaluate the total project costs (which are higher) and the existing project revenues (which are unchanged) and thus charge higher rates on the blended issue—as the financial condition of the total package is weaker than a Thruway Authority–only set of projects.

These bonds, if issued by a government-backed entity, may share the favorable status of being triple tax exempt (tax free at the state, local, and federal level). The issuing agency provides financial assurance through certain revenue and financial practices to provide security to the bondholders.

The bonds in general also have an implicit backstop of the general taxing authority of the sponsoring agency, state, and region. This decreases the expected risk on these issues and may lower the cost of borrowing.

Governmental entities may also issue revenue bonds to support private projects that have some form of government backing, such as housing, transportation, and economic development. The private revenue of the project is dedicated toward the bond payments, and the governmental entity has a limited role in repayment. The key role of the governmental entity in this case is to establish the structure and terms of the bonds such that they satisfy the public mission and risk profile desired by the issuing agency.

General Obligation Bonds

Bonds that are backed by the general taxing authority of a governmental entity are considered general obligation bonds. These bonds are paid out of the general tax levy of the governmental entity, and the bonds are rated based upon the general level of risk, debt level, and tax base that backs the bonds. General obligation bonds are then subject to payment based upon the general tax collections of the governmental entity and tend to be a priority expenditure for the issuing governmental entity.

General obligation bonds are useful for projects that do not have a dedicated revenue stream to pay for the borrowing. That does not replace sound judgment as to a long-term plan of generated revenues needed to ensure the repayment of the bond debt.

Rule: Look to the bond offering statements, which provide valuable information and insight into the finances of the governmental unit seeking bond financing. The bond offering statement is an official statement that presents the details of the offering and is a critical document in analyzing the debt. Understanding the ability to pay of the parties behind the revenue generation is critical, whether it's funded through taxes, fees, rents, tolls, or other government revenue generators.

 CORE ISSUE: GOVERNMENT SPENDING

Governments spend money based on a broad range of needs and interests. It is here, where value and people meet, that these often-conflicting interests need to be examined with a high level of professional skepticism. Political goals, special interests, social desires, and critical needs all play into the spending patterns of various levels of government. The ongoing national and regional debates that go on around government spending, taxing, and subsidy policies reflect various political orientations and beliefs about what the federal, state, and local governments' responsibilities should be and how to adequately fund them. Some political entities adopt a low spending/low service model while others adopt a high spending/high service model. Simple things such as trash collection, which seems a basic government service, can be provided through municipal service, with municipal trucks, staff, fuel, and disposal. The private contractor is hired by the town and paid from the collected taxes to provide the necessary trash collection services. The private contractor is given a fixed-fee contract that would require a public bid. This relieves the governmental entity from providing the services and incurring costs beyond the agreed upon fixed fee.

There is no clear right or wrong level in terms of government services. They are merely a reflection of the political will of the regional voters. However, certain services are naturally the providence of government. These services are generally defined as public goods. Public goods are goods where the use of the good or service is nonexcludable[21] and also nonrivalrous.[22] With these goods, it is difficult to impossible to exclude an individual from the use of the good. The use of the good by one individual also does not exclude another from its consumption. Streetlights and fireworks are examples of public goods. Since it is impractical to try to exclude people from using streetlights on a given street, charging for their use is also impractical. Thus, provision of such goods may naturally fall to government. However, fireworks are a useful example in that a given service is not always required. So just because a good is public, it does not mean it has to be provided by a governmental entity. In the case of public fireworks displays, we find it is common to provide the service via general public venue and they are typically funded by corporate and/or other donations.

Most goods and services provided by government are not public goods, so they can be provided in many ways. Everything from parking lots to public pools to golf courses are provided via public services. Most of these goods are not public goods in the pure sense, in that they are rivalrous and also are excludable—just look at your average golfer jockeying for a tee time at the local municipal course to see a great example of rivalry and excludability. Yet considerable pressure exists to provide these nonpublic goods as public services.

CONCLUSION

The sources and uses (inflows and outflows of funds) of government revenue are varied and controversial. Knowing how these inflows and outflows occur and knowing where the value exists by examining the inflow and outflows of cash and monitoring the people in the government system that have access to these funds is a critical preventive measure to avoid fraud and mismanagement. Developing new soft skills such as personality testing and Deviant Behavior Risk Modeling (discussed later in Chapter 7), along with maintaining higher levels of professional skepticism by brainstorming, we have further enhanced our soft skill tool kit that will aid in mitigating fraud and mismanagement.

The desire for government services and capital products is strong, so it is likely the need for government revenue sources will persist. It is these behavioral desires that create the environment in which fraud can remain undetected and ongoing. These types of demands will place continued pressures on taxation and government borrowing schemes. Examining the external pressures in a governmental unit's process is as important as examining its inner workings. We always have to be aware of the intense pressures placed on governmental entities to provide services and subsidize various private and public projects.

There will always be an ongoing debate about who or what should pay for government services, with no final resolution in sight. Given the interest in various forms of government finance, expect continued interest in user fee systems and alternative revenue sources, such as taxes on new goods and markets like marijuana, as well as the privatization of government services. The government's use of existing financing tools, such as bonds, cannot continue unabated. There is a distinct need to reduce the expansion of bond use without revenue sources to pay for the bond costs.

"He who promises runs in debt." — The Talmud

Government sets the tone at the top and needs to stop the credit card–type thinking and short-term approach to solving problems that were created over years. Rule: Promise less, deliver more.

The governmental entity should not need rules like the Dodd-Frank legislation, which created the Consumer Financial Protection Board (CFPB),[23] to implement a law that requires a mortgage lender to consider consumers' ability to pay before extending credit. That should be the expected behavior by the party responsible for the lending transaction. Citizens need to examine behavior and develop public servants who are principle-based rather than those who need governmental entities to implement rules. The oversight people need to have the ability to make the right choices. There needs to be people in the public entity who make sure other employees are doing the right thing. Rules do not make people do the right thing; other people do. People will only follow rules they understand and perceive as being fair.

Public-entity units that have debt should be held to a standard that obtains majority consensus and serves the majority interest. A high level of skepticism and complete transparency need to be applied to any public-entity debt financing. The justification for the need to finance should be based on a reasonable person's standard thinking and should make common sense. These types of financing should not be one-time fixes without examining what led to the need to finance a resolution to the problem.

The concept of centralizing debt must be accompanied by an assurance that the proceeds are not being spread across multiple public entities. Cross-collateralization needs to be followed up with a determination that there is a strong ability to pay. Such public entities should be able to clearly demonstrate to the public that there are sufficient cash flows within the entities to pay the debt. No leveraging should occur among related-party public entities. The public entity must maintain the proper maturity matching. A verification system must be in place that matches the term of the debt to the appropriate life span of the asset being financed.

Understanding current and long-term cash flow needs for the incurred debt is necessary to prevent fraud and mismanagement as well as ensuring solvency (current assets exceed current liabilities to create sufficient working capital to operate) to avoid exacerbating the problem. The fact that the U.S. federal debt is at $18 trillion and growing is evidence that there is an area that requires a clear understanding of the behavior surrounding such a significant debt obligation.

With the ongoing crisis in public capital concerning roads, bridges, and other public infrastructure, our need for public funds is immense and the traditional revenue sources have all but dried up. With the ongoing gridlock in Washington, D.C., and in many state capitals, the future of public finance seems murky at best. Preventing fraud and mismanagement requires Albert Einstein–type thinking. Solve problems by applying different levels of thinking by understanding the personalities and deviant behavior surrounding the value. This helps us develop solutions that can be applied to past history. Learning from our past mistakes can help us in the every-evolving systems and structures needed to prevent fraud and mismanagement.

Remember to look for potential external changes in circumstances. The successful entity continually develops people and policies that foster unified ethical behavior and common interests, which are two of the strongest defenses in measuring and implementing an effective fraud prevention measure.

NOTES

1. http://www.history.com/topics/interstate-highway-system.
2. http://taxfoundation.org/article/options-fix-highway-trust-fund.
3. http://taxfoundation.org/article/gasoline-taxes-and-user-fees-pay-only-half-state-local-road-spending.
4. http://www.nytimes.com/1991/05/03/nyregion/new-florio-fiscal-move-selling-a-stretch-of-i-95.html.
5. Jonathan R. Peters and Jonathan K. Kramer (2003), "The Inefficiency of Toll Collection as a Means of Taxation: Evidence from the Garden State Parkway," *Transportation Quarterly* 57(3), 17–31. Also Jonathan R. Peters and Jonathan K. Kramer (2001), "A Model of the Total Cost of Highway Toll Collection," *Proceedings of the Association of Pennsylvania University Business and Economic Faculties*, 39–42.
6. **Tax evasion** (typically criminal) is an illegal practice whereby a person, organization, or corporation intentionally avoids paying his, her, or their entity's true tax liability. **Tax avoidance** (civil) is the practice of reducing the amount of tax by means that are within the law.
7. http://www.encyclopediavirginia.org/poll_tax.
8. John O. Everett, Cherie Hennig, and Nancy Nichols, *Contemporary Tax Practice: Research, Planning and Strategies* (CCH, 2008).
9. http://www.bankrate.com/system/util/print.aspx?p=/finance/taxes/8-tax-breaks-cost-uncle-sam-big-money-2.aspx&s=br3&c=taxes&t=story&e=1&v=1.
10. Ibid.
11. Ibid.
12. http://www.zerohedge.com/news/2015-07-20/why-americas-first-national-supermarket-chain-just-filed-bankruptcy-again-spoiler-al.
13. Arthur J. Keown, John D. Martin, and J. William Petty, *Foundations of Finance*, 8th edition (Pearson, 2014), 460.
14. Eugene F. Brigham and Michael C. Ehrhardt, *Financial Management: Theory and Practice*, 13th edition (South-Western, 2011), 808. Italics from the original source.
15. http://taxvox.taxpolicycenter.org/2009/09/30/what-is-a-tax/.
16. http://www.ttb.gov/tax_audit/atftaxes.shtml.
17. *IRS Tax Data Book*, Table 29, Collections, Costs, Personnel, and U.S. Population, Fiscal Years 1980–2013.
18. The regulatory agency charged with overseeing financial products and services that are offered to consumers.

19. http://www.acainternational.org/cfpbarticle-cfpb-fines-ge-capital-225-million-for-deceptive-credit-card-practices-32311.aspx.
20. http://www.sec.gov/news/pressrelease/2014-285.html#.VRrKp_nF98E.
21. Nonexcludable: means that it is not practical to exclude from the benefit of receiving the good those people who do not pay for a good. A simple example is more pedestrians on a well-lit street does not add to the costs of providing the streetlights.
22. Nonrivalrous: means the consumption of the good does not add anything to the costs of production. Streetlights are a good example.
23. The regulatory agency charged with overseeing financial products and services that are offered to consumers.

CHAPTER THREE

Accounting for Government

"No man is good enough to govern another man
without the other's consent."

—*Abraham Lincoln*

Topics:

Regulatory Standards and Structures
Due Professional Care
Financial Reporting Practices
Following the Money and the Policies

Key questions:

Who's guarding the hen house?
Who audits the auditor?
Who's watching?
What personalities are involved in the accounting functions and the behavior
　　that surrounds these functions?

GOVERNMENTAL ENTITIES have certain standards and practices in terms of accounting. Government Auditing Standards (aka "Yellow Book") from the Government Accountability Office (GAO) provide a set of standards for accounting in public agencies. *The problem is that standards mean something only if the people held to the standards apply them. There remains differences of opinions and leeway in applying any standard.* Yet there is considerable *interpretation and application of these standards* in accounting practice between governmental agencies and divisions. How do these standards play out in the real world? How do they create the opportunity to divert resources from their intended purposes? This chapter explores the general operating practices of governmental entities and the common pitfalls that one encounters in operations and accounting for governmental entities.

In this chapter think of the authors as government accounting guides intent on demystifying government accounting. *In order to create demystifying aids, it is important to develop the appropriate levels of professional skepticism in order to prevent fraud and mismanagement in government. Understanding the personality behavior of the people identifying, recording, and communicating the transaction will help in designing effective systems and structures.*

The first step in *demystifying the accounting for the governmental entity is to formulate* a common language between government professionals and the public. Unfortunately, there are not a lot of courses offered at the college level that help a student develop a clear and practical understanding of the accounting processes and structures for governmental entities. Typically, these accounting functions are incorporated into the advanced accounting course curriculum in college, where the majority of the material is focused on *private corporation* accounting. Thus, most accountants get very little guidance with respect to government accounting. *The key to any effective accounting is the ability to communicate the numbers to the intended readers in ways that they can understand. The complexities that may arise within the accounting standards in government can mask long-term problems, as the financial statements are a historical perspective. These same financial statements are based on people understanding the proper reporting requirements and having the appropriate established oversight in place.*

Before discussing the differences in government and commercial accounting, it is necessary to understand that measuring the results of service provided by a governmental unit's activities is key in developing sound policies and procedures for accounting systems. The measuring approach requires an ongoing analysis, unlike financial reports, which are often annual, based on past activity, and taken as a whole. One of the best mechanisms to detect fraud and mismanagement is to watch the people in the process visualize and verbalize the results they are communicating.

SERVICE EFFORTS AND ACCOMPLISHMENTS (SEA) REPORTING

The reporting of the measured results of government programs and services is referred to as service efforts and accomplishments (SEA) reporting. This is the type of reporting needed to develop information beyond the basic numbers. Included in this type of reporting is information about the acquisition and use of resources, the *outputs* and *outcomes* of the services provided by the governmental unit, and the relationship between the use of resources (costs) and those outputs and outcomes. These are efficiency measures (cost-output and cost-outcome) of performance that tell the reader how well the government agency is doing in managing the government's resources. These measures are needed to assist citizens, elected officials, and other interested parties ("users" of the information) in assessing the governmental unit's performance. These measures include measures of service efforts (inputs), measures of service accomplishments (outputs and outcomes), and measures that relate service efforts to service accomplishments (cost-outputs and cost-outcomes).

The overall process of using and reporting SEA performance information is to assist in increasing public accountability and to determine the effectiveness of the management of the governmental unit based upon a performance measurement. This is a management approach that focuses on selecting, defining, and then working to achieve results that are important to the users of government services. Government transparency in communicating performance information—with respect to setting goals and objectives, managing, and allocating resources—and maintaining a scorecard of performance metrics is critical in giving its users an understanding of the value of government enterprise. For SEA to be effective, management must execute **planning, directing,** and **controlling** of the government resources through communicating results to the end users and sharing the foundation of the often judgment-based decisions that will be encountered. Requiring management to report performance can help the governmental unit in measuring the attainment of key desired results. Through this process, government's management skills can be improved to attain those results via more productive, prolific government activity. These metrics and management controls represent a more proactive response to organizational needs. They also help to create a more clear-sighted, more accountable governmental unit that is responsive to citizens, elected officials, and other interested parties. The financial information can now be placed into an additional measurement context that identifies the degree to which desired performance goals were achieved and the costs associated with those performance levels. These results then become the basis for future cost/benefit analysis and/or service delivery planning.

Expectation Gaps

Gaining an understanding of the similarities between government and commercial accounting will fill in some of the accounting gaps that commonly exist when one first examines governmental enterprises. One gap that needs to be examined is the differences that have developed between public expectations and the ability of the governmental unit to effectively provide the services. That understanding will help the accounting professional design processes to assist in evaluating the service results of the governmental unit that close these expectation gaps. The basic premise is that "numbers don't lie, people do." With a results-based approach, it's hard to fudge the numbers without a distraction, diversion, or division being created. However, as we have learned, need creates greed, and with greed you give a fraudster the potential to gain access to the government value.

This type of service accounting examination is all about the performance of management. If the results are good, the parties get reelected. Sound familiar? If a stock pays dividends or appreciates, people buy the stock. If people buy the stock, the company continues to have working capital. These pressures are what expose any entity, government, or private company to potential mismanagement and fraud. The concept is touched upon this early in the chapter to serve as a reminder that the numbers are only as good as the people behind them. Also, it is to remind you that accounting, whether internal or external, only provides reasonable assurances, not 100 percent guarantees. Management may engage in improper activity in order to meet expectations that lie outside even the strongest accounting systems. It is important to monitor the personality behaviors surrounding the programs and who is guarding the henhouse. This remains one of the reasons why value and resources are exposed.

Management-Driven Motivations

In terms of government accounting, it's important to remember that the motivations are somewhat different, with upper management elected to office as opposed to corporate boards of trustees, who are generally selected due to their investments in the enterprise or for their association with the executive pool. The elected official may have little to no expertise in running a large organization and very limited knowledge of accounting. How government runs and by what method its management decisions are made are important considerations. Listen and visualize the communications of the people making a critical decision and their motivations behind them. Make sure these decisions serve as the support for the reasonable assurance conclusion that is reached and ensure that intended objectives are met.

Double-Entry Accounting

Both government and commercial accounting use a double-entry accounting (debits and credits) system, maintain general ledgers (accumulated account totals in specific time periods), record journals (record transactions and events either needing adjustments or not run through the bank accounts or that need separate subsidiary accounting detail), record trial balances (adjusted period ending total accumulations), prepare financial statements (communicating the results for a given time period), and employ internal controls (strong internal controls create credibility in the numbers). However, there are major differences between the two systems of accounting.

A clear difference is that government does not operate to generate profit but, rather, to meet the needs of its citizenry. Government also has legal restrictions, with respect to both raising revenue and spending. Government also fails to maintain the match in revenue with expenditures, as often the parties funding the spending are persons other than the ones receiving the service benefit. In government accounting, the ethics, responsibility for planning, and management of the funds (resources) are entrusted to public officials.

Modified Accrual Basis

In Governmental Fund accounting, the modified accrual basis of accounting is used, rather than the GAAP-based accrual method used in private industry. Proprietary and fiduciary funds use the accrual basis of accounting. GASB Statement No. 6[1] explains the purpose of modified accrual accounting as a measurement of the flows of current financial resources into the government funds' financial statements. In the interpretation, the required standards for modified accrual recognition for certain liabilities and expenditures are clarified. These same standards open up the government to some strange reporting as to actual long-term costs. For example, governmental entities cannot record certain types of costs in the current year. For instance, long-term indebtedness (other than specific fund debt of proprietary and trust funds), liabilities for compensated absences, claims and judgments, special termination benefits, and landfill closure and post closure care costs are, in many cases, not recorded in the current year. These represent liabilities or expenditures that are not expected to be funded within the current period but, rather, upon maturity. So these future costs are not carried in the current period—the same period in which the decisions to incur these costs are being made by the elected officials; for example, the political costs of giving extra time off to government workers, in many cases, accruing zero costs in the current year, but you have one less person, which can lead to overtime and other costs as a result. This gap between reporting of costs on the government books and the decision point in spending creates a massive problem in the incentive structure in government. By allowing a governmental entity to incur cost—say, to guarantee a retiree health care—without funding any part of the implied costs in the current period essentially lowers the political pain of the costly decisions. It also creates less incentive to economize with government resources. Future governments have their hands tied by past administrations' decisions to increase future outflows of resources without identifying additional resources to fund these unfunded mandates.

Full accrual basis accounting is used on entity-wide financial statements and on Proprietary funds. Modified Accrual is only used for Governmental (General, Special Revenue, Capital Outlay, and Debt Service) funds.

This gap in reporting practices creates further problems in that it produces a structural underreporting of costs so that any elected official who tries to raise the issue of the long-term costs and underfunded liability may, in fact, be shut down by the other officials who operate with a current-year expense mind-set. That current-year thinking is not representative of the true financial picture. Only after long floor debate on a particular policy are the true costs identified and exposed and only if one party considers the longer-term impact of short decisions.

In general, a modified accrual accounting system records revenues when they become measurable and available. Expenditures are recorded when liabilities are incurred. Government is required to account for flows into funds separately within the organization to ensure that the money is being spent on the purpose for which it was intended.

Government utilizes fund accounting reporting, which reports specific revenues and expenditures in special purpose funds. Last, the governmental unit is required to create and adopt a budget in the general fund. It is an understanding of these differences in accounting treatment that enables an understanding of accounting for government operation.

Government Final Reporting

The Governmental Accounting Standards Board (GASB) was created in 1984 to establish standards for state and local governmental units' financial reporting. In 2010, GASB Statement No. 62[2] formulated authoritative information regarding accounting and financial reporting that unified and harmonized all Financial Accounting Standards Board (FASB) statements and interpretations, Accounting Principle Board Opinions, and Accounting Research Bulletins issued on or before November 30, 1989. What was good about GASB Statement No. 62 is that it developed major topics and standards for local and state government. Many of them are similar to those in general business accounting and financial reporting.

GASB Statement No. 55[3] established the hierarchy for generally accepted accounting principles for state and local governments. In GASB Statement No. 1, one of the core initial concepts was that three primary users of the government financial statements are identified: citizenry, the legislative and oversight bodies, and investors and creditors. In GASB Statement No. 4, the seven elements of financial position are further outlined and defined. These elements are assets, liabilities, deferred outflow of resources, deferred inflow of resources, net position, outflow of resources, and inflow of resources.

Assets represent government resources available to pay liabilities and carry on the intended purpose for which the entity was formed. Basically, these assets present servicing capacity that the government has in its current control. The liabilities represent committed resources that represent present obligations for which government has little or no discretion to avoid. Both of these are controlled by the elected officials. It is where the elected official and value meet that a high level of professional skepticism needs to be applied. The deferred outflow—with a focus on the mere word *deferred*—is a term that naturally creates opportunity to distract, divert, and deceive by delaying the outflow so the money can be redirected. As will be shown in examples in later chapters, these deferred and accruing accounting functions are, in many cases, the very things that create the opportunity for fraud and mismanagement to transpire. Similarly, deferred inflows of assets that are intended to benefit future reporting periods are treated as quasi-liabilities until that future period occurs. This would be the equivalent of unearned revenue in the commercial accounting world. In moving unearned revenue—a liability in the statement of net position—to the statement of activities, a revenue is created and a liability removed, giving the appearance of a stronger financial position.

Net position is the leftover element of the statement of net positions that represents the difference between the assets and deferred outflows of resources less the liabilities and deferred inflows of resources. Refer to the basic accounting equation: Assets minus liabilities equals equity. In government, it is not equity but, rather, net position that is discussed in greater detail in this chapter. How net position is utilized and what motivates elected or appointed officials' desire for and use of net positions is much more complex than the motivation of the directors of profit-making firms.

The remaining two of the seven elements are actual outflows of resources occurring in the reporting period and actual inflows of resources in the reporting period: incurred and paid, and earned and recognized. Deferred inflows and outflows are only recorded in full accrual basis financial statements.

Operational and Fiscal Accountability

Government accounting focuses on operational and fiscal accountability. The operational accounting aspects are government-wide financial statements that reflect how well the resources are being used and whether there are resources available to meet future obligations. Examine the personalities and behavior involved in the resource usage. Do they show how effectively and efficiently the elected official and his or her management team are managing operations? Closely examining and communicating with the elected official will assist in understanding the abilities of the elected officials and their management to create a solid visual and verbalized understanding of the reported transactions. The fiscal accounting aspect is reflected by the fund financial statements, which reports the funds operations as compared to its budget and provide assurances that the governmental unit is complying with the applicable laws and regulations. Again, what are the personality and behavior of the people generating the numbers that ultimately are being reported? Is there sufficient evidence to support the amount reported? The government financial statement standards require that the operational and fiscal accounting disciplines be reconciled. It is this reconciliation process that needs a high level of skepticism applied to make sure that there is no misuse or misapplication of the resources and that the funds are being used for the intended purposes. Understanding the levels of trust of the people developing the numbers and who have access to the value will guide you in where to place the appropriate 800-pound friendly gorilla oversight. Effective systems and structures need to be designed for specific communications. The more clear those communications are with detailed supporting documents, the harder it will be for fraud and mismanagement to take place.

Management Discussions and Analysis

Too often, the auditor gets comfortable or is concerned about getting reappointed. The fact that the public official decides on who performs the audits is, in itself, a potential conflict. As we continually state, management is responsible for the financials, and the auditor only gives reasonable assurances. Developing the right discussion points and strengthening the auditor's ability to formulate the right questions are important in strengthening the reliance on management representations.

The auditor needs to watch the reactions as well as the verbalizations of the representing parties. How well prepared are they? Is what they are saying well documented? Can what they are saying be third-party verified? Are required minutes available for public viewing of the discussion? How often did the group meet? What type of documentation was used in formulating an opinion? The more the right questions are asked, the greater the chance to prevent fraud and mismanagement. Auditors rarely prevent fraud, at best they identify frauds that have already occurred in the process.

External auditors are only required to plan their engagements based on consideration of the risk of fraud. The real responsibility falls on the management of the public entity to prevent fraud. The larger scale public units are usually appropriate to develop an internal audit function. With respect to all public entities, management is required to ensure the development of strong internal controls to prevent fraud and create reliable financial reportings.

The following sidebar identifies the minimum requirements for reporting the basic financial and required supplemental information. It helps to develop an understanding of how government reports the results from its various activities. The GASB defines the standard for a reporting entity. It also provides a context in which to evaluate the potential for fraud and mismanagement. A primary governmental unit is either a state government, a general-purpose local government, or a special-purpose local government with a separately elected governing body that is legally separate and fiscally independent of other state or local governments. A component unit is a legally separated organization to which the elected officials of primary government are financially responsible or exert control over.

GASB STATEMENT NO. 34 (AMENDED BY GASB STATEMENT NO. 62) GENERAL PURPOSE GOVERNMENTAL UNITS (I.E., STATES, CITIES, COUNTIES)

Management Discussion and Analysis (MD&A) - Required Supplementary Information

Government-Wide Financial Statements

	Statement of Net Position
Full Accrual	Similar to Balance Sheet
	Formula (Assets + Deferred Outflows of Resources less Liabilities + Deferred inflows of resources)
	Statement of Activities
	Reports Revenue and Expenses on a full accrual basis.

Fund Financial Statements

	Governmental Funds
Modified Accrual	Balance Sheet
	Statement of Revenue Expenditures, and Changes in Fund Balances
	Proprietary Funds
Full Accrual	Statement of Net Position
	Statement of Revenue Expenditures, and Changes in Fund Net Position
	Statement of Cash Flows
	Fiduciary Funds
Modified or Full	Statement of Fiduciary Net Position
	Statement of Changes in Fiduciary Net Position

Government Employees' and Officials' Responsibility to Find Inconsistencies and Irregularities

GASB Statement No. 61 goes on to further clarify financial accountability for a legally separate organization. It is often in government that the parties in the process fail to recognize the responsibilities they are required to fulfill. These government employees and officials fail to recognize that the buck stops with them when inconsistences or irregularities are found. Examining the personality behavior surrounding these failures is necessary to develop effective systems and controls. Where the government resource value meets people, controls can be left unchecked or they can be overridden. This is where errors, irregularities, and potential fraud come into play. To reiterate, the idea is that rules and standards cannot legislate ethical behavior; only with continued vigilance, using proper accounting practices, can fraud and mismanagement be prevented. The salient point: Accounting is not absolute. Accounting only provides reasonable assurance that everything having a material effect on the reported information is reflected within an acceptable measure of risk. That assurance is that the accounting is materially correct, consistent, and in accord with appropriate standards for the purpose of performing an external audit. Accounting remains management's representation of the Net Position of the entity on a date certain and changes in net position for the fiscal period then ended. This leads to expectation gaps. Accounting is also required to present fairly in accordance with the applicable accounting standards and practices, nothing more. This however, does not mean 100 percent guarantees. It is all about having the right people in the right positions with a full understanding of their responsibilities and the associated risks they face by failing to establish solid policies and procedures that ensure compliance with these and other types of established standards. The authors have watched lawsuit upon lawsuit unfold. Each of those lawsuits, in their opinion, was the result of poor human resource policies compounded by bad operational practice. The end result has usually been a significant dissipation of taxpayer dollars that could have been better utilized to benefit residents. One of the reasons this can occur is that there is the potential for tolerance or incompetence and malfeasance on the part of the administration, due to lack of effective internal controls and monitoring oversight. The incompetence and malfeasance are often manifested in a self-interest conflict. The governing body becomes more concerned with self-serving politics, while the employees feel a sense of entitlement (greed).

Parallel Interest Conflicts

Clearly, aligned groups with separate, but parallel, interests create the potential for conflicts of interest. Unions want more money and better work conditions. Administrators or elected officials may want to avoid political backlashes. As a solution, public money may be expended to buy peace and quiet with the unions or aggrieved workers.

The loser in this case is the taxpayer, who is left with future liability and was not represented properly by an elected official. Instead, the hypothetically bad politician, who should have been advocating for the taxpayer, is more interested in securing long-term political power for his or her party or the advancement of his or her own political career.

It does not mean giving raises to unions is inherently a bad practice if they are underpaid in comparison to similar size and geographically located unions and private sector workers—both union and non-union—in jobs of similar skill. As long as the reason for the raises is maintaining all interested parties interests.

Any established policy or rule must be applied consistently, contain the proper language, and clearly establish a no-tolerance policy that is applied to everyone without bias, or these and other lawsuits will proliferate. The best defense against employees' political retribution, sexual harassment, or any similar lawsuit is documentation, communication, and a zero tolerance policy for violation of rules. To accomplish this end, there must be well-written handbooks, well-communicated policies, and complete documentation of policy, training, and procedures.

ASSET AND LIABILITY RECOGNITION IN GOVERNMENT

Assets and liabilities can be manipulated to perpetrate fraud and mismanagement. The reason is that an asset in the former Statement of Financial Position, now the Statement of Net Position (Balance Sheet in the governmental entity), is a good thing. Move it to the Revenues and Expenditures and Changes in Fund Balance or Statement of Activities (Government's statement of Revenues), and it reduces the government resources as it becomes an expenditure. Similarly, a liability in the Statement of Financial Position is not good, as it requires resources to pay. Move it to the Revenues and Expenditures and Changes in Fund Balance or Statement of Activities and it is income. A simple allocation between related entities where one incurs the expense and charges an inappropriate allocation percentage to generate inflated revenue or inflows is an example of a potential manipulation of funds and misstatement of the true financial picture. Deferring, reserving, transferring, journalizing, and other accounting mechanisms are available to the fraudster. Knowing the rules is a fraudster-training requirement. Fraudsters must know the standards and ways to make them appear as if they've been fully complied with. Remember that accounting only needs reasonable assurance, not 100 percent guaranteed accuracy.

GASB Statement No. 65 (Table 3.1) clarifies each concept of asset and liability recognition, a key area of analysis to create greater efficiencies and evaluate management effectiveness.

To clarify, anything with Fund Balance are Governmental Funds and utilizes the modified accrual accounting method. Anything with Net Position is used in Entity-Wide or Proprietary funds accounting, which utilize the full accrual accounting method.

 ## STATEMENT OF NET POSITION

The Statement of Net Position requires the full accrual accounting of all operational and capital assets, including depreciation and amortization, and including infrastructure. Net position is broken down into three categories: net investment in capital, restricted, and unrestricted. Net investment in capital (the value of the capital) is calculated by figuring the sum of the assets minus accumulated depreciation, reducing that by the debt associated with the acquisition or any improvement made to the asset. The term *restricted assets* defines assets that are subject to imposed covenants or other externally imposed requirements by creditors, laws, regulatory bodies, or other governmental entities. The unrestricted is a plug figure arrived at by subtracting the net investment in capital and restricted resources from the net position.

For illustrative purposes, the authors use New Jersey's financial structure. It serves as a good example of the points being highlighted throughout the text. It's presented to illustrate the complexities associated with developing effective financial reports. New Jersey's various governmental agencies have multiple funds across all governmental entities and operate many services and business activities under the banner of government services.

One of the key areas in identifying gaps in fiscal controls is the concept of reconciling operational and fiscal accounting funds. This will identify many areas that have been subject to a diversion of the funds from their intended core purpose—for example, the state's handling of the Energy Tax and Consolidated Municipal Property Tax Relief Act (CMPTRA) funds or the Atlantic City luxury tax. Both are redirected and distributed based on what

TABLE 3.1 GASB Statement No.65, Concepts in Asset and Liability Recognition

All Reported in Full Accrual Based Financial Statements	
Examples of Deferred Outflows of Resources	**Examples of Deferred Inflows of Resources**
• Grant expenditures paid in advance to meet time requirements • Deferred amounts of debt refundings (debits) • Costs associated with the right to future revenues • Deferred loss from sale and leaseback • Negative fair value of government hedge of a future transaction	• Grant funds received in advance of meeting time requirements • Deferred amounts of debt refundings (credits) • Proceeds for the sale of future revenues • Deferred gain from sale and leaseback • Positive fair value of government hedge of a future transaction • Advanced revenue from imposed nonexchange transactions
Examples of Items That Continue to Be Reported as Assets	**Examples of Items That Continue to Be Reported as Liabilities**
• Prepayments of appropriations (expenditures) • Net pension plan positions in excess of employer total liability • Capitalized incurred costs for regulated activities	• Advances of derived tax revenues • Grant amounts received in advance of meeting requirements other than timing • Receipt of prepayment of revenues • Loan commitment fees • Refunds imposed by a regulator
Examples of Items Reported as Current Outflows	**Examples of Items Reported as Current Inflows**
• Debt issuance costs • Indirect costs incurred by lessor for operating leases • Fees related to purchased loans	• Loan origination fees related to lending activities • Commitment fee charged to make a loan • Loan origination fees for mortgage loans held for investment

the state decides is appropriate at any given time. These are required reconciliations of the governmental unit and thus must hold management accountable to sound accounting practice. In order to understand and justify these types of redirection, it is necessary to establish high levels of accountability for the judgments that are made with respect to the allocations of these funds. The voters' approval should be required for significant modifications to the use of the public monies that are collected in a fishbowl-like manner and redistributed disproportionately based on political whim or power.

During the authors' discussion of government practice, extracts from the State of New Jersey Financial Report are provided for the fiscal period ending June 30, 2014. These selected examples of the financial reporting communications for New Jersey provide a visual perspective to aid in understanding the financial communications.

The Statement of Net Position is broken into four columns: Government Activities, Business Type Activities, Total, and Component Unit. On the next two pages is the State of New Jersey's Net Position for the fiscal year ending June 30, 2014 (Figure 3.1). Familiarity with the basic components of the government reporting documents is critical moving forward. While Net Position is number-based, it is more important to gain a perspective of whether or not the servicing results are being met.

Where does one look to gain that understanding? To understand what the various aspects of the financial statement reporting are, first look to the liquidity of the assets to meet the current 12-month outflow needs. Are these assets sufficient in meeting current operational liabilities? Do they need to float anticipation notes since they do not have the cash on hand? Then look at future liabilities. Are they going to require future payments? What deferred expenditures do they have to meet and how long will they take to satisfy? Remember that the words *defer* and *accrual* create timing differences and are potential enablers of fraud and mismanagement. Finally, look to the capital structure being employed to generate the needed cash flows to operate the governmental unit. Is it primarily debt that funds operations? Do the revenue sources adequately cover the expenditures necessary to fund operations? Compare the cash flows to measures of the service results being achieved. In accounting there are three means to fund any entity: monies raised by the activities provided, by financing, or by investing. Understanding how the money flows into the various governmental entities is a strong control for preventing fraud and mismanagement.

If you were to review the Statement of Net Position for New Jersey, you would see that a good portion of current operations are funded through issuance of more debt, other assets, and not funding pension obligations but rather deferring the obligations. Simply look at the assets compared to the liabilities. If the liabilities are greater, you will have a negative fund balance of structural deficit, which is an imbalance against having enough revenues to pay necessary expenditures. To see the full 2014 Net Position Statements for New Jersey, enter http://www.state.nj.us/treasury/omb/publications/14cafr/pdf/fullcafr2014.pdf into your browser.

STATE OF NEW JERSEY
STATEMENT OF NET POSITION
JUNE 30, 2014

| | Primary Government | | | |
	Governmental Activities	Business-type Activities	Total	Component Units
ASSETS				
Current Assets				
Cash and cash equivalents	$ 221,387,556	$ 583,161	$ 221,970,717	$ 4,193,680,261
Investments	3,440,272,589	255,284,058	3,695,556,647	6,883,727,711
Receivables, net of allowances for uncollectibles				
Federal government	1,063,571,535	276,880,852	1,340,452,387	297,137,937
Departmental accounts	3,665,948,664	832,929,669	4,498,878,333	-
Loans	1,813,862,998	-	1,813,862,998	267,827,041
Mortgages	-	-	-	92,984,000
Other	740,351,948	114,713,838	855,065,786	695,450,529
Internal balances	144,707,427	(144,707,427)	-	
Due from external parties	10,623,042	-	10,623,042	179,809,967
Inventories	-	-	-	165,876,986
Deferred charges	-	3,027,054	3,027,054	-
Other	8,464,371	-	8,464,371	275,855,631
Total Current Assets	11,109,190,130	1,338,711,205	12,447,901,335	13,052,350,063
Noncurrent Assets				
Investments	-	245,502,273	245,502,273	4,452,010,399
Receivables, net of allowances for uncollectibles				
Loans	-	-	-	3,712,110,423
Mortgages	-	-	-	2,378,023,880
Other	-	-	-	142,595,938
Pension assets	4,022,726	-	4,022,726	-
Capital assets - nondepreciated	8,000,697,158	-	8,000,697,158	7,290,733,561
Capital assets - depreciated, net	17,531,319,656	-	17,531,319,656	18,305,916,139
Derivative instrument asset	-	-	-	7,553,000
Other	248,267,249	-	248,267,249	172,891,927
Total Noncurrent Assets	25,784,306,789	245,502,273	26,029,809,062	36,461,835,267
Deferred Outflows of Resources	1,121,885,236	-	1,121,885,236	490,937,548
Total Assets and Deferred Outflows of Resources	38,015,382,155	1,584,213,478	39,599,595,633	50,005,122,878

FIGURE 3.1 State of New Jersey financial statement, FY ending June 30, 2014

STATE OF NEW JERSEY
STATEMENT OF NET POSITION
JUNE 30, 2014

	Primary Government			
	Governmental Activities	Business-type Activities	Total	Component Units
LIABILITIES				
Current Liabilities				
Accounts payable and accruals	2,327,222,125	167,356,861	2,494,578,986	1,295,688,137
Due to external parties	123,863,888	-	123,863,888	273,759,368
Interest payable	262,897,761	-	262,897,761	323,765,499
Unearned revenue	456,512,178	-	456,512,178	490,994,443
Current portion of long-term obligations	2,453,202,328	50,768,499	2,503,970,827	1,062,442,656
Other	335,325,519	52,358,726	387,684,245	524,535,709
Total Current Liabilities	5,959,023,799	270,484,086	6,229,507,885	3,971,185,812
Noncurrent Liabilities				
Net pension obligation	15,949,329,630	-	15,949,329,630	51,218,784
Net OPEB obligation	23,573,700,000	-	23,573,700,000	821,798,749
Pollution remediation obligation	73,964,569	-	73,964,569	52,660,384
Derivative instrument liability	326,226,608	-	326,226,608	129,713,262
Other	42,817,670,443	246,189,172	43,063,859,615	25,006,401,948
Total Noncurrent Liabilities	82,740,891,250	246,189,172	82,987,080,422	26,061,793,127
Deferred Inflows of Resources	-	-	-	288,204,642
Total Liabilities and Deferred Inflows of Resources	88,699,915,049	516,673,258	89,216,588,307	30,321,183,581
NET POSITION				
Net investment in capital assets	8,038,178,174	-	8,038,178,174	9,861,171,479
Restricted for:				
Capital projects	-	-	-	209,089,529
Public safety and criminal justice	27,436	-	27,436	-
Physical and mental health	3,122,144	-	3,122,144	-
Educational, cultural, and intellectual development	408,129,775	-	408,129,775	-
Community development and environmental management	2,622,572,484	-	2,622,572,484	-
Economic planning, development and security	393,223,591	-	393,223,591	-
Transportation programs	2,374,581	-	2,374,581	-
Debt service	-	-	-	1,103,107,236
Unemployment	-	1,066,720,937	1,066,720,937	-
Prize awards and State contributions	-	819,283	819,283	6,205,783,766
Unrestricted	(62,152,161,079)	-	(62,152,161,079)	2,304,787,287
Total Net Position	$ (50,684,532,894)	$ 1,067,540,220	$ (49,616,992,674)	$ 19,683,939,297

FIGURE 3.1 (Continued)

GORDON GECKO ACCOUNTING

A scenario comes to mind from the first *Wall Street* movie that demonstrates the flawed kicking-the-can-down-the-road approach to financial mismanagement. It's a cautionary tale that can be applied to government finance. In the film, aspiring Wall Street corporate raider Bud Fox (Charlie Sheen) pitches an idea to senior corporate raider Gordon Gekko (Michael Douglas) to buy Blue Star Airlines and expand the company, with Bud as president. The idea, applied to government, is that any savings achieved through union concessions and the raiding of the cash value of an overfunded pension is replaced with a minimally funded plan. In New Jersey, Governor Chris Christie continuing a long-term practice of not funding the state employee pension plans and using the funds elsewhere is applying a similar concept in attempting to hold the line on taxes. "The unfunded liability has been climbing since the turn of the 21st century, largely because of investment losses, increased benefits and chronic underfunding. In a National Association of State Retirement Administrators' study of states' contribution from 2001 to 2013, New Jersey had the worst record."[4]

That same article points out that, despite New Jersey having the worst record, the state portion of the pension system was worth about $42.5 billion at the end of the 2014 fiscal year. The price tag to meet retirement promises was estimated at $82.6 billion, which results in the ratio of assets to liabilities of 51.5 percent. For every fifty one and a half cents of assets there is a dollar of debt. The article also states that a pension fund with an 80 percent funding ratio is considered healthy. This allowance of some underfunding may be reflective of a model of funding where economic and population growth would provide future revenue growth for governmental entities—an assumption that may be out of line for developed states with aging infrastructure. One only has to look to Michigan to see that population and economic growth is not assured for any state. These sorts of policy decisions are what create conflicts and cause poor financial choices by elected officials. With respect to fraud, manipulation of debt is a key way to gerrymander financial results. For example: Enron. Andrew Fastow (Enron's CFO) reduced the balance-sheet debt, maintained the credit rating, and reduced the cost of capital while simultaneously growing the balance sheet. This appears to have been facilitated in part by the ineptitude of the bond rating agencies, who fell prey to financial manipulation. Sound familiar? Using other related entities—such as authorities, bi-state agencies, and federal, state, county, and municipal government—spins on the same basic mode of financial manipulation can be applied. It's another way to fund government that may or may not be so transparent to citizens. Understanding net position is extremely useful in analyzing the assets, liabilities, and related-party transactions of a governmental unit to create accountability and preserve the governmental unit's resources.

There is good news in that the GASB recognized the problem and has formulated the new GASB Statement No. 68, Accounting and Financial Reporting for Pensions, amending GASB Statement No. 27. The summary: "The primary objective of this Statement is to **improve accounting and financial reporting** by state and local governments for pensions. It also **improves information** provided by state and local governmental employers about financial support for pensions that is provided by other entities. This statement results from a comprehensive review of the effectiveness of existing standards of accounting and financial reporting for pensions with regard to **providing decision-useful information**, supporting assessments of accountability and interperiod equity, and creating additional transparency."[5] The reason these key words in the summary are highlighted is to drive home that the numbers and information are not circumvented with political spin. The actuaries provide the appropriate funding to be made even if the oversee-ing government body decides not to fund. Even the best financial reporting means nothing. Numbers mean nothing if they are manipulated or the ethical standards in place are not followed. There is no way to regulate bad decisions to advance self-interest at the expense of creating potential conflicts of interest. High levels of professional skepticism need to be applied.

Interfund Transfers

Another governmental accounting practice that needs to have attention called to it is interfund transfers. Look for journal entries involving transfers when they involve related public entities, and monitor them closely. While it is recognized that using the money in the short term to pay obligations can result in interest savings, anytime there are transfers, or the use of interfund money to fund operational or other unrelated purposes, a policy should be in place that requires proper authorization. The other important consideration is to make sure the entity that the money was transferred to has the liquidity to return the funds.

If the funds are not used for their intended purpose, the citizenry should be reimbursed. Raising funds for unrelated purposes is unethical. It seems that government, in some cases, can justify approving regulations, passing resolutions, or adopting ordinances to circumvent the purpose for which funds were intended. These types of deviations should require the citizens' (voters) approval. Yet agencies again and again prove that political influence and meddling will cause agencies to transfer funds for inappropriate purposes.

Recently, the Port Authority of New York and New Jersey (PANYNJ) has been in a fight with bondholders and is currently subject to a Securities and Exchange Commission investigation over the diversion of $1.8 billion in funds to New Jersey Department of Transportation projects which are not owned or operated by the PANYNJ. This was motivated by pressure from Governor Chris Christie to fund these projects. No authorization of these fund transfers was required other than PANYNJ board action.

All governmental units should prepare a simple reconciliation report that demonstrates there is sufficient liquidity to clear all interfund transfers between these entities and/or related-party balances across the governmental units. Doing this will bring to light how the governmental unit funded its operations and how the funds interact with each other. It will also bring to light the governmental entities that are ending up with positive cash flows and ones that are not. Determining liquidity is an important part of the reconciliation of operational and fiscal accounting (fund).

In addition, there should be a plan in place for how future expected obligations will be funded. An example is an expiring grant that funds a current operational expense, such as expiring employment grants even though the employee expense will continue. Another example is the unfunded accrued sick-time deferring of liabilities that require expending of resources out of the current operations rather than reserving for them prior to payment. Any deferred future obligation should be met with long-term planning, not relying on current period operational funds (pay as you go thinking) to satisfy.

Inflow and Outflow of Cash

With all the potential areas of accounting for government, the focus will be on the inflows and outflows of cash to learn to develop a follow-the-money feel, paraphrasing the signature slogan from the movie *Jerry McGuire*, "Show me the money!" Notice that the word *feel* is used. The reason: Simply checking the numbers in an after-the-fact verification process does not replace thinking about whether or not a transaction **feels** right. How is this transaction being reported? When, where, and why? Such questions are critical in professional development and ensuring the money is being used for its intended purpose. It is all about following the money trail, whether it is the receipt of money or the spending of money.

Related Statements

Reconciling the fund balance sheet to the Statement of Net Position by analyzing a governmental unit like New Jersey or any public entity tells a lot about the governmental unit being examined. For instance, we have taken a look at

New Jersey's June 30, 2014,[6]Reconciliation of the Governmental Funds Balance Sheet to the Statement of Net Position. The governments are required to provide a summary reconciliation of total governmental fund balances to net position of governmental activities in the statement of net position. Let's examine the State of New Jersey's June 30, 2014, Reconciliation of the Governmental Funds Balance Sheet to the Statement of Net Position. In Figure 3.2 we have only showed the top portion of the statement, but we have provided the link where the full statement can be obtained below the figure.

The Fund balance taken from page 35 of New Jersey's Comprehensive Financial Reporting statement dated June 30, 2014, is $7,119,274,763; the statement reflects that there is $625,961,657 timing difference, capital assets net of accumulated depreciation of $25,532,016,814 not liquid, unearned tobacco settlement of $121,030,000, and other deferred outflows that are not current resources of $1,121,885,236, so the total assets-related fund balance sheet is roughly $33.3 billion. The current liability is $2,716,100,089. The noncurrent liabilities total $82,740,891,250. So the total liability is

---

STATE OF NEW JERSEY
RECONCILIATION OF THE GOVERNMENTAL FUNDS
BALANCE SHEET TO THE STATEMENT OF NET POSITION
JUNE 30, 2014

Total fund balances of governmental funds	$7,119,274,763
Amounts reported for governmental activities in the statement of net position are different as a result of the following items:	
Some of the State's revenues will be collected after year-end, but are not available soon enough to pay for the current period's expenditures and therefore are deferred in the funds.	625,961,657

FIGURE 3.2 "Reconciliation of the Governmental Funds Balance Sheet to the Statement of Net Position,"
http://www.state.nj.us/treasury/omb/publications/14cafr/pdf/fullcafr2014.pdf
(see page 35 of the pdf for the full statement).

roughly $85.5 billion. Insolvency is when liabilities exceed assets, so, by definition, New Jersey is insolvent. Assets are likely to be significantly understated in terms of value less than liabilities by $52.2 billion. There is a $12.5 billion depreciation expense, which is noncash. Where is the result of non-cash-type spending, which should be available for actual paid expenditures? You cannot look just to the bottom line numbers.

Let's examine what the numbers are really saying and the mistruths inherent in what is often heard from elected officials and administrators.

The $25.5 million in capital assets, if they were to be appraised, calls into question the real value of the State of New Jersey's depreciated capital assets; one would think well beyond the net historical carried costs. With that in mind, the capital assets are understated.

Another concern in the New Jersey fund reconciliation and financial statements is the term *deferred assets*, which immediately brings one case study to mind: WorldCom. WorldCom was once the fifth most widely held stock in the country and, at one time, the number-one provider of shareholder returns over a 10-year period. The CFO, Scott Sullivan, was at one time the highest-paid CFO in the country and was presented the CFO Excellence Award from *CFO Magazine* for his work in mergers and acquisitions. When WorldCom had to restate its financials by $3.8 billion, related to improper accounting treatment of operating expenses, it was a prime example of how deferring items can clearly manipulate the financial cash flow of an entity. Remember, both assets and expenses have debit balances and, depending on which statement they are placed in, can manipulate the financial perspectives.

Anytime an expense moves to the Statement of Net Position (balance sheet), it becomes an asset. The fact is that this is not a liquid asset, like cash, but an expense/transaction that was funded prior to its required recognition in accordance with accounting practices. Assets that are perceived to be good are already expended and will reduce future periods' results. Similarly, a deferred inflow would be cash that was received prior to it being required to be recognized under accounting standards. This transaction is reflected as a liability until that required time or condition is met. This is something that looks like a liability but is really going to create additional revenue and be available once the condition leading to its deferral has been met and it becomes recordable.

Statement No. 63[7] of the Governmental Accounting Standards Board Financial Reporting of Deferred Outflows of Resources, Deferred Inflows of Resources, and Net Position explains, in great detail, reporting state and local governments entering into transactions that result in the consumption or acquisition of net assets in one period that are applicable to future periods. These are areas that require a higher level of professional skepticism.

With New Jersey, or any government/public agency that bases its capital structure on using debt, the financial position will appear insolvent since the assets are not assessed at fair value as well as net of depreciation and amortization, which are noncash expenses (not requiring actual outflow of cash). The debts and obligations are stated at the present value, as-of date, which represents the best estimate of money owed. The debt at a present value versus the assets remaining at their cost rather than fair value can create an appearance of insolvency in the public entity.

If New Jersey had a net position that was positive, it would probably be pretty hard to convince the public that a tax increase was justified and public workers were not entitled to increases in wages. These types of manipulations are those that lead to potential mismanagement and fraud. The question: What is the real position of the State of New Jersey? It is certainly not a "firm" with a $50.6 billion deficit as of a certain date, that is, unless everything is required to be paid at that date. Like a tech startup company with significant long term value, governmental entities are given a bit of a "bye" in terms of financial solvency as compared to commercial entities. But this favorable treatment can end; see the case of Detroit in terms of borrowing and bond ratings over the last 10 years. A good policy would be to require government and/or any public agency to achieve and maintain structural balance where recurring revenues are required to be equal to recurring expenditures in the adopted budget.

BUDGETING AND ONE-SHOT ACCOUNTING IN GOVERNMENT

To begin this discussion, it makes sense to first home in on the budgeting concepts that are taught in managerial accounting and finance. Again, these are typically integrated into managerial (cost) accounting and focus on the private sector. In this chapter, these and other accounting processes and structures from the government perspective are explored to develop the necessary working base of knowledge to prevent fraud and mismanagement in government.

Consider a municipal government. In standard commercial accounting practice, a current-year operating budget would be set and a future-oriented multiple-year planning budget would be developed. Typically, these budgets are set in the period prior to the actual operational period, with, for example, roughly a seven-month prior window for the budget process and the budgeting process starting in July of the prior year to establish a budget for the next calendar year. So the planning cycle would start in July 2015 for the 2016 operating budget, with a final budget set by mid-December 2015 for all months in 2016. The governmental unit then would operate and track against this budget in

2016—typically, on a monthly basis. The process is outlined here to illustrate standard corporate practice. This differs sharply from government practice. What is paramount in budgeting is having clearly defined assumptions that serve as the basis for management's numbers. Unsupported or unrealistic assumptions defeat the whole purpose of budgeting.

In government budgeting, this process may not follow the same logical path. In fact, it is common practice in some states for the budget process to not commence prior to the operating year. In New Jersey, the local governments typically adopt a budget roughly five months into the fiscal year. This means that the governmental entities provide their services without any true budgetary process for almost one-half of the fiscal year. Many states have histories of late budgets, and this creates the potential to have significant periods without proper budget-tracking documentation. Further constraints on spending are possible if a state or locality cannot pass its budget. New York State was famous for not passing budgets. The budget was late each year for a 20-year period from 1985 to 2004.

Further compounding the problem, in New Jersey, municipal government can alter the budgets in the three months in the beginning of the budget-year cycle and two months at the end. The first question that should be asked is: Where is the control in allowing such flexibility to the government's oversight? Does this thinking impose spending restrictions or encourage responsible spending? A simple increase in a budget appropriation/expenditure line that is not being spent and is later moved to another budget appropriation/expenditure line by this transfer mechanism (possibly to reward supporters who worked on the campaign or to influence the politician's potential reelection) says that it does not prevent potential fraud and mismanagement. Where is the responsible person saying that this does not **feel** right? It still happens every year: The same account transfers are being made between, or possibly to another, unrelated appropriation/expenditure. If the government was really formulating responsible and transparent budgets, then transferring of overfunded expenditure's to underfunded expenditures would be a limited practice instead of an annual occurrence.

Budgetary modifications should be the exception, not the norm. In cases where unexpected expenditures have occurred—for example, due to exceptional snowfall, a hurricane, or a tornado—then it is expected that the public-entity budgets would need modifications. In the planning phase of the budgetary process, plans are made for spending near the norm—not for the exceptional event. When these events occur, budgets can and should be modified as needed. That being said, consistent patterns of budget modifications in particular ways may well indicate financial manipulation.

BUDGET MANIPULATIONS

Here is yet another warning sign: The budget states that more people will be hired in certain departments and there is no hiring there. Padding expenses means revenue was raised that was not used for the represented purpose, indicating overtaxing. This begs the question of where that money is and for what, exactly, it was used.

Another potential manipulation that can occur is when the revenue estimates are intentionally lowered, so that more revenue is received in the current budget year than was needed to fund the operations. This means the governmental unit had more cash than it needed to operate. In government, the action of understating revenue estimates creates surplus, which becomes a potential one-shot future revenue. It creates a temporary sound bite that enables the politician to say, "We are not raising taxes," because the surplus is used as a revenue. Basically, the taxpayers, or users of the service, were overcharged in prior periods.

Surplus, simply stated, is the inflow of revenues and other sources of inflows that are greater than the outflows of appropriations/expenditures or other types of outflows. In accounting terms, the debits are less than the credits. One-shot revenues and/or appropriations/expenditures are going to occur only in the one budgetary period or for a period-specific time period. When budgeting this type of revenue, extreme caution should be applied, with a lot of transparency.

One example of a one-shot revenue that can cause a drain on future revenue or lead to potential layoffs is the Staffing for Adequate Fire and Emergency Response (SAFER grant). It was created by the Federal Fire Prevention and Control Act of 1974, 15 U.S.C. 2201 et seq.[8] Once again, there is a temporary political goodwill sound bite that public safety is being improved and it will not cost the taxpayers any money, which is clearly not the case, as it is not a permanent revenue stream. It offers temporary cash flow relief.

As with any of the numerous grants available, the intentions are always good. Unfortunately, the lack of systems and structures in place to manage these grants allows them to lead to significant future budget shortfalls. In this case, it allows for the hiring of more firefighters and funds beyond the amounts raised in the operational budget. These types of grants are meant to be a short-term solution to evolving government problems when budgets aren't equipped to support the needed manpower for fire safety. Since it's not permanent funding of the operational budget and will cease at a point in time, the governmental unit that accepted the grant will need to find other sources when the funds dry up. What are those other sources? Usually this leads to raising taxes. One potential solution is to prevent government from exceeding the budgeted appropriation without the proper justifications. This can be accomplished by bringing any need for transfers, or required modification to shift appropriation in an established budget, to the public's attention, with a remedy for future budget impacts. There is a real need for these public-sector entities to better plan, direct, and control this type of budgetary spending beyond one-year thinking if they are to control the costs associated with these government services and the impact on the taxpayer.

It appears that elected officials and/or bureaucrats are particularly poor at understanding the impact of short-term grants and in-year changes in spending on the long-term financial health of a particular governmental entity. For example, in the case of the aforementioned SAFER program, one of the authors engaged in a discussion about hiring additional police force members, in part, due to grant funding. This discussion was treated by a layman elected official as a short-run annual cost of $45,000 in the current year, as that was the expended item for a new-hire police officer, covering base salary only, not overtime or benefits. In terms of long-term financial condition, actually hiring a new police officer is roughly a $1 million decision. That reflects the salary increases that will occur over the potential 25-year working life of the officer, the pension cost, benefits, and equipment expenses for keeping an officer in place. Yet, from a political perspective, in many cases it is treated as a one-time $45,000 cost. This problem also relates to salary increases. When a percentage increase in salary is given, it is essentially an annuity, each and every year that the worker is in place, the percent salary increase for this year is paid next year and every year thereafter. Then there is the cost of promotions to consider. Check the paychecks. The money is paid out again and again each year. This gap in understanding between current-year and long-term impacts creates many of the problems of government mismanagement that are explored in later chapters.

The authors, while looking to expose potential fraud and mismanagement, also see opportunities to shed light on the financial weaknesses of these grants and other temporary, one-shot remedies. The approach: First, recognize that SAFER, or any grant, is a short-term operational fix. This puts significant emphasis on the governmental unit to develop the proper long- and short-term presumptions in formulating sound budgeting assumptions with respect to such grants. Accept the rule that budgets represent an estimate and are never going to be 100 percent accurate. It's no different than getting the public to recognize that accountants only provide reasonable assurances that the governmental unit is accurately reporting financial information. The bottom line: Nothing is 100 percent assured. However, that does not mean that reasonable financial decisions cannot be made that are reflective of prudent practice. Is there a backup plan in place to fund the expenditure prior to the inflow, or is the one-shot revenue drying up? Was the plan developed when the grant was accepted? The themes of fraud and mismanagement often have simple plots, as this book continually points out.

Public and Private Sector

There are two sectors in the economy of the United States, public and private. Although people tend to have the impression that there is a drastic difference in the accounting for each sector, accounting is, in fact, reasonably standard in practice. It all comes down to debits (outflows) and credits (inflows) and following the money. Accounting is defined by Merriam-Webster's online dictionary as "the system of recording and summarizing business and financial transactions and analyzing, verifying and reporting the results."[9] In the very first accounting class in college, students are taught in order to account for a transaction they must identify, record, and communicate (IRC) the transaction. Such transaction examinations revolve around the actual inflows and outflows of cash. Monitoring the timing of these transactions is critical for effective analysis. Through examining the inflows and outflows, it becomes clear that government and private sector financial accounting are the same in that there are two sides to transactions being recorded, either an inflow or outflow of funds. The key difference is often that the timings associated with each transaction do not coincide in governmental accounting, which creates opportunities to distract, divert, and divide and can potentially lead to fraud and mismanagement.

Consider the conflicting practices that involve the government attempting to find ways to justify its actions in employing private and public funding in combination. Remember that rationalization and justification are often the fraudster's mind-set for committing the act. An example that comes to mind is the Iran–Contra scandal, which revolved around the idea of government (public) and private partnerships. Webster defines a partnership as "a legal relation existing between two or more persons contractually associated as joint principals in a business."[10] The mere joining of two parties raises the conflict-of-interest bar. What is the motivation by the parties to engage in a transaction jointly? Hold that thought as the Iran–Contra scandal is discussed to see how the conflicts developed. The potential exposures to fraud and mismanagement will be identified, recorded, and communicated.

The Iran–Contra scandal occurred during Ronald Reagan's presidency in the 1980s. The White House had developed a secret foreign policy funding plan to circumvent Congress's unwillingness to support the administration's policy on military action in Nicaragua. The Reagan administration's self-interest and desire were in direct conflict with the Democratic Congress at the time. In fact, Congress passed legislation preventing the use of federal money to overthrow the Nicaraguan government (to prevent funding of a counterinsurgency—that is, the Contras). Congress did so by enacting various bills from 1982 through 1986 that became known as the Boland Amendments.[11] It was later found out that private citizens and private monies, funded in part by weapons sales to Iran, were allegedly being directed by the National Security Council's John Poindexter, national security assistant, and his subordinate Lieutenant Colonel Oliver North, deputy director of political military affairs, to achieve the foreign policy aim desired by the Reagan administration and to fund the Contras. This was done despite Congress's rules and regulations via the Boland Amendments. So much for rules and regulations and the importance of developing principled ethics at the top. It is important to define the morality of principles-based ethics. The basic premise of any principle-based approach is common sense and the assurance that all interested parties share the same views and interests within the associated group. Clearly, this was not the case in the Iran–Contra scandal, as the Reagan administration and Congress's views were completely at odds. These are the focus points that need further examination to ensure compliance and preservation of value.

The rationalization by the Reagan administration in supplying weapons to Iran, clearly regarded as an enemy, was to gain the release of American hostages held in Lebanon by loyal Ayatollah Khomeini supporter of Hezbollah terrorists while funding their foreign policy (Contra) objectives. Often the intentions by the parties involved in a potential fraud and mismanagement situation are perceived to be good. However, transparency and holding to principle-based decision making are key to maintaining the proper ethical tone at the top of any organization. The executive branch of the federal government seeking private funds when there is a clear unwillingness of Congress to fund a particular foreign policy objective certainly adds reasonable doubt concerning an undermining of Congress's ability to control and provide oversight of a given policy. It is with this type of behavior, in that gray area of conflict, that the question of whether or not it was improper to fund a cause with private funds arises.

Politics offers these sorts of distractions to allow for the diversions of funds and potential fraud and mismanagement to occur.

It is this Machiavellian thinking that may, in some cases, also cause elected officials to allow monopolistic and oligopolistic companies to control certain markets. Webster's online dictionary defines *Machiavellian* as "using clever lies and tricks in order to get or achieve something: clever and dishonest."

Parties in the private sector may have "special" relationships with various forms of government such that they receive favored and beneficial contracts to provide government-type or -funded services. These strong "special" relationships, which in many cases are actively cultivated by the private sector, may politically limit the scale and practice of governmental control over monopoly firms. Yet this control is both proper and required to manage monopoly power. Such situations expose the public to significant costs and risks.

 ## MONOPOLISTIC CONTROL

Monopolistic is defined as exclusive control by one group of the means of producing or selling a commodity or service. "Monopoly frequently … arises from government support or from collusive agreements among Individuals," Milton Friedman said.[12] Oligopoly is when there are limited competitors and any of the parties in the group can have a material impact on price. An example is cable or other utility companies.

To examine the movement of funds in the Iran–Contra scandal, one needs to examine the public statements and internal accounting of the scheme. Start with the simplest facts of the Iran–Contra scandal:

> The U.S. took millions of dollars from the weapons sale and routed them and guns to the right-wing "Contra" guerrillas in Nicaragua. The Contras were the armed opponents of Nicaragua's Sandinista Junta of National Reconstruction, following the July 1979 overthrow of strongman Anastasio Somoza Debayle and the ending of the Somoza family's 43-year reign.[13]

Approach: According to ushistory.com, during the Contra Affair the United States "took millions of dollars from the weapons sale … " Think skeptically. Were there tax filings of all the income from the millions of dollars in sales? Where did the proceeds go? While it was two parties that were purported to have diverted the funds, who were the private parties? What was their profit in this venture? The distraction was that something was politically wrong.

The political wrong likely revolved around some sort of financial wrong. With companies being fined millions for violating the Foreign Corruption Practice Act (FCPA),[14] were there any fines? Where was the accountability to the enablers of this funding? Was it any different than a lobbyist being funded by corporate or private funds to stop a policy that they do not want by creating a filibuster[15] action? Politicians having a specific self-interest need to be funded by private monies to get elected; later they may well horse trade[16] or appoint these same private individuals or their representatives to positions of power or advance a particular need from these individuals. Where was the "following the money" feel and needed oversight? Forget for a moment the distraction that the Reagan administration did something politically wrong. What structures allowed the potential fraud and mismanagement to occur? It is more important to gain an understanding of how these funds should have been accounted for and where the failed financial systems and structures were that need to be in place so that these types of acts are stopped from recurring in the future.

Areas of Concern: With respect to the Iran–Contra scandal, the question is one of where to place these needed systems and structures. There were numerous questions concerning financial controls that should have been addressed—aside from any question about the skirting of the law. These issues pertained to the use of government structures and private capital to create revenue that was then diverted for specific purposes. A wealth of financial and accounting questions come to mind: What entity types funded the transaction? Were they for-profit or nonprofit entities? Were the funds from these entities restricted (regulated) with respect to outside political activities and lobbying involving other countries' interests? What was the private funders' motivation (need) and perspective for funding the Contra efforts? Vendor **accounts payable** provide stricter oversight of weapons sales that are privately funded. Did these purchases require competitive bidding? What about regulated weapons providers' logs and/or records of who created the purchase orders and initiated the ultimate acquisition?

Examine the controls in place to prevent sales of weapons to other countries on all the sales of weapons at all levels. Examine the terms of shipping and receiving. Look to the source documents, such as bills of lading and delivery tickets, as these would have provided insight into the activity, revenue, and profits from these transactions. To ensure accountability, the oversight body (management) needs to make sure the appropriate controls are in place to safeguard the **inventory** and monitor the costs related to inventory acquisitions. Examining the source documents that facilitate these and other, similar transactions is critical in developing sound accounting policy. Keep in mind that all accounting systems are connected—through processes such as manufacturing of the inventory and the sale and collection **(accounts receivable)** of funds related to the sale of that inventory. These systems should have provided some form of control over the governmental activities. Yet they apparently were lacking or were easy to subvert. The trust that goes along with the responsibility and the level of authorization given to the trusted parties must be monitored closely.

Government Intervention (Override)

Take a moment to compare the private sector and the public sector. In the private sector, organizations are privately owned and are not part of the government. These usually include corporations (both for-profit and nonprofit), partnerships, limited-liability companies, sole-member proprietorships, and charities. A simple way to think of the private sector is that it comprises all organizations that are **not** owned or operated by the government. Examples of the private sector: nonprofits, local business establishments and service providers, manufacturers, retail stores, credit unions, and banks, to name a few.

The public sector, on the other hand, is made up of organizations that are owned and operated by the government. These include federal, state, and municipal governments, authorities, and agencies and can vary by location. According to privacy legislation, these organizations are typically called a public sector, a public body, or a public authority. Some examples of services that operate under the umbrella of the public sector, with public funds, are education, certain health care organizations, police and prison services, roads, and federal, state, county, and municipal (local) government.

The Odd and Unsettling Mix of Public and Private Capital

While government may not own private entities, it often controls these entities by developing various rules, regulations, taxation, fees, and other conditions. These often conflict with the government adherence to the set accounting principles and standards of practice. An example is the AIG bailout, and the "too big to fail" excuse. On September 16, 2008, the federal government gave the American International Group (AIG) an $85 billion bailout. In exchange, the U.S. government received 80 percent of the entity's equity. The situation was precipitated by the subprime lending crisis. It is interesting to note that AIG was chartered as an insurance company, and that sector is typically regulated at the state level—in AIG's case, New York State. Yet in the moment of financial crisis, the U.S. government, via its agent the Federal Reserve System, took on the role of financial overseer and funder of a massive bailout of this firm. This sort of gap between the appropriate regulatory and the final financial backstop is problematic. If in the case of financial institutions, the ultimate backstop is at the federal level, it seems appropriate to have the regulatory structures at the federal level.

AIG was considered too big to fail by the regulators. Its investors consisted of large institutional investors, mutual funds, pension funds, and hedge funds, and many of the assets owned or controlled by these same firms were also insured by AIG. In particular, many investment banks that had collateralized debt obligations (CDOs) insured by AIG were at risk of losing billions of dollars. A *New York Times* article alleged that Goldman Sachs had $20 billion in exposure related to AIG's related business dealings.[17] These CDOs were being used by large investment banks and other major financial institutions. The CDOs lumped various types of debt—from the very safe (high quality) to the very risky (low quality)—into one single security package. The various types of debt are known as tranches. The French word *tranche* means "slice." Tranches represent a portion of the structured financing. This left many large investors holding mortgage-backed securities created by the CDOs filled with these subprime loan tranches. These tranches have several related securities that are offered at the same time but have different risks, rewards, and/or maturities.

AIG offered a quasi-insurance product called credit default swaps (CDSs), which provided holders of CDOs, in particular, protection from price declines in their securities. The market was largely unregulated, and speculators were also allowed to purchase CDSs that would pay out in the event of a decline in market prices for financial assets—even if the investor did not own the assets (such as CDOs). With the collapse of the housing market in 2008 and the subsequent losses in CDO values, AIG found itself with literally billions in claims associated with its outstanding CDOs. AIG did not have the funds available to pay off these claims. Why would a state-chartered insurance company be allowed to issue what is essentially an unbacked insurance policy on financial assets? How could such a set of securities be issued in the marketplace on a large-scale basis with the implied guarantee as an insurance against financial loss, but without full and proper actuarial backing of the "insurance policies"?

Yet AIG had a history of financial trouble and questionable financial practices. A 2006 *New York Times* article noted that AIG apologized for past transgressions. "Apologizing for deceptive business practices extending as **far back as two decades** ago, American International Group, the global insurance giant, reached a **$1.64 billion settlement** yesterday with federal and state securities and insurance regulators,"[18] the story said. The article explored the alleged circumstances revolving around the settlement and the potential bid-rigging schemes at work: paying insurance brokers to steer business its way, the use of fraudulent insurance transactions to increase its earnings, and the underreporting to state insurance departments of the amounts of workers' compensation premiums it had collected. Taxes were owed on all of these things, yet the government stepped forward and bailed AIG out in 2008.

In the 2008 bailout, the government took an 80 percent stake in a company that may have committed fraud and set a terrible ethical precedent in preventing fraud and mismanagement in government. A January 2015 Reuters article reported that a non-jury trial was scheduled for February 24 in Manhattan court before State Supreme Court Justice Charles Ramos in a nearly decade-old case. The accused are former AIG CEO Maurice ("Hank") Greenberg and former AIG Chief Financial Officer Howard Smith, who allegedly arranged fraudulent dealings to conceal AIG's true financial condition. The defendants are facing claims that they orchestrated a $500 million transaction with reinsurer General Re, a unit of Warren Buffet's Berkshire Hathaway Inc., in efforts to boost loss reserves without the transferring of risk and a deal with Capco Reinsurance Company that hid a $210 million underwriting loss in an auto warranty program.[19] These accounting manipulations/irregularities often involve a simple shifting of assets and/or liabilities.

The AIG bailout has been widely touted as a financial success. AIG was saved, and the federal entities made money. In 2012, the U.S. Department of the Treasury reported that the Treasury and the Federal Reserve had fully recovered the $182.3 billion in loans and grants made to AIG, and by 2013 a $22.7 billion profit on the AIG transactions was reported. While this may seem wonderful, one must consider the true risk that the Treasury and the Federal Reserve took on in this process. They essentially loaned a large amount of capital for four years at very modest rates of return (essentially about 3 to 4 percent per year). It might seem like a happy ending to have the money returned at all, but consider the risk that was taken on—in this case, by the U.S. government for the American people—and the return realized. It is interesting to note that the private sector was unwilling or unable to provide the same backstop for this kind of return. As a simple benchmark, one might suggest that a very risky investment such as this would require a return of 30 to 50 percent per year in the private sector.[20]

Yet AIG operates in an extremely regulated industry; the accounting oversight associated with publicly traded companies is extremely high. So why does an AIG-type blowup happen? The root cause is, in part, that the "tone at the top" is not held accountable. With all the frauds that transpired, why are the board of directors of these various entities not held accountable? Now switch the focus from a board of directors to an entrusted elected official or government employee. Accounting systems with strong policies are needed. Such systems can potentially expose these types of fraud and mismanagement by holding people accountable. The 800-pound friendly gorilla oversight is needed wherever the trusted responsibilities meet value in the public entity. And these intersections should also include risks to the public from private activity, such as with AIG, where a massive private misstep led to significant public risk. Explore the idea of using accounting to develop systems and structures as they relate to preventing fraud and mismanagement in the public sector.

The more common type of frauds that you will encounter in the public entity are frauds against the public entity. An example would be a defense contractor colluding with DOD officials to get paid for work not done or not needed. This is opposed to frauds committed by the public entity, like the Iran–Contra scandal or leaving loopholes like the ability to divert tolls, assumed by the public to be for bridge and road infrastructure maintenance and not to build skyscrapers; while not illegal it is certainly not moral.

AVERT TOOL

The same enabler mentality that existed in the preceding AIG example also may exist in the public government sector. Start with a simple acronym, AVERT (Analyze, Verify, Evaluate, Record, and Translate), which is used to remind everyone that incorrectly reflecting a transaction can result in serious consequences. Throughout this chapter the AVERT principle is used to get to the necessary level of thinking to develop sound systems and structures to prevent fraud and mismanagement in any governmental unit. Again, in any fraud there are underlying conflicting interests that need to be examined closely. Using the AVERT tool, these areas will be exposed. That does not mean that fraud or mismanagement exists. It means there is an area to potentially evaluate more closely. Remember that only a judge and jury can find someone guilty of fraud.

Since they are public entities, governmental units can give the perception that, ethical behavior can be regulated within it and fraud or mismanagement cannot exist. Take a look at all the enforcement agencies the government has in place to manage such issues. That very same thinking that fraud cannot exist is commonplace in private organizations—a "not in my company" mentality. It is this simple sort of complacency that lies in one's own mind that allows fraud and mismanagement to continue to exist and remain undetected in today's private, government, and other organizational structures.

Could it be that an invalid cost/benefit analysis is being conducted by policy makers? There is no fraud in my organization, all my people are honest, and therefore there is no need to spend money to improve internal controls, since there cannot be a benefit since there is no fraud now. It's only when they get taken that they start to develop the appropriate level of thinking. As Albert Einstein said, "We cannot solve our problems with the same thinking we used when we created them." Now look at the areas of accounting in the government structure from an AVERT perspective and factor in potential exposure or miscommunications.

The first AVERT area to examine is revenue recognition. The revenue areas of the governmental (public) unit require significant internal control over financial reporting. These are areas where the professional skepticism should be extremely high. People love to get their hands on revenue. A close eye needs to be kept on funds as they flow into an organization. This is a good place to see the unsuspected 800-pound friendly gorilla lurking. Revenue is an extremely important area for audit consideration when analyzing governmental units. Revenue is value. Where people and value meet is where fraud and mismanagement can take place.

 GOVERNMENTAL FUNDS

Revenues have to inflow or outflow from somewhere for a transaction to be completed. Gaining an understanding of the various government funds and their purposes is a soft skill necessary to develop sound systems and structures. These systems and structures need to be in place to safeguard the government (public) entities' value. Understanding the government funds' purposes helps the reader of the financial statements understand and validate the intended purpose for raising these funds. Acquiring a soft-skill approach—for example, asking what the funds are being used for and whether they are being used for the intended purpose—is the level of professional skepticism necessary to prevent fraud and mismanagement.

Remember, this is all guidance. Nothing replaces experience and sound, practical common sense. This is not an audit being conducted in accordance with applicable standards. An auditor is not responsible for detecting fraud or mismanagement. That is the responsibility of the government officials and their management team. With that in mind, switch the focus of the examination to how these transactions appear to a reasonable person from the outside looking in. Do they conform to good practice? Nothing replaces the soft-skill commonsense thinking of asking oneself what the public would think of the transaction in question.

In government accounting, the financial statements and reporting are typically built on fund balance accounting analysis. Although they will be cited in this discussion, Governmental Accounting Standard Board (GASB) references are not being addressed to auditors but are being used to assist us in understanding the language of government accounting. GASB has expanded its thinking by requiring separate reportings in the fund sections of "all major funds" and providing a definition.

GASB Statement No. 34 sets up the basis for financial statement reporting. While there is no specific number of fund accounts that a government should use, National Council on Governmental Accounting (NCGA) Statement 1, paragraph 29, states that a government "should establish and maintain those funds required by law and sound financial administration" and that "only the minimum number of funds consistent with the legal and operating requirements should be established." Paragraph 30 of the same statement was amended to state that individual funds are not required for financial purposes unless required by law. So much for principle-based accounting thinking. Back to the idea that good financial statement presentation and ethical behavior can be externally legislated only if a law requires them. The statement was further amended to require a separate debt service fund for financial resources being accumulated for future debt principal and interest payments. This does not help in developing sound systems and structures from a cash flow perspective. For example, a simple refunding or refinancing of debt can create additional inflows from nonoperational sources with these same funds thrown into a general fund pot. So the debt is administered in one place, and the funds needed to repay the debt are raised in another. From the perspective of mismanagement, what needs to be considered is good financial practice and transparency as opposed to relying on the GASB rules to foster appropriate financial reporting. This is troubling for managers or external reviewers looking to control fraud, as organizations may work to confuse the public. They may obfuscate their actions by channeling resources into nonsensical financial accounts or comingle resources so that the question of resource inflows and outflows becomes hard to trace.

Developing the necessary soft skills to grasp the accounting standards and practices created by the GASB—particularly GASB Statement No. 54, Fund Balance Reporting and Government Fund Types Definitions, which was issued in February 2009—is an important resource. To develop the required knowledge base in understanding the government (public) entity financial structure, applying these principles with emotional intelligence is necessary. "The objective of this statement is to enhance the usefulness of fund balance information by providing clearer fund balance classifications that can be more consistently applied and by clarifying the existing governmental fund type definitions."[21] GASB Statement No. 54 at the fund level breaks the funds categories into restricted, committed, assigned, and unassigned. Restricted fund balances are for specific purposes that are within a constitution, in written legislation, or imposed by external resource providers. Committed fund balances are set-aside funds that result from the decision-making body's decision to set up the funds for specific purposes. Unassigned fund balance is the residual fund balance from the general fund and includes all spendables that are not otherwise classified—basically, any fund balance that is not restricted or committed. The unassigned fund balance would also be where any overspending that resulted in a deficit fund balance would be reflected. In fund accounting there is no deferral or overfunding of expenditures so they would lower unrestricted fund balance. They would first create negative budget variances, aggregating to a deficiency of revenues over expenditures and close to a negative net change in fund balance. The statement also provided guidance with respect to the intended controls associated with how these funds can be spent.

An effective government system, with respect to funds, should establish a policy of self-balancing sets of accounts that maintain the segregated specific purposes for the establishment of the fund. A peer review independent oversight body that monitors and provides guidance on these established laws and regulations or special restrictions and limitations is needed to ensure compliance. NCGA 1, as amended, and GASB Statement No. 34 divided the eleven fund types for reporting resources and activities into three broad categories:

■ Government funds
■ Proprietary funds
■ Fiduciary funds

Government Funds

Government funds provide information with respect to measuring the sources, uses, and balances of the related assets and liabilities. All resources not accounted for in other funds are pooled in the general fund, and there should be only one general fund. Basically, by analyzing the inflows and outflows of cash, one can develop the necessary feel of the cash flow of monies circulating in the governmental unit. Comparing the funds' cash and cash equivalents to related liabilities provides an ability to establish the necessary oversight needed to ensure that an adequate working capital base of the governmental unit is maintained. This is no different than a firm in the private sector needing to maintain a sufficient working capital base within which to operate. Government funds typically use the modified accrual basis of accounting, which means amounts must be measurable and available—availability is crucial as the funds must be on hand for use to liquidate year-end payable and commitments. Under this method, revenues are recognized in the period they become available and are measurable. This method is referred to as the modified cash basis of accounting.

In general, there is a bias in government leadership and practice with regard to financial issues. There is an enhanced focus on short-term matters with respect to government funds, with less discussion and emphasis on capital assets and long-term liabilities. This focus creates an opportunity for fraud and mismanagement—one in which managers can massage the financial statements to misrepresent the true financial condition of either the short- or the long-term operations. Since a simple moving of short-term liability to long-term will give the appearance of an increase to working capital, any such move offers the opportunity to create distraction.

Potential Fraud Detection Action: Calculate the cash flow available to fund the purposes and see if there is sufficient working capital resources available to meet the current commitments. Look closely for journal entries and adjustments and changes that effect the public entities ability to fund its commitments. Working capital is the difference between current (short-term) assets and current (short-term) liabilities, meaning liquid available cash needed to fund current commitments. Current assets must be higher than current liabilities or the governmental unit meets the definition of insolvency. The desired goal: current assets higher than current liabilities, the key being the availability of the necessary funds to pay current commitments out of dollars on hand, as this shows the governmental unit's ability to satisfy its current obligations. Making sure that the short-term needs of the governmental unit are met with short-term funding and liquid assets is an effective system and is important in building an effective governmental structure.

These funds are summarized as follows.

General (Current) Fund

The general (current) fund is used to account for the general operation of the governmental unit and related activities that do not require the use of other funds. This fund accounts for any inflows and outflows that are not reported in another fund. **There can be only one general fund.**

A high level of professional skepticism needs to be applied, which ensures that general funds are not commingled with other funds and the outflows that are paid are meeting the designed policies that they were intended to meet. If there is a mere inference that does not fit somewhere else (other fund types), it goes here. Examining these potential commingled funds is key in developing the necessary systems and structures to prevent fraud and mismanagement in government.

An Example would be the governing body establishes a pre/post school program and creates an enterprise (proprietary) fund to account for the program. However, fees are set so low that the general fund must fund a material amount of the funds needed to cover the operating costs using general fund resources. If the fund is not self-sufficient, should it be rolled into the general fund?

PFDA: Calculate the cash flow available to fund the purposes and see if there are sufficient working-capital resources available to meet current commitments. Look for journal entries, deleted entries, reclassifications, and any change that indicates that the inflow or outflow was adjusted or reimbursed to other funds or receiving monies from other funds or sources, grants, and other forms of federal and state aid. Were there transfers? Look for these subtle changes and evaluate whether they feel right and meet the intended policy and operational intent behind the transaction.

Special Revenue Fund

The special revenue (or special) funds are required to account for the use of revenue earmarked by law for a particular purpose. Thus is the intent of GASB Statement No. 54, which provides guidance in understanding the revenue sources that are committed, assigned, or restricted to specific expenditures for purposes other than debt servicing or capital projects. An example of this type of fund would be the state and federal fuel tax revenue, which is classified under special revenue funds, because federal and state laws restrict the use of these taxes for transportation appropriation/expenditure purposes only.

One or more specific-purpose-restricted or committed funds are necessary to establish the special revenue fund, and it should represent an expected continual inflow of revenues. Other potential inflow resources to this fund could be investment earnings and transfers, if those resources are restricted, committed, or assigned to the special revenue fund purpose.

PFDA: Calculate the cash flow available to fund the purposes and see if there are sufficient working capital resources available to meet current commitments. Look for journal entries, deleted entries, reclassifications, and any change that indicates that the inflow or outflow was adjusted or reimbursed to other funds, or receiving monies from other funds or sources, grants, and other forms of federal or state aids. Review the documents that created the special purpose. Are they being followed?

Capital Projects Fund

The **capital projects funds** are used to account for the construction and acquisition of fixed assets, such as buildings, equipment, and roads, that are restricted, committed, and assigned to expenditures that require capital outlay (outflow). Depending on the intended use of the fixed asset, the financing may take place in a special revenue fund, in a trust fund or a proprietary fund, if it does not directly benefit the governmental unit, but instead serves some other intended purpose.

A capital project fund is only in existence until completion of the project.

PFDA: Calculate the cash flow available to fund the purposes and see if there are sufficient working capital resources available to meet current commitments. Capital assets acquired generally should match the debt maturity to the life of the capital asset. Capital projects are accounted for in the government's general fixed assets and long-term debts. Internal Revenue Service (IRS) Publication 946, on how to depreciate assets, is a useful tool and can be obtained for free from the IRS website (www.irs.gov) to assist in developing an understanding of the useful life of the asset being financed. Look for journal entries, deleted entries, reclassifications, and any change that indicates that the inflow or outflow was adjusted or reimbursed to other funds or receiving monies from other funds or sources, grants, and other forms of federal or state aid. Review the documents (actual invoices). Were bids competitive? Were bids designed to be very narrow so that they represented essentially a sole-source contract? Are the resolutions or documents that created the capital project being followed? Think back to the Rita Crundwell story that involved a capital sewer project account that was discussed earlier in the book and the enabling ability it gave Rita Crundwell to embezzle monies. Be wary of attempts to charge operating costs to capital projects to avoid negative budget variances or to overstate unrestricted, uncommitted fund balances in the general fund, by applying higher levels of professional skepticism and review.

Debt Service Fund

The debt service funds account for money that will be used to pay the interest and principal of long-term debts of the governmental unit. Bond financing used by a governmental unit to finance major construction and improvement

projects that are to be paid by tax levies over a period of years require the governmental unit to establish a debt service fund to account for the repayment of the
bond debt. With any debt there are required principle and interest payments.
Property **ad valorem taxes**, which are taxes based on the value of property,
are a major source of revenue for funding state and municipal governments
debt obligations.

If the special assessment and proprietary funds incur debt, they are
required to be accounted for within those funds separately, rather than in the
separate debt service fund. The GSA's real estate leasing program would be run
under similar principles—where real estate is leased to federal agencies by the
GSA on a cost recovery basis.

Whether debt is limited by a percentage of the ratable base (fair market
value of the governmental unit) or other limits, it is typically well spelled out,
either in the bond debenture[22] agreement or the terms and conditions of any
financing arrangements. The covenants and restrictions are spelled out in these
agreements so that the terms, restrictions, and other applicable requirements
can be administered properly. All financial resources for the repayment of principal and interest should be accumulated in this fund, unless in the proprietary
or other special funds with other specific purposes.

PFDA: Calculate the cash flow available to fund the purposes and see
if there are sufficient working capital resources available to meet current
commitments. Calculate the cash flow available to pay the required interest.
The more reserves available for interest payments, the stronger the financial
ability of the governmental unit's ability to pay its debt. Examine the frequency
of the borrowings. Calculate the percentage of the debt in relationship to
the assets and funds balance within the fund. Are there sufficient revenue
sources for funding the debt to its maturity date? Do the financed capital
assets' terms match the length of useful life of the asset? Has there been a
shift in current obligations to long term to affect working capital in the debt
service fund or other related interfund transaction activity? Look for journal
entries, deleted entries, reclassifications, and any change that indicates that
the inflow or outflow was adjusted or reimbursed to other funds or receiving
monies from other funds or sources, grants, and other forms of federal or
state aid. Review the documents that created the intended purpose. Are they
being followed?

Permanent Fund

The permanent funds were developed through generally accepted accounting
principles (GAAP), to assist government with accounting for money, such as
dividends or generated monies from interest. The purpose of the permanent

fund is to preserve a principal sum of money as capital and use it to generate interest income to fund a specific obligation or benefit. Permanent funds can also be used to pay for services related to endowments of government-operated cemeteries or libraries. These funds are used to support a government program and provide a benefit to the government and/or its citizenry.

PFDA: Calculate the cash flow available to pay for the purpose. Is there sufficient working capital? Verify the principal and validate the generated earnings that have been received. Look for journal entries, deleted entries, reclassifications, and any change that indicates that the inflow or outflow was adjusted or reimbursed to other funds, or receiving monies from other funds or sources, grants, and other forms of federal or state aid. Review the documents that created the intended purpose. Are they being followed?

Another government fund (not included in the 11 fund type category in NCGA Statement 1) that the authors have observed are special assessment funds. The special assessment funds account for specific public infrastructure improvements are financed by special levys against the property owner, who will specifically benefit by the improvement, rather than global levy, which is applied to a broader base. Sidewalks, curbs, and sewers are examples of improvements that often rely on these sorts of special assessments.

Look at financial statements, written policy, and procedures, and gather whatever information exists about the fund and the ultimate funding requirements to meet current and further obligations to ensure that the necessary funds are available to meet current commitments within the fund itself and not require other fund intervention to maintain operation. If another fund is funding shortfalls it should be rolled into the fund that is subsidizing its existence to create accountability.

Proprietary Fund

The proprietary fund is the business-like fund of a state or local government or public agency. The two types of proprietary funds are enterprise and internal service funds.

Enterprise Fund

Enterprise funds are used for services provided to the public on a user charge basis, similar to the operation of a commercial enterprise. Water and sewage utilities are common examples of government enterprises. These funds require and permit the charging of a fee to the users of the goods and services.

GASB Statement No. 34, paragraph 67, requires the reporting as **enterprise fund** if **any one** of the following criteria is met:

1. The finance debt of the activity is secured by the commitment of the net revenues from the fees and charges of the activity.
2. Laws and regulations require fees and charges and not taxes and similar revenues satisfy the debt and depreciation costs.
3. The prices of fees and charges are to be designed to recover its costs, including capital costs. This is crucial policy that needs to be enforced in practice.

> Note: GASB Statement No. 34, paragraph 67, removes the requirement from the reporting as an Enterprise fund if it is immaterial. Immaterial is a standard by which the level of spending and revenue is assumed to be of minor scale as compared to other sources. However, that standard is somewhat subjective and subject to internal manipulations. These types of exclusions can create the opportunity for fraud and mismanagement to occur. All exemptions should be documented.

PFDA: Calculate the cash flow available to fund the purpose. Is there sufficient operating working capital? Verify the costs and ensure that inflows are exceeding outflows and obligations are being satisfied in accordance with the terms of the intended activities' purpose. Look for journal entries, deleted entries, reclassifications, and any change that indicates that the inflow or outflow was adjusted or reimbursed to other funds, or receiving monies from other funds or sources, grants, and other forms of federal or state aid. Review the documents that created the intended purpose. Are they being followed?

A fraud by government could be the establishment of an enterprise fund for a program that cannot stand on the revenues being generated by the program revenues. Moving programs out of the general fund improves budget variances. To improve fund balances, transfers from the general fund are classified as inter-fund loans rather than residual equity transfers, therefore reducing fund balances as there is no anticipated repayment.

Internal Service Fund

Internal service funds are used for operations serving other funds or departments within a government on a cost-reimbursement basis. When the government is the primary user of the activity, the goods and services are to be delivered on a cost-reimbursement basis with respect to reporting. A printing shop, which takes orders for booklets and forms from other offices and is reimbursed for the cost of each order, is an example of use for an internal service fund.

Fiduciary Fund

The **fiduciary funds** are used to account for assets held in trust by the government for the benefit of individuals or other entities. The employee pension fund, created by the state government to provide retirement benefits for its employees, is an example of a fiduciary fund. Financial statements may further distinguish fiduciary funds as either *trust* or *agency* funds. A trust fund generally exists for a longer period of time than an agency fund. The government should clearly report that these funds are held in trust or custodial capacity for the parties other than the government.

Pension (and other employee benefit) trust funds are to account for the resources that are required to be held on behalf of the members and beneficiaries associated with a benefit plan. These fiduciary funds are trusts that account for defined-benefit pension plans, defined-contribution pension plans, other postemployment benefit plans, and other employee benefit plans.

This is an area that should be scrutinized by serious fraud professionals. Simply adjusting the actuarial assumptions of the rate of return on fund assets may well produce the appearance of requiring lower contribution levels to fund the pension plan. This dirty little trick permits politically motivated delays in pension funding that allow for the diversion of these resources to balance the current year's state or local budget. Other financial tricks involve raising contributions to the participants or changing the design of the plan to cover shortfalls without detailed analysis of the actuarial past and present histories of the fund. Analyzing the actual benefits promised and the proper actuarially based estimates of true costs are critical areas to examine if fraud and mismanagement are to be prevented. It is inappropriate to underfund or overfund the plan. The diligent fraud analyst should look to find deviations from the true expected cost of providing such plans.

Again the question arises as to whether it was a fraud by the government or was it fraud committed by the folks that codified an abusive and misleading practice into permitted standards to make it legal?

A recent study by the Department of Labor's Employee Benefits Security Administration (EBSA) found that 39 percent of benefit plan audits had major deficiencies[23] with regard to auditing standards. The EBSA was created in 1974 to administer the provisions of the Employee Retirement Income Security Act (ERISA). ERISA is a federal statute that establishes standards for pension plans in private industry and provides for rules on the federal income tax effects of transactions associated with employee benefit plans.

The GAO website discusses the effectiveness of federal oversight of ERISA and the exposure as a result of underfunded pension plans insured by Pension Benefit Guaranty Corporation (PBGC). The "GAO found that: (1) the Internal Revenue Service (IRS) increased its examinations of plan operations; (2) the Department of Labor and IRS made substantial progress in improving the quality and timeliness of plan annual report data essential to effectively identifying violations; and (3) labor adopted an enforcement strategy for investigating financial institutions and welfare plan service providers that it characterized as having high potential for fiduciary abuse. GAO believes that: (1) labor's proposal to strengthen ERISA independent audit requirements would improve ERISA oversight and enhance the security of participants' benefits; and (2) auditors should be required to review and report on the effectiveness of plans' internal control structures and compliance with laws and regulations, in addition to reporting on plans' financial statements."[24]

The November 2014 National Conference on Public Employee Retirement Systems and Cobalt Community Research study of the public retirement system found that 46 percent of the respondents included overtime in the calculation of a retirement benefit and some provision of health care benefits. Who is making sure the calculations are correct? Who is auditing, the auditor or the actuary? After all, what's required is reasonable assurance that the numbers are correct, not beyond reasonable doubt.

In a press release dated August 17, 2011, by Office of the Comptroller of New York Thomas P. Di Napoli, the following is stated: "Port Authority employees accounted for 71 of the top 300 pension earners in the New York State and Local Retirement System, with top annual pensions ranging from $125,612 to $196,768. The audit revealed that most of these retirees were in positions that would receive a **large amount of overtime creditable to retirement pensions**. End of career compensation, which can be inflated by overtime, factors heavily into pension calculations."[25] Here is where the 800lb friendly gorilla oversight is needed, as these unchecked positions of value can lead to the need to raise the toll prices. Overtime is at time and half and double time rates and create higher annual salaries. That in turns leads to inflated pension calculations. It is these type of transactions that often exist that way on the system and lead to the need to raise tolls and put limits on the existing working base pay that are not retired. Pension should be based on base pay and not inflated values as a result of overtime.

Examination of the recipient health benefit and other benefits side of these dedicated employee funds is also needed. The appropriateness of the fund payments needs to be explored. Are people using two separate plans? Are benefits being paid twice, or are people who are no longer employed covered? What independent analysis of the benefits has been conducted? Was it an independent party review that is not receiving a commission or fee based on total insurance premiums? These are the unexpected areas of financial controls that need the highest level of oversight and skepticism. Judgment as to the rate of returns, benefits to reward political allies, and a host of other reasons make this one of the potentially most abused areas. Watch for things like sick-time buyouts, where the parties receiving the sick time are also the ones tracking the benefit. The need for sound systems and structures is critical, because benefits are significant appropriations/expenditures for governments and the flaws in this area may take a considerable amount of time to become evident to the general public. The expectation gap issue is that government is for the good of the public, elected official, its employees all with different self-interests. Do the laws, regulations, and internal controls provide suitations where self-interest can supersede the public good? These are the critical position points in which the 800-pound friendly gorilla professional skepticisms need to be placed.

Case Study: Multiple Jobs and Double Dipping

A Central Jersey article by Sergio Bichao and Steph Solis says that "Edward" is a guy with eight public jobs (he used to have nine), pulling down a combined salary of more than $360,000 last year and working as a part-time tax assessor in eight different towns in Somerset and Morris counties. That same article reveals that "throughout the state, 540 public employees boosted their salaries last year with multiple government jobs that topped $100,000—which will lead to sky-high retirement payments for years to come."[26]

A Fox business article headlined "Double Dipping Pension Bleeding NJ Dry" revealed a loophole in state law (or a scam, depending on whom you ask) that allows public employees to retire with a pension from one job then promptly rejoin the government payroll at a full salary while still collecting that pension, a practice known as double-dipping.[27] The same article said that "80 retired state police officers who landed other government jobs after retiring are collecting a combined $12.8 million a year, about $7 million in salaries and another $5.8 million in pension payments, 17 county sheriffs and 29 undersheriffs are taking home about $8.3 million a year via double-dipping—$3.4 million from pensions and $4.9 million in salaries. Forty-five retired school superintendents collect more than $4 million in pension while working at full salary for the state as interim superintendents."

Future Pension Issues

As for the public pension system was the fraud committed when the governors refuse to make the necessary contributions or is the fraud committed when state legislatures raised the benefits and lowered retirement ages without providing funding for these massive expenditure increase?

Without oversight and continued monitoring of these segregated fundings and continual segregated fund thinking, the opportunity for fraud and mismanagement will continue. Again this is not a fraud against the government as it is legal. But is government a fraud enabler by allowing it to be legal? These segregated funds are related and must be reconciled to ensure they are utilized for the independent purposes for which they were established. This is yet another example of a fund that, if funded properly, with managed oversight and the correct accounting policies and systems in place, would perhaps lead to adequate funding and reduced costs.

PFDA: Calculating the cash flow available to pay for the designed purpose and determining if there is sufficient working capital to pay for the obligation is critical to ensure the credibility of the financial communications. Verify the costs and ensure that inflows are exceeding outflows and obligations are being satisfied in accordance with terms of the intended activities' purpose. Monitor abuse closely, and establish a no-tolerance policy for it. Look for journal entries, deleted entries, reclassifications, and any change that indicates that the inflow or outflow was adjusted or reimbursed to other funds. Beware of interfund loans that cannot be repaid! Examine the receiving of monies from other funds or sources, grants, and other forms of federal or state aid. Will these funds continue? If not, what resources will be needed to maintain the operations? Review the documents that created the intended purpose, and look at the source support for the transaction to ensure that all was done in line with proper reporting and calculations.

Remember: The investment trust funds are external investment pools that are government-sponsored. GASB Statement No. 31 establishes accounting and financial reporting standards for *all* investments held by external government investment pools.

The private-purpose trust funds are trust arrangements in which the principal corpus and income benefits the individual, private organization, or other government agencies.

The agency funds are resources that are arranged for specific custodial purposes for individuals, private organizations, or other government agencies. How can they be manipulated?

PFDA: These three funds have similar types of financial actions. Calculate the cash flow available to pay for the designed purpose and determine if there is sufficient working capital to pay for the obligation. Verify the costs and ensure that inflows are exceeding outflows and obligations are being satisfied in accordance with terms of the intended activities' purpose. Look for journal entries, deleted entries, reclassifications, and any change that indicates that the inflow or outflow was adjusted or reimbursed to other funds, or receiving monies from other funds or sources, grants, and other forms of federal or state aid. Review the documents that created the intended purpose. Are they being followed?

GASB Statement No. 34, paragraph 86, lays out the format for these fund statements. A forensic examiner asks questions like: Is the revenue continuing? Does the revenue correlate with its intended and established purpose? Is the inflow being accounted for correctly? With respect to the expenditures, other questions are asked, such as: Are the expenditures/appropriations normal, reoccurring, and within the scope of operations? Are they one-shot? Are they related to the fund purpose? Do they meet the designed objectives and the rules and regulations attached to the fund? The revenue minus expenditures/appropriations results in excess revenue over expenses and is a positive fund balance if revenue exceeds the expenditures/appropriations. If the expenditures exceed the revenues, a negative-number fund balance occurs, meaning insufficient funds to fund the expenditures. The result: a deficit or structural imbalance in the fund.

The next area is **other financing sources and uses**, including transfers with details as to what, when, why, and how these transactions are related to the fund. This is why the inflows and outflows are examined. Understanding the relationship to the fund is critical in the analysis and reemphasizes the importance of the flow **feel** of the money into the fund.

The next category is **special and extraordinary items with details**. Here is where the aim is for the documents to speak for themselves as well as the other financing areas. These are potential diversions or distractions that allow for potential fraud and mismanagement to occur and remain undetected.

Take the beginning cash balance of the public entity and add or subtract the resulting excess of operations, add or subtract the other financing sources, look at non-cash items such as depreciation/amortization, increases/decreases in accounts receivables and payables (changes in current assets and liabilities–working capital) which could lower cash even with an operating excess and other uses, and add or subtract the special and extraordinary items to arrive at the ending cash balance. Examine what goes through the bank accounts.

TABLE 3.2   Financial Cash Inflow/Outflow Comparison Government vs. Private Sources of Funds

Government		Private
Statement of revenue, expenditures, and changes in fund balance		**Statement of cash flow**
Operations		Operations
Revenues	Inflow	Revenues
less Expenditures	Outflow	less Expenses
Other financing sources and uses (including transfers)	Inflow (Outflow)	Financing activities
Borrowings		Borrowing, stock issuance
Special and extraordinary items	Inflow (Outflow)	Investing activities
		Purchasing assets, investments

Table 3.2 compares the cash flow statements under the GAAP's direct method versus the statement of revenues, expenditures, and changes in fund balance. Whether in governmental (public) or the private entity, it all comes down to following the money going into the bank account. In the case of government, the terms are revenue less expenditures, plus or minus other financing sources and uses and special and extraordinary items. In the private cash flow statement, it's inflows and outflows, plus or minus financings, plus or minus any investing activities. Studying these two statements, whether from a private or a public perspective, shows where the real cash being generated or used is going.

The cash flows in the governmental (public) entity, as with a private entity, show the working capital structure and the financial strength of the entity. Fund balance or retained earnings represents the history of the entity. Fund balance and retained earnings reported as a credit balance means that assets are exceeding liabilities. The way cash in an entity grows is by maintaining an operation in which the revenue exceeds the expenditure/appropriations. The other means is through the issuance of debt. The fund balance created from debt issuances is almost always legally restricted. The problem with debt is that it costs money to carry debt in the form of interest. The concept of maturity matching and maintaining infrastructure on an as-needed basis to utilize debt as a way to justify annual operating is inefficient and leads to structural deficiencies. Special and extraordinary spending is one time or transaction-by-transaction based and, again, is not as stable as if maintained through the operations of the governmental (public) entity. Understanding the government financial statement of revenues, expenditures, and changes in fund balance is a soft skill that is needed in the assessment of the financial strength of the governmental (public) entity. Follow the money trail.

FIXED ASSETS AND LONG-TERM DEBTS: SELF-BALANCING ACCOUNTS

State and local governments have two other groups of accounts that are not considered funds: *general fixed assets* and *general long-term debts*. These assets and liabilities belong to the governmental entity as a whole, rather than any specific fund. Although general fixed assets would be part of government-wide financial statements (reporting the entity as a whole), they are not reported in governmental fund statements. Fixed assets and long-term liabilities assigned to a specific enterprise fund are referred to as *fund fixed assets* and *fund long-term assets*.

If you sell debt for a project, the government funds record a revenue and long-term debt goes up. Fixed assets do not go up until the proceeds are spread. If the fixed funds are financed through the budget no income is recorded in the fixed asset fund.

Understanding the way government is funded and how these funds are recognized is a good place to start, since without inflows of cash, government cannot operate, as evidenced by threats of government shutdowns and Chapter 9 bankruptcies, like the city of Detroit, Michigan, which had an estimated $18 billion to $20 billion in debt. This was the largest municipal bankruptcy in U.S. history.

Federal shutdowns take place when the executive branch and Congress create gaps in funding by failing to pass the necessary legislation to fund governmental operations, at that moment the government is out of money and the only remedy is to shut down.

Bankruptcies like Detroit's occur as a result of unfunded liabilities such as pension liabilities that exceed operating revenue needs typically coupled with large structural debt. Government insolvency can be defined by simply stating that the liabilities exceed assets and the revenue streams do not provide sufficient funds to meet the operating cash flow needs for a governmental unit to remain a going concern. But, as we saw earlier in the chapter, government default is not well predicted by a simple examination of assets and liabilities; rather, it is also linked to the going concern aspect of the government entity. The going concern accounting principle operates on the assumption that the governmental (public) entity will remain in business for the foreseeable future (another operating period, which is typically one year). By making this assumption, the accountant can justify deferring expenses and/or deferring revenues into the foreseeable period.

By mandating the governmental entity to identify areas of underfunding (pension, other postemployment benefits [OPEB], and infrastructure maintenance) in the Management Discussion and Analysis (MD&A) and any Service Efforts and Accomplishments (SEA) reporting should require disclosure of the lack of reasonable corrective actions being implemented.

On December 11, 2014, with a midnight deadline approaching, the U.S. House of Representatives voted to approve a $1.1 trillion spending package to keep the federal government open. This once again shows the divided thinking as to how government should spend, along with the failure to translate AVERT on a clear, accurate basis. These factors are strong ingredients in creating the deceptive forces that inspire deflection. It is often the self-interested thinking that causes these distractions. These types of distractions enable diversions from the real issue and keep the mass population politically divided. That issue being $18 trillion in debt and the need for a tax increase. The root cause is the dominance of limited political self-interest, or dictating spending and taxation policy, rather than maintaining interests of the common good as a whole and not special interest groups. These external pressures are what weigh heavily on the auditing and accounting functions. Auditing and accounting functions offer after-the-fact verification and confirmation processes. Unfortunately, good longer-term forecasting is not a required practice in government. Because of this, governmental units may continue to operate from one financial crisis to the next. Could this be done a better way?

Where are the planning and vision when the government waits until the last minute to pass a $1.1 trillion spending plan? What government needs to do is develop a decision-making process that weighs long-term financial impacts of short-term decisions. Government should have solutions in place prior to taking a back-to-the-wall, last-minute approach to providing for long-term capital improvements. Government needs more upfront **analysis** that becomes well documented by going through a stringent **verification** process and look-ahead thinking. Government needs to maintain extreme transparency during an **evaluation** process. Before creating a formal **record of action,** the governmental unit needs an easy-to-understand **translation** of the objectives being set forth in the spending plan or policy issue.

To develop a better understanding of the accounting function in government, let's review the 10 basic accounting principles: economic entity, monetary unit, time assumption, materiality, full disclosure, revenue recognition, cost principle, going concern, matching, and conservative principles. These serve as the core foundation of financial reporting and accountability and are often overlooked. To foster a better understanding of the workings of these principles, we will break them down into three categories: assumptions, principles, and judgment-based principles.

It is through these 10 foundation principles that sound systems and structures to prevent threats of shutdowns and governmental bankruptcies can be developed before they happen. Today's government needs to establish proactive rather than reactive thinking by holding all its people to the highest ethical standards. There is a lot of wisdom in the saying "Actions speak louder than words." Government needs to take actions that stay on task with the represented objectives and definitely use fewer words. Remember this Oscar Wilde quote: "I have learned this: it is not what one does that is wrong, but what one becomes as a consequence of it."[28] Adhering to the thinking of these 10 principles helps avoid potential consequences and systematic mismanagement.

The first group is the assumption-based principles. Each principle is first presented with the existing accounting perspective, followed by how it can be applied in the governmental organization.

 ## ASSUMPTION BASED

As you read through the assumption-based principle, keep in mind the three J's: justification, judgment, and judicial. What personality behaviors surround the people in these trusted positions and do they display visual abilities that are in line with their verbal representation? Can they talk the talk and also walk the walk?

The concept of an economic entity "assumes" that the operations of the governmental entity are kept separate from the economic interest of those who manage the government on behalf of the citizens. Revenue and expenditures should be kept separate from personal expenses of the management that runs the governmental entity. In the authors' minds, this is by far the most critical principle, as it calls for each business to keep its interests separate. This means that each entity structure, whether private or public (government), must keep the transaction separate, and where there are related-party transactions, the highest levels of professional skepticism and transparency must be maintained.

Related party is defined by the International Financial Reporting Standards as related to an entity if any of the following situations apply:

Associate
> The party is an associate of the entity, with common economic self-interests.

Common control
> The party is, directly or indirectly, either under common control with the entity or has significant or joint control over the entity.

Family member
> The party is a close family member of a person who is part of key management personnel or who controls the entity. A close family member is an individual's domestic partner and children, children of the domestic partner, and dependents of the individual or the individual's domestic partner.

Individual control
> The party is controlled or significantly influenced by a member of key management personnel or by a person who controls the entity.

Joint venture
> The party is a joint venture in which the entity is a venture partner.

Key management
> The party is a member of an entity's or its parent's key management personnel.

Postemployment plan
> The party is participating in a postemployment benefit plan for the entity's employees.

This rule is not to be absolute but provides a further understanding of why the economic entity assumption is critical in creating effective government systems and structures. The separate status of a corporation can be disregarded when a stockholder uses a corporation as a mere tool for the purpose of evading or violating a statutory or other legal duty, or for accomplishing some fraud or illegal purpose. Government should apply the same level of thinking.

Consider the massive levels of structural relationships that can and may exist in local, regional, and even state and federal government. The words *related party* are charged words in Washington and many state capitals. Political entities, by their very nature, tend to create related parties with political appointees, agency jobs, and political staffers in bountiful numbers in national, state, and local capitals. The authors could point the readers to numerous related parties at federal regulatory agencies and in the firms regulated by their actions. This includes blood siblings, parents, spouses, and political friends. Whether or not these relationships are at the core of corrupt or poor management practices is not proven in all cases. Yet the surface appearance of such intertwined relationships provides a strong suspicion of illicit practice. There needs to be balance when deciding on wanting someone to serve in a position on a board that you trust. Make sure you do background checks and maintain independence in your decision by ensuring that these reviews are performed by objective and integrity based parties, therefore resulting in sound selections.

In deciding whether or not a subunit of government should be treated as the alter ego of the bigger governmental unit it represents, it is useful to consider the following:

- The purpose for which the sub-governmental unit was formed.
- Whether the sub-governmental units books and records were kept, separately, with independent regular meetings of the management being conducted, and other legal formalities were observed and transparent to the public they serve and viewed as independent of the bigger governmental unit.
- Whether the funds of any governmental agency were comingled into other funds instead of being segregated as required.
- The activity or inactivity of others as government officials, appointed or elected, directors, and/or any government employee having business affairs with the subunit governmental agency are independent and not involved in the management decisions in both entities.
- Any other factors disclosed by the evidence and tending to show that the governmental unit was or was not operated as an entity separate and apart from its all related parties and parties of interest.

Assumes[29] is defined in Merriam Webster's online dictionary as "think(ing) that something is **true or probably true without knowing that it is true**." The whole debate between what is a principle-based versus a rule-based accounting approach is called into question as soon as a word like *assume, principle,* or *judgment* is interjected into the discussion. Clearly, there is never a guarantee that people will follow established rules. What is even clearer is that ethical behavior cannot be regulated. A well designed system relies on people with high levels of integrity overseeing the process. When the people in the process operate in an environment of objectivity and independence, the likelihood is that fraud would not be identified and exposed. When the perception of getting caught as a result of this environment becomes large enough to dissuade potential frauds, hopefully it will lead to people avoiding bad choices.

Going concern "assumes" that the public entity will be in operation, which in the audit new standard is one year for the release of the audit report.

This validates the methods of asset capitalization, depreciation, and amortiza-tion. As stated previously, it also serves as the basis that enables accountants to defer expenditures or revenues into the future. The business will continue to exist in the unforeseeable future. An entity will exist at least through the next operating cycle.

If one was to audit most governmental units, a going-concern opinion would not be given, as the authors feel that the only reason government does not go into bankruptcy is that the majority of citizens are successful, hardworking, law-abiding taxpayers and the government typically has the ability to raise taxes and fees based on that identified ability to pay. Add to that the fact that mostly all public entities are annually audited. With rising health care costs that cover less, the weakening of unions, failing pension systems, and the growing gap between the rich and the poor, where is the future revenue going to come from? At what point does a municipal government like Detroit create the fear in the financial lenders that their long-term viability is in doubt?

One of the key conflicts that exists in public entities is trying to do more without the funds to pay for the initiatives. Until there is a balance struck between funding and need, the continued conflicts will remain and fraud and mismanagement will thrive.

The raising of revenue is often based on some form of taxation. These tax increases can often go unnoticed. A simple example is the recent deduction threshold for medical expenses. The threshold used to be 7.5 percent of adjusted gross income (AGI). However, it was raised to 10 percent. This has the effect of reducing the deduction, which leads to an increase in taxes. So if you had an AGI of $10,000, the first $750 in medical expenses would not be allowed under the 7.5 percent limitation—and now it's the first 10 percent of the same $10,000 example, or $1,000. The ultimate effect is a reduction of $250 in deductible medical expenses, leading to additional taxes. The ability to deduct medical expenses is further limited by the fact that a taxpayer must exceed standardized set amounts before receiving an additional reduction in tax. In 2014, the standardized itemized amounts for married filers was $12,400 and single filers $6200. The limiting of deduction effectively increases taxes without changing tax rates, thus increasing government revenues.

It is these diversionary types of taxes that are used to raise the revenue that one day may no longer be there, since most people will not exceed the limitation based on the national adjusted gross income average. These one-time revenue (increasers) usually lead to potential gaps in funding government going for-ward. Relying on one-shot revenue ideas is risky in the government structure and should be examined closely. A clear effect on the economy is that taxpayers have less money to spend, which means they will cut their spending or borrow to maintain the existing lifestyle. If taxpayers are not spending you have a contributing factor to a potential economic slowdown. Taxes already account for 17.5 percent of the U.S. gross domestic product (GDP).[30] Keeping the money in the hands of the public provides economic stimulus and growth. The matching of the policy and the cost benefit or usage monitoring is critical in ensuring that these services remain a going concern. Any form of taxation has potentially dislocative impacts on households and businesses.

The **monetary unit** principle "**assumes**" that a stable currency is going to be the unit of record. The FASB accepts the nominal value of the U.S. dollar as the monetary unit of record unadjusted for inflation. Thus, we rely on a stable monetary unity as our measure of value—and inflation can confuse and cloud our political discourse.

Understand that nominal GDP is usually higher than real (inflation-adjusted) GDP, because inflation typically increases product values. Nominal GDP is used when comparing within the same year. When comparing different time periods, such as GDP for two or more years, real GDP is used, because by removing the effects of inflation, the comparison of the different years' focus changes to volume. So do the numbers the government communicates reflect nominal or real dollars? We know the fixed assets are nominal since they stay at the transacted costs on the day they were acquired. Normalizing for inflation is the only way to ensure that a real understanding of the financial position is being communicated and generate sufficient funding for future obligations.

The **time-period** principle "**assumes**" that the economic activities of an enterprise can be divided into artificial time periods: monthly, quarterly, annually, and so on. Moving assets and liabilities between periods creates a host of accounting problems. In government, the deferring of expenditures and revenues using surplus is no different than the deferral accounting treatments used in the Lehman Brothers, WorldCom, and Sunbeam frauds. Lehman moved debt from the balance sheet to a sale in the income statement. WorldCom moved expenses from the statement of revenue to the balance sheet to create a current asset. Sunbeam sold inventory in one period and returned the inventory in the next.

The cliché "Timing is everything" should be examined closely in politics. Look to see if there is an election or an event surrounding the increase in tax, a fee, or proposed spending. A sudden zero tax increase sound bite in an upcoming election campaign indicates irresponsible management by the elected officials and administration. The surplus will be lopped off and taxes will likely increase once they've been in office for a while. Examining the external pressures outside the revenue and expenditures of government (public) entities' books is very important. Auditors audit past transactions. While audited financial statements provide assurances as to the financial condition of operating results on a snapshot date, they intend to focus a reader on future needs or future consequences of current decisions. Such additional consideration should receive greater prominence in the financial examining reporting process. The focus needs to be on the future spending, such as unfunded liabilities that put a strain on future cash flows.

PRINCIPLE BASED

As you read through the principle- and judgment-based principle keep in mind the 3 J's—justification, judgment, and judicial. What personality behaviors surround the people in these trusted positions? Do they display visual abilities that are in line with their verbal representation? Now the concern is whether they are able to produce documentation, what the ethical tone at the top is, and whether the systems and structures in place are monitored and not being overridden. Look for journal entries. Look where the judgments are made and by whom they are made. Do the proper department level personnel make the decisions or does a higher authority override them?

The **historical cost** principle requires companies to account and report based on acquisition costs rather than fair market value for most assets and liabilities, which is only representative of value on the date of purchase. That is that fair market value and cost are identical. This principle provides information that is reliable (removing the opportunity to provide subjective and potentially biased market values), but not very relevant. Thus, there is a trend toward using fair values. Most debts and securities are now reported at market values.

While the fair market value of assets cures the net asset deficit, it does not provide funds needed to fund liabilities like pensions. Pensions are actually adjusted from future payout projected amounts to present day obligations. The problem lies in the fact that organizations with hard values, are left with assets that cannot be readily converted into cash. The ability to leverage the assets through borrowing, which requires principle and interest payments, becomes a way to fund expenditures.

As reviewed earlier, if a governmental entity like the State of New Jersey lists all of its projected liabilities at its present value on the balance sheet, the appearance of structural deficit will exist in the financial communication. Is it a fair depiction of the governmental (public) entities' financial communications if the assets are not required to be measured at fair (market) value? Hidden in assets can often be government misspending or past liabilities created by these assets that become non-performing. Some government-owned assets can have actual open market prices—like public art collections—while other assets may more appropriately actually represent future additional costs and liabilities—such as a nature area or recreational park.

The **revenue recognition** principle requires companies to record revenue when it is (1) realized or realizable and (2) earned, not when cash is received. This method of accounting is called accrual basis accounting.

Matching principle. Expenses have to be matched with revenues as long as it is reasonable to do so. Expenses are recognized not when the work is performed or when a product is produced, but when the work or the product actually makes its contribution to revenue. Only if no connection with revenue can be established can a cost be charged as an expense to the current period (e.g., office salaries and other administrative expenses). This principle allows greater evaluation of actual profitability and performance (shows how much was spent to earn revenue). Depreciation and cost of goods sold are good examples of the application of this principle.

A simple requirement that governmental (public) entities should adhere to is that money should be spent in the period in which it was raised and only for the purpose it was intended. Matching expenditures/appropriations with the revenue in the proper period creates accountability. Reserves, surpluses, unused budgetary appropriations, and so on, to fund operations with accountability lead to an imbalance in the funds. The result is that taxes go down after a good year when surpluses are high, and taxes go up after bad years when surplus is down. This is a bit of a yo-yo effect that can be smoothed out by establishing good sound budgeting policies. More importantly it is not a good idea from a cash flow perspective.

Full disclosure principle: Amount and kinds of information disclosed should be decided based on trade-off analysis, as a larger amount of information costs more to prepare and use. Information disclosed should be sufficient to make a judgment while keeping costs reasonable by the examination of the cost versus the benefit of the provided service. Information is presented in the main body of financial statements, in the notes, or as supplementary documentation.

With all the media, Internet, and available communications, why are there so many increases in taxes and fees, spending, and misdirection that come to light only when there is interest? The answer may be that these communications need to boil down to the concept of service efforts and accomplishments (SEA) reporting. Stating the numbers and making funds match the expectations of the public is full disclosure.

JUDGMENT BASED

What remains a mystery to the authors is why those paying taxes are so disinterested in the use and level of these taxes? A few thoughts we have had could start the discussion: is it possibly that the complexities of the taxation system is daunting to explore and tedious to examine? The massive too-big-to-fail, fail-safe argument? Perceptions that it is impossible or difficult to change? Divisiveness and separation?

In order to have effective oversight, this has to change, and we must remove the reliance to prevent fraud and mismanagement from only at the internal management level control and add unsuspecting 800-pound friendly citizenry to the formula as they are the real stakeholders. One of the best defenses is an informed constituency that surrounds spending and taxation policy.

Overarching all of this is a general consensus of good practice. These include:

Materiality principle: The significance of an item should be considered when it is reported. An item is considered significant when it would affect the decision of a reasonable individual.

Conservatism principle: When choosing between two solutions, the one that is least likely to overstate assets and income should be picked (see convention of conservatism).

Fredrich Nietzsche, a German existentialist, played a major role in contemporary intellectual development. He believed that the fundamental force that motivates all creation is the will to power. Nietzsche also believed people to be unequal in ability, which leads to the stronger being able to win the contest, while not causing a diminishment of his or her own self-interest. Whenever judgment is involved in planning, transparency and well-supported documentation must follow.

We discuss all the principles as they relate to government but in an order that makes sense when analyzing mismanagement and potential fraud, **revenue recognition** is at the top of our list. With the recent converged accounting standard on revenue recognition by the Financial Accounting Standard Board (FASB) and the International Accounting Standards Board (IASB), nearly all existing U.S. GAAP and IFRS guidance is being replaced. The new standard places significant emphasis on management judgment. One of the biggest misconceptions is the idea that independent auditors and/or external accountants are somehow responsible for detecting errors, irregularities, or fraud. Wrong. Management is the responsible party; it is imperative that a clear line be drawn in the sand as to the auditor/accountant's responsibility for the integrity and accuracy of the financial data. The elected officials and entrusted government employees are the ones who must validate the financial information. In the Introduction of this book we discussed the Rita Crundwell fraud. How is it that we accept that the mayor and/or the other elected officials are not responsible for a 20-year ongoing embezzlement? In this case, the excuse was that state aid revenue was not being paid on time. Did the mayor or anyone think to call and verify the reasons behind a 20-year problematic budget and financial system? Clearly the auditor was asleep at the wheel.

A revenue decline in government or in any organization may well expose fraud and mismanagement quickly and is **red flag #1**. Why? Because without revenue-related funds, people stop getting paid, the need for cuts becomes eminent, and other whistle-blower types of cries begin to raise concern.

The new FASB/IASB joint revenue recognition is required to be implemented by January 1, 2017. Organizations under contract to provide goods or services to a customer will be required to follow a five-step process to recognize revenue:

1. Identify contract(s) with a customer.
2. Identify the separate performance obligations in the contract.
3. Determine the transaction price.
4. Allocate the transaction price to the separate performance obligations.
5. Recognize revenue when the entity satisfies each performance obligation.

So let's look at the government revenue accounting process, which still comes down to the simple thinking of what's coming in and what's going out. Rather than use words like *debits* and *credits*, we are going to examine the various types of inflows and outflows of funds.

Going concern: Auditors/accountants should look to the existing requirements with respect to evaluating whether there is substantial doubt about the government's ability to continue as a going concern for its intended purposes. Legal budgets and long-range planning are often contrary propositions, but the budgets are no less legal. Let's apply this thinking to the government revenue streams. Are they one-shot streams? Did the citizenry really get their fair share? Were the funds spent for the designed purposes? Are the numbers being represented? Is there wishful thinking as to whether revenue estimates will be met and expenditures controlled? Are these things well documented and supported? It is these questions matched with the proper levels of skepticism that avoid a going concern and/or avoid potential structural deficits in government.

Government seems to assume you know the old adage "When you assume, you make an ass out of you and me." Unfortunately, whenever you budget you have to make hypothetical assumptions. Examining these hypothetical assumptions closely is important in the development of systems and structures. There is a level of uncertainty associated with any assumption, creating the need for objective measurements, which are formulated with an extreme relation to economic, social, and fiscal conditions that exist during the formation process.

When developing revenue and expenditures in the government accounting process, there is a need to separate the new policy initiatives from existing ones. Examples would be to justify increases in total spending or to identify funding sources. Such accounting is not often well documented and as transparent as it should be.

 ## PRESIDENT OBAMA'S 2015 PROPOSED SPENDING

Let's take a look at President Obama's 2015 proposed spending and compare it to the GDP in the United States. Taxes represented an estimated 17.7 percent of the GDP in 2015.[31] Learning ratios such as the total government tax collections divided by the country's GDP is like comparing a company to its peer groups in comparison analysis. For example, Denmark had the highest tax-to-GDP ratio in 2013 (48.6 percent) and Mexico the lowest (19.7 percent).[32] When tax revenues grow at a slower rate than the GDP of a country, the tax-to-GDP ratio drops. These serve as a measurement to project future budget impacts. Since projections are estimates, the budget estimate's credibility hangs on the ability to correlate variables for comparison purposes, which in turn helps in formulating sound budgetary assumptions.

Taxes paid by individuals and corporations often account for the majority of tax receipts, especially in developed countries, and would serve as useful information in formulating budgetary assumptions for forecasting purposes. Table 3.3 shows U.S. taxes as percentage of GDP.

While 17.7 percent looks low, one has to consider that the United States has an estimated GDP of $18 trillion in 2015. A government may increase the tax-to-GDP ratio by a certain percentage in order to cover deficiencies in the budget revenue or shortfalls. The GDP can be used as a means to measure the government's ability to pay since a government's income is largely taxes or user fees. The taxes that can be collected depend on the total of all economic activity. These are simpler measurements that a citizen will be able to understand.

TABLE 3.3 Receipts by Source as Percentages of Gross Domestic Product: 1934–2020

Fiscal Year	Individual Income Taxes	Corporation Income Taxes	Social Insurance and Retirement Receipts		Excise Taxes	Other	Total Receipts		
			(On-Total Budget)	(Off-Budget)			(On-Total Budget)	(Off-Budget)	
2014	8.1	1.9	5.9	1.7	4.3	0.5	1.1	17.5	13.3	4.3
ESTIMATES										
2015	8.2	1.9	5.9	1.7	4.3	0.5	1.1	17.7	13.4	4.3

Source: Office of Management and Budget, Historical Tables, Table 2.3; http://www.whitehouse.gov/omb/budget/Historicals/ (last accessed February 4, 2015).

In fiscal year 2015, the federal budget was $4.2 trillion. The National Priorities Project broke down how much of the $4.2 trillion federal budget last year was allocated to areas like defense, housing, education, science, and interest on the debt. Then it applied those percentages to the average American's federal tax bill.[33]

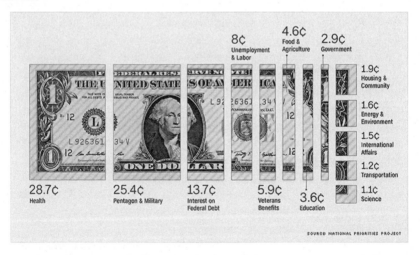

The average household paid $13,000 in income taxes to Uncle Sam for 2015. Of that, the federal government spent:

$3,728.92 (or 28.7%) on health programs
$3,299.13 (or 25.4%) on the Pentagon and the military
$1,776.06 (or 13.7%) on interest on the debt
$1,040.93 (or 8%) on unemployment and labor programs

$771.26 (or 5.9%) on veterans benefits
$598.74 (or 4.6%) on food and agriculture programs
$461.59 (or 3.6%) on education programs
$377.50 (or 2.9%) on government expenses
$250.03 (or 1.9%) on housing and community programs
$207.68 (or 1.6%) on energy and environmental programs
$194.29 (or 1.5%) on international affairs programs
$150.68 (or 1.2%) on transportation funding
$143.20 (or 1.1%) on science funding

Examining the United States budget using ratios and comparisons with peers (like data from other countries) gives a different perspective. Formulating additional financial information that creates citizen awareness by communicating the numbers effectively through tools like common sizing the numbers to enable comparison with other countries creates benchmarks and basis to compare. The preceding dollar bill breakdown chart is a further example available to enable the citizens to gain the proper perspectives on spending and stay informed. This is the real accountability that is beyond governmental legislative oversight and regulatory thinking, and it is the true measure needed to prevent fraud and mismanagement and enhance accountability. Efforts to produce clear and concise financial statements and overviews for governmental entities are ongoing. The authors have considerable experience in the field, and we are both hopeful of the progress we have made and also discouraged by the distance we still have to go. Perhaps the next section will provide some insight and suggestions for progress.

 ## RATIO AND TABLES FROM A GOVERNMENT PERSPECTIVE

Financial Ratios

Table A.3 in the Appendix provides a broad list of financial ratios that may be useful for elected officials, government watchdogs, and public policy wonks. Financial ratios are useful in assessing the performance of a given entity in a number of ways. They provide standardized measuring sticks which allow the user to identify individual results that deviate from the norms for a government's cohort. This in turn provides a focus for additional investigation relating to the accuracy of the financing information or efficiency of the government's operations before finalizing your opinion.

First, they provide the ability to compare organizations at a point in time using a normalization that allows comparisons across entities. Say we are looking at the amount of debt an organization holds. In a direct comparison, we are unable to assess the financial condition of two organizations of radically different size. A given level of debt may be very reasonable for a large organization with strong revenue sources and completely unsustainable for a small organization with limited funds.

Second, we can examine the same organization over time to see if its financial condition is improving or declining. So, for example, we may examine the self-paying percentage to see if a municipality is relying more or less on grants to sustain municipal spending. A growth in reliance on grants may foretell financial distress in the future, as grant support is not a local source of funds and, as such, is subject to external political changes.

Finally, we can use ratios to benchmark and find comparisons in costs across public and private entities. In the world of privatization and public-private partnerships, it's wise to examine and compare the costs of providing the same types of services between public-sector and private-sector costs. The public sector has certain advantages such as tax-free borrowing and the ability to tax to provide strong revenue protection for a project through the use of general obligation bonds. The private sector is typically stronger in the areas of operating efficiency and in the ability to manage and complete projects.

The authors provide a useful portfolio of metrics (below) that may be applicable to the questions raised here. It's important to understand what you are looking at and dive into the details. Here are some areas of caution in using ratios, statistics, and averages when developing a forward-looking perspective.

Regression Analysis Tool

While regression analysis is a statistical modeling, process for estimating the relationships among variables. Any regression analysis and data-mining technique needs to be supported with divergent brainstorming sessions with the right people to reach document-supportable conclusions of fact.

Mean is the weighted average of a set of numbers.

versus

Median, which is the middle value of a set of numbers.

Example: Given the numbers 1, 2, 3, 4, and 5: The **mean** is $(1+2+3+4+5) = 15/5 = 3$. The **median** is 3, since there are two numbers below it and 2 numbers above it. Here, the mean and the median are equal; no harm, no foul.

The issue with only using the mean is that outliers can distort the result, making things appear different from what they are. Hypothetically, in a governmental unit where there are three employees who make $30,000, $40,000, and $50,000 and the manager makes $200,000, the mean salary would be $80,000. However, everyone besides the manager makes less than $80,000, so the mean distorts the financial picture. The median would be $45,000 (average the two middle values if there's an even number of items). This number is closer to the salary that most people make in the governmental unit, with half making less than $45,000 and half making more than $45,000. This serves as a reminder that any analysis requires judgment and a close examination of the data set and information being relied upon in coming to a logical conclusion.

Ratios serve as opportunities to capture variation that needs further examination. The fact that a ratio yields abnormal results means a higher level of skepticism needs to be applied to understand why there is a deviation. Thus, the detailed documentation and support need to be examined before reaching a final opinion.

Developing relationships between variables enables you to develop an ability to compare large- and small-scale activities, referred to in accounting as *common sizing*. The value achieved in common sizing the public-entity statement is in being able to express numbers as percentages of a stated component, such as revenue. This can establish relationships between large- and small-scale public entities. Public entities don't report their statements in common-size fashion, yet it is beneficial to compute these percentages if you want to analyze two or more entities of differing sizes against one another (or two variables or varying amounts).

Be reminded that data can be manipulated to support pre-existing positions of the entity by people developing these statistics. Samuel Clemens quoted "Figures don't lie, but liars figure." People looking to commit fraud know the true figures need to be to remain undetected. You need to be the unsuspecting 800-pound friendly gorilla applying the appropriate level of professional skepticism to catch them.

Formatting financial statements or variables in different ways reduces the bias that can occur when analyzing entities of differing sizes or reasons. This type of examination allows for the analysis of entities over various time periods, revealing, for example, what percentage of revenue is for public safety and whether or not that value has changed over time. How does that value compare to other public entities? Financial ratios and ratio analysis help in drawing comparisons.

The hope is that readers will develop their own tools for comparison beyond those that the authors have suggested. There are many public ratios that could be developed in the future. The ones in the appendix are a good start. Remember there is not a single right or wrong way to prevent fraud and mismanagement; it all comes down to creative and proactive thinking on a case-by-case basis.

GOVERNMENT-WIDE FINANCIAL STATEMENTS SUMMARY

Government-wide financial statements provide a broad view of the government's (public entity's) operations in a manner similar to private-sector business standards, as well as both short-term and long-term information regarding the government's overall financial position for the year-end period. The governmental (public entity) financial statements represent financial communications through numbers. The numbers tell a story. By understanding these financial statements, we learn a new language. But one thing is certain: No matter what the language is, the overall objective remains the determination of whether or not the value of the services being provided makes sense considering the dollars spent, and that the public is aware of government spending practices.

Table 3.4 is a broad overview of the government financial statements of a state.

The government-wide financial statements include the following two statements:

Statement of Net Position
Presents all of the government's assets and deferred outflows of resources and liabilities and deferred inflows of resources, and calculates net position. Increases or decreases in the state's net position over time may serve as a useful indicator as to whether or not the government's overall financial position is improving or deteriorating.

Statement of Activities
Presents how the government's net position changed during the fiscal year. All changes in net position are reported when the underlying event occurs, giving rise to the change, regardless of the timing of related cash flows. This statement also presents a comparison between direct expenses and program revenues for each government function.

TABLE 3.4 Major Features of the Basic Government Financial Statements

Features	Government-wide Financial Statements	Fund Financial Statements		
		Governmental Funds	Proprietary Funds	Fiduciary Funds
Scope	Entire state government (except fiduciary funds) and the state's component units	State activities that are not proprietary or fiduciary	State activities that are operated similar to a private business	Instances in which the state is the trustee or agent for someone else's resources
Required Financial Statements	Statement of Net Position, Statement of Activities	Balance Sheet Statement of Revenues, Expenditures, and Changes in Fund Balance	Statement of Net Position Statement of Revenues, Expenses, and Changes in Net Position Statement of Cash Flows	Statement of Fiduciary Net Position Statement of Changes in Fiduciary Net Position
Accounting Basis and Measurement Focus	Accrual accounting and economic resources focus	Modified accrual accounting and current financial resources focus	Accrual accounting and economic resources focus	Accrual accounting and economic resources focus
Types of Asset/Liability Information	All assets and liabilities, both financial and capital, and short-term and long-term	Only assets expected to be used up and liabilities that come due during the year or soon thereafter; no capital assets included	All assets and liabilities, both financial and capital, and short-term and long-term	All assets and liabilities, both short-term and long-term
Types of Inflow/Outflow Information	All revenues and expenses during the year, regardless of when cash is received or paid	Revenues for which cash is received during or soon after the end of the fiscal year Expenditures when goods or services have been received and payment is due during the year or soon thereafter	All revenues and expenses during the year, regardless of when cash is received or paid	All revenues and expenses during the year, regardless of when cash is received or paid

Both the Statement of Net Position and the Statement of Activities have separate sections that report these activities: Annual decreases in net position could be indicating several issues in troubled funds, including the growth of unfunded liabilities for future pension and OPEB costs on the back-loaded debt maturity schedules, which results in annual depreciation expenses (non-cash) excluding long-term debt maturities pay downs.

Reconciliation of Government-wide and Government Funds Financial Statements (GFFS)

The comprehensive annual financial report includes two schedules that reconcile the amount reported on the government funds' financial statements (modified accrual basis of accounting) with government-wide financial statements (accrual basis of accounting). The following summarizes the major differences between the financial reporting impacts of transitioning from a modified accrual basis of accounting to a full accrual basis of accounting:

▨ Capital assets used in governmental activities are not reported on government funds' financial statements.

▨ Capital outlay spending results in capital assets on the government-wide financial statements, but is reported as expenditures on the government funds' financial statements.

▨ Bond and note proceeds result in liabilities on the government-wide financial statements, but are recorded as other financing sources on the government funds' financial statements.

▨ Certain other outflows represent either increases or decreases in liabilities on the government-wide financial statements, but are reported as expenditures on the government funds' financial statements.

▨ Long-term liabilities including debt instruments are not reported in the GFFS.

▨ Some short-term liabilities including accrued interest are not dues and payable in the current period and are omitted from the GFFS.

▨ Net Pension Liabilities are not reported on the GFFS.

▨ Short-term liabilities as a result of being self-insured for health care costs are omitted from the GFFS.

To find more information and to get a full understanding of the data provided in the government-wide financial statements and governmental funds financial statements, see the "Notes to the Financial Statements" that are generally included with the financial statements. The notes contain valuable information and are often not read by the average person.

Financial Statement Communications

A fund is a fiscal and accounting entity with a self-balancing set of accounts recording cash and other financial resources together with all related liabilities and residual equities or balances, and changes therein, which is segregated for the purpose of carrying on specific activities or attaining certain objectives in accordance with special regulations, restrictions, or limitations. The government fund financial statements reflect financial reporting practices in accordance with this definition. The government's funds, which exclude component units, are divided into three categories: governmental, proprietary, and fiduciary.

 # KNOW MANAGEMENT

By keeping in mind the 3 J's, justification, judgment, and judicial, understanding the personality behaviors surrounding the people in trusted positions and whether or not they display visual abilities that are in line with their verbal representation is important in gaining an understanding of the systems and structures needed to help people to continue to make good ethical choices.

OMB Circular A-123

A helpful tool in understanding the importance of internal control in government is OMB Circular A-123,[34] which was issued by the U.S. Office of Management and Budget (OMB) government circular. While applicable to federal entities only, they also serve as good guides for other government and public agencies to follow, as many states have adopted this standard for state level entities. The circular defines the management responsibilities for internal controls in federal agencies. It was issued by OMB's Office of Federal Financial Management on December 21, 2004. Whether in the public or the private sector, the strengths and weaknesses of the entities' financial statements reliability are based on the internal controls and oversights in place to ensure compliance. The circular was developed to improve the accountability and effectiveness of federal programs and operations. Establishing, assessing, correcting, and reporting on internal control in an entity is the only way for an accountant to develop credible financial statements. Knowing the elected officials, and the parties involved in the day-to-day operations, is critical to creating reliability in the financial communications that are being presented.

An excerpt from the Office of Management and Budget establishes the real responsible parties for the reliability and credibility of the financial communication. "**Agencies and individual Federal managers** must take systematic and proactive measures to (i) develop and implement appropriate, **cost-effective** internal control for results-oriented management; (ii) assess the adequacy of internal control in Federal programs and operations; (iii) separately assess and document internal control over financial reporting consistent with the process defined in Appendix A; (iv) identify needed improvements; (v) take corresponding corrective action; and (vi) report annually on internal control through management assurance statements."[35] Notice that nowhere does it mention the accountant. Yet, often, the presumption is that the accountant is responsible, because the financial statements are audited and prepared by the accountant. Accountants assist management in presenting financial information, however it is ultimately management's responsibility for the financial information presented for the entity. This is evident by the required "Management Representation Letter" required to be provided from management to the accountant who has been engagement to provide the services. There should be no expectation gap as management is the responsible party. The problem with setting these standards is that we may be setting up the people who have been put in these positions to fail. The question that needs to be asked we should ask is whether or not elected officials have the necessary soft skills to ensure that they understand the representations they are responsible for making and that they are accurately represented to the accountant's engaged to provide the services. If not, how does the governmental unit ensure that the proper skill levels are in place to build strong internal controls and policies? In Joe's first book, *Detecting Fraud in Organizations*, he talks about the people put in these trusted positions and the need for creating 800-pound friendly gorilla oversight.

OMB 123 is a well-written and helpful tool in developing the necessary procedures and policies to prevent fraud and mismanagement. But without developing a base of employees who can identify, record, and communicate the daily issues that arise and are able to implement corrective actions, the financial statement, whether for a public or a private entity, will remain open to mismanagement and fraud.

Looking at the auditor's recommendation and findings and reports on these internal controls is very important in gaining an overall understanding of the financial communications. Reading these findings and recommendations and then looking for the public officials and their management actions to remedy any deficiencies that might exist show that management is involved and being proactive. The governmental (public) entity must establish the necessary policies to ensure that procedures and the proper ethics are maintained and that reliable financial communications are being provided to the general public.

 ## CONCLUSION

Having a thorough understanding of the numbers being communicated and the application of the service efforts and accomplishments (SEA) goal is critical in determining if mismanagement or fraud exists in the government or public agency entity. Look beyond the numbers and apply different levels of thinking to the generated numbers. Look at the objectives of the governmental unit and see if a good costs/benefit mix exists to provide proper management incentives. Assess the relationship between the cost of a governmental (public) entity's undertaking and the resulting benefit's value goal. Examine the communications surrounding the transaction. Having the proper levels of skepticism and assurance in place that provide full public accountability only results from understanding the inflows and outflows of money.

Auditors often identify control deficiencies, but these do not get reported unless they rise to a level of significant deficiency or material weakness. The same reason is why most fraud exists; fraud is only of interest if it is material or it happens. As long as there is another control policy or procedure in place to mitigate the deficiency it does not rise to the necessary level to get reported. As long as the cash is coming in, no one may question the process. All this is based on judgment! Unfortunately some people have better judgment than others.

It comes down to watching the actions of the people in positions of trust for deviations from the established policies and procedures with the appropriate levels of professional skepticism in place and used. The way to accomplish that is to develop sound systems and structures monitored with the well-informed, unsuspecting 800-pound friendly gorilla oversight positioned next to potential exposed value that can be converted to cash.

 ## NOTES

1. http://www.gasb.org/cs/BlobServer?blobkey=id&blobwhere=1175824062
   796&blobheader=application%2Fpdf&blobcol=urldata&blobtable=
   MungoBlobs.

2. http://www.gasb.org/cs/ContentServer?pagename=GASB%2
FPronouncement_C%2FGASBSummaryPage&cid=1176158119446.

3. http://www.gasb.org/st/summary/gstsm55.html.

4. http://www.nj.com/politics/index.ssf/2015/04/nj_pension_fund_gap_
widens_to_40b.html.

5. http://www.gasb.org/jsp/GASB/Pronouncement_C/GASBSummaryPage&
cid=1176160219492.

6. http://www.state.nj.us/treasury/omb/publications/14cafr/pdf/fullcafr2014
.pdf.

7. http://www.gasb.org/cs/BlobServer?blobcol=urldata&blobtable=Mungo
Blobs&blobkey=id&blobwhere=1175824063336&blobheader=application%
2Fpdf.

8. https://www.cfda.gov/index?s=program&mode=form&tab=core&id=
7573598ab8ef8816b17284ec6538f2d3.

9. http://www.merriam-webster.com/dictionary/accounting.

10. http://www.merriam-webster.com/dictionary/partnership.

11. Congress passed the Boland Amendment, which prohibited U.S. assistance in training, equipping, or advising the anticommunist rebel Contras in
Nicaragua. A second and third Boland Amendment, passed in 1983 and 1984,
closed loopholes in Boland, which allowed for humanitarian aid and further
limited U.S. government support for the Contras. http://www.gilderlehrman
.org/history-by-era/age-reagan/timeline-terms/boland-amendment.

12. http://www.thefreedictionary.com/monopolistic.

13. http://www.u-s-history.com/pages/h1889.html.

14. Legislation signed into law in 1977 that prohibits U.S. firms from engaging
in bribery and other unlawful and fraudulent practices when conducting
business in foreign countries. The legislation assigned responsibility for FCPA
enforcement to the U.S. Department of Justice with supporting roles played
by the Securities and Exchange Commission (SEC) and the Office of General
Counsel of the Department of Commerce. http://www.businessdictionary
.com/definition/Foreign-Corrupt-Practices-Act-FCPA.html. Read more at
http://www.businessdictionary.com/definition/Foreign-Corrupt-Practices-
Act-FCPA.html#ixzz3TiICpaOB.

15. An effort to prevent action in a legislature (such as the U.S. Senate or House
of Representatives) by making a long speech or series of speeches; http://
www.merriam-webster.com/dictionary/filibuster.

16. A clever and often secret agreement made by powerful people who are usually
trying to get an advantage over others; http://www.merriam-webster.com/
dictionary/horse%20trade.

17. http://www.nytimes.com/2008/09/28/business/28melt.html?_r=1&
pagewanted=all.

18. http://www.nytimes.com/2006/02/10/business/10insure.html? pagewanted=all.

19. http://www.reuters.com/article/2015/01/30/amer-intl-group-greenberg-lawsuit-idUSL1N0V823020150130; the case is People v. Greenberg, et al., New York State Supreme Court, New York County, No. 401720/2005.

20. http://www.treasury.gov/initiatives/financial-stability/TARP-Programs/aig/Pages/status.aspx http://www.treasury.gov/connect/blog/Pages/aig-182-billion.aspx.

21. http://www.gasb.org/st/summary/gstsm54.html.

22. A Bond Debenture is a debt instrument that is not secured by physical assets or collateral, that is reliant on the creditworthiness and reputation of the issuer only.

23. http://www.pionline.com/article/20150528/ONLINE/150529873/some-39-of-benefit-plan-audits-show-major-deficiencies-8212-ebsa-study.

24. http://www.gao.gov/products/T-HRD-90-37.

25. http://www.osc.state.ny.us/press/releases/aug11/081711a.htm.

26. http://www.mycentraljersey.com/story/news/local/new-jersey/2015/04/13/new-jery-workers-six-figure-salaries-pensions/25625719/.

27. http://www.foxbusiness.com/economy-policy/2014/03/13/double-dipping-pensioners-bleeding-nj-dry/.

28. Oscar Fingal O'Flaherty Wills Wilde was an Irish playwright, poet, and author of numerous short stories and one novel.

29. http://www.merriam-webster.com/dictionary/assume.

30. http://www.taxpolicycenter.org/taxfacts/displayafact.cfm?Docid=205.

31. http://www.taxpolicycenter.org/taxfacts/displayafact.cfm?Docid=205.

32. http://www.oecd.org/ctp/tax-policy/revenue-statistics-ratio-change-latest-years.htm.

33. http://money.cnn.com/2016/04/18/pf/taxes/how-are-tax-dollars-spent/.

34. https://www.whitehouse.gov/sites/default/files/omb/assets/omb/circulars/a123/a123_rev.pdf This is a link to get you to OMB Circular A-123.

35. https://www.whitehouse.gov/omb/circulars_a123_rev.

CHAPTER FOUR

Who Works in Government and What Is Their Motivation?

"You'll never get ahead of anyone as long as you try to get even with him."

—*Lou Holtz, retired football coach, sportscaster, author, and motivational speaker*

Topics:

Politicians
Bureaucrats
Political Appointees
Union Workers
Virtuous Public Servants
Political Operatives

Key questions:

Who are these people and whose interests are being served?
Who can help us connect the dots?
When was the last background check performed?

G OVERNMENTS AND THEIR RELATED ENTITIES are established to promote many common goals. The public entity and structure of governmental agencies play a large part in how they operate on a day-to-day basis. However, the most important ingredient in the final mix of governmental entities is to remember the fact that the staff and leadership are human beings placed in charge of the workings within these public entities. This chapter gives a guided tour through the various types of beasts that one may encounter in the government service jungle. Some of these creatures are like the most stunningly beautiful kings of the jungle—such as lions—who wield power with grace, skill, pride, loyalty, and survival-of-the-fittest ethics. Others are the most vile, dangerous creatures that one may find anywhere in the world. Creatures of evil substance, bad intentions, and malicious behavior are unfortunately just more common on the forest floor. They are the poisonous snakes that sneak up and strike with a venomous bite when you least expect it. Join us on a safari into the world of the government staff, as you continue to develop the necessary soft skills you will need to examine these areas. But be forewarned: It is likely to be an unsettling ride through this dangerous terrain.

UNDERSTANDING PEOPLE

A social unit of people needs structure and management to meet a need or to pursue collective goals. Any entity, whether private or public, has some form of management structure that determines relationships between the different processes and the people charged with managing those processes. It is further subdivided with the assignment of specific roles and responsibilities. The key factor to be evaluated is the level of trust given to the various people within the public entity. The POP Joe talked about in his previous book, which examines the Perspectives, Occupations, and Positions, is critical in the formation of any public entity's structure.

Here are some basic formulas to consider for reference in this chapter:

$$\text{Value} + \text{ or } - \text{People} = \text{Fund Balance}$$

The maintaining of resources is an important responsibility and it will result in a deficit fund balance, if not properly monitored.

$$\text{People} - \text{Level of Trust} = \text{Balance}$$

The greater the level of approval authority created by a position, the higher the level of skepticism and the stronger the systems and controls need to be. The weaker the oversight and controls, the less likely the fund balance will be maintained and the greater the chances for deficits, fraud, and mismanagement occur.

Public Employee < Public Interest

The public employee's interest should never conflict with the public interest in which he or she serves. Preservation of the proper self-interests removes greed and the ability for conflicts of interest to develop.

People in these positions need to be reminded that these positions are publically funded. Whenever the funds are public funds, a fiduciary responsibility is imposed on the management of these entities. That responsibility requires that the people in these positions maintain integrity, transparency, and the proper controls to ensure that citizens' interests are preserved.

Government Workers

Many individuals work in governmental entities. They have various titles and positions with varying degrees of power and influence. These individuals work within and around the boundaries of that particular governmental entity which provides the basis, or core, of their power. They can be classified as elected officials, appointed officials, administrators, staffers, and public employees. These are the general public employee classifications that are commonly found in government. We will provide you with a bit of a tour of the various classes to start your education and to help you identify them in the field.

Elected Officials

Elected officials are government leaders who are elected to office by the public or some subset of the public as a whole. They generally have a geographic relationship to the community that they are elected to serve and represent. The question as to how they serve their voter base, or constituents, can and does fill volumes in political science texts. We have made a general assumption that elected officials want to keep their title as *elected* officials. As such, they are expected to continue to look for ways to attract votes from their constituents through popular policies and funding of voter-supported projects and services.

Elected officials should generally seek to find projects that provide direct services and benefits to their constituents. "Senator Robert Byrd (D-W.Va.), who is often called 'King of Pork' by his detractors, said Members of Congress have a responsibility to represent the interests, concerns, and needs of their constituents." In the same article, the Senator was quoted as saying, "One man's pork barrel spending is another man's job."[1] Let's take this idea but substitute *critical project* in for "job." This desire to fund projects in a home district is common in politics, as is the practice of trying to spread these same costs over the widest possible tax base to avoid charging one's own constituents for the same service. This tends to lead to the common practice of logrolling: swapping votes on projects the politician cares little about to gain votes on a particular project that benefits the politician's district. This process is continuous with each legislative session. The result is that massive amounts of funds are allocated to various pet projects around the states, the nations, and the world.

Elected officials generally have a role in the formation of governmental entities and the laws and regulations that govern them. As such, the role of the elected official is much broader than that of many others explored later in this chapter. The development of new agencies and staff positions is generally managed and capped by elected officials. While staff bureaucrats control a tremendous number of government functions, the ultimate control usually rests in the hands of an elected official or a committee of elected officials as policy makers. Whether or not the elected officials exert their power over agencies and bureaucrats is subject to their political will and whim. However, all players know that elected officials can have the final say if there is enough focus and desire on their part to manage a given situation.

This pattern of direct management and bureaucratic drifting is common in governmental agencies, with the line staff running the public entity for long periods with some degree of elected official control at key junctures and periods. The ability of bureaucrats to make and/or implement policy will be discussed later. But it is important to realize that a staff may get very limited supervision from the elected officials on a day-to-day basis. This creates an open situation for corruption and mismanagement, as the members of the line staff can execute what they perceive to be the mission of the governmental agency according to their own standards and whims. If that happens, the mission may drift away from the core values that were written into the enabling law by elected officials.

One major role of elected officials is the selection of political appointees to lead and work in governmental entities. This is one significant extension of political power that moves control away from the general public. In many cases, the appointed official has significant latitude in terms of operation once appointed to his or her role at a particular agency.

Delegate Model Versus the Trustee Model of Representation

Politicians are typically elected for a given term of office. Once elected, the elected official, in most cases, has considerable latitude in his or her decisions and legislative actions. This creates the somewhat odd situation in which elected officials can deviate from the general will of their voting base. They also face the second challenge of party politics. In terms of elected officials' actions as they relate to their constituents, the actions of an elected official are derived from either the delegate or the trustee model of representation.

In the delegate model, the elected official is expected to follow the will of his or her constituents and serve as a conduit of their will to the governing body on which he or she serves. The elected official is, essentially, the mouthpiece of his or her constituents and has limited to no authority to make independent decisions.

In the trustee model of representation, the elected official is entrusted with exercising good judgment in the decision making and may, in fact, make decisions that are in conflict with the current will of constituents if he or she feels that the decision serves the common good or future needs of those constituents.

From a practical perspective, elected officials will jump between these two models based upon the issue at hand, changing their decision process as they see fit. Few if any politicians follow either of these models exclusively.

Outside forces, such as party politics, may impose additional pressure on the political system and delegate voting.

In parliamentary systems, elected officials may be subjected to calls from their political parties to vote according to party position on a given topic. This voting call will be enforced typically by a senior and/or powerful party leader who will look to foist penalties on members who do not comply with the call for party line vote. This person may have the telling title of party "whip," which indicates the structural relationship of the elected official to his or her political party. In other words, politicians who do not follow the party line may well be whipped into shape.

In other cases, members of the British Parliament are not pressured and are given the option to vote on a given topic independently and objectively. This is typically granted for an issue that is subject to considerable debate and controversy within a given party—such as animal rights or the death penalty—where no clear party consensus has emerged. In the United States, elected officials may well find themselves subject to a call to vote along party lines as well. Members who fail to follow party instructions may well find their next election more challenging—seriously lacking in party support and funding.

Elected officials who vote in opposition to their constituents' interests or opinions may be labeled as poor representatives or out of touch with their constituents. This places a second constraint on elected officials' actions and behavior. By continually monitoring the opinions of their constituents, the elected official may gain a sense of what issues are likely to cause local unrest, and they may be able to avoid voting against the voters' interests. Failure to do this may result in a politician losing his or her position in the next election cycle.

These competing pressures, as well as political donations from wealthy individuals, industry groups, and special interests, create a swirling pool of pressures that are exerted upon a given politician at various times and can bend the voting process to a particular outcome. How they vote and how reliably they vote a given way may be subject to momentary and trending issues.

A SIDE NOTE ON PUBLIC GORILLAS

In his first book, Joe outlined the need for organizations to have "800-pound friendly gorillas." In public entities these friendly gorillas are known as watchdogs to the entity itself and gadflies to the fraudsters. They hold the management of these public entitles accountable. The mere presence of these gorillas tends to reduce fraud, as the fraudsters will generally want to avoid situations where a dangerous opponent is in place and poised to stop fraud. The idea of how a public entity can care for and feed the gorilla and how the activities in the public entity can discourage the creation and retention of gorillas will be explored further. Gorillas can come from any of the groups outlined in the introduction. Some groups have inherently more power, and some differ in terms of the types of power that they possess. The use of media outlets and information leaks can be a potent tool for all groups that lack official power or clear control over a given situation.

Information creates awareness and newspaper articles, television news, and other media outlets are great sources of information that are publicly available. Knowing where to look for this information is another soft skill to add to our tool kit, to assist in helping us determine sound systems and structures to prevent fraud and mismanagement.

Political Appointees

There is a broad range of officials at national, state, and local agencies who do not serve the interest of the voters, but who are, in fact, appointed to their positions by elected officials or the majority vote of a governing body as a whole. These political appointees serve in various roles in agencies. Some are more ceremonial in nature. Others have more direct and functional roles.

International ambassadors exemplify political appointees who may have largely ceremonial responsibilities, while other officials with similar titles provide critical services to the nation and the foreign country.

In the United States, there is currently a mixed pool of individuals who serve in the role of ambassador. Some are career staffers in the U.S. State Department while others are political appointees. In some instances, the ambassador selected for a more stable, desirable location is a party loyalist, top fund-raiser, or someone appointed for other political reasons. Where conditions may be unstable, political issues are greater, and diplomatic needs are more pressing, the ambassador is usually selected from the pool of career diplomats within the State Department. Here are some examples of these and other appointed ambassadors:

- Career diplomats Robert S. Beecroft and Stuart E. Jones are serving as ambassadors to Egypt and Jordan.
- Charles C. Adams, co-chair of political fund-raising group Americans Abroad for Obama, is ambassador to Finland.
- Caroline B. Kennedy, daughter of former President John F. Kennedy, is ambassador to Japan.

In spite of their level of qualifications and experience in their area of appointment, these political appointees may hold considerable power and discretion concerning the actions of their respective unit or agency. Smart political appointees commonly rely on the career bureaucrats that serve under their leadership to provide continuity, agency knowledge, and guidance with decisions and actions.

As a prime example, one can point to the various political appointees that were in charge of major agencies when the events of September 11, 2001, transpired. Look back at the case of Environmental Protection Agency (EPA) Administrator Christine Todd Whitman, who was an appointee and former governor of New Jersey. Whitman was subject to a major set of decisions related to the safety of the cleanup workers and residents of New York City.

As a person who was not an environmental expert, she was faced with serious questions about air quality and other environmental hazards in the wake of 9/11 that she knew little to nothing about. She had to rely on the expertise of her EPA staff to confront an ever-shifting environmental crisis that required quick decisions and policy action. Her 9/11-related actions and policies were the subjects of considerable debate and a lawsuit in 2007 that claimed she had inappropriately declared the air safe in the area around the World Trade Center site.

Bureaucrats

Bureaucrats serve as the backbone of governmental institutions and agencies. Unfortunately, they are often concerned more with procedural correctness, and less interested in the expenses related to meeting the needs of people. Bureaucrats play a vital role in society, as they hold the administrative and managerial positions throughout all governmental institutions and agencies.

Many career bureaucrats develop over time as they serve for extended periods of time in their given agency. The public entity structures of the agencies may give cover to these staffers from outside influence or pressure that may have created oversight by monitoring the visual and verbal actions of these people in trusted positions with abilities to access value.

A career bureaucrat may well differ from a given random employee selected from the private sector or the population as a whole. It is likely that bureaucrats have a great respect for institutions, authority, and structure as compared to the population as a whole, as they often have a sense of patriotism and altruism.

It is likely that the pool of career bureaucrats will suffer from what is dubbed self-selection bias in statistics. Self-selection bias is the statistical property that dictates that individuals who self-select into a given group create the potential for bias. In statistics, self-selection bias arises in any situation in which individuals select themselves into a group, causing a biased sample with nonprobability sampling. It is commonly used to describe situations where the characteristics of the people which cause them to select themselves in the group create abnormal or undesirable conditions in the group. It is closely related to the non-response bias, describing when the group of people responding has different responses than the group of people not responding. These select people in government service may be radically different than individuals who engage in the political process either as a candidate for office or in the role of political fund-raiser, party leader, or other position that may lead to political appointment to some agency. People in these positions may see these elected officials come and go, since they are often tenured or protected from the politics surrounding the public entity.

Even if people are in the same field, they are likely to exhibit different behaviors in those jobs, depending on whether or not they're working in the private or public sector. For instance, a staff statistician at the U.S. Census Bureau is likely to have a different disposition than that of a statistician at Google. In part, that's because public entities are not as subject to change as organizations in the private sector. Public entities are serving the public, while Google is serving the shareholders to provide a return on their investment. Again, understanding these conflicting external views and meeting them with the proper oversight and understanding will mitigate the risks of fraud and mismanagement.

Career bureaucrats are likely to be more risk averse and focused more on process as opposed to outcomes, since they have to get reappointed or reelected by the people they serve. As one career bureaucrat, who remains anonymous, told the authors about Washington, D.C., "Process is our product." With any process comes delays and other abilities to distract and, as with any process, once people know the system they know how to work around it. Bureaucrats are known to avoid paths of action that deviate from historical patterns of activity.

In many cases, these bureaucrats are charged with implementing laws and policies of their respective agencies, and they sometimes have significant latitude in terms of the interpretation of the statutes or laws. This activity can expand or contract the roles of a given agency beyond the actual letter of the law, causing different interpretations that may lead to the potential for fraud and mismanagement. Being involved in the policy and regulating the policymaking gives the bureaucrat the ability to delay implementation of a policy. These delays may be required until the bureaucrat gets the needed support or necessary funding. Giving the bureaucrat's opinions too much weight may shape the policies that dominate the operations of a given agency, which may be serving the bureaucrat's interests rather than the intended interests.

Again, people, economics, technology and other external factors change, and what worked 50 years ago may not work in today's society. The risk-averse bureaucrat is exposed in many ways when the operations of these various agencies are examined and there has been a failure to adjust to the times. Since bureaucrats tend to make decisions based upon prior practice and the letter of the law, deviations outside the norm represent risk to them. By sticking to past practice, the bureaucrat can reduce the potential for outside review. The bureaucratic culture is one of coloring within the lines, as opposed to thinking outside of the box. Large bureaucratic agencies tend to dislike staffers who ask difficult questions or want to radically change policy. Allowing bureaucrats to follow the same old trail is essentially providing the potential fraudster with a road map of where they can maneuver and not get caught.

Complacency and a lack of oversight result when there are no surprise visits, duties are not segregated, soft skills are not applied, and there is a failure to adjust to change. This creates bias that could enable fraud. Putting 800-pound friendly gorillas in places where these bureaucratic positions exist, and examining these positions with a "POP" skepticism will strengthen your fraud and mismanagement detection systems.

Nurturing Homegrown Gorillas

Agencies will hire a range of individuals to work in their public entity. As discussed, governmental agencies may suffer from some self-selection bias in terms of the applicants, with more conservative and rule-based candidates appearing more frequently in the applicant pool. Intelligent managers should look to recruit a certain percentage of workers who are more likely to serve as 800-pound friendly gorillas in the future. This may mean that they look for workers who have a greater potential for independent thought and a strong sense of right and wrong. It would be helpful if these staffers were also given an opportunity to develop the soft skills and institutional knowledge necessary to enable them to serve in the role of fraud detector/examiner.

Certain staff members may encounter challenges in their careers and personal lives that may make them more independent or function with a greater sense of purpose. These staffers can also serve in the role of fraud detector inside the public entity, provided that there are adequate training vehicles and communications and they recognize the risk that fraud can exist within the entity. These staffers may have arrived with the starry-eyed ideals of youth and been tempered by political or corrupt activities, but they have the potential to become gorillas. The reason being that these young examiners bring a new, current day perspective to the brainstorming sessions necessary when developing a fraud system.

Once the public entity has to identify its pool of potential 800-pound friendly gorilla monitors, the next question is what the public entity should do with these gorillas. How does it treat them? How does it react to the actions of these gorillas? Supporting these gorillas by applying all policies and rules consistently to all people in the public entity is a critical ingredient in a successful fraud and mismanagement risk plan.

The Care and Feeding of a Gorilla

In identifying a potential gorilla, a manager has to decide how to guide it and build a career path that will allow the new gorilla to gain weight—that is, ethical credibility—and reach that 800-pound goal. Gorillas, by their very nature, may cause stress on the public entity by identifying problems and issues that beg for analysis and solutions. The public entity needs to be very careful in how it reacts to budding gorillas that have identified problems and issues. There are two extreme paths and a range of in-between responses. Gorillas are known to be stubborn and have a strong sense of purpose, so they can step on toes as they move around the public entity.

The first path is when the organization provides encouragement and nurturing of the new gorilla. Here the management takes the issue raised by the gorilla seriously and deals with the problem in a creative and decisive way. This reinforces the value of gorillas to the public entity, encourages further actions by new gorillas, and may well go a long way toward encouraging other silent gorillas to come forward with other issues. These actions may also contribute to the public entity being perceived by gorillas outside the organization as a good place to work and one that encourages gorilla activity, attracting more gorilla applicants.

The second path is to treat the gorilla as a problem. Some public entities treat a whistle-blower, or someone with a critical eye on organization policy or operations, as the problem, not the solution. The reaction can range from no response to an outright attack on the individual who identified and reported the issue. The attack and/or retaliation can come in a wide range of punishments. These can include a reduction or removal of responsibility, assigning the individual to unpleasant tasks or to work in unpleasant locations, limiting or nixing promotion potential, or a salary downgrade. Both authors have seen all of these penalties applied to individuals who report suspicious or problematic activity within public entities that have little tolerance for gorilla activity.

Of course, choosing the second path will discourage existing gorillas from acting in future cases, and from joining the public entity. This can lead to a culture that avoids dealing with current fraud and mismanagement. Remember that tips are the number one way fraud is caught and encouraging people to come forward strengthens your systems of control.

Some of these negative actions are policed in the private sector, motivated by the desire for profit and performance. Corruption can cost the private organization profit and increase costs; there is more pressure to reduce waste. In governmental agencies, there may be limited competition for the service provided and significant protections afforded by the bureaucratic structure to prevent discipline of poor leadership. So the agency can create and protect a culture of corruption that persists for decades or longer.

Gorilla Hunting, Capture, Control, and Banishment

Public entities that have general practices that encourage or enable gorilla hunting will find themselves with fewer gorillas and more open to fraud and mismanagement. Why an organization would tolerate or even encourage gorilla hunting is perplexing on the surface. It is only when the motivation of the managers of bureaucratic public entities is unearthed that insight is gained into the short-term personal benefit of gorilla hunting.

By catching a gorilla, a manager can attempt to stamp out dissent and critique of his or her own actions. This may prove to be a valuable personal tool for maintaining control and power. By removing the gorilla, the problem in question is not brought forward for discussion or resolution, and the manager is not subject to questioning or sanctions.

Once the gorilla is caught, the manager needs to consider how to manage and control the gorilla's behavior. Some gorillas may be extremely competent and, as such, useful as functionaries in various roles in the public entity. Perhaps the manager can control the pesky behavior of fraud detection by providing the gorilla with additional benefits with the tacit agreement that these will encourage them to stay vigilant when performing their key roles within the public entity. Doing so steers the gorilla away from time spent on trying to rectify mismanagement issues. Too frequently, the authors have seen respectable colleagues enter public entities that use *golden handcuffs* to control potential gorillas.

Golden handcuffs basically provide superior compensation and benefits to employees with an expectation of loyalty and compliance to rules in return. The employee in the golden cuffs is getting a lot. What else could they want? Yet, the gorillas in the organization may still want to make changes and report mismanagement while educating other gorillas.

A gorilla that continues to report mismanagement issues and fraud may be targeted for some form of retribution. Firing this employee may be difficult, so other forms of punishment are used to discipline the actions of the gorilla. This may include verbal abuse or argument, assignment to unpleasant tasks, reassignment, and perhaps relocation to another facility. All of these techniques may be very effective and tailored to the particular individual who has stepped outside of management-defined boundaries.

Banishing the gorilla by moving it to a remote location or to a position with little to no power, control, or access to information can also serve to blunt the power of gorillas. Other gorillas seeing the punishment that is meted out to gorillas that are out of line may cause them to limit their activities and become less viable policers of fraud and mismanagement. Other gorillas may seek to work within the system to effect change by limiting the kinds of actions they will take to control inappropriate activity, but continuing to work toward change. In this case, the gorillas are only able to address a limited list of problems.

The Carrot and the Stick

One commonly hears of using a carrot and stick to control the behavior of individuals. Carrots are the rewards that are passed out to employees for the desired behavior and successful outcomes. The stick is the rod of discipline that is applied to individuals to punish poor behavior. Carrots and sticks can be applied to the workforce in many ways—some for good reasons and some for nefarious.

One has to examine how the public entity uses carrots and sticks and whether or not they are appropriately applied to reduce fraud and mismanagement. Corrupt public entities may apply sticks to gorillas in an attempt to beat them back into submission. They may, on the other hand, reward bad behavior with carrots, leading to a culture of immorality and corruption.

Certain individuals are not carrot-eaters. In a public entity that is corrupt, these individuals continue to do the right thing in spite of the incentives to break the rules or commit corrupt acts. There may be intense pressure placed on these individuals to begin to eat carrots and/or avoid any actions that would reduce the number of carrots that are provided to others.

> Find out just what any people will quietly submit to and you have the exact measure of the injustice and wrong which will be imposed on them.
>
> —*Frederick Douglass*

Likewise, there are some individuals who are *stick-resistant*. These individuals are not responsive to threats, punishments, or retribution. In a corrupt public entity, these individuals are highly problematic, as they do not fall prey to intimidation and, as such, are viewed as loose cannons that have the potential to cause massive disruption to the public entity. If the public entity is corrupt, stick-resistant individuals are key players in the detection of fraud and mismanagement. They will work to right wrongs in spite of the risks to themselves and their careers. It is also likely that they will leak information to the press, or another source outside the public entity, if they identify fraud or mismanagement and feel the public entity is not doing its part to address the matter.

Many workers are both carrot-eaters and afraid of the stick, so they will usually not report corrupt actions to appropriate authorities when a situation arises. The public entity builds an insular culture with respect to corrupt practices. The culture is reinforced by management behavior and practice and can lead to a management culture like Enron's.

A CASE STUDY IN TOO MUCH CARROT EATING

A great example of this problem of having too many carrot-eaters or stick-averse workers were the traffic jams caused on Interstate 95 at the George Washington Bridge. In this incident, when the staff at the public agency the Port Authority of New York and New Jersey closed various traffic lanes in what was termed by some to be a politically motivated attack by Governor Chris Christie's administration on the mayor of Fort Lee, New Jersey.

The fact that a public agency was used for political gain and retribution is not the most interesting aspect of this case. People tend to expect bad behavior from politicians, political appointees, and political operatives. The more interesting aspect came when the decision to close the traffic lanes was made. The bureaucratic staffers at the Port Authority apparently executed the lane closures with great expertise, but no staffers reported this illogical practice to anyone outside the public entity.

Because of that, the lane closure and resulting massive traffic delays went on for four days in September 2013. The police, bridge operations personnel, traffic engineers, and workers executed their functions with military precision. Only after enduring it for four days did the actions finally get leaked to the press. In the ensuing weeks, a number of staffers also committed fraud in their attempt to cover up the actions by claiming that the lane closures were part of an alleged traffic study.

Robert Durando, director of the George Washington Bridge, made a very telling statement to the New Jersey Assembly Transportation Committee. When asked why he followed the instructions of political appointee David Wildstein to close the lanes for no apparent reason, he said, "I was concerned about what Mr. Wildstein's reaction would be if I did not follow his directive."[2] Durando was clearly concerned that some form of career retribution would be handed down to him if he did not comply, and he did not want to risk any personal impact. Durando is apparently a stick-averse carrot-eater.

Such corrupt activity shows the level of actions that may be taken by political operatives to achieve their personal political goals through the use of a public agency. The leak after four days and the resulting press and broader knowledge of the situation imparted to the public caused the agency director to take action to stop the lane closures. The political operatives apparently had other plans. They had planned to keep the traffic delays going for 30 days if no one had caught them. When one becomes aware that most managers at the Port Authority are long-term staffers, with an average 22-year length of service, it does not seem surprising that they followed orders in this case without question. They were looking to protect their positions, compensation, and perks as opposed to questioning authority and politics. A few big gorillas were needed in this case to keep this agency on track and prevent an abuse of the public.

Union Workers

Public unions generally have a strong vested interest in preserving existing jobs and positions and maximizing salary and benefits for their members. These workers may be politically active and attempt to bend public policy and laws to favor their members. In some cases, there are state laws that protect their special status and rights. These include rules on internal promotions only (police departments: no outside hires for leaders), generous health benefits, union-only worker provisions (agency shop rules), binding arbitration on wages, and other such provisions.

Unions may be resistant to change and may not want to address evolving work conditions and technology innovations. This creates an environment in which innovative practice can be supplanted by existing rules. One may wonder why unions can create an environment that is opposed to change and innovation. By establishing and maintaining operational and work practice rules, union members can progressively negotiate for marginal improvements in their compensation and benefits. By continually working on an existing framework of practices, they can continually look to identify additional sources of work hours, compensation, and benefits for their members. It is important to also note that many municipalities have multiple unions across various work categories, and each union has its own peculiarities.

It is also important to consider that various unions may coordinate bargaining with governmental entities. However, at the end of the day, the contract that is struck with a given union that provides certain compensation and benefits is the key component of value for the union workers. This may be highly formalized. For instance in New York City, the AFL-CIO has an organized group, the New York City Central Labor Council. Within the council, about 40 unions coordinate negotiation practices and contract terms across a broad range of municipal workers to promote union workers' rights and benefits.

In terms of union form, there are unions that represent workers in a singular type of work. These types of unions are traditionally called craft unions: The organization of the union reflects the sole type of work that the union members perform. Electricians, carpenters, steamfitters, masons, and elevator installers may all be in different unions with different work rules and practices. Yet one key aspect of municipal projects may be the need to have all of these workers participating on a given project. The coordination and standards of practice that seem innocuous on the surface may create significant operational issues and costs when working with various unions.

As an alternative to this model of union structure, the industrial unions organize the workers on the basis of employer, not on the basis of craft. This creates a situation in which the workers in a particular organization are all members of a single union and working under one contract. These contracts may have various pay scales for various job categories and may have separate work rules for the different classes of workers. A prototypical type of industrial union was the United Mine Workers: No matter what particular job anyone had in the mines, he or she was a mineworker. In many cases, government workers have been organized under various unions, but they tend to have both industrial and craft organizational form. In municipal government, it is common to find craft unions such as police, teachers, and firefighters alongside more industrial types of unions that may have organized the clerical and operational functions of a given government.

The organizing unions may also be somewhat strange in terms of original purpose. It is not uncommon to find traditional public-sector unions such as AFSCME (American Federation of State, County and Municipal Employees) alongside other municipalities organized under other parent unions, such as the Teamsters or the Communication Workers of America, as the national union affiliates.

National municipal unionization has come under criticism in a number of cases, with the most pronounced activity in Wisconsin in 2011. There, Governor Scott Walker proposed a broad package of union bargaining reform that included a cap on pay raises for public workers to be in line with the rate of inflation, removal of the ability of various unions to bargain collectively, and ending the practice of automatically collecting union dues from public workers. Act 10 of 2011 passed and Wisconsin severely curtailed the rights of unions in bargaining, basically leaving wages as the only key item of discussion and capping the increase in wages to match the inflation rate.

It is interesting to note that Wisconsin was the first state to legalize collective bargaining in the public sector in 1959. The series of reforms proposed by Governor Walker has had a profound effect on public-sector unions in Wisconsin and in legislative proposals in state capitols across the nation. In reality, the ability of the public sector to tap the resources of the general population via the use of taxes and user fees creates a strong revenue source that can be used to fund public union membership interests based upon political pressure and ineptitude.

In many states, the practice of pattern bargaining is widespread. In pattern bargaining, the union attempts to get a favorable contract from one given municipality or private-sector employer and then uses the terms of the contract to attempt to get a similar settlement from other employers. This can also be applied across worker groups, or when unions negotiate for similar patterns of raises not directly addressing the matter of salary levels by union. This allows worker groups with very different salary levels to essentially maintain parity in terms of relative salary. That method is widely applied in many municipal unions, and, in fact, the unions may look to the municipal government to keep their contract terms at least as favorable as other union contracts that have been settled in recent periods.

Yet, municipal governments are wise to consider the value of having known terms for their labor contracts. An intelligent elected official looks to resolve labor issues in a timely and practical way, if reasonable contract terms are possible. Leaving many labor contracts open is not a painless or purely academic exercise.

For example, starting in 2010, former New York City mayor Michael Bloomberg adopted a very tough negotiating strategy with city labor unions. Local municipal unions countered with limited interest in bargaining. This resulted in 100 percent of the 152 unions working with expired contracts in November 2012, according to a *Wall Street Journal* story published on November 12, 2012.[3] While this may be symbolic of hardline negotiation on the part of New York City, given the high levels of unionization in municipal services, this creates an open-ended liability for the municipal government. New York City, through this practice, created a large unfunded liability of indeterminate size. Once the liability was created, organizations in the public finance sector became concerned about the city's ability to manage and pay for the liability. It was not even the level of liability that was of paramount concern, but also the fact that the size of the liability was unknown.

However, in some cases, unions may identify that the pool of resources to compensate workers is limited; this may create competition among various unions for the resources of the municipality and for the most beneficial contract terms. It may also create opportunities for corrupt practices and donations to elected officials, as unions jockey for beneficial relationships.

Public unions also will attempt to intervene in the political process to help sympathetic politicians get and stay elected to various offices. They will also attempt to undermine and defeat politicians who are opposed to their objectives.

While one would like to stand back and get into a political debate about how political leadership should serve all constituent groups, the fact of the matter is that when the unions back elected officials, those officials usually are expected to give the unions more favorable compensation and working conditions. Often these conflicting interests create an unpleasant reality where an elected official who desires to get reelected or elected is probably not serving the needs of his or her constituents.

We, again, have introduced the conflicting needs of interested parties surrounding a particular value. It is these types of external third party influences that need to be examined with the appropriate level of skepticism. If this was Wall Street it would be the investor demanding higher returns, or the consequences would be selling the stock and driving the price of the shares down and draining the organization's liquidity. Examine these and other third-party influences to strengthen your fraud and mismanagement detection systems.

There has to be a healthy level of balance from elected officials in their dealings with public unions. The services provided must be considered along with the cost of the union contract and the ability of the taxpayers to fund the union contracts. The only way to create balance is through oversight and independent, objective review.

The individual benefit of a strong union contract settlement by a worker who is also a local resident—and thus a constituent—is generally much greater than the payment that same worker makes into the tax system. So a contract settlement that increases union wages by 5 percent would increase the income of a worker household by 5 percent—but the tax burden would be shared among all taxpayers in the district. So the tax impact for the constituent union worker household would be relative to their portion of the taxpayer base. Table 4.1 shows a best-case (union workers contribute as large a share of taxes as possible) example of how little the workers actually pay—even if they are residents. Here, we have a public workforce that is 10 percent of the constituents of a district. They win a 5 percent salary increase for a worker pool of 500 who earn $65,000 on average. The cost per household for that tax increase would be $325—or $1,625,000 in total. If all union workers were also residents (a broad and most favorable assumption), they would only pay 10 percent of the tax cost—and receive all of the benefits—thus yielding a net increase in household income for union worker households of $2,925. This clearly skews the cost/benefit ratio for worker households toward favoring generous expenditures of public funds on public union workers—where they receive nine times the benefits as compared to their personal costs.

An elected official could be corrupt in any way, but if the union leadership thought the official could be useful in contract negotiations, then the union

TABLE 4.1   Union Benefit Impact (Union Member vs Non union Member Household)

Factor	Worker Household	Taxpayer Household	Worker Who Is a Resident
Original Wages	$65,000		$65,000
Number	500	5,000	500
Total Cost—Households		($1,625,000)	($162,500)
Wage Increase	5%		
New Wages	$68,250		$68,250
Household Impact	$3,250	($325)	$2,925
Total Cost/Benefit	$1,625,000	($1,625,000)	($1,462,500)
Household Cost/Benefit	Infinite	zero	900%

would support that official. By the same token, if the official was virtuous in all ways and clear-thinking in terms of issue analysis and that led the official to support changes in process that were a threat in any way to the status quo of the existing unions, then that official would likely be subject to a pitched effort by unions to unseat him or her. This political quagmire creates the common situation in which elected officials are unlikely to challenge union power and/or reform existing municipal employee practice.

This desire to have compliant public officials who will serve their needs and the desire to maintain the status quo create two strong areas where public unions can lead to corrupt practices and mismanagement. Their general intransience in terms of reform and their desire to maintain their power and position at all costs create an environment where 800-pound friendly gorillas are needed—and despised. In deciding how to provide a municipal service, an elected official should be able to consider various options. But powerful public unions would prefer to remain in marginal mode: not considering broad reforms and focusing on additional marginal changes.

While the goal of the union is to protect its worker base, there must be consistency in the treatment of employees across all unions by the public entity, with a common theme of protecting the rights of all public employees. The unions have to consider the taxpayers' interest (cost) and the taxpayers have to understand public employees' needs (earnings needed to provide support). The real control is getting those two parties on the same page.

What needs to be monitored are obvious realities like the fact that people are living longer. A result of people living longer is that there needs to be an actuarial pension adjustment. Similarly, health care costs cannot be allowed to rise 12 percent a year on average, when the inflation adjustment increase for social security and earnings is 2.7 percent on average. These are the real outliers, but the perception of the taxpayer is that the public unions and the elected officials are in bed together. Add to these items the idea of a cap on the amount to taxation. All a cap does is put pressure on these two groups to find other ways to fund the required services or write exclusionary regulatory language. The successful fraud examiner and development of sound systems and structures requires all divergent facts be gathered to be brain stormed and formed into convergent conclusions. The solution is not in telling me it's raining, but providing me with an umbrella.

Only by standing back and considering the various ways to provide public service—including privatization and contract services—can we realize the true cost of municipal worker and union contracts.

Unions as Gorillas

Unions represent the employers and negotiate on behalf of their membership to secure better wages and working conditions. The union is the 800-pound friendly gorilla that looks for the interest of the worker. Again the public entity is trying to hold down taxes and fees, clearing conflicting interests with the union that is trying to get better working conditions and higher wages for its membership.

Unions run large job-training services that maintain and develop the members' skills. Public entities are typically not equipped to develop large labor pools to operate in the various disciplines needed to operate the public entity.

Unions partner with other organizations to perform various community services. Union workers get better wages and benefits for their membership than nonunion workers. Unions provide workforces that are trained and ensure that health and safety conditions are maintained. Unions can deter nepotistic hiring processes by the public entity, as labor members are expected to meet certain efficiency standards and maintain skill levels.

The problems arise when the unions become threatened and their interests are not served. The taxpayers and users are reaching tipping points with the rising labor union costs. Therefore, unions resist everything from improved technology and management techniques to public-private partnerships. Trying to get a union to change is often subject to vigorous resistance and attempts at quashing analysis and review—not even adoption—so that the status quo can be preserved. Allowing public servants to be funded through union donations and support without checks and balances creates an environment that allows fraud and mismanagement to exist. You have two conflicting

800-pound friendly gorillas, one serving its membership, the union, and the public servant watching out for the taxpayer and/or user. All divergent facts must be considered before reaching any conclusion, as previously discussed. Examine the people approving the contracts and wage increases to ensure that the process is fair and open and serves all interested-parties needs.

Virtuous Public Servants

Compared to others in government, this group of public participants is probably the most fascinating. It is basically a group made up of all gorillas. These virtuous public servants have a strong sense of public duty. In the United States, these folks actually, in most cases, believe in the Constitution and the fact that people have to be ever-vigilant to protect the basic liberties and rights it affords. These public servants are generally career staffers who have committed themselves to serving the people. Good and virtuous public servants exist in most governmental agencies.

Currently,[4] 15.7 percent of workers are employed by federal, state, or local governments. Understanding productivity and efficiencies in governmental agencies is key to developing effective systems and structures. Without efficient labor, your costs are going to increase. Knowing the virtuous public servants' relative scarcity, it is important to consider the scope and activities of public entities. The limited supply of high-quality staff is a reason to suggest that limited goals for a governmental agency are probably appropriate in that an agency with limited goals and operations is more likely to have the right ratio of virtuous public servants to general bureaucrats to accomplish their given tasks. Agencies with expansive goals are likely to have difficulty deploying a good contingent of virtuous public servants to a given project, absent employees with the necessary skills to accomplish the tasks. Meeting the need with the proper resources, well-communicated objectives, and consistent application of the necessary controls is important in preventing fraud and mismanagement.

PFDA

Remember people are your greatest assets when they can get the job done and your greatest liability when they cannot. Know whether or not you have the proper staffing to provide your service in the most efficient manner possible. To examine whether or not labor is efficient, monitor usage of public entity programs, investigate any cost spikes, follow up on frequent that are solicited through an effect whistle-blower hot-line and/or develop and environment that encourages the reporting of labor abuses.

In 2009, the U.S. government implemented the American Recovery and Reinvestment Act with an expansive set of goals related to public spending on infrastructure that was intended to stimulate the U.S. economy. The program was then funneled to the various agencies of the federal government for project approval and funding. This presented a significant expansion of activity at agencies with a desire to spend the $105 billion in grant money associated with the act as soon as possible. The spending fury resulted in the common description of these projects as "shovel ready." At the U.S. Department of Transportation (DOT), there was a considerable need to shift bureaucrats to administer these new funds. This strained the pool of virtuous public servants at the U.S. DOT and created the odd situation where more funding resulted in greater agency difficulties.

Virtuous public servants, in many cases, may hold a significant portion of the institutional power and memory—and governmental entities are lucky if they do. By having a strong sense of the long-term goals of a given organization, they can guide policy in a positive way. If they have the ability to guide the organization toward more sensible outcomes, then the chance that the right decision will be made or the right action will be taken is enhanced. These public servants are usually well established in their organizations, and sensible political appointees allocate a significant amount of power to them. When a wise and creative political appointee uses the skills of the virtuous public servants in his or her organization and combines their own political power with the operational skills of the virtuous public servants, the outcomes can be astounding and the benefits to the public great.

Political Operatives

Political operatives are the lowest form of government insiders. This worker has strong political connections and has gotten a position for the main purpose of having a political arm in a public agency. Political operatives may have motivations that go way beyond the scope of their actual role in the governmental agency, and the current position may serve as a way station for a politician who lost an election. This storage of political power within the public agencies can create massive conflicts of interests for the operation of the agency.

First and foremost, an agency with a strong degree of politicization may find decisions on staffing driven, in part, by the desire to create more opportunities for political hires. Thus, the agency may overstaff and create massive bureaucracies with little purpose other than to employ down-and-out politicians. This incurs excessive costs and may spur higher long-term government expenditures for pensions and retiree health care costs. These unneeded staff positions may crowd out legitimate hires who become unaffordable in the existing budget due to the other staffing costs.

Second, the locating of political operatives within a public entity may be done with structure and intent; the political arm that secured the position for the staff may use that staffer to bend agency policy toward politically connected outcomes. For example, they may use the resources of the agency to support *special* projects that are outside the normal operating range of the given agency. These costs create political goodwill, which can be applied to achieving some greater political goal. This type of political pressure will seat political operatives in as many locations as possible. The potential then exists to exert political pressure on as wide a range of situations as possible.

Ever wonder why certain appointments or staff positions are sought out by certain politically active groups? Think about the value of these positions to achieving certain goals. Think of an elected official on a school board, an appointed member on a land use board, and a political hire in the state department of transportation. Any one of them may be useful in gathering information, obtaining some systematic advantage, or bending a particular decision in favor of some organization or group.

Political operatives are somewhat differentiated from incompetent nepotistic hires in that a political operative is, to some degree, expected to retain party or group loyalty within the public entity, and that political loyalty can be exploited at some point in time by the politically powerful. That power may be used sporadically or not at all. But the employee has some knowledge of the political relationships that have helped him or her along in the process.

A nepotistic hire is a hire of an incompetent or poorly skilled candidate over a more qualified candidate based on political or social connections. Here, for example, is where a local city councilperson may use his or her political connections to, say, get his or her son-in-law who has a substance abuse problem hired by the state highway department. This is accomplished by limiting the pool of outside candidates and/or hiring a manager using a political lens in the hiring process. For instance, jobs may not get posted, or jobs may be posted in odd venues (papers, websites, and such) so that viable candidates are not aware of the position. Candidate screening can be politicized. Decision makers may have a vested interest in certain job candidates and jobs being filled prior to being posted. A further wrinkle would be to bring in a few really bad candidates in the final pool to make the nepotistic candidate look "good" or like "the best of a bad lot."

Political operatives can also be put in place by political appointees, who, once they have attained their position, can stay in power and control of the agency for decades. This creates a deeper power base for the political appointees over time, as their span of control is extended as more and more staffers have a connection to the political appointees. Once the staffers have been put in place, their power and control may well be longer in duration than the terms of the political appointees. The shifting of political parties may clean a house of the political appointees, but if the appointees have been active at adding operatives, the power and control of the agency may remain controlled from afar by members of the political minority.

 ## HUMAN RESOURCES: THE FIRST LINE OF DEFENSE

It's all about people. Fraud starts and stops with the people in the public entity or those closely related to the public entity on the outside (e.g., contributors, vendors)—the external influencers. By examining the human resources, many of the essential fraud forces are brought together, as HR focuses on people, and one of the biggest motivational tools any public entity has to offer is compensation and benefits. Also, fundamentally speaking, people perpetrate fraud, and HR is responsible for facilitating the selection and continued engagement of these people. This puts HR on the front lines of the ability to combat fraud and mismanagement.

Human resources can be viewed as a prime obstacle for public authority. At the same time, HR is a critical control facilitator that can help to deter fraud or, if not adequately managed or neglected, can add significant fuel to the fraud fire. Many times, people and public entities as a whole underestimate the influence and impact of policies and decisions made in or communicated through HR on the building blocks of fraud within the public entity. Understanding HR plays a big part in determining if the public entity is more or less susceptible to fraud.

Human resources play a vital role in establishing, monitoring, and facilitating the social contract between employees and the public entity. The social contract is complex, but some of the principles underlying the concept are fair work for fair pay, the right to be heard, equality, following through on promises and trust, to name a few. Essentially, management needs to manage the mind-set of the employees within the public entity and their attitudes utilizing HR. It is interesting that these building blocks of employees' mind-sets can influence them to perpetrate fraud, but can also influence the people who perform control actions, depending on the variables in place.

Human resources' cousin is payroll. Payroll does not have as many intricate implications on the building blocks of fraud as human resources does. But all people in the public entity come into contact with payroll on a regular basis, and payroll usually involves expending a significant portion of public funds.

Ask how many people in the public entity would have worked in the public sector if the public worker did not get paid. The answer would be few, if any. The paycheck is a major motivator for people, as are benefits. For many public entities, payroll and benefit expenditures comprise the largest chunk of line item spending in the budget. This is the perfect recipe for fraud. Where there are people and value, fraud is a threat. Because of the value and number of people involved (not to mention the ramifications of not paying people or paying them correctly), payroll is critical when considering fraud potential, as defined by the people and value model that follows.

As in the previous chapters, to understand where fraud may occur, one must understand the public entity processes themselves, including where value resides and where people come into contact with that value and properly position the friendly 800-pound gorilla's oversight.

Going point by point through the process in Figure 4.1 shows that value and people are interwoven, even in ways that may not be readily identified and considered. Each public entity is slightly different, and some of these HR examples may not apply. Regardless, this is an exercise in identifying the value, people, and where they come into contact, thereby understanding where fraud could occur.

Hiring Process

Value: People/tone of public entity hiring.

People: All employees, hiring managers, and human resources hiring specialists.

The first element of HR is the hiring process. If a fraudster could be identified somehow and in some way, it would be the ultimate prevention: Simply don't hire them. It would be really nice if HR people were mind readers or if those who are prone to fraud had a big red "X" on their foreheads. Unfortunately, this is not the case; fraudsters look just like everyone else. So to get to know them is to make an informed decision. Unfortunately, getting to know someone is difficult and takes time. People are generally not good at getting to know one another. Look at the divorce rate! Also, factor in the fact that people change over time in a public entity.

Many officials heading public entities have been heard espousing that their employees are their biggest asset. In doing so, they are recognizing the value of people. It's interesting that fraud occurs where people meet value; in this case, the people are identified as value. People are a double-edged sword. If you hire people, you will be susceptible to fraud. If you don't hire people, you will not be able to provide certain services. People are a public entity risk simply

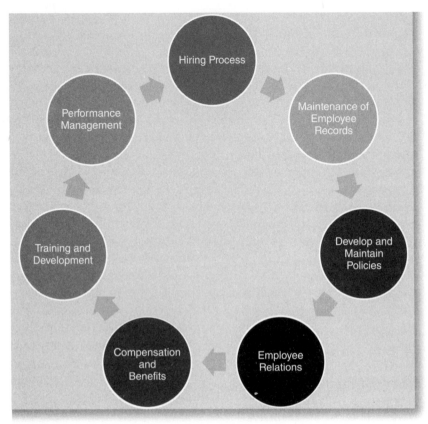

FIGURE 4.1   Human Resource Cycle

because they may be motivated to perpetrate fraud against a public entity. Want to get rid of fraud? Get rid of all employees! But that's not a reasonable solution. People are our most valuable resource, but they can also be our biggest liabilities. So how do we keep people engaged in their work and not motivated to perpetrate fraud? There is no simple answer, but it does have to do with the concepts discussed at the beginning of the chapter, the employees' mind-set, and the relationship between the employees and the public entity. Effective communication with appropriate monitoring is a good start.

An employee and public entity come into contact for the first time during the hiring process. This can be likened to dating. The employee and the public entity get together, questions are asked, and they try to get to know one another, ultimately to determine whether the relationship will work out.

Sometimes people who date someone who they meet for the first time immediately hit it off right away and they don't keep their guard up.

In a Forbes article,[5] "Seven Seconds to Make a First Impression," by Carol Kinsey Goman, it establishes an idea that people formulate a first impression within 7 seconds of meeting someone. This "Love at First Sight" often happens when someone is hired who ends up committing fraud. Because these first impressions can be misleading and often cause management to let their guard down, these hires have the potential to find ways to become immediately trusted by building upon their first impressions.

These first-impression fraudsters will have mastered the ability to display the necessary educational level required to do the job. They will have an uncanny ability to articulate their past successes. Their abilities will include an ability to maintain a high level of sophistication and etiquette. They will continue to adhere to a strong sense of social heritage. In addition to all that, they will often have a great personality and sense of humor. These same traits that lead them to getting past HR and hired, are the same characteristics that will get them to become a trusted employee, which in effect gives them an opportunity to access value.

It is very easy to fall into the trap of looking at a potential employee superficially, especially when entities are shorthanded and people are being required to do more as a result of budgetary constraints and/or other monetary limitations. Making hiring decisions without taking the time and effort to delve deeper into them creates a greater risk for potential fraud and mismanagement. This brings to mind the adage "Don't judge a book by its cover."

You need to be diligent in the hiring process. You cannot hire the first person you meet or hire them because of who they know, because without the proper oversight, they can gain access to the value. In a society built on technology, document alterations and exaggerations are a key stroke away. You can verify references and educations verbally, by making a simple phone call.

You need to continually monitor your hiring process with annual background checks. Match work lifestyles with outside work lifestyles by making inquiries. Institute mandatory vacation polices. Implement job rotation. Enforce the segregation of duties. Make sure there is an updated and regulatory employee handbook and secure sign off by the employee (witnessed). Make sure to examine areas where these trusted people have access to the value and match the level of trust with the appropriate level of oversight. Proceeding cautiously with any new hire and developing your opinion after some time and when all the facts are in is a critical defense in preventing fraud and mismanagement.

Think of how hiring decisions play a role when evaluating a public entity's fraud risk. When someone is hired, the aim is for that person to be technically competent and ethical. The employee should also fit in with the personality of the entity and share the same values as the boss and the public entity. Being successful in hiring positively impacts the public entity. The right hiring means the entity has the necessary skills to perform the services in a cost effective manner. When people believe in the same mission and come together to achieve a common goal, you have created positive motivation. The effective HR resource management team vets out people than can cause friction and only hires workers that fit in with the team. Utopia!

When there is too much friction within a public entity, bad things happen, such as fraud. It is similar to two married people who fight all the time. Eventually one or both are more likely to cheat or do something detrimental to the relationship. That being said, it is impossible to get into people's minds. Usually the assessment of a person's fit in the public entity does not become evident until sometime after he or she has been hired. The hiring process is a relatively short one, during which there is little time to accurately read someone. There are many tests out there that human resource departments use to gauge people's personality, and to determine whether they will fit in a public entity or specific position. Implementing these tests can be quite costly, and, frankly, we're not completely sold on their effectiveness. The effectiveness of such tests is dubious because skilled fraudsters are usually good actors. It is not a reach to suggest that a talented individual will be able to manipulate test answers to skew the results to match what they know the human resources department wants to hear. So how does one get to know people to determine whether they are a good fit in a particular public entity's environment? It's simple: Talk to other people to the extent permitted by the public entity. Luckily, getting to know people has gotten a little easier because of social media like Facebook, where people usually reveal themselves publicly over a period of time.

A simple but effective tool that can be used to weed out bad employees is the good old background check. Too often, though, background checks are performed only once, during the hiring process itself. Monitoring employees must be an ongoing process. People change over time. Much research that the authors have reviewed shows that frauds are often perpetrated by people who have worked at the public entity for a long time. The reason for this is simple: They become trusted and have access to more things of value. But that person has changed. The individual probably would not have gotten into the position over a long period of time if he or she did not fit in and share similar values with others in the entity. So what has changed and why? What are the circumstances? Remember, people change. Everyone must be cognizant of changes in public employees' behavior or actions, as they could be predictors of friction somewhere in their lives, which could result in negative consequences to the public entity, including the occurrence of fraud. In general, everyone in a public entity needs to get to know each other to maintain the appropriate robust working relationships over long periods of time.

A WORD OF CAUTION ABOUT TOO MUCH RELIANCE ON BACKGROUND CHECKS

Only a small amount of fraud is actually reported and prosecuted. Public entities have a tendency to simply terminate fraud suspects to avoid costly investigations and/or perhaps negative publicity. Entities that do not follow through on allegations of fraud and simply terminate suspects put future employers in jeopardy. Failing to fully prosecute fraud simply results in alleged perpetrators going somewhere else to perpetrate another fraud. Until there is sufficient outrage against fraudulent behavior by all employers, some fraudsters will continue their behavior, wreaking havoc against the next unsuspecting victim. Help other public entities and units get to know their potential employees and those who should not be considered.

During the hiring process, many promises are made by both parties. These promises and assertions shared during the process make up a quasi-contract between the employer and employee. This quasi-contract forms a bond of understanding between the two parties. When one party perceives that a part of the commitments made during the process has been breached, friction occurs. As we have discussed, when friction occurs, bad things can happen, including fraud. It is essential that the employment process be as transparent and honest as possible. The initial transparency and honesty will have a positive impact on the employee/employer relationship in the long run. Although this seems like a simple concept to follow, people generally have problems being truthful, particularly when money is at stake. In today's tough economic environment, with higher rates of unemployment, jobs are at a premium, particularly higher-paying jobs. This circumstance provides the incentive for people to embellish their achievements and credentials. In fact, credential fraud (e.g., college degrees and professional designations) have become popular topics. It is happening with greater frequency. With this being said, it is not just the applicant who may be motivated to mislead. Public entities sometimes employ professional recruiters who get bonuses based upon filling positions. In that scenario, they have an incentive to say whatever they have to say to get those positions filled. Last, but not least, there is the simple misunderstanding that may occur that can also lead to friction in the workplace.

The first step of the employment process, bringing the right people into a public entity, is critical in maintaining the culture desired by any public entity's senior management. This plays a vital role in minimizing friction within the public entity, which plays a role in minimizing fraud. However, this step is probably the hardest in the entire HR process, because there are two parties coming together who do not know one another. It is impossible to guarantee success in this phase, but it is helpful to maintain transparency, honesty, and fairness throughout the process. Conducting background checks is also a very helpful resource, but a limited one. Getting to know a person by asking others about them is the most effective approach, but it is limited by all the privacy laws that have been enacted. There is also the Employee Retirement Income Security Act (ERISA), as well as other labor law protections. However, there is always social media. Remember the old adage "An ounce of prevention is worth a pound of cure." Take time during the hiring process not only to protect the public entity, its culture, and other aspects, but also to help minimize the potential for fraud.

Personnel Data

Value: Data.

People: Those with legitimate access to the data, perhaps working in HR, such as an employee benefit specialist or retirement plan administrator; consultants with whom you share employee data for things such as pension valuation; or even an outsider who gains access to the system illegally or intercepts files being transmitted among legitimate parties; database managers or IT personnel.

The public entity maintains critical information about employees all the way down to their bank accounts. In the hands of the wrong people, this information could be used to steal identities and perpetrate a multitude of fraud schemes against those employees. Remember, it is not only those systems that should be a concern, but also vendors. Employees' personal data may be shared with several different outside parties, such as actuaries for pension calculations and payment, 401(k) administrators, and even auditors for different types of employee benefit or payroll tests. Many cases of lost employee data stemming from vendors can be found on the Internet. Just perform a search for "employee data" and "lost laptop," or similar words, to see how much disruption these events can cause within a public entity. There are a number of articles written on lost employee data, and much negative publicity. There are also additional steps to be taken after the fact, such as subsequent encryption of data and credit monitoring for the employees whose data was lost.

There are also various websites and agencies that track these events. One such database that is worth a look is http://datalossdb.org. This website is full of information about incidences of lost data, how the data was lost, applicable laws, and much more.

The bottom line: Employees' personal data is worth a considerable amount of money and, in the hands of skilled criminals, can be sold or used to perpetrate countless frauds. Fortunately, people who come into possession of this data often do so unknowingly, as a result of, say, simply stealing a computer for the purpose of getting their hands on a new laptop. However, data sensitivity is becoming more of a problem, with which all companies will struggle.

There is no easy solution to data security. Data compromise will always be an issue. It is similar to fraud. No matter how stringent the prevention measures taken, it will still happen. The following are some simple, starting-point steps that can be used to protect data:

This is not an all-inclusive list, as almost every situation varies.

- Understand what data exists in the particular public entity and where it resides.
- Establish data use and security policies and enforce them.
- Don't forget simple security protocols, such as requiring strong passwords and password-enabled screen protectors that turn on within a couple of minutes of computer inactivity.
- Physically secure data with security cables, devices to locate lost equipment, and by simply locking doors where they are kept.
- Limit access to data to those individuals who absolutely need it, and continually update access lists for people who have left the public entity.
- When data is needed for analysis purposes, use the least amount of data possible to accomplish the analytic objectives, such as not including names, Social Security numbers, salaries, bank account numbers, and addresses in developing analytical payroll testings.
- Encrypt data so it is meaningless to those without the encryption key.
- Secure remote access to data, such as cloud-hosted programs that can be accessed through the Internet using a browser from any computer.

Using these tips, in tandem with others that are applicable in any particular situation, will help reduce the risk of data loss and abuse as well as possible fraud. Remember: Data is power. The value of data will continue to grow and will probably eclipse the value of the actual assets as stated on a number of public entities' balance sheets. Remember that fraud occurs where people meet anything of value. Don't overlook the value of information within a public entity.

Policies and Job Descriptions

Value: Establishes expectations, accountability, rules.
People: All employees.

Public entities usually have plenty of policies and procedures, but, to be effective, they need to be updated regularly to reflect changes in the public entity and they need to be adequately communicated. Often, people who perpetrate fraud do so in an environment where there are no clear lines of responsibility and rules are not communicated or enforced. Usually these boundaries are established in documents such as job descriptions, policies and procedure manuals, codes of conduct, and countless other documents. Fraudsters typically thrive in public entities that are overly relaxed when it comes to establishing, communicating, and enforcing policies, because they can push, and even manipulate, limits set forth to help facilitate their fraud. A talented fraudster will take advantage of the looseness and thrive by exploiting informal boundaries to perpetrate their scheme. A good example of this is when a fraudster perpetrates a fraud under the auspices of helping others but is doing so only to take advantage of the situation and the access it gains him or her. People will also take advantage of ambiguity or lack of communication by using it as an excuse to cloud potential fraud investigations.

Example Policy: Cash Handling

Any public entity's policy should be to lock all cash received in a safe place at the end of the day. A new office employee is aware of the policy, but it is not formally communicated and acknowledged. The new office employee slowly takes over the role of interacting with walk-in citizens delivering payment. No one likes the distraction of handling this, so they let the new person take care of it. This often occurs when people in these processes are there for long periods of time, and they let the new employee handle important responsibilities like the collection of cash. In reality, everyone in the office should participate in the activity and duties should be segregated with proper checks.

The new person at first places receipts in the unlocked cash drawer that is located at the payment window, which is standard protocol. Over time, the new employee knowingly fails to move the receipts to the safe, since no one is watching and there is no segregation of duties. Funds continue to accumulate in the unlocked drawer, but no one says anything.

Finally, one evening after everyone leaves, the new employee walks out with the cash in the unlocked drawer. When confronted, the new employee argues that he was never trained to move the cash to the safe and contends that he/she would never steal money. The new employee points out that everyone in the office had access to the cash drawer. In a case like this, it is difficult to prove who actually misappropriated the cash.

The point is that without adequately establishing accountability and clearly defining responsibility for the walk-in cash receipts in this case, it is very hard to prove who is responsible for the wrongdoing if and when it does occur. The authors have also seen this many times when nonfraud issues are identified in a public entity as part of an audit or internal audit. Employees who are caught violating public entity policy plead that they simply did not know about it in the hope of leniency, which is usually unjustly forthcoming. This is very similar to people who get caught speeding or violating another law and responding to the authorities that they did not realize what the speed limit was. This is where the saying "Ignorance of the law is no excuse" comes into play. Often, public entity policies and procedures become outdated or are not communicated to employees who are responsible for a public entity's process. These oversights provide the loophole needed to exploit situations and potentially perpetrate fraud. Public entities must keep their policies up to date and ensure that all employees sign acknowledgments that they are aware of the policies and procedures and will comply with them.

One mistake public entities make when it comes to policies is failing to maintain consistency throughout the public entity. How does a person feel if treated unfairly? How about when one person can do something and another cannot? In these cases, people feel wronged or hurt, and more friction is created. When people are distracted by these feelings, they are more likely to overlook small details that could be indicators of fraud and may even be more likely to perpetrate fraud themselves. What type of inconsistencies?

Look at a hypothetical public entity scenario in which the public employee or authority is either explicitly or implicitly given "gifts" or "wined and dined" to, say, gain influence or get a contract. However, other people in the public entity follow rules and do not to take any type of "gift," even during the holidays. It is these conflicts that generate the perception that if one person is doing something unethical and not getting caught, then why shouldn't another?

Consistency in policy is a must in a public entity. Failing to maintain consistency in these areas will leave the door open to potential lawsuits and fraud. In the courtroom, having a consistent policy applied and well documented is the public entity's best defense against grievances, political retribution, sexual harassment, and any sort of employee-related lawsuits.

Job Descriptions

A related topic is that of job descriptions. When was the last time a job description was updated? This seems to be one of those things that public entities overlook. In reality, one's responsibilities probably change frequently, especially when the public entity has turnover or downsizing. It is essential for the underlying job descriptions to change with one's responsibilities. If the job description is not accurate, how are people held accountable? How are goals established? How is fair compensation determined? How does the boss know if someone is actually doing his or her job? How does a manager perform an evaluation? An accurate job description is critical to every other part of the compensation equation, along with making sure that the objectives of the public entity itself are going to be accomplished. Without accurate job descriptions, it is difficult to create a fair compensation system, which can result in resentment and unhappy employees. It creates more friction, which will, again, increase the likelihood of fraud in the public entity.

When we discussed hiring, we also mentioned the values of the public entity and the concept of hiring people who share these ideals. One of the most important documents, when it comes to establishing this tone, is that which sets a code of conduct or ethics. There has been a lot of emphasis on these documents, especially since the rash of financial statement frauds in the late 1990s and early 2000s. However, a code-of-conduct manual takes a public entity only so far. After all, it is only a piece of paper, like a policy or a job description. The real issue is what is done with the guidance set forth in the document. Remember: If the code is not communicated properly, it is worthless.

The funny thing about this is that people get the code of ethics on their first day, at the same time they receive their benefits forms and payroll forms, meet coworkers, and get acclimated. They are getting the code at one of the busiest and most overwhelming times in their career. The employee signs a piece of paper acknowledging that they received the code and that they will abide by it—and it is placed on their shelf, never to be looked at again.

Lead by Example

Having a written document in and of itself does absolutely nothing to help a public entity's fraud profile. That document must be advertised and discussed continually to remain relevant to employees. Ongoing training, using real examples of possible conflicts or issues, is best for the learning and reinforcement process. The more a person is faced with something, the more relevant it becomes to them. This is why leading by example is so important. A public entity can have all of the rules it wants, but real practice usually comes down to a "monkey see, monkey do" mentality.

Example of Lead by Example

A public entity manager occasionally has a spouse who calls and needs an item from work at home, such as, say, copier paper. The manager sometimes grabs what is needed off the shelf and runs out the door. However, the employees working the late afternoon shift see the manager leaving without paying for paper. It is not too long before the employees themselves are walking out the door with paper, and they are not paying either! Before long, shrinkage (paper shortages) are plaguing the public entity.

Employees are constantly watching their supervisors and managers for guidance on how to act with respect to what is right and what is wrong. Leaders need to understand that they are always under their employees' microscope and must do what they want everyone else in the public entity to do. *Leaders can even influence people to perpetrate fraud or theft!*

For now, assume that the code of conduct or ethics is properly communicated to employees. What are some of the important attributes of an effective code of conduct/ethics?

Think back to values: the need to identify people who share similar values during the hiring process. So what are the public entity's values? A code of conduct/ethics provides guidance on values, ethics, and how the public entity expects its representatives to conduct business. There is a lot of great guidance out there on how to write an effective code of conduct/ethics manual.

Here are some essential points to keep in mind while writing or evaluating these codes:

■ Codes of conduct should be written so they can be easily understood by everyone in the public entity.

- The document should be brief and to the point, as no one is going to read a lengthy document.
- The values and ethics displayed by the public entity should be consistent with the code.
- The code should provide relevant examples.
- Discussion of potential ethical dilemmas, or the relevant examples, should be encouraged.
- Careful consideration must be given when a public entity has international operations, as people of different cultures share different values and norms.

Employee Relations

Value: Tone of the public entity.
People: All employees.

Employee relations is concerned with the contractual, emotional, physical, and practical relationship between employer and employee. It's a function that is usually best positioned within the public entity to survey the pulse of the people, or the tone—how people are feeling about the public entity. Essentially, the function serves as a conduit for employee feedback and provides a venue in which differences between employees and management can be aired. Providing such a venue can help mitigate damage when there is a real or perceived breach in the social contract between the employer and the employee or between employees. As discussed previously, when there is a breach in the social contract between employer and employee, friction is created within the public entity. This friction could result in a supervisory employee becoming less engaged, providing the opportunity for a fraudster (or an employee) to be pushed over the edge and perpetrate fraud.

One of the most important tools used to detect fraud or noncompliance and maintain ethics is an independently established hotline. The perception of the hotline has to be that there is no overriding potential by people within the public entity. In order for the hotline to be successful it must be autonomous so the people who use the hotline remain free from retaliation from the public entity. Rewarding the people who bring these situations to light would be an effective way to encourage reporting and take fraud prevention one step further. Not only is a hotline used to report allegations of fraud, but it is often used to report other improprieties within the public entity that can lead to friction, such as favoritism or sexual harassment. Although hotlines were not initially intended for those sorts of complaints, they have morphed over the years and are now providing valuable insight into what is going on within a public entity. After all, the employees are reporting actual instances of friction within the public entity. Furthermore, it does not really matter if the actual event or friction is real or perceived, as many times perception of an injustice does as much damage as if a wrongful event had actually occurred. As discussed, friction is not an actual fraud, but it is a building block that can contribute to someone making the decision to commit fraud. As the hotline continues to morph, providing a window into the public entity, public entities need to be certain that the right parties are at the table to respond. As described here, employee relations fit nicely into the role of following up on policy and human resources issues surfacing through the hotline.

Much information can be found about hotlines and how to maintain them. One resource is a report published online by The Network at http://www .tnwinc.com/index.aspx. The Network publishes Corporate Governance and Compliance Hotline Benchmarking reports, which provide excellent insight into reporting statistics to assist in assessing risk. The reports are a great way to see how one hotline matches up to others. Another important point related to hotline practices is to perform periodic internal audits of the hotline to validate results and whether allegations and complaints are being adequately followed up. Last, but not least, results of allegations should be communicated to employees or at least the employee(s) who have made an allegation. If no action is ever seen as a result of using the hotline, over time people will see it as a useless waste of time and stop using it. This will pull the blinds on your valuable window into the public entity.

Employee relations goes beyond an HR function and percolates down into the public entity to every supervisor, from top level to immediate. Management's approach to maintaining human relations is essential. So how can management influence this process?

- ◼ Leading by example
- ◼ Encouraging dialogue and practicing an open-door policy
- ◼ Displaying characteristics established in the code, such as being transparent in decision making, and being fair and honest
- ◼ Engaging employees in dialogue, showing that their input is important
- ◼ Holding all employees accountable

Management's people skills can have a big impact on the building blocks of fraud. Anyone who is responsible for leading people, whether formally or informally, must demonstrate personal characteristics consistent with the values of the public entity.

Remember, although we're talking about management technique, that has a direct influence on people within a public entity. Failing to pay attention to the people will result in an increase in the potential for fraud.

Compensation and Benefits

Value: Payroll and value of benefits.
People: All employees.

Compensation and benefits are where the financial needs of employees are weighed against the fiscal position of the public entity. This is where talent is paid. It is also where a lot of power and money reside within the public entity.

During the Sarbanes-Oxley push, there was a big deal made about executive compensation in business. What about the public employees? Indeed, public employee compensation is an important variable to consider. The conflicting interests begin when trying to justify paying huge salaries to a handful of people when others are struggling to pay their bills. The other side of the argument is that different workers perform in more demanding disciplines and thus should be paid more. This is another point that causes friction within the public entity. It can create an entitlement mentality among employees. The individuals responsible for determining compensation in a public entity and those controlling the selection process for these positions hold great power. These people in positions of trust need to be monitored.

Most companies make a strong argument for the need to pay top dollar for top talent. Understood, to a reasonable extent. A reasonable person also needs to ask him- or herself how much money is enough and how much impact a handful of top management people can really have on a public entity versus the many people who actually help identify and execute corporate strategy. Executive compensation, right or wrong, can be viewed as an illustration of greed. It is interesting that the same people who have those same premium executive compensation packages perpetrated some of the largest frauds in history. Perhaps those individuals are the ones who least need the money, but they are also in the best position to take advantage of a situation to generate more money for themselves. These are indeed examples of greed at its best.

The fact of the matter is that executive compensation does cause friction within the public entity. During labor negotiations, it is quite common for workers and their representatives to point out the discrepancies between the haves and the have-nots within the public entity. Executive compensation has gotten much publicity, which has resulted in it being included in the Dodd-Frank legislation passed in 2010 in response to the most recent financial crisis. Here are some of the key elements of Dodd-Frank:

∎ Executive (key) compensation receives stockholder approval (nonbinding).
∎ Independent directors are on the public entities' compensation committees.
∎ Differences between executive pay and those of ordinary employees are disclosed.

Where is the comparable legislation in the public entities' compensation structure?

The AFL-CIO provides some tools and monitors the pay discrepancies between employees and executives. It has developed the "pay disparity ratio," which provides great insight into how much friction compensation disparity may cause within a public entity.[6]

People get satisfaction from their jobs in many different ways. Satisfaction does not always come from the actual paycheck, but the vast majority of people need their paycheck to survive. There are some folks who are lucky enough to work for a good cause or, perhaps, work for an excellent benefits package that compensates for lower pay. This being said, more often than not, it comes down to employees getting that check every payday so they can pay the bills. Probably more so today than ever before, employees are living paycheck to paycheck. But recently, paychecks have not stretched as far as they did years before. Many employees have seen their pay frozen during the latest economic downturn. Paychecks are remaining the same size while the basic cost of living has increased significantly (think of rent, utilities, and groceries). Pay rates staying the same while the necessity costs increase puts pressure on people, particularly in a "keeping up with the Joneses" society.

Under these circumstances, one would think that fraud would skyrocket. Not necessarily. Not all people are fearful of jeopardizing their jobs to fulfill an economic need. During these tough economic times, many people feel lucky just to keep their jobs and benefits. If they are caught committing fraud, the paycheck and benefits stop. This simple reality keeps a lot of people in check. The paycheck and benefits in this case are fraud deterrents in and of themselves.

How do pay rates, pay cuts, and wage freezes impact a public entity? Let's talk morale. As discussed earlier, the human resources department is a great place to monitor the morale of a public entity, which is very important. When people are not able to keep up with their peers financially, they will start to feel resentment, perhaps focusing that resentment upon the public entity itself.

This resentment typically sparks distraction both at work and at home. At work, pay becomes a frequent topic of conversation at the watercooler. People sit at their desks and stew over the fact that the family is not going to have as much money to spend on vacation this year. That is never a good discussion to have at home. It becomes a distraction at work. When people are distracted and feel resentment in the workplace, they simply do not pay close enough attention to their work. Distractions lead to bad things in the workplace, including fraud. Supervisors don't follow up on those anomalies, because they simply don't feel that there will be a reward for doing so. When wages are frozen in a public entity, the consequences of the action could be much more costly than the bottom-line savings.

Unemployment itself can have consequences in terms of fraud. As noted earlier, people may not want to become involved in a fraud scheme because they need their job. They are not going to take the toner cartridge, write it off, and sell it on Craigslist, because they need the security of the paycheck. But layoffs mean a couple of different things. One, the remaining employees are left doing more than ever. This creates the imbalance that not only is their paychecks not growing but they are being called on to do more. This is a double blow to the morale discussed earlier. Now more things are not being done; furthermore, what is done is not being done well, due to the cramming of extra work into the workday. The second problem with high unemployment and layoffs arises from changes in the public entity structure. Layoffs will impact internal controls within a public entity, which are critical in controlling fraud. Public entities generally have a tough enough time with internal controls. Having to reshuffle the deck to maintain the controls when significant cuts have been made is extremely challenging. Keep in mind that more is probably being asked of the people who remain without paying them more. This is not a good recipe for preventing and detecting fraud.

The subject of fraud does extend beyond what one would think, to include things like wasting time and resources. When employees are not motivated, they have a tendency to goof off. This includes surfing the Internet, taking long lunches, hanging out at the water cooler to complain about work conditions, watching the NCAA tournament, shopping online, emailing friends, spending time on social media outlets, and perhaps reading this book. The cost of not doing their jobs is yet another loss and a consequence of low moral. As discussed before, one way to show employees that they are receiving good value for the work they perform is to provide them with a total compensation statement. This will show the true value of their employment.

Employee compensation and benefits help fulfill the economic needs of workers. When workers are satisfied economically, logic says that they are less likely to perpetrate fraud. Yet the greed factor always remains. What is enough? So much fraud literature simply refers to people living outside of their means or spending extravagantly, but few pieces, if any, actually define what that means. Know how people spend their money. This is helpful not only for public management to understand what "living within one's means" equates to, but also for employees to understand how others spend their money. It is essential for employees and managers to understand personal fiscal responsibility. It is often these financial pressures that are widely publicized as being critical factors when individuals commit fraud. Employers have a hard time influencing people's personal lives outside of work directly, nor should anyone's privacy be violated. But turning a blind eye to significant lifestyle changes in a public employee's financial situation is a sign of significant weakness in public entity management. The solution is maintaining strong interviewing soft skills, observing behavior, and seeing the signs that will often be there. The successful entity creates an environment where people can have open and effective communication. Not to mention the annual background check.

All the internal controls in the world will not stop someone from encountering financial hardship. As already discussed, establishing stringent internal controls and other preventative steps are not foolproof antifraud measures. Financially motivated, intelligent employees will likely be able to find some way to perpetrate fraud to get the money they want.

Information like this, showing average family spending patterns, is excellent to share with employees. This can influence people to start a budgeting process at home. Depending on funding, and how far the public entity is allowed to go with assisting with things like providing access to reputable financial planners to help with this process, the offering of such help could contribute to a positive financial mind-set and stability in the workplace. The idea of providing financial planners' help with 401(k)s and other retirement planning, investments, saving, and budgeting is a good benefit to offer. Giving people an understanding of how to better spend and manage their paychecks is a good tool for keeping them from falling into financial difficulties that can potentially lead to them making bad ethical choices.

This could also be good information to include in a total compensation statement. A total compensation statement should show all the value the public entity provides to an employee. The total compensation should not only show the base wages, which are obvious, but other expenditures such as

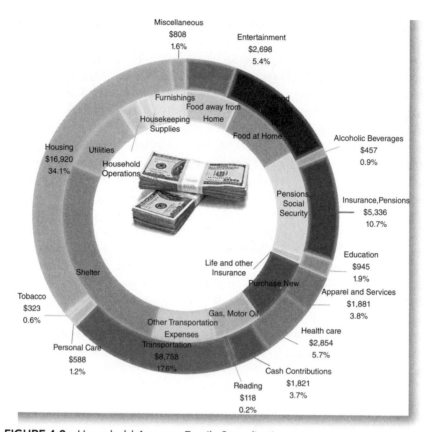

FIGURE 4.2 Household Average Family Spending's
Percentages are based on the average U.S. consumer unit. The average consumer unit consists of 2.5 persons, with 1.3 earners, and is age 48.8.
Source: Consumer Expenditures (U.S Dept. of Labor, U.S. Bureau of Labor Statistics).

the employer's required tax matchings, unemployment and disability taxes, contributions to retirement plans, health care and other related benefit perks, as well as the amounts contributed to worker's compensation insurance plans. The total compensation statement shows employees how much money a public entity actually expends for them to work there, which is much more than just a salary. Many employees will feel that they are better appreciated when they are involved in the bigger picture. The total compensation statement is a great vehicle to inspire people to become more fiscally knowledgeable. Many companies also include retirement projections and other financial tools.

Remember, a financially responsible, happy, satisfied employee will be less likely to perpetrate fraud.

Employee benefit plans involve a lot of money and are very complex. To explore fraud from the perspective of looking where people meet things of value, look no further than employee benefit plans. Think pension and 401(k) plans and the related trusts that hold their money. Companies can easily have billions of dollars in these plans. Benefit trusts are gold mines to motivated fraudsters. Interestingly, a control over HR in some public entities is less than stellar, and this is where some of the largest assets within a public entity reside. Remember: Internal controls are a finance or audit function. It is amazing that more fraudsters have not taken advantage of the corporate HR function. In addition to having considerable amounts of money in benefit trusts, a lot of money is spent for ongoing health and welfare benefits. Again, where people and value meet, fraud is usually lurking. Benefits and benefit payments are ripe for fraud. Everyone's heard about instances in which medical providers have submitted false or manipulated claims for payment. There are those employees who knowingly enroll people in their public entity benefits plans who are not eligible for coverage (or have duplicating coverage with a spouse). The more blatant fraud is when people who have passed away or leave the public entity remain covered.

Wedding Plan Benefits

A public entity needs to verify the eligibility requirements prior to providing any benefit. Any program, benefit, or other subsidy that involves public funds that have eligibility requirements attached to them must be verified prior to the issuance of funds.

Example: Not ready to get married yet, but your significant other needs medical coverage? Fake the wedding and get him or her added to your benefits plan. After all, it's not hurting anyone.

Frauds like this should not be a surprise, seeing how much benefits cost a public entity or would cost people without coverage, and it is easy to see the basis for rationalization to circumvent the rules.

Investment Management within the Public Entity

For fun, find out if your public entity manages its own investment portfolio in the pension trust. If they do, ask about "commission recapture dollars" or "soft dollars" and how they are accounted for.

Commission recapture dollars are funded by making trades on the in-house portfolio. For example, a trade costs a public entity $.04; however, the brokerage deposits $.01 out of that $.04 into an account, and that account can be used for research materials and training.

The benefit of the funds must benefit the plan, not the public entity. This includes earnings such as commission recapture dollars. They must be accounted for just like interest earnings.

Last but not least, it is our experience that the most risk lies in areas that span boundaries between the public entities' processes. This is seen a lot, and it is a great place for fraudsters to perpetrate their schemes because they don't have to work as hard to conceal the losses. Frankly, no one is looking.

Retirement Assets

Many times, the assets of retirement plans reside with the U.S. Department of Treasury, but their administration lies within human resources. The question may arise as to who should be reconciling the trust accounts. The answer is not black-and-white, because each public entity function has part of the information needed to complete the task. Treasury gets the statements and knows about returns but may not have the information about payouts, which is handled through HR. One public entity process needs the information from the other to complete the control, but no one takes the responsibility, and the trust reconciliations go incomplete or are not performed. This is a lack of control, but it is also a potential breach of fiduciary duty.

Compensation and benefits are where people and value come into direct contact. It is essential to balance the needs of employees with the financial needs of the public entity in a fair and equitable manner that helps to counter the weight of potential feelings of inequity, particularly among highly compensated employees and those who are in the lower-income bracket.

Training and Development

Value: Tone, capabilities, efficiencies, best practices.
People: All employees.

Training provides people with what they need to succeed. To be competitive, public entities need to have talented people who are well informed on current technology and methodologies. Again, fraud is about people. Make sure people can compete in the marketplace. It will help maintain morale and bolster the control environment. However, this book is not as much about management as it is about fraud. Unfortunately, fraud and fraud prevention are not taught in most management classes or schools. Internal controls, for example, are the responsibility of management to establish and maintain. Where have managers learned about what these controls should look like? They have not. Not only have they not been educated about internal controls, but they are not familiar with fraud schemes, scenarios, and red flags in their area of responsibility, simply because they have never been educated. Fraud will not be found unless the person looking knows what to look for. Many managers and employees within the public entity simply do not know what to look for.

It is essential to educate everyone within a public entity about fraud in order to get as many people involved in the fight as possible. The first hurdle is to get them to recognize that fraud can happen in their process. So many times, detection of fraud is thought to fall onto internal audit or some component unit of finance, or, perhaps, compliance, until there is an event that causes sufficient outrage that changes ownership for fraud and internal controls and is appropriately distributed throughout the public entity to its rightful owners, management.

Example

Internal auditors perform a limited-scope audit of a corporate disbursement process. Approximately 300 hours are allocated to the internal audit. The internal auditor reviews corporate policy and its application, authorization limits, matching of purchase orders to receiving reports and invoices submitted for payment (three-way match), limited disbursement testing, and performs a comparison of the vendor master to the employee master to determine whether there might have been any conflicts of interest or shell companies established by employees to perpetrate fraud against the public entity. The internal audit results were rather clean. There was some splitting of transactions to circumvent authorization limits, but seemingly for legitimate purposes. Four weeks after the audit, it is determined that a freight carrier had been overpaid, because it submitted duplicate invoices for payment. The invoices amounted to $560,000. The CFO is enraged that internal audit did not discover the alleged fraud during its audit.

Some background facts:

- The freight carrier was paid in excess of $12,000,000 in the prior year, making any analytical review results inconclusive.
- Management reviewed and approved each allegedly fraudulent (duplicate) invoice, allowing them to pass through the system (the invoice number was different).
- Certain payments to the carrier were automated, so when a load was delivered, the public entity automatically paid without a carrier invoice.

What was revealed was that management was not reviewing paper invoices thoroughly enough and was essentially rubber-stamping them because of the relationship with the carrier and the volume of transactions. This was not a breakdown in the internal audit approach; it was a breakdown in control within the public entity. This scenario illustrates that a control is only as good as the person performing it. Training and reinforcement of the importance of management reviews of these transactions in order to prevent the overpayment or perhaps attempted fraud. It is not practical for everyone to think like an auditor, nor do we suggest that. But it is essential for operational employees to understand the fundamental control points within their particular public entity's process and the potential impact of failing to adequately perform the control actions. In this case, failing to understand the risk of duplicate payments because of an automated system probably should not have been beyond the expectations of management. Antifraud and internal control training needs to encourage critical thinking about risk, controls, and safeguarding corporate assets. To be effective, the training needs to go beyond simply understanding control points and to the underlying rationale of their existence.

Perhaps one of the most important opportunities to prevent and detect fraud in a public entity is to train people in what fraud looks like. One of the reasons fraud is so prevalent is that public entity employees are not trained on how to prevent it or detect it. Unless one is an accounting or criminal justice major, the dynamics of the crime and how to prevent or detect it are not taught in college. No wonder many people think fraud is the auditor's problem alone. In reality, as noted numerous times, fraud is everyone's problem within a public entity. Instead of the public entity being the victim and taking a passive approach to fraud, to truly lessen the blow of potential fraud and losses, public entities should insist that their employees go on the offensive to combat fraud and those who perpetrate it. Face it: Auditors—and even managers—can only be so many places at once. Empower everyone to have his or her eyes and ears open. This, along with a robust reporting mechanism, will go a long way in preventing and detecting fraud in a public entity.

Performance Management

Value: Employee satisfaction, efficiency, competency.
People: All employees.

Performance management is always an interesting subject, and one that often can negatively impact a public entity's tone. Performance management usually has an impact on employees' bank accounts. Performance management systems, not to mention the evaluations themselves, are difficult to create and administer in real terms. Yes, people set goals themselves. However, there always seems to be some element of subjectivity that creeps into the process, for either the good or the bad. Regardless, when people are judged by others, there is usually some type of resentment or disagreement. People like to look upon themselves positively, and to hear that they are "average" is a hit to the ego. No one gets excited about receiving criticism, whether warranted or not. Remember that all public entity processes are related. Failing to meet one's objectives might not be that employee's fault.

Some things that could impact performance include unclear job descriptions, a lack of leadership, and a dependence on other departments or individuals for support. The perceived fairness of a performance management system is critical to maintaining balance among your people. Losing this balance will create an incubator for fraud.

Example

A public entity hires the best and brightest graduates, many of whom maintained very high GPAs throughout their college career. The new hires were accustomed to being at the top of their class. It is a shock to them when they are placed into a performance management system where overnight they go from being at the top of the class to an average employee with an average performance score within the corporate public entity environment. It is difficult to convince a high performer that overnight he or she has become average, due to a lack of experience and public entity knowledge, among other things. Being recognized as a star student has been a fundamental part of their conditioning for years. Breaching that conditioning causes friction within the public entity, and where there is friction, the public entity culture suffers and there is an increased likelihood of fraud.

Performance management problems span generational differences, though. Anyone would be hard pressed to find a public entity where there is no animosity among people when it comes to someone being promoted over another. It is a logical argument that if there is someone who can be relied on to get a job done, it serves a manager well to keep that person in place. Those who really can't be relied upon will be encouraged to move on to other positions or even get promoted out of the positions in which they are not productive. Many readers are thinking that performance management would penalize the individual who cannot do the job. Correct, only if the manager is strong enough and willing to face conflict to make the point. Furthermore, if the manager was responsible for hiring the individual, that manager must face the fact that he or she made the wrong hiring decision. People follow the path of least resistance more often than not. It is much easier to transfer or promote. When this happens, the culture is impacted because people see it and resent it. This element could be a deciding factor when someone is contemplating fraud.

Human resources is a unique area in a public entity. It is an area where considerable value resides. Furthermore, human resources can do a lot to prevent fraud in a public entity, because its purpose is people. People are half of the fraud formula (fraud occurs where people and value meet).

Payroll

Payroll responsibilities in human resources include:

- Maintenance of payroll master data
- Accumulation of time and related data
- Administration of sick and vacation time
- Calculation and payment of salaries and wages
- Reporting and payment of taxes and related withholdings

FIGURE 4.3 Human Resource Responsibility Cycle

The payroll process is a little like an ex-spouse to the HR process: The public entity needs to keep the two separated. A public entity can lose a lot of money quickly if it fails to segregate HR from payroll. Human resources is mostly where the soft elements of the process reside. Payroll directly touches people, because everyone enters their time or is accountable for what they did on a day-to-day basis to some degree. Payroll is where value is delivered to employees. There goes that fraud recipe of value and people coming together.

Payroll (employee) master data consists of data used to pay employees, report earnings, and manage withholdings along with benefits. A person's pay rate is also a critical element. Again, it is important to secure the data in payroll, not only because it can be used against the public entity and employees in scams like identity theft, but also because it can be altered to give people more money simply by changing the rate of pay. It is essential not only to secure this data, but to also keep a log of changes that can be reviewed by the appropriate level of management (preferably someone who does not have access to files).

Accumulation of time and related data is a process in which employee interaction picks up. In many cases, employees make assertions about what they have worked on and for how long. People can fudge these numbers to meet project budgets and accomplish other objectives, such as hiding the fact that they are consistently late for work. Again, this is another example of employees providing information that results in their looking out for their own best interests. Remember, people are generally very self-serving, especially when a paycheck or bonus is on the line.

Example

A manufacturing public entity installed a badge reader at the entrance to the plant to automatically record employees' work times. However, when employees knew that they would be late, they would give their badge to a coworker to "swipe" them in. The same thing could be accomplished with most other time entry systems. However, some systems are now moving to biometrics to verify the identity of the employee clocking in.

Sick and vacation time is a valuable commodity to employees. If there are not good controls in place to monitor how people classify their time, employees could misclassify their work to extend the amount of time that is available for vacation or sick leave. The first line of defense against this happening is thorough supervisory review. Once again, dependence on people who could be distracted or have a multitude of other priorities perceived as more pressing than reviewing time entries or classifications is not productive.

The payment method of salaries has changed rather significantly over the past decade or two. Many employees now have direct deposit, where their salary is placed directly into their bank account. This is generally safer than having negotiable instruments floating around (like checks). However, now companies have the bank account numbers of their employees on file, a risk explored earlier in the section "Personnel Data." A fraudster changing bank account numbers to collect someone else's salary would probably not last long unless the employees at the public entity don't need the money.

Example

A public entity hired an individual for a salaried, higher-level management position. The individual accepted the offer and was scheduled to start work. All the paperwork was forwarded to payroll and HR and the individual was set up in the system in advance of actually starting. The public entity was finally being proactive! Unfortunately, the individual received a second offer from a competitor the day before starting and decided to take it. The employee called the public entity on the anticipated start date and informed HR. However, no one thought about the fact that the individual was already set up in the system. A manual payroll check was cut and mailed to the individual, since direct deposit information was not entered into the system. Luckily, the individual was honest and returned the check.

An area of possible concern for public entities is the payment of taxes and withholdings from employees' checks. Many public entities have been surprised to find out that the payments have not been made and that they have significant liabilities to the government. Employee withholdings is a great place for a fraudster to manipulate the system. All employees have withholdings, so the money is legitimately available. Payment to the entity that is expecting the withholding is not always tracked as closely as it should be. There must be checks by the public entity administering the payments throughout the year to determine if the taxes that are being withheld from the checks are remitted in a timely fashion to the proper taxing agencies. Typically, from an employee perspective, failing to accurately report payroll withholdings will show up at the end of the year when W-2 forms are issued and/or tax returns are filed, and the IRS matches up what the employee has reported as being paid versus what was actually reported or deposited by the employer. This is not good for morale, to say the least. Not to mention that it creates liability for the public entity.

TYPICAL TYPES OF FRAUDS

Now that the HR and payroll processes and how some of the intangibles can influence fraud are understood, it's time to look at the traditional fraud models impacting these processes.

Segregation of Duties among HR, Payroll (Hiring and Paying), and Accounting

Who's involved: Anyone with access to HR and payroll functions (with the ability to set up and/or pay employees)

Classic no-no's

- Don't allow a single individual to hire employees, set them up in the system, and also have the ability to pay them. The risk is that this individual could create a fictitious ("ghost") employee and pay him or her, with the fraudster collecting the fictitious paycheck.
- Never mix general ledger accounting with any other function such as payroll accounting because of the potential to hide a fraud.
- When filling out the tax matters for payroll taxes and other withholdings, do not list the person responsible for the actual withholdings or disbursements. If they are perpetrating a scheme and absconding with payroll taxes or withholdings it will be found out much faster if they don't call the perpetrator.
- Don't give payroll clerks the ability to change hours or rates. A payroll clerk could inflate an individual's hours for a kickback.
- Never return checks to the preparer (this goes for all checks). They could convert the check themselves, and if it is for a ghost employee or a terminated employee, the check could be getting handed right back to the perpetrator.

Common tip-offs

- An employee without benefit selections (if you don't exist, you don't need benefits).
- An employee whom nobody knows (they don't exist).
- An employee without an HR employee file (no application, W-4, I-9, etc.).
- More checks/direct deposits than employees.

- Employees working more hours than physically possible (remember, there are only 168 hours in a week, 336 in a two-week period, and 720 in a 30-day month).
- Checks coming back with strange endorsements.
- Budget to actual numbers out of line with what was expected.
- Employee complaints about incorrect withholdings or other payroll issues.
- A payroll clerk who never goes on vacation.
- Year-end payroll reporting and reconciliations not tying out.

Time Entry

Who's involved: Almost all employees, particularly hourly employees, but salaried employees may also need to keep track of projects they worked on

Classic no-no's

- Allowing people to record their time manually or override the system (people will usually round off the time and not rat themselves out if they are late).
- Employees having friends clock them in because they are always late or have an appointment.
- Having employees tally their own timecards.
- Allowing time to be changed after it has been approved by a supervisor.
- Not having budget numbers that can be easily compared to actual numbers, both in total and on a budget line-specific basis.

Common tip-offs

- Employees working more hours than physically possible
- Someone being clocked in but nowhere to be found
- People never missing work because of doctor appointments or any other conflicts
- Budget to actual numbers out of line with what was expected

Management/Supervisory Review and Approval

Who's involved: Supervisors and managers responsible for other employees

Classic no-no's

- Allowing employees to tally their own timesheets without the supervisor or someone else checking them. An employee could knowingly miscalculate hours, giving themselves a bigger paycheck.

▧ Giving employees the ability to change hours worked. This needs to be restricted to management. A clerk could overpay someone in order to get a kickback.

▧ Not reviewing the *final* payroll register. A fraudster could change it after the review, making the control useless. This review is a critical control. Management should look at the names as well as hours worked and withholdings and possibly compare results to prior payrolls for consistency. The management performing the review should be knowledgeable about the people and operations.

▧ Not comparing the numbers in the payroll register to the general ledger. The numbers in the general ledger are critical, because that is what is actually paid out. The detail in the payroll register can be manipulated. But, provided good accounting controls are in place, the actual cash disbursed is what counts.

▧ Not keeping track of how much vacation or sick time an employee has already used versus what is available in a given period. It is common for supervisors to approve vacation time without knowing how much time the employee actually has available. If employees are working remotely, the manager may not know whether they are working or on vacation.

Common tip-offs

▧ Employees are working more hours than physically possible.

▧ Budget to actual numbers are out of line with what was expected.

▧ Projects are falling behind schedule unexpectedly.

▧ Employees are accumulating large amounts of vacation time, even though they have been off work.

▧ Year-end payroll reporting and reconciliations are not reconciled.

Security and Access Controls

Who's involved: Everyone in the HR/payroll process

Classic no-no's

▧ Not adequately securing or locking up employee files.

▧ Not implementing IT controls to restrict access within the system. Areas of particular interest include segregating HR and payroll functions (pay attention to the employee master file), payroll and general ledger functions, and time entry and edit functions (see segregation of duties, above).

▧ Failing to secure check stock and/or signature stamps or plates.

- Signing blank payroll checks in advance because of an upcoming vacation.
- Putting paychecks on people's desks when they are out of the office or on vacation.

Common tip-offs

- Employee identity theft.
- Missing checks or checks used out of order.
- Employee not getting a check.
- Unusual endorsements on canceled checks.

Human Resources

Who's involved: Employees in HR and related functions, such as treasury and accounting

Classic no-no's

- Not reconciling the trust accounts in a timely fashion.
- Not paying attention to payouts from the trusts.
- Giving one individual the ability to make investment decisions or select investment managers that may result in kickbacks or preferential treatment.
- Failing to validate the eligibility of dependents for benefits.

Common tip-offs

- Unusual trends in payouts from retirement plans.
- Employees who have added new dependents and do not have pictures of them in their office/cubicle or have not discussed them in the past.
- Investment managers or investments that do not fit the risk/return profile of the entity.

 CONCLUSION

In this chapter the various people found in governmental agencies have been explored. A full explanation of the human resource and payroll areas of the accounting process has been given and is the best line of defense in preventing fraud and corruption as well as mismanagement. The characters range from the virtuous to the vile, and everything in between is the challenge.

Governmental agencies represent the best and the worst of human behavior; their frailties are the frailties of mankind. Yet we can aspire to better government. Improvements in government practices and policies would yield a more just and functional public sector, and that would be good for society. But the structural nature of these problems needs to be explored and systems need to be developed that encourage positive change.

The politics of the public sector can incite various types of behavior, and only good structures and policies, coupled with strong action by an ethical staff, can yield better outcomes. The need to be endlessly vigilant and focused on agency success is a key component in better government. Don't be afraid or discouraged if you are an agency staffer. Look to find those virtuous public servants in your public entity and work with them to create positive change.

To all of you public-sector gorillas or wannabe gorillas: Good luck, and keep the faith. Look to find other gorillas in your public entity and try to learn their ways. But the best way to develop these gorillas is through sound human resources and payroll administration.

If you are an 800-pound friendly gorilla in charge at any of these agencies, make sure that rewards and punishment systems are maintained to encourage the strong growth of an outstanding troop of gorillas. They will be needed to resist the wide range of political and social pressures that occur within public agencies.

 NOTES

1. John Rossomando, "One Man's Pork Is Another Man's Job," July 7, 2008, http://www.cnsnews.com/news/article/one-mans-pork-another-mans-job.

2. http://www.northjersey.com/news/transportation/democrats-call-for-resignation-of-christie-appointee-after-assembly-hearings-on-gwb-lane-closures-1.705032?page=all.

3. http://www.wsj.com/articles/SB10001424127887324439804578113091166283364.

4. http://blogs.wsj.com/economics/2014/11/07/the-federal-government-now-employs-the-fewest-people-since-1966/.

5. http://www.forbes.com/sites/carolkinseygoman/2011/02/13/seven-seconds-to-make-a-first-impression/#3d39de0f645a.

6. http://www.aflcio.org/Blog/Corporate-Greed/Conference-Addresses-CEO-to-Worker-Pay-Disparity.

CHAPTER FIVE

Fraud in Public Agencies: Horse Trading or Stealing?

"Everybody is a political person, whether you say something or you are silent. A political attitude is not whether you go to parliament; it's how you deal with your life, with your surroundings."

—*Paulo Coelho, Brazilian novelist*

Topics:

Kinds of Fraud
When Is It Fraud?
Nepotism and Knowing Whom to Know
No-Show Jobs
Fraud in Purchasing—No-Bid Contracts
Fraud in Employment—LIRR, Pension Padding, Timekeeping

Key questions:

Is it still stealing if I don't take the money (in cash, in kind, in spirit)?
How do you know when a fine line has been crossed?
Where are the gray areas and value exposures?

T HIS CHAPTER EXPLORES the complex interactions and policies of the public serving agencies. The focus here is on the potential to commit individual fraud and the methods used by fraud perpetrators. Understanding the motivation for fraud and the various aspects of public corruption is key in recognizing and preventing them. The use of case studies illustrates the broad portfolio of fraud and corruption practices in the United States. This chapter introduces readers to government fraud and will help them understand why fraud can happen. Gaining a solid foundation of how to prevent, deter, and detect fraud is key in understanding how it happens despite public scrutiny and legislative body and multiple agency oversights, not to mention the media attention it generates when discovered. Fraud is first and foremost a people problem. Flawed processes may support its propagation, but processes are only part of the environment in which fraud occurs.

UNDERSTANDING GOVERNMENT FRAUD AND MISMANAGEMENT

Countless government investigations have been performed over the years, yet mismanagement and fraud continue. There are the Senate Governmental Affairs Committee's 2001 Government at the Brink, the Congressional Budget Office Budget Options book, studies published by the U.S. Government Accountability Office (GAO), and a host of other reports and investigations, yet fraud and mismanagement persist. One big problem is a lack of informed skepticism and procurement of the necessary details and support to better understand the sources and uses of public funds. The Freedom of Information and Open Public Records acts have helped to make these records more available, yet that's not enough. A high level of skepticism in thinking will aid in fraud and mismanagement analyses, but the proverbial devil is in the details. These governmental and public agencies are often large, and the amount of paperwork and attention to detail involved can get cumbersome. Add to that a simple change in the legislation policy, and a wrong can become a right. Welcome to the ultimate rule: that only a judge and jury can find someone guilty of fraud.

Thinking divergently and developing as many findings as possible surrounding the government or public agency is an effective method in formulating an opinion. Speaking to documents that support your findings (such as a Bank Statement) is a key factor in developing an overall supportable analysis. The *Black's Law Dictionary* definition of *affinity fraud* is the best to apply. It is defined as "a fraud in which the perpetrator tailors the fraud to target members of a particular group united by common traits or interests that produce inherent trust." There are many types of fraud, but affinity fraud is the one that best describes the public entity as targeted to serve a common group sharing self-interests.

The lightbulb over your head should have come on by now, as these core competing self-interests create conflicts of interest, which is one of the main sources of fraud activity in government and public agencies. We think knowing the standards of legal fraud in the context of government and public agencies will assist you in gaining an overall understanding of when an action rises to legal fraud. Being able to establish these fine lines helps in understanding when they might have been crossed. In our experience, people often cross these lines without realizing it, which unfortunately may be too late to correct or prevent the action.

Let's try to understand this in a legal context. Fraud is being defined as a material **misrepresentation (M)** that was done **intentionally (I)**, that someone **relied (R)** on, and that resulted in **damages (D)**. We like to use the acronym MIRD. The term *fraud* covers numerous activities that would fall under the MIRD umbrella. Fraud has so many faces and flavors that a guided tour is valuable to begin our discussion of the topic. All types of fraud have facets of the four MIRD elements, and the fraudster will combine these aspects through various institutional structures to create particular types of material damage, ranging from direct attempts to obtain revenue through illicit means to dissuading action that may have long-term benefits. Use of the acronym MIRD is helpful in understanding the necessary burden of proof associated with fraud.

- Affiliate click fraud is a form of fraud in which the number of clicks an ad gets on a hosted website is fudged when payment is based on that number of clicks.
- Bank fraud is knowingly defrauding a financial institution by making false representations.

■ Bankruptcy fraud usually involves some type of concealment of assets, destruction of the assets, or misrepresentation. Until the cities of Detroit's and Scranton's bankruptcy filings and New Jersey governor Chris Christie's appointment of an emergency manager in Atlantic City, did we have to start considering examining this type of potential fraud?

■ Civil fraud is an intentional act that was *not* done willfully. If it was done willfully, then it is considered criminal. A simple example is tax avoidance.

■ Tax avoidance is completely legal, as one is reducing his or her tax liability by legal means; it is a civil fraud.

■ Tax evasion, on the other hand, is an attempt to reduce tax liability by fraudulent means and is a criminal fraud.

■ Fraud on the court is when misrepresentations occur in a judicial hearing. An example would be bribery of a juror.

■ Fraud in factum is when a legal instrument is different from the one executed.

■ Fraud on the market (securities and stock fraud) is when an issuer of securities leaks information that ultimately affects the security.

■ Extrinsic fraud is deception that is used to persuade someone not to pursue something or from knowing about certain rights.

■ Intrinsic fraud is fabricated evidence involving the original case, such as false testimony.

■ Insurance fraud is when the insured makes misrepresentations to the insurance company that meets the MIRD criteria.

■ Mail fraud is a false representation that was made using the U.S. Postal Service and that meets the MIRD criteria. While this seems to be a very basic and bland matter, the fact is that mail fraud is a federal crime: The use of the mail system to commit acts of deception may shift the crime from a local matter to a federal matter. It is common to find mail fraud or wire fraud (discussed below) as one of the charges in a federal corruption case. The statute is quite clear:

> Whoever, having devised or intending to devise any scheme or artifice to defraud, or for obtaining money or property by means of false or fraudulent pretenses, representations, or promises, or to sell, dispose of, loan, exchange, alter, give away, distribute, supply, or furnish or procure for unlawful use any counterfeit or spurious coin, obligation, security, or other article, or anything represented to be or intimated or held out to be such counterfeit or spurious article, for the purpose of executing such scheme or artifice or attempting so to do, places in any post office or authorized

depository for mail matter, any matter or thing whatever to be sent or delivered by the Postal Service, or deposits or causes to be deposited any matter or thing whatever to be sent or delivered by any private or commercial interstate carrier, or takes or receives therefrom, any such matter or thing, or knowingly causes to be delivered by mail or such carrier according to the direction thereon, or at the place at which it is directed to be delivered by the person to whom it is addressed, any such matter or thing, *shall be fined under this title or imprisoned not more than 20 years, or both.* If the violation occurs in relation to, or involving any benefit authorized, transported, transmitted, transferred, disbursed, or paid in connection with, a presidentially declared major disaster or emergency (as those terms are defined in section 102 of the Robert T. Stafford Disaster Relief and Emergency Assistance Act (42 U.S.C. 5122)), or affects a financial institution, such person *shall be fined not more than $1,000,000 or imprisoned not more than 30 years, or both.*[1] (emphasis added)[2]

■ Another favorite is wire fraud: fraud committed using electronic communications. In this technologically oriented world, everything is electronically transmitted: texts, emails, Skypes, phone calls, and anything using computers, iPads, and other devices. Wire fraud involves communicating any fraudulent act that meets MIRD:

Whoever, having devised or intending to devise any scheme or artifice to defraud, or for obtaining money or property by means of false or fraudulent pretenses, representations, or promises, transmits or causes to be transmitted by means of wire, radio, or television communication in interstate or foreign commerce, any writings, signs, signals, pictures, or sounds for the purpose of executing such scheme or artifice, *shall be fined under this title or imprisoned not more than 20 years, or both.* If the violation occurs in relation to, or involving any benefit authorized, transported, transmitted, transferred, disbursed, or paid in connection with, a presidentially declared major disaster or emergency (as those terms are defined in section 102 of the Robert T. Stafford Disaster Relief and Emergency Assistance Act (42 U.S.C. 5122)), or affects a financial institution, *such person shall be fined not more than $1,000,000 or imprisoned not more than 30 years, or both.* (emphasis added)[3]

These penalties are significant, and the elevation of a crime to the federal level may remove the potential benefit of local policing, prosecution, judge, and jury. Certain states and regions may be more tolerant of activity that is seen as corrupt in a broader context. Juries and judges as well as prosecutors may choose to pursue a given course of action in a fraud case based upon political issues or local support. Moving the crime to the federal level removes that local layer of prosecution and subjects the crime to potentially greater fines and penalties. In terms of tools, the federal government has additional statutes such as the Racketeer Influenced and Corrupt Organizations (RICO) statutes to pursue ongoing corrupt organizations.

JUST HOW PERVASIVE ARE FRAUD AND CORRUPTION?

The ACFE 2014 Global Fraud Study provides us with an excellent overview of the core issues and also lists the main activities identified in cases of corporate, government, and agency fraud. Corruption cases top the list:

Corruption	36.2%
Billing issues	19.1%
Noncash frauds	17.7%
Payroll issues	15.6%
Expense reimbursement	12.8%
Check on hand	12.1%
Skimming	11.3%
Cash larceny	10.5%
Check tampering	5.7%
Financial statement fraud	5.0%
Register disbursement	0.7%

(These items exceed 100 percent in total, as the report highlights that multiple methods may be used in a given fraud incident.) The report also highlights the shocking scale and duration of fraud activity. Many cases appear to go on for extended periods of time, and the cost of these frauds is great. The report highlights that 20 percent of fraud cases last more than 36 months and that these long-duration cases are the most expensive for the firms—averaging $650,875 in losses as compared to the average fraud loss of $220,859—representing 59 percent of the value lost to firms due to fraudulent behavior.

ACFE further reports that more than 25 percent of cases they studied were in government (15.1 percent) or not-for-profit entities (10.8 percent) in 2014. Thankfully, that is much lower than the incidences in publicly held (28.5 percent) or private commercial firms (37.9 percent), but some of that may be due to a lack of control or reporting in not-for-profits or public agencies. Perhaps this is also linked to the downside of following up on a fraud case in the public sector—where significant potential exists for bad press and the value of recovery is minimal—as the owners are the people in general and the funds would be returned to the entity, and that has little to no value to the managers. This is in stark contrast to a privately held firm, where any recovered value is the property of the owners, so pursuing the money is of great value to the owner/managers.

A critical piece of information with regard to how to detect fraud is included in the ACFE report: 42.2 percent of the detected cases come from a tip to the firm, far exceeding the impact of management review (16 percent of cases) or internal audit (14.1 percent of cases). These tips are generated by employees almost half the time (49 percent), and a significant portion come from customers (21.6 percent) or are anonymous (14.6 percent). Most important, firms with a reporting hotline for tips experienced significantly more tips (51 percent of cases) as opposed to firms without a hotline (33.3 percent). In both cases, tips remained the top way fraud cases were identified—but the firms without a tip line were much less effective in collecting that information.

While statistics are used, they do not represent an absolute view of how fraud is detected. A lot of fraud is not reported or the public entity has insured the risk or does not want it found out, to avoid public scrutiny. A whistle-blower line is a tool that gives people a place to go when faced with inappropriate behavior. It does not replace catching the fraud before it happens by educating people about the consequences and having them guided by unsuspected 800-pound friendly gorilla monitoring and mentoring of ethical behavior.

Hopefully, this has you thinking about the potential risks surrounding day-to-day transactions that you might be doing and, if they are found to be fraudulent, the type of sentencing that can be imposed. By always remaining objective and independent in your thinking and applying sound principles, you have the magic formula for staying above the fray.

We have looked at data through forensic language. Let's take that language and formulate typical schemes in language beyond Enron, Rita Crundwell, Bernie Madoff, ACFE, and so on. Following are some examples of fraud schemes that might occur in the public entity, using simplified language. There is lot of wisdom in KISS: "Keep it simple, stupid."

- People's greed enables: conflicts of interests
- The accrual method enables: premature revenue recognition
- Failing to test 100 percent enables: made-up revenue records
- Failing to verify or value assets enables: asset overstatement
- People making judgments enable: estimation manipulations
- People, lax controls, and poor ethical tone at the top enable: asset misappropriations
- Greed from external self-interest enables: Ponzi schemes
- The environment that allows people to put little or no money down and the speculative nature of the rise in home values enable: asset flips
- Power and ego enable: bribery
- Accounting reporting standards enable: journal entries and adjusting entries to be made. This can create misrepresentations as they are after the fact recording to correct or adjust transactions. Unlike a physically written check that is processed through the bank and recorded at the time the check is tendered.

Every fraud in a public agency is not necessarily filed with complex accounting thinking and should not be confused with creative accounting concepts that circumvent sound practices and standards. Examining schemes such as those outlined here can assist you in designing effective systems and controls to mitigate fraud and mismanagement, as you gain an understanding of what fraud looks like in a public entity.

WHY DO AGENCIES DO WHAT THEY DO?

Agencies are typically formed to address particular problems or issues. At the federal level, the classic breakdown of power is by presidential cabinet members. Starting with George Washington, the secretaries of state (foreign affairs), treasury, and defense (war), and the attorney general have provided a core of knowledge and also a division of labor for the leadership of the national government. Other cabinet-level posts have been added over time, so today the president has 16 major departments represented at the cabinet level. Additional specialty agencies have been established at the federal level as well as myriad agencies at the state and local levels. Each of these entities typically has a particular focus and mission. Providing a division of mission and also specifying the key topics of concern should provide for a knowledgeable agency staff that supports the goals of the entity. They should also be able to establish procedures and methods to help them accomplish their key tasks.

For instance, the U.S. Census Bureau, an agency under the Department of Commerce, is charged with maintaining and developing data in the areas of population and the economy. The mission statements of the entities are as follows:

Commerce Department mission statement
The mission of the Department is to create the conditions for economic growth and opportunity.[4]

Census Bureau mission
The Census Bureau's mission is to serve as the leading source of quality data about the nation's people and economy. We honor privacy, protect confidentiality, share our expertise globally, and conduct our work openly. We are guided on this mission by scientific objectivity, our strong and capable workforce, our devotion to research-based innovation, and our abiding commitment to our customers.[5]

You can clearly see that the mission of the Commerce Department is very broad and could encompass myriad tasks and functions. The Census Bureau, one could argue, has used the clarity of its more focused mission to actually develop a staff that in many cases consists of the leading experts in the fields of demography, economics, and social trends and behavior. We have had the opportunity to work with staffers at the Census Bureau, and we can assure the reader that a deep level of understanding of technical matters exists in that agency.

To the degree that we can refrain from politicizing the activities of technocratic agencies and also maintain a long-term mission with sufficient clarity, we believe that there is an opportunity to develop real expertise and depth in public agencies. Entities with broad and loose missions as well as organizational goals that are motivated more by politics or policy are by their structure prone to more questions of corruption.

Fraud and mismanagement are generally linked in their misuse of funds or resources. The level and intensity of the misuse would dictate whether a particular action is actual fraud, and, as we indicated earlier, this depends upon the letter of the law as well as internal rules and policy. The U.S. Congress is well known for both setting laws and excluding itself from the same oversight. This creates a gray area in legal terms as to the content of a particular action—but it does not absolve the action from any ethical standards. A common action taken that could fall into the range of fraud or mismanagement is the use of the concept of earmarking in the federal budget. An earmark is a legislative provision that approves funds to be spent on specific projects or can allow for specific exemptions from taxes or mandated fees. There are two types of earmarks: hard earmarks, which are found in legislation and are legally binding, and soft earmarks, which are found in the text of congressional committee reports and are treated as if they were legally binding. It is evident that legislators are going to advance their constituency's interests over those of other legislators by directing projects to their own home state or district.

Earmarks are commonly defended as important spending initiatives that are placed into the budget by a concerned elected official who has expert local knowledge and thus can guide the federal government to a better and more targeted solution to a particular problem. In reality, earmarks are an opportunity to divert resources to a particular purpose—and that may be done for both good and bad reasons.

One of the most massive examples of earmarking was the famous Bridge to Nowhere project. Formally known as the Gravina Island Bridge, it was intended to link the city of Ketchikan, Alaska (population 8,900) with Gravina Island (population 50). There is ferry service to the island, but some town residents complained about the 15- to 30-minute wait and the $6-per-car fee. Proposed at a cost of $398 million, and backed by Alaska congressman Don Young and Alaska senator Ted Stevens, the project sailed through the allocation process and wound up being a direct hard earmark in the SAFETEA-LU federal transportation bill. The earmark was criticized for being a massive waste of government resources.

According to a CNN online article, Senator Stevens, a Republican with a long history in the Senate, had been indicted on seven counts of making false statements on Senate financial disclosure forms. Notice that long history and also what we have learned about people who serve in given elected or appointed positions for a long time. They become trusted and gain the ability to influence. Senator Stevens had been criticized by observers of congressional spending for his lack of fiscal control. In spite of the criticism, in 2005 he backed the legislation to build the "Bridge to Nowhere."[6] Now, the reader may wonder why a well-placed and powerful senator would go out on a political limb to obtain funds for a questionable project. The answer to that question provides us with great insight into why governments might mismanage funds on a regular basis—especially in big capital improvement projects.

Basically, the key issues are: When should government resources be used to construct major infrastructure projects, and how do we decide what projects to build? As with any form of government spending, there is a general consensus that spending should be allocated under some form of cost/benefit analysis, whereby the public costs of a project are balanced with the public benefit. The expectation is that public investment should provide a broad base of public benefit and also perhaps add to the economic vitality of a given region, such that the tax system is able to collect additional revenue that will provide for the resources to build the project. Clearly, with the existing tax system, it is not clear that the economic benefit of the Bridge to Nowhere would have been captured and recycled to the agency that was supposed to build the facility. In particular, the federal dollars were largely assumed by many localities to be "free," and thus the project essentially had a lower, or no, cost.

As we have highlighted earlier, private individuals often attempt to get public funds to support their own private needs. In the case of the Gravina Island Bridge, the argument was made that the regional economic impact of the bridge would have been too limited. Thus, it was considered a "pork barrel" project. One wonders how such a project could make it into the final authorization bill while more deserving and valuable projects languish without funding. The answer lies in the reality of the legislative process. By allowing an official, elected by a local pool of voters, to set budget priorities and spending for a budget where the local costs are practically zero, we create an inherent opportunity to pass on costs to others while directing resource investment back to the local constituent base. In Congress, the seniority of a given representative or senator gives them additional power to direct legislation. Senator Stevens, with a lengthy 37-year term of seniority at the time (2005), clearly had the political clout and desire to move the project forward—and he did.

Here is yet another example of mismanaged funds in government that revolves around targeted specific interests, which only upon significant outrage was ultimately caught and resolved. In a *Washington Post* online article that helped put an end to earmarks, a $400 million project became the symbol of Washington pork. The bridge was an earmark, one of those projects lawmakers slip into bills to direct money to politically important causes back home. But in the hands of opponents, the bridge became The Earmark—one of the worst of Washington waste stories.[7]

This is where the 800-pound friendly gorilla oversight is critical in order to prevent fiscal irresponsibility by Congress. Yet it stands as an example of the breakdown in the monitoring of the money (value) that Congress is entrusted with by the taxpayer. Observe the behavior surrounding these earmarks with a high level of skepticism and gather all citizen input—not just from those who would benefit from the earmarked funds.

WHO MOTIVATES POLICY?

We will explore the broad range of power sources that lean upon agencies and attempt to steer them in certain directions. These sources of power might be within the government bureaucracy, within the agency, inside the elected realm of government, or totally outside of the government structures. Any attempt to change policy can create political pressures to retain the existing policy. There are typically industries or individuals who will perceive themselves to be on the losing end of a particular policy change. If the impact of the change is very concentrated—say, a change in the hours of work for drivers of 18-wheel trucks—then it is likely to be vigorously opposed by the industry that is impacted by the change—the trucking industry in this case. If the change is made to address some concerns that are broadly diffused in the public, it is unlikely that a broad coalition of the beneficiaries of the policy will form, as the benefit that is accrued to any one individual is very small and likely to be difficult to perceive—say, a slight improvement in traffic congestion or accident rates. Those broadly benefited or hurt thus tend to remain on the sidelines, and the strongly impacted tend to jump into the political fray. So laws that target specific industries, interest groups, or social movements have a greater likelihood of either being strongly supported by, for example, the mining industry, the National Rifle Association, or abortion rights groups.

Alternatively, as we highlighted earlier, agencies tend to collect like-minded individuals and "birds of a feather." Whether it be due to the required educational criteria or political patronage. We often find a great concentration of like-minded economists at the Bureau of Labor Statistics, demographers at the Census Bureau, environmentalists at the Environmental Protection Agency, engineers at the Department of Transportation, and such. These individuals may have strong feelings about the direction in which their particular agency should move and also may attempt to expand or contract the letter of the law on a particular matter. Thus, the agency staffers can form a potent core of interested parties who continually look to modify policy to their liking.

Finally, we cannot discount the important impact of regional matters on national and regional agency behavior. In the western United States, much of the land is owned by the U.S. government—in the five southwestern states (California, Nevada, Arizona, New Mexico, and Utah) more than 40 percent of the land is owned by agencies of the U.S. federal government—in Nevada it's more than 84 percent! The residents of these states have a strong national interest in federal land use policy and, as such, they are personally more engaged with federal land policy than, say, in a state like Iowa, where the federal government owns 0.76 percent of the land. Issues such as mining, ranching, recreational use, and forestry loom large in these communities. Similarly, farming policy and subsidies are of keen interest and are critical hot-button issues in the Midwestern states. Elected officials from these same states are likely to have a disproportionate interest in these programs—and, given the population skew in the U.S. Senate, these matters may get more national time than is the average interest level of an American voter.

GOVERNMENT AND PUBLIC AGENCY FRAUDS AND MISMANAGEMENT—WHY?

Governmental entities suffer the pain of being responsive to the electorate. At the end of the day, the expectation is that a governmental agency will serve the people. It is unlike a corporation, where the goal is profit, and unlike a household with close personal bonds. Governmental entities respond to the cultural and political norms of their region and country. This creates the unpleasant situation where the governmental entity may be subject to changing social goals and policies. This leaves the entity to develop practices and metrics of performance that are linked to meeting those goals. Yet today in Washington, D.C., we see the intense factionalism of the elected officials. For example, the ideas espoused by radical community development groups to greatly change our existing systems are active and promoted to address issues such as social and economic justice. This is in sharp contrast to the radical right perspective of libertarianism, whereby all problems can be solved by market mechanisms and the private sector will provide the socially optimal outcomes. Libertarians see no range of market failures or externalities that create gaps in the market system as identified by Pigou and Marx more than 100 years ago.

We then have an entire accounting system that is built on a common set of assumptions about knowledge, a continuing world of empirical studies, and the relationship between theory and practice. This particular panoramic view, with its emphasis on testing of the consequences of hypotheses and technical control, creates a range of problems. Yet our agencies may be led or guided by individuals who do not share their agency's core mission—for example, the famous appointment by Ronald Reagan of James G. Watt in 1981 to lead the Department of the Interior was viewed by the environmental community as a massive mistake. They felt his support for oil and gas drilling and mining on public lands was completely at odds with the core mission of the department. Correspondingly, Jimmy Carter's appointment of Joan Claybrook as head of the National Highway Safety Administration was also viewed as a radical choice, because she was seen as a pro-regulation reformer with strong ties to Ralph Nader and other anti–auto industry advocates.

Yet the agencies have to move forward and attempt to meet their core mission and goals. We thus have to begin by understanding the assumptions, and the often fundamentally different conflicting interests that occur in these organizations, and then we can gain much more meaningful insight for arriving at a conclusion about the right course of action.

Understanding views and their underlying assumptions clears the way to interpretive policy and procedure. The "same" policies (problems) cannot have two different alternative perspectives. These policies (problems) need to be dealt with through effective communication and finding solutions that address all common interests. Yet finding common ground is not always easy; the fact is that some questions or problems have a broad range of potential governmental responses. These responses can range from intense direct action by a governmental entity to a laissez faire model where we expect the markets to solve the problem. From housing to poverty to jobs to the economy, our political will has swung back and forth from interventionist to libertarianism.

During our research, an interesting read came up involving Hillary Rodham Clinton, who, as a student at Wellesley College,[8] wrote a thesis entitled "'There Is Only the Fight': An Analysis of the Alinsky Model"[9] (hereafter referred to as the "Saul Principles," referencing community organizer Saul Alinsky). This follows some of the arguments in the use of diversionary tactics that can cause a useful distraction that can then lead to a diversion and causes division. Three of the ingredients a fraudster relies on in remaining undetected.

When people develop logical constraints or political views early in life, these constraints can impact future opinions, leadership styles, and moral standards. One of the most prominent public leaders in the Unites States is former Secretary of State Hillary Rodham Clinton. Secretary Clinton has held a number of elected and appointed government positions since the 1980s, yet her early writings may offer some insight into how she views and viewed the world. One may want to consider if her own personal experiences and educational experience color her views and decision making. Like all of us, she is a product of her life experiences, and her case offers us an opportunity to explore the mind and cultural norms of a powerful public leader. Do her early political writings indicate a worldview that may or not be reflective of a administration or political office?

Fraud and mismanagement occur because the people committing them understand the self-interests and needs of the people who create the value. Need can be equated to demand or interest, value creation being a central mission of the public entity. As an example, people need to cross a bridge to get to another state; that need generates value. Greater value is created when the need is in demand or there are limited choices available. These are the external factors that create an opportunity for fraud and mismanagement to exist.

Greed is nothing more than one person advancing his or her self-interest at the expense of another's. In Alinsky's writing, we are looking at external influences and areas that create conflicts or divisive behavior. Anywhere a fraudster sees the opportunity to create debate they succeed in diverting attention from themselves. This can take the form of extended studies (costs) that cause confusions and lead to delays. It can be identified lobbying that goes on for specific self-interest. All of which create an environment in which the potential for fraud and mismanagement can exist.

Based on Alinsky's books *Rules for Radicals* and *Reveille for Radicals*[10] and the political media, an idea surfaced that eight levels of control are necessary for creating a socialist state.[11] These are issues that distract, divert attention, and cause division. They are discussed here, as they are often intertwined with long-term fraud and mismanagement. We would argue that the political whip-sawing that goes on over these issues and programs creates an environment of policy uncertainty that likely adds to the potential for fraud in these areas.

The eight levels of control are:

1. Health care: Control health care, and you control the people.
2. Poverty: Increase the poverty level as high as possible. Poor people are easier to control and will not fight back if they are being provided with everything needed to live.
3. Debt: Increase the debt to an unsustainable level. That way, taxes can be increased and there will be more poverty.
4. Gun control: Remove the ability of people to defend themselves against the government. That way, a police state can be created.
5. Welfare: Take control of every aspect of their lives (food, housing, and income).
6. Education: Take control of what people read and listen to. Take control of what children learn in school.
7. Religion: Remove the belief in God from the government and schools.
8. Class warfare: Divide the people into the wealthy and the poor. This will cause more discontent, and it will be easier to take taxes from the wealthy with the support of the poor.

Keeping the idea within the context of controlling the citizenry, we can define domestic policy as all issues and activities within the nation's borders that require governmental or public entity intervention. Domestic policies regulate business, education, energy, health care, law enforcement, money and taxes, natural resources, social welfare, and personal rights and freedoms.

Poverty is a source of conflict. What policies are in place to eradicate poverty? Why does the Second Amendment, giving the citizenry the right to bear arms, cause divisive debate? Does radical community development cause effective social change or conflicts of interest? Government starts out to structure policy. Does government at all levels have supermajority support or small centralized special interest and localized support of the citizenry? Is the policy attempting to suppress existing rights with the potential to render itself out of control? With any domestic policy debate, the concern over the application of the appropriate level of government intervention remains with respect to economic and social issues.

The classic class debate provides further areas for dissent and room for the political pendulum to swing. We like to call it a conflicting-interest perspective. Conservatives believe that the government should not play a major role in regulating business and managing the economy. Most conservatives believe that government action cannot solve the problems of poverty and economic inequality. The existence of wealth inequality supports that statement. According to an analysis of Federal Reserve data by the Economic Policy Institute, the wealthiest 1 percent of Americans controls 35.6 percent of the total wealth of the country—more than one-third.[12] Even more incredible is that the richest 10 percent of Americans control 75 percent of the wealth, leaving only 25 percent to the other 90 percent of Americans.

Most liberals, however, support government programs that seek to provide economic security, ease human suffering, and reduce inequality. Many liberals also believe that the government should regulate businesses to ensure safe and fair working conditions and to limit environmental pollution. Add the complexity that domestic policy issues are especially controversial among people of different cultures, religions, and personal beliefs. Examples of such issues include abortion rights, the rights of homosexuals, the role of religion in public life, and the place of cultural diversity in education and employment. The process of shaping and implementing domestic policy becomes a breeding ground for fraud and mismanagement.

A nation's form of government largely determines how its domestic policy is formed and implemented. Under authoritarian governments, a ruling group may pursue its domestic policy goals without the input or consent of the people being governed. But in democratic societies, the will of the people has a much greater influence. In a democracy, the formal design of domestic policy is chiefly the responsibility of elected leaders, lawmaking bodies, and specialized governmental agencies. But a number of other factors also play a role in the process. Voters, for instance, determine which individuals and political parties have the power to determine policy. The mass media reports present information about domestic issues, laying out the facts from which public opinion is formed. People then tend to band together in support of those opinions based on fact. Lobbyists, activist groups, and other organizations also work to influence policy through a variety of methods. Such methods may include monetary donations, promises of support, advertising campaigns, or demonstrations and protests.

The effectiveness of domestic policy depends on the government bureaucracy (system of agencies) that puts laws and programs into action. In some cases, bureaucracies act slowly or inefficiently, or fail to apply policies as they were originally intended. Domestic policy may also face challenges in the courts that delay or change the policy. In many countries, courts have the power of judicial review, which allows them to strike down any legislative or executive action that they find in violation of the nation's constitution.

Better Call Saul is an American television drama series based on the story of small-time lawyer Saul Goodman six years before his appearance on the successful *Breaking Bad* series. Saul is the lawyer who wants to avoid court at all cost with his classic "I know a guy." In government it's all about "I know a guy." The fraudster and managers know a guy, or they would not be able to perpetrate fraud or mismanage. As examples of the types of fraud, mismanagement, and waste in government and the public entity are explored, look for their Saul.

TYPES OF GOVERNMENT AND PUBLIC AGENCY FRAUD

Fraud and mismanagement wander about in our agencies, cropping up on an all-too-frequent basis. When internal controls are lax or policies conflicting, the opportunity to bend the systems of an agency to personal gain increase and fraud practitioners are ready to open for business. There are a multitude of tactics that fraud perpetrators can use. Their tactics and methods morph and change as policies and policing tactics change. As with the question of who is the best forger in the world, the answer is that we do not know, as his or her forgeries have not been detected yet. We will outline some of the known practices of fraudsters and attempt to explain their methods.

On the mismanagement side, the tests of when an agency has poor management practices are many. In addition, mismanagement does not have to rise to the level of criminality to be dealt with. It is expected that employees will do their jobs in an appropriate and "workmanlike" manner. Thus, the threshold where management can move in and stop a practice is much lower than the point at which management will be able to prove criminal fraud. Practices that are sometimes tolerated but are still bad operational standards are common in many organizations. Everything from poor time reporting to improper breaks and lunch periods to general shirking of duties can be found across the agency and corporate world.

CASE STUDY: SOCIAL SECURITY SYSTEM

Massive systems create massive opportunities for fraud and misman-agement. They also offer the opportunity for economies of scale. Thus, we need to strike a balance between the efficiency of a large-scale organization and the need to implement appropriate measures of management to combat fraud and waste. Further, agencies that focus on the distribution of funds may tend to have less incentive to deny funds, as the large scale of the beneficiary class may create a sense of power and importance for a federal program. The Social Security system was established with lofty goals to create a more just society, where the elderly and the disabled would not become destitute.

The benefits received are based on a number of factors, and the evaluation of the benefits to be paid and the categorization of the recipients opens the door to significant opportunities for fraud and mismanagement. Fraud may be committed on an individual basis or in a coordinated ring of fraud activity. The fraud may occur due to misrepresentation in the benefits application process or misdirection of the resources after the benefits are paid. Given that the program distributes more than $1.4 trillion in benefits each year—or about one-third of federal spending—it is not surprising that this benefit program has attracted its fair share of criminals and cons. Table 5.1 provides the Social Security expenditures by spending category for 2014.

TABLE 5.1   Social Security Payments, by Category, from Each Trust Fund in 2014 (in billions)

Program Cost	Old Age and Survivor	Disability Insurance	Hospital Insurance	Supplemental Medical Insurance	Total
Benefit payments	$706.8	$141.7	$264.9	$339.6	$1,453.0
Railroad Retirement financial interchange	$4.3	$0.4	–	–	$4.7
Administrative expenses	$3.1	$2.9	$4.5	$4.4	$14.9
Total	$714.2	$145.1	$269.3	$344.0	$1,472.6

Source: https://www.ssa.gov/OACT/TRSUM/index.html

According to the Office of Inspector General (OIG), fraud, waste, or abuse[13] with respect to Social Security includes making false statements on claims. Remember MIRD.

Making false statements occurs when people apply for Social Security benefits and they state that all information they provide on the forms being submitted is true and correct to the best of their knowledge. If a person reports something they know is not true, it may be a crime. Similarly, on tax forms, the taxpayer's declaration is signed under penalties of perjury: "I declare that I have examined this return and accompanying schedules and statements, and to the best of my knowledge and belief, they are true, correct, and complete." There are authorizations in all of the fraud, mismanagement, abuse, and waste examples. Someone is responsible for safeguarding the exposed value.

Concealing material facts or events that affect eligibility for obtaining Social Security benefits is a form of fraud. Social welfare is the giving of a value by a governmental agency. It may be considered to be a fraud if a person makes a false statement on an application intentionally or does not tell the Social Security Administration (SSA) certain facts that might affect benefits. *Intent* is an important, and the most difficult, proof burden that must be overcome in developing facts and findings. Remember, a judge and jury are the only ones that can find someone guilty of fraud.

Misuse of benefits by a representative payee is a form of fraud. Misdirection and redirections are areas to examine. Often, people who receive Social Security benefits are not able to handle their own financial affairs. The Social Security Administration (SSA) allows for the appointment of a relative, friend, or another individual (guardian) or organization to handle the disabled person's Social Security matters. It's important to remember that it might be a crime if a representative payee misuses a person's Social Security benefits.

Buying or selling counterfeit or legitimate Social Security cards. Being able to manipulate documents and alter records is an area ripe for fraud. The buying and selling of counterfeit or legitimate Social Security cards is a crime. "Identity theft is one of the fastest growing crimes in America. A dishonest person who has your Social Security number can use it to get other personal information about you."[14] It is important to safeguard Social Security numbers, passwords, identifications, and critical documents in the governmental or public entity workplace.

Social Security numbers involving people linked to terrorist groups or activities. The SSA/OIG is committed to protecting the security of the nation, including maintaining a fraud hotline.

(continued)

(continued)

Crimes involving SSA employees. The SSA employees are public servants, and, as such, they are required to maintain a high level of integrity. Some of the scams involve impersonating an SSA employee. The OIG has received reports about individuals who have been contacted by someone impersonating an SSA employee. The intent of this type of call may be to steal identity and/or money from bank accounts. Never provide any information to these or other individuals unless you can ensure they are legitimate.

Bribery of a SSA employee is offering a government employee anything of value, such as money or gifts, in exchange for government services, and it is illegal.

Fraud or misuse of grant or contracting funds. The SSA is responsible for overseeing a significant amount of dollars in contracts and grants. As mentioned, a fraud hotline is in place to process allegations of fraud, waste, or mismanagement related to contracts and grants.

Standards of conduct violations. Public service involves public trust. All SSA employees are bound by the Standards of Ethical Conduct for Employees of the Executive Branch. Violations should be reported to the OIG Fraud Hotline.

Workers' compensation fraud generally involves Social Security disability benefits that are received by parties who are collecting workers' compensation. It could be fraud if the person receiving Social Security disability did not inform the SSA.

These are types of fraud that were identified by the OIG to assist in explaining the areas of fraud to be discussed. *Black's Law Dictionary* defines government fraud as "all multifarious means which human integrity can devise and which are resorted by one individual to get an advantage over another by false suggestion or suppression of the truth. It includes all surprise, trick, cunning or dissembling and any unfair way by which another is cheated." In simple language, it's the taking of money or property by cheating someone. In government, the fraud is depriving the government or the public entity of funds by using deceptive or unfair actions.

CRIMINALITY AND INTENT VERSUS INEPTITUDE

When we look at the operational activities in a private or governmental enterprise, we generally find standards of practice that help the organization work in a productive and sensible way. Individual workers or groups of workers may work outside of these normal practices and thus be noncompliant with firm rules. In some cases, these actions may happen due to a lack of knowledge about good practice or due to an inadvertent breach of policy. Other times, workers may actively seek to violate the rules of the firm for many reasons. Firm rules may be cumbersome, archaic, and impractical—and this tends to encourage workers to skirt the rules.

If the workers are evading the rules on purpose to achieve certain outcomes, a smart manager should consider both the outcome and the range of rules violated. In some cases, workers are attempting to achieve key goals and promote efficiency. In those cases, smart managers will examine the rules and look for opportunities to modify them if possible and sensible. Other times, workers are evading the rules for personal gain or other illicit reasons. Proper management will examine the situation; determine whether the violation is due to ineptitude, good intent, or malicious intent; and act accordingly.

In some cases, the evasion crosses the line into a range of activities that are beyond the scope of firm rule violation and actually cross into the realm of criminal activity. In those cases, the next appropriate step for the managers is to contact law enforcement.

Given the need to understand where the line is in terms of the moment when contacting law enforcement is an appropriate action or when legal proceedings may be needed, it is useful to distinguish fraud from waste, and mismanagement from criminal fraud.

When is it fraud that is intentionally dishonest, misleading, or deceitful conduct and deprives the government (public agency) of its resources or rights?

Examples:

- Manipulation, falsification, or alteration of accounting records or supporting documents to conceal theft or an entity's true financial condition
- Submitting false vouchers for reimbursement
- Intentionally misrepresenting the costs of goods or services provided
- Falsifying payroll information
- Use of state equipment or property for personal gain
- Bid rigging

Waste and mismanagement, on the other hand, involve the needless, careless, or extravagant expenditure of funds, or mismanagement of government (public entity) resources or property. Waste does not necessarily involve private use or personal gain, but it almost always signifies poor management decisions, practices, or controls.

Examples:

- ▪ Failing to administer programs according to state or federal laws and regulations
- ▪ Purchasing unneeded supplies or equipment
- ▪ Purchasing goods at inflated prices
- ▪ Permitting serious abuse of paid time, such as significant unauthorized time away from work, or significant use of paid time for personal business
- ▪ Allowing a travel reimbursement system to be abused

As you can see, there is a wide range of activities that could fall into the range of waste and mismanagement that actually may be fraud. One of the classic ways for fraudsters to avoid capture and prosecution is to claim that they were inept and the activity was just waste or mismanagement. By claiming to not know the rules, the fraudster essentially looks to lower the penalty—just as manslaughter (unintentional killing of an individual) is generally a lower-penalty crime as compared to first-degree murder (intentional, willful, and premeditated killing of an individual). Thus, unless the individuals take action to conceal their activities, it may be hard to prove criminal intent in a fraud case. As a former U.S. prosecutor told the authors, "You don't catch the crime—you catch the cover-up."

CASE STUDY: LONG ISLAND RAILROAD RETIREE FRAUD

In a case of widespread corruption, the federal prosecutors pursued more than 1,500 Long Island Railroad (LIRR) retired employees for participating in a scam where they were declared to have been injured on the job and thus eligible for enhanced disability retirement benefits. Two doctors were convicted in their role of falsifying medical records and reports to support claims of disability for the commuter railroad workers. Both Dr. Peter Ajermian (who pleaded guilty to the charges) and Dr. Peter Lesniewski (who fought the allegations and was convicted) were sentenced to eight years in prison, and the U.S. Railroad Retirement Board (RRB) rescinded the disability pension subject to further medical review. Two former LIRR employees, Marie Baran and Joseph Rutigliano, were also convicted for their roles as "consultants" who would fill out forms and arrange "treatment" for the workers prior to retirement to form a paper trail that would support the claim. Another 29 workers were convicted of fraud and given various sentences and penalties related to the case.

The U.S. Department of Justice summed up the methods and scale of this fraud in their March 8, 2013, press release:[15]

Hundreds of LIRR employees have allegedly exploited the overlap between the LIRR pension and the RRB disability program by pre-planning the date on which they would falsely declare themselves disabled so that it would coincide with their projected retirement date. These false statements, made under oath in disability applications, allowed LIRR employees to retire as early as age 50 with an LIRR pension, supplemented by the fraudulently obtained RRB disability annuity. From 2004 through 2008, 61% of LIRR employees who stopped working and began receiving RRB disability benefits were between the ages of 50 and 55. In contrast, only 7% of employees at Metro-North who stopped working and received disability benefits during the same time period were between the ages of 50 and 55.[16]

Clearly, in this case, the workers exploited a gap in the certification process and poor managerial control over the awarding of disability pensions created a strong financial incentive to locate medical personnel who were willing to create fraudulent behavior on a massive scale. Having two separate pension-granting agencies may have contributed to the problem, as each may have been relying on the other to supervise the process.

Amazing as it may seem, this practice apparently continues today. The Government Accountability Office (GAO) reported that in March 2013, the RRB indicated that it approved 96 percent of the disability claims submitted by LIRR workers (496 of 519). This is five years after the scandal broke, and the GAO report indicates that the RRB has a long way to go to achieve good practice in financial management of its program. Of course, one wonders what the goal of the RRB is—and one could consider that a bureaucracy may desire to grow and more pension would justify the role of the RRB on the federal government landscape. So what is actually controlling fraud may be seen by the agency to be a reduction in mission. Clearly, the RRB is not in a rush to reform its practices.

Source: https://www.fbi.gov/newyork/press-releases/2013/twenty-thirddefendant-pleads-guilty-in-long-island-railroad-disability-fraud-scheme

CASE STUDY: NO-SHOW/LOW-SHOW JOBS

Politicians often have the ability to command public resources and benefit their own pockets via compensation and perks. However, in some cases, politicians may want to help friends, family, or key supporters with benefits. A classic method of political corruption is using the power of

(continued)

(continued)

an office or elected post to place your family member in a "no-show" or "low-show" job. These jobs could be in the actual public sector, on a board that is appointed by the government, or in a private firm that has strong political ties to the government or has a high level of public regulation on the industry or firm. The firm benefits from a "special" conduit to the elected official—and, of course, the hope that this connection will lead to favorable legislation for the industry. Because the level of competency of the worker is not the deciding factor in the hiring decision, these jobs may have limited responsibilities or requirements. In the classic model, the individual does not even have to show up to work—the no-show job.

In a recent case in New York state, Adam Skelos—the son of powerful state senator Dean Skelos—was hired by a medical malpractice insurance company, Physicians' Reciprocal Insurers (PRI). During testimony in a corruption trial of the father and son in federal district court, the executives of PRI outlined how the junior Mr. Skelos was hired by PRI and that in fact he did not show up for work for days on end. In one incident, the manager reported that Adam Skelos threatened to "smash" in his supervisor's head after the supervisor questioned his work habits. In spite of all of this, the firm retained him, paying him $78,000 a year. After additional incidents, the senior Mr. Skelos called the CEO of the firm and demanded to know why Adam Skelos's supervisor was "picking on him," finally telling the CEO of PRI, "Well, just work this out." PRI finally moved the junior Mr. Skelos to a job that did not require him to come to the office at all but to just make 100 sales calls a week, and paid $36,000 for this service. The CEO in court testimony indicated that he did not make the calls.[17]

 ## AUDITOR VERSUS ACCOUNTANT UNDERSTANDING

To comprehend why fraud and mismanagement are difficult to uncover, an understanding of what is really involved in auditing is important. As with many accounting functions, there is a need to accumulate information to enable it to be put into a verifiable form. It is through the accumulation of this evidence that one is able to determine the degree of correspondence that is necessary to develop competent findings as perceived by an independent person.

Quantifiable Evidence

To perform an audit, one must find quantifiable evidence. Typical evidence revolves around financial statements, tax returns, bank statements, and other sources of third-party verifiable information support. The problem is that there are many oversight bodies. As an example in the United States, what we call the standards, Generally Accepted Accounting Principles (GAAP), differ in application of accounting from International Financial Reporting Standards (IFRS). These types of conflicting-rules situations with accounting oversight bodies often cause some of the problem. As you have already learned, government accounting rules have their own additional standards under the supervision of the Government Accounting Standards Board (GASB). An example is GASB Statement No. 68: Accounting and Financial Reporting for Pensions. Given the impact that pensions have on taxpayers, it's been necessary to create more accountable records for them. Problems often arise when there are different ways of doing the accounting, such as GAAP, IFRS, and GASB. With these different accounting methodologies or differences in approaches to a given accounting item, the degree of subjectivity involved and the information itself become more difficult to verify.

A key component of any successful audit is the evidence that is available. Evidence consists of any records that an auditor could use in establishing a mechanism to verify the accounting records or practice. In today's world, such evidence could come in the form of electronic and documentary data, written or electronic communication outside the governmental or public entity, physical observations of activity that the auditors might see in the course of their work, oral communications from management and/or the employees within the public entity, as well as any other means that one might reasonably use to provide substantiation.

As with any discipline, the auditors must fully understand the necessary evidence they are examining in order to reach the appropriate conclusion. Whether it be the audit, an agency matter, or a government official, the person examining the data must approach the issue with the mental attitude of independence. The higher the level of independence, the more confidence the party relying on that information will have. One issue that usually arises concerning auditor independence is that the auditor's fees are paid by the governmental entity and/or public agency. Then add the fact that the internal auditors who are in place are also paid by the government and/or public agency. This type of conflict of interest must be examined in order to maintain a high level of independence.

The first area of audit practice to examine is the order by an IRS agent for a review of an entity's tax and operational practices. The accumulation of evidence revolves around examining what was filed on the tax return. The taxpayer then becomes responsible to verify that the items have been properly reported. Evidence acquired in this way would be canceled checks, invoices, deposits, contracts, and other forms of support to create a verifiable position. The established criteria are the Internal Revenue Code and all the interpretations that have been established over time.

"More Likely Than Not" Standard

Interestingly, when a taxpayer has a position that will likely *not* successfully survive an IRS examination by greater than 50 percent—even succeeding 50.01 percent of the time—the taxpayer should not reflect the transaction without proper supporting evidence. Again, assuming that 50 percent or greater will ultimately result in 100 percent accuracy fosters gray-area thinking. Fraud and mismanagement will continue, as we are dealing with estimation (judgment) and conflicting interests (the taxpayer, who wants to reduce the tax, versus the IRS agent, who wants to collect more taxes for the government).

In order for the taxpayer to be successful in an IRS audit, the taxpayer needs to convince the auditing agent of the veracity of his or her position. The tax position requires a significantly higher degree of evidence than just *barely* proving your case to a 50.01 percent, "more likely than not" standard, as the taxpayer needs 100 percent hard evidence to satisfy the IRS auditor. A more appropriate level of proof to prevail, in the authors' experience, is using the standard of "beyond reasonable doubt" or, as is commonly used in the fields of statistics and finance, "moral certainty."

Failure by the taxpayer to convince the examining agent of the validity of the claim often leads to the assessment of penalties and interest. Again, this can vary depending upon the IRS auditor's personality and view with respect to whether the required burden of proof has been met.

"Reasonable Person" Standard

Simple comparison of policy measured from the viewpoint of a reasonable person with a majority ownership position in a firm often sheds light on the reasonableness of the spending decisions. Obviously, the minority in any situation is the net benefactor of any inappropriate spending that they may obtain for their own use, while the majority owner only wants spending that directly benefits himself or herself or the firm. The question again becomes what evidence is available, who is responsible for testing the evidence, and what are the specific results in meeting the designed objectives of the spending policy. Unfortunately, there is not an Internal Revenue agent verifying and testing these spending choices.

Often the confusion arises due to the differences in perspective of the user of the services of an auditor versus the general public's perception of what an auditor does. Let's apply this thinking to "auditor" versus "accountant." Clearly, Xerox is not the only copier and Google is not the only search engine, just as an auditor represents one type of accounting function, but not *all* of the accounting functions. It is these broad societal inferences that cause public confusion as to who should be doing what, and there is no greater point of confusion than calling an auditor an accountant.

Identify, Record, and Communicate

Let's clarify the difference between auditing and accounting. Accounting is the identifying, recording, and communicating of economic events in a logical manner so that financial information can be developed for decision makers. This means an accountant must have a thorough understanding of the principles and rules that are necessary to prepare accounting information that is expected by a reasonable person as well as doing what another professional would do, given the same facts and information.

The first and foremost principle of accounting is that *whatever is being examined in accounting remains a going concern.* The whole theory behind accruing, deferring, and other accounting practices hangs in large part on the premise that the entity will continue as an entity ongoing into the future. The facts and circumstances surrounding the federal government (and some state and local government) policies that cause a need to accumulate significant debt should be closely analyzed. This debt accumulation should be met with "where do we go from here?" thinking and not "how did we get here?" The problem is that the officials who may go down these paths will eventually no longer be in office. Such inconsistencies that arise allow debt to accrue into the future and fraud and mismanagement to remain undetected. With any inconsistencies comes the ability to create distractions that allow for finger-pointing and pass-the-buck assigning of blame. At some point the government cannot be expected to remain an ongoing concern, because, as with any debt accumulation, cash flows eventually dry up and reach an unsustainable level.

We can examine the financial situation of Puerto Rico, which had been borrowing massive amounts for the past 40 years, as the territory used debt issuance as a way to balance its budget. Since 1973, the commonwealth has accumulated more than $71 billion in debt, and in August 2014 it defaulted on a $58 million payment on that debt. This growing overhang of debt caused the bond-rating agencies to downgrade the Puerto Rican debt in February 2014 to a non-investment-grade bond—"junk bond" status.

The second most important accounting principle, in the view of the authors, is the idea of economic entity assumption. It is key to keep each entity independent of the others in order to establish true accounting results. No greater evidence of this problem exists than when a firm such as Enron can create multiple corporate entities and thus formulate large off-balance-sheet debt. *Off-balance-sheet financing* means a governmental or public entity does not include a liability on its balance sheet. In accounting terms, that action masks the government's and/or public entity's true level of debt and liability. Common forms of off-balance-sheet financing are operating leases and public-private partnerships, overlapping and duplicating services, and other creative finance initiatives to horse-trade self-interests.

CASE STUDY: DIVERSION OF RESOURCES

Even in cases where the governmental entity operates with good intent, the opportunity exists to thwart the initial goals of a given legislative statute and divert resources. A good example is the use of funds that are raised for transportation purposes in general and particularly from and for road users. These funds form the core of the famous Highway Trust Fund. Into this central fund pour the proceeds of the federal gasoline and diesel taxes. This money is then allocated back out of the fund to highway, mass transit, and underground storage tank programs. States maintain similar funding sources and central trust funds to support particular government services. Yet even with a clear purpose and dedicated revenue source, the opportunity to divert resources is too tempting, in many cases, for politicians to resist. Further, it can be difficult to gather the political will to increase these taxes and fees to support the regional and national infrastructure. Thus, our existing sources of revenue have weakened with regard to purchasing power as inflation has chipped away the real value of the fund.

In many countries, tax resources are not allocated to a specific spending category when the governmental entity establishes the tax. Thus, in many European countries, for instance, tax levy funds flow into the general fund—the central pool of resources that the government collects. The budgetary process in these countries is completely separate from the sources of funds.

The United States has a history of establishing dedicated trust funds in governments for specific purposes. In the case of roads, there was a strong movement in the 1870s through the 1920s to build improved roads across the nation to support the growing number of automobiles and the need for improved commerce. This new investment was funded by the implementation of taxes on fuel—gasoline and diesel. These funds collected at the state level flowed, in most cases, into dedicated funds for building and maintaining roads, bridges, tunnels, and such. This was the so-called Good Roads Movement.

These taxes were wildly popular, as road users paid a fee and also got an investment in a public resource that they both desired and valued. Road users could not pay for improved roads individually, as the value of the network was in the scale and options for travel destinations. Thus, any one user could not pay for his or her individual use of the road—although the prior funding mechanism before 1900 was largely road tolls and local taxes and that attempted to exclude nonpaying travelers. Road networks are generally usable by all—a classic public good—so the road that can be used by all is supported by all most effectively via a broader tax mechanism—and thus the implementation and popularity of fuel taxes as a road-funding source.

In 1956, the federal government took a strong role in this process by establishing a dedicated fund to receive federal fuel taxes and providing a subsidy for the construction of road assets across the nation—the Highway Trust Fund. Yet we now have apparently lost steam due in part to the diversion of resources away from the core mission of the Highway Trust Fund.

With the federal Highway Trust Fund drying up, government borrows money from other funds to pay for a minimum level of maintenance and few, if any, improvements. So instead of paying with revenue generated by the tax, the diversion is to fund through some combination of income and business taxes and deficit financing. "The Highway Trust Fund is projected to face a $58 billion deficit over the next four years, according to the Congressional Research Service."[18]

According to *Equipment World,* to make matters worse, as much as 25 percent of the federal motor fuels tax goes to projects other than roads and bridges—things like public transit, bike paths, and beloved projects of certain politicians. And the states use the fuel taxes they collect for all kinds of debts and obligations unrelated to transportation. A 2014 *Wall Street Journal* story reports that:

- ▪ Texas spends 25 percent of its fuel tax revenue on education;
- ▪ Kansas has allocated some of its gas tax revenue to pay for Medicaid and schools;
- ▪ New Jersey will set aside $516 million of its gas tax revenue to help pay down its $1 billion in debt interest;
- ▪ Washington State will spend 70 percent of its fuel tax revenue paying off the debt for past projects.[19]

(continued)

(*continued*)

This diversion of resources away from their stated purpose produces the opportunity to misrepresent the financial conditions of the general governmental entity and also provides a mischaracterization of the financial status of the given trust fund.

These off-balance-sheet gimmicks and creative accounting are what beg the question: Where are the auditors? The auditors are independent external parties. Yet these and many other poor management decisions, subprime lending failures, recessions, and fraud and mismanagement continue to plague the government and public entities. As stated earlier, the auditor needs to accumulate and evaluate the evidence and determine the degree of reporting to enable effective communication between the information (transactions) and established criteria (policy objectives). Where is the quantifiable audit information? Where are the effectiveness and efficiency evaluations? Where are the internal controls over the reports?

This constitutes professional skepticism, and these are the questions that need to be asked in order to address the matters at hand.

While here we are talking about risk in a government or business setting, we commonly discuss many types of risk in a firm—business risk, event risk, default risk, interest risk, and the like. One of the largest risks that an auditor can face is information risk. Government and public entities face that same risk. Auditors may base their opinions on the information that is presented—but that information might be in error or incomplete. Over time, the true information usually gets out, thus awareness is created and the outrage begins. Then, after the fact, we try to fix years of poor judgment.

So what does the auditor do with the information, and what are the procedures that are chosen to gather this evidence? How are the tests being performed to substantiate the evidence, examining unusual, nonrecurring, one-shot revenue/expenditures, unexpected information, whistle-blower communications, and off-balance-sheet transactions? Where is the information necessary to prevent fraud and mismanagement from occurring? Where are the names of the people who authorized the actions that led to the deficit? What measures have been implemented to address the weaknesses that enabled the fraud? What were the failed internal controls? The auditors are required to provide sufficient reliable information to support an opinion within a reasonable degree of accountant certainty or reasonable assurance. When that relied upon information generates conflicts of interest, the level of professional skepticism and needed documentary supports are elevated significantly. What information did the auditor use in making their judgment or decision to look past these potential conflicting interests between the public good versus the individuals in the government process?

Why do fraud and mismanagement happen? They happen because people find ways around rules and regulations. Sam Antar, the felon and former certified public accountant who helped perpetrate one of the largest securities frauds of the 1980s at Crazy Eddie, said when asked why one commits fraud, "Because I can."

Crazy Eddie's advertising campaign was unprecedented. For 17 years, the company marketed its products to the whole northeastern U.S. market with seemingly nonstop television, radio, and newspaper advertisements. Sound familiar? It seems similar to elected officials using public money to provide unfunded services—which, of course, they then use toward the record spending they need to get elected. Crazy Eddie was the go-to place to get appliances and was turning over large sales volumes and generating cash as a result of these strong marketing efforts. When the cash is coming in no questions are being asked.

The politician needs public support to get elected. This often requires large special interest support to fund the larger political office campaign. A campaign is an organized and active way to achieve a particular goal. These efforts circulate information and stances that often do not happen. But, if you market a product or person with the right pamphlets and advertising you become trusted and people tend to rely on what they see and hear.

It is not until we establish a proactive "Too Good to Be True" mind-set, rather than a reactive, after-the-fact approach with interested parties that we will have the proper environment to prevent fraud and mismanagement. Add to that auditors with higher levels of skepticism who hold management to task, then we will have the necessary system in place to create checks and balances.

The auditor focus remains on snapshot financial and operational matters, and a full reliance on the management of the organization. When was the last time that an auditor focused on external information such as taxpayers' needs or that user (essentially, the shareholders of the government/public agency) information was reviewed or examined? This is relevant information for making an informed opinion about the operating practices of an agency, yet the auditors never see in an audit report that the residents or taxpayers have concerns.

With the primary focus of an audit being on the operation of the government and/or public entity, compliance, and the ability to complete a financial communication, it is important to gain a full understanding of such audits. Payroll is an area where government and/or the public entity needs to move into the twenty-first century. Let's take the Port Authority of

New York and New Jersey (PANYNJ) as an example—a bi-state agency with multiple operations. The Authority runs airports, marine ship terminals, bridges and tunnels, a mass transit system, and real estate investments. What evaluations do the auditors perform to determine whether these different areas are operating efficiently and effectively? In our experience, asking for payroll information is a time-consuming task and almost always fraught with error. So if we were designing an operations audit for the payroll, we would need to have the precise number of payrolls that have been processed, the union contracts, health care costs, pension records, developed cost by department, accumulated sick pay tracking, and any information on other benefits. Given the number of employees, the different contractual arrangements, the hiring and termination, and the requirements and accounting necessary to manage time attendance, the lack of well-established standards with respect to payroll is astounding. Human resources is the gatekeeper and first line of defense against fraud and mismanagement, with the available evidence in the form of canceled checks, processed payrolls, established contracts, and existing records. In an audit these are generally not examined closely, beyond tying the payments to the general ledger and examining required payroll filings to ensure that budgets are not exceeded and that there is compliance with required tax filings. Auditing human resources competence in the government and/or public agency is the first system/procedure that reduces mismanagement and fraud. Many bad decisions that are made are the result of incorrect payroll information. Payroll remains the public entity's most significant cost, as it would be for any service provider.

The next major component of the auditor's role in establishing compliance within the payroll accounting function is examining the payroll process. The auditor must examine whether the administratively established payroll procedures are being followed as prescribed. That examination should include a review of compliance with the applicable minimum wage laws, ensuring contractual obligation compliance with legal requirements, and that all newly enacted regulations (e.g., the Affordable Care Act) are being complied with. Is the auditor relying on the human resources management team of the government/public entity to provide the information? How much testing has the auditor performed to confirm the information? What is the auditor's competence with respect to the labor laws with which he or she is expected to ensure compliance? Noncompliance in these areas is but one of the reasons that fraud and mismanagement can occur in these areas of accounting.

Add to this already highly complex area of accounting the additional compliance requirements imposed on the unit. Some of these complexities are the result of complying with the mandates of federally funded grants to subsidize other forms of revenue. The burden of such compliance is placed on the governmental unit, and this is often expensive to implement. We are faced, again, with the dreaded cost/benefit analysis thinking. The government/public entity now has to find additional dollars in the budget. Therefore, the public thinking is that the auditor is the new policing agent to ensure compliance. Given the time constraints to produce these financial presentations and the external influences and pressures, it is often these areas that produce the opportunities to perpetrate potential fraud and mismanagement.

These issues are at work in the federal government as well. Even though government operations may not be subject to an external audit, the internal controls of the Government Accountability Office (GAO) function in a similar manner. A government accountability officer works for the U.S. GAO, according to the nonpartisan legislative branch of the federal government that is headed by the comptroller general, who reports directly to Congress. This GAO office examines the various federal governmental agencies and reports the findings to Congress (the oversight). The checks and balances do not work if people are able to go around the congress, like in the case of the Iran–Contra Scandal. Since the basis for the expenditures and receipts of the governmental agency is defined by law there is a considerable amount of compliance testing that is required in these audits to ensure compliance. The GAO's efforts are largely based on a desire to understand the operating efficiency and effectiveness of various federal programs. Unfortunately, due to the immense size of many federal agencies, the GAO audits, and the resources available, there is a lot of emphasis placed on sophisticated statistical sampling and computer risk assessment techniques as opposed to a heavy amount of hands-on analysis. Therefore, we have to be careful that the data sampled is valid—to avoid the "garbage in, garbage out" outcome that may occur if we blindly apply rule-based analysis methods. If there is no verification of the source documents, how can the GAO accountability officer provide the necessary assurances that the opinions reached are supportable?

Government employee fraud is when employees use their position to advance their own interest. We refer to the root cause in many cases as being linked to perspectives, occupations, and positions (POP). In this situation, the employee is in a trusted position and may have considerable autonomy and authority—so it is a given that his or her actions need to be closely monitored. The types of fraud can include such things as using government intellectual property to disclose personal data; misappropriating assets (inventory and equipment), which can be both cash and noncash items; misstated financial statements; and various corruption frauds.

 ## CATEGORIES OF WASTE

Understanding the potential for waste and matching the need (benefit) with the cost can be managed only if there is an understanding of how the waste is allowed to transpire. Why does fraud happen? Because someone decides it can? Waste is no different.

Here are five principles that potentially create waste in government and public agencies:

1. Government can perform and meet a need better than the open (private) market can. We call this the "We know better" principle.
2. Government and the associated public entities can ensure that all the intended benefactors receive the benefit and others not entitled to the program benefits are excluded. This is the "Big Brother can watch all" principle, the belief that the government can monitor all behaviors in all situations that can arise, which is a big leap of faith.
3. Government and the public agency update and remove unnecessary programs as warranted based on program success. This is not supported by history. We call this the "No downsizing" principle.
4. Government and the public never duplicate programs and efforts. We call this the "Overlapping" principle.
5. The federal government delegates to state and local programs. We call this the "Pass-the-buck" principle.

Opportunities where there is a potential for wasteful and unnecessary spending:

- Programs that the federal government should delegate to state and local governments
- Programs that could be better performed by the private sector rather than the public sector

- Misdirected programs where the parties not entitled to government benefits receive them
- Programs that do not meet the desired goals on a regular basis
- Overlapping or duplicate programs

These categories are all based on subjectivity in that they involve judgment, and reasonable people can have conflicting opinions as to whether or not a program failed or is effective. The last listed waste potential area (overlap and duplication) can be easier to identify. We need to look for the potential for waste and unnecessary spending so as not to enable diversion of funds to unintended purposes, duplicative programs, and discretionary versus mandatory and divisive policy types of decisions to avoid conflicts of interest.

Yet by their very nature, government programs may have winners and losers resulting from the program policies. In many cases the winners are the beneficiaries of the program and the losers are the taxpayers—who face increased taxes to pay for the programs. Thus, the winners have the incentive to maintain their winning, and the losers may try to end the program. Conflicts of interest may thus arise on a regular basis in government programs or policies, and the actions of government are not always dictated by an objective measure of success but, rather, by the political power of the players. Take, for instance, the highly controversial new firms of Airbnb and Uber. Both provide people with alternatives means to traditional services—Airbnb provides hotel-type room rentals, and Uber provides taxicab-like services. Both have been subject to regulatory pushes from the government, and there have been pitched efforts by the existing players to protect their business models—as opposed to the new services. Government has been brought into these decisions about whether to pass laws to preserve the existing providers or change laws to accommodate the new services. Political horse trading is very active in these situations, and it is not clear who the final winner will be—but you can rest assured that the decisions will not be based *only* on the best public policy.

 ## CENTRALIZATION

The *centralization of government* creates decisions that can be applied all over the country within all agencies (and even in the private sector) from that central focal point of Washington, D.C. The problem faced by thinking that a one-size centralized policy fits all is that there will always be unforeseeable or uncontrollable factors. One of these unforeseeable or uncontrollable events can be Mother Nature. The more spread out the population base that you are attempting to control, the greater the potential for waste in programs as it becomes difficult to put the necessary controls in place to safeguard the value. The better idea is to determine who has the better pool of resources to deal with the problem and the ability to create efficiency in meeting the policy/program objective: the open market or government? Maintaining a free open-market way of thinking, with principle-based people who have the proper resources, rather than a centralized, one-size-fits-all approach, creates diversity and a more cost-effective means to meet the objective.

In cost accounting, a manufacturing nightmare is a bottleneck that causes a delay in product creation and an ultimate loss in revenue. Successful organizations have the critical capabilities to make split-second decisions and adjust accordingly. An important factor is that putting the decision making in the hands of capable people who ultimately know better and operate in an open market with proper segregation of duties and controls in place leads to greater efficiency in the process and ultimately increases the bottom-line profits. Government and public entity thinking tends to create monopolization and a centralization of control and limits choice, which is never a good thing. Any economy that allows a public entity to grant a monopoly by giving exclusive privilege to a private individual or firm to be the sole provider of a good or service drives potential competitors away by law, regulation, or other mechanisms of government enforcement. This creates the power to influence and the ability to potentially corrupt, as there are no competitive checks and balances. The definition of a government monopoly is "a forced form of market domination whereby a national, regional, or local administration, agency, or corporation is permitted to be the only provider of a certain product since any competition with their product is legally prohibited. A government monopoly is generally created and run by a government, rather than by a private business."[20]

These points of centralization need to be examined with the appropriate level of skepticism and understanding of the personality behaviors they are surrounded by to prevent fraud and mismanagement.

One need only examine the government's response to critical natural disasters to see that a centralized program may not have the flexibility to adapt to changing conditions or needs. The federal government responses to Hurricane Katrina on the Gulf Coast and Superstorm Sandy in the New York metro region were sharply criticized due to their overly bureaucratic nature and slow response. In our experience, it is fascinating to watch a federal program in a disaster area change the method of filing for emergency aid in the midst of the crisis. We know of several cases where the federal program requested certain paper documentation and forms for requesting aid, then requested resubmission using a new online system, during the follow-up to Superstorm Sandy. Homeowners, business owners, and local government needed help quickly to mitigate the impact of the disaster—but it was clear that the federal government and its agents were not rushing to move aid dollars out to the final recipients. In some cases, the federal agents were asking for documents and paperwork that were likely destroyed in the extensive flooding; yet these agencies were inflexible about alternative documentation that could have provided the same or similar information.

Yet how engaged are our citizens in providing guidance to our leaders? We hope that the citizens would provide a strong core of influence so that politicians would craft laws and policies that are reflective of the community values of our country. The record is mixed on this point. The founding fathers were clearly of the mind-set that the central government would not perform all functions of government; they instead would leave a significant role for the states in many matters.

The original perceived advantage of centralized political systems was that they were economy-based. The thinking is that government has the ability to unite markets, develop a uniform fair taxing system, fund defense, maintain foreign relations, and regulate commerce to ensure economic growth. Table 5.2 shows that since the Great Depression, the winner of the presidential election accumulated, on average, 30.74 percent of the *eligible* vote. The highest percentage attained was with Lyndon B. Johnson at 37.64 percent, and the lowest was with Eisenhower, at 25.03 percent.

Without the proper levels of interest, the minority vote can lead to majority rule. How is there accountability with this type of interest in Presidential elections? This allows concentration and targeted areas and causes one of the three D's to happen—the division discussed in Joe's previous book, *Detecting Fraud in Organizations* (Wiley). Once again, why is there no interest? We suggest that it may be because of the electoral vote system. If you live in a Democratic or Republican dominated state your vote only matters if you vote the party in control of that state. If you do not agree with the in-control candidate choice why vote? Where there is complacency, there is opportunity.

Is there true participation in the various programs that exist in the governmental entity? By applying Service Efforts and Accomplishments (SEA) reporting requirements you are removing complacency and developing

TABLE 5.2 Presidential Election Results, 1932–2012

Year	Democratic Candidate	Republican Candidate	% of registered voters who participated	Winners % of votes cast in election	Percentage the Winner has of Eligible Vote
1932	**Franklin S. Roosevelt**	Herbert Hoover	52.6%	59.2%	31.15%	0.5%
1936	**Franklin S. Roosevelt**	Alvred Landon	56.9%	62.4%	35.50%	0.6%
1940	**Franklin S. Roosevelt**	Wendall Wilkie	58.8%	54.9%	32.31%	0.6%
1944	**Franklin S. Roosevelt**	Thomas Dewey	56.1%	53.8%	30.17%	0.6%
1948	**Harry Truman**	Thomas Dewey	51.1%	52.3%	26.71%	0.5%
1952	Adlai Stevenson	**Dwight D. Eisenhower**	61.6%	55.4%	27.48%	0.6%
1956	Adlai Stevenson	**Dwight D. Eisenhower**	59.3%	57.8%	25.03%	0.6%
1960	**John F. Kennedy**	Richard Nixon	62.8%	50.1%	31.45%	0.6%
1964	**Lyndon B. Johnson**	Barry Goldwater	61.4%	61.3%	37.64%	0.6%
1968	Hubert Humphrey	**Richard Nixon**	60.7%	50.6%	29.96%	0.6%
1972	George McGovern	**Richard Nixon**	55.1%	61.8%	21.04%	0.6%
1976	**Jimmy Carter**	Gerald Ford	53.6%	51.1%	27.37%	0.5%
1980	George McGovern	**Ronald Regan**	52.8%	57.0%	22.71%	0.5%
1984	Walter Mondale	**Ronald Regan**	53.3%	60.4%	21.08%	0.5%
1988	Michael Dukakis	**George H. W. Bush**	50.3%	53.9%	23.18%	0.5%
1992	**Bill Clinton**	George H. W. Bush	55.2%	53.5%	29.51%	0.6%
1996	**Bill Clinton**	Robert Dole	49.0%	54.7%	26.79%	0.5%
2000	***Al Gore	**George W. Bush**	50.3%	**50.2%**	25.27%	0.5%
2004	John Kerry	**George W. Bush**	55.7%	51.4%	27.05%	0.6%
2008	**Barack Obama**	John McCain	57.1%	53.8%	30.70%	0.6%
2012	**Barack Obama**	Mitt Romney	57.5%	51.9%	29.86%	0.6%
				Average	28.19%	

Source: www.history.com/topics/us-presidents/presidential-elections

Source: US. Census Bureau, Statistical Abstract of the United States, 2012

accountability. Are there controls in place that ensure the funds are being properly disseminated to the interests they are designed to serve? When there is no interest, there will be waste.

There is no mandate when only one-third of eligible voters decide the person who sets the tone at the top. Establishing control requires majority agreement, an all-in buy in. Requiring 75 percent agreement establishes safeguards against waste and overspending. How often is there this degree of approval with regard to allowing debt to accrue to the current federal level of an estimated $18 trillion? Creating awareness and interest among the citizenry is the best way to safeguard government and public agency assets and ensure accountability.

The United States has 50 states, and each has its own governor, legislature, and judiciary branch. The idea is that each state serves as a smaller version of the federal system, with each branch empowered to develop its own state's laws which require all branches to be in agreement to become law. This concept has drastically changed as differences in opinions on how to deal with same-sex marriage, immigration, and a host of other conflicting situations have arisen. With the need for all levels of management (in this case governor, legislative, and judicial branches) to agree, the views of all interested parties are presented, which creates debate and skepticism. We have created balance.

With the idea that there are one-size-fits-all solutions, which is centralized thinking, the problem remains that the multiple levels of approval still exists. Depending on the makeup of the governing body, decentralization offers the flexibility to address infrequent and unusual transactions that are not planned. The State of New Jersey as an example breaks down into multiple layers of government—for example, New Jersey has 522 municipalities, 21 county governments, and 605 school districts. With each segregation the focus becomes broader based and dilutes the centralized power. In accounting we often break the revenues and expenditures into profit centers to better account and identify potential break downs and inefficiencies.

While some powers are reserved for the states and federal government, these overriding precedences become problematic in many areas. By diluting the powers of the state and allowing local decision making, it reduces the power at the centralized state government level and affords the local governmental unit the opportunity to solve the local issue. The advantage of a decentralized political system is that different problem-solving proactive approaches can be tried, which create higher levels of thinking and the potential for more effective solutions. As the power and choice is being spread out, the people closest to the issue at hand are looking for resolutions and more accountability to the interests that are directly being affected.

With the federal government's power to override state authority, the individual state's majority rule control is superseded. This is the mentality that the government at the federal level knows what is better for the state than the persons attempting to solve the problem at the state level. Often the federal direction comes without factoring in costs associated with these mandated decisions, not to mention that the state and local people's voice becomes muffled.

The concern with the idea of decentralized power is that this decentralization will create inefficiency. If that's the case, why does the federal government set up multiple locations across the nation to provide the same services in various areas? Does having 50 different centers of power actually create responsibility centers and thus greater accountability closer to home? Are similar functions being duplicated? One has to ask why. If the state creates programs which are under both federal and state administration, is that not a duplication of efforts and more red tape bureaucracy, leading to greater costs and more people that can be blamed? Different states have different types of crime and different needs—and policies should reflect those differences. Marijuana legalization is a great example of a social norm that varies among states and in terms of calls for local control as opposed to national policy. Allocating the federal resources to the states to administer is not decentralizing but, rather, centralizing at the point of value and the point at which the program and policy value is exposed. No matter what the thinking is at the time, these policies are created, and, whatever their lofty goals, we need to have well-informed elected leaders who represent the total voice of the citizenry and whom we can trust, in order to create a self-governing system to avoid waste.

Without interest, there can be no control. Unsuspecting people provide the best accountability with respect to creating efficiency. Whistle-blower hotlines, suggestion boxes, and the virtual checks and balances that come from people outside looking in constitute the next set of principles up for discussion with respect to establishing controls that lead to potential efficiency.

CENTRALIZATION VS DECENTRALIZATION OF GOVERNMENT/PUBLIC AGENCY INTERNAL ACCOUNTING CONTROL

Centralization is the concentration of decision making in the hands of a few. The concentration of the established internal controls is set by the people in power. All the important internal control decisions and actions are actually occurring at the lower levels of personnel. These actions occurring at the lower levels are subject to the approval of top management. The idea of centralization is that responsibility at a central point in the governmental or public agency unit can be systematically and consistently created. The problem with this thinking is that the decision-making power at the top level generally causes delays. The desire for the ultimate decision makes middle managers and the employees with the executing authority hesitate and wait for direction. The phrase *red tape* comes to mind, which means "an excessive bureaucracy" or "adherence to rules and formalities." This is especially common and well known in the governmental and/or public agency process. One could argue that governmental red tape is so bad today that when one approaches a local government to conduct a standard business function—say, open a factory—it is common to have an undetermined number of permits and forms to fill out, it will take an undetermined amount of time to complete the process, and it will cost an undefined amount of money. The red tape may also exist at multiple layers of government, and these layers might not coordinate policy—even in the same area of concern, for example, in environmental issues.

Keeping important and key decisions at the top management level and leaving the other levels dependent on those decisions to implement is not principle-based thinking. It's rule-based. For example, in a military transaction, the general knows that he has an opportunity to end the war by executing an action. He has the experience and has trained for this all his life, but he must call the president to execute the action. This means the president, or whoever is at the top, is making the decision. Split-second decisions can save lives. Split-second decisions can reduce costs. Leaving the decisions in the hands of the people performing the services, with well-defined policy, is the key to centralization. Centralization that relies on rules rather than believing that the people in the governmental or public entity unit will maintain integrity by being objective and independent is the real key to having efficiency and sound systems and structures. An ongoing daily checks-and-balances mentality at the service-performing level is the only assurance in establishing sound internal controls. Centralized, mandated, red-tape regulatory oversight thinking is not.

Putting the choice in the hands of the people executing, rather than those who think the few know more than the many at high levels of an organization, is being proactive and steers away from the need for reactive thinking. Two heads are always better than one. One should also consider proper audit review and controls of the people executing agency decisions to ensure compliance with policy and avoidance of corruption.

This idea of decentralization is achieved by systematically delegating authority at all levels of government and/or public agency management and in all functions of the organization. With decentralization comes the need to segregate duties, create mandatory vacation policies, make surprise and unannounced site visits, and utilize outside-looking-in perspectives. By creating these individualized values, there is greater accountability and less red tape. The public entity needs to create a preventative and more proactive approach by assigning the value points with well-defined and -communicated policies that hold people accountable. We need to solve problems at the levels in which they were created. We need to raise the level of thinking at these creation points of value where the risk exposures are created, if we are going to achieve the designed objectives of the taxpayers and users or public entity services.

In decentralization, the approvals are maintained at the point of service performed or objective obtained. Top management always retains the authority, as long as the people performing the approvals are trained and there is always open, transparent communication. Major decisions and framing policies concerning the whole problem should have been addressed well before the implementation of these services or actions. The delegated authority has the planned action and is executing accordingly. In fact, the delay in getting an approval adds potential bias and lessens the opportunity for management override. Human resources is the area within any organization that provides the best assurances that the people put in these trusted positions are qualified and best suited to handle the decisions. Remember POP (perspectives, occupations, and positions)—knowing these trusted people and the positions they are in with exposure to the value is critical in safeguarding the government and/or public agency assets.

Any determination of degree of centralization and decentralization depends upon first understanding the responsibility and the potential outcomes of poor decisions. This is part of the continued risk assessment to maintain proper operations. The lowest level of authority executing the policies needs well-communicated policies and procedures and a full understanding of the authority and the potential consequences. Basically, that 800-pound friendly gorilla oversight needs to be in place to create a sense that someone is watching.

Decentralization is the same as delegation. Complete decentralization can be achieved only when the moral and ethical standards of the people in the daily process are extremely high. When a Social Security application is processed, the manager of the area is responsible for approving the application for the whole of the concern. The manager delegates this work to the subordinate who is now responsible for approving the applicants. In this situation, delegation of authority has taken place; but, left unchecked and given to an employee who is not as qualified, this is a potential exposure to fraud. This is why the new thinking needs to be to gain an understanding of the personality behaviors of the people who are entrusted with authority

Refocusing that the lower-level delegated authority is not transferable and can be changed only by higher-level approval is maintaining centralized power thinking, and is a safeguard against low-level overrides. Job rotation and unannounced checks and balances are needed with decentralized operations. This idea of increasing the role of subordinates is at the core of decentralization policy, and that decreases the role of the centralized control. The delegation remains partial, with the managers from an accountability perspective still reporting on performance to the higher levels; however, it is expected that by the time review has occurred at the upper level, any fraud or mismanagement has already taken place. Technology, cameras, and other readily available deterrents can be put in place at these value points that create accountability. Decentralization and delegation are ways of life in any process and require developing people who are have high moral standards.

The benefit of decentralized thinking is that the focus is on principle-based thinking. The people performing the daily responsibilities are empowered and understand there are consequences attached to that responsibility. It is impossible for any person in power to be involved in every detail of all the action under his or her authority. This gives the people executing the daily responsibilities an opportunity to think and act independently. This is how true talent is developed. Imagine an athlete not able to act on instinct rather than design. The key components of a successful decentralization could be codified as follows.

Key Principles for Successful Decentralization:
- Effective communication.
- Formalized and documented procedures.
- Specific goals and objectives.
- A well-coordinated plan for implementation.
- Adequate training and staffing.
- The "Trust Responsibility and Persons" moral tone is well established via agency culture and is correct in terms of focus; it also must remain subject to checks and balances. Examine the "Tone at the Top."

The greater the responsibility and risk, the higher the level of established internal control required.

Numbers don't lie, people do. The best way to prevent lying is to develop talented people in decentralized positions who will make the right choices. It is this thinking in the development of systems and structures that prevents fraud and mismanagement. Rules are made to be broken and always will be. There needs to be people in place who are of high ethical standards in these trusted positions to counter that inevitable, unfortunate, bad thinking that continues to occur. People need to help others to not make bad choices by ensuring that they are not put in positions that create the opportunity for them to make those unfortunate choices and then have to deal with the extreme consequences as a result of their actions.

 ## MONEY AND POWER

One principle to consider is that of constant power. This idea boils down to two areas of thinking: money and people. Start considering the idea that although the money seems to be plentiful, it seems to be controlled by the few.

How Wealth Distribution Leads to Fraud

Wealth inequality can be best described as the unequal distribution of assets within a population. Unfortunately, in the United States inequality between the rich and the poor has widened more than in any other developed nation. In the United States, wealth is defined as net worth, which, in basic accounting terms, is assets less liabilities.

Assets typically include a personal residence, cash in savings accounts, investments in stocks and bonds, real estate, retirement accounts, collectibles, and more. Liabilities generally mean debt. Examples of liabilities are a mortgage loan, car loan, credit card balance, student loan, or any other debt that is owed and remains unpaid.

In the United States, wealth inequality is greater than income inequality. A good source for household wealth is the official U.S. source of data on household wealth distribution that is produced by the Federal Reserve's Survey of Consumer Finances (Figure 5.1).[21] This is an in-depth survey of the finances of American families that is conducted every three years. The latest federal survey results reflect data collected in 2013. In that data, the wealth share of America's top 3 percent, Fed researchers calculate, rose from 44.8 percent in 1989 to 51.8 percent in 2007 and 54.4 percent in 2013. This means that *the top 3 percent holds more than double the wealth of 90 percent of America's poorest families.*

The vast majority of American families (94.5 percent), in the latest Federal Reserve survey, showed some sort of financial asset (savings, checking, stocks,

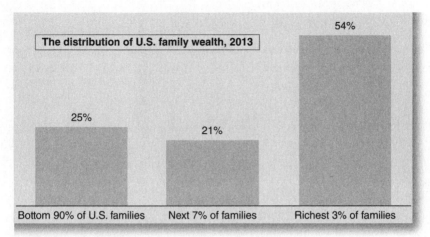

FIGURE 5.1 Distribution of U.S. family wealth, 2013
Source: Federal Reserve Board Survey of Consumer Finances, 2014

and cash-value life insurance policies) being held. But *significant* ownership of these financial assets has become more and more concentrated in the United States' richest 10 percent, which now holds nearly 85 percent of these assets. The Federal Reserve data shown in Figure 5.2 reflects the surveyed responses from households given the triennial Survey of Consumer Finances questionnaire.

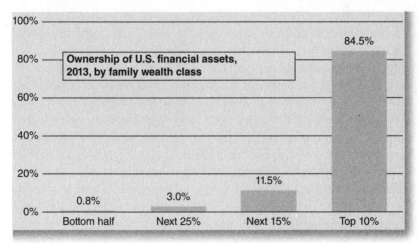

FIGURE 5.2 Ownership of U.S. financial assets, 2013, by family wealth class
Source: Federal Reserve Board Survey of Consumer Finances, 2014

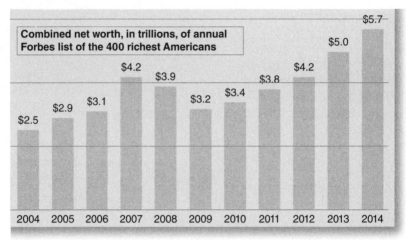

FIGURE 5.3 Combined net worth of annual Forbes list of 400 richest Americans (in trillions)
Source: *Forbes*, 2014

Statistics on the nation's 400 richest, according to *Forbes Magazine* (Figure 5.3), provide another indicator of wealth inequality in the United States. In 1982, *Forbes* began annually listing America's 400 richest people. To make the 2014 *Forbes* 400 list, one needed to have a net worth of at least $1.55 billion. This shows the widening disparity in net worth.

The division of wealth, revealed in a Pew Research Center analysis of Federal Reserve Survey of Consumer Finances data (Figure 5.4), showed a further widening in the longstanding racial and ethnic wealth divide in the United States. The typical white family held a net worth six times greater than the typical black family at the end of the twentieth century. That gap has now doubled. The wealth gap between white and Hispanic households has widened as well.

Unfortunately, income inequality can worsen wealth inequality. The reason is that the income people have available to save and invest (disposable income) is being eaten up by rising health care costs, people living longer, and other everyday necessity spending. "Focusing on private income, such as earnings and dividends, plus cash government benefits, we see that families near the top had a 70 percent increase in income from 1963 to 2013, while the income of families at the bottom stayed roughly the same."[22]

An article by Priceillusion.com[23] says it is important that the numbers be reflective of the current economics. When sampling is used we are attempting

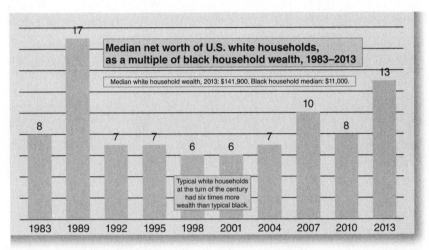

FIGURE 5.4 Median net worth of U.S. white households, as a multiple of black household wealth, 1983–2013
Median white household wealth, 2013: $141,900; black household median: $11,000. Typical white households at the turn of the century had six times more wealth than typical black ones.
Source: Pew Research Center analysis of Survey of Consumer Finances data, December 2014

to determine individual risks by testing the data. As we have previously stated, data involved in a sampling or any matter can be manipulated. Understand, that if we change the variable in a sample the result will change, and this should call into question why the need to change a specific variable took place. Let's apply the same sampling mentality to determine economic indicators like the Consumer Price Index (CPI). It seems the government changes the items that go into the calculation. It's called the "basket." The CPI formula:[24] The CPI is calculated by collecting the prices of a *sample* of representative items over a specific period of time.

- The CPI can be used to index the *real value of wages, salaries, pensions, and price regulation*. Note: It is one of the most closely watched national economic statistics.
- The equation to calculate a price index using a single item is:

$$\text{Current CPI} = \text{Current item price} \times \text{Base year price}$$

$$\times \ (\text{Current CPI} \div \text{Base year CPI})$$

■ The equation for calculating the CPI for multiple items is:

CPI for multiple items = (Cost of CPI market basket at current

period prices ÷ Cost of CPI market basket at

base period prices × 100)

These calculations are used to determine real salary and wages. What if they are incorrect or manipulated? Do they result in stock market crashes, people losing homes, and accumulation of debt leading to insolvency? Understanding the formulas and the numbers behind the formulas, and the people gathering the data, are key elements in giving the decision makers the necessary information to make proper decisions. This is real control. Is .006 percent a good sample?

Peters, King, Gordon, and Santiago in their 2015 paper, "For Whom the CPI Tolls: Reporting of Road Pricing in the Consumer Expenditure Survey," explored the data limitation and analysis issues that surround the CPI market basket as it is developed to estimate household expenditures. The Bureau of Labor Statistics collects data on household expenditures using the Consumer Expenditures Survey (CEX). With 124,412,000 households in the United States in 2012, one wonders how large a sample is necessary to accurately reflect the portfolio of goods that households purchase on a regular basis. The CEX surveys between 6,000 to 7,000 households on a quarterly basis. The BLS data records household expenditures in over 1,800 categories—from cemetery plots to laundry detergent to canned corn to downloading video expenses. These consumption weights are then used in calculating the CPI market basket. Any limitations in the collection of this data would alter the weight of goods that are used in the CPI—and thus the overall level of price changes. If an expenditure is not reported reliably in the BLS CEX data, then it would not be reflected reliably in the CPI.

Hiding behind numbers and not truly understanding what the numbers indicate is allowing mismanagement and fraud to continue to exist. The fact that rating agencies missed Enron and did not catch the subprime lending crisis shows that statistics and formulas are subject to judgment and are only as good as the people who are supplying the variables needed to determine the results. Just ask Bernard Madoff's victims about the magic formula for returns no one else was getting at the time but, somehow, his formula was able to achieve. The world needs to be seen beyond the numbers.

The amount of money that households have available for spending and saving after income taxes have been accounted for is disposable income. It is

TABLE 5.3 Food Plan for a Family of Four, per Week

	2003	2013	Average annual increase
Thrifty-cost plan	$108	$146	3.5%
Low-cost plan	$139	$191	3.7%
Moderate-cost plan	$173	$239	3.8%
Liberal plan	$208	$289	3.9%

the only economic indicator that matters. Disposable personal income is used in monitoring many key economic indicators that are in turn used to gauge the overall state of the economy. Is the economic measure the real numbers, or is it what people want to hear? There are numerous economic indicators that are used to define the state of the economy or economic conditions. Some of these indicators are the unemployment rate, levels of current account and budget surpluses or deficits, GDP growth rates, and inflation rates. This economic data is released on a regular basis, typically weekly, monthly, and, sometimes, quarterly. The unemployment rate and GDP growth rate are watched closely by market investors, as they can help to make an overall assessment of current economic conditions.

A *USA Today* article[25] reports that the U.S. Department of Agriculture numbers show food costs have gone up (Table 5.3).

The cost of each plan increased by an annual average of at least 3.5 percent; the cost of food in general went up 3.2 percent per year. During the same time period, *inflation averaged about 2.6 percent per year*. These two items alone are eating into disposable income. The real measure is what people can afford to spend. Government and its public agencies are learning that taxes, and other mandated necessities (insurance, shelter, gasoline, etc.) are now impacting what people can afford to pay. Another example is toll fares, which are now rising to unsustainable levels for the average person. People faced with having capped salaries and wages are being asked to spend more on everyday necessities, with corresponding increases in income to offset. What happened to disposal income when a necessity like fuel cost rose in the past? Let history be a great lesson.

How Donations Can Lead to Fraud

Government and the public agency rely on appealing to the people, which often revolves around monetary and economic considerations—what we have mentioned as the cost/benefit analysis and what are the real dollars that the people funding these policies have available. We, therefore, call this principle "Money and people": Where money goes, people often follow or, better yet, get what they want. In a capitalistic society, the signature chorus of a song in the musical *Cabaret*, "Money makes the world go round," is the fuel formula for a political person getting elected. Take any campaign and follow the money: from special interest groups to people looking for jobs, and, essentially, people wanting something under the "good for humanity" banner.

According to a *Business Insider* article, Barack Obama indicated in his 2004 financial statements that he had three sources of income.[26] One was an $80,287 salary for being an Illinois state senator. Another was a $32,144 salary from the University of Chicago Law School, where Obama was a lecturer while he was in the statehouse. The third was Michelle Obama's salary from the University of Chicago Hospitals, where she was an administrator.

The same article reports that Obama said in 2006 that he got $147,490 for his book *Dreams from My Father,* and $425,000 from Random House for *The Audacity of Hope*. In 2007, as his presidential run made him a household name, book sales skyrocketed; he then got $815,971 for *Dreams* and $3.28 million for *Audacity*. When there is this much value available to the people put in office, the incentive develops to return favors to the people who raised the necessary funding to get the person elected. Greed remains the main component of mismanagement and fraud. Why is the president not required to return the funds to the taxpayers from the sale of the book, as his salary as president is paid by the taxpayers? If you're paid by a company and invent a formula, it's the company's formula. Much of the reason for buying his book is a result of the popularity of being the president. The criminal who writes a book has to give the proceeds from the book and any related movie based on it to the victim of his or her crime. Where there is this much money and power, it is easy to see the potential for fraud.

Is the presidency up for sale? A 2015 article in *The Hill* estimated that $5 billion would be spent on the 2016 presidential campaign.[27] Many countries do not even have a $5 billion gross domestic product. In raising that kind of money, there will often be strings attached. With that type of money, the net worth and wealth concentration, the unions, and other interest groups recognize the fund-raising needs to get the person elected. This is where monitoring measures need to be in place. Who really has the power? When was the last time any substantive action resulted from a probe into the contributions to the presidential campaign? When was the last time there was an IRS audit of the significant donors focused on where the political contributions were reflected in the financial statements or on the tax returns filed.

Politically active nonprofits—principally 501(c)(4)s and 501(c)(6)s—have become a major force in federal elections. The term "**dark money**" is often applied to this category of political spending because these groups do not generally have to disclose the sources of their funding. There are instances where a minority does disclose some or all of their donors, but it is by choice or in response to a specific request. This enables these organizations to receive unlimited corporate, individual, or union contributions that they do not have to make public, and though their political activity is supposed to be limited, the IRS—which has jurisdiction over these groups—by and large has done little to enforce those limits. Again, who is the fraudster? Is it the elected official benefitting? The failed rules that prevent the manipulations? Or is it the IRS who can come after a small business owner but look the other way when it comes to enforcing the limits?

Examining election reports at the federal and state levels is following the money, and is a useful tool to see where the funds are being raised. Understanding the revenue, whether political contributions, taxes collected, and so on, can yield beneficial information in your fact-finding examination.

Every state prohibits bribery as a means to obtain government contracts. There are only a few states that restrict campaign contributions from businesses seeking government contracts. Why is there not an executive order requiring federal contractors to disclose their political spending?

A June 23, 2015, letter from the House of Representatives[28] urged President Obama to execute his 2011 order entitled "Disclosure of Political Spending by Government Contractors." The order requires all federal contractors to disclose political contributions. It also addresses concerns with respect to funneling campaign contribution money through nonprofit entities. It also states that, based on the analysis by Public Citizen, less than half of all corporations fully disclose their contributions to 501(c)(4)s—social welfare organizations. In order for a social welfare organization, described in Internal Revenue Code (IRC) section 501(c)(4), not to be taxed, the organization must not be organized for profit and must be operated exclusively to promote social welfare. These groups are allowed to participate in politics as long as it does not become their primary focus.

President Obama's campaign operation, Obama for America, turned into Organizing for Action after the 2012 election. These organizations typically have multiple arms including nonprofit and super PAC affiliations. These 501(c) nonprofit groups are not required to disclose their donors. The groups are spending money on independent expenditures and electioneering communications by using funds from undisclosed donors.

New Jersey has a strong pay-to-play law:

P.L. 2005, c. 51 (codified as N.J.S.A. 19:44A-20.13 et seq.) and Executive Order 117 Since October 14, 2004, pursuant to P.L. 2005, c.51, the State (or any of its purchasing agents, agencies or independent authorities) is generally prohibited from awarding a contract for goods, services or for the sale, acquisition or lease of land or buildings worth more than $17,500 to "business entity" that has made certain "reportable" political contributions. Election law defines a reportable contribution as a contribution greater than $300 per election in the case of a contribution to a candidate committee (e.g. greater than $300 for a primary election and greater than $300 for a general election) and greater than $300 per calendar year in the case of a contribution to a party committee, legislative leadership committee or continuing political committee.[29]

"Wheeling" is the practice of redirecting large sums of campaign money from wealthy political sources through an intermediary that funnels it to a targeted political purpose. In New Jersey, leadership PACs, created in 1993, allow each party's leader in the state senate and assembly to operate a political action committee (PAC) that can receive contributions up to $25,000 from a single source. That's 10 times the maximum allowable contribution for an individual candidate. These same PACs can make unlimited contributions to candidates and party organizations. Leadership PACs concentrate enormous power in a few hands, with absolute control over the legislative agenda, reducing the role of individual legislators.

Do contributions buy results? Do contractors/vendors see this as a cost of doing business? Is there a difference between a bribe and a campaign contribution, except that a bribe is deemed by law to be illegal? Are political contributions made because over the years it was learned that not making them would result in potential loss in revenue?

Connecting political affiliations is like connecting dots—they serve as potential conflicts of interests. Understanding these potential conflicts that may involve family, friends, and political affiliation removes bias and creates independence when transparent. The fact remains that there was a failure to disclose and, without transparency, fraud and mismanagement will continue to exist.

Open Secrets, a website[30] that lists top donors, yields interesting information but nothing surprising. Under the category All Election Cycles, the number one contributor was Service Employees International Unions, with 99 percent of the contributions going to Democrats and liberals. In the top 50, Blue Cross Blue Shield is at number 43, with 66 percent of the contributions going to Republicans and conservatives. And Goldman Sachs is at number 22, with 76 percent going to Republicans and conservatives. Monitoring these potential external influences is always a critical area of focus in a forensic accountant examination. Applying this same thinking about external influence by the public is creating professional skepticism and is the interest that is needed to create accountability and ensure the greater good is served. It is important in understanding needs. Why are these industries contributing? What are they asking for? Which legislation has changed? Recent Dodd-Frank banking legislation, the Affordable Care Act, the repeal of the Glass-Steagall Act, deregulation of energy, and many other examples, were all thought of as means to better serve the public good. The fraudsters used them to create a financial crisis centered around subprime mortgage lending, the Enron scam, and a host of other fraud scams, which can be tied to similar political regulatory decisions. Health care costs are going up. Where are the Republicans asking Blue Cross why? Is it because Blue Cross is a campaign fund provider to the Republican Party? These potential conflicts are examples of what must be examined closely.

Media, legislators, and presidents all have one thing in common—the realization that money is needed to operate. These are the things in the public entity that are not going to be found on the balance sheet, because they are external, intangible influences. Auditors do not audit these types of intangible influences.

Political Principles to Prevent Fraud

The next principle is the "Never underestimate the enemy" principle. Keep the enemy from allowing irrelevant arguments to create uncertainty, insecurity, and panic, which are necessary to create a smokescreen of confusion that sidetracks the thinking and can lead to fraud and mismanagement. Often, it is very difficult to detect who the enemy really is, whether due to internal or external pressures and demands. As the famous quote from the movie *The Godfather* goes, "Keep your friends close, but your enemies closer."

Wherever competing forces are combined with competing interests, conflicting perspectives can breed. Being able to create balance among these competing interests often leads to dissent as a win-win situation for all interests cannot be achieved. Maintain credibility by showing enemies that you are living up to the same commitments that they are alleging you failed to achieve. Do not avoid issues, face them head on.

This leads to the next principle: the "Find me a solution, don't restate the problem" principle. Clichés like "I told you so" or "Monday morning quarterback" capture this tendency. In the world of government and the public agency, with everyone looking to advance self-interests, it should be a required rule that every time a problem is aired and complained about, there is a solution proposed to remedy it. There is no greater distraction than creating sound-bite politics or economics.

This leads to the next principle: the "sound bite" principle used to ruin reputations, filibuster bills, lobby for other interests, and cause division. These sound bites are often completely open-ended; they are typical political cheerleading types of quotes. The opposing factions always know how to advance their self-interests, playing to the prospective audiences. Understanding the voter interest in presidential elections or a specific group interest enables you to see the base they are targeting. Fraudsters understand this and use it to gain value or create value for their own benefit. Fraudsters target or redline selected interests, which causes divisions that can lead to wars, hate, and mistrust in government, but for them, these are diversions that they can use to convert value for their own selfish interests. The tax imposed on tea started the Revolutionary War. It is when citizenry feels rules are not fair that we see the necessary interest and develop the majority needed to effectuate change. What is the next issue that will be needed to bring the water to a boil to establish effective control? Are inefficient programs and fraud uncovered only when interest brings the water to a boil? Proactive thinking is critical in developing systems and procedures that create balance. What we do not want to happen is action based solely on public interest or outrage. An effective monitoring system avoids fraud and mismanagement before the water boils. Examine the sound bites surrounding the value points, and if they are too good to be true, then be skeptical.

To do this, another principle needs to be applied: "Matching the expertise with the need." In accounting there is the general standard rule 201, which requires that an accountant show due professional care, adequate planning and supervision, demonstrate professional competence, and maintain sufficient documentation (evidence). Without the government and/or public agency developing similar thinking, mismanagement and fraud will continue to exist. A level of professional skepticism needs to be reestablished in these policies. Nothing replaces skepticism in creating accountability.

Successful matching of responsibility with proper levels of trust at the points of the created value is a catalyst to efficiency and, ultimately, to preventing fraud and mismanagement.

The final principle is the "Polarize principle" or the melting pot dispersion, the Crayola crayons of all colors rather than blended as one. The single divisor at the root of many failures is this polarization concept. Webster's online definition of *polarization* is: " … to cause (people, opinions, etc.) to separate into opposing groups"; the definition in physics is "to cause (something) to have positive and negative charges: to give polarity to (something)." At a very early age, we learn the concept of winning versus losing, who is wealthy versus poor, classifications like honors student versus underachiever and stereotypical thinking. These types of divisive thinkings develop the elements necessary to distract, divert, and divide and weaken majority approval.

 ## HEALTH CARE DIVERSION

Talk about a polarizing, hold-the-gun-to-the-head kind of policy, think of health care. You must have insurance. You must pay said amount to get care. The different prices for different people in different areas demonstrates inconsistently applied standards, which has the potential to lead to fraud and mismanagement. People are afraid and confused. Never underestimate their potential enemies. Insurance companies are not anyone's friend.

In January 2015, "UnitedHealth Group, the largest health insurer, reported ... that it made $10.3 billion in profits in 2014 on revenues of $130.5 billion. Both profits and revenues grew seven percent from 2013. United impressed Wall Street so much that investors pushed its share price to an all-time high," according to Publicintegrity.org.[31]

According to *Consumer Reports*, "Person for person, health care in the U.S. costs about twice as much as it does in the rest of the developed world. In fact, if our $3 trillion health care sector were its own country, it would be the world's fifth-largest economy."[32] A simple look at the cost of health insurance versus the salary increases over the past ten years shows the disparity. Read any public contract negotiation. There is always a need and requirement for employees to contribute to health care. "Since 2000, incomes have barely kept up with inflation and insurance premiums have more than doubled. The average employer family health plan that cost companies $6,438 per staffer in 2000 shot up to $16,351 by 2013."[33]

Earlier in this chapter, we referred to Saul Alinsky's books *Rules for Radicals* and *Reveille for Radicals*[34] in conjunction with the idea that there are eight levels of control in creating a social state. Look at them as diversionary tactics to cause distractions. According to the National Health Statistics Group, in 2013 national health care expenditures (NHE) grew 3.6 percent to $2.9 trillion,[35] or $9,255 per person, and accounted for 17.4 percent of gross domestic product (GDP). It's scary that a significant cost of living to safeguard against getting sick or providing medical care when sick is taking away income for other necessities. The "average deductibles rose from $518 in 2003 to $1,025 in 2010 and

$1,273 in 2013. Deductibles comprised 2 percent of median income in 2003, rising to 4 percent in 2010 and 5 percent in 2013," reports *U.S. News*.[36] With more out-of-pocket expenses and rising costs, once again the potential for abuse and mismanagement is ramped up.

Just a few examples show that when there is a lot of value, profit, and centralized power, that creates monopolistic thinking. We begin hearing about the record profits and stock prices achieved by UnitedHealth and others in the insurance industry—the Wall Street influence effect. American International Group (AIG) "reported a 5.7% increase in net income for the nine months ending Sept. 30, to $10.61 billion. For the third quarter, the insurer reported a 142.1% increase in net income, to $4.22 billion,"[37] according to *Business Insurance* in a story dated November 9, 2006, just prior to the collapse in the financial markets and the ensuing bailout.

Where is the Dodd-Frank Wall Street Reform and Consumer Protection Act type of legislation for insurance that the banking industry is enduring? This is needed to control insurance profits, commissions, and bonuses to safeguard the public interest. Hopefully, such controls would create better competition as well as keep the cost of insurance down for the public. These sorts of selective regulatory standards are what breed the opportunity for mismanagement and fraud. We regulate the mortgage industry, why not the insurance industry to the same extent? It is such inconsistencies in policies that create the potential for fraud and mismanagement. Look at the fraud in the health care industry. Apply the health care cost to the public entity and public employee. It's not hard to see that there is a lot of value with a lot of people who have access to that value. This is the sort of environment that is ripe for the thriving of greed.

According to a review by a Tennessee law firm, "Healthcare fraud continues to roil the industry, as a steady stream of doctors, practice owners, suppliers and even executives are charged weekly with ripping off patients and payers alike. In 2014, the federal government recovered nearly $5.7 billion in healthcare fraud cases, up $1.9 billion from the prior fiscal year. Of that amount, $2.3 billion was tied to healthcare fraud against the federal government."[38]

Typical Health Care Frauds

The following are examples of the types of scams that plague society through application of the Saul Principles, whereby health care can effectuate control over society as it is accepted as a necessity and required by federal law.

Services are not performed but are billed. This scheme is common not only in health care fraud but in all areas of services, and there's no better target than the public servers of good that are put in place to serve the interests of their constituency, whoever that may be. In this scheme, the medical provider or its facility submits claim forms to government health care plans and/or insurance companies for services and care that were never provided and for which the corresponding patient files have no supporting documentation. The self-insured governmental agency is a prime target for duplicate payments, insuring people who are no longer employed, double insuring, and, of course, getting billed for services not performed. The failure to require the governmental or public agency to operate like an enterprise fund or internal fund and develop operating profits and losses and full accrual of all liabilities creates the perfect scenario for burying the ills of the past, hiding funds, raising budgets, and blaming it on employees and the cost of health care. These legal accounting diversions create perfect sound-bite principles to justify raising taxes and generating revenues. "We didn't have to reserve, we didn't have to accrue," should be replaced with what's responsible and not merely what is required by rules and regulations. A bit of planning and supervision, some extra dates and codes on the claim forms, and there is the creation of value the fraudster is looking to fabricate. Take away the fraudster and call it just a government employee not paying attention, and there's, at a minimum, waste and mismanagement.

Another scam is when the **services are not covered** or **are billed under an incorrect diagnosis**. All it takes is a few strokes of a pen or taps on a keyboard, and the doctor submits claim forms and still gets paid for the treatment that was not covered or for a treatment that reimburses more money. This can be accomplished by coding the service as something other than what was actually performed, something that is covered by insurance plans and policies or that generates a higher reimbursable amount.

Insurance is built on billing as much as one can and seeing what the insurance company will pay. If anyone else inflates bills for services, it's called mail fraud or wire fraud—just ask Tom Cruise's character in the movie *The Firm*. "Mitch McDeere" claimed that by mailing the falsely inflated legal bills to clients, his prestigious firm committed mail fraud and he exposed them to RICO charges. When the industry sets the thinking that it is okay to bill amounts in excess of what we expect will be paid, the opportunity for fraud is created. Why not bill, knowing what the actual charges are so that manipulations and adjustments are not required. "Let's bill and see what we get paid" is the exact type of thinking the fraudster needs to gain access to the value and divert it. How is it possible to control these types of fraud? Insurance companies are reducing reimbursements and denying coverage, and people wonder why fraud and mismanagement continue to occur. It comes down to the need for well-defined policies and procedures.

Another potential breeding ground for abuse is found in the ACFE's 2013 Fraud Examiners Manual. It showed that a correctly billed procedure for a hysterectomy would cost $1,300. If that medical provider were to unbundle that procedure, it might charge the $1,300 plus $950 for removal of ovaries and fallopian tubes, $671 for the exploration of the abdomen, $250 for an appendectomy, and $550 for "lysis of adhesions"—for a total of $3,721 (not to mention anesthesiology and lab costs). Once again, these conflicting methodologies can be synced and righted only by creating consistent, deviation-free, agreed-upon procedures.

Add to these examples the patient's mind-set, which is to feel better, and the added stress of how much that patient will have to pay out of his or her own pocket for the services. As long as the insurance companies are paying the bill, plenty of rationalizations and justifications are going to take place.

Providers may also **manipulate the date and extent (or overuse and misuse) of services provided**. Add an extra date, and a doctor's appointment becomes another, separate billable event. When this happens, the services indicated on the claim forms will be correct, but the dates of service will be false. Overuse and misuse of services involve billing for services that aren't really necessary. Unneeded tests and exams can go on indefinitely, or at least as long as a patient still has coverage or is able to make payments. Alcohol and drug rehabilitation facilities are ripe for such overuse. A staggering statistic from the U.S. National Survey on Drug Use and Health in 2011 showed that "21.6 million persons aged 12 or older needed treatment for an illicit drug or alcohol use problem (8.4 percent of persons aged 12 or older). Of these, 2.3 million (0.9 percent of persons aged 12 or older and 10.8 percent of those who needed treatment) received treatment at a specialty facility."[39] Obviously, there is a lot of potential for fraud in this area. When these types of diversionary events surround treatment, a high level of professional skepticism needs to be applied. In mental health treatment, careful scrutiny also needs to be applied so that the people who really need the treatment are afforded the opportunity.

Where the patient goes for the services is also often misrepresented: home visits versus a clinic; the number of times the services were performed at a location; billing for services when the doctor is not even at that location.

In the movie *Catch Me If You Can*, Leonardo DiCaprio's character posed as a doctor. Believe it or not, **people impersonate physicians and bill for treatment**. It does happen. Medical doctors sign insurance claim forms showing that they had provided all the care, but, in reality, less-qualified professionals administered the procedures. In these cases, the insurance companies would have paid less for the less-qualified medical professional, assuming he or she maintained the appropriate credentials. Some care facilities hire people to be therapists or other medical professionals who have never been trained to provide those services. A part-time doctor can come in a few days a week to review treatment files and sign claim forms under the assumption that he or she is the supervising physician, or it's someone else's responsibility, such as the owners of the facility.

Not collecting deductibles or copayments is another problem. Most government health care plans and insurance companies don't allow medical providers or facilities to waive patients' deductibles or copayments. But they're prohibitive costs, blocking the path to getting needed care, for some. The thinking behind copayments and deductibles is that if patients have to pay something to see doctors, they may not seek the care. Think of it the other way. How many people who might need care don't get it because of the deductible and/or copay cost and end up with a snowballing medical issue and more cost in the end? Neglect of a medical issue because the copay and/or deductible is unaffordable only leads to more medical care and expense incurred at a later date for a bigger, untended problem. The rationalization for providers to not collect the costs might be that they are helping the patient. It's shortsighted thinking, as someone ultimately pays.

As with any industry, the potential for corruption in health care is great. Providers have been known to unlawfully pay for and/or receive **payment for referrals**. The illegitimate referrals are made for services that aren't even needed, such as X-rays, MRIs, or prescription drugs. To establish that a bribery/kickback scheme is under way, quid pro quo ("this for that") must be established. However, remember the rule: Only a judge and jury can find someone guilty. Remain the fact finder. Substantiating that the provider paid or received something of value in return for referrals boils down to intent and is not easy to prove. These kickbacks or bribes are often hidden or masked in the form of luxury vacations, discounts on facility rentals, or hidden gifts, as compared to a check or cash being given under the table.

One of the biggest areas where this has been seen is prescription drugs and the rising addictions associated with them. The drugs being prescribed by the physician are not always used for their intended purpose. Worse than that are illicit prescription providers who write scripts for profit rather than for medical purposes. Supporting the concern is a report entitled "Under the Counter: The Diversion and Abuse of Controlled Prescription Drugs in the U.S.," a 2005 analysis by the National Center on Addiction and Substance Abuse (CASA) at Columbia University. According to this report, the number of U.S. citizens who abuse controlled substance prescription drugs nearly doubled, from 7.8 million to 15.1 million in 11 years, from 1992 to 2003. Painkillers are the most commonly abused prescription. The street value of these drugs is almost 10 times the legal prescription value.

Patients "doctor shop" to obtain drug prescription painkillers. The doctors usually have no idea that the patients have already visited other physicians to obtain the same or other drugs. Fraudsters can easily recover the cost of the doctors' visits and filling of prescriptions by selling some or all of the drugs on the street. One can make pen-and-ink changes to the quantity and/or authorized refill numbers on the paper prescriptions. Using electronic prescriptions from providers to pharmacists will mitigate this fraud.

According to the CASA report, 28.4 percent of pharmacists surveyed reported that they didn't regularly validate the prescribing physicians' DEA numbers (assigned to them by the U.S. Drug Enforcement Administration, which permits them to prescribe drugs) before dispensing controlled drugs, and one in 10 pharmacists rarely or never did.

Daraprim is a 62-year-old drug that is the standard of care for treating a life-threatening parasitic infection. It "was acquired in August [2015] by Turing Pharmaceuticals, a start-up run by a former hedge fund manager. Turing immediately raised the price to $750 a tablet from $13.50, bringing the annual cost of treatment for some patients to hundreds of thousands of dollars."[40]

A fraudster can simply include a few low-dollar false billings on several different patient claim forms to stay under the radar: 200 false prescription claims at $50 each often will get less scrutiny than one false claim for $10,000. Don't dismiss small-dollar claims listed under individual patient names, because they could be part of a much-higher-dollar fraud scheme.

A dishonest pharmacist could also change the quantity listed on legitimately received prescriptions for painkillers (or other drugs), easily manipulate the patients' paperwork and receipts, or make the copayments. The possible schemes are endless.

When drug price ranges can jump from $13.50 to $750 on a 62-year-old drug, when there are different prices for different plan participants and patients, allowing billings to be significantly **written down** for what's been billed, it's a recipe for fraud and mismanagement.

Almost every aspect of the health care field is overseen by one regulatory body or another, and sometimes by several, yet fraud and mismanagement continue. Until there are consistent policies and procedures and they are applied to everyone equally, costs will continue to rise. To the government/public entity, these costs, along with pensions and other benefits, are what have driven tax increases and reduced other needed services to balance budgets. The Saul

Principles point to the impact on society and the importance of understanding the prospection surrounding the value and ensuring that there are adequate systems and controls in place.

IMPROPER PAYMENTS

The following examples of inappropriate and unnecessary spending are presented to help the reader gaining an understanding of where the systems and structures are necessary. With any payment, there is a required process. Without controlled oversight and specific accountability, these types of improper payment fraud will continue to occur.

According to a *Federal Times* story, a GAO report found that "the federal government racked up more than $124 billion in improper payments in 2014, $19 billion above the previous year. Washington spends $25 billion annually maintaining unused or vacant federal properties."[41] According to the same article, Medicare, Medicaid, and Earned Income Tax Credit programs accounted for 75 percent of improper payments across the federal government. Compliance is a key area of controlling this type of spending. The article further stated that since 2003, the GAO estimated that $1 trillion in federal funding has been lost throughout the federal government.

MEALS AND ENTERTAINMENT: DIRECTLY CONNECTED TO A PUBLIC ENTITY'S OPERATIONS

It is interesting that Section 162(a) of the Internal Revenue Code defines "business expenses" as the "ordinary and necessary" expenses of carrying on a trade or business. Business expenses are usually tax deductible. However, the IRS does not provide a detailed collection of generally accepted business expenses, leaving it up to the taxpayer to decide from its definable criteria between ordinary and necessary. In fact, the terms *ordinary* and *necessary* were not defined in the original statute establishing the Internal Revenue Code, leaving it to the tax courts to establish their meanings through case law. Again, a key word that creates the conflict is *judgment*. What one may think is ordinary and necessary may be different from another's definition. The key words associated with the term *necessary* are *convenient, useful, essential, appropriate,* and *helpful,* while those associated with the term *ordinary* are *habitual, normal, usual, customary, common, accepted,* and *expected.* The facts and circumstances surrounding the transaction, the intention of the taxpayer, as well as the degree of the ordinariness and necessity of the transaction in carrying on one's business or trade are all involved in the determination of whether an expense is ordinary and/or necessary. These same standards are applied in public entities' policies and processes to prevent inappropriate payments.

From the IRS rules, for the meals and entertainment to be considered directly connected to business purpose, the meal or entertainment event must meet several conditions:

■ It must have been scheduled with more than a general expectation of deriving future income or a specific business benefit from the event. In other words, a meal or dinner date arranged for general goodwill purposes does not qualify.
■ A business meeting, negotiation, or transaction must actually occur during the meal or entertainment, or immediately preceding and following it. In other words, business actually must be discussed.
■ The main character of the event, considering the facts and circumstances, is the active conduct of the company's trade or business.
■ The business owner or one of the supervising employees must be in attendance. It is not possible to give away tickets to an event or money for meals and still claim a tax deduction.

Expenses incurred by an employee who treats a client to a golf game in order to discuss the general parameters of a business deal in an informal atmosphere and who engages in conversation directly connected to the business may *qualify as partially tax deductible* if documentation requirements are met. Similarly, a manager who discusses sensitive business plans with a subordinate employee over lunch at an off-premises restaurant may also be partially tax deductible.

Applicable Limitations

Reasonable travel and lodging expenses associated with a business purpose are fully deductible. Only 50 percent of expenses incurred for meals and entertainment are deductible (including while traveling), and must be properly documented. A limited exception applies to entertainment or on-premises meals provided to employees. Travel, lodging, meals, and entertainment expenses for family members are not deductible. For tracking purposes, it is advisable to separate travel and entertainment expenses into three buckets:

those that are fully deductible, those that are 50 percent deductible, and those that are not deductible for tax purposes.

There is also an optional per diem allowance method, in lieu of the actual cost method, for lodging, meals, and incidental expenses while traveling away from home for work related matters. The IRS regularly publishes per diem rates for certain locations inside and outside the United States. The IRS also publishes standard mileage rates that may be applied to work-related auto travel.

Expenses with respect to entertainment facilities are not deductible at all. Country club dues are not deductible, although the meals purchased with business clients at the club are, up to the 50 percent limitation. Deductions for tickets or luxury boxes at entertainment or sporting events are limited to the face value of a non-luxury box seat ticket, plus contemporaneously prepared documentation must be kept showing compliance with the meals and entertainment and record-keeping rules.

Record-Keeping Requirements

Even if a meal or entertainment expense qualifies as a business expense, none of the cost is deductible unless strict and detailed substantiation and record-keeping requirements are met. Some relief is available due to the tax law that waives the otherwise rigorous substantiation rules when a particular expense is below a certain minimum dollar level. Simply put, the public employees don't technically need receipts for non-lodging expenses under $75 that are reimbursed by their employers. Although this is a big break, it doesn't mean that all record keeping can be ignored. Receipts are still needed for all lodging expenses (even if the cost is under $75), unless the public entity pays traveling employees the IRS-approved per diem rate. Those incurring the expenses must record the

- time
- place
- persons in attendance (including business title)
- business reason
- amount

of each travel expense, including lodging, meal, and entertainment expenditures. If a per diem is used, amounts don't have to be recorded at all. Businesses should note that an expense for more than $75 unaccompanied by a receipt does not receive a $74.99 deduction by default; an IRS examiner will treat such unsubstantiated expense as $0.00 instead.

CHURCHES AND POLITICAL CAMPAIGN ACTIVITY

Churches and other nonprofits are strictly prohibited from engaging in political campaigning. This prohibition stems from the requirements of Section 501(c)(3) of the Internal Revenue Code. This is directly from the IRS website:

> In general, no organization may qualify for section 501(c)(3) status if a substantial part of its activities is attempting to influence legislation (commonly known as lobbying). A 501(c)(3) organization may engage in some lobbying, but too much lobbying activity risks loss of tax-exempt status.
>
> For this purpose, legislation includes action by Congress, any state legislature, any local council, or similar governing body, with respect to acts, bills, resolutions, or similar items (such as legislative confirmation of appointive office), or by the public in referendum, ballot initiative, constitutional amendment, or similar procedure. It does not include actions by executive, judicial, or administrative bodies.
>
> An organization will be regarded as attempting to influence legislation if it contacts, or urges the public to contact, members or employees of a legislative body for the purpose of proposing, supporting, or opposing legislation, or if the organization advocates the adoption or rejection of legislation.
>
> Organizations may, however, involve themselves in issues of public policy without the activity being considered as lobbying. For example, organizations may conduct educational meetings, prepare and distribute educational materials, or otherwise consider public policy issues in an educational manner without jeopardizing their tax-exempt status.[42]

The following is from a *Think Progress* article by Zaid Jilian entitled "12 Tax-Dodging Corporations That Spent $1 Billion to Influence Washington Over the Last Decade":

> EXXON MOBIL: The oil giant that was the world's most profitable corporation in 2008 has spent $5.7 million in campaign contributions over the last ten years and $138 million in lobbying expenditures. What was its federal corporate income tax liabilities for 2009? Absolutely nothing. Not only did it pay nothing, but it also received a tax rebate the same year of $156 million.
>
> CHEVRON: Chevron spent $4.4 million in campaign contributions and $91 million in lobbying expenditures over the last decade. It

received a tax refund of $19 million in 2009 while making $10 billion in profits and $324 million in government contracts in 2008.

[The list continues with ConocoPhillips, Valero Energy, Bank of America, Citigroup, Goldman Sachs, Boeing, FedEx, Carnival, Verizon, GE, ...]

The amount of money that taxpayers are losing from the tax dodging by these major corporations is enormous. For example, if five of the nation's biggest banks paid their taxes at the full rate, we could re-hire every single one of the 132,000 teachers laid off during the recession—twice.[43]

Who sponsors churches and nonprofit groups? Understanding the sources of this money is key in developing sound systems and structures to prevent fraud and mismanagement. Following the money and how it can be circumvented is a critical component in preventing fraud and mismanagement.

Government auditors spent the past five years examining all the federal programs and found that 22 percent of these programs cost the taxpayers a total of $123 billion a year. With these staggering GAO auditor findings, systems need to be developed. There is a concept referred to as "zero-based budgeting." In a zero-based budget, managers are required to justify all of their budgeted expenditures, rather than the more common approach of requiring justification only for incremental changes to the budget or the actual results from the preceding year. A manager is theoretically assumed to have an expenditure base line of zero, hence the name of the budgeting method.[44] The zero-based budget concept is designed to force prioritization, require an evaluation of the adequacy of the funding levels, and compare them to the intended performance levels, and to ensure the clearly identified objectives.

The Congressional Budget Office (CBO) published a "Budget Options" series identifying potential for spending cuts. The publications revolve around defense, energy, natural resources and the environment, commerce, transportation, community and regional redevelopment, education and social services, health, income security, veterans' benefits and services, administration of justice, and general government. From that and other sources, Heritage Foundation fellow Brian M. Riedl developed a list of "50 Examples of Government Waste," which included the following:[45]

"A GAO audit classified **nearly half of all purchases** on government credit cards as improper, fraudulent, or embezzled." "Examples of taxpayer-funded purchases include gambling, mortgage payments, liquor, lingerie, iPods, Xboxes, jewelry, Internet dating services, and

Hawaiian vacations. In one extraordinary example, the Postal Service spent **$13,500 on one dinner** at a Ruth's Chris Steakhouse, including 'over 200 appetizers and over $3,000 of alcohol, including more than 40 bottles of wine costing more than $50 each and brand-name liquor such as Courvoisier, Belvedere and Johnny Walker Gold.' The 81 guests consumed an average of $167 worth of food and drink apiece."[46]

"Federal agencies are delinquent on nearly 20 percent of employee travel charge cards, costing taxpayers **hundreds of millions of dollars** annually."[47]

"The Federal Communications Commission spent **$350,000** to sponsor NASCAR driver David Gilliland."[48]

"Members of Congress have spent **hundreds of thousands** of taxpayer dollars supplying their offices with popcorn machines, plasma televisions, DVD equipment, ionic air fresheners, camcorders, and signature machines—plus **$24,730** leasing a Lexus, **$1,434** on a digital camera, and **$84,000** on personalized calendars."[49]

"Over one recent 18-month period, Air Force and Navy personnel used government-funded credit cards to charge at least **$102,400** on admission to entertainment events, **$48,250** on gambling, **$69,300** on cruises, and **$73,950** on exotic dance clubs and prostitutes."[50]

"Members of Congress are set to pay themselves **$90 million** to increase their franked mailings for the 2010 election year."[51]

"Taxpayers are funding paintings of high-ranking government officials at a cost of up to **$50,000 a piece**."[52]

"Congress appropriated **$20 million** for 'commemoration of success' celebrations related to Iraq and Afghanistan."[53]

"Homeland Security employee purchases include 63-inch plasma TVs, iPods, and **$230** for a beer brewing kit."[54]

"Washington recently spent **$1.8 million** to help build a private golf course in Atlanta, Georgia."[55]

A top official at the Office of Thrift Supervision was paid $10,000 in relocation expense reimbursements to move from Los Angeles to San Francisco—but she didn't actually move. Instead, according to the *Washington Examiner*, the official stayed in LA and billed the agency $87,047 over four years for the cost of commuting to SF, which the government paid. According to the Treasury Department inspector general, "supervisors were aware of the wrongdoing, but did nothing to correct it."[56]

COMMON TRAVEL AND EXPENSE REIMBURSEMENT FRAUD SCHEMES

Employees decide to defraud a public entity by submitting fraudulent expenses. This typically involves their submitting a few low-dollar expenses to see if they will get caught. If they are not caught, they gradually increase the dollar amount and eventually start adding new expense reimbursement schemes. The fraudulent expenses are submitted in each individual expense report and may not seem material, but the total amount of overtime can prove to be significant, especially if several employees are involved.

The following are a few scheme types common to many organizations:

Unassigned or unused credits

This scheme involves the personal use of credits owed to the public entity. Employees who undertake this scheme usually do so unknowingly at first. They might have been issued a credit from a refunded or returned item and notice a credit balance on their account. A few months pass and they notice no one has questioned the credit balance. They begin to charge a few personal items to decrease the balance. Over time they make more purchases until the entire credit has been used. Since they were successful and no questions were asked, they might get into the habit of intentionally making purchases, expensing them, and then having them refunded to obtain the credit. Airline tickets work well in this scheme, especially if an employee travels a lot on government business. For example, a public employee books an international flight and charges it to the company credit card. The employee later cancels the flight, and a credit for the amount of the ticket is issued to the card. The public employee now has a credit balance on his card. Instead of submitting the credit on an expense report or returning it to the public entity, the employee charges personal items on the card to offset the credit balance.

Duplicate or fictitious expenses

In this scheme, a second (or third or fourth) claim is submitted for reimbursement for a single transaction. Public employees involved in this scheme might submit duplicate expenses using the same receipt or collude with another employee or third party to submit a duplicate expense. These fictitious expenses are usually submitted in separate expense reports so as to not raise suspicion. For example, a public employee could have a legitimate business meal with a coworker. One employee pays for both meals using the company credit card. The coworker submits a request for reimbursement using a copy of the original receipt as supporting documentation, and the public employees split the proceeds.

Cash advances

In this scheme, a company-issued credit card is used to withdraw cash directly from an ATM or bank for personal use. The public employees involved in such schemes generally do not intend to pay back the funds. For example, a public employee might travel several times a month on government business. While traveling, he or she likes to use some down time to shop, and he or she uses the company credit card to withdraw cash at an ATM to purchase personal items. When the cash advance payment is due, the employee submits fraudulent cash expenses to offset the cash advances taken. In order to not raise suspicion, the public employee may also include legitimate business expenses in this same expense report.

Here are some expense reimbursement schemes you should be aware of that may be impacting the public entity:

Mischaracterized expense reimbursement

A public entity typically reimburses its employees for out-of-pocket expenses that policies identify as reimbursable, such as travel, lodging, and meals. In a mischaracterized expense reimbursement scheme, the perpetrator simply requests reimbursement for an expense that is not actually government purpose–related.

For example, a public employee takes his or her family on a vacation and requests reimbursement for their hotel stay. The employee submits the receipt and falsifies the expense report to indicate that the costs incurred were for government purposes. The false report prompts the public entity to issue a check, reimbursing the public employee for personal expenses, and a vacation becomes a free one for the public employee and his or her family.

Fictitious expense reimbursements

In a fictitious expense reimbursement scheme, a public employee submits a request for reimbursement for totally fictitious expenses. The individual makes up a false expense report and submits it for reimbursement, as opposed to overstating real business expenses or seeking to be reimbursed for personal expenses.

Multiple reimbursements

In the case of a multiple reimbursement scheme, the public employee submits a request for reimbursement for the same expense multiple times. Most often, the fraudster will submit several forms of documentation as support for the same expense.

For example, the public employee purchases an airline ticket for government travel and submits the receipt generated at the ticket counter to the supervisor for reimbursement. A month or so later, he or she submits a second form of proof of payment, such as an email confirmation (different form of documentation) of the reservation or a credit card statement to a different supervisor so that neither would see both expense reports. The public entity ends up reimbursing the perpetrator for the travel expense twice.

Overstated expense reimbursements

In an overstated expense reimbursement scheme, the public employee inflates the cost of actual government expenses. This can be perpetrated in a variety of ways, including altering receipts or overpurchasing and benefiting from some sort of a refund, discount, or sale of the items. In many cases, this scheme may not be carried out by the public employee but by the associate (enabler) who handles or processes expense reports.

For example, an accounting assistant (enabler) who processes expense reports may alter the expense report of his or her coworker and insert a larger dollar amount for reimbursement. He or she then passes on the reimbursement to the other public employee for the amount requested and keeps the remaining amount.

SYSTEMS AND STRUCTURES THAT CAN POTENTIALLY PREVENT EXPENSE REIMBURSEMENT SCHEMES AND ABUSE

Having a well-established, clearly written, and concise reimbursement policy within the organization's public employee handbook with written sign-off from the public employees that they have received the handbook and read it lays a good foundation.

- Ensure that supervisors are familiar with the public entity's expense reimbursement policy and require two approvals that are independent of one another. An example would be two signature authorizations, where the supervisor and an independent person in accounting with signature authority who is bonded be required to sign off. A surefire way to mitigate risk is bonding people who can write checks or receive funds and putting an insurance policy in place that insures against the risk of theft or malfeasance. Public entities can bond public employees to protect against employee theft and dishonesty as well. The bonding will reimburse the entity in cases of property loss due to the acts of the public employee. When employees have access to money or valuable property, bonding protects the organization. Many key financial positions require bonding.

▪ Allow reimbursement only after the expense has been incurred, not prior to it as a cash advance. If an advance is given, it should be subject to two-person sign-off and followed up on with established procedures in place. Another step to mitigate the scam is to give the supervisor reviewing the expenses only the task of confirming that it meets the IRS Order and necessary standard, but no authority in approving the dollar amount, which should be standardized. This same supervisor or approving party should not distribute funds.

▪ Have someone conduct an independent, unannounced audit of the travel and entertainment and other expense reimbursement accounts.

Bribery, Kickbacks, and Gratuities Frauds

This happens when, for instance, a contractor offers money for preferential treatment during the contract awarding process. For example:

▪ The contracting official or approving public employee then accepts money, gifts, or favors from a bidder in return for awarding a government, or public, contract.

▪ An employee in the contracting office, who has no actual authority to award contracts, promises to ensure award of a contract to a bidder if the bidder pays the employee money.

Making or Using False Statements Frauds

This happens when there is falsifying, concealing, or covering up of a material fact by any trickery, scheme, or device; false, fictitious, or fraudulent statements or representations are intentionally made; any false document or writing is created or used; or creating or altering a document. For example:

▪ Types of things that are falsified by the vendor/contractors are altered employee time cards or inflating the number of hours allegedly worked, thereby increasing costs on a cost-reimbursement contract.

■ The vendors or contractors of a manufacturer's proposals for bids uses the names of several other vendors/contractors without their knowledge or approval to meet the qualifications or add to the other areas of the request for proposal (RFP). These proposals are then submitted in an effort to obtain various contracts.

■ The contracting officer's representative falsifies a DD250 Material Inspection and Receiving Report for receipt of goods and services.

Companies Conducting Business under Several Names

This happens when the company's officials are trying to conceal a poor reputation for poor contract performance or poor past financial history (bankruptcies) by conducting business under several different names or other parties' names simultaneously. Such companies may also submit more than one bid or offer in response to a solicitation.

Collusive Bidding

A group of bidding companies with the capability of providing the same goods or services conspires to exchange bid information on contract solicitations and then takes turns at submitting the low bid, effectively defeating competition. These actions may be carried out in collusion with procuring officials. Following are some indicators of bid rigging:

■ Identical bids are received.
■ A number of the bids received are much higher than published costs of previous RFPs for the same type, or of previous bids by the same firms for similar services or goods.
■ Fewer firms' bids are received than would normally be expected from that industry.
■ There is a large gap between the winning bidder and all other bidders.
■ The successful bidder subcontracts work to companies that submitted higher bids on the same project.
■ Competing contractors regularly socialize, or contractors and government procurement personnel socialize.

Conspiracy to Defraud

This happens when two or more persons agree to commit a criminal act, such as making false claims or submitting false statements. One or more of the persons make an overt act. The overt act could have been as simple as drafting a fake proposal, even if the document was not submitted. For example:

■ The public employee submits false receiving documents on behalf of a contractor/vendor indicating that a specific amount of materials on a contract had been received when, in fact, the materials were never delivered.

■ An individual contacts a contractor/vendor and requests that it prepare several different proposals for one individual contract. The individual specifically asks the contractor/vendor to prepare one in the individual's name and one in the contractor's/vendor's name, and to "invent" another one. The contractor/vendor then prepares the proposals as requested.

Disclosure of Proprietary Source Selection Sensitive Information

This happens when a contracting office official illegally discloses information regarding an upcoming request for proposal (RFP), providing an unfair advantage. The contracting official then discloses one offeror's information to another offeror.

Insufficient Delivery of Contracted Items

This happens when the contractor/vendor operates under two separate contracts, for example, to deliver 10,000 pairs of boots under each contract and delivers only a total of 10,000 pairs of boots. Two contracts is no different than two sets of boots; it provides a means of separation and with it, the ability to divert.

Failure to Meet Specifications

This happens when a contractor increases profits by providing goods or services that do not meet contract specifications. Such action is often difficult to detect, because materials omitted from end products are not readily identifiable. The contractor/vendor may, for example, use one coat of paint instead of two, use lower-compression-strength concrete, install cheaper memory chips in computers, or use inferior replacement parts.

COMMON SCHEMES

Rigging Specification

This happens when the requesting public entity tailors the specifications to meet the qualifications of one particular company, supplier, or product.

Small Purchases Pattern

Patterns in small purchases may indicate that a buyer is awarding contracts to favored vendors without soliciting competitive offers from additional firms. The buyer may also be entering fictitious competitive quotations and consistently awarding a favored vendor at inflated prices. Many governments will have thresholds. These thresholds can create these schemes.

Breaking Large Requirements into Smaller Ones

The public entity contracting or requiring activity personnel may split the requirements into small purchase orders to avoid the scrutiny required for larger dollar value contracts. Splitting the requirement may waste funds by losing the economic advantage of volume purchasing. Favoritism or other forms of fraud are easier to conceal when small purchase methods are used.

Duplicate Payment

A vendor submits the original voucher for payment, while the public employee purchaser, acting alone or in collusion with the vendor, collects for the same item from the cash.

Overstatement of Weights and Numbers Ordered

Carriers may be defrauding the government by artificially inflating the weight of a shipment. Possible ways to create overstatement:

- Fuel bumping: getting the tare weight with less than a full tank of gas and the *gross weight* with a full tank.
- Double billing on small shipments (500 to 3,000 pounds): getting two *tare weight* tickets for the truck, picking up the two small shipments, getting two gross weight tickets for the combined weight of both shipments, then submitting both tickets for payment.
- False tickets: paying the weight master to provide a false weight ticket or having a supply of blank or false weight tickets. If blank tickets are used, the weight will usually be handwritten rather than printed.

Patterns in Expense Frauds

What are the situations that enable this fraud and mismanagement to occur, based on the types of fraud listed here? What are the commonalities? Some of the phrases that come to mind are "lack of," "failure to monitor," "authorization process," and "not segregated." Keeping these phrases in mind, know that in any fraud or mismanagement there is typically a failure to properly monitor and oversee contract performance. Without adequate inspection (qualified inspectors) or through collusion, contractors providing goods and services have an opportunity to be paid for more work or supplies than they ever actually performed or provided. Let's say there are work orders for the removal and installation of leasehold improvement, to put up partitions, and to install electrical outlets, telephones, plumbing, etc. These work orders can be compromised by simply inflating the quantities of items removed or installed.

Two of the major concepts that author Joe talked about in his other book are failing to maintain solid controls with unsuspecting acquisition checks and balances at the point of value and the receiving of the goods and services and the payment for those goods and services. The four key areas defined with respect to these concepts are the receipt of money, the receipt of goods and services, the payment to vendors, and payroll. Examining the point where the value can be exchanged is where the systems and structures need to be closely monitored.

Failing to segregate duties by having the same individual authorize the order and receive goods and services presents a critical problem. No one person should be given the authority to control both the ordering and receiving functions. This creates the ability to divert the supplies or services for their own benefit or sign for "phantom," incomplete, or technically inferior shipments in exchange for money or favors from the contractor/vendor.

The controls need to be strong when contract services include bid items that are one-time or non-recurring or with a recurring contract provider. Individuals working with requirements or contracting activities may be in collusion with the existing contractors/vendors by including such items in bid solicitations. This gives the existing contractors/vendors an unfair advantage on future work that has previously negotiated prices for the items, thereby restricting competition.

Poor physical security controls, such as poor warehouse lighting, unsecured storage areas, and allowing private permitted vehicles to park adjacent to storage areas are examples of weaknesses that encourage or contribute to theft of government property.

Control procedures should be in place that require items received to be traced to a valid requisition that could have been ordered for personal use or resale, especially when there is no paperwork. All unreconciled items need to be documented and explained by an independent reviewer who is not involved in the authorization process.

 ## CONCLUSION

When you prepare a report for testimony, it will be "within a reasonable degree of certainty" that you arrive at an opinion. The accountant only provides reasonable assurance in determining if the financial statements are presented fairly. The government and/or public entity needs to raise that standard to beyond a reasonable doubt or an appropriate skeptical level that ensures compliance. The intended purpose is to arrive at a fully documented and supportable position to ensure that there has not been a distraction that led to a diversion of the public entity resources.

The established standard needs to be raised by examining the intent and what a reasonable person thinks of the act. There needs to be a balance between the laws put in place and forceful controls to safeguard the value in these public entities. We need to develop principle-based people for these positions who do things not because of rules, but because it's the right thing to do.

Examine the conflicts of interest that are present, with the proper level of professional skepticism; gather all the documentary supports for your findings; and maintain independence, integrity, and objectivity when analyzing. Remember that only a judge and jury can determine if someone is guilty of fraud. The idea behind any sound system and structure is that it should be designed to help people avoid making bad choices, by communicating responsibility.

Proactive thinking involves forward, forecasted planning with testing of these assumptions and monitoring. The best test is the "get to know your unknown subject" test. The test requires observing the subject's habitual characteristics in all environments and in the company of different people. This will assist you in gaining an understanding of the unknown party or parties. Hanging out at the watercooler, getting to know their friends, going to political functions and fundraisers, and observing who they are influenced by and who their funding sources are can help prevent fraud and mismanagement.

Remember the "no interest, no outrage" formula. Without interest and awareness, fraud and mismanagement will continue. Keeping all people involved and engaged is a strong defense against this. No one is above the law. There should be no tolerance for illegal, or potentially illegal, actions.

 NOTES

1. https://www.law.cornell.edu/uscode/text/18/1341.
2. https://www.law.cornell.edu/uscode/text/18/1342.
3. https://www.law.cornell.edu/uscode/text/18/1343.
4. https://www.commerce.gov/page/about-commerce#mission.
5. http://www.census.gov/about/what.html.
6. http://www.cnn.com/2008/POLITICS/07/29/stevens.history/.
7. http://www.washingtontimes.com/news/2015/nov/8/alaska-kills-bridge-to-nowhere-that-helped-put-end/?page=all.
8. http://www.thepoliticalinsider.com/breaking-newly-discovered-letters-hillary-clinton-saul-alinsky-marxist-community-organizer/.
9. Carl Bernstein, *A Woman in Charge: The Life of Hillary Rodham Clinton* (Knopf, 2007), p. 57.
10. http://www.amazon.com/Reveille-Radicals-Saul-Alinsky/dp/0679721126.
11. http://www.educationviews.org/levels-control-create-social-state/.
12. http://www.epi.org/files/page/-/BriefingPaper292.pdf.
13. http://oig.ssa.gov/what-abuse-fraud-and-waste.
14. https://www.fbi.gov/newyork/press-releases/2013/twenty-third-defendant-pleads-guilty-in-long-island-railroad-disability-fraud-scheme.
15. http://www.ssa.gov/pubs/EN-05-10064.pdf.
16. The U.S. Department of Justice summed up the methods and scale of this fraud in their March 8, 2013 Press Release.
17. *New York Times*, December 4, 2015, A28, http://www.nytimes.com/2015/12/04/nyregion/testimony-at-trial-details-no-show-job-of-dean-skeloss-son.html.
18. http://www.washingtonexaminer.com/article/2551384.
19. http://www.equipmentworld.com/toll-roads-p3s-and-creative-financing-will-bring-short-term-gain-long-term-disaster-for-the-road-building-industry/.
20. http://www.businessdictionary.com/definition/government-monopoly.html.
21. http://www.federalreserve.gov/pubs/bulletin/2014/pdf/scf14.pdf.
22. http://datatools.urban.org/Features/wealth-inequality-charts/.
23. https://priceillusion.wordpress.com/2014/11/18/cpi-market-basket-determined-by-only-0-006-of-americans/.
24. https://www.boundless.com/economics/textbooks/boundless-economics-textbook/measuring-output-and-income-19/cost-of-living-95/defining-and-calculating-cpi-360-12457/.

25. http://www.usatoday.com/story/news/nation/2013/05/01/grocery-costs-for-family/2104165/.
26. http://finance.yahoo.com/news/how-barack-obama-made-his-fortune.html.
27. http://thehill.com/blogs/ballot-box/presidential-races/230318-the-5-billion-campaign.
28. http://eshoo.house.gov/wp-content/uploads/2015/06/06.23.15-House-Letter-to-President-Obama-on-Contractor-Disclosure.pdf.
29. http://www.njbia.org/docs/default-source/fast-facts/Fast_Facts_Complying_with_NJ_s_Pay_to_Play_Laws.pdf?sfvrsn=0.
30. https://www.opensecrets.org/orgs/list.php?cycle=2014.
31. http://www.publicintegrity.org/2015/01/26/16658/health-insurers-watch-profits-soar-they-dump-small-business-customers.
32. http://www.consumerreports.org/cro/magazine/2014/11/it-is-time-to-get-mad-about-the-outrageous-cost-of-health-care/index.htm.
33. http://www.consumerreports.org/cro/magazine/2014/11/it-is-time-to-get-mad-about-the-outrageous-cost-of-health-care/index.htm.
34. http://www.amazon.com/Reveille-Radicals-Saul-Alinsky/dp/0679721126.
35. https://www.cms.gov/Research-Statistics-Data-and-Systems/Statistics-Trends-and-Reports/NationalHealthExpendData/NHEA-Related-Studies.html.
36. http://www.usnews.com/news/blogs/data-mine/2014/12/09/workers-are-spending-more-of-their-income-on-employer-health-insurance.
37. http://www.businessinsurance.com/article/20061109/NEWS/20008785.
38. http://www.healthcarefinancenews.com/slideshow/biggest-healthcare-frauds-2015-running-list.
39. http://www.icpsr.umich.edu/icpsrweb/ICPSR/studies/34481.
40. http://www.nytimes.com/2015/09/21/business/a-huge-overnight-increase-in-a-drugs-price-raises-protests.html.
41. http://www.federaltimes.com/story/government/management/budget/2015/10/01/government-burns-125b-improper-payments-gao-says/73162178/.
42. https://www.irs.gov/Charities-&-Non-Profits/Lobbying.
43. http://thinkprogress.org/economy/2011/04/13/158264/tax-dodging-lobbying-congress/.
44. http://www.accountingtools.com/zero-based-budgeting.
45. http://www.heritage.org/research/reports/2009/10/50-examples-of-government-waste.
46. Government Accountability Office, *Government-wide Purchase Cards: Actions Needed to Strengthen Internal Controls to Reduce Fraudulent, Improper, and Abusive Purchases*, GAO-08-333, March 2008, at http://www.gao.gov/new.items/d08333.pdfnew.items/d08333.pdf (October 5, 2009); Marc Stewart, "Federal Gov't Questions TVA Spending," WBIR.com, February 27, 2009.

47. Robert Brodsky, "Report Paints Agencies as Deadbeat Travel Card Holders," *Government Executive*, May 28, 2009, at http://www.govexec.com/story_page .cfm?articleid=42837&dcn=todaysnews (October 5, 2009).

48. Ira Teinowitz, "FCC Goes NASCAR Racing to Publicize DTV," *TV Week*, October 2008, at http://www.tvweek.com/news/2008/10/fcc_goes_nascar_racing_to_publ.php (October 5, 2009).

49. Louise Radnofsky and T. W. Farnam, "Lawmakers Bill Taxpayers for TVs, Cameras, Lexus," *The Wall Street Journal*, May 30, 2009, at http://online.wsj.com/article/SB124364352135868189.html (October 5, 2009); Jonathan E. Kaplan and Mandy Kozar, "Lawmakers Spend on Big Screens, Popcorn," *The Hill*, November 8, 2005.

50. Government Accountability Office, *Travel Cards: Air Force Management Focus Has Reduced Delinquencies, but Improvements in Controls Are Needed,* GAO-03-298, December 20, 2002, p. 4, at http://www.gao.gov/new.items/d03298.pdf (October 6, 2009); *Travel Cards: Control Weaknesses Leave Navy Vulnerable to Fraud and Abuse,* GAO-03-148T, October 8, 2002, p. 8.

51. Emily Yehle, "House May Get Big Boost for Election-Year Mailings," *Roll Call,* May 4, 2009.

52. Christopher Lee, "Official Portraits Draw Skeptical Gaze," *TheWashington Post*, October 21, 2008, at http://www.washingtonpost.com/wp-dyn/content/article/2008/10/20/AR2008102003627.html (October 6, 2009).

53. Anne Plummer Flaherty, "Congress Ready for Its End of War Party," *Associated Press*, October 4, 2006, at http://www.presstelegram.com/news/ci_4443037 (October 6, 2009).

54. Government Accountability Office, *Purchase Cards: Control Weaknesses Leave DHS Highly Vulnerable to Fraudulent, Improper, and Abusive Activity,* GAO-06-1117, September 2006.

55. Kevin Duffy, "Why Did the Federal Government Help This Golf Course?," *Atlanta Journal-Constitution*, November 13, 2006.

56. http://www.washingtonexaminer.com/top-treasury-employees-swindled-thousands-of-dollars-in-the-know-bosses-did-nothing/article/2544743.

CHAPTER SIX

Corrupt Policies and Actions

"Power doesn't corrupt people, people corrupt power."

—*William Gaddis, American novelist*

Topics:

Corruption: Agency Thinking and Inbreeding
Corrupt Acts
Limits on Corruption
Public Policies That Encourage Corruption
Regulation and Supervision

Key questions:

Do corrupt acts, rationalized behavior, or a combination of both breed fraud (and/or mismanagement) in the public entity?

What is the appropriate level of thinking with respect to determining a corrupt act?

Where are the potential overrides of the controls?

Who are the enablers and detractors?

THIS CHAPTER EXPLORES the structural forms of corruption that can exist in organizations and how agency policies can help or hinder fraud and corruption. Patterns of behavior and policies that promote fraud are discussed as well as the regulatory structures that are intended to limit fraud. We break down the fraud risks that any government and/or public entity can face. Understanding how risk pressures can influence the systems within structures give the reader vital information to ask the right questions and avoid corruption. The 3 J method—Justification, Judgment, and Judicial—is a tool to keep in mind as someone trying to develop systems and structures to mitigate fraud and mismanagement in the public entity.

 CORRUPTION: AGENCY THINKING AND INBREEDING

Fraud, in the minds of the authors, is all about greed. The 3 J approach is a helpful tool, as it develops an understanding of the personalities that revolve around the public entity. The reason corruption exists is that there is a concentration of power and the ability to override, circumvent, and spin in order to create diversions that distract and cause division. Political corruption is created by the concentration of power in the hands of a few. Home-rule thinking, multiple oversight bodies with conflicting policies, and a self-interest focus create a "perfect storm" for corruption.

Let's apply 3 J thinking to the concentration of power as an example. Power gives the people with trust the ability to start justifying why it is okay, or why they are entitled, and any other thought process to enable them to perpetrate fraud. Examining the rationalizations and the personalities of the people making these justifications helps the examining party gain an understanding of the perspectives and thinking surrounding the public entity process. Then we proceed to the second J, which is the judgment they are making and the level of exposed value they have access to. Again, what are the estimations and underlying assumptions? Have they been tested well and is there a majority opinion or are there conflicting interests? This examination develops the understanding and intent behind the action of the parties in these trusted positions.

We continue to develop our soft skills by understanding the prospective reasoning behind the justifications, and the real intent and the basis behind the intent that leads to fraud and mismanagement. Finally, we come to the third J, judicial, which asks what are the consequences if not legal, or if legal but not acceptable by the constituency? The third J is very important, as you need sound factual evidence and supports for your opinions and conclusions. While hard evidence is needed for the first two J's, you're still in allegation thinking and developing a case for whether fraud or mismanagement has taken place. With the third J, judicial, you're attempting to formulate a factual conclusion, and when doing that you better be able to back it up. A key reminder is that we do not find people guilty of fraud; only a judge and jury can convict someone of fraud. With the 3 J's soft skill under our belt, let's examine the thinking that often goes on in the public entity.

Kleptocracy is the formation of a government made up of people who seek status and personal gain at the expense of the governed. It sets the tone for corruption. Not to pick on anyone in particular, but in Nigeria, Saudi Arabia, and modern Russia a good chunk of the economy is based on the proceeds of oil in the hands of the few. The "Belgian Congo" was built as a colony, yet all the profits went to the King of Belgium. The classic colonial models under the conquistadors and/or other imperialists were built in part on a model of personal gain for the "parent" country.

Let's examine term limit laws that restrict the number of years that someone can serve in an elected office. Right now, the president is the only elected federal official who has a limit placed on his term of service: two terms, or eight years. The longer people are kept in trusted positions, the greater the risk for corruption—because the longer people are in positions of power, the more time they have to rationalize and develop the necessary situations to circumvent the process. Public office needs to be a public service, not a means for satisfying one's own self-interest or a career.

Chris Cillizza of the *Washington Post* writes: "There are many more people populating our state legislatures and U.S. Congress who have never done anything outside of being a professional politician than there were even a few decades ago."[1] His blog entry presents a chart by David Mendoza showing just how large a shift it actually has been; the chart categorizes senators' and representatives' job backgrounds from 1965 through 2013. The volume of data makes it impossible to add to this book. However, it remains a helpful resource in developing 3 J thinking, as it tells you the occupational makeup of Congress for almost four decades. This also helps your "O" (occupation) analysis when determining if the POP (perspectives, occupations, and positions) is present to enable fraud and mismanagement.

However, term limits for members of Congress would have to be passed by Congress. It is the positions of power that are misaligned with the ability to formulate the proper constraints, as that position creates the ability to remain in power. Remember that the POP is necessary to enable fraud and misman-agement. The longer one is left in power, unchecked, the greater the potential for fraud and mismanagement. The premise of the legal system is a jury of your peers, and that seems to get lost when we allow people in power to remain in those positions without restriction. This remains a clearly identifiable risk.

Understanding the probability of loss created by political power in gov-ernment is key in developing an understanding of how to manage the risks. These political risks are not insurable and, with the possibility of force majeure (or "superior force") risks, are often deemed to be insurmountable. *Power* is defined by Webster's online dictionary as "the ability or right to control people or things."

The exercising of power is the root cause of political risk. How this power is exercised creates the agency and inbred thinking. Do the government's actions threaten real value? Does creating laws to develop correct behavior really solve the core problem? Prohibition is a perfect example.

Prohibition in the United States was designed to reduce drinking by elimi-nating businesses that manufactured, distributed, and sold alcoholic beverages. The Eighteenth Amendment was added to the U.S. Constitution to take away the license to do business as wholesalers and retail sellers of alcoholic beverages. The leaders (centralized power) of the prohibition movement were concerned by the drinking behavior of Americans at the time. Their agency thinking was that there was a grave concern about a drinking culture filtering into some sec-tors of the population.

The prohibition movements grew after organizations like the Anti-Saloon League were formed. These types of organizations supported enacting local pro-hibition laws. Eventually, the prohibition campaign became a national effort. The prohibition leaders felt that once the license to do business was removed from the liquor traffic, the churches and other reform organizations could con-vince Americans to give up drinking.

Prohibition leaders then began enforcing the ban in order to eliminate supplies of alcohol. But the leaders educating the public on the ills of alcohol never got the support needed for their lesson. The law enforcers were never able to persuade government officials to mount enforcement campaigns against illegal suppliers of alcohol. While there are many photos and stories about the law smashing barrels, the law was ignored. This is a perfect example of why regulations cannot create moral behavior, only people can. The bottom line is the public majority wanted to drink. The new generation of Americans began to disregard the law and the idea of self-sacrifice, which served as the basis for winning support in the fight against the law as they do not feel it is fair. We may well be facing the same tipping point with regards to marijuana legalization. The Pew Foundation reports that 53 percent of Americans supported marijuana legalization in 2015—and for 18–34 years olds (the Millennials) that rate rises to 68 percent (http://www.pewresearch.org/fact-tank/2015/04/14/6-facts-about-marijuana/).

It is the task of every chief financial officer to evaluate whether government action poses a threat to the financial well-being of his or her organization. Prohibition is an example of government thinking they thought that they knew the market better than the entities that provided the goods and services, and underestimated the will of the majority of the people. This same premise can be applied to the individual needing laws to ensure his or her well-being. The first level of thinking to measure political risks is to compare a macro, country-specific level of political risk to the micro, public-entity local levels. Examine correlations and the effects these variables have on one another. It's important to understand what the majority of the people want in order to develop laws that people will follow.

For example, when considering the political risks to a bi-state agency, one must look at what each state-level political risk is and how it will impact the agency. A simple example is New Jersey Governor Chris Christie's nullification of the infamous ARC tunnel project. Cezary Podkul's ProPublica article posed the question "Why did Christie kill the tunnel, and what did he do with the money afterward?" The article reported that "Christie diverted a total of $3 billion of highway toll increases and Port Authority of New York and New Jersey money originally earmarked for the tunnel to bail out New Jersey's finances—the biggest one-time budget fix of his administration." Was it in the best interest of individuals commuting to and from New Jersey? What about the fact that it would relieve stress on aging infrastructure? It is when these types of political risks inherent in decisions are examined that a balance is created to avoid the potential for corruption.

 ## SYSTEMATIC RISK

To better understand corruption, let's approach it in familiar accounting/finance terms: unsystematic and systematic risks. Unsystematic risk is a specific type of risk that is due to some type of uncertainty that comes with that particular entity or industry; call it individualized risk. Systematic risk is the potential for political risk to corrupt economics; it's market-based risk where the uncertainty is inherent in the entire market, or segment, posing a group risk. Ironically, both of these risks are directly attributable to people's actions. In the world of the stock market, people can make the market extremely stable or unstable. Similarly, people can make the government more or less stable. Balancing the individual and group interests reduces the opportunity for systematic corruption.

Probable cause is really being able to establish reasonable grounds to move forward with an investigation. Keep in mind that systemic is something that affects the whole, not just the individual or parts. So, when systematic corruption is discussed, we are discussing corruption that extends throughout the entire government rather than one or two people.

Another distinction is government risk versus the instability risks that may exist in government. Government risk arises out of the trusted authority that they are given, legal or not. Take, for example, a legally enacted tax increase versus a drug ring operated by a local police chief. Both are government risks. It is clear that they both have inherent legal and illegal characteristics.

Instability risk arises when there is division among political individuals and/or groups—such as Congress fighting over seats to control power, or mass riots over a police shooting. It is when risk is analyzed that the bigger picture is better understood.

A simple formula that helps in gaining an understanding of any governmental unit risk is the audit risk formula. Audit risk is the risk that an auditor may assess a financial report that fails to detect material misstatement due to either error or fraud. There are three risks associated with **Audit Risk**: **Inherent Risk** (IR), **Control Risk** (CR), and **Detection Risk** (DR). One can determine audit risk by applying the following formula: $AR = IR \times CR \times DR$.

IR involves the risk associated with the specific transaction. Example: Anytime cash is involved, there is more IR than if a check is given. That's because the check needs to be cashed or deposited through a third party.

CR refers to the risk associated with internal controls failing to detect or determine a misstatement that should have been prevented or requires correction. One of the simplest control risks is segregation of duties. The less the segregation, the higher the control risk.

DR is the designed audit procedures which often fail to detect the existence of a material error or fraud. Often there is confusion when comparing DR and CR. With CR, we are looking at the strength and weakness of the internal control procedures with 800-pound friendly gorillas and proper oversights that create effective checks and balances. With DR, the auditor's samplings are examined for potential errors or human risk factors. Again these are samplings and not 100% verifications as the auditor is only providing reasonable assurances. These risks and other risk assessment tools afford the opportunity for better management of potential risk.

 ## WHY DOES WRONGDOING CONTINUE TO HAPPEN?

Let's make it clear, people commit fraud and wrongful acts, and we often forget that people are human and make bad choices. We are taught to forgive and understand from the time we first enter kindergarten and throughout our lifetime. That is why the best defense is a good offense that watches the behavior and personalities with friendly 800-pound gorilla monitoring and remains proactive. The effective public agencies create policy, communicate, and train people to understand the consequences of making bad choices and the collateral damage it can cause.

Imagine an encounter with a criminal, drug abuser, or agitated or aggressive person. Focus on the effect one of those altered-state personality types may have on your own thoughts, behavior, or actions.

Everyone has an attitude, force field, or aura surrounding them. It is the reason why some people make others feel good and others prompt feelings of frustration or anger or just push others off their game.

People often react to one another's thoughts or actions with their own negative reactions. The job of an auditor/examiner is to learn not to react to negative behavior, by being unassuming, calm, and happy, yet firm enough and skillful enough to defuse a given situation. The auditor, like the person affected by the negative aura of a criminal, must not be taken in by the bad behavior vibe and continually remain an independent and objective observer: clear-visioned and uninfluenced. The problem with corruption is proving the intent associated with it. Failing to act when not in one's best interest is moral behavior. In the minds of the criminals or fraudsters they are rationalizing the behavior and its deviance from societal norms. The problem can be that not all societal norms are acceptable to the mass population. The story of Robin Hood comes to mind: "robbing from the rich and giving to the poor" alongside his band of Merry Men. Organized crime, gangs, democracies, and republics, to name a few, all gather for a purpose, and that is to advance their interests.

Criminal, or bad, behavior is not the norm to society, but is the norm to the individual or groups acting out their self-interested behavior. Often people behaving this way are acting with some varying degree of mental stress or for their own needs and wants. The brain's health has a tremendous impact on attitude. Picking up bad habits from friends, relatives, or close associates also has an impact. Corruption is a learned behavior, because when susceptible people (enablers) come into contact with corrupt people it stimulates a latent behavior in themselves. They start thinking that corruption is normal, and they take on the thoughts and behaviors of the people who are in charge. The sense of thrill and excitement emanating from the corrupt person over the success of their actions associated with the bad behavior becomes contagious. So how do we reduce the chance of corruption?

It starts at the employment training level. Create a culture in which speaking the truth is highly prized, and reward people who tell the truth no matter what the consequence. Third-party whistle-blowers provide the potential third party independent reporting mechanism. No white lies. A lie is a lie. Give people training so they can learn not to be affected by other people's negativity.

Removing thoughts of hate from authority figures and colleagues by creating majority rather than one-person enforcement. Do not allow decisions to be made in the midst of anger. No violence. Imposing consequences is the last resort to be used only when all else fails. Devise a method for brainstorming about these bad reactions and use it as a training tool. Provide a venting outlet so that people can let out their own level of negativity and negative reactions to others naturally, in ways that they know are consequence-free.

Encourage public servants who think for themselves, are individuals, and take responsibility for their own actions—not those who just follow the leader. Create a work environment in which people look out for one other. If someone's behavior is becoming negative, remove them from the situation. Give them support and/or training. Promote people based on ability, not because they agree with you or they're your friend or family member. Don't cover up the truth, pick it apart. Admit what is wrong and use it as a learning experience that benefits everyone.

If the public servant's reaction is "I am always right," "I will not take that," "I am angry," "I'll teach you a lesson," and "The law gives me power to do what I want," he or she is engulfed in negativity that can precipitate a corruption culture. The public servant is there to serve the public's interest. He or she must learn to be calm, not agitated or frustrated; happy and tolerant, not angry; helpful, not abusive. The general public will react completely differently to a calming influence.

The health and fitness of the body have a huge impact on attitude and the ability to handle different situations and create an environment where there is normalcy, productivity, and calm. Improve the environmental health of the workplace with plants, cleanliness, positive images, empowering posters, fresh-smelling air—and having 800-pound friendly gorillas hanging out at the watercooler or wherever negativity and vulnerabilities potentially exist.

When corruption is found, nip it in the bud and do not ever let it manifest itself. Corruption is not normal. Integrity, trust, and honesty are. The better the people in these key public entity positions behave, the better society will behave. People are watching, and there's no better behavior to demonstrate than leading by example.

TYPES OF CORRUPTION FOUND IN GOVERNMENT

There are several types of political corruption that occur in government. Some are more common than others, and some are more common to local governments than to larger segments of government. Local governments may be more susceptible to corruption, because interactions between the private individuals and public officials happen more frequently and often lead to a greater relationship than more decentralized or removed levels of oversight.

The typical forms pertain to money, since it's the quickest exchange of value and the most difficult to trace. The typical local government corruption schemes are bribery, extortion, embezzlement, and graft. Other forms of political corruption are nepotism and patronage systems.

Bribery is when someone is offering something—in most cases cash, but this can also be goods or services—in order to gain an unfair advantage. Common advantages can be to change a person's opinion, action, or decision; reduce the amounts of fees collected; speed up government grants; or change outcomes of legal processes.

A commander in the U.S. Navy pleaded guilty to federal bribery charges, admitting that he provided a government contractor with classified ship schedules and other internal U.S. Navy information in exchange for cash, travel and entertainment expenses, and the services of prostitutes.[2] Information has a value. Know who controls the information and put the proper control procedures in place to prevent bad choices from being made.

According to ESPN, "[Governor Chris] Christie's spokesman, Kevin Roberts, told ESPN.com on Monday that Jones (Dallas Cowboy Owner) paid for Christie's previous trip, including travel and tickets, so no New Jersey taxpayer funds were used."[3] Cindy Boren wrote in a *Washington Post* article, "The trip, however, is proving to be controversial. Christie flew to Dallas and accepted the ticket to the game at the expense of the Cowboys' owner, who just so happens to have a business relationship with the Port Authority of

New York and New Jersey."[4] This again shows the importance of applying the three J's to ask where the conflicting opinion arises. It is what occurs at the top with regard to tone that creates gray areas. This is not intended to formulate an opinion as to whether it's bribery, but rather to put forth what creates bad justification, judgments, and judicial—if it's okay for the behavior at the top, it must be okay. Once again, the problem is the conflicting interest of Jones's business relationship with the Port Authority and Christie's ability to potentially influence the six Port Authority commissioners whom he appoints to the agency.

Extortion is the practice of threatening or inflicting harm (not necessarily physical harm) on a person, their reputation, or their property in order to wrongfully obtain money, actions, services, or other goods from that person. Blackmail, shakedown, and extraction are forms of extortion.

An IRS report provides an example: "On August 21, 2013, in Brownsville, Texas, Abel Corral Limas, a former 404th State District Judge, pleaded guilty on March 31, 2011 to racketeering charges. According to court documents, Limas used his office [...] as a criminal enterprise to enrich himself and others through extortion."[5] He accepted money and other consideration from attorneys in civil cases pending in his court in return for favorable pretrial rulings. Extortion is the practice of obtaining something, especially money, through force or threats. The judge in this case uses the power forces he is afforded to obtain monetary benefit. People often think extortion involves physical force. That is not always the case. Here is an example without using physical force. Someone with AIDS, who needs certain drugs to survive, creates a no-choice need and power for the people that satisfy the need. This is the type of force that allows for price gouging, which is not violent yet enriches the company at the expense of the party with the no-choice need.

It is these situations that necessitate that a company like Valenta (a pharmaceutical company) to answer the 3 J's. What is the company's justification, what were the judgments and motivations behind the judgment, and did the company do anything judicially wrong. With proper preventive legislation and oversight these injustices can be prevented. Unfortunately, unless enough outrage is created, no one is interested, and without interest these injustices will continue.

A *New York Times* article discusses how Bruce Mannes has been taking the same drug, Cuprimine, for 55 years to treat Wilson disease. Then Valenta more than quadrupled its price overnight. According to the article, this impacts Medicare, which now has to cover about $35,000 for the 120 capsules (the required dose each month), and Mannes must pay about $1,800 a month out of pocket, compared with the $366 he paid prior to the increase.[6] These gray areas need to be looked at with a high level of skepticism and well-defined policies with the appropriate levels of 800-pound friendly gorilla oversight. Once again, that conflicting-interest dilemma rears its ugly head: the company-interest profit motivation versus the survival interest of the party in need who has limited choices.

Embezzlement is the illegal taking or appropriation of money or property that has been entrusted to a person but is actually owned by another. In political terms this is called graft, which is when a political officeholder unlawfully uses public funds for personal purposes. Indonesian dictator Suharto, whose rule from 1968 to 1998 has been called the "most brutal and corrupt [dictatorship] of the 20th century,"[7] enriched himself by somewhere between US$15 billion and $35 billion using graft and other corrupt practices.

In general, the longer someone is in power (or in a process), the greater their ability to use absolute power–based force. This can mean that they can use that power to override and circumvent, if there is a lack of interest and weak oversight controls. These are red flags indicators of a potential environment, ripe for embezzlement, fraud, and/or mismanagement. Too often the excuses for a neglectful work ethic are that employees have been there a long time, they would never steal, and classic lines such as "But that's the way we've always done it." The level of thinking needs to be changed to one that employs surprise checks of those trusted employees, good segregation of duties of these trusted responsibilities, and mandated vacations, which means someone else has to be involved in the responsibility while that trusted person is on vacation. All of these create checks and balances within the public entity operational processes.

Nepotism is the practice of people in power favoring their own relatives, friends, political donors, or related party's interests, when giving jobs, promotions, raises, and other benefits to employees. It is often based on the concept of familyism, which is the study or promotion of family relationships. Some political officials give privileges and positions of authority to relatives based on relationships rather on their actual abilities.

The Delaware River Port Authority (DRPA) is a two-state agency (Pennsylvania and New Jersey) that operates four bridges and a train line. According to an NJ.com article, "The DRPA has long been criticized for patronage hiring and spending money for non-transportation projects. It stopped some of its most controversial grant-giving" in 2008. But the agency came under scrutiny again in 2010 after an official resigned, "admitting his daughter used a free E-ZPass transponder from one of his colleagues."[8]

President John F. Kennedy appointed his brother Robert as attorney general. Every president and governor is going to name close associates to key cabinet positions. Mayors choose who they know and trust on citizens committees and commissions. Related parties can usually be counted on for loyalty and maintaining the officeholder's interests.

Patronage is the practice of granting favors, contracts, or appointments to positions by a local public officeholder or candidate for a political office in return for political support. Many times patronage is used to gain support and votes in elections or in passing legislation. Patronage systems disregard the formal rules of a local government and use personal instead of formalized channels to gain an advantage. As noted in Chapter 5, "Former New York State Senate majority leader Dean Skelos, along with his deputy Thomas Libous, both garnered lucrative positions for their sons in exchange for a litany of favors being rendered."[9]

Grand corruption comprises acts committed at a high level of government that distort policies and create economic instability. This corruption typically takes place at the formulation of policy, the end of the political process, or where the value is able to be converted into cash. It starts with policies that have not been correctly cost-assessed. As with any process, managing the costs and effectiveness of the process is key in developing a sound performance-based public entity. The grand corruption tone is set at the top levels of the public entity's organizational chart. These public officials are no different from the board of directors that formulates policies and rules that dictate the moral compass of the entity. The fraudster needs to know the policies and rules so he or she can figure out how to circumvent them to gain access to the value.

Political corruption is any transaction between the private and public sector through which collective goods and services are provided illegitimately. In incidents involving corruption, an illegitimate conversion of the value of the goods and services is, in some instances, translated into cash payoffs. Political corruption usually involves a high level of approval and decision-making authority. The bureaucratic version of corruption involves political decision makers.

The scenario: The people at the top of the political process begin rationalizing that they are entitled to something. Once the thinking has begun to occur, the politicians and state agents fail to enforce the laws of people they were elected or appointed to govern so the fraud and mismanagement can occur. Typically, scenarios like this occur when they need to use their authority to sustain their power, status, and wealth.

Political corruption not only leads to misuse of resources, it also creates the thinking on which future decisions will be based. When the laws and regulations are ignored by the political leaders, sidestepped, not monitored, or massaged to fit their interests, there is a critical need to institute a system of checks and balances. Legality involving practices surrounding purported corruption can be determined only by the triers of facts—the judge and jury. The problem then lies with the potential influence these political leaders may have on a judge or jury. That influence is especially powerful when political leaders and supporters are involved in the appointment of these legal decision makers.

Failing to maintain independence in any system will lead to potential corruption.

Petty corruption involves everyday acts perpetrated by low- and midlevel public officials in the normal course of public process. It is small-scale, bureaucratic, or petty corruption that takes place at the implementation or end of the policy or the point where the value is created. Examine where public officials meet a public need, and apply the appropriate oversight. Petty corruption can be bribery in connection with the implementation of existing laws, rules, and regulations, resulting in small sums of money being exchanged. Areas to examine are anywhere there is public administration and services, like hospitals, schools, local licensing authorities, police, taxing authorities, and other entities in which individuals are given authority to alter or change the rules and regulations that are in the political leaders' interests and not the interests of others. No corruption, small or large, can be tolerated. Often, fraud or mismanagement starts out small and continues to grow. Systems and structures need to be designed to capture both the small- and large-scale corruption incidents. One of the problems in the accounting testing performed to determine risk involves the sample selection. If known by the potential fraudster or mismanaging party, the sample can be altered to reflect results that are not a true representation of the sample.

Legal and moral corruption are forms of corruption in which the law is clearly broken. It is not so easy to prove in the world of politics with the ability of the powerful to seal and withhold information. The problem is that all laws are not always clearly stated, leaving opportunities for doubt about meaning, inadvertently relegating more interpretation discretion to public officials. What is a corrupt activity and what is not? According to John Gardiner, "If an official's act is prohibited by laws established by the government, it is corrupt; if it is not prohibited, it is not corrupt even if it is abusive or unethical."[10]

Any legal approach provides a neutral and static method of adjudicating potentially emotive and perception-determined concepts of corruption. Attacking corruption from a law perspective undermines self-regulated behavior and a dependence on the legal approach to determine right from wrong. Legislating behavior does not increase morality. It's basing morality on law rather than having faith in self-regulated behavior. A corrupt act can, in fact, be camouflaged by lawful justification: the Fifth Amendment right to avoid self-incrimination, forgetting to read someone their rights, and other technicalities. These mitigating factors, as well as what the reasonable juror perceives, are all factored in when deciding a verdict.

Undue influence over public policies, institutions, laws, and regulations by vested private interests at the expense of the public interest is the worst form of corruption, whether legal or illegal. Cultural change, rather than legal change, may be a better way to stop corrupt behavior. If the citizenry remains complacent (enablers), it will eventually give rise to the repeated re-election of compromised politicians, with the same related interest being maintained. Add to that one party rule as a result of citizenry complacency, you have the potential ingredients for absolute control.

While non-corrupt actions may be undertaken within the letter of the law, they do not always account for the spirit of the law. The legal approach diminishes the role of moral discretion and is constrained by clearly defined proclamations. Moral behavior cannot be legislated. Only with an engaged 800-pound friendly gorilla citizenry can we bring to light fraud and mismanagement.

EXAMINING DEMOGRAPHIC FACTORS FOR CORRUPTION POTENTIAL

Socioeconomic characteristics and the size of the population of people who make up the public entity (people in the agency and the size of its constituency) can be factors public officials may see as opportunities to engage in corrupt practices. Homing in on where political corruption has existed, it is evident that it often has been found in places where there are similar demographics. Demographics create factors that have been known to lead to or increase the likelihood of corruption in a government system. These factors often revolve around religion, race, class, size of the public entity, local economic conditions, education, political culture, and gender. These factors are interrelated and can lead to other factors that may cause more corruption.

Size of a Municipality

Smaller public entities tend to be good breeding grounds for corruption within local governmental units. That is because smaller public entities require more local officials to represent and run the local government arm. At this size, interest is not present to create an accountable environment. The more officials there are, the harder it is to keep tabs on each one and establish sound administration-monitoring systems to track their activities. Small public entities may also lack the proper policing and prosecution of corrupt local officials. Lack of enforcement, allowing corruption to take place, increases the public official perception that there is less likelihood of either getting caught or being prosecuted. Therefore, more officials may become dishonest, or at least be tempted, as a result of not having adequate controls in place to make sure their approval and decisions are not left unchecked. No matter what the size of a public entity, the appropriate systems and structures to stave off corruption need to be put in place.

People within small public entities tend to put greater trust in the people who operate within the processes. The management within these smaller entities more likely than not interacts with more of the constituency than in municipalities with large populations. The Rita Crundwell embezzlement discussed earlier in the book took place in a small town, where people knew Crundwell and her long-standing history created trust. People that can perpetrate a fraud have POP—Perspective, Occupation, and Position, all of which were present in the Crundwell embezzlement. The perspective was she was trusted, the occupation was controller, and position was authority to access value (funds). Examining the potential POPs within the public entity will reduce the risk of fraud and mismanagement.

Whether small or large unchecked power, failing to perform background checks, and failing to observe the outside lifestyles of people in these trusted positions with access to the value, exposes the public entities to potential fraud and mismanagement.

Putting in place the proper policies, systems, and structures that create accountability, along with having people who understand the risks and have the means to address them regardless of the size of a public entity, is important. This can be accomplished by having consistent application of the policies and procedures in all processes without bias or override, regardless of size. Even large public entities break down processes into subunits. Developing an understanding of trust and value accesses is critical in smaller entities or subunits with fewer resources to manage these risks and, therefore, the need for a higher level of skepticism and unsuspected monitoring to be proactive. Again identifying the risks before they are allowed to occur will assist in developing the necessary systems and structures.

Another good example is John Merla, former mayor of Keyport, New Jersey. According to the *Asbury Park Press*, "Merla, 45, was one of 11 men—mayors, councilmen, former elected officials—arrested on Feb. 22, 2005, as part of Operation Bid Rig, the FBI's long-term probe into political corruption in Monmouth County."[11] Merla is an especially good example, as he insisted on his innocence until pleading guilty two years later. The potential fraudsters often do not think they did anything wrong and continue to rationalize their actions.

Mayor Merla got 22 months in prison, a tougher sentence than the other two defendants, as a result of staying in office for two years after his arrest according to the U.S. Attorney's office.

Simple controls, independent third-party reviews, background checks, reference checks, and review of past performance with other parties are all essential tools to alert an entity about the potential existence of fraud.

Condition of the Local Economy

Understanding the potential distractions that can enable fraud is a critical view that needs to be applied regardless of what the distractions might be. Low economic development has been found to be an encouraging factor for political corruption. Why? Because the initial design of the policy is generally to serve the greater good via economic growth in the region, yet it involves cash and potentially lucrative contracts that can be manipulated for private gain. Put people and value together and, left unchecked by the friendly 800-pound unsuspected gorilla oversight, you have the ingredients for fraud and misman-agement. Economic events create more personal economic distraction, be that job loss, reduced hours, or lower wages. During good times people are often less interested than during down times when you have the distractions. An example is the lending crisis that led people to lose their homes, created the need for taxpayer-funded bailouts, and other assorted sound bites that create an environment that provides for justifications for needy parties not to follow or to work around the rules. Remember: Need rhymes with greed.

The concept of a redevelopment agency is ripe for corruption, as it's a great sound bite, but it's yet another subdivision of government created to improve blighted, depressed, deteriorated, or otherwise economically depressed areas. The intention is to assist the property owners who are displaced by the redevelopment and to issue bonds or other instruments necessary to fund the programs. These goals are normally accomplished in partnership with private developers. But they don't always serve the greater good of the public for which they were created.

A good example is the sale by Long Branch, New Jersey, of Pier Village, an Oceanside redevelopment area. The city of Long Branch tried to use eminent domain to build the project. "The Institute for Justice represented the Long Branch homeowners who fought their City's effort to forcibly take their homes and hand the land over to private developers who planned to make tens of millions of dollars building upscale condos for the wealthy."[12]

In another example from an NJ.com article, a redevelopment agency that has a separate functioning board is being examined. The Jersey City Incinerator Authority "is one of six city autonomous agencies that operate with city funding but are governed by their own boards, including the Jersey City Redevelopment Agency and the Municipal Utilities Authority." In July 2015, Jersey City police arrested four men, including Clayton Dabney, assistant executive director of the JCIA and brother of the executive director, accusing them of "accepting construction debris for cash and co-mingling the trash with Jersey City garbage."[13]

Dependencies on certain industry needs in these redevelopment areas, which are often laden with poverty, generally leads to less stable governments and less money available to fund them. Weak economies lead to increased levels of poverty and lessen the opportunities for people to get out of poverty. Poverty in itself can often encourage corruption in local governments. Places with failing economies and poverty get loans or start aid programs to support the local economy and the people, and public officials are often able to unlawfully take the money or goods for private gain. While there are many public officials who volunteer or get very little compensation for serving on a governing body, others are not so altruistic.

With less money available, local officials are more likely to get lower wages, which creates the entitlement rationalization and can be seen as another potential factor that leads to corruption. Officials who earn lower wages may begin to develop rationalized thinking that they are entitled to an extra job-affiliated benefit or paybacks for favors, cash, or other value. Allowing rationalization entitlement thinking creates the potential for corrupt acts such as embezzling money that may be entrusted to them in the local treasury. Low wages can cause economic insecurity and encourage politicians to take advantage of opportunities as public figures of authority to advance their own interests in the pursuit of higher office and other opportunities. The more money government has to spend, the greater the tendency it will have to do so inefficiently, which can lead to corruption. Poorer municipalities are often perceived to be more susceptible to corruption than rich ones because of the public monies that are readily available to the lower-income communities.

Education

The less educated the population demographic, the greater the chances of increasing poverty and encouraging corrupt government practices. Those with less education are not as informed about how the government works or what rights they have under the government. It is easier for corrupt officeholders to conceal corrupt activities from a poorly educated public. Uneducated or ill-informed citizens are less likely to be aware. When people are unequipped to recognize and stop corruption or the potential for it, corruption is more apt to flourish.

The key to successful policies is knowledge. Educating the citizenry about the need for change is no different than trying to get most public entities to believe fraud can exist in their organization. If the citizenry don't see the change coming, it will cause confusion, and where there is confusion you have the potential distractions that can lead to fraud and mismanagement. The government entity must recognize that the citizen body being affected needs to see the value in the change, and the government entity needs to communicate that the policy change is not creating competing self-interests. The citizens also need to be made to feel that waiting to implement a policy can create potential consequences. This is equivalent to making sure people understand that a bad choice like committing fraud has consequences. The policy being proposed needs to be clearly communicated at all levels of education by being transparent and well documented.

Without political awareness, citizens are not able to distinguish between honest and dishonest candidates or recognize signs of bad politics to help prevent corruption from taking place in their governments. This often leads governments to be continually governed by one or more corrupt local officials who use patronage or nepotistic practices to stay in office or keep influence in the government for long periods of time. Given that there is considerable variation in the ratio of local taxes to total local expenditures, it makes logical sense that political officials would be very proactive in preserving local programs that are largely paid for by state or federal sources. Perhaps an examination of the ratio of local revenue sources over total expenditures would illuminate this issue.

Local political leaders who lack the education required to run a public entity must have the necessary support system surrounding them to enable them to find legitimate ways to make the public entity productive, well-structured, and successful.

Political Culture of the Municipality

Many governments have established political cultures with certain expectations and practices. These cultures often determine what is acceptable and not acceptable in local politics. In government, when faced with an undeveloped or underdeveloped political culture, accountability and credibility principles are difficult to establish. An example of educating political culture is the "Municipal Financial Disclosure," which is framed as a monitoring device, serving as a communication tool between the municipal government and interested users of that information. Political culture is principally a measure of the interaction between a government and its citizenry.

This can encourage corruption to take hold in the governmental unit, because citizens do not know what is considered corrupt, and local officials are not afraid to be corrupt because of the limited accountability. This goes back to what makes something right or wrong—if the question is posed to three people, you may get three different answers.

The issues are that one municipal goal—housing, as an example—is traded off against another municipal goal, which is consistency in the planning for housing development. The problem is that there is often no relationship established between them. These costs are then passed on to the taxpayers and are not always easy to quantify. Municipal planning cannot be allowed to be arbitrary and or unprincipled. The problem is that most of the public are unaware of these ongoing political cultures. Even relying on council members or other public officials to uncover potential schemes may well be beyond their skill set. Again, the situation should be monitored by independent analysis and oversight that informs the entire constituency and not just the limited areas affected.

In some places, governments may be corrupt because the citizens think that is how it is supposed to work, only because they've always been exposed to corruption and, for them, it's the status quo. The longer political instability is allowed to go on, the more likely it will lead to corruption in a government. When people are unsure of how the government should operate and do not know what corrupt practices look like or how to stop them, it will continue to exist. We are missing the 800-pound friendly gorilla oversight control to mitigate fraud when we do not give the citizenry the proper understanding of how public entities operate. Where distractions, diversions, and divisions become common occurrences in the public entity, corruption can exist. Structural corruption exists in many developing countries due in part to limited expectations on the part of the general public with respect to the actions of public officials—as corruption is so embedded in the process and just a part of life.

CORRUPT ACTS

What is corruption? *Black's Law Dictionary* defines corruption as "illegality; a vicious and fraudulent intention to evade the prohibitions of the law. The act of an official or fiduciary person who unlawfully and wrongfully uses his station or character to procure some benefit for himself or for another person, contrary to duty and the rights of others." The past offers the opportunity to learn and continually improve. The following are things that can potentially precipitate corrupt acts and are areas requiring a high level of skepticism. Examining the differences between policies and the personality behavior surrounding these varying polices needs a higher level of professional skepticism. Next, perform a review of whose self-interests are being served and whether there is a conflict of interest. These key analyses are the beginning steps in formulating the allegation of corruption and determining whether there is material misrepresentation present (remember MIRD), intentionally done, that causes the damages present.

Corrupt Act 1: Money Makes the Government/Public Agency World Go Round

People forget that when they were in kindergarten, they were taught to share. All that people are encouraged to do now is to make money and spend—spend money that they do not have. Buying into the idea that everyone needs to work and spend leaves no time to do simple things, like give back. The need to make money to survive creates division. An ever-present danger looms: that class warfare with respect to existing wealth inequalities, less-than majority approvals needed to pass legislation, and the ability to use the media/public relations will camouflage mismanagement and fraud.

Is a new form of global government in the future? Will it be one in which there is a world monetary dictatorship system, making the existing savings worthless? People being led to invest money in multinationals and banks will only give the powerful more power and control over the wealth. The U.S. Federal Reserve controls interbank interest rates, which stood at 0.12 percent at the end of 2014. The U.S. government paid 2.03 percent on money it borrowed,[14] but the average interest on a residential mortgage was 4.17 percent, which means the average person pays twice as much to finance a residential home.[15] Why is the rate for the individual so much more than that for the group? A U.S. banking sector or government default is far less likely than an individual's default, but the rates are in fact a reflection of expert evaluation of the comparable risks or the cost of capital.

Government that borrows and mortgages the future revenue systems without adequate controls in place will continue to allow systematic corruption to continue. Money doesn't make the government and public agencies' worlds go 'round, people do—and people need to have the ability to make money and be less reliant on public assistance and entitlements.

Webster defines *entitlement* as "the state or condition of being entitled, a right to benefits specified especially by law or contract, a government program providing benefits to members of a specified group, funds supporting or distributed by such a program, belief that one is deserving of or entitled to certain privileges." The mistake is to provide too much financial assistance to a person without the proper controls in place. The motives are usually good. Government and the public agency want to help the people get started in life or assist when a financial need rises or public need is critical. Unfortunately, the result is often the opposite of the one desired. Instead of helping people become self-sufficient, they often become dependent or expect the entitlement. Rather than sparking initiative and discipline, people may become idle and expectant. Instead of being achievement/entrepreneurial-minded, they may become entitlement-driven, ungrateful, and demanding. If people always gets what they want, they will always want, as long as they live.

The true unemployment rate is much higher than the officially recorded rate. The official rate does not include workers who have dropped out of the labor force, nor does it account for the underemployed. What about the jobs that are subsidized? There are people on pensions, students, and many small businesses that are on government subsidies. There are employees on government benefits while working other jobs. There are retired superintendents making well into six figures doing interim gigs, adding to pensions and getting more, plus double benefits. There have been good investigative stories on this. False government figures mask the ability to pay and thus feed systematic corruption. What would the public outrage be like if the real numbers were revealed? Certainly, this is a factor in creating political risk.

Corrupt Act 2: Entitlement versus Earned (Rights)

Rights are something that other people can take away. Rights of citizens can be defended, not granted, by one another. Rights revolve around the freedom to do as one pleases and the opportunity to excel, achieve, and succeed. These rights grant us the right of protection from harm or undue burden or inconvenience by the government and others, as well as the privilege to serve or give in any way that one chooses.

Rights under the U.S. Constitution's Bill of Rights—such as the freedom of speech, religion, and assembly; the right to bear arms; and the freedom from double jeopardy, self-incrimination, and unreasonable search and seizure—are established in writing for citizens. Not equated to these rights are the money, material items, or services required to maintain them. It's important to understand the government cost/benefit analysis, which places costs on these rights.

What are these cost drivers? Public safety (terrorism), infrastructure (roads and bridges), health and welfare, pension (retirement), and education are some.

In a well-established system and structure there is no right to forcibly take these rights from others or authorize the government to perform this kind of seizure of one person's rights when it is for the benefit of another. Rights are no different than something earned, which is a by-product of someone's action or effort. Examining the efforts, whether well- or ill-intended, is the only way to maintain efficiencies and preserve these rights. Think of the spending associated with the Islamic State of Iraq and Syria (ISIS) terrorism. ISIS is very skilled in the area of social media. It uses the Internet to publicly post videos of beheadings of soldiers, civilians, journalists, and aid workers, prompting outrage and looking to destroy other cultural interests not aligned with its own self-interest, which would be "cultural imperialism" or "religious imperialism." These create unequal relationship balances between the powerful nations and weaker nations. Again, the conflicts create the opportunity to distract and divert that the fraudster is looking to gain access to the value and remain undetected. No interest can be advanced without money. Who is providing the funding support? Follow the money. Without it, bombs and the tools needed to advance ISIS's interests cannot be bought. Securing borders and military strikes cost money. Finding out what it is they really want and understanding how they are funded are no different than determining how a business funds its operations. Developing cost-minded people in the government structure and citizenry and understanding where the money is coming from is developing sound systems and structures.

Entitlements, on the other hand, are established by governments via the politically elected representatives or by direct vote of the people. They include money, material items, services, and various forms of aid and assistance. Entitlements can be fully or partially earned. Examples of earned entitlements are Social Security and Medicare, to which the recipient generally contributes while he or she is working and those contributions pay for a significant portion of the benefits received. However, there are many entitlements that are completely unearned. Food stamps, welfare, and Medicaid, and emergency aid, such as that provided by the Federal Emergency Management Agency (FEMA), are some examples. Some would argue that these things are earned via the fact that we pay taxes, but the inequality in who pays the taxes makes the argument questionable, since many of those who receive these kinds of entitlements often pay little if any taxes. The highest tax brackets will likely never receive anything from these entitlement programs, which creates a potential class conflict.

SOCIAL SECURITY

First we need to start with a very basic financing and investing example. If you had $1,000,000 at 2 percent you would earn $20,000. If the investment was $20,000, you would need a 100 percent return to earn the same $20,000. As the base increases you need less risk, as the rate of return is directly related to the risk an investor is willing to take.

Where is the large base of money earning reasonable returns? Salaries are greater, more people are working longer, and Social Security benefits can be taxed. The counter is that people are living longer and health care costs are rising. The public entity always creates two sides to an argument, with the distractions necessary to allow fraud and mismanagement to exist.

Social Security is one of the biggest government programs in the United States. All wage earners pay 6.2 percent of their pay and their employers pay a matching 6.2 percent; self-employed individuals pay the whole 12.4 percent themselves. Most of the population is subject to this tax. Although there is a cap

TABLE 6.1 Future Value of Social Security Tax Revenue

Year	Salary**	Social Security Tax*	FV of Tax at Year 40 (Inflation**)	FV of Tax at Year 40 (Stocks***)
1	$20,000.00	$2,480.00	$7,009.69	$31,796.97
2	$20,540.00	$2,546.96	$7,009.69	$30,587.75
3	$21,094.59	$2,615.73	$7,009.69	$29,424.53
...				
37	$52,187.44	$6,471.24	$7,009.69	$7,874.33
38	$53,596.50	$6,645.97	$7,009.69	$7,574.87
39	$55,043.60	$6,825.41	$7,009.69	$7,286.80
40	$56,529.78	$7,009.69	$7,009.69	$7,009.69
			$280,387.71	$658,805.16
Average monthly SS received			$1,335.00	$1,335.00
Months the amount collected will last			282	Forever
If retired at age 67, will last to age			90	Forever

Source: https://www.irs.gov/taxtopics/tc751.html Internal Revenue Service
*SS tax is 12.4 percent of salary.
**Assumes wages and SS fund grow at the 30-year average *price* inflation rate of 2.7 percent.[16]
***Assumes SS fund grows at the growth rate of the S&P 500 in 2014, which was 6.76 percent.

on the income taxed, most earners do not exceed the statutory exempt amount, so 85 percent of the population is paying 6.2 percent of their wages.

So 12.4 percent of every paycheck goes to retirement. Assume that someone starts out earning $20,000 and, over their lifetime, receives the average cost of living increase during the 40 years they work. Table 6.1 factors in those assumptions.

Using the money collected from this person at a 2.7 percent inflation adjustment rate and an average $1,335 payment,[17] they would be covered until average age 90.5 with the money they and their employers contributed. If the money was invested in the market, the monthly amount would increase to $4,629.49; thus, *if* Social Security tax funds grew at the *assumed* rate of stock market growth, at this benefit level they would last forever. Rate of returns (cost of funds) and understanding the time value of money are critical with respect to meeting projected future liabilities.

Understanding the time value of money is critical in the effective management of these entitlements and any future government or private entity obligations. Anytime there is a future liability, there must be an ability to understand it in present dollar value. That means knowing what that liability costs today so there are sufficient funds to pay the future obligation. As evidenced via this book's examples and theories, it seems government and public agencies too are not good at it. So what is the time value of money? The time value of money (TVM) is the concept that a dollar that you have today is worth more than a dollar in the future.

There are a number of reasons why there is a need to apply present value in order to provide accurate accounting of financial transactions. Anytime money is to be paid back in the future, it is subject to the risk of default and the party at risk will want to be compensated. Present value is also needed to address price inflation, which reduces the real value of money over time. That same money given up could have been invested over the same period of time it remained unpaid. Two identifiable risks associated with any future liability are the inflation and default risks.

One of the hardest parts of maintaining a control system is ensuring that typical monitoring is continued. Failing to update controls or rechecking the established foundational basis, like meeting the ever-changing needs associated with the entitlement, leads not only to potential fraud and mismanagement but to insolvency as well. Failing to monitor assumptions and the variables that go into an actuarial analysis and ongoing validation of the assumptions involve judgment. Just look at the underfunded pensions that most states are dealing with.

Management in any organization can manipulate expected returns and they would have a windfall, as the pension expense would be reduced. The returns in government should be in line with the reasonable returns that an individual would be able to earn in a free market. Putting the responsibility on these highly compensated managers that public entities employ to invest and generate fair return rates, then using the funds for other government funds, leads to potential fraud and mismanagement.

Forget returns. The base of dollars is shrinking, and without dollars to invest there is no return. Social Security is broken down between FICA and MEDI. The FICA is for retirement and the MEDI is for Medicare. One simple question is: Why are the funds commingled? The answer is that they need to combine dollars to meet the expected outlays.

If government was to set aside each individual's invested (FICA) contributions for retirement, people who worked longer, more hours, and/or more jobs would have a separate accounting for their retirement. Why should it not operate like a 401(k) (subject to all the same regulation and requirements as a private entity) and be accountable to provide more reasonable returns to grow the retirement fund needed to meet inflationary costs over time. Why are all the funds put in one pot? Add to that the risk that the funds are declining, and you can see that the reason the government wants to control returns is because the funds that are invested are not liquid. A Ponzi scheme is taking people's money knowing that you're never going to pay them. How is not requiring a fixed return to people who contribute over the course of their lifetime proper structure?

Remember that the amount subject to the Social Security tax rate has increased from 3 percent in the 1930s to 12.4 percent in 2015. The taxable wage base subject to tax increased from $3,000 to $118,500 in 2015. With these types of tax rates and changes to the taxable base there should be increasing cash flows. With the shifting of funds and the use of Social Security funds elsewhere in the government funding cycle, it is critical that the parties' resources be properly invested with reasonable returns to ensure their funds are there at retirement to meet the inflation-adjusted numbers. As one can see the contribution amounts have been continually increasing, going from $3,000 to $118,500 of income per year and the rate applied to that income has increased from 3 to 12.4 percent.

Another simple perspective is that 6.2 percent of every dollar a citizen earns is put away, matched by the 6.2 percent employer share, totaling 12.4 percent with the government. The workplace retirement saving nationally is significantly lower than the Social Security contributions. "Government

Accountability Office (GAO), states around 29% of households age 55 and older have neither retirement savings nor a pension."[18]

"Under the intermediate assumptions, the Trustees project that annual cost for the OASDI program will exceed non-interest income in 2013 and remain higher throughout the remainder of the long-range period. The projected combined OASI and DI Trust Fund asset reserves increase through 2020, begin to decline in 2021, *and become depleted and unable to pay scheduled benefits in full on a timely basis in 2033.*" (emphasis added) This is taken directly from the 2013 Annual Report of the Board of Trustees of the Federal Old-Age and Survivors Insurance and Disability Insurance Fund.[19] It is important to remember that these reports are based on actuarial estimates.

In that same report, the projected deficit in 2013 is $75 billion and will be reimbursed by the general fund. These are the areas that have to be examined and be extremely transparent to the citizens. Allowing transfers and moving of budgeted line items for different purposes creates an environment for potential fraud and mismanagement. Did the government take a loan of these funds? The over accrual was due to demographic trends—driven by the Baby Boomers in their prime working years—much like the school boom in the 1950s and the college enrollment boom in the 1960s and 1970s. Segregation of the funds is the only structure that should be tolerated if the ever-growing tax burdens people are facing are to be managed. The proverbial "robbing Peter to pay Paul" is not the solution.

In the National Council on Governments (NCGA) Statement, interfund balances are classified separately from fund revenues. The four basic types of transfers are loans between funds (interfund loans, services provided and used, interfund shared services between units), reimbursements for expenditures attributable to another fund, transfers that were previously residual equity, and operating transfers. So the receipt of money, the receipt of goods and services, payroll, and vendors are the four key areas where fraud and mismanagement will be found.

Another concern is that government's state and or local units can legally incur expenditures up to the amounts included in the government's budgeted appropriation. Here again is a conflict that arises and creates the need to apply the proper skepticism. Anytime money needs to be transferred, or there is an allocated loan, it means one thing—the money was not properly budgeted. In the example from the 2013 Annual Report (of the Board of Trustees of the Federal Old-Age and Survivors Insurance and Disability Insurance Fund) there was a shortage in 2012. Why was the 2013 budget not adjusted? In GASB Statement No. 54, Fund Balance Reporting, the traditional entry is under Debit Encumbrance and Credit Reserve for Encumbrance, since reserves are no longer part of fund balance. The key is to remember that the offset to

Encumbrances is only a budgetary account offset. If items remain outstanding in the following year, they will be reflected in the restricted, committed, or assigned to fund balance, as they are appropriated.

Most governments do not record expenditures until goods are received or the services are rendered. However, in an encumbrance accounting system, the amounts of the purchase orders issued for those goods and services or spending commitments are recorded at the time commitments are made, despite the goods and services not being delivered or performed.

Examining the encumbrances and appropriations and the need for transfers to ensure they have the proper documentary supports is having a sound system structure in place. There is always a financial impact when money is taken from one place and put into another. Understanding that impact is also having a sound system in place. Think of personal finances and the impact. For example: If your car broke down and the mortgage was due at the same time, you would have a financial impact. If you do not fix the car, you cannot go to work and make money to pay future bills, but you have to pay the mortgage.

These are everyday conflicting decisions. A sound financial system provides for the worst and hopes for the best instead of just continuing to kick the can down the street until you arrive at Armageddon. Government needs to address the problems and plan changes today, not tomorrow, even if decisions made to address those problems are unpopular.

People are taught that if pain is felt, then whatever is causing the pain is bad and should be avoided. This concept is contrary to that which says that when good work ethics are applied, savings are earned. It is important to teach oneself and clients in a professional finance environment to continually work past the point of comfort. One of our favorite sayings is "A LITTLE BITE MORE." Not many reach this point regularly, but it is here that we create people of character. Learning good work ethics takes perseverance through the uncomfortable and beyond the pain of work. Creating spirit and proper thinking are critical.

 ## HOW THE U.S. GOVERNMENT SPENDS

According to the conservative site USgovernmentspending.com, "In 2010, welfare spending decreased, but healthcare and pensions spending increased. In 2015, pension spending is estimated at 6.8 percent of gross domestic product (GDP), healthcare spending is estimated at 7.5 percent of GDP, and welfare spending is estimated at 2.6 percent of GDP."[20] Look at the 2016 spending graph (Figure 6.1). The numbers are supported, and it shows the contribution the government makes to the GDP. The value created by the government's need creates a competition between the private need of the goods and the government

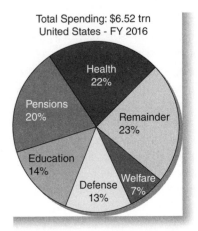

FIGURE 6.1   U.S. federal spending, FY 2016
*Percentages are based off of the average U.S. Consumer Unit. The average consumer unit consists of 2.5 persons in the unit, with 1.3 earners and is age 48.8.
Source: http://www.usgovernmentspending.com/piechart_2016_US_total

and yet another identifiable conflict. Why does government get lower cost of funds, or the ability to go around established controls? Examining these types of transactions is critical to maintaining control.

People need to make money to maintain the necessities of everyday life.

People are making a big mistake when they ignore or underestimate political risk. There are crises all around us. The Eurozone negotiations, the debt ceiling debate in the United States, and the Arab Spring protests throughout North Africa and the Middle East are all crises that arose with very little warning time. Then there are the Iranian government–type threats to close the Straits of Hormuz, which would likely have a direct effect on oil prices. These are theories of constraints, and any government and/or public entity—better yet, any organization—needs to understand what affects its operations. Our system needs to run as if any of the above scenarios could occur—and plan for these possible outcomes. Our overall financial plans should not be based on the best case scenario.

HOW PEOPLE SPEND

Understanding the necessity for spending helps in determining lifestyle changes. The core personality analysis needs to go beyond the findings related to the entity to include an analysis of the public employee's or official's spending behaviors outside the public entities. Understanding the norm, or what we like to term "benchmarks" or "average spending levels," creates a metric to measure when someone experiences a significant change in cash flow or income level. Too often no one pays attention to the money public employees or officials raise as a result of the position of power they find themselves in. If we know what are the norms in terms of spending, we can potentially detect employees and staff living outside the norm.

Knowing the averages or standards for people gives you the ability to monitor and establish a baseline perspective.

Let's make the following assumptions:

- New Jersey's 2013 median household income[21] of $71,637 a year
- Federal and state taxes at 20 percent rate
- Resulting in net pay of $57,309.60

and see where the spending is affected based on U.S. averages (Figure 6.2).

In Table 6.2, there are four primary themes: food, insurance and pensions, transportation, and housing (shelter).

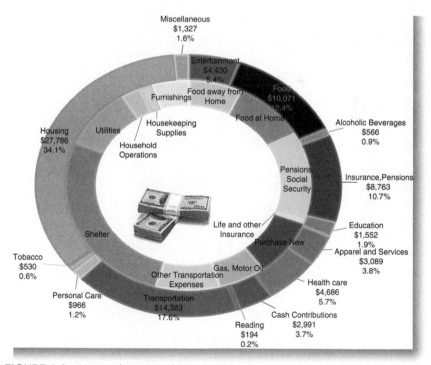

FIGURE 6.2 National Average household budget

Source: Consumer Expenditures (U.S. Dept. of Labor, U.S. Bureau of Labor Statistics)

TABLE 6.2 New Jersey Household Budget

(a) Outer Circle Main Categories	
Entertainment	$3,115
Food	$7,081
Alcoholic Beverages	$527
Insurance, Pensions	$6,161
Education	$1,091
Apparel and Services	$2,172
Health Care	$3,295
Cash Contributions	$2,103
Reading	$136
Transportation	$10,112
Personal Care	$679
Tobacco	$373
Housing	$19,535
Miscellaneous	$933
Total	$57,309

(b) Inner Circle Subcategories		
Food	$3,081	Away
	$4,000	Home
Insurance, Pensions	$5,788	Pensions, Social Security
	$344	Life, Other Personal Insurance
Transportation	$3,725	Purchase New
	$2,751	Gasoline, Motor Oil
	$3,611	Expense, Other Trans.
Housing	$11,577	Shelter
	$4,012	Utilities
	$1,146	Household Operations
	$745	Housekeeping Supplied
	$2,063	Household Furnishings, Equipment

Food is a necessity, and entertainment and alcohol are discretionary spending. Food obviously eats up more of the after-tax income. After-tax income represents the amount of disposable income that a person or entity has to spend on present consumption needs. The Bureau of Economic Analysis (BEA) has many useful tables, articles, and data, including personal income and outlay information, as well as many other tables critical in developing a sound, supportable finding.

With respect to *insurance and pensions*, insurance is required on automobiles, and obviously safeguards a person from liability, so, once again, it generates a lot of money for insurance companies, and with a lot of money comes a lot of power. The global insurance sector is worth $3.3 billion.[22]

The next primary theme is *transportation*. Again, people need to drive to earn or go places, or they need to have other forms of transportation. The final theme is *housing*. One common theme running through all four categories is captured in the word *need*. When people need something, manipulation can come into play. When one can manipulate, one can corrupt. Examining the chart, it is evident that an average family needs to order its spending priorities. A logical order is to secure a safe environment to live in, have an adequate supply of food, have a means of transportation to work, and address other needs and provide for future needs like retirement.

The more income the government needs, the less disposable income the individual has and the less spending and savings abilities available to maintain the necessities. Total federal revenue in fiscal year 2015 was expected to be $3.18 trillion. This revenue breaks down into three major funding sources:[23]

Income taxes paid by individuals	$1.48 trillion	47 percent of all tax revenue
Payroll taxes paid jointly by workers and employers	$1.07 trillion	34 percent of all tax revenue
Corporate income taxes paid by businesses	$0.34 trillion	11 percent of all tax revenue

Government generates 47 percent of its revenue from individual taxes and, once again, there is an apparent conflict. Do people pay their taxes or eat? Driving soaring health care costs and taxes means taking away disposable spending. Government has to establish a similar protocol of what is necessary to maintain health and safety and prioritize its spending so it does not keep reducing the average to the middle class's disposable spending. Priority and pay-as-you-go spending are frugal methods for not only individuals to maintain, but government and public entities as well. It's a salient motif: Knowing what people want and being able to provide it leads to having greater control over them. When the need is a basic necessity, the controller needs to create desperation. Basic necessity needs are defined as needs one cannot do without, and they can alter behavior.

Knowing the spending habits by having a handle on the normal necessity spending can generate red flags that warrant further skepticism and examination.

 POLITICAL RISKS

In Chapter 5 we spoke about audit risk and then behavioral risk. This chapter is about corruption, and we felt it would be more fitting in laying the groundwork for seeing how power can corrupt or enable wealth inequalities all around politics. Let's define politics as activities in our world transactions associated with the governance of a country or other area that create debate or conflict among individuals or parties having or hoping to achieve power. Once given the power, they have the ability to advance specific interests at the expense of others.

Today's political risks (constraints) are taking new and different forms. In advanced economies, governments are dealing not only with real and perceived income inequalities but also with high levels of sovereign debt, as illustrated by the Eurozone discussions and a cap on the U.S. debt. In general, there are macro and micro perspectives when examining the political risk—the macro being the global perspective of the policies and the micro being who is directly affected by a political policy.

Most people will typically claim that their money and income are not sufficient and that they need more. The public entity operates with a similar mind-set. This means there is a need to influence the actions of many more people in order to develop the necessary value needed to drive the desired objective.

These types of limitations result in budget constraint. Scarcity of resources imposes limits and ultimately changes behavior. People maxing out at some optimal capability with a time limit constraint in which they can earn income presents another restriction. In order to earn income, people have to sacrifice leisure time. In general, the mere existence of constraints shows that people cannot satisfy all their wants, but must choose to forgo some needs in order to accomplish others. The public entity is no different. A trade-off is to get more of one thing, which, in turn, means something else must be sacrificed. The public entity needs to understand the impact of these trade-offs as part of the internal control structure of the system and to structure, plan, and manage these imminent risks. Excessive borrowing may allow government entities to avoid facing some of these trade-offs for a period of time—as we are borrowing resources from future tax payers and spending them now. That may be a fair trade-off—if we are spending the resources on long-term capital assets—such as a water supply system, parks, transit systems, or bridges—where the lifespan of the asset is long and the value for future tax payers is great. Look at the New York City water supply system, which is massive and very old. Today's city residents are still benefiting from capital investments and real estate purchases made over 100 years ago.

A sample of simple political risk is a state action that promotes state-owned companies. Once again you have conflicting interests creating the opportunity for fraud and mismanagement, as this removes free market and competition thinking. These types of actions affect the cash flow of companies operating within national borders where these actions are to take place. Building of trade barriers that are ongoing will eventually cause significant problems to many companies in the United States that have international/overseas operations. Trade-offs like these need to be measurable, recordable, and well communicated.

Typically, government focused its attentions on financial, market (economy), and operational types of risk, especially since the economic crisis of 2008. Most companies neither measure nor manage political risk and the constraints that they impose on the management of these public entities. Organizations tend either to accept (or ignore) these risks, or to avoid situations that seemingly pose large political risks altogether, even if those risks present a significant opportunity or the potential for disaster. Political risk may have many different characteristics than other types of risk. But all risks need to be managed. Effective management of political risk creates opportunities to enter new and improved policy environments, creating approvable and supportable legislation that drives efficiency, improves costs, and manages the trade-offs with which the public entity is often presented. Planning, directing, and controlling these risks can be tied into managing the risk and seizing opportunity risk associated with meeting the defined objective.

So how is political risk identified? At best, when dealing with local, state, national, and other public entities, having an understanding of the geographical impact of the objectives is necessary to formulate the right system and structure design. Is there a tone indicating centralization or decentralization? Is there home-rule- or self-interest-driving motives? What are some of the identifiers associated with political risk? Look for an increase in taxes, wars, and terrorism, sit-downs, and strikes—things that stir interest. From a financial perspective, the identifiers are forms of deregulation that create oligopoly thinking.

The Teapot Dome Scandal was one of the largest scandals in the United States and occurred in Wyoming during the Warren Harding administration. The Teapot Dome is an oil field located on public land in Wyoming that was reserved for emergency use by the U.S. Navy. The issue was that oil companies and politicians claimed that there was no need for reserves and that the oil companies had enough inventory supply for the Navy in the event of shortages. The need was oil in case of shortages. The public entity gained control to serve the public good, and for the private entity, profit motivated need. Where these meet you have an environment that allows fraud to exist.

The *Wall Street Journal* exposed the bribes. The person in charge was Secretary of the Interior Albert B. Fall, who was found to have accepted gifts and loans from oil company executives in return for leasing the rights to the oil at Teapot Dome to Mammoth Oil and Pan American Petroleum without asking for competitive bids. The leases were legal, but the gifts/kickback were not.

The identified risk: the influence to circumvent Secretary Fall (unchecked approval authority), the value he had in access to the Teapot Dome Fields (the value creator was leases), and the lack of competitive bids leading to the breakdown of the systems and control that were in place. The Supreme Court ultimately ruled that the oil leases had been illegally obtained, and the U.S. Navy regained control of Teapot Dome and other reserves. Fall was ultimately found guilty of bribery, fined $100,000, and sentenced to one year in prison.[24] He was the first cabinet member imprisoned for his actions while in office. President Harding was not aware of the scandal, but it contributed to his administration being considered one of the most corrupt in history.

An *International Business Times* article reports, "Private or publicly listed firms received at least $138 billion of U.S. taxpayer money for government contracts for services that included providing private security, building infrastructure and feeding the troops."[25] The same article reveals that "the company (Haliburton) was given $39.5 billion in Iraq-related contracts over the past decade, with many of the deals given without any bidding." The public entity gained control to serve the public good and private entity profit motivated the need. Again, remember need and greed rhyme. Examining the specific interests is a good place to position your unsuspected 800-pound friendly gorillas.

According to a 2010 PolitiFact article,

> Government officials have raised many questions about KBR's (Halliburton's) fulfillment of its contracts, everything from billing for meals it didn't serve to charging inflated prices for gas to excessive

administrative costs. Government auditors have noted that KBR refused to turn over electronic data in its native format and stamped documents as proprietary and secret when the documents would normally be considered public records. Over the course of several years, the Defense Contract Audit Agency found that $553 million in payments should be disallowed to KBR, according to 2009 testimony by agency director April Stephenson before the bipartisan Commission on Wartime Contracting in Iraq and Afghanistan.[26]

The identified risk: potential to influence, potential to circumvent—Vice President Cheney (enabler). The value he had access to was due to the need for goods and services in a wartime setting war zone (distraction) leading to limited providers, creating the appearance of a no choice need. There were no competitive bids, leading to a breakdown in the systems and controls that were in place.

After risk is identified, the political risk impact needs to be measured. One way to do this is to perform a discounted cash flow (DCF) analysis. The DCF analysis method is used when determining the intrinsic value of an entity (asset or liability). As with the time value of money, discounted cash flow tries to figure out the value today, based on projections of all of the cash that could or would be available or required to be paid out to or by the public entity in the future. Discounted cash flow is based on the "time value of money" principle that cash in the future is worth less than cash today. To measure risk, managers need to create models of the public entity as a network of various interdependent units. For example, when buying goods the public entity might have manufacturing, packaging, and distribution providers across countries bid on the project.

An important aspect of measurement is the translation of past projected transactions into readily identifiable and comprehensible metrics, such as dollar figures, an impact index, or an ability-to-influence index. These metrics should lay out all the risks. In Halliburton, Cheney's former company, there were no-bid contracts, and no policies in place to prevent loopholes and the steering of taxpayer dollars to selected contractors. There were regulatory circumventions and political parties involved in the selection process.

The DATA.gov/metrics site is a great site for the results of government gathering of statistical data. One study, "Widespread Time and Attendance Abuse," analyzes findings and serves as the basis on which a system and structure can be corrected. In the summary report,[27] results of the Census Hiring and Employee Check (CHEC) were investigated. The report found various abuses by the CHEC, and the OIG qualifies that data was interpreted in the most favorable light. "From January 1, 2010 to September 20, 2014, the 40 current and former CHEC office employees whose time and attendance were analyzed resulted in 19,162 hours, which is equal to 2,395 eight-hour days in discrepancy between recorded hours and hours worked. The estimated cost to the taxpayers was $1.1 million," the report says.

While it's hard to get a handle on the losses caused by time theft, one study estimates that it costs U.S. employers more than $400 billion per year in lost productivity.[28] Allowing 10 and 15 minutes here and there add up to big losses over time. The average employee steals four hours and five minutes every week, according to the American Payroll Association.[29] Measuring is a critical area of control. Without maintaining data and continual monitoring, fraud and mismanagement will continue.

Now that the risk has been identified and measured, an effective system for active political risk management can be put in place. The first element in managing political risks is to map potential risk management methods against the priority risks. Once a public entity establishes a course of action, the risk management team needs to assign responsibilities and establish a schedule for consultation, reporting and review, and alignment with other risk controls. A public entity will have multiple options for addressing identified risks, but often one is dealing with unionized labor contracts, nepotism, and other underlying political complications. A public entity that is operating in an environment where there are signs of perceived corrupt labor practices, for example, may seek to review its overall code of conduct and step up local training activities to ensure that all rules are thoroughly understood and a no-tolerance standard is set.

Public entities can gain significantly from recognizing and managing political risk. Effective management of political risk can enable public entities to improve revenue streams and reduce costs.

 ## PUBLIC CORRUPTION

Public corruption means the abuse of power by a political leader to extract and accumulate for private enrichment or to maintain his or her hold on power. Concentration of power in the hands of a president, violence unleashed by security forces and/or devastation under the cover of a state of emergency, and deepening economic inequality, social injustices, and corruption are political tools used to destroy reputations, advance self-interests, and allow fraud and mismanagement to exist.

With the multiple modes of opposition—including political mobilization and street protests by concerned citizens, strikes and sit-ins by workers, and cyber-launched efforts to enhance awareness of state repression and corruption—conflicts also exist that enable corruption.

Abuse of political power for other purposes, such as repression of political opponents and general police brutality, is not considered political corruption. Political corruption takes place at the highest levels of the political system; hence, it can be differentiated from administrative or bureaucratic corruption. It can also be distinguished from business and private-sector corruption.

Political corruption can be approached from the accumulation and assigning of accounting costs. The first is one that includes accumulation and extraction—where government officials use and abuse their hold on power (accumulation) to extract from the private sector, government revenues, and the economy at large to develop a base. With the extracted resources (and public money), they have the ability to preserve and extend their power base. This can be accomplished using nepotism and patronage politics. It includes jobs and politically motivated distribution of financial and material inducements, benefits, advantages, and spoils to supports and other interested parties.

Political scandals are as old as politics itself. Things like sex, greed, and self-importance often go hand in hand with power, money, and cronyism, causing many a politician to stray from the straight and narrow. Scandals have taken the form of extramarital affairs and are personally embarrassing for the parties involved. Others involve abuse of power at the highest level of bestowed trust. These types of scandals destroy reputations and even the most promising careers.

Any system that can be developed relies on the credibility and the reputation of the individual at the top.

DEREGULATION

Deregulation is when the government reduces or eliminates restrictions in order to improve the ease of doing business. Deregulation occurs when Congress repeals a law or the president issues an executive order and the enforcing agency removes or stops enforcing the regulation.

The positive is that the market is free to set prices. It creates an opportunity for smaller players to compete who could not afford the compliance costs and overhead to conform to the laws and the regulated industries that built themselves into monopolies. The negative is that it creates the opportunity for fraud (Enron, gas deregulations) by forming asset bubbles that ultimately burst, creating financial crises and recession as well as the need for bailouts. It prevents industries with large initial infrastructure costs, like electricity and cable companies, from being able to get started. It exposes people to fraud and excessive risk taking by entities that will do anything to gain higher profits. Social concerns are often lost. As an example, a social concern might be to ignore damages to the environment by an entity, since the costs often are not paid by the entities. The social concerns in underserved rural and other unprofitable populations remain.

Banking Deregulation

People have to be required to understand their investments and not rely on the government to fight their battles when risky types of investments later fail, if future crises are to be averted. The idea must change that regulation can prevent profit innovation that creates investments like credit default swaps (CDSs). Credit default swaps are contracts that insure against default of municipal bonds, corporate debt, and mortgage-backed securities. Banks sell CDSs. Remember, the banks' function is to provide liquidity needed for families and businesses to invest for the future. Insurance companies that collect a premium for providing the insurance also sell CDSs. Privately owned hedge fund companies that pool investors' dollars and then reinvest them into all kinds of complicated financial instruments sell CDSs as well. The hedge fund's primary goal is to outperform the market averages. Value and self-interest are the two key ingredients in greed. Understand that collateralized debt obligations (CDOs) are structured asset-backed investments based on the payment stream continuing. Anything that involves structuring and relies on the ability to pay needs to be approached with the appropriate level of skepticism and adequate collateral or protections to safeguard the asset. Creating these types of perceived high-return investments stimulates the external needs and wants. Sound familiar? Bernard Madoff supposedly generated returns no one else could produce. Approach anything that sounds "too good to be true" with caution. Financial regulations are designed to protect investors from financial risk and fraud. In the 1930s, the Glass-Steagall Act was enacted, prohibiting retail banks from using deposits to fund risky investment purchases. In the 1980s, the banking industry sought deregulation to allow global competition with other, more profitable financial firms.

The funny thing is that a bank functions because people trust it. The key words are "functions" and "trust." People give a bank money to keep it safe for them, and then the bank turns around and gives it to someone else in order to make money for itself. The reason most people keep their money in banks is because banks typically pay interest, and they're insured and safe. Well, after the financial crisis one has to wonder how safe banks really are.

The U.S. banks were deregulated in the 1980s. The savings and loans were allowed to invest deposits in commercial, not just residential, real estate. Many of these savings banks began making risky investments. The Federal Home Loan Bank Board (FHLBB) tried to stop them from making these loans. These views were in direct conflict with the policy direction of the Reagan administration, which was to prevent government from interfering with business. The examining of these conflicts is a key tool in developing an overall understanding of what systems and structures are needed.

In 1989, Lincoln Savings and Loan Association, of Irvine, California, collapsed. The Lincoln chairman was Charles H. Keating, who was accused of asking for political support to get the banking regulators to back off. FHLBB former head Edwin J. Gray testified that five senators had asked him to back off from the Lincoln investigation. Those senators, four Democrats and one Republican, in alphabetical order, are Alan Cranston (D-CA), Dennis DeConcini (D-AZ), John Glenn (D-OH), John McCain (R-AZ), and Donald W. Riegle, Jr. (D-MI). They became known as the Keating Five after it was revealed that they received a total of $1.3 million[30] in campaign contributions from Keating. While the investigation determined that all five acted improperly, all of them defended themselves by claiming that this was standard campaign funding practice.

Jeffery Load wrote in the *American Spectator* about the "IRS Ten: The New Keating Five" and compares the two scandals.[31] The Keating Five were accused of corruption in 1989 as part of the larger savings and loan crisis. They all insisted they had done nothing improper. Sounds like a familiar position taken once exposed. The Senate Ethics Committee ultimately concluded in 1991 that none of the Keating Five had violated laws—surprise, surprise. Yet the Senate Committee did say that Senators Cranston, DeConcini, and Riegle had interfered with the bank board's inquiry. Senator Glenn and Senator McCain were cleared but criticized for "poor judgment." Senators determining senator behavior is not independent thinking.

So what's the corruption recipe? Take an independent agency, like the IRS, and pair it with senators' and congressmen's influence. Add to that their powerful contributors (the value) and their self-interested need of wanting something in return. Put it all together, and there's the same formula that created the Keating Five. A report by the House Oversight and Government Reform Committee concluded that the IRS had been biased in targeting taxpayers based on political beliefs.[32]

The independent authority (IRS) + public officials' influence (elected officials) + contribution money for a need they want satisfied, and the potential for fraud and mismanagement exists. With bias comes favoritism and unfair advantage, which, in turn, creates the opportunity for corruption.

Examine who the potential enablers are of illegal targeting by the IRS, based on the authors' examination:

- Barack Obama, President of the United States: tone at the top
- Colleen Kelley, President of the National Treasury Employees Union (NTEU): contributor (enabler)
- Douglas Shulman, U.S. Commissioner of the Internal Revenue Service (IRS), and Lois Lerner, Exempt Organization Director of the IRS: parties that can carry out the act (enablers)
- The IRS Ten, all Democrats (influencers): Charles Schumer (D-NY), Michael Bennet (D-CO), Sheldon Whitehouse (D-RI), Jeff Merkley (D-OR), Tom Udall (D-NM), Al Franken (D-MN), Jeanne Shaheen (D-NH), Carl Levin (D-MI), Max Baucus (D-MT), Peter Welch (D-VT)[33]

Having the power to use a government agency to investigate and having the power to deregulate create the overrides that are necessary to allow fraud and mismanagement to occur. The commonality, from a fraud and mismanagement perspective, is that the IRS Ten, the Keating Five, and Glass-Steagall all involved external motivations and objectives. There is clearly a conflict in any one of these decisions that are put in the hands of a few.

In 1999, the banking industry secured what it wanted, and the Gramm-Leach-Bliley Act repealed the Glass-Steagall Act. The banking industry had promised to only invest in low-risk securities that would diversify their portfolios and reduce risk. Instead, traditional banks invested in risky derivatives to increase profit and shareholder value. The result of the repeal was the financial crisis of 2008 and the near-failure of the entire financial system. The blame at first rested solely on deregulation, but that's not where it belongs. If fraud and mismanagement are to be mitigated, the blame has to be on the people who invested with unchecked trust. The people enabled the investment and, when the investments went bad or the manipulations took place, they became the victims. The real 800-pound friendly gorilla is a public with interest and one that is well-informed, not the one-size-fits-all regulatory thinking.

People create fraud and mismanagement, and only people themselves have the true means to stop them. All regulations are reactive responses, often enforced after the fact or when the act is ongoing. Why not use the fight-your-own-battles thinking? If you develop people who will gather all the information and understand the risks before they act, then it seems like a battle that they can fight on their own. One wonders what sweeping changes in regulation have occurred post 2008 to address the behavior of banks in light of the financial blowup. Unfortunately, we have to disappoint the reader, as changes in regulations and bank supervision have been slow and marginal.

Energy Deregulation

Dr. Wendy Gramm, in her capacity as chairwoman for the Commodity Futures Trading Commission (CFTC) (enabler), is the independent authority that exempted Enron's (contributor wanting something) (influencer) trading of futures contracts in response to a request for such action by Enron in 1992. At the time, Enron was a significant campaign funding source for Wendy Gramm's husband, Texas senator Phil Gramm,[34] the influence. Does Senator Gramm sound familiar? Senator Gramm is the Gramm of the Gramm-Leach-Bliley bill that deregulated banking by repealing the Glass-Steagall Act.

After passage of Gramm's energy commodity deregulation bill, Enron took advantage of the lax oversight that followed deregulation. "Mr. Gramm was one of the ringleaders who engineered the stealth like approval of a bill that exempted energy commodity trading from government regulation and public disclosure," according to a *New York Times* article by Bob Herbert.[35] In the same article, a report from the *Public Citizen* stated that Enron paid Wendy Gramm between $915,000 and $1.85 million in salary, attendance fees, stock options, and dividends from 1993 to 2001. These relationships between the public entity and the entities with which they do business are areas that need to be closely examined.

Enron's manipulation of the energy market was filled with cooked books, lack of oversight, and lack of transparency, and is a classic example of where regulations make sense. Energy is a necessity that people demand; competition needs to be ensured, not monopolistic or oligopolistic entities. Government needs to ensure that it is not supporting these forms of markets that develop absolute control over the public so that people have no choice.

Enron's fraud ultimately led to the Sarbanes-Oxley Act, which was intended to crack down on corporate fraud.

Airline Deregulation

Whenever we have a need, as we have seen in health care and as we move to transportation, we have to be careful with deregulation. Do we have a choice with respect to a bridge with a toll if that's the only way to get to our destination? Similarly, if the airlines create oligopolies with respect to routes is there not the potential for price fixing and coming up with new fees—for example, for bags that weigh more than 50 pounds. Does this not lead to targeting routes that are more profitable and leaving other areas underserved? The point is that these events cause distraction, diversion, and division and need to be monitored with 800-pound friendly gorilla oversight.

In the 1960s and 1970s, the airline industry was being targeted for deregulation. In the 1978 Airline Deregulation Act, U.S. federal law intended to remove government control over fares, routes, and all new airline market entries from commercial aviation. The Civil Aeronautics Board (CAB), at the time, regulated routes and set fares that were guaranteeing airlines a 12 percent return on flights that were 55 percent full.[36] During this era, airline travel was so expensive that 80 percent of Americans had never traveled by air. The Airline Deregulation Act solved the problem; the CAB's only responsibility to regulate was safety. Competition rose, fares dropped, and more people flew.

Companies that could no longer compete were merged, acquired, or went bankrupt. As a result, a limited number of airlines control the U.S. market, creating a near-monopoly. Deregulation has led to some problems. Small and even midsized cities are underserved. It's just not cost-effective for the major airlines to keep a full schedule. The result: Smaller carriers serve these cities at a higher cost and less frequently. Airlines are now charging for things that used to be free, such as changing a ticket, meals, and luggage. Flying has become an unpleasant experience, between the security searches, crowded flights, and long waits. However, the consumer expectations are driving the costs, and the public can choose and manage the flight costs as a result of availability of information via the Internet or other means. Ultimately, one must consider the benefits and costs of regulation. While universal air service may be desirable, a regulatory regime changes the costs and flow of resources in the system. Thus, travelers from hub cities with high volumes would be paying more to provide service to routes that had weaker traveler patterns. With rate regulation, the carriers were guaranteed a profit and had a lock on certain routes. Today we live in a world of more competitive prices—and much greater air travel.

The decline of small and midsized airports and the potential for underserved smaller cities should not be viewed. The view should be the economics, such as the trend in rising fuel costs, industry consolidation, and better management at the big airlines. The small and midsized companies have to develop a cost-effectiveness measure and not make the perception flat for everyone. First class costs more than coach, and if people can pay for it, they fly first class. If they can't, they fly coach to live within their means.

CONCLUSION

As we've shown, there is a value in seeing the past factors associated with corruption. It takes all shapes and sizes and affects all industries. The required formula for corruption to work is: Independent authority + Public officials' influence + Contributions of money for a need they need satisfied = potential corruption, fraud, and mismanagement. Monitor the personality behavior, match the self-interests, and, most important, remember to apply 3 J thinking to the process and the people overseeing the process in the public entity. Be reminded that intent is a key element needed to call it a corrupt act, and often remains very difficult to prove. Also, the final deciders of whether it's a corrupt act or not are the judges and jurors of those facts, not you as an examiner.

Planning, direction, and control matter. Accumulation and assigning the levels of responsibility to those who can access the value matter. Monitor the areas where there are conflicting interests with the unsuspected 800-pound friendly gorilla.

Introducing unsuspected checks, requiring term limits, and job/position rotation, which create accountability, matter. Maintain a well-informed and educated citizenry. Ensure transparency, by having readily available information that keeps the interested parties informed, that is disseminated to the public in easy to understand communication. The system must establish an independent level of approval process prior to the act taking place. These lead to developing a proactive rather than regulator-reactive approach. These remain key tools to be put in place in formulating a sound system and structure that can prevent fraud and mismanagement. It comes down to responsible management with the proper levels of oversight and a clear understanding of the personality behaviors surrounding these responsibilities where the trust levels can gain access to the value and convert it to cash.

NOTES

1. https://www.washingtonpost.com/news/the-fix/wp/2014/05/22/the-rapid-rise-of-the-career-politician-in-2-gifs/.
2. http://www.justice.gov/opa/pr/us-navy-commander-pleads-guilty-international-bribery-scandal.
3. http://espn.go.com/dallas/nfl/story/_/id/12143556/new-jersey-gov-chris-christie-attend-dallas-cowboys-playoff-game-green-bay-packers.

4. Cindy Boren, "Chris Christie's Trip to Dallas on Jerry Jones's Dime Raises Ethics Concerns" in *Washington Post* (Jan 5, 2006). https://www.washingtonpost.com/news/early-lead/wp/2015/01/06/chris-christies-trip-to-dallas-on-jerry-jones-dime-raises-ethics-concerns/.

5. https://www.irs.gov/uac/Examples-of-Public-Corruption-Investigations-Fiscal-Year-2013.

6. http://www.nytimes.com/2015/10/05/business/valeants-drug-price-strategy-enriches-it-but-infuriates-patients-and-lawmakers.html.

7. http://www.therichest.com/rich-list/most-shocking/10-most-shocking-cases-of-government-embezzlement/10/.

8. http://www.nj.com/news/index.ssf/2010/08/major_changes_might_be_on_way.html.

9. http://jewishvoiceny.com/index.php?option=com_content&view=article&id=11792:new-york-corruption-cases-swirl-around-nepotism-and-patronage&catid=112:new-york&Itemid=295.

10. John A. Gardiner, "Defining Corruption," in *Corruption and Reform* 7 (1993).

11. http://archive.app.com/article/20070118/NEWS/701180387/EX-KEYPORT-MAYOR-BRIBE-PLEA-GUILTY.

12. http://ij.org/case/city-of-long-branch-v-gregory-p-brower/.

13. http://www.nj.com/hudson/index.ssf/2015/07/fulop_moves_to_eliminate_agency_where_workers_were.html.

14. https://www.treasurydirect.gov/govt/rates/pd/avg/2014/2014_12.htm.

15. http://www.freddiemac.com/pmms/pmms30.htm.

16. http://data.bls.gov/cgi-bin/cpicalc.pl?cost1=100&year1=1985&year2=2015 ; 100 dollars in 1985 is 220.36 in 2015 (30 years), solve for the yearly inflation rate and you get 2.66%.

17. https://www.ssa.gov/news/press/basicfact.html.

18. https://smartasset.com/retirement/average-retirement-savings-are-you-normal.

19. https://www.ssa.gov/OACT/TR/2013/.

20. http://www.usgovernmentspending.com/entitlement_spending.

21. http://www.nj.com/news/index.ssf/2013/12/nj_has_second_highest_median_household_income_according_to_census.html.

22. http://www.richestlifestyle.com/richest-insurance-companies-in-the-world/.

23. Office of Management and Budget, President's Budget for Fiscal Year 2016, Budget Authority.

24. http://www.encyclopedia.com/topic/Teapot_Dome.aspx.

25. http://readersupportednews.org/news-section2/308-12/16561-focus-cheneys-halliburton-made-395-billion-on-iraq-war.

26. http://www.politifact.com/truth-o-meter/statements/2010/jun/09/arianna-huffington/halliburton-kbr-and-iraq-war-contracting-history-s/.

27. https://www.oig.doc.gov/OIGPublications/OIG-14-0790-I_Summary.pdf.

28. Terrance Daryl Shulman, "Biting the Hand That Feeds: The Employee Theft Epidemic," *Kentucky CPA Journal* (Fall 2007).
29. http://www.americanpayroll.org.
30. http://spectator.org/articles/55417/irs-ten-new-keating-five.
31. https://www.google.com/url?sa=t&rct=j&q=&esrc=s&source=web&cd=1& cad=rja&uact=8&ved=0ahUKEwi5p_KGl-nKAhVJJx4KHQLvBX0QFggd MAA&url=http%3A%2F%2Fspectator.org%2Farticles%2F55417%2Firs- ten-new-keating-five&usg=AFQjCNEkb_QO8cM9urjUEb-o1eWcZt97Ig& sig2=8G7d4zpvovlH7wTBmdHqOQ.
32. https://oversight.house.gov/release/issa-releases-report-irs-targeting-113th- congress-concludes/.
33. http://www.foxbusiness.com/government/2013/05/23/how-political- pressure-on-irs-began/.
34. https://www.citizen.org/documents/Blind_Faith.PDF.
35. http://www.nytimes.com/2002/01/17/opinion/enron-and-the-gramms .html.
36. http://www.huffingtonpost.com/david-morris/airline-deregulation-ideology- over-evidence_b_4399150.html.

CHAPTER SEVEN

Policing of Public Corruption and Fraud

"Honesty is the best policy."

—*Benjamin Franklin*

Topics:

Key Regulations—Gaps in Federal, State, and Local Rules
Enforcement—Who Are the Police?
Enforcement Gaps—Do They Police?

Key questions:

Is there consistency in the application of the law, or do some get a "get out of jail free" card because of their affiliations?
Why are there these expectation gaps?
Can you legislate ethical behavior?

THIS CHAPTER ADDRESSES the key regulations over government corruption and the operational aspects of these laws and policies. The authors explore variation in laws, rules, and practices by states and compare them with federal law. In addition, the aspects of enforcement and policymaking by regulatory agencies are considered. Finally, a holistic view of government practice by type of agency is examined, with comparisons to international standards. Unfortunately, today's auditors need to understand the personalities of fraudsters, and, equally unfortunate, is that most do not have the required skills to determine the people who are likely to perpetrate a fraud. Proactive thinking is the skill needed to prevent fraud.

This chapter homes in on the Generally Accepted Accounting Principles (GAAP) and regulation. We do not require you to memorize rules but, rather, that you change your thinking that rules can prevent fraud. Can moral behavior be legislated? The authors employ a "reasonable person" standard. That standard is defined as whether people with different experiences and levels of knowledge who are tasked with determining whether or not the party being examined displayed moral behavior all come to the same conclusion.

Put three independent people in a room. Will they all come to the same conclusions given their different experiences and levels of knowledge? If they all conclude, given the possible diversity in their backgrounds, that something is ethical, then it likely is.

However, most circumstances do not operate from the perspective of a majority. Most standards are, instead, built on more-likely-than-not scenarios or a preponderance-of-the-evidence, which are based on the 50.01 percent rule. If something is probable, it requires recording. In government secrecy spending (the $52.6 billion black box budget),[1] interfund transfers and creative policy maneuvering—whether through shuffling of debt or by creating sound-bite policies that target the few but are not applicable to government—there are huge gaps in how rules are applied. There are one-size-fits-all policies and the mentality that if you know someone powerful, you will get more lenient treatment. The foremost rule is that objectivity and integrity lead the heart to independent thinking. Until this foundation principle is adhered to at all levels of the government and/or in public entities, fraud and mismanagement will persist. Let's take a look at how the gatekeepers lose their way and what must be done to improve the necessary systems and structures to create accountability that stops mismanagement and fraud before it happens.

First, develop an understanding of the regulatory gap. Where there is an absence of adequate laws (including regulations and monitoring and enforcement systems) to govern an activity, there is a regulatory gap. These gaps sprout where there are competing issues in which one person in the conflict has an unfair advantage over another.

Look at observable governance gaps that occur in public entities. Where there are no mechanisms in place to ensure coordination and cooperation within and across sectors—between federal, state, local, and public agencies and institutions—gaps are created in federal rules. Where there is a lack of agency oversight or process necessary for the proper administration of principles and policies associated with activities, there are federal regulatory gaps.

Failing to maintain a process that ensures consistent application of governance principles—such as transparency, accountability, public citizen participation, and adequate funding mechanisms—also creates a gap in the federal rules. Failing to assess existing and future uses of the public entity resources, in terms that protect and preserve the intent of the regulations, will spur gaps in the federal rules. Having no systems in place that safeguard a public entity's resources and manage the costs associated with providing the activity will also create gaps in the federal rules.

A public entity's failure to have effective compliance and enforcement in place will precipitate gaps in federal rules. A lack of clarity in the intended purpose of a policy and regulations which the general public does not understand is also a springboard to gaps in federal rules.

If a public entity's policy and/or program lacks participation and there is a failure to properly implement, a perceived lack of enforcement (monitoring), a feeling of unsustainability, and general disinterest, regulatory gaps will continue. The saying "The squeaky wheel gets the grease" comes to mind. These gaps become evident when a lot of noise is made over them.

BACKGROUND ON INTERNAL CONTROL

In order to close the gaps in regulation, there must be controls that establish consistency, independence, reliability, and relevance. Internal control is the key to ensuring that government standards are properly being applied and maintaining the overall integrity of the governmental unit's financial reporting and accounting to establish numbers that don't lie. Without reliability, independence, and consistency by the management of the public entity, the financial information being reported may not tell the real story. Throughout this book there have been examples of how a breakdown in communication or a circumvention and lack of internal control can enable fraud and mismanagement to occur. Remember, accountants test the internal control system;

they do not run them or sign off as the party responsible for the internal controls—management does.

In order to understand internal control from a forensic auditor's view, the auditor needs new skills that we call *personality audit testing*. Like the *Audit Risk Model* (inherent risk times detection risk times audit risk [IR x DR x AR]), the *Deviant Behaviors Risk Model* is built around abnormal types of behavior. The *Deviant Audit Behavior Model* (FRB x RFB x PSER x AER) is **Financial Reporting Behavior** times **Risk Found Behavior** (behavior surrounding a found risk) times **Planning and Supervision Engagement Risk Behavior** (how well the examination was planned) times **Audit Execution Risk Behaviors** (whether the proper tests and procedures were performed or whether there were shortcuts or gray areas overlooked). If during the examination or review of any public entity's process there are deviant behaviors or diversionary behaviors encountered in the financial reporting, found risks, planning and supervision, and execution you should require further documentary evidence to support the findings. This ensures that the public entity is free of Material misrepresentation, which may have been Intentionally done, that created a Reliance and resulted in Damages (MIRD)—the four elements of fraud.

In 1992, the Committee of Sponsoring Organizations of the Treadway Commission (COSO), a group of auditors and accountants, issued a report that reestablished internal control as a broad management tool. Here is the important point that has to be established: This is *management's responsibility, not the accountant's. Without management integrity (proper personality behavior) and oversight within the governmental or public entity, there is no credibility in the financial reporting.* In the 1940s, internal control was the idea of coordinating procedures that lead a business to protect its assets and check the accuracy and reliability of the accounting data. As Joe stated in his previous book, internal control is only as strong as the people who are coordinating and ensuring compliance.

This definition of internal control was viewed as being too broad. So, in 1963, the American Institute of Certified Public Accountants (AICPA) broke the controls into two categories: administrative controls and accounting controls. These two controls were to establish operational efficiency in addition to safeguarding the assets and maintaining the reliability and accuracy of the accounting records. Accounting controls revolve around the physical controls over assets and reporting, while administrative controls are more about analyzing through training, quality control, and studying the performance of the established controls.

In 1972, the AICPA reduced the auditor's responsibility. It should be reiterated that an auditor only provides *reasonable assurances* (not *beyond reasonable doubt*), so if the management integrity is not there, the financial reporting entity is exposed to mismanagement and fraud.

The authors follow Joe's idea that the COSO model is like a Rubik's Cube. Requiring twists and turns to bring all the colors into line, the Rubik's Cube is a reminder of how the faces of political environments are exposed to those same twists and turns.

The five main components of the COSO model are:

- the control environment
- risk assessment
- control activities
- monitoring and information
- communication

In 1996, the AICPA recognized it as an acceptable framework. Unfortunately, Enron, WorldCom, Tyco, and a slew of other financial frauds occurred, and, in 2002, the Sarbanes-Oxley (SOX) Act required management to certify the internal control system. It also established the Public Company Accounting Oversight Board (PACOB) to set auditing standards and regulate the firms performing the audits—more regulation in an attempt to create ethical behavior. Auditor rotation, audits of the auditor, and peer review are a good start. But who audits the audit of the government?

A January 2013 report from the GAO regarding the state of the U.S. government budget process to the president, the president of the U.S. Senate, and the speaker of the House of Representatives said, "Material weaknesses resulted in ineffective internal control over financial reporting for fiscal year 2012."[2] If the government of the United States does not have strong internal controls, how does it expect other organizations to recognize the importance of well-established internal controls? Regulations need to be equally applied to everyone if they are expected to create accountability.

The good news is that the COSO model was updated in 2013. Unfortunately, it remains a voluntary private-sector initiative. For this or any model leading to control to work, it needs to be integrated into the culture that exists within the public entity. These initiatives have to be voluntarily embraced by the top decision makers and a lead-by-example tone has to be set at the top—one that is self-policing.

Table 7.1 shows the changes in the updated 2013 COSO model. This is an ever-evolving model that will continually need redefining to set up the appropriate internal controls. The reason? There is always change.

In government and/or the public agency, there is either new management with a changing of the guard or management that seems to be a permanent

TABLE 7.1 Updates to the COSO Model

What changed	What did not change
Core definition of internal control	Changes in business and operating environments considered
Three categories of objectives and five components of internal control	Operations and reporting objectives expanded
Each of the five components of internal control are required for effective internal control	Fundamental concepts underlying five components articulated as principles
Important role of judgment in designing, implementing, and conducting internal control, and in assessing its effectiveness	Additional approaches and examples relevant to operations, compliance, and nonfinancial reporting objectives added

Source: http://www.coso.org/documents/coso%20mcnallytransition%20article-final%20coso%20version%20proof_5-31-13.pdf

political fixture with the same old same oversight. One type of fraud that comes to mind is the one in which write-downs after acquisition give the new takeover management the ability to blame others for the ills of the past. Hewlett Packard (HP) purchased Autonomy for $11.1 billion in 2011. A year later, HP announced an $8.8 billion write-down and blamed $5.5 billion of that loss to accounting fraud at Autonomy before the sale. Autonomy founder Mike Lynch claimed that HP determined that U.S. and international accounting practices permitted certain revenues to be reported at later dates than from when they were initially earned. HP then recorded the Autonomy 2010 and 2011 revenue in future periods. The accounting term for this is "deferring revenues," which is a liability until the revenue is later recognized.

Where were the internal controls? Why is a simple accounting change capable of having a devastating effect on the true financial picture? Because all decisions are judgment-based. Is government borrowing to fund operations or spending beyond what it expects to collect any different? What needs to be different is that the internal control needs to also apply to the external issues and influences, not just the internal. That way, people outside the management entity see the appropriate levels of control in place. How is that done when it's labeled voluntary? When the external activities create the value, via taxes, fees, or borrowing, the necessary 800-pound friendly gorilla oversight needs to be in place. The COSO model of control needs to develop an external perspective of what's not in the internal processes and off book, or outside the accounting systems.

The Financial Managers' Financial Integrity Act of 1982 was politicians' reminder to the government officials of where to maintain internal controls. The core objectives of the act were to provide "reasonable assurance" of the following:

1. Obligation and costs complied with the applicable laws. If the act was meeting its objective, why are government officials allowed to underfund pensions? Whenever policies are able to be overridden and a diversion of funds is allowed to occur, the result is one public entity policy benefiting at the expense of another. A one-shot-fix creates opportunities for mismanagement and fraud. A sound system does not allow for dictatorial decisions and should require the approval of a majority and reasonable thinking.

2. Assets are safeguarded from waste, misappropriation, and loss. Clearly, in the examples cited in this book the internal controls are not working.

3. Revenue and expenditures are recorded properly to enable the preparation of reliable financial statement presentations to the reader.

The bankruptcy of Detroit comes to mind and hundreds of other government and public entities that use debt, modified accounting, and other accounting gimmicks. Other examples of potential accounting gimmicks are not reserving funds for future liabilities like sick time accruals, underfunding required pension contributions liabilities, and funding other areas of the budget by raising one budget line item with less interest and then transferring to other line items that may draw further scrutiny by exposing cost overruns.

The public body can create resolutions and other documents to cover the trail, rationalize the expenditure, or justify the revenue. OMB revised its provisions and embraced COSO and the SOX provisions with respect to internal controls. The key concept these revisions embrace is that of additional assurances. What assurances? The "assurances" have been in place for a while, yet the federal debt lingers above $18 trillion. A 2012 *Reuters* article reported that "America's 50 state governments owe $4.19 trillion, including outstanding bonds, unfunded pension commitments and budget gaps, according to a new report. At $617.6 billion, California had by far the biggest total debt, more than twice the total of No. 2, New York, with $300.1 billion owed, according to State Budget Solutions, a research and non-partisan advocacy group. Texas, with $287 billion owed, New Jersey, with $282.4 billion, and Illinois, with $271.1 billion, ranked next among states with the biggest total debt, according to State Budget Solutions. Vermont had the smallest debt load at $5.85 billion."[3]

Debt liability and allowable overspending create outstanding bonds, unfunded pension liability, and budget gaps. With the ability to use liabilities to fund rather than an adequate revenue base as working capital, insolvency is created. Where are the internal controls to manage these runaway obligations? A system cannot have solid controls when the assurance is being entrusted to a few individuals—especially when language like "reasonable" and "judgment" is added to significant financial decisions. There is also the blame-it-on-the-other-guy mentality of politics. People love putting the blame on one fraudster such as Bernie Madoff or gangsters like Al Capone. Until the culture that breeds the type of thinking that allows these fraudsters to exist is held accountable and the people who fuel these fraudsters' ability to perpetrate fraud are held responsible, fraud and mismanagement will continue.

As long as society perceives behavior as acceptable, that enables the fraudster to operate. Investors will be getting returns that no one else could generate. Here are some scenarios that create environments where fraud can exist: people wanting to drink (Prohibition), deregulation of the gas industry (Enron), and the repeal of the Glass-Steagall act (subprime meltdown). Understand who these potential enablers and detractors are. They are a means to create a gap in regulations.

The Rubik's Cube should come to mind when you look at Figure 7.1 and the idea of twists and turns caused by people in the control process. By applying the new soft skill testing technique, the Deviant Behaviors Risk Model, you begin

FIGURE 7.1 Committee of Sponsoring Organizations (COSO) 2013 Internal Control Framework Cube

Source: http://www.coso.org/documents/coso%20mcnallytransition%20article-final%20coso%20version%20proof_5-31-13.pdf

gaining an understanding of the people's personalities involved in applying the framework. The systems are management systems enforced by people and this is a new tool that will prevent fraud and mismanagement. Like a Rubik's Cube it requires the right twisting and turning to solve the puzzle and align all the colors. It's no different in aligning all the public entities' responsibilities.

Only through people following models like the Committee of Sponsoring Organizations (COSO) 2013 Internal Control Framework, will these deviant behaviors begin to be controlled and identified. The people involved in any framework need to have skills that look beyond generating numbers themselves. Without proper oversight with the appropriate level of professional skepticism they will not be effective.

Environment changes that have driven Framework updates:
- Expectations for governance oversight
- Globalization of markets and operations
- Changes and greater complexity in business
- Demands and complexities in laws, rules, regulations, and standards
- Expectations for competencies and accountabilities
- Use of, and reliance on, evolving technologies
- Expectations relating to preventing and detecting fraud
- Financial transaction complexity and managed finance

Developing effective interviewing techniques is critical when opening channels of communication in a fraud investigation. An important question to ask is what kind of information is necessary? Think about things like what happened, where it happened, when it happened, why it happened (intent is difficult to determine independently), how it happened, how much was taken, who has the opportunity, and who helped it happen.

When an organization is formed, the thinking is all about how to make a profit. When the organization hires its employees, the assumption is that these people will have the organization's best interests at heart. This is where there is a need for controls and/or an understanding that a lack of controls can create conflicts of interest.

 ## DISTINGUISHING AMONG DETERRENCE, PREVENTION, AND DETECTION

Much has been written about what fraud is, how fraud occurs, trends among those committing or trying to commit fraud, and the importance of the "Tone at the Top" principle in an effort to stem the flow of fraud. Antifraud programs are typically defined as deterrence, prevention, or detection tasks. But what exactly do these task terms mean, and how are they distinguishable from each other?

Fraud deterrence refers to tasks or barriers designed to discourage those with a temptation to commit fraud from doing so. The threat of imprisonment and the fear of becoming a social outcast are examples of deterrence.

Fraud prevention refers to methods and strategies used to prevent those not deterred from succeeding in committing a fraud. Requiring two signatures on checks is an example of fraud prevention.

Fraud detection describes the methodologies deployed to investigate allegations when deterrent and preventive approaches have not been successful in thwarting a fraudster's efforts.

The goal of a fraud investigation is to obtain sufficient and relevant information surrounding the event or allegation to come to a credible conclusion as to whether or not a fraud occurred and identify the perpetrator.[4] The American Institute of Certified Public Accountants' Code of Professional Conduct says that sufficient and relevant information must be obtained to support conclusions reached.[5] This requirement is not only necessary for compliance with many organizations' professional standards; it also makes a lot of sense, because it establishes acceptable practices within the industry standards.

Entities that rely on reactionary postures and wait for suspicions to arise are more susceptible to fraud. Sound fraud risk policy requires that standing and ongoing procedures are in place to address deterrence, prevention, and detection simultaneously. Unfortunately, there are no systems, procedures, policies, or other mechanisms one could deploy that would provide a 100 percent guarantee against fraud. Good and bad economies provide motivation for the potential fraudster. As long as there are people with access to money and other items of value that belong to someone else, there will be a risk of fraud that must be managed. This is a key point of this text. It is these vulnerable areas within an organization that need to be exposed and understood in order to deter, prevent, and detect fraud. Proactive rather than reactive fraud management is critical in the fight against organizational fraud.

The only way to manage fraud risk effectively is by identifying value within an organization and protecting that value using a methodology or approach *specific* to that organization. There is no way to definitively predict who among an organization's stakeholders is likely to try to commit fraud, and there is no generic, or one-size-fits-all, method to prevent its occurrence. Organizations are unique in terms of structure and staffing. Individuals are unique, and there

is no uniform system designed to capture each fraud before it is c
Each organization's situation needs to be examined on its own merits, and a
solution devised to meet its needs based on its unique characteristics and the
characters involved.

 BACK TO ANALYZING THE RISK BEYOND NUMBERS

The risks beyond the numbers and the gaps in regulatory caps in the prevention of fraud and mismanagement are evident in analyzing the risks associated
with finances.

Financial Reporting Risk

Financial reporting risk includes more than just fund balance management
(e.g., overstating assets or revenues, understating liabilities or expenditures).
These are the types of potential financial misconduct by public officials that are
perceived to fund their policy decisions. Maybe these manipulations are needed
to create numbers that are not backed by the liquid value required to fund current operational costs and mask the real necessary tax increases in an election
year. These are not numbers. They're external pressures. Again, what are the
personality traits of the people surrounding the financial risk? Remember that
the examination of any deviant behaviors or abnormal behaviors is the skill to
be applied. While numbers don't lie, people often do, so examine the personalities of the people involved in the process.

If the government did not let the roads deteriorate or divert highway
resources to other purposes, it couldn't justify raising tolls or gasoline taxes.
Examining the behavior and the personalities is accomplished by knowing the
right questions to ask and understanding the personalities behind the decisions.
For example, why are they not fixing the roads, where are the funds flowing,
and what is causing the abnormal or deviant behavior are simple questions
that need to be asked in order to create transparency and create accountability.

If people didn't need health care, the government could not justify raising
taxes or creating new taxes around the Affordable Care Act. If there were no terrorists, government would be unable to justify spending so much on security
and the military. The point is that the real financial risks are not in the public entity processes, but in the external forces that drive them. These are all
driven by deviant or abnormal behaviors and the advancing of one interest at
the expense of another.

Where are the real financial risk behavior abnormalities? The risk is in
the spending that is redirected. Look for spending items that continually go

over budget. Look at journal entries to see who is making them and why the entries are being made. What level of authority is making the journal entry or the decision to override?

Monitor any increases from year to year over 10 years, if the information is available. It takes five years, at minimum, to start analyzing a meaningful trend. Look for spending items that can be transferred to fund other purposes. Getting answers as to why a transfer is needed and why money is left over in that certain line item is managing the risk. Look at the revenues. If they increased, how is the money being used? The more money government has, the more it spends. What is the year-over-year change? What is the 10-year trend, if available? Getting answers to explain these variations is managing the risk. One-shot revenues, using surpluses, and borrowing money all have inherent financial risks, as funds will need to be replaced or paid back. Unfunded liabilities and transfers between funds to related public entities all present financial risks. None of these risks should be allowed. A plan for how to handle them in the future should be in place. Often these risks are allowed by a particular elected official's vote, which, as discussed, does not represent a majority, since not everyone votes.

The longer a public entity does business with a particular vendor and/or contractor, the greater the financial risk. Again, look at the personalities surrounding the procurement process. The longer the decision-making approval authority has been making the decisions, the greater the financial risk. Experience can be beneficial most of the time, unless the ethics change and the rationalizations begin.

Operational Risk

Operational risk is found by understanding where the assets and revenues came from and how and where they are funded within a public entity. Apply the internal control deviant/abnormal behavior model. Have there been overrides, diversions, and unusual behavior that you have encountered? If the revenues and assets were obtained by fraudulent or misrepresented means or through the use of illicit tactics to avoid incurring expenditures (e.g., not funding accumulated sick time or pension liabilities to give the perception of not raising taxes to the public), the result will be a need to raise taxes and incur debt. Who are the people behind the numbers and what behaviors are demonstrated in arriving at the final asset and revenue numbers? What caused a negative fund balance and an inability to continue to provide the service? Whether or not it is fraud, misstating facts or poor judgments of the past create operational risks; the numbers are the damage after the fact. While the financial status in the present period is important, even more important is how we got to their point.

It's all too common to hear that it's the last guy's fault, with years' worth of warning signs. There are higher taxes, huge debts on the books of the federal and state governments, fewer services, municipal bankruptcies. Yet, no one is saying anything about any operational risk fixes being in place to prevent a recurrence.

Operational risks are the fiscal risks inherent in the practice of people at the top advancing their own interests at the (budgetary) expense of the public. Understanding the behavior of the people in public entities is a critical skill needed to prevent fraud and mismanagement. Operational risk lies in the assumptions and judgments made. Those assumptions and judgments should be checked as frequently as needed to ensure that the underlying assumption holds true and the fiscal objectives and goals are being met. Forget generally accepted accounting principles of any kind and develop reports that tell the real story. All regulated financials come after the fact and in uniformly presented formats. Management accounting is based on performance and efficiency and is not annually presented, as is currently the case with government and public entities. The operational risk is not found in the final financial numbers, but by gaining an understanding of the people who are behind the numbers and responsible for developing the assumptions that these reports are based on, as that is not always evident. Only with continual testing of these judgments will fraud and mismanagement be mitigated.

The accounting regulations are in place, yet the government continually finds ways to deviate from them and get by without consequences. Clearly, there are huge loopholes in federal rules, and the policing of these rules is, at best, sparse.

Compliance Risk

Compliance risk exists when no one follows the required controls and procedures and expenditures or liabilities are incurred for improper purposes (e.g., corrupt practices), or there is asset misappropriation through embezzlement of funds or other resources of the public entity. There are myriad rules and agencies in place, yet taxes are out of control, tolls increase, wages have not gone up to maintain purchasing power, and wealth inequality grows. The Deviant and Abnormal Behavior Test developed in this book is likely to result in more findings in this area of risk than others, the reason being that people with power often believe that the rules do not apply to them and they have the ability to override them.

Yet, we're led to believe there is compliance testing and regulatory oversight that prevent fraud and mismanagement. Defined simply, compliance is a rule that is followed by all and applied to everyone uniformly. With all the government forms, there needs to be one uniform form of compliance throughout the nation. It should be called the ICS form—the "I Can Steal" form. This is the biggest risk of all. If there is compliance, there will be no financial or operational risks. In fact, compliance is the great enforcer. If every public employee were in compliance, there would be no fraud or mismanagement, other than outright stick-'em-up-and-give-me-the-money robbery. Examining behavior of the people involved in ensuring the compliance is one tool to reduce financial and operational risks. Again, know the people behind the numbers and develop the appropriate oversight necessary to maintain proper ethical behavior.

 ## WORMS

Planarian worms are tiny freshwater flatworms that are about the size of fingernail clippings and can re-form from slivers 1/300th of their original size. To do this, planarian worms use stem cells, called neoblasts, which have the ability to become almost any cell type in the body. Webster's online dictionary defines a stem cell as a simple cell in the body that is able to develop into any one of various kinds of cells (such as blood cells, skin cells, etc.).

The risk in the public entity is very similar to the stem cell. Its starts out as a sliver and morphs itself into whatever form is necessary to remain undetected.

Warnings Operations Revolve Management System (WORMS)

Since the public entity is based on authority (power), there needs to be an accumulation of the process positions where the accumulation of value takes place and an understanding of how management assigns these accumulation of value points. These accumulation of power positions should apply the POP principle to see if there are proper levels of oversight surrounding the potential risk exposure. Without the Warnings Operations Revolve Management System (WORMS) and the understanding of how management morphs its cell through the many slivers of change that occur, risks will not be quantifiable.

So what are the risks faced by management in public entities?

1. *Support risk (SR)* takes on the funding support that is in place. Can the management support the people needed to execute and carry out the policy? Is the scope well-defined? Support Risk = Underfunding + Unskilled + Undefined.

2. The next risk is *change risk (CR)*, where the management can be changed because of the association of political or nepotistic ties: Change Risk = Relationship + Time + Skill.
3. *Design risk* is the feasibility analysis of the plan to determine whether it will be a success: Design Risk = Research and Development + Talent to Develop + Time to Set up + Cost to Set up. In the accounting world, this is called a cost/benefit analysis.
4. *Technical risk* is what's available, what's changing, the usability, and the security issues involved, such as identity theft and preserving information privacy and credibility. Technical Risk = Cost + Change in Technology + Sophistication of Users + Security Breaches.
5. *Integration risk* is the risk in delivering these designed services, which is subject to interruptions, cultural changes, and economic, social, and political factors, and needs to be monitored closely. Integration risk = Cost + Change + Communication. It is managing the costs and resources within a public entity's process, factoring in the fact that all processes in the public entity are connected.

Timing is everything. Most things can be measured in time. It is in the manipulation of time where the major risks lie. If a project is not completed on time, it means more cost. The longer something takes, the more complexities, or the more resistance, the greater the chance that the necessary distractions are in place to potentially manipulate the numbers. For example, the economy is booming, property values appreciate, and the government that bases taxes on property values thrives. With all these external distractions, the people often have no interest. Take away the economic concerns and the appreciating property values, and the interest level rises, often allowing the inefficiencies and fraud to come to light. During that period of growth, restraint needs to be put into the design, because what goes up (property values) eventually comes down. Not having built reserves into these potential down turns or unexpected events leads to pressure and potential short-term fixes when the funds begin to dry up. Again, examining the personalities of the people in the positions of authority and the types of behaviors they are displaying is important.

Atlantic City is a perfect example of value shift. For years, the taxpayers of Atlantic City paid very low taxes due to the fact that the casinos comprise much of the property value. With gambling expanding into other states surrounding Atlantic City, and the Revel Casino bankruptcy—which was built for $2.4 billion and sold for $82 million—which helped substantiate the drop in property values of surrounding casinos and thus reducing their property tax burdens, the tax base shifted to the residents. New Jersey Governor Chris Christie called it a financial crisis; finance experts called it poor management.

Think of project Xanadu, a multi-billion-dollar megamall funded by taxpayer money. An NJ.com article says, "Triple Five, the company that took control of the project in 2010, plans to invest $2.5 billion into the site, about $800 million of which will be raised through bond issuances."[6] The East Rutherford, New Jersey, mayor, James Cassella, according to that same article, pushed to raise the proceeds by utilizing a $675 million bond debt offering on Triple Five's behalf. This is debt collateralized on the backs of the Rutherford taxpayers. Another NJ.com article reports, "As shopping malls across the country are dying, New Jersey is attempting to add another giant complex to its already crowded landscape, even as other tourist destinations, such as Atlantic City, continue to wither."[7] It is always hard to determine who would get a "haircut" (also known as a financial loss) in the event of a default or financial failure in a publically financed private deal. The claim is usually made that the government entity faces no risk—but as we will see—many times the state is encourage making a public investment or forgoing tax revenue. These are very questionable investments at best.

The subject of a *Bloomberg* article[8] is the Revel Casino in Atlantic City, in which Christie invested public resources. "Technically, the state didn't invest any money in Revel," the story says. "Instead, it agreed to reimburse $261 million in sales, hotel and corporate taxes that Revel might collect over the next 20 years. In exchange, the state will get 20 percent of any profits received by Revel's owners. This structure mimics an equity investment without requiring the state to put up any cash." The same story points to the fact that "Construction on American Dream (Xanadu) has been off and on since 2004, and in 2011, New Jersey put up $200 million to allow the $3 billion project to be completed."

Timing is everything, and risks like these need to be better managed. Understanding these past accumulations of bad investments or assistances that are ongoing will help in developing the necessary systems to handle and mange such risks and prevent them in the future. In cost accounting, costs are accumulated and associated with a particular product. Depending on the product being made, accounting for those costs can be a simple or complex process. It is an important philosophy to recognize when you are throwing good money after bad money. Tax dollars should be risk averse, not subject to elected officials' decisions to spend millions. The problems often take years to create, and risky short-term fixes are not often the best answers.

To encourage a better understanding of risk concepts, Figure 7.2 was developed as a reference tool. The first area is the idea of accumulate and assign. What are the proper documentary pieces of evidence needed to gain the proper understanding of these risks? Once there is an understanding of the potential risks, they can be assigned the proper oversight controls.

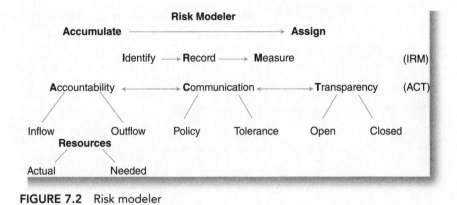

FIGURE 7.2 Risk modeler

The basic relevant principles are those of evidence (accumulation) and determining what weight to assign them. By assigning weight, consider whether the evidence is the smoking gun, convincing (beyond reasonable doubt), or circumstantial (still needs development). The word *relevant*, itself, means that it meets the admissible test as sufficient evidence to support findings. It's no different than the CPA general standard (AICPA Rule 201) of sufficient documentary evidence. Irrelevant principles, on the other hand, tend to be when the evidence neither disproves nor approves the fact or position being taken.

There are different standards depending on the elements of proof. In a criminal matter, one must be 100 percent convinced. This standard of evidence is referred to in criminal law as "beyond a reasonable doubt." Since the accused are innocent until proven guilty, the party seeking to charge only needs to have probable cause. This goes back to the application of reasonable standards of care—that one only needs a reasonable basis to act on a situation. The facts in any decision often start as either direct or circumstantial evidence. Direct evidence proves the position, and circumstantial evidence relies on whether or not intent can be established.

POLICING AND UNDERSTANDING THE ENFORCEMENT GAPS

In the corruption and fraud cases that we have seen or experienced, both direct and circumstantial evidence exists in the accumulation of the facts and findings. For example, in a case in which one of the alleged defendants admits paying a cash bribe to a government official, and there is no other direct evidence, the party trying to prove the allegations needs to gather further proof. That proof might include circumstantial evidence to corroborate the direct evidence.

Here is an example of an approach that could be taken in an accumulation process. Again, in accumulation, accusers are being fact finders, not the ultimate deciders of the guilt or innocence. That's the judge and jury's responsibility.

1. Make a record with extreme detail (when, where, how, why, etc.). During the interview, have a second person, and videotape the witness's statement that he or she has paid the government official in cash (this is the direct evidence).Videotaping and recording, securing a signed affidavit that the witness was not coerced and is making the statements of his or her own free will, and establishing the proper chain of custody maintenance are critical.

   Circumstantial evidence is subject to intent—it requires allegation verification with hard and direct evidentiary proofs.

2. To prove that the government official spent or deposited a significant amount of cash shortly after he or she allegedly received the cash bribe, one needs the canceled checks, deposits, and other direct evidence to corroborate the statement and support the direct statement that he or she paid the bribe. It's all circumstantial until the physical checks, bank records, and invoices are in hand—originals. Copies can be altered. The original source documents must show chain of custody and be secure.

   Chain of custody is the preservation of pieces of evidence in chronological order: all documentation or paper trails, showing the seizure, custody, control, transfer, analysis, and disposition of all direct physical or electronic evidence as well as all circumstantial evidence.

   The O.J. Simpson trial is a reminder of how critical this can be in a trial. "From the beginning, there were issues involving evidence collection. An important bloody fingerprint located on the gateway at Nicole Brown's house was not collected, secured, and entered into the chain of custody when it was first located. Although it was documented by Fuhrman, one of the first detectives on the scene, in his notes, no further action was taken to secure it."[9] This single fingerprint created reasonable doubt. Make sure each piece of evidence is original and unaltered.

3. Perform a net worth and/or lifestyle change analysis. Simply start eliminating all other potential sources of revenue for the official's cash expenditures or deposits, to the extent possible. Look for acquisitions of assets and no corresponding liabilities: passports, homeowner insurance policies, motor vehicle registrations in their name or the names of others. Yes, the

perpetrators often think putting assets in other people's or entity's names will shield it from discovery. Wrong!

4. Two people should interview. Interviewing the subject official with another interviewer on hand to ask questions as well may show that the official cannot explain the source of the cash expenditures or deposits, or lied about it. That creates circumstantial evidence. Close-ended questions require yes-or-no answers. These questions should not be asked without direct evidence in hand or without you knowing the answer.

Everything is an allegation. Figure 7.3 is a simple, step-by-step approach to follow when developing facts and findings. The evidence should create the flow and should be maintained independently and objectively. Again, this is a fact-finding process involving only the fact finder. Fact finders do not get to determine if someone is guilty of fraud. The authors' premise is to stop fraud and mismanagement before it happens by making people aware of the bad choices and the consequences of their actions. Alleged fraudsters remain innocent until the evidentiary proofs show otherwise and they are convicted by a judge and jury. Assume no one is innocent until the facts prove them innocent or they are no longer determined to be a person of interest when gathering your evidence.

Figure 7.3 is a guide to the facts and the direct and circumstantial evidence that needs to be brainstormed in a conclusive finding. A 2003 *Journal of Accountancy* article says: "Research has shown that auditors are much more likely to correctly identify fraud risk conditions if the audit team engages in open-ended, nontraditional considerations of them. Responses from numerous stakeholders, such as forensic accountants, internal auditors, external auditors and other fraud experts, have reaffirmed the benefits of auditors engaging in such discussions."[10]

The problem in a public entity structure is that there is often a cloak of silence, and, unfortunately, the brainstorming needed to develop sound systems often is not involved. Imagine asking the president to attend such a brainstorming meeting so a couple of people in the private sector can assess his or her opinion on the internal controls over budgetary spending. Unfortunately, the system does not allow it, as he or she is working in many directions and, accordingly, delegates. It's ironic, because it is his or her budget, but his or her involvement is a 10,000-foot view-from-above perspective and often involves short-term fixes—the ultimate tone at the top. So much for top-to-bottom budget initiatives.

Brainstorming is a group divergent technique in which efforts are made to find a conclusion for a specific problem through gathering a list of ideas spontaneously contributed by everyone involved, both internally and externally.

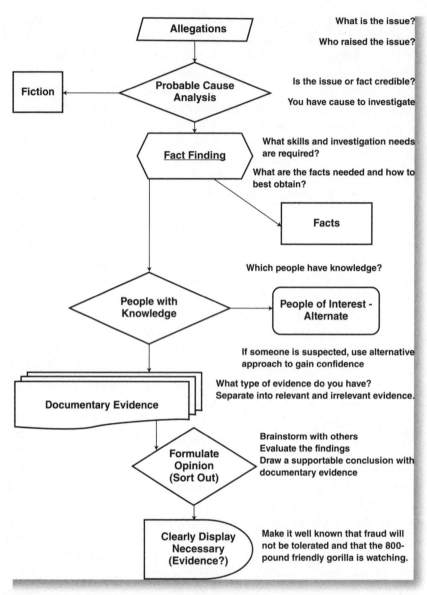

FIGURE 7.3 Flowchart for allegation follow up

One of the best ways to narrow regulatory gaps is by brainstorming the accumulated facts and understanding to whom they were assigned. The hardest aspect of enforcement of the regulation is to prove that the subject *knew* he or she intended to defraud another party. This is an essential element in all fraud and corruption cases. When someone cannot say that he or she unintentionally bribed someone, or does state that they did it by accident or in error, it is difficult to prove intention to defraud. Again, it's not so easy to prove malicious intent.

Dealing with knowledge and intent as states of mind (of the person who committed the alleged act), the courts allow the use of circumstantial evidence, gathered from all of accumulated facts and circumstances, as a form of proof.

U.S. jury instructions typically state, "Intent may be proved by circumstantial evidence. Indeed, it can rarely be established by any other means. We simply cannot look into the head or mind of another person. But you may infer the Defendant's intent from all of the surrounding circumstances. You may consider any statement made or act done or omitted by the Defendant and all the facts and circumstances in evidence which indicate the Defendant's state of mind."[11] That is why the authors have developed a crucial standard for arriving at conclusions about fraud and mismanagement: What a reasonable person being asked to judge thinks of the findings.

The people who judge whether or not these constitute strong evidence are reasonable people. The sentiment that no two people think alike creates gaps in the enforcement of rules and regulations.

Examples of circumstantial evidence of knowledge and intent in a fraud investigation might be relevant documents that are deliberately altered, forged, or destroyed. In addition, the evidence may be improperly withheld from the investigator by the fraudster, the fraudster may lie to investigators or to another party about a material point to hide guilt, and/or the fraudster may attempt to obstruct an investigation. The IRS maintains a list it calls the Badges of Fraud. In reviewing the list, we have formulated our own list, which has categories that are applicable to any potential fraud in a public entity. It is not a full and complete list, but one that will aid in a better understanding of where there is potential for fraud and mismanagement to occur.

Potential Public Revenue Badges of Fraud

- ▣ Omissions of specific revenue items where similar items are included.
- ▣ Omissions of entire sources of revenue.
- ▣ Unexplained failure to report substantial amounts of revenue identified as received.

- Substantial unexplained increases in net worth of the public employee, especially over a period of years.
- Substantial personal expenditures exceeding reported available resources.
- Bank deposits from unexplained sources substantially exceeding reported revenue.
- Concealment of bank accounts, brokerage accounts, and other property.
- Inadequate explanation for dealing with large sums of currency, or an unexplained expenditure of currency.
- Consistent concealment of unexplained currency, especially in an entity not routinely requiring large cash transactions.
- Failure to deposit receipts in an entity account, contrary to established practices.
- Failure of the public employee to file a tax return, especially for a period of several years, despite substantial amounts of taxable revenue being received.
- Cashing checks, representing revenue at check cashing services and at banks where the entity does not maintain an account.
- Concealing sources of receipts by false description of the source(s) of disclosed revenue, and/or nontaxable receipts.
- Unreconciled or untimely bank and cash reconciliation reports.
- Delays in required financial reporting.
- Understated and/or overstated budgeted revenues.
- One-shot revenues.
- Timing differences in revenue recognition.
- Transfers between related public entities.
- Shared debt between public entities.

Potential Public Badges of Fraud Related to Expenditures
- Substantial overstatement of expenditures.
- Substantial amounts of personal expenditures deducted as public entity expenditures.
- Claiming fictitious expenditures.
- False expenditures claimed for nonexistent, deceased, disabled, suspended, or other nonpublic workers.
- Providing false or altered documents, such as birth certificates, lease documents, or school/medical records, for the purpose for obtaining a position or promotion.
- Trust fund and/or other interfund loans disguised as expenditures.
- Continual transfers of the same budgetary expenditure lines.

- Improper allocations between public entities with respect to shared costs.
- One-shot expenditures.
- Contingent expenditures for future periods.

Public Entity Books and Records

- Maintaining multiple sets of books, or no records outside the computerized system (failed integrations).
- False entries or alterations made on the books and records, backdated or post dated documents, false invoices, false applications, false statements, or other false documents or applications, multiple journal entries, lacking detailed supports.
- Invoices irregularly numbered, out of sequence, unnumbered, or altered.
- Checks made payable to third parties that are endorsed back to someone else. Checks made payable to vendors and other business payees that are cashed by someone else.
- Failure to keep adequate records, concealment of records, or refusal to make records available.
- Variances between treatments of questionable items, as reflected on the required filings and representations within the books.
- Intentional under- or overfooting of columns in journals or ledgers, as well as failing to reconcile in a timely way.
- Amounts on required filings not in agreement with amounts in books.
- Amounts posted to ledger accounts not in agreement with source books or recorded supports.
- Journalizing of questionable items in order to correct account.
- Recording items in suspense or asset accounts.
- False receipts to donors by exempt organizations.
- Failing to clear interfund loan balances for a 30-day period during the 12-month accounting period.

Allocations of Public Entity Badges of Fraud

- Distribution of fund and surplus balance to fictitious or unrelated entities.
- Inclusion of revenue or expenditures on one related party because one entity is operating in surplus and the other in deficit.

Conduct of Public Entity Badges of Fraud

- False statements about material facts pertaining to any examination.
- Attempts to hinder or obstruct the examination. For example, failure to answer questions, repeated canceled or rescheduled appointments,

refusal to provide records, threatening potential witnesses, including the examiner, or assaulting the examiner.

- Failure to follow the advice of an accountant, attorney, or consultant.
- Failure to make full disclosure of relevant facts to the accountant, attorney, or consultant.
- The public employee has knowledge of the entities' practices that resulted in numerous questionable items appearing on the filings and books and records.
- Testimony of public employees concerning irregular entity practices by the public employee responsible.
- Destruction or failure to keep books and records, especially if just after examination was started.
- Transfer of assets for purposes of concealment, or diversion of funds and/or assets by officials or trustees, diverted for other pet projects.
- Patterns of consistent failure over several years to report revenue correctly.
- Proof that the financial filings were incorrect to such an extent and in respect to items of such magnitude and character as to compel the conclusion that the falsity was known and deliberate.
- Payment of improper expenditures by or for officials or trustees.
- Willful and intentional failure to execute pension plan amendments.
- Backdating applications and related documents.
- Making false statements on Tax Exempt/Government Entity (TE/GE) determination letter applications.
- Use of false Social Security numbers.
- Submission of false federal IRS Forms.
- Submitting a false affidavit.
- Attempts to bribe an examiner.
- Submission of tax returns with false claims of withholding (Form 1099-OID, Form W-2) or refundable credits (Form 4136, Form 2439) resulting in a substantial refund or nonexisting public employees.
- Intentional submission of a bad check resulting in erroneous refunds and releases of liens.
- Submission of false federal IRS Form W-7 information to secure Individual Taxpayer Identification Number (ITIN) for self and dependents.

Badges of Fraud Regarding Methods of Concealment

- Inadequacy of consideration.
- Insolvency of transferor.
- Asset ownership placed in other names or shifted to other related entities.

- Transfer of all or nearly all of debtor's property.
- Close relationship between parties to the transfer.
- Transfer made in anticipation of an assessment or while the investigation of a deficiency is pending.
- Reservation of any interest in the property transferred.
- Transaction not in the usual course of business.
- Retention of possession or continued use of public entity assets.
- Transactions surrounded by secrecy.
- False entries in books of transferor or transferee.
- Unusual disposition of the consideration received for the property.
- Use of secret bank accounts for revenue and proceeds.
- Deposits into bank accounts under nominee names other than the public entity.
- Conduct of public entity transactions in false names.

These Badge of Fraud indicators raise the potential for allegations to be made. Before proceeding with any allegation, however, all facts should be investigated. Again, this is not a full and complete list but, rather, one comprehensive enough to aid the examiner of the facts in recognizing the potential areas where fraud and mismanagement can exist.

HOW TO PRESERVE THE EVIDENCE OF FRAUD AND CORRUPTION IN THE PUBLIC ENTITIES

As previously stated, material, intention, reliance, and damages (MIRD) are needed to meet the burden of proving fraud: a material misrepresentation of facts that was intentionally perpetrated that is there as a reliance by an innocent party who was damaged. All four factors must be present for fraud to exist.

The evidence must be beyond a reasonable doubt when proving any intentional act or omission, including a misrepresentation, that was intentionally (knowingly) or recklessly misleading, or even attempts to mislead, a party that is to obtain a financial or other benefit or to avoid an obligation for their own benefit. Intent remains a difficult hurdle to overcome in proving fraud.

Some of the acts could include forging a document, forging a signature, or altering (backdating, etc.) a document. An omission in fraud cases refers to knowingly and willfully failing to disclose a material fact. A simple example is a contractor failing to disclose that he lost his license. This is a material fact that the contractor omitted in order to obtain an improper benefit or avoid an obligation. The misrepresentation refers to making a false statement of fact and generally may not be an opinion. A simple example of a misrepresented fact is a company representing that it employs 10 people with computer experience for the public entity work, when it, in fact, employs one. An exception to this is an opinion with respect to the correctness of a financial statement, issued by an accounting firm, which it does not know to be false or intentionally misleading. An accountant's opinion only provides reasonable assurance.

"Knowingly" means that the fraudster acted with actual knowledge that a statement was false and with intent to mislead the recipient. "Recklessly" means that the fraudster acted without knowing whether the submitted facts were true or false, nor did he or she make adequate inquiries to determine the truth. The fraudster typically acts with a willful blindness with regard to the truth or falsity of any statement. The fraudster will deliberately fail to determine the correctness of the facts or to put in place policies and procedures that would enable it to remain undetected. If the act was due to negligence, then it would not likely be fraud and this is a defense that could be raised.

Examples of obtaining a financial benefit would be to have a prequalified bid to receive a contract award or to inflate a payment request. Examples of avoiding an obligation would be to avoid performing work to the contract specifications or to avoid returning overpayments received under the contract.

 ## HOW TO PRESENT THE EVIDENCE IN A PUBLIC ENTITY FRAUD OR CORRUPTION CASE

The first thing that the accuser is trying to prove is that the fraudster made a "representation"; he or she is not yet concerned with proof of guilt. The focus is to develop fact findings and not be the judge and jury. Obtain all the originals or an accurate copy of the alleged misrepresentation. Examples are the bid or proposal, a resume, an invoice, or a supporting document that is contained in the alleged false statement or misrepresentation. Brainstorm and carefully examine the document for all potential misrepresentations and look for any potential inconsistencies that could create doubt about the fraud.

Make sure the chain of custody and authenticated evidences are documented by showing who created them. Verify the recipient or another person with direct personal knowledge of its preparation, submission, or receipt. Make sure the chain of custody of the original evidence is safe and make a copy with a notation in a corner, recording from whom the document was received, the date and place, and your initials. The originals always should be secured and free from potential contamination.

In the event that the accuser will be relying on verbal misrepresentations, they must closely question the witness who heard the representations and document the findings well. Cover your back, since you are only as good as the party making the representations. Examine the personality of the witness and look for any unusual or deviant behavior. Make sure all the relative information is obtained, and immediately prepare a memorandum for all parties confirming their understanding of the interview; have the party making the statement sign it (or an affidavit).

Record each and every relevant representation by the subject, separately and in clear and easy-to-understand language. The authors say, "Write it for a kindergartener to understand where possible." It is always harder for the party making the statement to recall it at a later date.

Try to see if anything in the statement can be found to be false. To prove that the representation was false, you need to locate witnesses with direct personal knowledge of the truth or falsity of the alleged or suspected false representation—direct and circumstantial evidence. This takes care of the relevant risk modeler as the highest burden of proof beyond a reasonable doubt or as an absolute. One of the problems in stopping fraud and mismanagement is that these accumulations and assignments do not test all transactions and provide absolute assurance. There has to be a higher level of proof whereby there are conflicting interests and exposed public entity value, and the power is absolute.

The identification process needs to happen at the starting point of the transaction. Examine the controls that are in place. Too often it's not until the transaction has been recorded in the public entity's books and records that an understanding of the controls that are in place is formulated. Examine the trust at the point of the transaction and the surrounding oversight. Make sure there is a clear segregation surrounding the ability to commit those resources. The measuring should take place as each resource is committed and not be an annual revisit. Variances in spending need to be at the point of spending or incurring. The measuring should be benchmarked in accordance with similar-sized public entities and the overall public marketplace.

The accountability needs to be more frequent, not when the fraud breaks (after the fact), but before the fraud occurs. The key step in creating accountability lies in the formation of communications that people can understand and improve upon. No one is perfect, but catch the problem sooner rather than later, and the damage is mitigated. If someone brings an issue up and questions cannot be answered without a detailed analysis, transparency is probably lacking. That's the first hint of a problem.

Accountability is about the inflow and outflow of resources and matching them to the intended purpose of the spending and receiving of revenues. Communication is about the policy and the tolerance level with which it is applied consistently to all parties involved. Transparency can be both open and closed. When a door is open, there is no need for the Freedom of Information Law (FOIL), Freedom of Information Act (FOIA), or other open public records requests. A closed door means these measures need to be used.

CONCLUSION

Following the risk modeler diagram will assist in developing conclusive findings with respect to where the risk for fraud and mismanagement exists. Regulation of government corruption and the operational aspects of these laws and policies are contingent upon having ethical people in place to ensure adherence.

Know the qualifications of the people in place to oversee the necessary controls. Make sure consequences for bending or breaking fiscal rules are well-communicated and fully understood. Ensure that the protocol for enforcement of the policies is in place and applied to everyone equally. Regulatory agencies will be considered. Whether communicated by principle, rule, or any other means, the rules are only as good as the people who follow them. These rules need to be balanced between the interests that are being preserved and the interests that are being oppressed. These are the conflicts that need to be managed to avoid the potential gaps that can be created by rules and regulations.

NOTES

1. http://www.washingtonpost.com/wp-srv/special/national/black-budget/.
2. http://www.gao.gov/products/GAO-13-271R.
3. http://www.huffingtonpost.com/2012/08/28/state-debt-report_n_1836603 .html.
4. The investigator's role is to develop facts sufficient to enable the Court to determine an accused person's guilt or innocence, and not to proclaim an individual innocent or guilty of the subject offense. Facts and other information developed may indicate that guilt resides with a particular party; however, that

guilt or innocence is a determination for the legal system and not for antifraud professionals.

5. The American Institute of Certified Public Accountants' Code of Professional Conduct Rule 201 states in part: "Sufficient Relevant Data. Obtain sufficient relevant data to afford a reasonable basis for conclusions or recommendations in relation to any professional services performed."

6. http://www.nj.com/bergen/index.ssf/2015/06/american_dream_bonds .html.

7. http://www.nj.com/insidejersey/index.ssf/2014/11/dream_land_canadian_ developers_take_on_meadowlands_megamall_project.html.

8. http://www.bloombergview.com/articles/2012-08-10/chris-christie-s-failed-state-capitalism.

9. http://www.crimemuseum.org/crime-library/forensic-investigation-of-the-oj-simpson-trial.

10. http://www.journalofaccountancy.com/issues/2003/dec/aprimerforbrain stormingfraudrisks.html.

11. "The Basics of Evidence for Fraud and Corruption Investigators," *Guide to Combating Corruption and Fraud in Development Projects*, http://guide.iacrc.org/the-basics-of-evidence-for-fraud-and-corruption-investigators/.

CHAPTER EIGHT

Final Thoughts

"Knowledge will forever govern ignorance; and a
people who mean to be their own governors must
arm themselves with the power which knowledge
gives them."

—*James Madison*

Topics:

Final thoughts, tools, and techniques that will assist in developing sound systems and structures within the public entity, and that identify the potential
fraud risk and mismanagement that may exist.

Key questions:

How can government be made more accountable?
Why does knowledge create transparency?
How do we develop lists or other potential warning signs of fraud and
mismanagement?
What are the proper levels of oversight and professional skepticism needed to
monitor the trusted person where the value is exposed for manipulations?

OW CAN PEOPLE MOVE FORWARD to make their agencies and government more functional and just? This chapter draws together the information from prior chapters to assist in the development of a synthesis of practice that can guide agencies, staff, and government officials in rooting out corruption and isolating problematic practices. It all starts with gathering the right facts and having informed checks and balances with the proper levels of skill and skepticism.

People have perspectives. Ask this question: Are the expectations and *perspectives* of the potential fraudster aligned with those of the organization?

People are classified within an organization by occupation (title). Ask this question: Is the potential fraudster in the right *occupation* to commit fraud?

People get put in positions of trust based on occupation and title. Does the fraudster's *position* within an organization give him or her the ability to commit fraud?

From the presidential authority to the mailroom, there are people who have the Perspective, Occupation, and Position (POP) to commit fraud. At the top, people—even presidents—are in a position to commit fraud. Public entities are expected to deliver targeted budget numbers, which, of course, puts a lot of pressure on a public employee to meet the targeted expectations, whether they are attainable or not. This, in turn, gives the public employee a perspective from which to commit fraud. Public employees by nature have the occupation (title) and are well positioned (POP) to manipulate information in order to meet expectations (because they are in power positions).

But it's also good to remember that even people who are not part of a public entity can commit fraud within it. Imagine that the public entity uses a third-party consulting service (occupation). The employees of this consulting service might be in the public entity building after everyone else has left. They have the opportunity to look at files and documents that are not locked up. They are in charge of the computer data and can access files that were not secured properly, and thereby obtain confidential information. All of these things create the environment needed to commit fraud. Even though they are outside the public entity, these people have access to the public entity's value (the position) and have the opportunity to commit fraud.

A cursory application of principles (rules), models, checklists, or computer-generated analyses without consideration of the limitations, assumptions, and conditions associated with them often creates a false sense that fraud has been eliminated. However, one must not assume that having fraud deterrents in place will stop all fraud. It is important to always remain proactive and focus on understanding the perspectives, occupations (title), and positions of the people inside and outside of an organization to see who has access to organizational value. Pay attention to these people, and the fraud "POP" can be avoided.

SIX SYMBOLIC SHAPES OF GOVERNMENT: ORGANIZATIONAL SYMPHONY

We explained the workings of governmental entities and provided information to help you further understand how to search for unusual behavior that might signal fraud or corruption. It is useful to think about how unusual behavior is handled within a public entity. By their very nature, fraud and corruption will attempt to hide within the main structures of an entity. How do you detect and sense behavior that is out of character? How do you understand when an organization is focused on its key goals and mission? When can you detect that an organization is off track?

Much like a professional symphony performing a great piece of classical music, the functioning of the governmental entity should flow and change with varying actions and motion in the activity. Jarring and off-tone elements, as well as subtle changes in inflection, can be the warning signs that set off your fraud "radar" and draw you toward an off-pitch action. Is a particular musician, at one point in the score, playing off-key? Is a musician late to enter after a rest in the music? Is a player too loud or strained and overwhelming the tone of the piece? Using these musical metaphors to build a framework for discussion, we look to explore some of the emotional aspects of fraud detection that lie at the heart of a skilled fraud examiner. These subtle cues can speak volumes to a trained professional, and they have the potential to expose well-disguised fraudulent or corrupt activities.

In some ways, the authors wish they could provide the reader with concrete methods to detect fraud. But, in many cases, new techniques in fraud are created by an ever-changing world of activities to study. The fraudsters and bad managers continue to find new ways to perpetrate fraud and to mismanage every day. The best advice to give to a budding fraud detection expert is to continually look for those *off* notes. Vigilance is key, as is a trained "ear" to hear the breaks in the score. Why does that sound different? What can be done to prevent people from hitting that sour note and making a bad choice? What are the people waiting to hear? Understanding these perspectives is a continuing skill that only comes with practice (experience).

Shane Adams, nicknamed "Your Majesty," was one of Joe's music professors at Berklee College. Professor Adams taught him the important role shapes play in the development of a song. Let's use musical shapes to illustrate government policies and political people, as they serve as good pictorial references.

The first shape is **parallel** ————————. The straight line. It represents a steadiness in feeling. In government it is the idea that because something has always been done a certain way, that it is the right way. We can tell you firsthand that times, laws, and political environments change, as do people's interests. Thinking back to the categories of waste mentioned in Chapter 6, it's this parallel thinking that allows mismanagement and fraud to continue to exist in today's government.

The second shape is the **zigzag** /\/\/\/\/\. Up-and-down motion creates a confused feeling. In the context of government, flip-flopping, going with the "flavor of the month," and thinking that "the squeaky wheel gets the grease" causes this up-and-down policy-making to occur. Anytime you fail to maintain consistency in policy decisions, expect mismanagement and fraud. One key element in preventing mismanagement and fraud is the consistent application of policy and rules to all people in government by establishing no-tolerance policies. In the world of accounting, it's called internal control. If management overrides these internal controls, then mismanagement and fraud can occur. The same applies in government. Failing to maintain rules and order for all, equally, is a major flaw in our existing government system and structure.

The third shape is the **ascending** shape ↗. It represents a happy, upbeat feeling. Think of this in the context of a policy or political sell—terms like "too good to be true," special interests, horse trading, overreaching, red tape, and fishbowl (commingling) come to mind. Why does it take a massive fraud like Enron to happen to make the signing off on internal control policies by the CEO and CFO a requirement? Why did we need to regulate ethical responsibility through Sarbanes-Oxley legislation? This supports the claim that government is reactionary. Add Dodd-Frank as an example of the result of the subprime lending crisis, and the point is clear. If there is outrage, government acts. How else can these elected officials get elected if they are not spearheading the hot issues? In order to get ahead of the mismanagement and fraud curve, government needs to replace reactionary thinking (thinking of today and not tomorrow) with proactive (projecting out into the future) systems and structures.

The fourth shape is the **descending** shape ↘. It represents a down, or negative, feeling. Think in the context of government failures such as deficit, debt, and being driven by specific interests. These shapes are the most damaging to the politician, as this is what the public sentiment embraces. There is no greater example then George W. Bush going from being the 9/11 superleader to falling out of favor when the economy fell on hard times. As Prefab Sprout's 1980s song "Moving the River" says, " … you're only as good as the last great thing you did." People trust, and people forgive. As these authors see it, and as history has shown, the American public is composed of generally trusting and forgiving people. It is this sort of trust and forgiveness that often is the impetus for dropping the guard just enough to let mismanagement and fraud trickle into government.

A Rasmussen report shows 53 percent of voters think neither political party represents the American people.[1] One problem is the idea that 50.01 percent—also the standard for surviving an Internal Revenue Service tax position or in financial reporting—is the necessary percentage requirement for reporting a contingent liability.[2] Unfortunately, if public opinion is evenly split on policy issues, the country will remain divided and government will stand still. A supermajority percentage of 66.67 (2/3) percent is needed to head in a more agreed-upon direction. In government, it is this type of division that causes the three D's: *distract, divert,* and *divide.*

The fifth shape is the **arch** ⌒. The arch represents the rainbow where it continues to rise and then comes back down. Of all the shapes, the arch seems to be the way to establish policy, as it represents a step up toward getting to a good place—the end where the pot of gold sits, or reaching the objective. Beginning with an understanding of what the objective is remains the key to formulating effective policies and structure. However, policies and structure are two separate things: One is philosophical and the other concrete. An example is the welfare concept. It was designed to help people get back on their feet. Welfare programs need to raise people to the top of the arch and then have them come back down by reestablishing themselves without needing further government support. Proactive thinking follows the proverbial idea that "if you give a man a fish you feed him for a day, but if you teach a man to fish you feed him for a lifetime." Programs need to have specific timeframes in which to establish structure. Programs without an endgame in mind will fail to meet the defined objective, as more and more people will be dependent on government intervention.

The sixth and final shape is the **inverted arch** ⌣. The upside-down arch represents legislation being approved without the necessary forethought as to how it will be implemented, or measured, resulting in highs and lows and a continued draining of resources. Using this model can hinder legislative policy. Unfortunately, thousands of taxpayer dollars are spent trying to correct the fact that there was no thought put in to the creation of legislative policies as we attempt to rise back to the top of the inverted arch. The final accomplished policy goal is met with a significant financial tax burden and/or debt being shifted to citizens, and the importance of attaining the goal is lost. This would serve as an example of mismanagement, unless it was intentionally or willfully done, which raises it to potential fraud. Government needs to formulate proactive thinking by implementing better cost/benefit analyses and not acting solely on impulse to try to solve problems with knee-jerk responses to advance particular political interests. In order for government to be effective in accomplishing policy objectives, it needs to keep its eye on the core mission and not deviate. Diversion is a distraction that causes division, as you have seen throughout this book. If one sticks with his or her core moral beliefs, integrity will not be compromised. Even though people can be forgiving, one intentional unethical act, and one never fully recoups his or her integrity. The public entity must maintain the highest level of integrity in setting the tone at the top. Unfortunately, government involves people, and people make bad choices because they're human. Sound ethical standards and solid core beliefs must be established for government or any organizational structure to prevent mismanagement and fraud.

These six symbolic shapes of government can be used in the development of effective systems and structures for the detection of fraud and mismanagement by creating a symphony that plays all its compositions in unison. Proactive (transposing) thinking is necessary for effective governance at all levels. The people at the top need to create transparency that leads to trust that must be established through effective communication. To be effective, this communication must be established at all levels. These shapes help us to better understand how organizations can communicate their mission to the public and other entities in a symbolic way. It is public involvement and oversight that creates a well-orchestrated symphony—and a well-defined mission that involves a public that hears the music.

FRAUD CAN HAPPEN AT ANY TIME OR PLACE

A very good friend of Joe's, Walt Pavlo, author of *Stolen Without a Gun*, provided the following three stories to help you understand that fraud can happen at any time or place. Fraud often happens because people think that it can't happen to them. Walt and Joe continually discuss fraud and the idea of controls. Here are Walt's thoughts on the subject. If you think about fraud controls, they are mostly meant to prevent otherwise good people from crossing the line. It reminds me of why we have locks on doors.

A small percentage of the population are sociopaths. They will lie, cheat, and steal their way through life. No matter the controls put in place, they will find a way around them. Think of a homeowner who invests in locks on the doors. Those locks are good and will keep out most people, but to the person bent on committing a crime they are just a small obstacle. So why invest in locks at all?

The reason is that just about everyone, and we mean everyone, knows that homes have locks on the doors. So when otherwise good people walk by, and they are in a desperate situation (greed, jealousy, or rage), they know that the locked doors prevent them from getting into the home. The locks are the deterrent. It is the same with financial controls. They are there for everyone in the company.

There is fraud in almost every organization (public or private), and there is a potential for fraud in every organization. The purpose of books like this is not to eliminate fraud but to reduce instances of fraud by increasing the awareness that it could happen. Keeping one's guard up for fraud is the best way to prevent fraud.

Here are three stories that Walt provided that remind us of the importance of continually analyzing fraud risk before fraud actually happens. Each of these story descriptions have been written by Walt.

First Story: Embezzling from Churches

In 2013, the *Washington Post* did an investigation on fraud in nonprofit organizations which revealed that incidents of corruption are either not reported at all or are reported but not directed to authorities. What is puzzling is why entities that are set up to do "good" would hide actions that are bad. Nonprofit organizations often mask fraudulent activities in their annual reports to the government by using terms such as "mismanagement" or "inefficiencies" when in fact fraud was the root cause of missing assets or funds. Walt Pavlo at Forbes.com looked at corruption inside church operations, and the problem there was even worse. Unlike nonprofits, churches are not required to do an annual report to the government on whether fraud was found during the period, but it most assuredly was there.

According to the U.S. Tax Code: "Every organization exempt from federal income tax under IRS 501(a) must file an annual information return except: (1) a church . . . ." When the reporting is missing, so is accountability.

There were three separate cases of Catholic priests in Connecticut who got prison time for drug trafficking, obstruction of justice, and embezzlement. However, even when these types of frauds are reported, there are pressures to keep them private. Take the case of Catholic priest Rev. Michael Jude Fay, who pleaded guilty to stealing $1.3 million from congregation collections in Darien, Connecticut. According to a *New York Times* article,[3] a bookkeeper and an assistant pastor at St. John's Church discovered the theft and showed their findings to the Catholic Diocese of Bridgeport, but nothing happened. The two then took matters into their own hands, hired a private investigator, and took their case to authorities. While Fay would go on to be sentenced to 37 months in prison, the duo that reported the fraud quit their jobs at the church under pressure from diocese officials for alerting outsiders to the problems.

Gordon Conwell Theological Seminary in Hamilton, Massachusetts, has conducted research on all aspects of finance related to Christian churches around the world through its Center for the Study of Global Christianity. The director of the center, Todd M. Johnson, PhD, said that "there is a lack of research on fraud within the church," but that is something he has been trying to change. Johnson teamed with David B. Barrett to write the book *World Christian Trends*, which represented a statistical view of the Christian churches of the world. Barrett, who passed away in 2011, was a pioneer in collecting data on churches and noticed a significant increase in embezzlement fraud during the 1980s. In one of Johnson's studies, *Status of Global Mission 2013*, there is a line item for "Ecclesiastical Crime," which is projected to be $37 billion worldwide, or nearly 6 percent of the total $594 billion given to churches. Losses due to mismanagement of funds are also a line item totaling $8 billion. In contrast, the total spent on mission work to introduce Christianity to more people throughout the world is $32 billion.

"Much of the fraud goes unreported," Johnson said. "Barrett worked with accounting fraud experts on his initial study who estimated that as much as 95% of fraud within churches goes undetected or unreported." Similar studies of corporate fraud have determined that upward of 66 percent of frauds go unreported. But why not report them? Johnson told me that "part of it is a reluctance to see the bad side of a nice pastor, a secretary or a board member of the church." Johnson even cited one quote from a church member who knew of an embezzlement and said, "I know he stole my money but I still think he's a wonderful person."

Seminaries like Gordon Conwell have incorporated ethics training into their curriculum as a commonsense approach to combating fraud in the church. "Simple lessons about two signatures on a check can avert many problems," Johnson said. However, small churches that have spun off from other congregations or are just starting from scratch are a growing part of the Christian church, and the funds they receive can also grow quickly. "A number of these churches get big fast, and their message can send mixed signals," Johnson said. The "Prosperity Gospel," a theological message that implies that God wants you to be rich, has taken root. "A church can raise a lot of money when parishioners are encouraged to give more for their own good," Johnson said.

In Alabama, Alton Sizemore, who is now a forensic accountant after a 25-year career with the Federal Bureau of Investigation, was asked to participate in a presentation for church leadership in the Shelby County area. The local sheriff's department, the federal government's Bureau of Alcohol, Tobacco, and Firearms, and Sizemore presented on issues facing churches including lone gunman scenarios, theft protection, and procedures for handling cash donations. More than 60 church leaders attended, and when it came time for questions only one topic was brought up by the attendees: concern over the lone gunman. The audience had been assured that the chances of such a tragedy playing out would be "remarkably slim, but better to be prepared." The pastors showed more concern over the unlikely scenario of gun violence than over the high likelihood of fraud within their own churches.

"Nobody wants to believe that the person they trust, the person they respect, is stealing from them," said Sizemore. "But that is exactly what I'm seeing in our practice." Each year, his firm receives three or four cases of a church or nonprofit that has discovered or suspects fraud. Typically, when they investigate, they find few if any accounting controls and most financial procedures in place are based on "trust."

From the looks of it, fraud does happen to churches, and there are plenty of facts that prove it. There's even a website dedicated to writing about fraud in religious institutions. We just need the courage to face it and then do something more to prevent it, other than saying a prayer.

Second Story: Dixon, Illinois[4]

We put a lot of trust in our government officials. Once we cast our ballot and our candidate is elected, we believe the last message told to us in a commercial or stump speech. "I can do the job," "You can trust me," or "It is time for a change" are all common slogans for candidates from city councilmen and -women to the president of the United States. We tend to believe that these campaign themes will translate into similar actions, but sometimes they fall short, way short.

Take the case of Rita Crundwell, who worked for the small town of Dixon, Illinois. Crundwell pleaded guilty to embezzlement in November 2012 and has been cooperating with authorities since her arrest in the recovery of assets to repay the city. She knew the jig was up in April 2012 when she was first approached by the FBI, and she soon thereafter confessed to stealing the money over a 20-year period. The process by which Ms. Crundwell was able to obtain the funds was not extremely complicated. She created an account at Fifth Third Bank and named it RSCDA account (Reserve Sewer Capital Development Account). That account appeared to be for the benefit of the city of Dixon, but Ms. Crundwell was the only signatory and the only person who wrote checks from that account. She would then cause Dixon funds to be deposited into another account, the Capital Development Fund and after creating false invoices she would write checks from that fund payable to "Treasurer" and deposited those checks directly into the RSCDA account—really her account. The bank assumed the money was for the city as well.

Rita Crundwell had to be one of the most trusted people on Dixon's payroll. She started working for the city's finance department while still in high school in 1970. In 1983, she was appointed as the comptroller/treasurer; seven years later she would begin her scheme that would span 22 years. The initial thefts started out small, amounting to $181,000 in 1991. By 2008, Crundwell's thefts resulted in a diversion of $5.8 million for that year alone; this was also at the height of the financial crisis. All the while, Crundwell not only participated in budget meetings for the city with other city council members, but she voiced a need for Dixon to make spending cuts due to a lack of sufficient funds. Her horse business thrived. The government, in a motion to the court, stated that Crundwell and her horses won numerous awards at national quarter horse competitions including being named the leading owner by the American Quarter Horse Association for eight consecutive years prior to her arrest.

How could a person abuse her post in such a way? While not an elected official, she was accountable to the citizens of the town and she took advantage of the trust everyone had in her. That trust translated into little or no oversight. It is easy to see how government officials can abuse their positions when people do not ask them to back up the words they say on the campaign trail.

Third Story: Nick's Roast Beef

Some private businesses get so frustrated with government that they avoid taxes by operating strictly on cash. That was the case of a small deli north of Boston. Nick's Roast Beef celebrated 40 years of being in business during 2015, an amazing accomplishment for small business owners/partners Nicholas Koudanis and Nicholas Markos. Its single location in North Beverly, Massachusetts (about 20 miles north of Boston) is as noted for its sliced roast beef sandwiches as it is for the arduous navigation of its tight parking lot. The place is packed from 10:00 a.m. until closing at 10:00 p.m., and patrons not only rave about the food, they are evangelical about spreading the word globally. Photos throughout the restaurant depict tourists holding their "Nick's Roast Beef" bumper stickers at locales ranging from Mt. Everest to the Sydney Opera House. It is "cash only" at Nick's and an ATM in the corner accommodates the modern customer who carries more plastic than currency.[5]

On December 10, 2015, things took a bad turn for the restaurant's owners. They were indicted on 17 federal criminal counts. Koudanis, his wife, his son, and Markos were arrested for diverting cash to themselves and not paying taxes to the Internal Revenue Service. Based on the indictment, not only were they paying themselves in cash, but also the suppliers and employees. Over the past seven years the government said that Koudanis and Markos avoided paying nearly $2 million in taxes. An IRS audit in 2013 showed sales of about $1 million, when the government claims that it was really over $2.3 million. There were similar ratios of real income versus the alleged doctored amounts in other years.

According to defense attorney Joel Androphy, who is not involved with this case, the federal government can easily target small businesses, which tend to be less sophisticated in their business practices and financial controls. "Businesses like this are low hanging fruit for prosecutors," Androphy said, "which is a shame because large corporations are skating around paying taxes because of the inefficiency of the IRS whistleblower program." That program is supposed to reward whistle-blowers who tell on companies and individuals who are avoiding paying taxes. Androphy says there are hundreds of millions that the government could go after, but those cases can be complicated. He has a point: In a report from Watchdog.org, the IRS program is mired in delays and the majority of the cases they work are for claims under $2 million—that hits small businesses hard.

While everyone should play by the rules, the rules seem to be enforced more on those who can least afford to fight. Defending a criminal case is expensive and the U.S. government has the resources to go as long as it takes to get a conviction. The charges, in the case of Nick's filing false tax returns and obstruction, do not carry long prison terms, but prosecutors are known for adding more charges later in order to pressure defendants into a guilty plea. In cases involving large amounts of cash that could mean money-laundering charges, and that could lead to more than a decade in prison. "Nobody should cheat," Androphy said, "but the rich and large corporations can fight the government in a way the small businessman cannot."

Accepting credit cards for business transactions comes with convenience but also high fees that can cut into the bottom line of mom-and-pop shops. Having open invoices and clients who take a long time to pay are also heavy burdens for small businesses that are often paying money out as fast as they are taking it in. So cash-based businesses are the best solution, but that comes with increased scrutiny from the government and risks being associated with crossing legal lines. The Bank Secrecy Act from 1970 is getting renewed interest for fighting terrorism, drugs, and money laundering, but it also catches up with small businesses like Nick's. Banks have become the watchdogs that are supposed to monitor large cash deposits and withdrawals. While the indictment did not state how Nick's investigation progressed, one can be sure that the popular restaurant was being monitored. At the time of their arrest, the Koudanises had $1.6 million in cash in a safe in their home.

Cases like this play out across the United States; however, we should hope in this case that justice would also take into consideration the larger impact that the outcome will have on the people in the surrounding community. If banks are too big to fail, then businesses like Nick's are too essential to fail. However, the small businesses are much easier to prosecute.

The Warning System

Each of these stories serves as a lesson that trust, rationalization, and failing to hold people accountable with 800-pound friendly gorilla oversight will allow fraud to happen. Thanks to Walt for sharing these stories in our quest to create awareness and to help good people avoid bad choices.

The Arc of Exposure Defcon warning system tool depicted in Figure 8.1 is useful in assessing the risks associated with the people you come in contact with

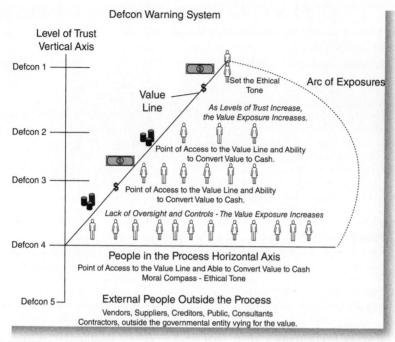

FIGURE 8.1 Arc of exposures

when examining suspected fraud or mismanagement. After reading the stories, your thinking should be focused on learning to examine where the conversions of cash can take place and where the conflicting interests lie. Let's now examine the categories of fraud.

 ## FIVE CATEGORIES OF FRAUD

These are some places to look for fraud, which will be described in the sections that follow:

1. Misstatement of revenues
2. Misstatement of expenditures and/or appropriations
3. Misstatement of assets/liabilities
4. Inadequate disclosure
5. Misappropriation of assets and failing to provide for future liabilities

Understanding the five categories of fraud helps us learn where the necessary systems and structures should be put in place.

Misstatement of Revenues

Revenue manipulation is one of the most common schemes employed by fraudsters when they commit financial statement fraud. In this scheme, the fraudster manipulates the different types of revenues. Clearly identifying the different types of revenues present in an organizational process can help in the identification of the potential risk for revenue misstatement.

Here are some types of revenues that may or may not be applicable to the public entity that can be manipulated.

Types of Revenue (See Table A.2 in the appendix for types of taxes and fees)

1. Tax-based
2. Fee-based
3. User-based
4. Other

Knowing where the revenue comes from and determining if it is sufficient enough to fund the expenditures to provide the expected services of the public entity is an important place to place the 800-pound friendly gorilla oversight. Don't forget to follow the money.

Advance or Deferred Recording

The public entity and its accounting methodologies create a lot of opportunity to delay or advance the recognition of revenues. Advanced or deferred recording by a fraudster could intentionally recognize revenues before they are allowed to be recognized or defer them to a later time than the rules allow. There is a need for people in the public entity with the knowledge or experience of the overall control environment, conditions, and circumstances of the public entity's revenue streams to determine whether a fraudster could commit the following fraudulent actions:

1. Recording revenue before all terms are completed.
   The fraudster is recording grant revenue or other specific revenues before regulations allow it. This is usually done by incurring expenses that are not in conformity with the specific terms of the agreements or that are not one of the allowable expenses.

2. Improper charging of fees.

   A user is billed or not billed for services; the user is overcharged, and the public entity fails to comply with all the requirements for recording the billing and charging for the transactions.

3. Services are claimed to have been provided that have not yet been provided.

   Transactions are recorded, even though they involve unresolved contingencies or terms that are often amended by unauthorized side agreements that gave a user some unauthorized right.

   An example is tracking all fire or police calls to justify the costs when the public entity sends out extra manpower.

4. Consignment revenue.

   Revenue is based on the sharing and allocating of services when evidence indicates that the obligation to pay for the services and goods is contingent upon the actions of another (third) party.

5. Improper matching of revenues.

   Revenues are recognized without matching them with their associated expenditures in the time period to which they apply. An example is the "cap" banking term in municipal government under which expenditures are accumulated and available for future periods.

6. Improper revenue cutoff period.

   Revenues before or after the period-end are not recorded in the correct period—uncollected taxes, reserve for taxes, or any reserve that is ultimately collected in a future period. This reduces the revenue for one year to possibly justify a tax increase and creates surplus in another to give raises or fund another service that the public employee deemed necessary with transparency.

7. Improper use of the percentage of completion.

   The percentage of completion method of accounting for long-term contracts is intentionally manipulated to misstate revenues and profits. Using the percentage of completion gives you the ability to recognize that projects are more complete than they actually are in order to justify the spending. Remember, debt is a credit and its counter is an asset, which is a building or structure. Assets increase when liabilities increase.

8. Shipments not requested by the public entity.

   Goods and services are billed and are improperly recorded for items that have not been ordered by the public entity. A term in the fraud world is *channel stuffing*, or when a company inflates its sales and earnings figures by deliberately sending its customer distribution channels more products than they are able to sell to the public. In the public entity, the idea of buying bulk to save money comes to mind. Wherever there is an inventory or storage need, there is the cost of moving the items to a facility, which means labor and potentially trucking and additional freight costs. There's no better place for the vendors to channel stuff than the public entity, which often buys in bulk. This enables the public entity to potentially inflate spending or overbudget and create convertible value.

Fictitious Revenues

There are different ways a fraudster could intentionally record fictitious revenues. There needs to be people in the public entity with the knowledge or experience of the overall control environment, conditions, and circumstances of the organization's revenue streams to determine whether a fraudster could commit the following fraudulent actions:

- Giving bogus fees to fictitious customers or inflated or unauthorized users
- Implementing non-arm's-length transactions, such as (services provided) to affiliates and undisclosed related parties
- Misclassifying gains, or manipulation of gains and losses between ordinary and extraordinary items
- Not recording noncharges, exceptions, and allowances
- Not recording returns and credits

Misstatement of Expenditures

There are different ways that fraudsters could intentionally understate or overstate liabilities and their related expenses. There needs to be people in organizations with knowledge of or experience in the overall control environment, conditions, and circumstances of the organization's expenses to determine whether the following fraudulent actions could be committed by a fraudster:

Understating or overstating recorded liabilities and their related expenses
Liabilities and their related expenses are recorded, but the amounts are intentionally overstated or understated.

Failing to record some liabilities and their related expenses, including some contingent liabilities
Liabilities (including contingent liabilities that are required by accounting standards to be recorded) and their related expenses are intentionally not recorded.

Recording revenues instead of a liability for payments received for certain transactions

Revenues are recorded instead of a liability for deferred/unearned revenue when payment has been received for goods or services that have not been provided by the seller; *or* revenues are recorded instead of a liability for payments received for customer deposits, client funds, advances, loans, or other nonrevenue cash flows.

Public Entity Cash Flow Analyzer Tool

Figure 8.2 is a tool to analyze the inflows and cash flow within a public entity and a broad overview to assist in examining the fund balance and cash flows.

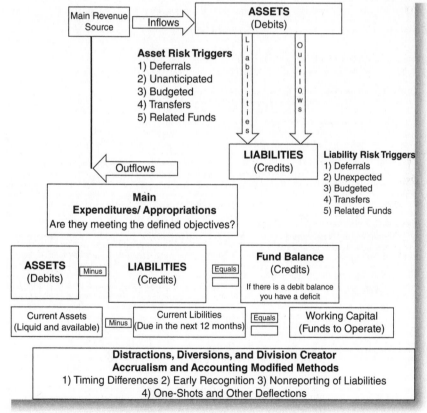

FIGURE 8.2 Public entity inflow and outflow analyzer tool

Follow the Revenue and Where It Leads You

Figure 8.3 is a tool to analyze the effects of revenue generators within a public entity and a broad overview to assist in examining the fund balance and the related cash flows.

Misstatement of Assets

In financial statement frauds, assets are usually overstated rather than understated. However, assets may be understated as part of a scheme to understate reported earnings (for example, when earnings targets have already been met to reduce taxable income and/or to boost earnings in future periods). Assets can be overstated in three ways:

■ Overstating existing assets
■ Recording fictitious assets or assets not owned
■ Capitalizing items that should be expensed

Note, however, that the fraudster often uses multiple schemes to overstate assets.

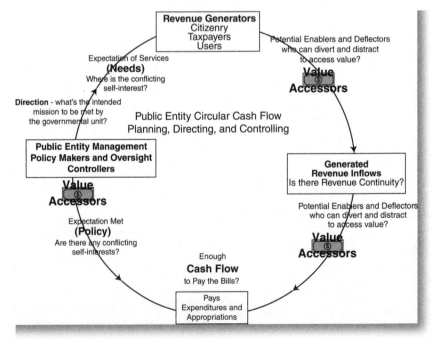

FIGURE 8.3 Public entity revenue generator tool

Assets may be overstated by manipulating the processing of transactions within the accounting system or by creating unusual transactions, such as large journal entries that increase income and overstate net assets. Any account may be changed by such journal entries. They do not have to make sense.

Existing assets are most often misstated initially, because financial statement frauds often start out small. Frauds tend to grow quickly in size, making it difficult to conceal a large fraud only among existing assets. So large fictitious assets, or assets not owned, may be required to continue the cover-up.

Particular assets may be selected for misstatement because it is easier to conceal a misstatement due to the size of the asset, the complexity of the determination of the asset's value, the judgment involved in determining the asset's value, or the relative difficulty of auditing that asset.

Ways Fraudsters Intentionally Misstate Assets

Assets can be intentionally misstated by fraudsters by:

- Manipulating the quantity of the asset received
- Manipulating the price paid for the asset
- Manipulating allowances (for example, bad debts or excess and obsolete inventory allowances write-offs)
- Manipulating or avoiding write-downs for permanent diminution in value of older assets
- Improperly writing up assets to claimed appraisal or market values
- Recording of real assets that are not owned by the public entity or transferred to other related entities
- Recording fictitious assets
- Improperly capitalizing expense items (or expensing capital additions).

Common Schemes of Misstating Assets

Here are some common schemes.

Cash Misstatement Schemes

a. Manipulation of bank reconciliations. Potential red flags are untimely or unreconciled accounts.
b. Failing to disclose cash balances that are pledged as collateral for loans or not properly allocated for restricted or committed purposes. Potential red flags are large cash balances, with undisclosed future or existing liabilities.

c. Failing to disclose cash balances that are interfund balances by other related public units.

d. Creation of fictitious cash balances and/or bank accounts in a public employee's name formed jointly with the public entity.

Investments/Marketable Securities

a. Manipulating the price of the assets or investments in a private entity. The American International Group (AIG) bailout and New Jersey governor Chris Christie's investment in the Revel casino are examples of investments that can provide entities with the ability to manipulate the asset's price.

b. Manipulating or avoiding write-downs for permanent diminution in value. Examples are defunct or devalued public entity properties or inventory that have not been valued at current fair-value amounts and are kept on the books at original cost; properties with environmental concerns and liabilities, the liabilities for which are not recorded properly; landfills and old military storage arsenals.

c. Improperly writing up assets to claimed appraisal or market values, such as selling a roadway to an authority at unsupported value. (See the New Jersey Turnpike/Florio example from Chapter 2.)

d. Recording real assets that are not owned by the public entity, such as assets owned by the public entity for the benefit of the public employee.

Example 1: A public employee runs a side business. He or she uses the public entity computer to type and reproduce the schedules for the workers in the side business.

Example 2: Lynn works for a federal agency and is an avid runner in her spare time. She needs to have pens and paper pads on hand for note takers at the runners' club meetings at her house, so she "borrows" some from her agency's supply cabinet.

e. Recording fictitious assets.

Example: The public employee is ordering a lawn mower for the fields in the town. An additional order for a mower goes in, and the vendor who the public employee purchases hundreds of thousands of dollars in equipment from delivers it to the public entity employee's home. The lawn mower is on the public entity's books, but was purchased for the public employee.

Accounts Receivable Misstatement Schemes

a. Premature or late revenue recognition (see revenue recognition section).

b. Manipulation of allowance for bad debts for taxes.

c. Creation of fictitious accounts (tax) receivable.

Inventory Misstatement Schemes

a. Manipulation of allowance for excess and obsolete inventory.
b. Manipulation of write-down to lower than cost or market value.
c. Manipulation of physical inventory counts.
d. Manipulation of inventory pricing paid for goods.
e. Creation of fictitious inventory.
f. Manipulation of costs capitalized into inventory. Accumulating cost on construction and long-term project tracking. Cost overruns, being over budget, excess change orders are some red flags.

Fixed Asset Misstatement Schemes

a. Improperly capitalizing expenditures as fixed assets. Remember that an expenditure is a debit in the statement of revenues and expenditures and is also a debit in the balance sheet. In one statement it reduces assets, and in the other it increases them. In the balance sheet, debits increase fund balance, and in the statement of revenues and expenditures, debits reduce fund balances.
b. Creation of fictitious fixed assets. All it takes is fictitious invoices and a long-term project that they can be buried in.
c. Improperly writing up fixed assets to claimed appraisal or market values. All it takes is an overstated appraisal that ignores the facts, such as environmental issues and other functional obsolescence.

Loans or Notes Receivable Misstatement Schemes

a. Manipulation of allowance for loan losses between related public entities and funds.
b. Creation of fictitious loans or notes receivable between related public entities and funds

Patents (and Other Intellectual Property) Misstatement Schemes

a. Improperly writing up or failing to write up assets to claimed appraisal or market values of a public entity's intangible assets.
b. Recording real assets that are not owned by the public entity.
c. Recording fictitious assets.
d. Improperly capitalizing expense items (or expenditure capital items).

Oil, Gas, and Mineral Reserves

a. Improperly failing to write up assets to claimed appraisal or market values.
b. Recording real assets that are not owned by the company.
c. Recording fictitious assets.

Other Asset Misstatement Schemes

a. Recording fictitious assets.

Inadequate Disclosures

There are various areas where fraudsters could intentionally withhold or provide inadequate financial information to commit financial statement fraud. A fraudster could commit the following fraudulent actions:

Liabilities

Failing to disclose commitments, contingent liabilities, loan covenants, loan defaults, and other key facts that may give rise to liabilities and impact a company's financial condition. Examples: unrecorded sick time, pension, environmental and contingent liabilities that are probable and estimated able to be paid in the future.

Significant events

Failing to disclose significant events impacting a company, thus making financial statements misleading.

Related-party transactions

Failing to disclose transactions between one public entity and a second that is under the control or significant influence of the first public entity or a common third party. Although not necessarily fraudulent, transactions with undisclosed related parties are likely to be fraudulent. Look for journal entries and interfund balances between the public entities that are ongoing and/or for which there are no available funds to clear balances.

Legal and regulatory compliance violations

Failing to disclose violations of laws and regulations that may have a significant adverse impact on a public entity's financial position or on its ability to continue to operate, without the need for significant increases to taxes and fees.

Significant changes in accounting policy and estimates

Failing to disclose significant changes in accounting policy and estimates, which renders the public entity's financial statements misleading.

False statements

Making false or misleading statements, orally or in writing, which may mislead people about a public entity's financial condition or prospects.

Misappropriation of Assets

Based on knowledge or prior experience of the public entity's overall control environment, conditions, or circumstances, consider whether the fraudster could commit material embezzlement in a particular organization:

Material embezzlement
A substantial amount of money or other assets are stolen, and the theft is concealed such that the financial statements are misstated in a way that is material to a company as a whole. Note that it is extremely rare for embezzlement to be material to a large public company.

WHY PUBLIC ENTITIES' AUDITORS/ACCOUNTANTS FAIL TO DETECT FRAUD

The following is a quick list of reasons why auditors and accountants often fail to detect fraud:

- They are fooled or influenced by the fraudsters.
- They did not apply the appropriate level of professional skepticism.
- They are too trusting of employees, executives, and managers in the public entity. There is the potential turning of a blind eye to observable abuses.
- They do not pay attention to the red flags that may indicate fraud.
- They do not know what fraud looks likes in a public entity.
- They base the current numbers on past or other relevant information instead of actual documentary evidence. They test to substantiate and do not provide a 100 percent verification of the evidence.
- They accept it when clients explain away findings they have uncovered.
- They accept explanations for fraud symptoms without verifying facts with 100 percent assurance that they are accurate.
- They put too much emphasis on evidence obtained through inquiry rather than the 100 percent documentary support for red-flagged items.
- Their only responsibility is to provide reasonable assurance, not 100 percent accuracy.

Red Flags Indicating Potential Fraudsters

■ Fraudsters appear to have total control and do it all. Observe the level of authority and what controls are in place in the public entity.

■ Fraudsters do not take vacations. Institute mandatory vacation policies within the public entity.

■ Fraudsters complain about others in the process (employees, vendors, etc.). Hang out at the watercooler and observe who knows what; monitor the ethical spirit surrounding the public entity.

■ Fraudsters exhibit morale and attendance changes. They have to be perceived as model public employees to remain above suspicion.

■ Fraudsters exhibit lifestyle, habit, and behavior changes. Know what the financial changes are, and examine the financial disclosures for significant changes and/or undisclosed items.

■ Fraudsters operate on a crisis basis. Superstorm Sandy and Katrina provided all the diversions needed to distract and divide any public entity and open the door to fraud and mismanagement.

■ Fraudsters cannot explain variances in numbers. Control and monitor variances and unusual numbers readily, not annually but, rather, as needed. Financials to end users are not as effective as management-generated financial reports internally. These management reports should be done on an as-needed basis and be detailed in ways to aid the managers in making informed decisions. The historical perspectives of the normal public entity's financial reporting, while useful, are not as effective a system and structure as an ongoing, well-designed reporting system, because they are a snapshot view. Information creates efficiency when it is timely.

■ Fraudsters will have missing and altered documents. A simple control to prevent alteration and create accountability is to maintain a chain of custody of original documentation and require signing off on copies and originals. Not allowing one-person approval over a document is another simple control. Prenumbering forms, creating multiple-copy forms, date-stamping when received, and centralizing the mail opening by independent parties add further safeguards.

■ Fraudsters will make duplicate payments or not maintain the original documentation. Not allowing one person to approve and pay is the type of safeguarding and segregation of duties required to prevent fraud and mismanagement. Look for altered entries in the books and records, unreconciled cash accounts, larger-than-expected variances in the budgetary line items, budgetary transfers, and unexplained journal entries. Examine the approval authority and the length of time the person has been in that position.

■ Fraudsters will use management overrides. Examine the position and the authority that goes along with it. Is there a potential for conflicting self-interests?

■ Fraudsters will not reconcile. No account should be left unreconciled. Sloppy and orderly record maintenance are irrelevant factors if the accounts are not reconciled. Accounts should not be reconciled by the same person who oversees the approval or has the ability to override. Any reconciliation that is not done independently of the approval authority is at risk for fraud and mismanagement.

■ Fraudsters will not fully investigate. All fraud, regardless of size, should be treated with a no-tolerance management mentality. A separate, independent party should conduct the investigation, and the appropriate legal oversight should be put in place.

■ Fraudsters circumvent approval processes. Two signatures, required independent party sign-off, surprise checks, job rotation, and proper levels of skills and training should be placed at the points of access to value.

■ Fraudsters have inappropriate relationships with vendors and suppliers. "Watch their friends," Joe's grandma would say. Look at the bidding process. Do these vendors go to conventions? Are they political contributors? Do they frequently meet with the public employee outside the public entity's facility? Are there other parties involved in the relationship? And how long have they been doing business with the public entity?

■ Fraudsters process transactions outside the normal organizational channels.

■ Fraudsters maintain adversarial attitudes toward control functions. Any resistance to time recording clocks, dual signature requirements, adequate accounting software, and transactional oversight should serve as a warning sign. An unwillingness to put in further systems and structures to provide a higher level of control is a red flag that should be investigated. Claims that it costs too much, the contract says that "we don't have to comply," and other excuses should be met with putting the proper policies in place at the top to prevent excuses for nixing the controls.

A SIMPLE FRAUD RISK PLAN FOR THE PUBLIC ENTITY

This is a basic plan of action for detecting fraud in any organization. Here is a foundation for an organization's fraud forces. Remember that every organization is different and that circumstances often require different actions. Use this list as a guide, but also consider the particular organization and its specific circumstances to develop the most effective ways to detect, deter, and prevent fraud. Put the 800-pound friendly gorilla to work and improve controls by implementing continuous auditing and monitoring over the organizational process.

■ Always strengthen controls over the transaction authorization process and use continuous unannounced (unpredictable) auditing and monitoring tests to validate the effectiveness of the controls in place. An organization needs to use simple repetitive analysis for fraud detection means by setting up the necessary algorithms to run against large volumes of data to identify potential fraud, like abnormalities, as it occurs over a period of time. Using computers can drastically improve the overall cost benefit, efficiency, consistency, and quality of a fraud detection risk plan. Running these created algorithms against data to get periodic notification when an anomaly occurs in the data is creating that necessary notion that someone is watching. This is critical in detecting, deterring, and preventing fraud. This not only assists in mitigating fraud but provides the users of the financial communication with more accurate and reliable findings, since not all abnormalities are fraud-related. The findings often lead to greater efficiencies in the organizational process, since you are working with more accurate information.

The 800-pound friendly gorilla can run the created algorithms every night by going through all those transactions to develop timely notifications of trends and patterns and exceptions in the reporting that can be provided to management. For example, this algorithm could run specific tests against all employee expense transactions as they occur to ensure they are in accordance with controls and in line with past history.

■ An organization must make sure the 800-pound friendly gorilla has communicated the monitoring activities that are in place throughout the organization.

■ An organization must communicate the fraud prevention program across all organizational processes. An inch-by-inch fraud prevention communication is equal to inch-by-inch fraud detection. Everyone inside and outside an organization should know there are systems in place that alert to potential fraud or a breach of controls. This is accomplished by communicating that every transaction that is being run through the company's systems is monitored. This is a measure to exceed reasonable assurance and have more significant, preventative fraud approaches.

The sooner an issue is identified and documented, the better the outcome will be. An organization needs to have the necessary reports with recommendations on how to enhance the existing controls or make the necessary changes to an organizational process to reduce the risk of fraud. Remember the example of the worm from Chapter 7 and do not take even the smallest potential risk lightly.

■ Perform full tests of transactional data to see if there is a potential for fraud risk around the value created in the organization.

Fraudulent transactions do not occur randomly, so complete testing should be performed. While some fraudulent transactions may fall within the boundaries of sample-type testing, others may not. Many smaller inconsistencies may be missed and add up over time, resulting in very large instances of fraud, if left unattended.

Make sure weaknesses in the controls are fixed immediately.

■ Identify any overlapping of responsibilities (segregation of duties). Make sure people in the organization cannot initiate, approve, and/or be the receiver of the goods from the transaction.

■ Continually expand the fraud risk plan and continually enhance it over time to account for changes in the organization.

Update databases by staying on top of trends in fraud. Make sure the profiles of key people are updated annually. Know the most common fraud schemes and those that pose the greatest risks to the organizational process. Keep the 800-pound friendly gorilla investigations on the move and make them unpredictable. Use analytics (algorithms) to find out where controls are not working. Maintain trusted people in overseeing responsibilities and safeguarding the public entity value within the process. Investigate suspicious patterns and watch for the red flags of fraud that may emerge from the fraud detection tests and continuous auditing and monitoring that are in place.

■ Maintain a database of the types of fraud and profiles of the stakeholders and decision makers both inside and outside the organization with access to its value.

■ Compile and maintain a database of the types of fraud that have occurred in the past in the organization and see if the organization is still exposed to these types of fraud risks. In doing this evaluation one needs to look at the people in an organization from top to bottom and see if the organization's value is exposed and, if so, where. Emphasize the areas that have the potential to cause the greatest reduction in organizational value.

 FRAUD AND MISMANAGEMENT TYPES, SIGNS, AND SUGGESTED ACTIONS

Approval

Defalcation fraud is the misappropriation of funds by a person trusted with oversight of them.

Fiduciary duty fraud is when the public employee fails to act within the law and does *not* act in the interest and for the benefit of the public entity.

Influence fraud is the sale by public officials of their authority or influence, to obtain a favorable outcome for a particular party or interest.

Pilfering fraud is the theft of physical goods such as office supplies or inventory.

Trust fraud occurs as result of one party's reliance on another's discretion and/or a breach in a relationship of trust resulting in financial loss. It is a knowing misrepresentation of the truth, or concealment of a material fact, to induce another to act to his or her detriment. Trust is a key element in the success of a fraudster.

Types/Signs of Fraud and Mismanagement:
- ☐ Look for single-sourced procurements (requests for proposal—RFPs) when there is an available pool of potential bidders to compete for goods or services.
- ☐ The awarded contract requirements were not reviewed and/or approved by management.
- ☐ Look at the public employee who has the authority to sell publicly owned property. Is that party selling the items at less than market value to receive a future kickback or to sell the property back to the public entity at a higher price at a later date?
- ☐ Examine the payment to determine if the public entity is paying high prices or purchasing unnecessary or inappropriate goods/services.
- ☐ Public entity personnel responsible for awarding contracts are living beyond their personal means.
- ☐ The public entity approval employee declines promotion from his or her current position.

☐ The public entity approval employee is in discussions with a current or prospective provider about employment.

☐ The public entity approval employee frequently socializes with the provider and accepts inappropriate gifts, such as travel or lunches, or the winning award is high compared to cost estimates, published price lists, similar jobs, or industry averages. Benchmarking to similar projects, goods, and services is a good way to check for reasonableness.

Establish the proper code of conduct in writing to set the proper ethical and behavioral standards that are adopted by the public entity to which *all* employees of the public entity are required to adhere. This code of conduct, if not extended, should be extended to include contractors, consultants, suppliers, and customers if the system and structure is to be successful in mitigating fraud and mismanagement.

Billing

Billing fraud involves a public employee who causes the public entity to issue payment by submitting invoices for fictitious goods or services, inflated invoices, or invoices for personal benefit.

Purchases for personal use or resale fraud occurs when the public employees purchase items through the public entity that are intended for personal use, such as tools, personal computers, or automobile parts. The public employee intends to resell the items as part of a side business.

Types/Signs of Billing Fraud and Mismanagement:

☐ The public employee creates a shell company and bills the public entity for services not actually rendered.

☐ The public employee purchases personal items and submits invoices to the public entity to be paid.

☐ Unclear reasons for using a particular service provider, and the appropriate documentation concerning the goods/services are not provided.

☐ The service provider is not generally known to other public employees and is not being handled in a customary way; the provider is being dealt with exclusively by a particular public director or manager.

☐ Large number of invoices for a particular provider just beneath the established approval thresholds.

☐ Numerous correcting entries or other adjustments on books and records.

☐ Numerous entries held in suspense accounts needing to be classified.

☐ Providers don't offer the usual industry discounts or terms.

☐ Duties are not segregated between the processing of invoices and updates to provider master files, between check preparation and posting to the provider account, and between check preparation and mailing of signed checks.

☐ Provider does not have the proper documentation of additions, changes, or deletions to the vendor master file.

☐ There are excessive credit adjustments to a particular party and/or credit issued by an unauthorized department in the public entity.

☐ An employee takes advantage of the lag time, which typically occurs during book closing, to get false invoices approved and paid.

☐ Frequent, undocumented, and/or unapproved adjustments, credits, and write-offs to the accounts receivable subledger.

Suggested Actions:

☐ Examine invoices that are incomplete (i.e., no phone number), on odd-sized paper, or altered in some way.

☐ Examine unfolded invoices, as they may indicate that they have not been mailed.

☐ Examine invoices from various providers that appear to be on the same type of stationery.

☐ Look for recurring identical amounts from the same provider who is not under contract.

☐ Look closely at different provider remittances that indicate one address for a particular provider.

☐ Look for provider payment increases given for no apparent reason and without adequate documentation.

☐ Observe checks that are directly handed to the provider by the approving public entity party.

☐ Look for a potentially false email payment request combined with a hard-copy printout with potentially forged approval signatures. Be alert to requests for bonded signatures, notarization, or in-person signing before issuing payments.

☐ Look for the potential for a public employee to submit invoices for payment from a fictitious company.

☐ Look for the potential for a public employee to arrange for overpayment to providers and/or pocket overpayment when returned to the public entity.

☐ Look for the potential for a public employee to submit invoices or use the public entity credit card for personal purchases.

☐ Look for providers that make undisclosed payments to a public entity in order to aid in overbilling schemes.

☐ Look for providers with which the public employee might have financial interests. Look for related-party and other hidden relationships that are being used in an attempt to hide the affiliation.

☐ Look for a lack of segregation of duties between processing of the accounts receivable or accounts payable notices and recording to the books and records.

☐ Look at the lack of policies and procedures regarding write-offs and other required procedures.

☐ Look to see if reconciliations of accounts receivable and accounts payable are performed to the general ledger control account and other required reporting.

☐ Make sure there is sufficient supervisory review of accounts receivable and accounts payable aging. Anything over the terms of payment should be examined.

☐ Look to see if there is unrestricted access to general ledgers and records and if the proper levels of authorization are in place for those accesses.

☐ Examine items to determine if they are unaccounted for or missing from inventory.

☐ If there is any missing or altered documentation, a detailed inquiry should be made.

☐ Make sure that any orders are reviewed and approved by the proper levels of authority, with an independent party being included in the approval process.

☐ Examine all excessive inventory shortages.

☐ Any items to be dropped off, shipped, or delivered to another location need to have the proper public employee on the receiving end of the documentation.

☐ Require physical approval control for any off-site provider services.

Cash

Skimming
Cash is stolen before it is recorded on the books and records.

Cash Larceny
Cash is stolen after it has been recorded on the books and records.

Check Tampering

A public entity's funds are stolen by intercepting, forging, or altering a check drawn on one of the public entity's bank accounts.

Check Kiting

A scheme that utilizes multiple bank accounts, in which the money is deposited from account to account. This is made possible by the float that is generated via the process of collection. The float arises as the one account has been given credit for the funds before it clears the account in the other financial institution upon which it is drawn.

Overbilling Fraud

A scheme that involves a provider charging more time and/or more materials and/or at a higher rate or for substandard work/time/materials than what was originally contracted for.

Negative Invoicing Fraud

A scheme that involves the public employee using an invoice of a negative amount in some form of credit-type adjustment to reduce a provider's receivable balance. This is done to cover up the theft of a received payment.

Padding Fraud

A fraud that involves the provider or the public employee adding fraudulent expenses to an invoice or request for reimbursement.

Paperhanging Fraud

A fraud perpetrated by checks being written on closed accounts.

Purchasing and Billing Fraud

A scheme involving a public entity's funds being stolen by the interception, forging, or altering of a check drawn on one of the organization's bank accounts.

Types/Signs of Cash Fraud and Mismanagement:

☐ Failure of the operation to separate key functions to ensure adequate separation of duties and responsibilities

☐ A public entity employee buys goods and services from the provider it is working with. Not all illegally exchanged value will be cash between fraudsters.

☐ Collecting cash, but not recording the transaction. There are various licensing fees such as dog licenses, public pool, and other fee-based collections.

☐ Collecting cash, keeping a portion of cash, and underreporting the transaction amount.

☐ Collecting a citizen/user's payment, but not crediting the amount to his or her account.

☐ Stealing incoming cash or checks through an account set up to look like a bona fide account of the public entity.

☐ Skimming of cash before recording revenues or receivables on the public entity's books.

☐ Stealing cash and checks from the daily receipts before they can be deposited in the bank.

☐ Stealing cash receipts posted to revenue and receivable accounts.

☐ Stealing cash from bank deposits.

☐ Stealing cash at the point of the transaction.

☐ Forging an authorized signature on a public entity check.

☐ Forging the payees' signature on a public entity check.

☐ Altering the payee on the public entity check.

☐ A public employee steals blank public entity checks, then makes them out to him/herself or an accomplice.

☐ The public entity steals the outgoing check to a provider and then deposits it into his or her own bank account or uses it to pay his or her own creditors.

☐ The public employee orders duplicates for the public entity.

Suggested Actions:

☐ Document any shortages or overages on the daily cash record.

☐ Look for voiding transactions and pocketing of the cash.

☐ Match cash deposits to the bank statements to determine if there are any deposits not received by the bank.

☐ Look for multiple payments to a single provider on the same date.

☐ Look for insufficient supervisory review over the daily cash activities.

☐ Examine the public employees who have the opportunity to pocket.

☐ Have a control that requires the public employee to work out of an open cash drawer.

☐ Cashiers have access to the register's read and reset keys. A cashier can potentially clear registers, determine sales figures for the day, and accumulate/remove overages at the end of the day.

☐ Determine if there are weak cash handling procedures and cash accounting records.

☐ Look for checks issued to the provider that bounced or caused the cash account to reflect the transaction as having insufficient funds.

☐ Look at how the public employee conducts him- or herself outside the public entity.

☐ Look for public employees who are living beyond their means.

☐ Look for public employees who never or rarely take time off.

Complaints

Types/Signs of Records Chain-of-Custody Fraud and Mismanagement—Complaints/Whistle-Blowing:

☐ Make sure all complaints are reviewed at the appropriate levels of management within the public entity. Having a separate complaint hotline along with a whistle-blower hotline is a good control. It is similar to the municipal clerk controlling the information and recording it, then requesting that the public employee be responsible for handling it. With the hotline, there is the added evidence of a recording of the phone call, the clerk's office documentation, and the witnessing of the party that is required to respond, making this a sound control that establishes accountability.

☐ Complaints from unsuccessful bidders that a particular bidder is being favored over others.

Conflicts-of-Interest Risk

The authors believe that all greed is the result of conflicting self-interests, and studying these conflicts will greatly reduce the risk of fraud and mismanagement. Conflicts of interest can arise if the public employee maintains undisclosed interests in or with vendors/consultants/contractors. As previously noted, these public employees often accept inappropriate gifts, favors, or kickbacks from these parties and engage in unapproved discussions and arrangements.

The personal conflicts arise when an individual is in a position (POP) to perform his or her job and make decisions in ways that may enhance his or her financial standing. When there is a conflict of interest, the public employee's interests are advanced at the expense of the public entity. This often occurs when a public entity is part of some big development or construction project, and/or with the acquisition of goods and services.

Employee fraud means to take money or other property from an employer by fraudulent means. The employee performs an act that enables the conversion of the public entity's value into cash and the position that they are in allows them to remain undetected.

Federal Employees Compensation Act fraud is when public employees falsely claim injury or illness, making them unable to work, and receive monetary compensation from the government.

Workers' compensation/disability fraud is any practice that uses the workers' compensation insurance in any way that is contrary to the intended purpose of either the program or the law. Fraud occurs when someone in the public entity knowingly and with the intent to defraud, presents or causes to be presented any written statement that is materially false and misleading to obtain some benefit or advantage. It can also include doctoring records to secure a benefit that they would not otherwise have been provided.

Types/Signs of Conflict-of-Interest Fraud and Mismanagement:

☐ The provider receiving the public entity contracts is also hired by public entity personnel to perform work on their personal property.

☐ The public entity official fails to file conflict-of-interest or financial disclosure forms.

☐ The provider fails to file conflict-of-interest or financial disclosure forms.

Suggested Actions:

☐ Look for the public employee who has the potential to add or does add ghost employee(s) to the public entity's payroll.

☐ Establish procedures that will not allow for public employees to alter base pay based on falsified hours or rates.

☐ Establish procedures to ensure that commissions are not paid on inflated numbers or commission rates. The health insurance or insurance paid by the public entity for insurance commissions should be fully disclosed.

☐ Look at all changes in salary levels and make sure they are accompanied by the proper documentation.

☐ Require that all holiday leave or time-off entitlements be documented and properly tracked by an independent party and not by a public employee within the same unit of the public entity.

☐ Examine all workers' compensation (disability) claims. Hire an independent third party.

☐ Examine all employee contributions to benefit plans.

☐ Mandate that all requests for reimbursement of personal expenses claimed as a necessary expenditure get approval by an independent party in the public entity and by a supervisor.

☐ Mandate that any overstated cost of actual expense and reimbursement be met with a no-tolerance consequence.

☐ Look for multiple reimbursements of the same expenses submitted by the public employee.

☐ Look for the same support being utilized by multiple people seeking reimbursement from the public entity.

☐ Look for the public employee who invents an expenditure and seeks reimbursement that is not ordinary and customary to the public entity.

Contract Bid Award Process: Request for Proposal (RFP)

Collusive bidding occurs when the bidders have a secret understanding to submit competing high bids that allow a preselected contractor to win. These secret agreements are designed to prohibit or limit competition and manipulate prices to increase the amount of business available to each of the participants.

An example of bid collusion is highlighted in a U.S. Senate Committee on Commerce, Science & Transportation press release, which says, "The Committee has significant questions about whether conduct surrounding the bidding strategies employed by DISH Network and two affiliates adhered to both the letter and intent of the law."[6] The same press release discusses the strategy that involved multiple subsidiaries to develop the necessary patterns to win the bids by colluding.

Information leaking is the illegitimate practice of the public entity personnel involved in the process sharing information to help a favored bidder formulate a proposal.

Unfair advantage bidding happens when a public employee, who is likely in collusion with a corrupt bidder, excludes other qualified bidders. This can be accomplished by imposing narrow or unduly burdensome prequalification criteria on the other potential bidders. This is often accomplished by establishing unreasonable bid specifications, splitting the purchases or items requested to avoid competitive bidding, making unjustified single-source awards, and other potential diversions.

Manipulation of the bid occurs when a public employee, probably as the result of corruption, manipulates the bidding process in a number of ways to benefit a favored service provider. Bids are manipulated by leaking information regarding competing bids, accepting late bids, changing bids, rebidding work, and other diversions and distractions. Another form of bid manipulation is when a provider submits a low bid with the understanding that the corrupt public employee will approve later contract amendments and price increases. That is why it is important to examine and change orders or adjustments to the original proposals without the proper approvals and supporting documentation.

In bid rigging the specification, the public entity employee who is given the authority to purchase/procure work with the provider drafts a request for bids or proposals that contains specifications that are either too narrow or too broad. The unduly narrow specifications allow for the favored contractor to qualify. The broad specifications can be used to disqualify an otherwise qualified contractor to bid. Broad specifications can also be used in connection with later contract amendments and change orders to facilitate a corruption scheme and create value.

A bidding scheme accomplished among bidders is one in which the winning bidder and the winning bid are decided before the bids are submitted. This allows the winner to artificially inflate the bid without the chance of overbidding. The terms of the scheme may vary when providers take turns on the contracts according to the size of the contract by allocating equal amounts to each conspirator or allocating volumes that correspond to the size of each conspirator's company. The other scheme involves larger awards being broken into a number of smaller awards to avoid some of the controls or oversight that apply to larger awards.

Failure to meet specifications happens when the provider intentionally fails to meet contract specifications but indicates that the specifications have been met in order to increase profits. Specifications are not met when a provider is allowed to use goods or perform services that cost less or are not of the same anticipated quality as required by the contract.

Bid suppression happens when one or more competitors who otherwise would be expected to bid, or who have previously bid, agree to refrain from bidding or withdraw a previously submitted bid so that the designated winning competitor's bid will be accepted.

Missing term bidding occurs when the public entity employee favors a bidder by creating specific line items in a bid request that will not be included in the initial contract. The public employee then proceeds to provide the favored bidder with information to meet the vague or ambiguous terms in the bid request so they fall within the public entity's estimated budget. Then, they later receive additional money for items that were not included.

Single-source bidding is defined as a fraudulent act involving the public entity personnel who, in collusion with a supplier, improperly award a contract without securing competitive bids and/or prior review.

Single-selection fraud happens when the contracting officer is required to select the proposal that represents the best value to the government. While the contract award process has been designed to efficiently ensure the delivery of goods and services, the complex procedures involved in source selection may provide an opportunity for fraud.

The price is not right bidding is defined as the arrived-upon pricing by a provider that involves the inflating of costs in order to increase profits or limit losses.

Truth-or-dare bidding: In 1962 Congress passed the Truth in Negotiations Act, which requires, among other things, submission of complete and current cost and pricing data to the government during pre-award negotiations for contracts valued over $100,000. The Cost and Pricing Data Provisions of the Act are contained in 10 USC 2306 (a). A key document in the contract file relating to disclosure of cost and pricing data is the price with respect to government bidding. Fraudsters love when the contract has a benchmark. So if the contract is for $99,999.99, do the rules not apply?

Joe experienced a fraud early in his career. An owner left a signature stamp with a $1,000 approval authority to sign checks. So the employee stamped $999.99 checks made to him/herself and entered them in the computer as legitimate expenditures. When the embezzlement was found, the perpetrator had taken in excess of $250,000. Similar purchasing limits are set throughout public entities. So these below-the-radar amounts require closer examination.

Mismatch bidding as a result of cost mischarging is defined as the improper allocation of costs being charged to the contract. It also includes charging the contract at higher rates than the contract allows. The accounts those charges should be directly applied to are charged against other contracts. The result of cost mischarging is an improper overcharge to another area of the public entity for goods and services. That is why examining the variances and understanding why line items can be transferred is an important step in the process of mitigating these risks.

Labor substitution as a result of mischarging costs occurs when a provider misrepresents the cost of labor charged to a public entity contract.

The provider can also substitute poorly trained staff and bill at the agreed-upon rate. Examining the rate cost structure of labor looking for large variations in the billing rates will help to mitigate fraud.

Product/service substitution fraud as a result of mischarging occurs when the provider delivering goods or services to the public entity does not conform to contract requirements and does not inform the public entity.

Misrepresented progress payment fraud is a form of contract bid fraud that involves the submission of contract progress payment requests based on falsified direct labor charges, material costs for items not purchased, or a falsified certification of a stage of completion attained or work accomplished.

Commingling of contracts by cross-charging costs is when the provider can submit multiple bills on different contracts or work orders for the same work performed. A public entity employee can facilitate the scheme and share in the profits by writing similar work orders under different contracts and accepting the multiple billings.

False statements and claims fraud and mismanagement can be applied to all areas of fraud. False statements and claims can be defined as when a provider and/or public employee has *knowingly and willfully* falsified, concealed, or covered up by any trick, scheme, or device a material fact related to bids or contracts. The provider and/or public employee will have made materially false, fictitious, or fraudulent statements or representations. The provider or public employee will have made or used any false documentation knowing that it contains materially false, fictitious, or fraudulent statements or data entries to perpetrate fraud or mismanagement. The False Claims Act is the federal government's primary litigation tool in combating fraud against the government.

Types/Signs of Bidding Process Fraud and Mismanagement:

- ☐ If all losing bids did not comply with the bid specification, or only one bid is competitive while the others are poorly prepared, this needs to be further investigated and documented.
- ☐ Fewer competitors than usual bidding on a contract. Examine the situation further, as it may indicate a deliberate scheme to withhold bids for some reason that creates the opportunity to get access to the value.
- ☐ The request for proposal (bid) contract is unnecessarily rebid.
- ☐ Failure of original bidders to rebid, or an identical ranking of the same bidders upon rebidding when original bids were previously rejected as being too far over the public entity's estimate.

☐ Undocumented acceptance of late bids.

☐ Any appearance of identical calculations or spelling errors in two or more competitive bids may indicate direct collusion among the providers.

☐ The late bidder is the winning low bidder.

☐ Change orders issued soon after the contract was awarded, deleting or revising the original contracted item requirements.

☐ A failure by the provider to correct known deficiencies in the scope of goods and services to have been provided.

☐ There is a repeated denial by the provider of the existence of historical records that are later found.

Suggested Actions:

☐ Look for correspondence or other indications that may exist, where the providers have exchanged pricing information, divided territories, or other acts that established informal agreements.

☐ Look to see if certain providers are always bidding against one another or, conversely, if certain providers do not bid against one another.

☐ Examine jointly submitted proposals by providers that usually bid alone.

☐ Look at the qualified providers that did not bid and became subcontractors.

☐ Look at winning low bidders that withdrew and later become providers.

☐ Examine when bid prices drop when a new bidder enters the competition.

☐ Make sure all bids are date stamped, recorded, and received by a neutral party to maintain chain-of-custody documentation.

☐ Look for identical bid amounts on a contract line item by two or more contractors. It may be acceptable in some instances for lines to be identical, as suppliers often quote the same prices to several bidders. However, a large number of identical bids on any service-related item should be further reviewed.

☐ Examine any potential indications of falsification or alteration of supporting data.

☐ Investigate any provider's nonresponsiveness, delays, or inability to provide supporting documentation for costs attributable to goods and services claimed to have been provided.

☐ Look at records with respect to rebates, discounts, and other price breaks that the provider may have withheld. Examples are prescription and energy efficiency rebates to which the public entity may have been entitled.

☐ Look for long-term agreements not requiring fair and open bidding that renew continually.

☐ Examine all agreement terms and conditions to make sure there is no preferential wording.

☐ Look at contracts that are awarded to the same providers over multiple years for which bidding was no longer required.

☐ Examine for mathematical accuracy all overhead calculations that are reimbursable costs. Any work that is provided on a time and material–emergent basis should be subjected to a higher level of skepticism.

☐ Investigate any lack of reporting of residual or excess materials by the provider.

☐ Look for new cost centers appearing on supporting documentation that are not part of the contract awarded.

☐ Look for transfers/write-offs to scrap accounts or inventory write-off accounts.

☐ Look for employee reclassification in billing rates.

☐ Look for time postings and charges that do not jibe with the provider's billing to the public entity.

Procurement/Purchasing—Bribery and Kickbacks

When investigating potential kickbacks and bribes, any overly friendly interaction between a public employee and the vendor/consultant/contractor should be looked at closely. Monitor the public employee for any increase in wealth or expensive hobbies (see the Rita Crundwell story earlier in this chapter). Watch public employees who accept inappropriate gifts or entertainment. The New Jersey League of Municipalities observes who the convention sponsors (party throwers) are and whether or not they are political donators or have political affiliations. This is an example of a place to monitor potential kickback and bribe relationships. Findings don't come to fraud investigators; they have to find ways to catch such conflicts. Look at any discrepancies in a report and match them to the vendor/consultant/contractor invoices through a segregated, independent party prior to payment.

Verify that the necessary documentation for any vendor/consultant/contract violations exists and that those actions are being monitored by a system that is in place.

■ Examine reputations of contractors/providers in the industry known for paying kickbacks. Other competitors love to be whistle-blowers.

■ Are there middlemen or brokers involved in the services provided or goods purchased?

- Were requests made or designed for a one-party procurement when there was a pool of other potential vendors/consultants/contractors eligible to compete for the contract?
- Look for undocumented or frequent requests for change orders being awarded to particular vendors/consultants/contractors. Legal is an area that warrants further skepticism as well. Fixed fees, well-scoped-out terms, and work descriptions tighten up the availability of funds for kickbacks and bribes. Time and cost billing needs detailed scrutiny and is an area with which all public entities should be concerned. Instituting proper policies and examining why the litigation costs are excessive is a solid control. If litigation damages transpire, institute policies that prevent recurrence.
- Check to see if a certain industry has a reputation for corruption.
- Check to see if a contractor/provider (or is it the public entity?) has a history of giving favorable treatment to a particular party.
- Look to verify whether or not there has been improper (noncompetitive) or repeated selection of a contractor/provider aligned with a particular party.
- Watch for a public employee who sells public entity–owned property at less than market value to get a kickback or to sell the property back to the public entity at a higher price in the future.
- Watch for lengthy, unexplained delays between the announcement of a winning bidder and the signing of the contract award. There is the possibility that the party might be refusing to pay the bribe.
- Are the payments being made at higher than the market value? Are purchases made or services rendered necessary or do they have inappropriate characteristics? Is there continual late delivery, high-priced, low-quality work being accepted by a particular approval party with limited oversight in place?
- Look for an unusually high volume of purchases or services exceeding budgetary or pre-established dollar amounts and/or a need for changes in the scope of services.
- Cross-reference the vendor's address, telephone number, or zip code to see if there are matches to the suspected public employee's address, outside business, or relatives. Use data mining, which is a computer science process for discovering patterns in large data sets (big data) by designing algorithms. Algorithms are designed sets of rules to be followed in calculations in order to problem-solve massive amounts of transactions (data). In this case, one would compare addresses from the list of public employee information with the vendor/consultant/contractor information and look for matches.

- Examine those vendors/consultants/contractors with an incomplete address or a P.O. box.
- Examine the vendor/consultant/contractor's identification numbers for possible matches with the public employee's identification number.

Setting sound policy and procedure systems and structures around any official procurement and any purchasing actions will mitigate the risks of fraud and mismanagement. Having people in the public entity who notice whether or not these parties are following protocol and are acting within the normal scope of their responsibilities associated with awarding or administering a purchase or contract procurement is creating the necessary awareness to reduce these risks. As an examiner, look to see if the procurement/purchasing employees declined any promotions or other non-procurement positions in the past. Look at their financial disclosure statements and see if they have been filed and look for changes or items not disclosed. See if the procurement/purchasing employee continues to lobby for hiring certain suppliers and subcontractors. Note the length of time he or she has been in the position. Note whether or not he or she takes vacation time. All these mitigation measures contribute to the development of a sound fraud risk assessment plan.

Never ignore complaints from vendors, consultants, or subcontractors reporting that they have received pressure from a public employee to pay kickbacks, make political contributions, and/or other gratuities. All public employees should always be aware of the potential for violations of the anti-kickback statute or others. The imposable legal consequences should be effectively communicated in developing an ethical culture. It is necessary to have the appropriate whistle-blower policy/procedure in place that enables public employees to feel free from threats of job loss when alerting the public entity that a public employee is being paid kickbacks by a provider.

The establishment of a no-tolerance policy that prohibits preferred agreements or other types of long-term arrangements is key. The longer there is an established relationship, the greater the risk for fraud and mismanagement. The auditor whose fees are paid by the client and who has been auditing for 10 years has developed a relationship with the principal parties. While not necessarily wrong, there is a greater chance that independent thinking has been impaired in such cases. Peer review, auditor rotation, and other checks and balances need to be put in place to mitigate the risks.

Another way to examine the process includes speaking with the unsuccessful bidders. Ask questions like this: Do you think it was a fair process? Did the winning bidder receive the work because he or she paid a kickback? A survey of customer satisfaction that asks what the bidders thought of the process and why they thought they were unsuccessful should be performed.

Types/Signs of Controls Fraud and Mismanagement:

- ☐ Poor internal controls over the bidding procedures.
- ☐ The winning provider participated in drafting specifications.
- ☐ Circumvention of the bid process.
- ☐ Bid due dates unnecessarily extended.
- ☐ Failure to allow a reasonable time period to bid. Do not allow short or limited time periods unless well-documented and justified.
- ☐ No partial awards where there is a splitting or otherwise limiting of the requested proposal amounts. Examine any partial awards closely.
- ☐ No unreasonable narrowing of bid specifications. If this has occurred, further examination is required.

Suggested Actions:

- ☐ Look for weak internal controls that create opportunities to adjust labor charges or lack the appropriate audit trail to verify whether or not the labor charges are proper.
- ☐ Look at the provider's employee turnover.
- ☐ Create reasonable bidding prequalification procedures (standardized qualifications) and do not impose unreasonable conditions to qualify to bid.
- ☐ Examine if the provider needs to hire large numbers of personnel quickly and/or if they have the required skills to perform the work.
- ☐ Examine the provider to determine if they have adequate personnel to work on different contracts/task orders in the required labor categories.
- ☐ Look for failures to enforce deadlines.
- ☐ Look for failures to maintain a public opening of bids.
- ☐ Look for adequately publicized requests for bids.
- ☐ Examine awards to a nonresponsive bidder.
- ☐ Look at winning bids voided for errors and jobs that are rebidded and/or awarded to somebody else.
- ☐ Examine disqualification of a qualified bidder for questionable reasons.
- ☐ Examine changes to bids after received.
- ☐ Investigate lost bids and surrounding circumstances.
- ☐ Investigate awards not rebid even though fewer than the minimum number of bids were received.

☐ Investigate requests for bids sent to an unqualified provider that previously declined to bid.

☐ Investigate any line item bids that appear to be unreasonably low.

☐ Match the line items on the request for bids to the actual contract to determine if any discrepancies exist.

☐ Look to subsequent change orders and match them to the bid line items to determine if those line items were initially bid low.

Favoritism (Nepotism)

Types/Signs of Favoritism Fraud and Mismanagement:

☐ Unexplained or unjustified special treatment of a particular bidder or provider.

☐ Numerous singularly awarded contracts to the same providers.

☐ Inadequate documentation of contract violations by the public entity personnel for provider violations.

☐ The public entity employee continually accepts the low-quality work and overrides problems brought to their attention.

Suggested Actions:

☐ Look for questionable, noncompetitive, or repeated awards to a particular bidder/provider.

☐ Examine any public employee with interest in using a particular provider.

☐ Look for apparent connections between providers, such as common addresses, personnel, phone numbers, family relationships, school, and/or any other associations that might indicate preferential treatment.

Information (Disclosure)

Communications fraud is a process in which information is exchanged using different forms of media. Thefts of wireless, satellite, or landline services are examples of communications fraud, which is often written off as being de minimis. But if the time that the public employee is not performing the normal job responsibilities is factored in and multiplied across the entire entity, the cost can become significant.

Cooking the books involves the intentional altering of the books of an entity's account or accounting records to deceive or confuse. This is done to distract and divert the attention away from the ongoing fraud.

Dumpster diving is the practice of rummaging through someone's trash to obtain personal information used to commit identity theft or other types of fraud. Make sure all personal and/or business information is shredded and/or appropriately discarded.

Expense reimbursement schemes involve the public entity employee making claims for reimbursement for fictitious or inflated expenses.

Journal entry fraud involves the creation or alteration of accounting entries to cover up fraud.

Inventory inflation occurs when the public employee prepares fraudulent journal entries to cover up the fraud that has been perpetrated.

Inventory shrinkage is a loss of inventory through theft. This can be the result of a provider billing for the goods and shorting the delivery. It can also result from the public employee selling the goods in a side business. Without physical oversight, such as surprise checks, periodic counts, and other policy procedures in place, this is an area in which a lot of fraud can remain undetected.

Payroll fraud is when the public employee causes the public entity employer to issue payment by making false claims for compensation. Hand scanners and other time and attendance control tools will significantly reduce the abuse of time.

"Employee fraud is on the rise, soaring from $400 billion in lost revenue for U.S. businesses in 1996 to over $600 billion in 2003."[7] "While many organizations have implemented background checks as a requirement for employment, the majority of employees who steal—68.6%, according to Association of Certified Fraud Examiners—have no prior criminal record. A study conducted by the University of Florida estimates that employee theft is the cause of about 48% of inventory shrinkage in business. That's equal to more than $15 billion per year. The study goes on to estimate that the average loss per employee is in excess of $1,300, which is significantly higher than the cost normally attached to individual incidents of shoplifting, which is just over $207."[8]

This is an important area in which the public entity can create systems of accountability and efficiencies that result in significant cost savings.

Phantom vendor/ghost employee fraud is a form of fraud that transpires when the public entity personnel within the payroll, or accounts payable or procurement responsibility, create and/or approve invoices or paychecks for fictitious companies or employees in order to embezzle funds or to personally appropriate the goods and/or services for their own benefit.

Phishing/spoofing are terms that refer to forged or faked electronic documents. Spoofing generally refers to sending an email that is forged to appear as though it was sent by someone other than the actual person sending it. Phishing, often used in conjunction with spoofed email, is the act of sending an email falsely claiming to be an established legitimate entity in an attempt to fool the unsuspecting recipient.

Renumbering fraud is when a pre-numbered instrument (receipt, check, invoice, etc.) from a pad of similar documents is removed in such a way that the removal can later be used to falsely document illegal activities.

Types/Signs of Information Disclosure Fraud and Mismanagement:

☐ The same provider appears to always be close to the independent public entity's estimate. This may indicate that the provider is receiving inside information relative to the public entity's estimate.

☐ Public entity personnel provide proprietary information (bid and proposal specifications) to one or a few competitors. Using an after-bid survey that asks if there was any bias in the process and other inquiries about the bid process is proactive thinking.

☐ The suspect bid contains data based on information in the public entity's official file but not available to the general public.

☐ Payroll checks are signed by the receiving party, despite an automatic deposit payroll.

Suggested Actions:

☐ Examine losing bidders that cannot be located in any business directories, have nonexistent addresses, and/or other suspicious required information. Check employee personnel files for completeness.

☐ Look for employees who have the opportunity to steal or misuse confidential citizen, financial, and general information.

☐ Update background checks.

Middleman Fraud and Mismanagement

Look for unnecessary middlemen or power brokers being involved in contracts or purchases.

Types/Signs of Middleman Fraud and Mismanagement:

☐ If there is poor or incomplete performance, but the provider continues to receive payments, more contracts, and positive past performance scores, further examination should be undertaken.

☐ A certain provider appears to be bidding substantially higher on some bids than on others, with no logical cost difference to account for the increase.

☐ The successful bidder repeatedly subcontracts work to companies that submitted higher bids, or to companies that received bid packages and could have bid as a prime provider but did not. Look at losing bids that were submitted that are similar to bids on different public entity requests for proposals.

☐ Look at the public employee who socializes or accepts gifts and favors from the provider.

☐ Determine if there is a pattern of providers that are qualified and capable of performing but fail to bid, with no apparent reason. Any situation in which there are fewer competitors than usual submitting bids should be examined closely and documented.

☐ A certain provider repeatedly wins contracts with one public entity but not with other public entities for similar goods or services.

Suggested Actions:
☐ Look for patterns of rotating winning bidders by job, type of work, or geographical area to see if any collusion is present.

☐ Look for patterns indicating regular low-awarded bids. An example would be a certain provider always being the low-awarded bidder in a certain geographical area, or in a fixed rotation with other bidders. If the other bidders commonly received the previous awards, an even higher level of examination should be performed.

☐ Examine unusual bid patterns that show bids that are consistently too high, too close, or too far apart, or have round numbers, are incomplete, or have other irregularities.

☐ Look for patterns of losing bids for which the bidders are unqualified, inappropriate, or unknown.

Reputation (Rumors)

☐ Does the party the public entity is doing business with have an ethical reputation? Have there been any rumors of kickbacks or other unethical behavior?

☐ Is the industry susceptible to corruption or unethical behavior?

Segregation (Overlap, Levels of Trust, Approval)

Look for a lack of segregation of duties to ensure a single public employee is not responsible for initiation of a requirement for award of a contract/order and receipt, inspection, and acceptance of supplies and services.

- ☐ Timing (delay, schedule, performance, delivery)
- ☐ Examine all lengthy delays that are not explained, between the announcement of the winning bidder and the signing of the contract.
- ☐ Look for variances (like when changes are unusually high)
- ☐ Look for questionable, undocumented, or frequent requests for change orders awarded to a particular contractor.
- ☐ Examine the continued acceptance of late deliveries of high-priced, low-quality work.
- ☐ Look for an unusually high volume of purchases.
- ☐ Match the provider's address, telephone number, or zip code with those of the public entity employees to cross-check whether any addresses are the same or an outside business or family relationship exists that might indicate a conflict of interest.
- ☐ Look at public employees who have a side business and make sure it does not conflict with their responsibilities to the public entity.
- ☐ Look at provider information that is vague, missing, or matches an employee's address, phone number, or zip code.
- ☐ Run a computer data mining search, looking for potential matches between the provider and public employees.
- ☐ Look for assessment progress reports that do not match the provider's invoices. For example, the assessment reports indicate contractor progress was greater than it actually was and the contractor has been paid for more than the work completed.
- ☐ Review payments that indicate undocumented higher prices.
- ☐ Review any unnecessary or inappropriate acquisition of goods or services that are not needed.

Change Orders, Unusual Volume, Late Delivery, Subpar Goods and Services

- ☐ Look for questionable, undocumented, or frequent requests for change orders awarded to a particular contractor.

☐ Examine the continued acceptance of late delivery and high-priced, low-quality work.

☐ Look for unusually high volume of purchases.

☐ Match the provider's address, telephone number, or zip code with those of public entity employees to see if the addresses are the same or an outside business or family relationship might cause a conflict.

☐ Look at public employees who have a side business and make sure it is not conflicting with the public entity job responsibilities.

☐ Look at the providers information to see if it is vague, missing, or matches an employee's address, phone number, or zip code.

☐ Run a computer data mining search, looking for potential matches between the provider and public employees.

☐ Look for assessment progress reports that do not match the provider's invoices. For example, the assessment reports indicate contractor progress was greater than it actually was and the contractor has been paid for more than the work completed.

☐ Review payments that indicate undocumented higher prices.

☐ Review any unnecessary or inappropriate acquisition of goods or services that are not needed.

RISK OVERVIEW AND PLAN

What are the public entity risk indicators and approaches?

☐ The management of the public entity must communicate an approach to all participants in the process that affords them an understanding of the potential risks. The public and the people in the public entity must understand that the risk of fraud and mismanagement can exist. The public entity must put in place the necessary strategic planning and performance measurements to guide their management in ways to address these potential risks.

What are the process risk indicators and approaches?

☐ The public entity must identify the risks. The strategies to address these risks must be put in place with the proper oversight to ensure the established systems and structures are not being overridden or ignored.

☐ Consideration should always be given to the risk, from the perspective of how this risk can affect the public entity's operations.

☐ Key risks within the public entity's operations should be documented to reflect how they are being managed and by whom. These risk occurrences should be transparent to the public and not kept secret.

☐ The risk management team and the management team of the processes should be working together and on the same page.

☐ A risk response strategy needs to be in place with the proper oversight to ensure that the appropriate actions are taken.

☐ All risks whether low- or high-level priority need to be addressed with the appropriate level of skepticism and independent oversight.

☐ All applications of the plan must be applied in a consistent manner across the public entity.

What are the behavioral risk indicators and approaches?

☐ Do not let the people in key positions of trust demonstrate unacceptable risk taking or react adversely to implementing risk policies and procedures.

☐ Do not let the public entity operate without planned systems and structures to monitor the behavior of people in trusted positions and those who have access to the value.

☐ Keep track of the behavior monitoring and look for deviations or changes in behavior, whether internal or external.

We have discussed common risk management failures with respect to fraud and mismanagement. The following are some flags that should trigger further investigation:

☐ Poor governance and ethical tone (Tone at the Top) at the public entity.

☐ The occurrence of unacceptable or excessive risk taking.

☐ Inability or unwillingness to implement an effective risk-monitoring system.

☐ No oversight records on whether the systems and structures in place are effective at handling potential risks.

☐ Failure of the public entity management to implement the necessary risk management setting strategies to effectively handle fraud and mismanagement.

Compliance Checklist

The following is a list that an examiner should use to verify that the management of a public entity is in compliance with their set-upon objectives.

- ☐ **Cash Management** – Checks to make sure all reimbursements are properly supported, all advance payments are properly managed, and that any interest earned on investments remains inconsequential and remitted to the intended grantor.
- ☐ **Program Income** – Any gross income earned and received by the public entity from whatever source must meet the specific terms and conditions attached to the generation of those revenues. These funds should be accounted for in the period in which they were earned and within the activity period in which they were designed to support, unless the terms require otherwise.
- ☐ **Eligibility** – All participants in any program that are eligible to receive funds from the public entity (benefit of the funds) must meet the programs criteria's fully, with no exception.
- ☐ **Procurement, Suspension, and Debarment** – Review the procurement for compliance with the applicable laws and regulations and other conditions attached to the funds, both post and pre-award. Determine if the public entity verifies whether or not the parties involved with the procurement comply and are qualified (not suspended, debarment or otherwise excluded).
- ☐ **Allocation of Cost (Cost Principle)** – Examine the specifics of the costs that can and cannot be funded under the program. Examine how they are calculated and what level of support there is for them.
- ☐ **Activities Allowed or Unallowed** – Examine the specific activities that can or cannot be funded by the program.
- ☐ **Matching the Level of Effort When Earmarking** – Any cost sharing or subsidizing should be matched to the level of use, checking the participation from period to period. Understand the earmarked rationale for setting aside funds.
- ☐ **Period of Performance** – Examine the allowable costs incurred during the period of performance. Verify the cost incurred to date and that the funds were authorized and within the scope of the written polices and/or agreements attached to those funds.

☐ **Equipment and Real Property Management** – Verify the public entity management is safeguarding the use and disposal of the real (real estate) or tangible property (equipment/other).

Do these sound familiar? **Time period assumption** (report activities and revenues in the proper periods), **economic entity assumption** (funds should not be used for any other purpose, except for what they were designed to fund), **monetary unit** (the costs have to be able to be measured in dollars), **historical cost principles** (the costs need to be recorded), **matching** (revenue and expenses are to be matched in the proper period of activities), **revenue recognition** (account for transactions as they are earned or incurred), **consistency** (all terms need to be applied equally on an ongoing basis), **full disclosure** (all terms for use of funds must be documented and in accordance with the specified terms and conditions for using and collecting the funds), and **conservatism** (always apply sound rational thinking to the use and collection of these funds). If you do not know them, they are the foundation principle for accountants. Any checklist or system development should apply these principles. While we have modified to support the compliance checklist, the overall character of these principles comes through. Keep these in mind when developing your system and structures to prevent fraud and mismanagement.

 CONCLUSION

The intent of Chapter 8 was to summarize the soft skill knowledge base outlined in the other chapters and to enhance your ability to examine for fraud and mismanagement. We attempted to provide these tools to prevent the one-dimensional thinking that often exists in public entities. In order to create the proactive preventative model, a new level of thinking has to be implemented. That means developing a culture within the public entity that believes fraud and mismanagement can and will happen in a public entity. Specifically, the eyes and ears of the people involved in an entity need to remain open to the potential signs of fraud and mismanagement. This chapter gives many warning signs and ideas. These lists of warning signs are not intended to be exhaustive, as the types of fraud and the tools available to create them, like technology, are forever changing. They are designed to help you evaluate whether fraud or mismanagement is occurring within a public entity. The successful examiner looks for these warning signs no matter how subtle they can be and follows up with the proper level of skepticism. The answers to developing sound systems and structures are not in reading about them but, rather, in actually performing them on an ongoing basis.

 FINAL WORD

The cost of fraud to a public entity goes well beyond dollars and cents. Along with the availability of insurance coverage to reimburse for fraud and the obvious embarrassment to the entity, there are a few reasons why not all fraud is reported. Fraud ruins reputations and lives, and brings down even the most successful political figures. Fraud is a significant business risk to the public entity and needs the immediate attention of citizens. Having a well-designed fraud detection system, based on the transactional data analysis of the public entity's operational systems, can significantly reduce the chance of fraud occurring within a public entity and lead to greater efficiencies. However, nothing replaces having the correct ethical spirit in place from top to bottom.

Here are some final things to consider when developing a public entity fraud prevention plan:

■ Ratings can be useful, but what good is a rating if it is falsified or inaccurate? Fraudsters can manipulate ratings. This is why using only one component to judge something is a bad idea. Ratings are great sanity checks when they are verified with the appropriate levels of documentary support.

■ When detecting, deterring, and preventing fraud, it is important for a public entity to consider *perception* (oversight), *ethics* (communication), and *trust* (assigned power). Public entity employees are fiduciaries, and as such they hold the interests of others in the decisions they make. Adequate systems can only operate effectively when the proper levels of trust are in place and the people who have been given the authority to act are putting the interests of others before their own.

■ The public entity needs to consider perception. Throughout this book, the importance of outrage and a willingness to fight fraud has been discussed. The way that people on the outside look at the potential for fraud in the public entity will have an impact on the public entity's susceptibility to fraud. If the people in the public entity believe in their organization and want to combat fraud, then that is a big step toward preventing fraud. If the people do not have any interest in the well-being of their organization, then it makes the public entity more vulnerable to fraud.

■ The public entity cannot afford to have public employees who think of fraud as something that is inevitable or commonplace. This is the wrong attitude. Still, the public employees should be made aware of or even expect fraud. The public entity must establish a no-tolerance policy. Furthermore, looking the other way or assuming that fraud will not happen can also be problematic. An attitude of "Oh, it will happen anyway" is likely to perpetuate apathy and prevent the necessary outrage and motivation needed to combat fraud.

■ The public entity needs to consider its ethics and work to create an environment where people are encouraged to do the right thing. One of the best fraud deterrents is having the right people on staff who have high ethical standards and can be trusted. Human resources is the first line of defense. Proper screening and follow-up on personnel is a way to ensure efficiency and safeguard public entity resources.

Trust is something that a public entity has to learn is earned. There is no room for nepotism, political favors, or other horse trading in place of putting the right people in key positions. If the public entity cannot trust its employees, then it cannot function effectively. While there needs to be trust in the public entity, that same public entity needs to think about putting in place the proper oversight, communication, and power assignments to fulfill the specific responsibilities needed to carry out the policy objectives.

Even in a trustworthy staff and environment there needs to be oversight. People need to be monitored by the unsuspected 800-pound friendly gorillas. These gorillas need to establish an open and communicative environment. An example of a proactive fraud prevention measure is to establish a third-party independent whistle-blower hotline. A system that encourages people to come forward is a strong system. Merely having a whistle-blower hotline within a public entity does not necessarily provide the reporting parties with the confidence that their privacy is being protected and that the problem is being investigated objectively.

If there is a lack of communication in the public entity or employees do not feel they have a voice that is heard and that matters, then it is likely to make it more difficult for the public entity to establish trust and, in turn, prevent fraud and mismanagement.

Finally, even in a trustworthy and communicative environment there needs to be a limit on power. The points where there is value and trusted people meet that value need to be examined closely. An appropriate level of independent skepticism is a critical element in effectively managing the risks of fraud and preventing fraud from occurring. As we stated, there is no 100 percent way to stop fraud and mismanagement, but this will significantly reduce the instances of them. No one in a public agency should be given too much power. As Lord Acton said, "Absolute power corrupts absolutely."

Remember to question everything, and if asked why you are asking, simply say, "Because I can."

 NOTES

1. http://www.rasmussenreports.com/public_content/politics/general_politics/april_2014/53_think_neither_political_party_represents_the_american_people.
2. Contingent liability is a liability that is reflected in the financial statements if it is probable and estimable and has not yet occurred.
3. http://www.forbes.com/sites/walterpavlo/2013/11/18/fraud-thriving-in-u-s-churches-but-you-wouldnt-know-it/#5ba913d06fea.
4. http://www.forbes.com/sites/walterpavlo/2013/02/14/fmr-dixon-il-comptroller-rita-crundwell-sentenced-to-19-12-years-in-prison/#5395ba355726.
5. http://www.forbes.com/sites/walterpavlo/2015/12/15/cash-only-small-business-targeted-by-irs-the-case-of-nicks-roast-beef/#8b4b283c844c.
6. https://www.commerce.senate.gov/public/index.cfm/pressreleases?ID=3A81DD76-56D4-47A1-955F-4846493CB4BC.
7. http://leadership-results.com/pdfs/white-papers/Fraud-Theft-Workplace-Violence.pdf.
8. http://leadership-results.com/pdfs/white-papers/Fraud-Theft-Workplace-Violence.pdf.

Appendix: Tables

TABLE A.1 State Top Income Tax Rates

State Income Tax Rate Top 10		Tax Rates			Income Brackets		Population
Ranking	State	High	Low	No. of Tax Brackets	High	Low	(July 1, 2014 est., in millions)
1	California	12.30%	1.00%	9	$519,687.00	$7,749.00	38.8
2	Hawaii	11.00%	1.40%	12	$200,001.00	$2,400.00	1.4
3	Oregon	9.90%	5.50%	4	$125,000.00	$3,350.00	3.9
4	Minnesota	9.85%	5.35%	4	$154,951.00	$25,070.00	5.4
5	Iowa	8.98%	0.36%	9	$69,255.00	$1,539.00	3.1
6	New Jersey	8.97%	1.40%	6	$500,000.00	$20,000.00	8.9
7	Vermont	8.95%	3.55%	5	$411,500.00	$37,450.00	0.7
8	District of Columbia	8.95%	4.00%	4	$350,000.00	$10,000.00	0.7
9	New York	8.82%	4.00%	8	$1,029,250.00	$8,200.00	19.7
10	Maine	7.95%	3.00%	3	$20,900.00	$5,200.00	1.3

Source: Federation of Tax Administrators and http://quickfacts.census.gov/qfd/index.html

458

TABLE A.2   Types of Government Revenue

No.	Government Revenue Sources: Taxes, Fees, and Others	Descriptions
1	Accounts Receivable Tax	Whether you collect sales or other income in a business transaction you pay taxes if you select the accrual basis of accounting. Accruals can be defined as the ability to maneuver, manipulate, and manufacture the necessary diversion, distraction, and divisions to materially misrepresent intentionally resulting in reliance and leading to damages of one's self-interest and unjustly enriching another's. It this ability of non-provable cash that leads to the potential for fraud and mismanagement.
2	Accumulated Earnings Tax	A tax imposed by the federal government upon companies with retained earnings deemed to be unreasonable. **IRS Publication 542**
3	Alcohol Tax	Alcohol tax is an excise tax. Excise taxes are indirect taxes on the sale or use of specific products or transactions. The tax is often passed on to people and organizations that purchase particular products or services. A tax based on the presence of alcohol in a product is an excise tax; other examples of excise taxes on products include tobacco, energy (oil and gas taxes), and waste (trash containers). Unlike value-added taxes and sales taxes, excise tax is usually not a function of the value of the product being taxed but, rather, a fixed-rate tax or specific tax, expressed as a monetary amount per quantity, not value, of the product. **IRS Publication 510**
4	Ad Valorem Tax (includes duties on imported items), also see Property tax	A tax based on the assessed value of real estate or personal property. Ad valorem taxes can be property taxes or even duties on imported items. Property ad valorem taxes are a major source of revenue for many state, county, and municipal governments.
5	Air Transportation Taxes (just look at how much you were charged the last time you flew)	Along with traditional income and payroll taxes, airlines and their customers (passengers and shippers) pay many special taxes and fees to a variety of authorities, both at home and abroad. Among the stated purposes of these taxes and fees are homeland (national) security, environmental protection, agriculture inspection, infrastructure enhancement, airport and airway operations and maintenance, and agency financing.

(continued)

TABLE A.2 *(Continued)*

No.	Government Revenue Sources: Taxes, Fees, and Others	Descriptions
6	Alternative Minimum Tax	The alternative minimum tax (AMT) is another federal income tax imposed on individuals, corporations, estates, and trusts. The AMT tax is basically imposed as a flat rate tax on an adjusted amount of taxable income above a certain threshold. It basically guarantees a minimum tax by preventing these entities from benefiting from certain exclusions based on income. **IRS Publication 556**
7	Aviation Fuel Tax	A Federal Excise tax imposed on aviation fuel. This is also taxed under other fuel measurement reporting requirements, i.e., heavy trucks and trailers, highway use, as well as kerosene.
8	Beach Badges Fees	Different state and municipality law allows towns to charge beach fees "in order to provide funds to improve, maintain and police the (beach) and to protect the same … and to provide facilities and safeguards for public bathing and recreation," including lifeguards.
9	Bike License	A bicycle license is required for bicycles operated on any public street or sidewalk, or upon any public path set aside for the exclusive use of bicycles. The laws regulating bicycles have a dual purpose, antitheft and safety. By registration of the bicycle serial number and the issuance of a license emblem, positive identification of ownership is enhanced. This alone acts as a deterrence to theft.
10	Biodiesel Fuel Taxes	Biodiesel may be sold without the motor vehicle fuel tax only if it is sold as dyed biodiesel. The sale of clear biodiesel must include the motor vehicle fuel tax.
11	Building/ Construction Permit	A permit required in most jurisdictions for new construction, or adding on to preexisting structures, and in some cases for major renovations. Generally, the new construction must be inspected during construction and after completion to ensure compliance with national, regional, and local building codes. Failure to obtain a permit can result in significant fines and penalties, and even demolition of unauthorized construction if it cannot be made to meet code.

TABLE A.2 (Continued)

No.	Government Revenue Sources: Taxes, Fees, and Others	Descriptions
12	Bulk Transfer Tax	According to regulation, the term "bulk sale" means any sale, transfer, or assignment in bulk of any part or the whole of business assets, other than in the ordinary course of business, by a person required to collect tax and pay it to the Department of Taxation and Finance.
13	Capital Gains Tax	The capital gains tax takes a percentage of all realized capital gains. This is an important distinction. A capital gain is said to be "realized" when the asset is sold. An unrealized capital gain is an asset that has increased in value, but has not been sold. **IRS Publication 409**
14	Car Vehicle Registrations	Your annual vehicle registration payment consists of various fees that apply to your vehicle. Your annual renewal notice and registration card itemize these fees. The following is a list of the various fees that may be included in your annual vehicle registration payment: registration fee, vehicle license fee, weight fee, special plate fee, county/district fee, owner responsibility fee.
15	Cement and Gypsum Producers License Tax	Montana producers and importers of cement and cement products are required to pay a quarterly license tax of 22 cents per ton. Producers and importers are required to pay 5 cents per ton for gypsum and gypsum products. Individuals retailing cement and gypsum products in Montana must pay a license tax of 22 cents and 5 cents, respectively, for every ton that has not been paid for under any other law.
16	Cigarette Taxes	Cigarettes are taxed at the corporate, federal, state, and local levels. The cigarette manufacturer pays taxes assessed at the corporate level, including corporate income taxes, property taxes, payroll taxes, etc. Then there are the taxes paid by the wholesalers, the retailers, the warehouses, and the taxes embodied in the products the manufacturer uses to make the cigarettes. In addition to the cigarette tax,

(continued)

TABLE A.2 (*Continued*)

No.	Government Revenue Sources: Taxes, Fees, and Others	Descriptions
		cigarettes are generally also subject to sales or use tax. Typically, a tax is imposed when a distributor receives cigarettes for the purpose of making a first sale in a state. A stamp must be affixed to each package. This is evidence that state tax has been paid. Persons who possess untaxed cigarettes may be assessed a penalty.
17	City Taxes	City-Local Tax—A tax assessed and levied by a local authority such as a county or municipality. A local tax is usually collected in the form of property taxes, and is used to fund a wide range of civic services from garbage collection to sewer maintenance. The amount of local taxes may vary widely from one jurisdiction to the next.
18	Coal Severance Tax	Jurisdictions use this tax on extracted resources such as gas, oil, coal, and timber from private land. There is also a gross production tax. Other jurisdictions tax royalties.
19	Coal Gross Proceeds Tax	A jurisdictional tax based on the natural resources gross proceeds value.
20	Consumer Counsel Tax	Council taxes were first introduced in 1993, replacing the Community Charge (poll tax), which in turn replaced local rates in England and Wales in 1990. The prior system was based on the rental value of your home, not the market value.://www.which.co.uk/money/tax/guides/council-tax/understanding-council-tax/
21	Consumption Tax	Consumption tax is also known as an expenditure tax is based on cash flow since it is taxed when people spend. States raise significant revenue through sales taxes, which are a consumption tax. There has been talk about a national sales tax or value-added tax to replace the personal income tax that is based on salary and wages, interest dividends, and capital gains. The federal gasoline excise tax is another example of a consumption tax.

TABLE A.2 (*Continued*)

No.	Government Revenue Sources: Taxes, Fees, and Others	Descriptions
22	Corporate Income Tax	The profit of a corporation is taxed to the corporation when earned, and then is taxed to the shareholders when distributed as dividends. This creates a double tax. The corporation does not get a tax deduction when it distributes dividends to shareholders. Shareholders cannot deduct any loss of the corporation.
23	Corporation License Tax (Fee)	Fee to register a corporation.
24	Court Fines (revenue from many activities)	A fine is an amount of money that the court has ordered to be paid as a penalty. Fines may be ordered in a variety of civil cases, such as traffic citations or drunk and disorderly citations. Fines can include court costs and other fees. A judge may order a fine as the whole or part of a sentence. Fines can be ordered for a wide range of offenses.
25	Customs Duty	Customs duty is a tariff or tax imposed on goods when transported across international borders. The purpose of customs duty is to protect each country's economy, residents, jobs, environment, etc., by controlling the flow of goods, especially restricted and prohibited goods, into and out of the country.
26	Disposal Fees	A fee charged for the amount of waste disposed of by customers at a landfill.
27	Dog License Tax / fee	A dog license is required in some jurisdictions to be the keeper of a dog. Usually a dog-license identifying number is issued to the owner, along with a dog tag bearing the identifier and a contact number for the registering organization.
28	Driver's license commercial renewal fee	A commercial driver's license (CDL) is valid for only so many years. Although each state sets it own life span on the license, it expires at regular intervals. This allows each state to periodically reevaluate your standing as the holder of a CDL, much like the licensing boards for other professionals including doctors, attorneys, and architects.

(continued)

TABLE A.2 (*Continued*)

No.	Government Revenue Sources: Taxes, Fees, and Others	Descriptions
29	Driver's license renewal fee	State regulated; renewal varies by State.
30	Double Tax (double taxation)	Double taxation is a term used to describe the way taxes are imposed on corporate shareholders and on corporations. The corporation is taxed on its earnings (profits), and the shareholders are taxed again on the dividends they receive from those earnings.
31	Electrical Energy Producers Tax	The electrical energy license tax is imposed on each person or organization engaged in generating, manufacturing, or producing electrical energy in Montana. This tax is in addition to the wholesale energy transaction tax.
32	Employer Health Insurance Mandate Tax	Obamacare's "employer mandate" is a requirement that all businesses with 50 or more full-time equivalent employees (FTE) provide health insurance to at least 95% of their full-time employees and dependents up to age 26, or pay a fee. The employer mandate is officially part of the Employer Shared Responsibility Provision. Under the Affordable Care Act, the federal government, state governments, insurers, employers, and individuals are given shared responsibility to reform and improve the availability, quality, and affordability of health insurance coverage in the United States.
33	Employer Medicare Taxes	Employers have numerous payroll tax withholding and payment obligations. Of the utmost importance is the proper payment of what are commonly known as FICA taxes. FICA taxes are somewhat unique in that there is required withholding from an employee's wages as well as an employer's portion of the taxes that must be paid: Social Security tax, Medicare tax. There is a Medicare surcharge if the wage exceeds a certain amount.
34	Employer Social Security Taxes	Employers have numerous payroll tax withholding and payment obligations. Of the utmost importance is the proper payment of what are commonly known as FICA taxes. FICA taxes are somewhat unique in that there is required withholding from an employee's wages as well as an employer's portion of the taxes that must be paid.

TABLE A.2 *(Continued)*

No.	Government Revenue Sources: Taxes, Fees, and Others	Descriptions
35	Electronic transmission of tax return fees	Fee to transmit tax returns.
36	Environmental Fees	The Environmental Fee is a fee on businesses in industry groups that use, generate, or store hazardous materials or that conduct activities related to those materials. In the past, the annual fee only applied to certain corporations.
37	Estate Tax, Inheritance	An inheritance tax is a state tax that you pay when you receive money or property from the estate of a deceased person. Unlike the federal estate tax, the beneficiary of the property is responsible for paying the tax, not the estate. However, as of 2014, only eight states impose an inheritance tax. And even if you live in one of those states, many beneficiaries are exempt from paying it. The key difference between estate and inheritance taxes lies in who is responsible for paying it. An estate tax is levied on the total value of a deceased person's money and property and is paid out of the decedent's assets before any distribution to beneficiaries.
38	Excise Taxes on Comprehensive Health Insurance Plans (Cadillac Tax)	The Cadillac Tax is an excise tax scheduled to take effect in 2018 to reduce health care usage and costs by encouraging employers to offer plans that are cost-effective and engage employees in sharing in the cost of care. It is a 40% tax on employers that provide high-cost health benefits to their employees.
39	Excise Tax on Charitable Hospitals (page 2001/Sec. 9007 of Obamacare)	Excise Tax on Charitable Hospitals (page 2001/Sec. 9007/Min$/immediate): $50,000 per hospital if they fail to meet new "community health assessment needs," "financial assistance," and "billing and collection" rules set by HHS (updated on page 364 of manager's amendment).

(continued)

TABLE A.2 *(Continued)*

No.	Government Revenue Sources: Taxes, Fees, and Others	Descriptions
40	Federal Income Tax	The most common form of federal taxation is the income tax. The income tax rules allow the government to collect taxes from any person or business that earns money during the year. The tax rules provide a broad and sweeping definition of taxable income to include any and all property you receive, regardless of whether you earn it at work, through a business, or from making good investments. Although this can seem overwhelming, the rules also provide a wide range of credits, deductions, and exclusions that reduce the amount of tax you must pay.
41	Federal Unemployment Tax	The Federal Unemployment Tax is a tax incurred by employers. The taxes are used to fund agencies that work on behalf of the workforce. In order to report these taxes, the employer submits a Form 940 to the IRS each year. Under some circumstances, the employer may be required to pay for the tax in payments that are spread throughout the year, rather than as a lump-sum payment. The Federal Unemployment Tax is used to pay for unemployment insurance for those who are unable to find work. It is also used to pay for half the cost of unemployment benefits. If the states need to borrow money to pay unemployment benefits, the federal government uses this tax to provide the money that the states borrow.
42	Fire Inspections (Fee)	Inspection services performed by fire inspectors.
43	Fishing License Tax	*Fishing* is defined as the act of angling, or to catch, take, kill, or remove, or the attempt to catch, take, kill, or remove, from any waters or other areas any fish by any means or method for any purpose whatsoever. *Casting* and/or *retrieving*, whether by rod, reel and line, or by hand line, for oneself or for others, requires a current license, unless specifically exempted by law.
44	Flush Taxes	In 2004, the Maryland Legislature took a major step toward protecting the Chesapeake Bay and its tributaries when it passed what has become known as the "flush tax."

TABLE A.2 *(Continued)*

No.	Government Revenue Sources: Taxes, Fees, and Others	Descriptions
45	Food Service License Tax	A public food service establishment is a building, vehicle, place, or structure open to the public where food is prepared, served, or sold for consumption at or near the establishment or as takeout, or is prepared and delivered to a different location for consumption.
46	Franchise Business Taxes	Franchise taxes are fees that companies must pay for the privilege of doing business in a particular state or city. (Despite the name, they don't apply just to franchises.) Franchise taxes are not based on profit, meaning that even companies that lose money or only break even must pay them. These taxes may be a flat fee or may be based on a company's net worth or its gross receipts—the amount of business that a company does in the state or city imposing the tax. Different states impose franchise taxes on different kinds of companies, but they typically aren't limited to corporations.
47	Fuel Permit License Tax	Fuel permit laws are governed by state laws, which vary by state. Generally, you must have a fuel permit or license to operate certain vehicles in the state and if you operate these vehicles on a public highway in a state without a required permit or license, you may be subject to fines and penalties, and your vehicle could be impounded.
48	Garbage Taxes	Garbage collection is dependent upon location. Residents in the Solid Waste Collection District pay a garbage tax to receive municipal collection. Residents not located in the district do not pay this tax and must arrange for a private hauler to collect their garbage.
49	Gas/electric bill fees & taxes	There are three types of charges on gas bills: fixed monthly fees, gas costs, and taxes and surcharges. The Gas Tax is imposed on persons in the business of distributing, supplying, furnishing, or selling natural gas for use or consumption (not for resale). Propane gas is taxed under this act providing it is delivered by pipeline to the consumer.

(continued)

TABLE A.2 *(Continued)*

No.	Government Revenue Sources: Taxes, Fees, and Others	Descriptions
50	Gas Guzzler Tax (Luxury Tax)	Congress established Gas Guzzler Tax provisions in the Energy Tax Act of 1978 to discourage the production and purchase of fuel-inefficient vehicles. The Gas Guzzler Tax is assessed on new cars that do not meet required fuel economy levels. These taxes apply only to passenger cars.
51	Gasoline Tax (8 to 35 cents per gallon) Per tank?	A gasoline tax is a sales tax imposed on the sale of gasoline. In the United States, the funds are dedicated or hypothecated to be used for transportation or roads purposes, so that the gas tax is considered by many to be a user fee. The federal government has levied a tax on gasoline since 1932.
52	Local Gasoline Tax	Similar to other Gasoline Taxes that is assessed at the local level.
53	Federal Gasoline Tax	The federal government has levied a tax on gasoline since 1932. For many years, the proceeds of the tax went into the general fund of the Treasury. Although at the time of enactment there was no earmarking of any kind, federal highway aid was continuously granted to the states. In 1956, the federal gasoline tax was increased and the proceeds paid into a trust fund set up to finance the federal government share the cost of the interstate highway system.
54	Generation-skipping Transfer Tax	The estate tax gets all the press, but if you are leaving property to a grandchild, there is an additional tax you should know about. The generation-skipping transfer (GST) tax is a tax on property that is passed from a grandparent to a grandchild (or great-grandchild) in a will or trust. The tax is also assessed on property passed to unrelated individuals more than 37.5 years younger.
55	Gift Tax	The gift tax is a tax on the transfer of property by one individual to another while receiving nothing, or less than full value, in return. The tax applies whether the donor intends the transfer to be a gift or not. The gift tax applies to the transfer by gift of any property. You make a gift if you give property (including money), or the use of or income from property, without

TABLE A.2 (*Continued*)

No.	Government Revenue Sources: Taxes, Fees, and Others	Descriptions
		expecting to receive something of at least equal value in return. If you sell something at less than its full value or if you make an interest-free or reduced-interest loan, you may be making a gift.
56	Gross Production Tax	A tax imposed by states on companies that generate their revenues by depleting nonrenewable resources such as oil and gas, coal miners, and miners of metals and minerals. Gross production taxes were introduced as a means of compensating the state for the pollution that results form the miners' efforts.
57	Gross Receipts Tax	The gross receipts tax, also known as the "turnover tax," has a simple structure, taxing all business sales with few or no deductions. Because it taxes transactions, this tax is often compared to retail sales taxes. However, while well-designed sales taxes apply only to final sales to consumers, gross receipts taxes tax all transactions, including intermediate business-to-business purchases of supplies, raw materials, and equipment. As a result, gross receipts taxes create an extra layer of taxation at each stage of production that sales and other taxes do not—something economists call "tax pyramiding."
58	Gun Ownership Permit	Licensing laws facilitate responsible gun ownership by requiring a person to obtain a license before purchasing a firearm. Although licensing laws vary, the most comprehensive laws require all gun owners to possess a license and regularly renew it. These licenses may only be issued or renewed after the applicant has undergone a background check and safety training, and has passed written and performance-based tests showing that the applicant knows how to safely load, fire, and store a gun, and has knowledge of relevant firearms laws.
59	Hazardous Material Disposal Fees	Persons who dispose of hazardous waste to land at an authorized hazardous waste disposal facility in California will pay a disposal fee directly to the disposal facility, and the disposal facility then submits the fee and a return to the BOE. The fee varies and is

(continued)

TABLE A.2 *(Continued)*

No.	Government Revenue Sources: Taxes, Fees, and Others	Descriptions
		determined by the waste category and the total tonnage of waste. Only the disposal facilities/operators are required to file returns with the BOE. (commenced 7-1-85, H&SC section 25174.1 et seq.).
60	Highway Access (Fees)	Fee on highway access.
61	Hospital Facility Utilization (Fee)	Fee on hospital utilization.
62	Health Department Inspection (Fees)	Local public health departments regularly inspect businesses serving food to ensure restaurants and other food retail outlets are following safe food handling procedures. Local laws regulate how frequently these inspections take place and what specific items the inspectors look for, but, in general, environmental health inspectors check that safeguards are in place to protect food from contamination by food handlers, cross-contamination, and contamination from other sources in the restaurant.
63	Health Insurers Tax (Page 2026/Sec. 9010 of Obamacare)	Section 9010 of the Patient Protection and Affordable Care Act (ACA) imposes a fee on each covered entity engaged in the business of providing health insurance for United States health risks.
64	Hotel and Occupancy Tax	Hotel occupancy is the use, or right to use, a room in a hotel. The room rate or rental charge is the amount that guests must pay to stay in the hotel room (or to have the right to use the hotel room). This amount is taxable at the full state and local sales tax rate.
65	Household Employment Tax	If you paid cash wages of $1,900 or more for 2015 (this threshold can change from year to year) to any one household employee, you generally had to withhold 6.2% of Social Security and 1.45% of Medicare taxes (for a total of 7.65%) from all cash wages you paid to that employee.

TABLE A.2 (*Continued*)

No.	Government Revenue Sources: Taxes, Fees, and Others	Descriptions
66	Hunting License Fee Tax	Fees required to hunt.
67	Import Taxes	In general, import duty is a tax that the importer has to pay to bring foreign goods into his or her country. Import VAT (value-added tax) is a tax charged on imported goods and services.
68	Individual Health Insurance Mandate Taxes	If you can afford health insurance but choose not to buy it, you must have a health coverage exemption or pay a fee. (The fee is sometimes called the "penalty," "fine," "individual responsibility payment," or "individual mandate.")
69	Inheritance Tax, see Estate Tax	An inheritance tax is a state tax that you pay when you receive money or property from the estate of a deceased person. Unlike the federal estate tax, the beneficiary of the property is responsible for paying the tax, not the estate. However, as of 2014, only eight states impose an inheritance tax. And even if you live in one of those states, many beneficiaries are exempt from paying it. The key difference between estate and inheritance taxes lies in who is responsible for paying it. An estate tax is levied on the total value of a deceased person's money and property and is paid out of the decedent's assets before any distribution to beneficiaries.
70	Innovator Drug Companies Tax (Page 2010/Sec. 9008 of Obamacare)	Tax on Innovator Drug Companies ($22B): $2.3 billion annual tax on the industry imposed relative to sales made that year. Began in January 2010.
71	Insect Control Hazardous Materials Licenses (Fee)	A fee on insect licensing.
72	Inspection Fees	Fee to perform inspections.

(*continued*)

TABLE A.2 *(Continued)*

No.	Government Revenue Sources: Taxes, Fees, and Others	Descriptions
73	Insurance Premium Taxes	An insurance premium tax is a tax upon insurers, both domestic and foreign, for the privilege of engaging in the business of providing insurance. The insurance premium task can be viewed as the insurance company's equivalent of the individual's income tax. In other words, the tax is calculated on the amount of premiums received or receivable by the insurance company.
74	Internet Transaction Fee (passed in California; being considered in other states and at federal level)	Tax on internet use.
75	Interstate User Diesel Fuel Taxes	The California Interstate User Diesel Fuel Tax (DI) License is issued only to persons who operate diesel-powered vehicles and whose interstate travel is restricted to Mexico and California, or to persons who are not based in an International Fuel Tax Agreement (IFTA) jurisdiction.
76	Inventory Tax	Some state laws, which vary by state, require that certain inventory, such as that of motor vehicles, boats and trailers, mobile homes, and heavy equipment, be appraised and taxed. Inventory tax is typically based on the total sales of the inventoried item in the prior year. Local law should be consulted for specific requirements in your area.
77	IRA Early Withdrawal Taxes	Traditional IRAs. The IRS will charge you a 10% early withdrawal penalty if both of these apply: 1. You withdraw money from your traditional IRA 2. You are younger than age 59 1/2.
78	IRS Interest Charges (tax on top of tax)	When you do not file and pay your taxes on time, you will be charged interest on any unpaid balance, and you may also be subject to penalties, such as the failure-to-file and failure-to-pay penalties. Interest charged on any unpaid tax compounds daily from the due date of the return (without regard to any extension of time to file) until the date of payment.

TABLE A.2 *(Continued)*

No.	Government Revenue Sources: Taxes, Fees, and Others	Descriptions
79	IRS Penalties (tax on top of tax)	When you do not file and pay your taxes on time, you will be charged interest on any unpaid balance, and you may also be subject to penalties, such as the failure-to-file and failure-to-pay penalties.
80	Jewelry Taxes and Surcharges	Tax and surcharges associated with jewelry.
81	Kiddie Tax	If the child's interest, dividends and other unearned income total more than $2,000, part of that income may be subject to tax at the parent's tax rate instead of the child's tax rate.
82	Land Value Tax	Land value taxation is a method of raising public revenue by means of an annual charge on the rental value of land.
83	Library (Fees)	Taxes and /or fees associated with libraries.
84	License Plate and Car Ownership Transfer Taxes and Fees	Tax and fees associated with vehicle registration.
85	Liquor License Tax	Retail liquor licenses are required for businesses or nonprofit organizations that retail or serve beer, wine, or spirits, such as grocery stores, restaurants, or bars. Nonretail liquor licenses are required for businesses or nonprofit organizations that manufacture, distill, wholesale, transport, import, or export alcoholic beverages.
86	Liquor Tax	The distribution of liquor is a state enterprise under the auspices of some state liquor authorities.
87	Local Tax	Cities, counties, and local government bodies in some U.S. states impose local income tax, in addition to state tax. Employers are legally required to withhold local income tax from employee wages as part of their overall federal income tax withholding obligations. While most states levy local income tax as a tax on wages, some levy it as a percentage of the state income tax. The states that charge local income tax

(continued)

TABLE A.2 *(Continued)*

No.	Government Revenue Sources: Taxes, Fees, and Others	Descriptions
		are: Alabama, Arkansas, Colorado, District of Columbia, Delaware, Iowa, Indiana, Kentucky, Maryland, Michigan, Missouri, New York, Ohio, Oregon, and Pennsylvania.
88	Local Corporate Taxes	Corporate income tax assessed at the local level.
89	Local Income Taxes	A local tax assessed at the local level.
90	Local School Taxes	School taxes support the schools in your local school district. All residents pay school taxes in one way or another, regardless of whether you have one child, seven children, or no children attending a public school in your district. The school tax is set by your local school board and assessed annually as part of the local taxes you pay.
91	Local or State Unemployment Taxes	A local assessed payroll tax in some jurisdictions.
92	Lodging Facility Use Tax	There are two taxes imposed on users of an overnight lodging facility (such as a hotel, motel, campground, dude ranch, or guest ranch, which are collected by the facility and remitted to the Department of Revenue. These two taxes are a 4% lodging facility use tax, and a 3% lodging facility sales tax, for a combined 7% lodging facility sales and use tax.
93	Luxury Tax	Luxury taxes are levied on luxury commodities. The intention behind imposing luxury taxes in the U.S. may be to tax the wealthy class, who can afford to pay some amount of their earnings to the state as a tax to help make the nation more prosperous. The U.S. luxury tax has been imposed on goods like perfumes, tobacco, luxury cars, alcohol, and jewelry.
94	Marriage License Tax	Every state requires a couple to obtain a marriage license in order to have a legally binding wedding ceremony. Some states require a medical examination or blood tests in order to obtain a license. All require proof of identification and a license application fee.

TABLE A.2 *(Continued)*

No.	Government Revenue Sources: Taxes, Fees, and Others	Descriptions
95	Medicare Tax	Taxes under the Federal Insurance Contributions Act (FICA) are composed of the old-age, survivors, and disability insurance taxes, also known as Social Security taxes, and the hospital insurance tax, also known as Medicare taxes. Different rates apply for these taxes.
96	Medicare Tax Surcharge on High Earning Americans under Obamacare	In tax years 2013 and later, additional Medicare tax applies to an individual's Medicare wages that exceed a threshold amount based on the taxpayer's filing status.
97	Medical Device Manufacturers Tax (Page 2020/Sec. 9009 of Obamacare)	The Obamacare Medical Device excise tax of 2.3% taxes manufacturers that profit under the law. The Medical Device excise tax went into effect January 1, 2013.
98	Metal Mines Gross Proceeds Tax	A tax assessed on mining.
99	Metal Mines License Tax	Every person who engages in or carries on the business of working or operating any mine or mining property in the state of Montana from which gold, silver, copper, lead, or any other metal or metals or precious or semiprecious gems or stones of any kind shall be mined, extracted, or produced, whether such person shall carry on such business or engage in such work or operations as owner, lessee, trustee, possessor, receiver, or in any other capacity, must for each year when engaged in or carrying on such business, work, or operations pay to the department of revenue for the exclusive use and benefit of the state of Montana and impacted local government units a license tax for engaging in and carrying on such business, work, or operation in this state.

(continued)

TABLE A.2 *(Continued)*

No.	Government Revenue Sources: Taxes, Fees, and Others	Descriptions
100	Miscellaneous Mineral Mines License Tax	The operation of any mine extracting micaceous minerals is subject to a quarterly license tax. Micaceous minerals are those that are generally classified as complex silicates, and include such minerals as vermiculite, perlite, kernite, Masonite, and bauxite.
101	Miscellaneous Mines Net Proceeds Tax	Tax on Mining.
102	New Car Surcharge	New car dealerships are responsible for collecting a 0.4% surcharge on the sale of new passenger vehicles, light trucks, SUVs, or vans for which either of the following conditions apply: 1. The gross sales/lease price of the new vehicle is $45,000 or greater, before trade-in, manufacturer's rebates, or additional Person(s) with a disability driver adaptive equipment; 2. The new vehicle has an average EPA mile/gallon (city and highway) rating of less than 19.
103	Nursing Facility Bed Tax	Forty-three states have a provider tax, also known as a "bed tax," on nursing homes, and states use provider tax revenue to help finance Medicaid. That in turn pays for a bulk of nursing home care.
104	Obamacare Individual Mandate Excise Tax (if you don't buy "qualifying" health insurance under Obamacare you will have to pay an additional tax)	Obamacare's individual mandate requires that most Americans obtain health insurance by 2014 or pay a tax penalty. The individual mandate went into effect at the beginning of January 2014 and continues each year. The penalty for not having coverage will be paid on your federal income tax returns for each full month you or a family member doesn't have health insurance or an exemption and is based on your modified adjusted gross income (MAGI).
105	Obamacare Surtax on Investment Income (a new 3.8% surtax on investment income)	The Net Investment Income Tax is imposed by Section 1411 of the Internal Revenue Code. The NIIT applies at a rate of 3.8% to certain net investment income of individuals, estates, and trusts that have income above the statutory threshold amounts.

TABLE A.2   *(Continued)*

No.	Government Revenue Sources: Taxes, Fees, and Others	Descriptions
106	Occupation taxes and fees (annual charges required for a host of professions)	To generate revenue, any class of city may collect a "privilege or license tax" on an occupation or business within its boundaries. The tax must be applied uniformly and fairly to the types of businesses on which it is imposed. The most common types of businesses affected are hotel operators, car rental companies, telecommunications providers, restaurants, and bars.
107	Oil and Natural Gas Production Tax	A tax is imposed on the market value of gas or oil produced and saved in the state by the producer.
108	Oil Storage/ Inspection Fees	The U.S. Bureau of Land Management would impose inspection fees for onshore oil and gas producers operating on lands under its jurisdiction under the Obama administration's proposed fiscal 2015 budget. The fees would be similar to those the U.S. Bureau of Safety and Environmental Enforcement charges offshore producers.
109	Parking Meter Tax	Tax to park in designated spaces.
110	Passport Application/Renewal Fee	A fee to renew passport and/or obtain a passport.
111	Payroll Tax	Payroll taxes are the state and federal taxes that an employer is required to withhold and/or to pay on behalf of employees. The employer is required to withhold state and federal income taxes as well as Social Security and Medicare taxes from the employees' wages.
112	Plastic Surgery Surcharge	Surcharge on plastic surgery.
113	Poll Tax	A tax levied on every adult, without reference to income or ability to pay.

(continued)

TABLE A.2 (*Continued*)

No.	Government Revenue Sources: Taxes, Fees, and Others	Descriptions
114	Professional Privilege Tax	The professional privilege tax is levied on the privilege of having an active license to practice certain professions, businesses, or occupations.
115	Professional License Fee (accountants, lawyers, barbers, dentists, plumbers, etc.)	Fees associated with profession licenses typical review in a specified period like annually, bi-annual or other designated time period.
116	Property Tax	Property tax is the annual amount paid by landowners to the local government or the municipal corporation of the area. The property includes all tangible real estate property, house, office building, and property rented to others.
117	Proxy Tax	In the United States, a tax levied on the political or lobbying activity of certain tax-exempt organizations. Subject to certain restrictions, the proxy tax applies to organizations under section 501(c)4, 501(c)5, and 501(c)6. Generally speaking, this includes labor unions, civic groups, chambers of commerce, and similar groups.
118	Public Contractor's Gross Receipts Tax	Contractors Gross Receipts Tax is a privilege tax imposed on persons, firms, and corporations engaged in the business of contracting to construct, reconstruct, or build public highways, roads, bridges, streets, or tunnels for the Alabama Department of Transportation.
119	Public Service Commission Tax	Tax associated with maintaining public utilities.
120	Public Utility Tax	This is a tax on public service businesses, including businesses that engage in transportation, communications, and the supply of energy, natural gas, and water. The tax is in lieu of the business and occupation (B&O) tax.
121	Real Estate Tax	Real estate taxes (or "property taxes") are imposed on immovable property—land and structures that are permanently attached to the ground such as houses, buildings, cabins, garages, barns, etc.

TABLE A.2 *(Continued)*

No.	Government Revenue Sources: Taxes, Fees, and Others	Descriptions
122	Real Estate Transfer Tax	Real estate transfer taxes are taxes imposed by states, counties, and municipalities on the transfer of the title of real property within the jurisdiction. They can also be used for specific purposes, such as affordable housing and open space development.
123	Recreational Vehicle Taxes	Tax on Recreation Vehicles.
124	Registration Fees for New Businesses	Not all levels of business structures are required to register with a state. Businesses that do face a registration requirement will find different fee structures from state to state and, depending on their operations, may need to file in several states as a "foreign" business entity. For corporations, registrations will be only the beginning of annual filings of board minutes, annual reports, and other forms. Registration with the state is only one of the costs facing business start-ups.
125	Rental Vehicle Sales Tax	When it comes to rental cars, most consumers know the price they start off with isn't always the price they end up with. A rental includes sales tax. If you bring your vehicle back with virtually no gas in it, the company will charge you a premium to fill it up (unless you opted for the prepaid tank option, which can work out unless you return the car with close to a full tank). Extra insurance from the rental car company will also increase your bill.
126	Resort Tax	Many hotels now charge mandatory "resort fees" ranging from $5 to as much as $30 per night. These fees can include all kinds of items and privileges, ranging from local telephone calls to Internet access to the coffeemaker in your hotel room.
127	Resource Indemnity and Groundwater Assessment Tax	All businesses engaged in mining or extracting mineral resources within this state are subject to an annual tax on the percentage of the gross value of the product, pursuant to 15-38-104. The tax rates are as follows: Talc, 4.0%; coal, 0.4%; vermiculite, 2.0%, quicklime, 10%, industrial garnet, 1%; all others, 0.5%. There is a minimum annual tax of $25. This tax is in addition to all other applicable fees and taxes.

(continued)

TABLE A.2 (*Continued*)

No.	Government Revenue Sources: Taxes, Fees, and Others	Descriptions
128	Retail Telecom- munications Excise Tax	A state-mandated tax imposed on the gross sales of telecommunication services. For example, the Montana excise tax of 3.75% is assessed on all switched voice services and features. Receipts of the retail telecommunications excise tax are deposited in the State General Fund.
129	Sales Tax	In the United States, most of its 50 states assess a sales tax, which is a tax on sales to the end user. For example, in Wisconsin a retailer must collect a 5% sales tax and perhaps another 0.5% for a county sales tax on specified goods and services. The retailer must remit the sales taxes collected within a prescribed time period.
130	Sales and Use Tax Seller's Permit	A seller's permit is required for every individual, partnership, corporation, or other organization making retail sales, leases, or rentals of tangible personal property or taxable services, unless all sales are exempt from sales or use tax.
131	School Tax (State)	State taxes used to fund schools.
132	Self-Employment Tax	Self-employment tax is a tax consisting of Social Security and Medicare taxes primarily for individuals who work for themselves. It is similar to the Social Security and Medicare taxes withheld from the pay of most wage earners. Both portions are paid: Employee & Employer.
133	Septic Permit Tax	The lot owner must fill out an application (a fee is required). This authorizes an Environmental Health Specialist to go to the property to evaluate it. The property will need to be properly marked. After the site evaluation, a letter will be sent to the owner from the Environmental Health Specialist to advise him/her whether or not the lot will support a septic tank system in its present condition. Recommendations for necessary site improvements will be made.

TABLE A.2 *(Continued)*

No.	Government Revenue Sources: Taxes, Fees, and Others	Descriptions
134	Severance Tax	Severance taxes help ensure that costs associated with resource extraction—such as road construction and maintenance, and environmental protection—are paid by the producers, helping to alleviate potential impacts on state and local taxpayers. States distribute revenues in various ways, but, typically, most of the collected taxes are deposited into the general fund. Many states also use the extra revenue to fund conservation and environmental cleanup projects and distribute portions of the collected taxes to local governments.
135	Sewer Fees and Tax	The sewer service fee is charged on all properties connected to the system of sewerage (*or having passed a deadline for connection to the system of sewerage*) for purposes of defraying the costs of operating, maintaining, and repairing the system of sewerage. The wastewater treatment plant charge is a component of the sewer service fee.
136	Soda/Fatty-Food Tax	A fat tax is a surcharge applied to a product that is deemed fattening (food, beverages). Examples of fattening food products are cookies, cakes, pies, chips, candy, chocolate, burgers, pizza, fries, and hot dogs. Fattening beverages are soft drinks, sodas, energy drinks, sugary fruit juices, and sports drinks.
137	Social Security Tax	The Social Security tax is applied to income related to labor. All employees and self-employed entrepreneurs pay into Social Security through the Social Security tax, which is also known as Old-Age, Survivors, and Disability Insurance (OASDI).
138	Special Assessments for Road Repairs or Construction	Special assessments are one way that property owners pay for the benefit they receive from construction or repair of streets, sidewalks, and alleys. The cost of a public improvement is usually divided on a front-foot or area basis. Public hearings are held to order the improvement and specify the special assessment amount for each property.
139	Sports Stadium Taxes	Taxes as result of stadium support such as police, potential financing and other taxpayer related subsidy.

(continued)

TABLE A.2 (*Continued*)

No.	Government Revenue Sources: Taxes, Fees, and Others	Descriptions
140	State Income Tax	State Income taxes, which vary by state, are a percentage of money that you pay to the state government based on the income you make at your job. Just like the federal government, states impose additional income taxes on your earnings if you have a sufficient connection to the state. Although each state has the authority to create its own system of imposing the tax, most jurisdictions use a similar structure as the federal government. However, a minority of states impose the income tax at a flat rate on all taxpayers or they don't even charge the tax at all.
141	State Corporate Taxes	A levy placed on the profit of a firm, with different rates used for different levels of profits. Corporate taxes are taxes against profits earned by businesses during a given taxable period; they are generally applied to companies' operating earnings, after expenses such as COGS, SG&A and depreciation have been deducted from revenues. Corporate taxes are usually levied by all levels of government (i.e., State and Country). Corporate tax rates and laws vary greatly around the world, as different governments and countries view corporate taxation in different ways. For example, those in favor of lower corporate tax rates point to the possibility for greater economic production if companies are taxed less. While others see higher corporate tax rates as a way to subsidize government spending and programs for the nation's citizens.
142	State Park Entrance Fees	The fees you pay stay within the parks to play an important role in protecting open space and wildlife, support recreational activities and nature education, and provide visitor assistance and safety.
143	State Unemployment Tax	Employers must pay federal and state unemployment taxes in order to fund the unemployment tax system. Unemployment compensation is designed to pay benefits to workers when they lose their jobs through no fault of their own.

TABLE A.2 *(Continued)*

No.	Government Revenue Sources: Taxes, Fees, and Others	Descriptions
144	Statewide Emergency Telephone 911 System Fee Tax	This is a monthly tax on switched access (wireline) lines, radio access (wireless telephone numbers) lines, and Voice Over Internet Protocol (VoIP) service.
145	Surtax Tax—Extra tax.	A tax levied on top of another tax. A surtax can be calculated as a percentage of a certain amount or it can be a flat dollar amount. A surtax is generally assessed to fund a specific government program, whereas regular income or sales taxes are used to fund a variety of programs. Thus, one unique feature of a surtax is that it allows taxpayers to more easily see how much money the government is collecting and spending for a particular program.
146	Tanning Taxes (a new Obamacare tax on tanning services)	Amounts paid for tanning services are subject to a 10% excise tax under the Affordable Care Act.
147	Tariffs—A tax on imports. Needed to protect all the industries we used to have.	A tariff or duty (the words are used interchangeably) is a tax levied by governments on the value including freight and insurance of imported products. Different tariffs are applied on different products by different countries. National sales and local taxes, and in some instances customs fees, will often be charged in addition to the tariff.
148	Telephone 911 Service Taxes	Tax on 911 services.
149	Telephone Federal Excise Tax	A statutory federal excise on telephone service.
150	Telephone Federal Universal Service Fee Tax	Since May 1997, this tax has helped provide affordable phone service and gives schools, libraries, and rural health care providers access to the Internet.

(continued)

TABLE A.2 *(Continued)*

No.	Government Revenue Sources: Taxes, Fees, and Others	Descriptions
151	Telephone Minimum Usage Surcharge Tax	Telephone minimum usage surcharges are charged by some telephone companies and vary by company. The usage minimum surcharge is based on usage and is not a monthly fee. If you spend less than the minimum in a given month in qualifying, your account will be charged the difference between what you use and the minimum.
152	Telephone State and Local Taxes	Taxes, governmental surcharges, and fees include sales, excise, other taxes, and government surcharges that telephone companies are required by law to collect from customers on behalf of local, state, and the federal government. These taxes, surcharges, and fees may change from time to time without notice.
153	Telephone Universal Access Taxes	Since May 1997, the Federal Communications Commission (FCC) requires telecommunications carriers to pay into the Universal Service Fund. This helps provide affordable phone service and gives schools, libraries, and rural health care providers access to the Internet. Telecommunications carriers are required by the FCC to pay a percentage of their revenues for state-to-state and international services into the Universal Service Fund.
154	TDD Telecommunications Service Fee Tax	Tax on telecommunication services.
155	TV Cable/Satellite Fees and Taxes	Tax on TV, cable and satellite services.
156	Tire Recycling Fees	The Environmental Conservation Law imposes a $2.50 per tire waste tire and recycling fee on sales of most new tires sold at retail within New York State. The Tax Department is responsible for administering the collection of the fee.
157	Tire Taxes	Fee on the sale of new motor vehicle tires, including new tires sold as a component part of a motor vehicle, either sold or leased, that are subject to New Jersey sales tax. The tire fee is imposed per tire, including the spare tire sold as part of a motor vehicle. The tire fee also applies to sales of new tires in connection with a repair or maintenance service.

TABLE A.2 *(Continued)*

No.	Government Revenue Sources: Taxes, Fees, and Others	Descriptions
158	Tobacco Products Tax (Other than Cigarettes)	The tobacco products tax is imposed upon the distribution of tobacco products based on the wholesale cost of these products at a rate determined annually by the State Board of Equalization (BOE). Tobacco products include all forms of cigars, smoking tobacco, chewing tobacco, and snuff, as well as any other articles or products made of, or containing, at least 50 percent tobacco.
159	Toll Road Fee Tax	Toll roads are roads for use of which tolls or fees are collected; the most common instance of toll roads is a toll road that is considered a motorway and infrastructure; these are roadways that lead to a tunnel or a bridge of some sort. However, there are a number of no infrastructure type roads as well.
160	Toll Bridge Fee	Fee for use of bridge.
161	Toll Tunnel Fee	Fee for use of the tunnel.
162	Tonnage Tax	The U.S. can charge tonnage tax, light money, and special tonnage tax on all foreign-flag vessels. However, the U.S. does not charge special tonnage tax and light money on the vessel of a particular foreign country if that country does not charge such special tonnage tax and light money on U.S. flag vessels. (Light money are charges imposed by government assessed against shipping entering a port, for the maintenance of lighthouses and light-ships).
163	Tourism and Concession License Fee	Tourism and concession fees.
164	Traffic Fines	The total amount of a traffic fine is made up of amounts required to be paid by state laws as well as county and city ordinances, which vary by jurisdiction. There are three levels of severity of traffic violations: infractions, misdemeanors, and felonies.
165	Trailer Registration Fee Tax	Fee to register a trailer.

(continued)

TABLE A.2 *(Continued)*

No.	Government Revenue Sources: Taxes, Fees, and Others	Descriptions
166	Use Tax	Use tax is a type of excise tax imposed on both businesses and individuals. Generally, you are supposed to pay use tax if you purchase an item without paying your home state's sales tax and you use, give away, store, or consume that item in your home state.
167	Utility Tax, see Public Utility Tax	This is a tax on public service businesses, including businesses that engage in transportation, communications, and the supply of energy, natural gas, and water. The tax is in lieu of the business and occupation (B&O) tax.
168	Vehicle Registration and License Tax	Registration fees for passenger vehicles are based on the class of vehicle and on the weight of a vehicle in cases of trucks, buses, and for-hire vehicles. In addition, some municipalities and boroughs levy a Motor Vehicle Registration Tax (MVRT.)
169	Vehicle Sales Tax	Whether you're buying a new car or a used car, or even leasing a car, you'll have to pay state sales tax. Nearly every state has a sales tax, ranging from under 3% to over 8%. The national average in the United States is 5.75%.
170	Waste Management Tax	The Environmental Conservation Law imposes a $2.50 per tire waste tire and recycling fee on sales of most new tires sold at retail within New York State. The Tax Department is responsible for administering the collection of the fee.
171	Water/sewer fees & taxes	A city in which a water-sewer district operates works, plants, or facilities for the distribution and sale of water or sewer services may levy and collect from the district a tax on the gross revenues derived by the district from the sale of water or sewer services within the city, exclusive of the revenues derived from the sale of water or sewer services for purposes of resale. The tax when levied must be a debt of the district, and may be collected as such. The district may add the amount of tax to the rates or charges it makes for water or sewer services sold within the limits of the city.

TABLE A.2 (*Continued*)

No.	Government Revenue Sources: Taxes, Fees, and Others	Descriptions
172	Watercraft Registration Tax	If your new boat (except kayaks or canoes) is longer than 16', your dealer will apply for title and registration (license) on your behalf, and is responsible for providing you with license materials.
173	Well Permit Tax	A Landowner Water Well Permit allows you to construct, alter, or abandon a water well on your own property. Any work you complete on the well must be in compliance with Oregon Ground Water Law and the Administrative Rules for Water Well Construction and Maintenance in Oregon (OAR Chapter 690, Divisions 200 through 230). The landowner must also obtain a bond or an irrevocable letter of credit in the sum of $5,000. A start card is a "notice of beginning of well construction" and must be submitted prior to constructing, altering, deepening, abandoning, or converting a well.
174	Waste Management Tax	The California State Board of Equalization (Board) administers the Integrated Waste Management Fee Program pursuant to section 48000 of the Public Resources Code and the Integrated Waste Management Fee Law beginning with section 45001 of the Revenue and Taxation Code. Each operator of a disposal facility required to have a disposal facility permit from the Integrated Waste Management Board shall pay a fee quarterly to the Board based on all solid waste disposed of at each disposal site on or after January 1, 1990. Each fee payer is required to file a return quarterly with the Board.
175	Wholesale Energy Transaction Tax	A distribution services provider who purchases its electricity directly from an agency of the U.S. government will self-assess the tax on the kilowatt-hours of electricity that it receives and will forward the tax to the department.

(continued)

TABLE A.2 *(Continued)*

No.	Government Revenue Sources: Taxes, Fees, and Others	Descriptions
176	Workers' Compensation Tax	Amounts you receive as workers' compensation for an occupational sickness or injury are fully exempt from tax if they are paid under a workers' compensation act or a statute in the nature of a workers' compensation act. The exemption also applies to your survivors. The exemption, however, does not apply to retirement plan benefits you receive based on your age, length of service, or prior contributions to the plan, even if you retired because of an occupational sickness or injury.
177	Yacht and luxury boat taxes	In 1990, George H. W. Bush passed a budget that included a "luxury tax" on yachts over $100,000 in addition to jewelry, furs, etc.
178	Zoning Permits	A zoning approval is required before starting a use, erecting a structure or building, obtaining building permits, or obtaining certificates of use and occupancy.
179	ATM Bank Transaction Tax	This is 1% tax on all transactions to or from any financial institution, i.e., banks, credit unions, mutual funds, brokers, etc.

TABLE A.3 Financial Ratios for Government

Ratio 1	**Actual Revenues versus Budgeted Revenues**

Explanation: The ratio will expose deviations between actual and budgeted revenues which will require further investigation and a follow up to determine the reason for the variance.

Calculation: $\dfrac{\text{Actual Revenue} - \text{Budgeted Revenue}}{\text{Budgeted Revenue}}$

Discussion: Simple ratio comparison can flag variances. How about if we add to the numbers perspective the servicing result concept. The servicing result concept. Percentage miss in terms of revenue target.

Ratio 2	**Percentage Change in Taxpayers**

Explanation: Ratio shows the percentage change in the number of taxpayers in a municipality or region.

Calculation: $\dfrac{\text{Actual \# Taxpayers} - \text{Expected \# Taxpayers}}{\text{Expected \# Taxpayers}}$

Discussion: Is the tax base growing or declining. Examining the servicing results associated with the revenues and utilizing the SEA concept, will help management become more efficient and ensures accountability. Pure numbers mean nothing until they are correlated with corresponding objectives.

Note: If a user based fee then the user would replace taxpayer. Example toll roads would be toll payers, which could be broken down further depending on by the available descriptions.

Ratio 3	**Self Paying Percentage - AKA - a Metric of Reliance on Grants and Subsidies**

Explanation: The ratio will reflect what percentage of revenue is funded by local sources as opposed to grants or subsidies further investigation and follow up to determine the reason for the variances.

Calculation: $\dfrac{\text{Total Revenue} - (\text{Grants and Subsidies})}{\text{Total Revenue}}$

Discussion: This metric provides an estimate of self-paying ability and the level of reliance on grants and subsidies for the year. Have the grants and subsidies been uniformly applied? Have they only disclosed equitable share and financial management grants? Have the grants and subsidies been uniformly applied? Have they only disclosed equitable share and financial management grants? Are they waiting to recognize grants under Chapter 159 or other later recording procedure?

(continued)

TABLE A.3 *(Continued)*

Ratio 4	**Actual Appropriations to Budgeted Appropriations**

Explanation: The ratio will expose deviations between actual and budgeted appropriations (expenditures) which will require

Calculation: $\dfrac{\text{Actual Appropriations}}{\text{Budgeted Appropriations}}$

Discussion: Actual appropriations will either exceed or be less than budgeted appropriations by a percentage. For example - positive ratios can occur when an entity spends less on health insurance. Negative ratios can occur when an entity incurs a onetime expenditure such as a retirement payout. The ratio above indicates that the actual appropriations were XXX% over (under) the entities budgeted appropriations.

Ratio 5	**Appropriated Personnel Expenditures Versus Actual Personnel Expenditures**

Explanation: The ratio will indicate the change in appropriated personnel Items as compared to Actual Personnel Item Expenditures.

Calculation: $\dfrac{\text{Appropriated Salary, Wages and Allowances}}{\text{Final Year Total Expenditures on Salary, Wages \& Allowances}}$

Discussion: The ratio above indicates that xxx% represented the amount attributable to personnel costs in relation to budgeted personnel costs. This ratio raises awareness of rising costs so that entities can address them. This ratio may be a flag for a budget that is padded in terms of expenditures - where extra personnel costs are budgeted for - but not expended. Further analysis may be warranted if the personnel funds are then reallocated to other discretionary expenditures or non-budgeted items.

Ratio 6	**Appropriated Personnel Expenditures as a Percent of Total Appropriated Expenditures**

Explanation: The ratio will indicate the percentage of total appropriations (expenditures) that is attributable to personnel costs.

Calculation: $\dfrac{\text{Appropriated Salary, Wages and Allowances}}{\text{Total Appropriated Expenditures}}$

Discussion: The ratio above indicates that xxx% represented the amount attributable to personnel costs in relation to total appropriated expenditures. This ratio raises awareness of rising costs so that entities can address them. This ratio may be a flag for a budget that is padded in terms of expenditures - where extra personnel costs are budgeted for - but not expended Further Analysis may be warranted if the personnel funds are then reallocated to other discretionary expenditures or non-budgeted items.

TABLE A.3 *(Continued)*

| Ratio 7 | **Interest as a Percentage Total Appropriation (expenditure)** |

Explanation: The ratio will indicate the percentage of total appropriations (expenditures) that is attributable to interest costs.

Calculation: $\dfrac{\text{Interest Paid}}{\text{Total Expenditures}}$

Discussion: The table shows that xxx% of total appropriations are attributable to interest costs. The ratio above indicates that xxx% represented the amount attributable to interest costs in relation to the Total Appropriations (expenditures). This ratio shows whether or not an entity is more or less dependent on borrowing.

| Ratio 8 | **Repairs and Maintenance as a Percentage of Total Appropriations (expenditures)** |

Explanation: The ratio will indicate the percentage of total appropriations (expenditures) that is attributable to repairs and maintenance.

Calculation: $\dfrac{\text{Repairs and Maintenance Expenditures}}{\text{Total Expenditures}}$

Discussion: The ratio above indicates that xxx% represented the amount attributable to repairs and maintenance in relation to the Total Appropriations (expenditures).

This ratio will show if an entity has improved in general. It will also assist in the preliminary evaluation of the effectiveness of an entity's overall asset maintenance plan. Delaying and deferring maintenance is an easy way to cut current expenditures - but at the expense of greater future expenditures on capital replacement

| Ratio 9 | **Acquisition of Property, Plant & Equipment : Actual Versus Budgeted** |

Explanation: The ratio is designed to identify by class whether or not there is a variance between the PP&E actual Versus the PP&E budgeted when the two are compared.

Calculation: $\dfrac{\text{Actual PP\&E Acquisitions} - \text{Budgeted PP\&E Acquisitions}}{\text{Budgeted PP\&E Acquisitions}}$

Discussion: The table shows that xxx% of unexpended, over expensed acquisitions were not acquired in accordance with the entity's budgeted capital plan. The ratio above indicates that xxx% of PP&E acquisitions were either more or less than the entity's budgeted acquisitions. Expenditures on PP&E are also subject to considerable discretion as to timing and amount - as such strong deviation in this expenditure item should be examined in detail to assure that long term capital assets are acquired appropriately.

(continued)

TABLE A.3 *(Continued)*

Ratio 10   **Acid Test Ratio**

Explanation: The ratio demonstrates the ability to meet short-term current liabilities (obligations) with short term liquid assets.

Calculation: $\dfrac{\text{Current Assets} - \text{Inventory}}{\text{Current Liabilities}}$

Discussion: The acid test ratio shows that there is 1xx dollar of assets for every 1 dollar of liabilities. The more asset dollars available to pay current liabilities the stronger the working capital base of the entity. The ratio above shows that there is/are XXX dollar(s) of assets to satisfy every 1xx dollar of current liabilities (obligations) incurred by the entity. This indicates the entity's ability to satisfy current obligations.

Ratio 11   **Total Liabilities as a Percentage of Total Assets**

Explanation: The ratio demonstrates the amount of assets that have been utilized in the past to incur debt.

Calculation: $\dfrac{\text{Total Liabilities}}{\text{Total Assets}}$

Discussion: The ratio above indicates the balance of liabilities to total assets. Organization with heavy liability burdens as compared to their asset holdings are at greater risk for financial distress.

Ratio 12   **Net Cash Flow From Operations Compared to Total Debt of the Municipality**

Explanation: The ratio demonstrates the ability to generate cash flow from operations that is available to pay off debt. The higher the ratio is the better the entity's ability to meet the outstanding obligations.

Calculation:

$$\frac{\text{Net Cash Flow from Operating Activities less Investing Activities}}{\text{Total Liabilities}}$$

Discussion: The ratio above indicates that there is/are XXX dollar(s) of net cash flow from operations to satisfy every 1 dollar of the entity's outstanding debts.

Ratios of Economic Vitality

TABLE A.3 *(Continued)*

Ratio 13	**Public Safety and Social Service Spending as a Share of Total Expenditures**

Explanation: The ratio explores the impact of public safety and social services on total budget.

Calculation: $\dfrac{\text{Police and Social Service Expenditures}}{\text{Total Expenditures}}$

Discussion: High spending on social services and public safety may indicate a community with a excessively short term and crisis focus as opposed to long term strategic investment.

Ratio 14	**Ratio of Collected to Billed Taxes**

Explanation: The ratio examines the ability of the municipality to collect billed taxes

Calculation: $\dfrac{\text{Tax Collections}}{\text{Taxes Billed}}$

Discussion: Strong collection rates are indicative of a region with strong valuation and performance - owners are unwilling to risk tax avoidance and tax leans. Indicator of overall economic attractiveness of a region and profitability. Can be evaluated both from a residential and a commercial perspective.

Ratios of Financial Independence and Flexibility

Ratio 15	**Debt Service as a Percent of Total Revenues**

Explanation: The ratio explores the cost of debt as it is related to the revenue of the municipality

Calculation: $\dfrac{\text{Debt Service Payments}}{\text{Total Revenues}}$

Discussion: Organizations with high debt service are generally considered more financially frail than organizations with less debt as compared to the revenue stream.

(continued)

TABLE A.3 (*Continued*)

Ratio 16 | **Federal and State Mandated Costs as a Percentage of Expenditures**

Explanation: In many local governmental entities, a large share of spending may be mandated by federal or state law - this metric explores the level of discretionary spending as a share of total expenditures.

Calculation: $\dfrac{\text{Federal and State Mandated Costs}}{\text{Total Expenditures}}$

Discussion: There are two aspects of this metric. First, it provides guidance as to how much local spending is actually subject to local political control and discipline. Second, it provides information as to the mandated level of spending based upon federal and state mandates - and as such, the level of revenue that must be maintained to support these expenditures.

Ratio 17 | **Long Term Debt to Population Ratio**

Explanation: Provides a measure of long term debt per capita for a municipality

Calculation: $\dfrac{\text{General Obligations Long-Term Indebtedness}}{\text{Municipal Population}}$

Discussion: High debt burdens place significant financial burdens on the taxpayers. This ratio combined with other measures of outside financial support such as state or federal aid provides us with guidance as to the long term ability of the community to shoulder the costs of municipal capital and operations.

Ratio 18 | **Ratio of Municipal (Public) Worker Productivity**

Explanation: This metric explores the level of staffing for an organization as compared to the population base

Calculation: $\dfrac{\text{Total Number of Municipal Employees}}{\text{Municipal Population}}$

Discussion: Municipal (public) employees provide many governmental services. The use of municpal (public) and scale of public operations needs to be considered in light of the population served. This ratio provides a measure of staffing relative to population and also provides guidance over time as to a sustainable level of growth in the municipal workforce.

TABLE A.3 *(Continued)*

Ratio 19	**Capital Expenditures as a Share of Total Expenditures**

Explanation: Provides a measure of long term debt per capita for a municipality

Calculation: $\dfrac{\text{Capital Outlays}}{\text{Total Expenditures}}$

Discussion: High debt burdens place significant financial burdens on the taxpayers. This ratio combined with other measures of outside financial support such as state or federal aid provides us with guidance as to the long term ability of the community to shoulder the costs of municipal capital and operations.

Ratio 20	**Ratio of Payments to Local Source Revenue**

Explanation: This metric explores the level of staffing for an organization as compared to the population base.

Calculation: $\dfrac{\text{Notes Payable} + \text{Accounts Payable} + \text{Vouchers Payable}}{\text{Total Own Source Revenues}}$

Discussion: Municipal (public) employees provide many governmental services. The use of municipal (public) staff and scale of public operations needs to be considered in light of the population served. This ratio provides a measure of staffing relative to population and also provides guidance over time as to a sustainable level of growth in the municipal workforce.

Ratio 21	**Revenue Realization - Projected to Actual Revenue**

Explanation: This ratio examines the ratio of actual to estimated revenue

Calculation: $\dfrac{\text{Actual Revenue}}{\text{Estimated revenue}}$

Discussion: Accurate revenue targets provide a measure of stability for spending and debt service. Projections of revenue that will be obtained from all sources should match well to revenue collected. The public entity should have good revenue projections methods and produce accurate forecasts. Appropriate estimates of uncollectables should be maintained.

(continued)

TABLE A.3 *(Continued)*

Ratio 22 **Physical Assets to Debt**

Explanation: This measure examines the level of debt as compared to net investment in physical assets.

Calculation: $\dfrac{\text{Net Investment in Physical Assets}}{\text{Physical Debts}}$

Discussion: Debt should be used to provide for funding for long term assets. As such, the level of debt that is on the balance sheet of a public entity should be covered compared to the net investments of the entity. If a entity has excessive debt due to borrowing for current. - this ratio will be low.

A good rule of thumb would be that this ratio should be 3 or above - to reflect a funding stream that is reflective of investment in physical assets.

Index